T0202897

# Lecture Notes in Computer Science  10911

*Commenced Publication in 1973*
Founding and Former Series Editors:
Gerhard Goos, Juris Hartmanis, and Jan van Leeuwen

More information about this series at http://www.springer.com/series/7409

Pei-Luen Patrick Rau (Ed.)

# Cross-Cultural Design

## Methods, Tools, and Users

10th International Conference, CCD 2018
Held as Part of HCI International 2018
Las Vegas, NV, USA, July 15–20, 2018
Proceedings, Part I

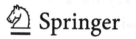 Springer

*Editor*
Pei-Luen Patrick Rau
Tsinghua University
Beijing
China

ISSN 0302-9743              ISSN 1611-3349   (electronic)
Lecture Notes in Computer Science
ISBN 978-3-319-92140-2        ISBN 978-3-319-92141-9   (eBook)
https://doi.org/10.1007/978-3-319-92141-9

Library of Congress Control Number: 2018944395

LNCS Sublibrary: SL3 – Information Systems and Applications, incl. Internet/Web, and HCI

Printed on acid-free paper

This Springer imprint is published by the registered company Springer International Publishing AG
part of Springer Nature
The registered company address is: Gewerbestrasse 11, 6330 Cham, Switzerland

# Foreword

The 20th International Conference on Human-Computer Interaction, HCI International 2018, was held in Las Vegas, NV, USA, during July 15–20, 2018. The event incorporated the 14 conferences/thematic areas listed on the following page.

A total of 4,373 individuals from academia, research institutes, industry, and governmental agencies from 76 countries submitted contributions, and 1,170 papers and 195 posters have been included in the proceedings. These contributions address the latest research and development efforts and highlight the human aspects of design and use of computing systems. The contributions thoroughly cover the entire field of human-computer interaction, addressing major advances in knowledge and effective use of computers in a variety of application areas. The volumes constituting the full set of the conference proceedings are listed in the following pages.

I would like to thank the program board chairs and the members of the program boards of all thematic areas and affiliated conferences for their contribution to the highest scientific quality and the overall success of the HCI International 2018 conference.

This conference would not have been possible without the continuous and unwavering support and advice of the founder, Conference General Chair Emeritus and Conference Scientific Advisor Prof. Gavriel Salvendy. For his outstanding efforts, I would like to express my appreciation to the communications chair and editor of *HCI International News*, Dr. Abbas Moallem.

July 2018                                                                 Constantine Stephanidis

# HCI International 2018 Thematic Areas
# and Affiliated Conferences

Thematic areas:

- Human-Computer Interaction (HCI 2018)
- Human Interface and the Management of Information (HIMI 2018)

Affiliated conferences:

- 15th International Conference on Engineering Psychology and Cognitive Ergonomics (EPCE 2018)
- 12th International Conference on Universal Access in Human-Computer Interaction (UAHCI 2018)
- 10th International Conference on Virtual, Augmented, and Mixed Reality (VAMR 2018)
- 10th International Conference on Cross-Cultural Design (CCD 2018)
- 10th International Conference on Social Computing and Social Media (SCSM 2018)
- 12th International Conference on Augmented Cognition (AC 2018)
- 9th International Conference on Digital Human Modeling and Applications in Health, Safety, Ergonomics, and Risk Management (DHM 2018)
- 7th International Conference on Design, User Experience, and Usability (DUXU 2018)
- 6th International Conference on Distributed, Ambient, and Pervasive Interactions (DAPI 2018)
- 5th International Conference on HCI in Business, Government, and Organizations (HCIBGO)
- 5th International Conference on Learning and Collaboration Technologies (LCT 2018)
- 4th International Conference on Human Aspects of IT for the Aged Population (ITAP 2018)

# Conference Proceedings Volumes Full List

1. LNCS 10901, Human-Computer Interaction: Theories, Methods, and Human Issues (Part I), edited by Masaaki Kurosu
2. LNCS 10902, Human-Computer Interaction: Interaction in Context (Part II), edited by Masaaki Kurosu
3. LNCS 10903, Human-Computer Interaction: Interaction Technologies (Part III), edited by Masaaki Kurosu
4. LNCS 10904, Human Interface and the Management of Information: Interaction, Visualization, and Analytics (Part I), edited by Sakae Yamamoto and Hirohiko Mori
5. LNCS 10905, Human Interface and the Management of Information: Information in Applications and Services (Part II), edited by Sakae Yamamoto and Hirohiko Mori
6. LNAI 10906, Engineering Psychology and Cognitive Ergonomics, edited by Don Harris
7. LNCS 10907, Universal Access in Human-Computer Interaction: Methods, Technologies, and Users (Part I), edited by Margherita Antona and Constantine Stephanidis
8. LNCS 10908, Universal Access in Human-Computer Interaction: Virtual, Augmented, and Intelligent Environments (Part II), edited by Margherita Antona and Constantine Stephanidis
9. LNCS 10909, Virtual, Augmented and Mixed Reality: Interaction, Navigation, Visualization, Embodiment, and Simulation (Part I), edited by Jessie Y. C. Chen and Gino Fragomeni
10. LNCS 10910, Virtual, Augmented and Mixed Reality: Applications in Health, Cultural Heritage, and Industry (Part II), edited by Jessie Y. C. Chen and Gino Fragomeni
11. LNCS 10911, Cross-Cultural Design: Methods, Tools, and Users (Part I), edited by Pei-Luen Patrick Rau
12. LNCS 10912, Cross-Cultural Design: Applications in Cultural Heritage, Creativity, and Social Development (Part II), edited by Pei-Luen Patrick Rau
13. LNCS 10913, Social Computing and Social Media: User Experience and Behavior (Part I), edited by Gabriele Meiselwitz
14. LNCS 10914, Social Computing and Social Media: Technologies and Analytics (Part II), edited by Gabriele Meiselwitz
15. LNAI 10915, Augmented Cognition: Intelligent Technologies (Part I), edited by Dylan D. Schmorrow and Cali M. Fidopiastis
16. LNAI 10916, Augmented Cognition: Users and Contexts (Part II), edited by Dylan D. Schmorrow and Cali M. Fidopiastis
17. LNCS 10917, Digital Human Modeling and Applications in Health, Safety, Ergonomics, and Risk Management, edited by Vincent G. Duffy
18. LNCS 10918, Design, User Experience, and Usability: Theory and Practice (Part I), edited by Aaron Marcus and Wentao Wang

**http://2018.hci.international/proceedings**

# 10th International Conference on Cross-Cultural Design

Program Board Chair(s): **Pei-Luen Patrick Rau, *P.R. China***

- Na Chen, P.R. China
- Zhe Chen, P.R. China
- Kuohsiang Chen, Taiwan
- Zhiyong Fu, P.R. China
- Toshikazu Kato, Japan
- Sheau-Farn Max Liang, Taiwan
- Dyi-Yih Michael Lin, Taiwan
- Juifeng Lin, Taiwan
- Rungtai Lin, Taiwan
- Cheng-Hung Lo, P.R. China
- Yongqi Lou, P.R. China
- Liang Ma, P.R. China
- Alexander Mädche, Germany
- Katsuhiko Ogawa, Japan
- Chun-Yi (Danny) Shen, Taiwan
- Hao Tan, P.R. China
- P.L. Teh, Malaysia
- Yuan-Chi Tseng, Taiwan
- Lin Wang, South Korea
- Hsiu-Ping Yueh, Taiwan

The full list with the Program Board Chairs and the members of the Program Boards of all thematic areas and affiliated conferences is available online at:

**http://www.hci.international/board-members-2018.php**

# HCI International 2019

The 21st International Conference on Human-Computer Interaction, HCI International 2019, will be held jointly with the affiliated conferences in Orlando, FL, USA, at Walt Disney World Swan and Dolphin Resort, July 26–31, 2019. It will cover a broad spectrum of themes related to Human-Computer Interaction, including theoretical issues, methods, tools, processes, and case studies in HCI design, as well as novel interaction techniques, interfaces, and applications. The proceedings will be published by Springer. More information will be available on the conference website: http://2019.hci.international/.

General Chair
Prof. Constantine Stephanidis
University of Crete and ICS-FORTH
Heraklion, Crete, Greece
E-mail: general_chair@hcii2019.org

**http://2019.hci.international/**

# Contents – Part I

**Cultural Differences**

**Culture, Emotions and Design**

# Contents – Part II

## Culture and Creativity

## Cross-Cultural Design for Social Change and Development

# Cross-Cultural Design Methods and Tools

# Applying Design Thinking in Real Estate Development

Li-Yu Chen[1(✉)], Wei Bi[2,3], and Yang Gao[2]

[1] Department of Interior Design, Chung Yuan Christian University, Taoyuan, Taiwan
chenly99@gmail.com
[2] Graduate School of Creative Industry Design, National Taiwan University of Arts,
New Taipei City, Taiwan
beebvv@qq.com, lukegao1991@gmail.com
[3] School of Jewellery, West Yunnan University of Applied Sciences,
Yunnan, People's Republic of China

**Abstract.** In recent years, real estate development has become an investment hotspot. However, behind the thriving development, we also notice that real estate in our country is subject to traditional development mode at present. Based on the interests of enterprises, the products are developed at a maximum estimated value. Therefore, in essence, the mode has neglected the important value of the design. The traditional development mode tends to be problematic and flawed. "Design-oriented" real estate development mode boasts the advantages of wide–range applicability, short time and fast replication. In other industries, the "design-oriented" development mode is not yet highly appreciated and widely used because of its current lack of in-depth understanding and awareness. As China's real estate industry leader, Vanke started early to explore the "design-oriented" development mode and this strategy gradually becomes clear in the challenging exploration. Through the actual cases of "design-oriented" development mode, the direction of a new real estate development mode is further verified to offer reference to other real estate companies in the future development process. In this way, "design" as the dominant means can essentially improve the development problems like waste of resources, inferior product quality, prolonged construction period and reduced design benefits, then give full play to the leading role of "design" in real estate development.

**Keywords:** Applying design thinking · Real estate development
Vanke Real Estate Co.

## 1 Preface

As we all know, the real estate industry has always been "the sunrise industry forever", which is an important force for our country's economic development. However, due to its recent rapid development, there have been a number of disadvantages, which brings difficulties to our real estate development. Information from the National Bureau of Statistics shows that since 2007, due to the improper real estate development mode, the resulting precarious situation is deteriorating year by year. It's mainly caused by

© Springer International Publishing AG, part of Springer Nature 2018
P.-L. P. Rau (Ed.): CCD 2018, LNCS 10911, pp. 3–17, 2018.
https://doi.org/10.1007/978-3-319-92141-9_1

superficial market analysis, neglected actual needs of consumers, inferiorly designed products, low products standardization, inferior building quality, low technical innovation of building, irrational design management and failure in forming economies of scale. Due to these problems, the development of China's real estate industry has been severely restricted.

At present, most domestic researches on real estate development mode center on management and sales and most of the research results mainly focus on procedural real estate management, scientific decision-making, specialized marketing and profit maximization to put forward reform and make adjustment, but rarely reflect on real estate development mode from the "design" perspective.

In such a severe situation, some real estate enterprises also put forward their own decisions to change the traditional development mode. However, most enterprises still rely on the traditional mode for improvement without any in-depth innovation. Vanke Real Estate Co., Ltd. (hereinafter referred to as: Vanke Real Estate) has gone deep in the study and found its own road to reform. It constantly improves and changes its traditional development model, and gradually transforms to "design-oriented" real estate development mode. It is this essential shift that makes Vanke's real estate development mode unique in the industry, far ahead of other real estate developers.

As a pioneer of real estate based on the "design-oriented" development mode, Vanke Real Estate has explored and researched a lot based on "design-oriented" and has continuously stepped up its research efforts in recent years. As the first "design-oriented" product developed by Vanke Real Estate, "City Garden" series has also proved correct in Vanke's real estate reform through its successful replication and promotion. The "City Garden" series is being extensively replicated throughout the country in this development mode and several projects have successfully replicated it (Fig. 1). This success marks that Vanke Real Estate's "design-oriented" real estate development mode is worth the recognition and learning by other businesses. Vanke Real Estate will also fully implement it in all its future products to explore and improve this "design-oriented" real estate development mode. However, this exploration is time-consuming and requires perseverance and effort.

**Fig. 1.** Vanke Research Center (source: self-photography, Vanke real estate official website)

Vanke Real Estate's "design-oriented" development mode is based on the "Six Design and Research Centers (hereinafter referred to as: Six Centers)" - design management center, design and industrialization center, design and standardization center, technology research and development center, new products R&D center and theory promotion center - as the core and decision-making in development. In reality, these "six centers" rely on each other and collaborate, making the concept of "design orientation" throughout the entire project development process.

Faced with the increasingly fierce competition in real estate market, real estate developers are also beginning to concentrate on improving their previous development model, thus enhancing their steady and rapid development in current real estate market with the fierce competition. In such situation, Vanke Real Estate adheres to the development mode of real estate from the "design-oriented" perspective and establishes its own "six centers" and puts "design" concept throughout the entire real estate development process. "Design-oriented" real estate development mode is constantly improving its design management, design standardization, industrial design, new products and technology research. Therefore, China's real estate development mode develops in accordance with the traditional mode. In the face of the bottleneck now, the use of "design" to integrate is an inevitable trend of China's real estate development mode with reference value (Fig. 2).

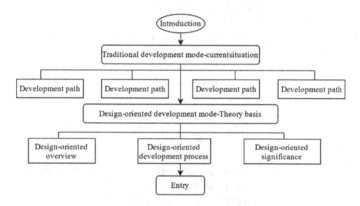

**Fig. 2.** Main research framework of the paper

## 2  Discussion of Traditional Real Estate Development Mode

Throughout the country, the traditional real estate development mode in real estate market progresses gradually. This mode begins to show various disadvantages in the fierce competition: such as the lack of design management, economies of scale, design specialization, design standardization, industrial design and many other factors, resulting in the severely restricted development of real estate enterprises. The main types of traditional development mode are as follows (Table 1):

**Table 1.** Types of real estate development mode

| Types of development mode | Characteristics | Representative enterprise |
|---|---|---|
| Longitudinal integration | Advantages: All-in-one service of construction, decoration, property management from a company. Disadvantages: Blind pursuit of profit maximization, blind development that lead to loss of development focus, deny the importance of design | R&F Properties |
| Mixed | Advantages: With the conceptual real estate, composite real estate, themed real estate as the starting point, house properties as vehicle, a variety of industries (agriculture, commerce, tourism, ecology, sports, education, science and technology) are integrated to create a new real estate operation mode. Disadvantages: lack of product reproducibility, deviation from the future real estate industrialization and standardized mode | Jinye Real Estate Development Co., Ltd. |
| Improvement and accumulation | Advantages: Through conceptualizing the house property from the original purpose of residence, finish a project then start anew, projects are operated individually. Disadvantages: Blind emphasis on sale restricts real estate development | Qifu, Everbright, Jinbi Real Estate |
| Innovation and market segmentation | Advantages: Well-built and quality-oriented. Pay attention to speed and innovation, individualization, clear target customers. Disadvantages: Narrow customer group, showy product characteristics and lack of overall consistency | Modern City, Times Property |

Based on this, we can clearly understand the current common types of real estate development mode in China, clarify all relevant aspects of its development and then grasp the dominant idea of each development mode and the fundamental development knowledge.

## 2.1 General Process of Real Estate Development Mode

In the era of rapid real estate development, more and more enterprises are involved in real estate development. However, no matter how complex the development is, the basic steps of the real estate development process must be followed. From investment to completion of property, the logical development procedures must be followed. However, with the advancement of the times and the continuous development of science and technology, innovation should be added to the original steps in each development mode. For example, Vanke Real Estate adds "design" as the prerequisite of each step based on the traditional development mode, which results in the excellent quality of the designed products.

If a single traditional development mode is used to discuss real estate development steps, it will be easy to neglect the importance of "design" in it. The traditional development mode is basically based on the following mode:

Stage one: investment opportunities search and screening. On the basis of deep understanding and occupation of much local market information, the developers explore the possibility of investment and seek more available investment opportunities in the market.

Stage two: Refine the investment program. Developers choose the land to be developed to explore the feasibility of the design and make a relative preliminary plan design of feasibility and then further explore the feasibility report of developing land.

Stage three: Design feasibility study. Real estate developers conduct a formal market research, preliminary estimates of market absorption rate and determine the feasibility of the project from the legal, technical and economic aspects.

Stage four: Contract negotiation and signing. Real estate developers based on market research and customer needs to finalize the program design and then negotiate the contract with developers, clarify the lease side of the contract and obtain government land, planning permits.

Stage five: Construction. According to the budget, the real estate developers conduct preliminary real estate cost control, approve the marketing and change the project demands proposed by development team, make the early payment of the project and promote the progress management program of the construction.

Stage six: Completion and use. Real estate developers are responsible for organizing property management team, marketing it and obtaining the approval of government for occupancy and the owner occupancy.

## 2.2 Problems in the Traditional Development Mode

With the constant reform of real estate industry in recent years and blind pursuit of the maximized commercial profits, real estate development has caused many problems. For example, in the development, the design products advantage of it is not established, the important role of "design" in the real estate development mode is neglected and the research on real estate standardization and industrialization is not perfect, which results in many problems exposed in the product design and construction in the development process.

The inappropriate development mode leads to the high energy consumption in real estate development process, low productivity of commercial housing, delayed construction period, high risk of construction. At this point, through the analysis from the "design-oriented" real estate development mode, it is concluded that there are some problems in the overall development of real estate in China. The problems are mainly manifested as follows:

(1) The analysis on real estate market fails to further explore: In the real estate industry development, market analysis is the basis of the entire business acquisition and plays a decisive role for determining the feasibility of real estate projects. If developers go directly to the design when they obtain the plot, instead of digging into what kind of "design products" are suitable for today's market, it directly neglects the in-depth understanding of the market.

(2) Neglect the customer demands: Most of our real estate enterprises have neglected the demand of customers, especially the individual needs. At present, the real estate investment return rate is significantly higher than other industry returns. As a result, many investors hold excessive expectation on the profits when operating projects, so that the market considers less about the demands of customers. The most concern lies in the sales of houses developed, followed by the profits earned. Others are all neglected.

As the customers remain relatively rational when purchasing the property, in addition to the price factor, they tend to pursue the quality of the product with design. If this cannot be satisfied, the results are obvious. In addition to quality, the symbol of individualization and quality of design products is also the goal pursued by customers. The vast majority of real estate companies in China find it difficult to manage it. However, Vanke Real Estate achieved it as it firmly adheres to the customer-oriented and "design"-oriented development mode, which makes Vanke unique in the real estate industry.

(3) Neglect the role of design standardization: Design standardization plays an important core role in real estate and saves cost from the design standardization. The lack of residential standardization system is the shortcoming of most of the current real estate. Most of the real estates fail to focus on product standardization and management standardization and so on, resulting in product variability, so that design costs soar. However, Vanke Real Estate takes product standardization as the core and top priority of corporate research. The excellent efficacy of Vanke Real Estate in management, products, services standardization enables the businesses to get more profits.

(4) Lack of professional design industrial research: At present, China's industrial research in real estate industry is minimal and real estate industrialization takes the demand for the product construction market as design orientation, design, materials, standardization as basis, factory mass production as the main mode of production.

However, in our country, the systematic research of real estate enterprises is still in its infancy, which fails to form a corresponding system of research and fails to fully develop industrial system. As a result, China's real estate product design and industrialization lags behind and fails to form a complete set of technology industrialization system.

(5) Backward technology research: Due to differences in the level of economic development around the different regions, the maturity of building technology has large difference and real estate is an industry with wide coverage, high correlation and the use of social resources. Developers' blind pursuit of speed in development projects makes it hard to guarantee the quality of houses. At present, there are still a few enterprises that insist on doing technical research which takes a long process.

In China, dangerous events due to nonconforming house quality occur every year. However, although the quality of some projects is high, the speed remains average, resulting in the slow return of funds and the inefficient use of funds. Only by accelerating technological research can we better solve the problems caused by building technology. Through technology upgrading, the construction cycle will be greatly shortened and the level of construction technology will be improved.

From the above problems, it can be seen that at present, we cannot stand out only by sales and advertisement. At the moment, China's real estate industry must rethink the existing real estate development mode problem and thus changing the direction of its development mode. It should also realize that in the future development, "design" will gradually move to the leading position and bring new impetus and direction to the real estate industry.

# 3 Design-Oriented Real Estate Development Mode

"Design-oriented" development mode was first proposed by Abernathy and Utter back in the design of industrial products before it's successfully replicated in the enterprise. "Design-oriented" development mode gradually penetrates into various industries and plays an important role in the real estate industry. "Design-oriented" mode has significantly changed the traditional real estate development mode and has a significant impact on the real estate development steps so as to promote the development of the real estate industry into a new era.

## 3.1 Design-Oriented Real Estate Development Mode Process

The core issue of the real estate development mode is to solve a complex, comprehensive and long-term development process that needs to address a wide range of issues arising from many development processes. The traditional development mode process is often described as developers obtain a piece of land, hire a "designer" before hiring sales planning expert for promotion. While the "design-oriented" real estate development mode is described as "product design" comes first before obtaining land to develop a series of feasible "design products" and combine it with the particularity in the specific projects and apply these characteristics in each single design programs and detailed design in the details design. Therefore, this "design-oriented" development mode has the advantages of a wide range, short time and fast replication.

The "design-oriented" development mode is not a one-way advancement in the real estate development process, but a hand-in-hand, three-dimensional and complete process concept. In this development mode, developers should timely integrate a variety of design content in advance to achieve an ideal state. For example, the research speed of new products, the rationality of the company's design and management, the design standard formulation, the convergence of design commercialization, the research results of new technologies in the technology research center, the actual state of implementation, the construction efforts of factories, the actual use in products, the final product industrial chain development and the establishment of final theoretical study to a nationwide replication and promotion. These development processes are different from the traditional mode of the development process. Only by properly linking these steps can we effectively implement the "design-oriented" real estate development mode.

"Design-oriented" development mode requires real estate enterprises to have a certain degree of co-ordination, integration, integration capabilities. To run the mode in enterprise, it should always put "design" as the core throughout the process and follow the development process to deepen the product (Fig. 3).

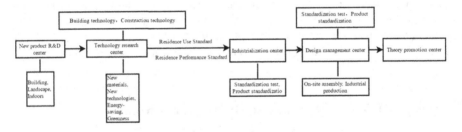

**Fig. 3.** Design-oriented standard process

(1) First, determine the basic content of real estate development. If possible, establish the enterprises' "residence use standards", "residential performance standards", "new product research" and other pre-development research and requirements and then further improve and transit to actual projects.

(2) Second, carry out product standardization of management, design, engineering of enterprise in light of the development of enterprise. Only by establishing a standardized system can enterprises achieve maturity, reduce unnecessary waste and standardize their own enterprises. Vanke Real Estate follows the standardization of housing to achieve the standardization of residential product system, while forming standardized design and design management system. Standardized residential product design and design management system are based on current market customer base and the actual need and continue to deepen understanding of the market and design requirements for product positioning and comprehensive upgrading.

(3) Thirdly, set up the relevant departments to study the product new technologies and products industrialized manufacturing. Through industrial transformation, real

estate development will become a standard process for digital lean management and it is a scalable, reproducible, sustainable and streamlined construction program that carries out industrialized manufacturing with standardization.

(4) In addition, after achievement of industrialized manufacturing, carry out integration of product series and overall combination of standardization and industrialized manufacturing, so that the "design" is merged in the "design-oriented" development mode and can be applied to the entire real estate development mode.

(5) Finally, under the condition of mature standardization and industrialization, the theoretical research is carried out and the feasible series of "design-oriented" development mode theory is put forward to fully replicate and promote the products so as to reduce the resources waste and improper development efforts brought by the development mode.

Only by managing the links among each step, focusing on "design-oriented" development mode process can design-oriented mode be gradually approached and ultimately improve development mode continuously.

## 3.2  Importance of Design-Oriented Real Estate Development Mode

In the future real estate development mode, real estate enterprises focus on "design-oriented" development mode to develop products and its important necessity can be presented from the following aspects:

(1) From the development environment, the real estate product can be described as a microcosm of the city and society. Its level of development and construction reflects the local people's pursuit of life and culture. It is an important benchmark for the development of social material civilization and spiritual civilization. In addition, people spend most of the time in residential area. Its design features, building quality are related to people's physical and mental health and safety. Therefore, improving the level of real estate development and improving the real estate development mode are of great social significance.

(2) Shorten the construction cycle, improve yield. With the substantial increase in land costs, the deepening of 7090, the policy of price-capped housing and threat of meager profits of real estate, the threshold for real estate access is getting higher and higher, making it increasingly difficult for SMEs to survive. With the rapid expansion of scale, the difficulty in design and construction will surely increase. It is possible to achieve rapid growth under limited conditions by adopting a "design-oriented" development mode to improve construction efficiency and construction time.

(3) The impact of "design" on the market is immeasurable. At this stage, emphasis on the "design" has become the basic idea of today's developers and a sound design system has become an important bargaining chip of real estate industry in the diversity competition.

(4) From the standardization, industrialization perspective, "design-oriented" development promotes resource integration, improves the efficiency of real estate development. One-time "design", factory-like production have brought insurmountable

quality problem of the design and construction. In the future, after all-round construction and implementation of industrialization, construction of houses and sale of houses are just like the purchasing in IKEA. The components are uniform standards and the building structure can be easily assembled. The assembly can be completed easily.

As the standardization and industrialization under "design-oriented" mode of development are the assembly of buildings and combination of components to some extent, it will be easier and convenient to manage, thus saving a lot of resources. Mature replication is conducive to ensuring the design level and reducing development risk.

(5)  From the sales level, the "design-oriented" development mode and the project success are directly linked. "Design-oriented" development mode can be designed to enhance the quality of products in essence and lay basis for achieving good performance in sales process of design products so that products constitute product line and form design brand benefits to increase the added value of design products.

(6)  From the profit point of view, "design-oriented" mode of development greatly reduces the cost of development, saves considerable funds for the project compared with previous construction methods. However, the real estate industry is a capital-intensive industry. The capital turnover rate and the speed of capital recovery play a decisive role. The "design-oriented" development mode can quickly improve the construction speed, which is directly related to the recovery of funds to enhance the efficiency of real estate (Fig. 4).

**Fig. 4.**  Residential industrialization implementation site

### 3.3  "Design-Oriented" Development Mode in Vanke Real Estate

"Making a house like building a car" is the dream of Wang Shi, chairman of Vanke Real Estate. Now this dream is gradually becoming clear in the difficult exploration.

As a leader enterprise in China real estate industry, Vanke Real Estate has long explored the "design-oriented" development mode and stepped up research efforts in recent years. The replication and promotion of its design products Vanke "City Garden" mark that the Vanke Real Estate has completed the initial exploration with "design-oriented" development mode. Nowadays, Vanke Real Estate is still continuing to study and improve its "design-oriented" real estate development mode. In the future, the "design-oriented" product development mode will be fully realized in Vanke Real Estate enterprises.

As a pioneer in the "design-oriented" development mode, Vanke Real Estate has persisted in using "design techniques" for many years to solve problems in real estate development and continuously explored and perfected the work. As early as November 1994, Vanke Real Estate set up a design platform for close communication with design units—Wanchuang Architectural Design Consultants Co., Ltd. to further refine design product competitiveness from the design. In 1998, a design engineering department was formed and a building research center was set up under the design engineering department. Vanke Real Estate at this time focused on the details of consumer demand and product design itself and greatly adjusted "design-oriented" mode. With the further specialization of Vanke Real Estate, in 2001, the design engineering department was further improved and the design engineering department was recomposed of design department and project management department. In 2002, Vanke Real Estate took the lead to start the housing industrialization, standardized production scale exploration nationwide. These are all researches carried out around "design".

With the unremitting efforts, Vanke Real Estate gradually clarifies a set of process to promote the construction industry and development with design, emphasizes the coordinated operation, so that the development process tends to simplified, industrial standardization, design controllable system. Therefore, "design-oriented" development mode further develops and strengthens in the Vanke Real Estate and becomes leading development mode system. Vanke Real Estate has always input "80% of the energy to do 20% of the products," spent lots of research and development efforts to design products to ensure the leading place of Vanke Real Estate in the industry. It is also the emphasis of Vanke Real Estate on the design and the accurate mastery that leads Vanke Real Estate to successfully explore "design-oriented" real estate development mode. At the same time, it also promotes the "design-oriented" development mode to be identified in Vanke Real Estate.

In order to further develop and improve the "design-oriented" development mode, Vanke Real Estate has preliminarily subdivided the "design-oriented" mode into six core components and set up six corresponding research centers - design management center and new products R&D center, technology research center, design standardization center, industrialization center, theory promotion center. These "six major centers" all focus on "design" as a prerequisite for research and exploration of real estate development. However, these "six major design research centers" are not "design" in the traditional sense, nor "design" that can be replaced by design institutes.

The core development functions of the "six major centers" in the "design-oriented" development mode in the real estate project development process are as follows:

(1) Design management center: that is, for the whole process tracking of each project design, use "design" to guide and manage the entire project design development and construction process.

(2) New product R&D center: To solve the relationship between Vanke Real Estate and customers and professional architects, the key point is to redesign a customer-oriented design-oriented design product system in the way of "design" according to customer needs and market demands, which covers the design of product

innovation and new product design as a whole, finally formulates feasible new product design report (Fig. 5).

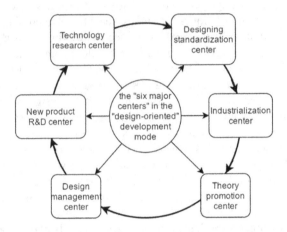

**Fig. 5.** Six design-oriented development modes

(3) Technology research center: Vanke Real Estate is researching the application of new materials, new technologies, energy saving and green environment in residential buildings. It puts forward the design-oriented research on materials, technology, energy conservation and green environmental protection to reduce the troubles caused by technology and work hard to improve the quality and technology of design products.

(4) Designing standardization center: The purpose of Vanke's establishment of this center is to start research on the premise of "design-oriented" development mode, to provide standard procedures and systems for the possibility of housing construction, and to establish a standardized and modeled modern design patterns that can be continuously developed, to achieve the simple programming and unity of product in the design and construction process.

(5) Industrialization center: On the basis of the standardized mode, carry out factory mass production on residential products and components. Through industrialization, products can be connected, replicated and promoted, so that product efficiency and quality are improved and guaranteed.

(6) Theory promotion center: Through the residence problems obtained from the successful cases developed by Vanke Real Estate, from the "design" point of view, it can solve the problem effectively and finally form the feasibility development system of Vanke Real Estate itself: "design-oriented" development mode, and then replicate and promote it nationwide (Fig. 6).

Vanke Real Estate "six centers" ideas are guiding the realization of "design-oriented" development mode, mainly from several aspects: First, solve the complex problems in the development process to make it simple through the design. Second, achieve the standardization of design, establish relevant design standardization and system to set prerequisite for industrialization through the research of new product design; third,

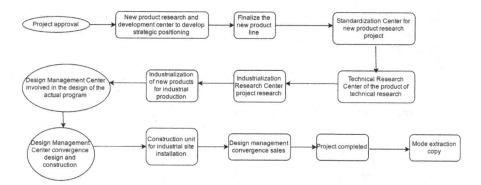

**Fig. 6.** Development model process

gradually realize the production and industrialization through standardized design, thus promoting the development of the industry, promoting industrialization. Fourth, apply the latest design forms to reflect the contemporary real estate product design. Finally, carry out theoretical research on product and carry out design management implementation and replication nationwide.

## 4   Conclusion

After years of strategic practice, Vanke Real Estate has preliminarily established a "design-oriented" development mode and taken "design strategy" as the core to gradually form its own development theory system, to give full play to commercial advantages and realize the rational allocation of resources. Vanke Real Estate's mature "design" theory also makes it a leader in the domestic real estate industry in the long run. "Design-oriented" mode of development will be the future development trend of the real estate industry. At present, in light of the current situation in China, the following issue need to be addressed to vigorously promote this mode:

(1) Expand coverage

"Design-oriented" development mode is applied in Vanke Real Estate to certain extent, but it's not popular in other real estate companies. The important reason for this is that the "design-oriented" research mainly focuses on the real estate enterprises like Vanke Real Estate, which has its own testing base. For other real estate companies without "design-oriented" development mode, the problem lies in only focusing on the current large investment and slow return, which leads to failure to actually establish the corresponding design research process in enterprises.

(2) Correct design awareness

Some enterprises assume that "design-oriented" is to manage "design" well, which is only suitable for the application of real estate development mode in a certain stage. In other aspects, the application will not have much effect, so that the mode can't be understood and applied in reality. Most real estate companies believe that the implementation of a "good design" is equal to the implementation of the "design-oriented" mode, so they fail to make any adjustment and improvement on the existing design methods and simply make good "design", ultimately failing to achieve the desired effect.

(3) Mechanical application

"Design-oriented" mode requires a certain degree of corporate awareness. When applying the mode, the real estate enterprises in our country fail to have a deep understanding of "design-oriented" and their specific application environment. Instead, they apply mechanically or in isolation, then the promotion of the development mode is just a mere formality.

(4) Lack of overall consistency

Many real estate enterprises in our country are divided by functional departments in implementation of design, project management, technological transformation and market research. They even set up specialized leading bodies, which is against the normal development of enterprises. The above work should be integrated with the "design" to form a unified enterprise process, establish the enterprise's norms of "design-oriented" development. Through continuous efforts and dedication to improve, the performance of the enterprise can be finally improved.

In short, the "design-oriented" real estate development mode in China is in the ascendant, plays a good supplementary role for the real estate companies with good prospects and great market potential, which is the new beacon for future development of real estate enterprises.

## References

1. Barthes, R.: Elements of Semiology. Macmillan, London (1977)
2. Fell, J.P.: The phenomenological approach to emotion. In: Emotion. Brooks/Cole, Monterey (1977)
3. Gamble, T.K., Gamble, M.W.: Interpersonal Communication: Building Connections Together. SAGE Publications, Thousand Oaks (2013)
4. Hillman, J.: Emotion. Routledge & Kegan Paul, London (1960)
5. Han, C.Y.: Image Communication. Wiseman, Taipei (2005)
6. Hsu, C.-H., Lin, C.-L., Lin, R.: A study of framework and process development for cultural product design. In: Rau, P.L.P. (ed.) IDGD 2011. LNCS, vol. 6775, pp. 55–64. Springer, Heidelberg (2011). https://doi.org/10.1007/978-3-642-21660-2_7
7. Huang, M.F.: Application of pet therapy to healing style design: a case study of LINE stickers design. (Unpublished master's thesis). Department of National Taipei University of Technology, Taipei (2004)
8. Kreifeldt, J., Lin, R., Chuang, M.-C.: The importance of "Feel" in product design feel, the neglected aesthetic "DO NOT TOUCH". In: Rau, P.L.P. (ed.) IDGD 2011. LNCS, vol. 6775, pp. 312–321. Springer, Heidelberg (2011). https://doi.org/10.1007/978-3-642-21660-2_35
9. Lin, R., Sun, M.-X., Chang, Y.-P., Chan, Y.-C., Hsieh, Y.-C., Huang, Y.-C.: Designing "Culture" into modern product: a case study of cultural product design. In: Aykin, N. (ed.) UI-HCII 2007, Part I. LNCS, vol. 4559, pp. 146–153. Springer, Heidelberg (2007). https://doi.org/10.1007/978-3-540-73287-7_19
10. Lin, R.: Cultural creativity, value-added design. Art Apprec. 1(7), 26–32 (2004)

11. Norman, D.A.: Emotional Design: Why We Love (or Hate) Everyday Things. Basic Books, New York (2004)
12. Norman, D.A.: The Design of Everyday Things: Revised and Expanded Edition. Basic Books, New York (2013)
13. Strongman, K.T.: The Psychology of Emotion from Everyday Life to Theory. John Wiley and Sons, Chichester (2003)

# User Defined Eye Movement-Based Interaction for Virtual Reality

Wen-jun Hou[1,2], Kai-xiang Chen[1,2(✉)], Hao Li[1,2], and Hu Zhou[1,2]

[1] School of Digital Media and Design Arts,
Beijing University of Posts and Telecommunications, Beijing 100876, China
noideaser@163.com
[2] Beijing Key Laboratory of Network Systems and Network Culture,
Beijing University of Posts and Telecommunications, Beijing 100876, China

**Abstract.** Most of the applications of eye movement-based interaction in VR are limited to blinking and gaze at present, however, gaze gestures were neglected. Therefore, the potential of eye movement-based interaction in VR is far from being realized. In addition, many scholars tried to define some special eye movements as input instructions, but these definitions are almost always empirical and neglect users' habits and cultural background. In this paper, we focus on how Chinese users interact in VR using eye movements without relying on a graphical user interface. We present a guessability study focusing on intuitive eye movement-based interaction of common commands in 30 tasks of 3 categories in VR. A total of 360 eye movements were collected from 12 users and a consensus set of eye movements in VR that best met user's cognition was obtained. This set can be applied to the design of eye movement-based interaction in VR to help designers to develop user-centered and intuitive eye movement-based interaction in VR. Meanwhile this set can be migrated to other interactive media and user interfaces, such as a Post-WIMP interface base on eye movement-based interaction, as a reference to design.

**Keywords:** Eye movement-based interaction · Gaze gesture · Virtual reality
Guessability · Intuitive interaction

## 1 Introduction

With the advent of multiple screen devices such as VR devices, interaction between human and computer has become more and more frequent and complex. Many interaction techniques in VR appearing with much challenge, most of whom have obvious disadvantages including low input bandwidth, weak adaptability and far away from natural interaction. Thanks to eye-tracking technology, eye movement-based interaction which can meet the requirements of VR interface design well is becoming more and more reliable. Nevertheless, there still exist some contradictions we still need to fix, for example, most of the applications of eye movement-based interaction in VR are limited to blinking and gaze at present, however, Gaze gestures was neglected. Therefore, the potential of eye movement-based interaction in VR is far from being realized. In

© Springer International Publishing AG, part of Springer Nature 2018
P.-L. P. Rau (Ed.): CCD 2018, LNCS 10911, pp. 18–30, 2018.
https://doi.org/10.1007/978-3-319-92141-9_2

addition, many scholars tried to define some special eye movements as input instructions, but these definitions are almost always empirical and neglected users' habits and cultural background. Therefore, this article focuses on studying intuitive eye movements that provide intuitive interaction between the real world and the VR world.

## 2   Related Work

### 2.1   Interaction in VR

The development of VR interaction technology is in its infancy, there hasn't any mature solution about how to design easy-to-use VR interaction. Different enterprises have different solutions. Some try to define VR interaction using traditional interactions, such as remote control, binding handle and touchpad. Others try to combine some new and natural interaction, such as gesture interaction and voice interaction [1].

However, these current popular VR interactions are neither natural nor easy-to-use, most of which can only be used in some special scenarios. Furthermore, most of these interaction methods simply replace keyboard-mouse operation on PC or the touch-screen operation on mobile devices. Most VR interfaces design is based on WIMP interface, but WIMP interfaces have many disadvantages that can service VR well. In a nutshell, there are still many problems when design VR interactions worth exploring.

Because of its advantages of high bandwidth, naturalness, clean, etc., eye movement-based interaction gradually began to show its heads. As early as 1993, Jacob had compared the eye movement-based interaction in VR with other three-dimensional interaction techniques and found that eye movement-based interaction is superior to other interaction techniques of pointing in most scenarios [2].

In general, if we want to improve the usability of AR interactions so that VR can reach more people, there is a way that we focus on improving or inventing new input mechanism of eye movement-based interaction for VR.

### 2.2   Eye Movement-Based Interaction

Studies have shown that there are three modes of eye movement, gazing, saccade and smooth pursuit [3]. Gazing is the process of aligning the foveal area of eyes with a particular object. In general, the fixation time is greater than 100 ms, which is usually 200–600 ms [4], Jacob defined that a gaze input is 1000 ms in order to avoid misuse [5]. Saccade is a rapid beating of the eyeball between two fixation points and lasts for 30 ms to 120 ms. A single saccade can cover a viewing angle of 1° to 40°, usually between 15° and 20°, with a maximum speed of 400–600°/s [6]. Hyrskykari began to use saccade as a new input type which is called gaze gesture [7]. Smooth pursuit refers to the continuous movement of the eyeball with the moving target, which is only generated during the tracking of the moving target. For rest targets, there is only eye movements. The purpose of a smooth pursuit is to keep the image of the moving target near the foveal area with a maximum speed of 30°/s [8].

Eye movement-based interaction is actually recorded through the device and identify the specific mode of eye movements as the input signal to control the specific task.

Blinking, gaze and saccade these three eye movements are usually used as an input signal that is called blinking input, gaze input and gaze gesture input in Human-computer interaction. Table 1 shows the difference between blinking input, gazing input and gaze gesture input.

**Table 1.** Comparison between blinking input, gazing input and gaze gesture input.

| | Blinking input | Gaze input | Gaze gesture input |
|---|---|---|---|
| Parameter | Blinking duration/ Blinking frequency | Fixation duration/ Fixation field | Saccade length/ Saccade duration/ Saccade velocity |
| Bandwidth | Low | Lowest | High |
| Efficiency | Fastest | Slow | Fast |
| Demand for interfaces' time- space characteristics | High | Very high | Low |
| Naturalness | Quite natural | Natural | Not very natural |
| "Midas contact" problem | Appears often | Appears very often | Appears rarely |

Blinking input is quick and easy. But for now, limited by the development of eye movement recognition technology, it has not been widely used. The main limitations are reflected in two points. First, the awareness system can't intelligently identify the difference between physiological and unconscious blinks. The second is that the blinking itself will affect the tracking of tracking devices. Blinking's corresponding parameters are: blinking duration, blinking frequency and so on.

Gaze input is now the most popular way of eye movement-based interaction, for a relatively simple interface, it is ideal for use. However, once the interface tasks become slightly complicated, due to its high requirements on sight stability and interface time-space characteristics, user experience will exponentially decrease, including slow efficiency, easy misuse, high cost of making mistakes, and more. Gazing's corresponding parameters are: fixation duration, fixation field and so on.

Gaze gesture input is fast. Low requirements on the time-space characteristics of the interface making gaze gesture not easy to misuse. First of all, the fastest speed of saccade up to 400°–600°/s which means that Gaze gesture input can reach 1° to 40° viewing angle within 30–120 ms which is much faster than a standard gaze input unit time 300–500 ms. Secondly, as gaze gesture input does not require the interface must be presented specific interactive controls and elements, the interactive time is also relatively high robustness and it does not necessarily require an accurate response time. Interface design will be easier and faster because of the low requirements of the interface time-space characteristics. Thirdly, because gaze gesture input is based on the sequence, it does not require a precise starting point and ending point. Therefore, for the "Midas Contact" problem, gaze gesture has more advantages than blinking and gazing. Of course, the application of gaze gesture input has not yet been matured because of its own very obvious disadvantages. For example, how to design a reasonable eye movement is a very difficult research topic. If the movement is too simple, it is easy to overlap with unconscious eye movements, resulting in misuse; once too complicated, but also increase the user's learning costs, memory burden and cognitive load, contrary to the original intention of natural interaction. Gaze gesture's corresponding parameters are: saccade length, saccade duration, saccade velocity and so on.

Most of the applications of eye movement-based interaction in VR are limited to blinking and gaze at present, however, Gaze gestures was neglected. Therefore, the potential of eye movement-based interaction in VR is far from being realized. This article attempts to let go of ideas and allow users to decide on what type of eye movement-based interaction to use.

## 2.3  Intuitive Interaction

In the concept of user-centered design, intuitive design is the most important part. Cognitive psychology believes that intuitive design is the process by which people can quickly identify and deal with problems based on experience. This process is unconscious, quick and easy. Blackler's research also confirmed this process [9]. Cooper also mentioned that intuitive interface design made people quickly establish a direct connection between functions and finish tasks only by relying on the guidance from interfaces [10].

Although intuitive design helps to improve the friendliness of interaction, but there are still many limitations in the practical application process. First, whether the user-designer experience is a match. If there is a difference or misunderstanding between the user's and designer's cultural background, level of education, etc., the outcome of an intuitive design may not be truly intuitive. Second, user's experience and unconscious behavior are harder to extract and quantify and most of past research is simply a qualitative description. Most or the intuitive interaction studies comes from literature research and user interviews, so that the semantic meaning of the user's definition of input symbols may not be good because it ignores habits and cultural background of the users. So that if we want to study intuitive eye movement-based interaction in VR, we must use a more scientific and more suitable method.

The speculative method proposed by Wobbrock can solve above problem well. By building guessability and level of agreement metrics, the results of user experience are quantified and can be well used to assess the degree of instinct of action design [11]. Later, Wobbrock applied this method to the research of large touch screen interaction [12]. Due to the merits of guessability method, many researches in this field were born later. For example, Ruiz et al. Studied the guessability of gesture interactions in smartphones [13]. Vatavu et al. Studied the guessability of air gesture interactions based on television manipulations [14]. Piumsomboom et al. Studied the guessability of gestural interaction in augmented reality [15]. Japanese scholar Slipasuwanchai et al. Studied the guessability of hands and feet interaction in the game [16]. Leng et al. studied the guessability of gesture interactions in VR music applications [17].

Intuitive design is of great importance to the good application of eye movement-based interaction, especially for gaze gesture interaction which has high-bandwidth but high cognitive cost. Guessability is a good method for the research on the intuitive eye movement-based interaction which deserves to be further study.

## 3    Experiment

### 3.1    Selection of Tasks

Combined with the literature review and reference to many VR applications on the market, 30 commands and tasks were derived from typical interactions in VR. This resulted in 30 task units that were grouped into 3 categories (9 sub-categories): object control (Selection, Deselection, Movement, Rotate, Uniform scale, Editing), scene control (View point transform), and system control (Global command, Temporary command). The following Table 2 shows the list of 30 selected task units under 3 categories.

**Table 2.**    Universal operating tasks in VR.

| Category | Tasks | Task units |
|---|---|---|
| Object control | Selection | Single selection/Multiple selection/Select all |
| | Deselection | Deselection |
| | Movement | Move up/Move down/Move left/Move right/ Move forwards/Move backwards |
| | Rotate | X-axis/Y-axis/Z-axis |
| | Uniform scale | Scale up/Scale down |
| | Editing | Copy/Paste/Delete/Redo |
| Scene control | View point transform | Upward view point/Downward view point/ Leftward view point/Rightward view point/ Zoom in/Zoom out |
| System control | Global command | Open/ Close menu/ Play menu |
| | Temporary command | Accept/confirm Reject/cancel |

### 3.2    Participants and Device

12 participants (6 males and 6 females) were voluntarily recruited, ranging in age from 21 to 25 years old (mean = 23.3 years old and SD = 1.44 years). All of the participants had visual acuity or corrected visual acuity of 5.0 or above. Participants must have minimal knowledge of experiencing VR eye movement-based interaction in order to avoid the impact of their prior experience on the definition of the set of eye movements. The experimental device is HTC Vive which running on the software we set up for the experiment. A video recording device was used to record what participants had said during the experiment. Experimental staff for the experimental including an operator, a recorded and a host.

### 3.3    Procedure

Firstly, the host introduced the basic concept of VR and eye movement-based interaction to the participants. Secondly, the host introduced the details of this experiment and all of the

30 tasks to the participants. In addition, participants were required that they do not need to take technical implementation issues such as the recognition accuracy of the eye movement into consideration, just try to imagine the most suitable eye movements that were best suited to the task. Finally, the participants were asked to wear the equipment in a sitting posture and start the experiment. Figure 1 shows the specific experimental scenario.

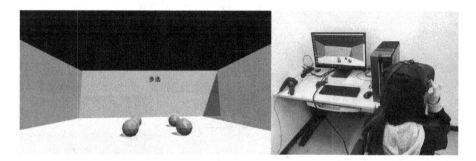

**Fig. 1.** The experimental scenario.

Participants started the experiment according to the Latin square experimental order in order to avoid interference caused by the legacy effect on the experimental results. For each experimental task, the VR equipment worn by participants was accompanied by the name of the task and an animation of the target scene to clearly convey the operation task to the participants. Target scenes were created by using Unity software and Steam VR, and finally applied to HTC Vive. Target scenes were made independent of any particular application such a football game which might influence the result.

During the experiment, participants were asked to define eye movements for 30 VR tasks. Meanwhile, a think-aloud protocol was used to let participants indicated the start and end of their performed eye movements and described the reason. A camera was set in front of the participant to record the experimental details, such as voice, for later analysis.

After each experiment, participants were also asked to immediately subjectively evaluate the performance of eye movements they defined from three indicators which are matching, easiness and fatigue: "The eye movement I performed is good match for its purpose"; "The gesture I performed is easy to perform"; "The gesture I performed is not tiring". The evaluation questionnaire was designed using Likert's 7-point scale, of which 7 for "very agree" and 1 for "very different agree." The entire experiment took about 40 min.

## 4   Results

A total of 360 eye movements were collected from 12 participants who performed 30 selected tasks. Then a consensus set of eye movements in VR that best meets user's cognition were obtained.

## 4.1 Designing User-Defined Eye Movements Set

Since different participants might defined different eye movements for a same task, the eye movements gotten from participants can't just put together and define the set. The eye movement symbols collected from the experiment can't simply be put together to form an action set, as different users may have different definitions of the input action. According

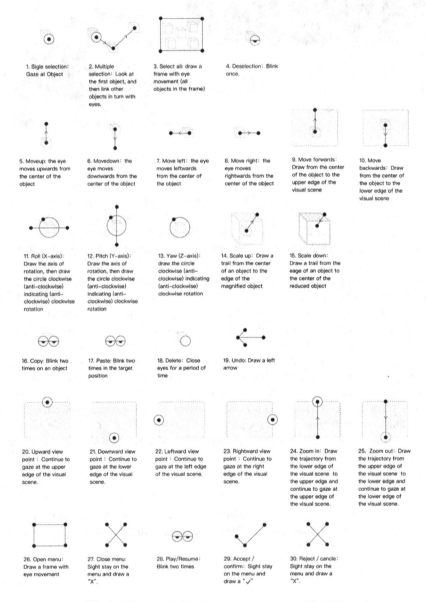

**Fig. 2.** The user-defined consensus gesture set for VR.

to guessability method, the action symbol with the highest frequency of occurrence is selected as the standard input symbol of the task, and its score is recorded as:

$$score = |symbols| \tag{1}$$

In Eq. 1, symbols are the appearance frequency of the standard input symbols, and the standard input symbols in each operation task are grouped together as a consensus set. Figure 2 shows the consensus set of eye-movement based interaction in VR acquired in this experiment.

In the consensus set, the blinking input accounted for 5/30 (closing eyes for a period of time were also taken for blinking input), the gaze input accounted for 8/30 and the gaze gesture input accounted for 20/30, of which there are 3 more complex gaze gestures using a circle symbol. It is noteworthy that there is a mixed input accounted for 3/30 in the consensus set.

$$G = \frac{\sum_{s \in S} |P_s|}{|P|} \cdot 100\% \tag{2}$$

In Eq. 2, G is the guessability score, P is the set of proposed symbols for all referents, and Ps is the set of proposed symbols using symbol s, which is a member of the resultant symbol set S. Figure 3 shows the guessability score for 30 tasks in descending order.

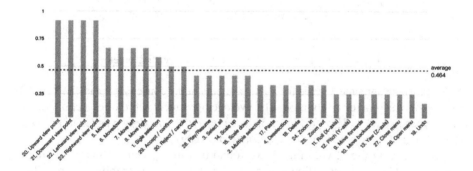

**Fig. 3.** Guessability score for 30 tasks in descending order.

The average guessability score for all movements in the consensus set is 46.39% (SD = 0.2292), which is relatively high. The average guessability score of object operation category was 40.35% (SD = 0.1673), of scene operation category was 72.22% (SD = 0.3012), and of system control was 38.33% (SD = 0.1264).

## 4.2 Level of Agreement

The agreement score was calculated by the Eq. (3) to evaluate the cognitive quality of the standard input symbols and the user group's level of awareness of the input symbols. The higher the score indicating that users can know more easily to know about what the symbols mean just by the characteristics of these symbols rather than learning these symbols. At the same time, the cognition between users is relatively close and the scattered levels of cognitive is low.

$$A = \frac{\sum_{r \in R} \sum_{P_i \in P_r} \left(\frac{|P_i|}{|P_r|}\right)^2}{|R|} \qquad (3)$$

In Eq. 3, A is the agreement score, $r$ is a referent in the set of all referents $R$, $P_r$ is the set of proposals for referent r, and $P_i$ is a subset of identical symbols from $P_r$. The range of Eq. 3 is $1/|P_r| * 100\% \leq A \leq 100\%$. The lower bound is non-zero because even when all proposals disagree, each one trivially agrees with itself. Figure 4 shows the agreement score for 30 tasks in descending order.

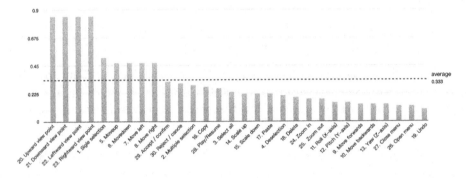

**Fig. 4.** Agreement score for 30 tasks in descending order.

The average agreement score for all movements in the consensus set is 33.27% (SD = 0.2369), which is relatively high. The average agreement score of object operation category was 26.83% (SD = 0.1394), of scene operation category was 62.50% (SD = 0.3442), and of system control was 22.69% (SD = 0.0972).

By comparing Fig. 2 with Fig. 3, we found that the agreement scores of single selection and multiple selection ranked higher than the guessability scores. The reason was that the eye movements defined by participants for these two tasks are more concentrated.

For single selection which was the most basic task in all VR scenarios (this task was also the leading task for most other tasks), the user's opinion divided into two groups that 7 users used gazing input while 5 users used blink input. For multiple selection, in addition to entering the consensus set of movement (look at the first object, and then link other objects in turn with eyes), the majority of users chose to repeat using the single action, which means blinking or gazing in turn.

Participants commonly find it hard to subconsciously think of appropriate movements to finish the task when the task is relevant with depth in the 3D scene. the design of these actions took more time during experiment. Judging from the results, the consistency levels of the movements such as zoom in, zoom out, move forwards, move backward, and the Yaw(Z-axis) were lower than those of the same category.

There were some abstract tasks such as "Undo" and "Open Menu" in the system control category and the object operation category. Though the agreement scores of these abstract movements were all lower than the others, the definitions were very similar to each other. This result indicating that these abstract movements may exist more appropriate definition. On the other hand, it may be that these abstract task instructions have a higher bandwidth of semantic, leading to different user preferences. High bandwidth of semantic for users provides more ways of movements design, which may be beneficial for users, it is worthy to go deeper to explore the definition of these abstract tasks.

### 4.3   Subjective Evaluation

In the experiment, participants were also asked to subjectively evaluate from three indicators which are matching, easiness and fatigue. For the convenience of description, we called the set which included all the standard eye movements as consensus set, and he set which included all the rest eye movements as discard set.

By comparing the consensus set and the discard set, we found that the performance of the consensus set was overall better than the other from the results of the descriptive statistics. In terms of matching indicator, the average score of consensus set is 5.61 higher than the discard set of 4.76. In terms of the easiness indicator, the average score of consensus set is 5.36 higher than the discard set of 4.88. In terms of fatigue indicator, the average score of consensus set is 5.07 higher than the discard set of 4.74. In general, the subjective evaluation of eye movements from the user-defined consensus set were better than the eye movements of the discard set (Fig. 5).

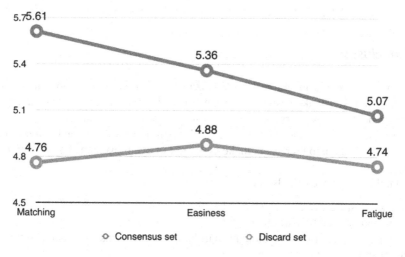

**Fig. 5.** Subjective evaluation of consensus set and discard set.

In addition, if the consensus set is classified into blinking, gaze, gaze gesture and mixed input according to the input type of eye movements, differences were found in all three indicators by the results of the descriptive statistics. As can be seen from the comparison in Fig. 6, the blinking input is optimal in terms of easiness and fatigue. The gazing input is optimal in the matching indicator, which was slightly higher than the gaze gesture input. The gaze gesture input performed well in matching but both easiness and fatigues of gaze gesture were lower than blinking and gazing, suggesting that gaze gesture interaction has great potential for intuitive design. Lastly, the mixed input is far lower than non-mixed input in terms of all indicators.

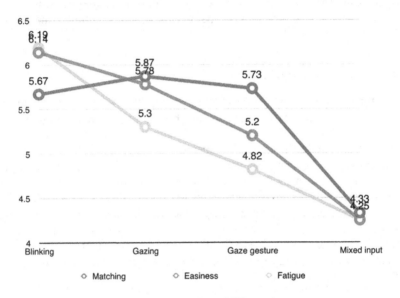

**Fig. 6.** Subjective evaluation of different input types.

## 5   Conclusion

This paper presented a guessability study focusing on intuitive eye movement-based interaction in VR. Thanks to the participants, the problem caused by the mismatch of experience between designers and users was effectively reduced, and finally a consensus set of eye movements in VR that best met user's cognition were obtained as a reference to the relevant design to help users make better use of eye movement-based interaction in VR.

From this study, we can also get these conclusions:

- The tasks that were relevant with depth in the 3D scene were more difficult to intuitive design and defined by participants.
- Participants subconsciously thought that the eye movements itself can show information about depth in 3D scene.
- Gaze gesture input for the expression of multi-dimensional information had a better overall performance.
- Abstract tasks had a higher bandwidth of semantic leading to different definitions of eye movements. These definitions are very similar to each other.

- Participants tended to repeat defining different tasks by using same simple eye movements.
- Gaze gesture input more easily led to fatigue with the eyes, so that the user always halfway changed into fuzzy input.

In the follow-up study, we will conduct a more in-depth study based on the above findings, so that the application of eye movement-based interaction in VR can be more natural and effective.

# References

1. Jerald, J., LaViola Jr., J.J., Marks, R.: VR interactions. In: ACM SIGGRAPH, Los Angeles, USA, pp. 1–105. ACM Press, New York (2017)
2. Jacob, R.J.: Eye movement-based human-computer interaction techniques: toward non-command interfaces. Adv. Hum. Comput. Interact. **4**, 151–190 (1993)
3. Haber, R.N., Hershenson, M.: The Psychology of Visual Perception, 1st edn. Holt, Rinehart & Winston, Oxford (1980)
4. Young, L.R., Sheena, D.: Survey of eye movement recording methods. Behav. Res. Methods Instrum. **7**(5), 397–429 (1975)
5. Jacob, R.J.K.: What you look at is what you get: eye movement-based interaction techniques. ACM Trans. Inf. Syst. **9**(2), 152–169 (1990)
6. Goldberg, J.H., Kotval, X.P.: Computer interface evaluation using eye movements: methods and constructs. Int. J. Ind. Ergon. **24**(6), 631–645 (1999)
7. Hyrskykari, A., Istance, H., Vickers, S.: Gaze gestures or dwell-based interaction? In: Proceedings of the Symposium on Eye Tracking Research and Applications, California, USA, pp. 229–232. ACM Press, New York (2012)
8. Shioiri, S., Cavanagh, P.: Saccadic suppression of low-level motion. Vis. Res. **29**(8), 915–928 (1989)
9. Blackler, A., Popovic, V., Mahar, D.: Investigating users' intuitive interaction with complex artefacts. Appl. Ergon. **41**(1), 72–92 (2010)
10. Cooper, A., Reimann, R., Cronin, D.: About Face 3: The Essentials of Interaction Design. Wiley Publishing, Inc., Indiana (2007)
11. Wobbrock, J.O., Aung, H.H., Rothrock, B., Myers, B.A.: Maximizing the guessability of symbolic input. In: CHI 2005 Extended Abstracts on Human Factors in Computing Systems, Portland, USA, pp. 1869–1872. ACM Press, New York (2005)
12. Wobbrock, J.O., Morris, M.R., Wilson, A.D.: User-defined gestures for surface computing. In: Proceedings of the SIGCHI Conference on Human Factors in Computing Systems, Boston, USA, pp. 1083–1092. ACM Press, New York (2009)
13. Ruiz, J., Li, Y., Lank, E.: User-defined motion gestures for mobile interaction. In: Proceedings of the SIGCHI Conference on Human Factors in Computing Systems, Vancouver, BC, Canada, pp. 197–206. ACM Press, New York (2011)
14. Vatavu, R.D.: User-defined gestures for free-hand TV control. In: Proceedings of the 10th European Conference on Interactive TV and Video, Berlin, Germany, pp. 45–48. ACM Press, New York (2012)
15. Piumsomboon, T., Clark, A., Billinghurst, M., Cockburn, A.: User-defined gestures for augmented reality. In: CHI 2013 Extended Abstracts on Human Factors in Computing Systems, Paris, France, vol. 8118, pp. 955–960. ACM Press, New York (2013)

16. Silpasuwanchai, C., Ren, X.: Jump and shoot!: prioritizing primary and alternative body gestures for intense gameplay. In: Proceedings of the 32nd Annual ACM Conference on Human Factors in Computing Systems, Toronto, Canada, pp. 951–954. ACM Press, New York (2014)
17. Leng, H.Y., Norowi, N.M., Jantan, A.H.: A user-defined gesture set for music interaction in immersive virtual environment. In: Proceedings of the 3rd International Conference on Human-Computer Interaction and User Experience, Indonesia, pp. 44–51. ACM Press, New York (2017)

# Cross-Cultural Communication in Design Collaboration

Rungtai Lin[1(✉)], Hong-lin Li[2], Jun Wu[3], and Wei Bi[3]

[1] Taiwan Design Center, Taipei, Taiwan
rtlin@tdc.org.tw
[2] Department of General Education, National Taiwan University of Arts,
New Taipei City, Taiwan
larryli@ntua.edu.tw
[3] Graduate School of Creative Industry Design, College of Design,
National Taiwan University of Arts, New Taipei City, Taiwan
junwu2006@hotmail.com, beebvv@qq.com

**Abstract.** Cross-cultural Communication is a relatively new terminology that has emerged over the last decade. The use of information technology in design is becoming more common and accessible to users. Designers apply a variety of multimedia, symbols and metaphors to independently create and design products that express their ideas and communicate their life experience. The products per se are the media which provide powerful and essential means of communication. If design is viewed as a process of communication, it follows naturally that how the designer's performances are conceived, developed, delivered and received, and how the user is attracted, accurately understanding the products, and affected by the design are worth exploring. By blending Science, Arts and Design (SAD), we can produce a higher impact on cross-cultural communication to reach Collaboration, Humanity, Empathy, Ecology and Renaissance (CHEER). Therefore, this study intends to probe how the relationship between the designer and the user is potentially altered in cross-cultural communication. The results suggest that the communication matrix approach would be validated through more testing and evaluating of designs in further studies.

**Keywords:** Communication matrix · Design research · Cross-culture design
Interdisciplinary

# 1 Introduction

## 1.1 Cross-Cultural Communication: An Emerging Concept

Cross-cultural communication is a relatively new terminology that has emerged over the last decade. It appears to be a new concept that is a regrouping of the previously known ideas of social interaction, communication and networking [1–3]. Cross-cultural communication has received increased attention in the academic and business communities over the past decade [4]. Both academics and practitioners have emphasized that the role of social networking in relationship development relates not only to the human community, but also to aspects such as business, management, arts, and even different fields of therapy [5–8].

## 1.2   Design as an Interconnected Dialogue

We must note that, with the advent of social networking, the world is becoming 'smaller', and people are now more inter-connected than ever. The use of informatics technology in multimedia which provide powerful and essential means of communication is becoming relatively common and accessible to users [9]. By grasping new opportunities in social networks, cross-cultural communication has transcended from a traditional to a technological approach. Specifically, companies nowadays are more focused on adapting new technologies and combining them in ways that create new experiences and value for customers. With the development of industrial tendencies, most companies have come to realize that the keys to 'word-of-mouth' communication rely on not only marketing and technology but also service innovation design [8]. Let us take as an example 'Design at the Edges: 2011 IDA Congress': the aim of the IDA Congress is to bring together the unified voice of designers around the world in a themed framework to advance the vision and mission of the IDA by engaging government leaders, INGOs, business, science and technology, education and social science. The IDA Congress is a primary event, so to speak, for dialogue between designers and non-design stakeholders in a summit format (http://www.gov.taipei/ct.asp?xItem=28391465&ctNode=54046&mp=100095). This event signifies the fact that design is a system combining diverse elements and the interaction within.

## 1.3   The Issues

From the viewpoint of communication, design is an activity of transforming the restrained into the exuberant preferred through communication. It reflects the concern of the process of creating useful things. As we concur that design is a way to understand communication and an approach for investigating the social world [10], it must be stressed that, for design to be effective in communication, it needs to be meaningful, understandable, memorable, etc. [11]. In order to evaluate design with respect to its effectiveness in communication, we must identify the cognitive factors affecting them, which can then be used as the basis for evaluating designs during the creation stage. In this connection, two points have to be made here. First, while most existing studies discuss design evaluation after the phase of completion, very few works address its status at the creation stage to ensure the design for communication [9]. Second, communication studies, as previous researchers have indicated, are effective in evaluating comprehension of human behavior. This position has been backed up by the capability of traditional evaluating tools, which is considered to depend on whether underlying rating factors have been chosen properly, as explicated in Communication Style Inventory [12, 13], Communication Matrix [14], and Cognitive Style [15, 16]. In a word, the importance of communication studies has repeatedly been shown in several researches on design evaluation. However, despite the recognized importance of social interaction between designers and users, a systematic approach is still lacking to provide a full description of it [9, 15–19].

Taking design as communication [10], how the designer's performances are conceived, developed, delivered and received, and how the user is attracted, accurately understanding the products, and affected by the design need to be studied. Therefore, the purpose of this paper is to capture the factors affecting the evaluation of design. Subsequently, these factors are analyzed and discussed in order to establish a cross-cultural communication matrix to understand the perception of designers and users [20].

## 2   Research Framework–From SAD to CHEER

### 2.1   SAD in Design Education: Has a Lost Piece Been Found?

Sciences and arts education have already been established in the general education system. In traditional education system, children have been required to study sciences and arts at a relatively early age. That is, design in general education has been a missing 'third area'. 'Design', as the report of Royal College of Art has emphasized, is not so easily recognized, because it has been neglected, and has not been adequately articulated [21]. The core value of design is the conception and realization of new things which concern the appreciation of 'material culture' and the application of 'the arts of planning, inventing, making and doing'. Indeed, design has its own distinct 'things to know, ways of knowing them, and ways of finding out about them' [21, 22].

Recently, educational reformation has proceeded, and the acronym STEM (science, technology, engineering, and mathematics) has been adopted by numerous programs as an important focus for renewed global competitiveness [23, 24]. As a follow-up on STEM, a theoretical model for STEAM education has been proposed for science educators and curriculum developers to execute STEAM, which is an acronym of Science, Technology, Engineering, Arts, and Mathematics [25]. The proposal to build an interdisciplinary connection gains support from Norman [26]. Norman [26] argues that the spirit of time is over going. In his view, in educational institutions, industrial design is usually taught in schools of arts or architecture granting the degrees BA, MA, or MFA. Science, mathematics, technology, or social science are rarely offered as required courses in design education; consequently, the skills of the designer are not well suited for modern demands.

As Norman [26] noted, the discipline of design has its long tradition rooted around fine arts. Thus, the backgrounds of most designers are primarily fine arts. It is no exception for Taiwan. Tsao and Lin [27] conducted a study at three highly rated design programs in the US, as well as five design programs in Europe. They made recommendations for the design training programs in Taiwan. Among these recommendations are teamwork among designers and other professionals, internship programs for students, diversifications of students' course work, design as a process of project management, transformation of culture features into design, and closer collaboration between academia and industry [27].

For the past decades, the field of design research has shifted from the aim of creating a 'design science' to that of creating a 'design discipline'. Cross [28] stated that the focus of design research is on understanding the design process through an understanding of design cognition, or the 'designerly' ways of knowing and thinking. In the book entitled

'The new ABCs of research: Achieving Breakthrough Collaborations', Shneiderman [29] used three elements S, E, and D to 'achieve breakthrough collaborations'. The A, B, and C in the title stand for 'applied and basic combined', whereas S, E, and D designate 'science, engineering, and design'.

## 2.2  CHEER in Design Practice

In his work of Design Thinking, Brown and Wyatt [30] noted that the increasing complexity of products, services, and experiences has taken the place of the legend of the lone creative genius with the reality of the enthusiastic interdisciplinary collaborator. That is, the best design thinkers are not those who simply work alongside other disciplines. Instead, many of them have significant experience in more than one field. Take IDEO as illustration: they employ professionals with interdisciplinary expertise those who are engineers and marketers, anthropologists and industrial designers, and architects and psychologists.

Taking design as interdisciplinary cooperation, 'design at the edges' is the theme of the 2011 IDA Congress, hosted by the Taiwan Design Center (TDC). In 2004, the Taiwan Design Center was founded under the full support of the government. It is now an independent national design center offering complete design services. TDC aims to spread widely the seeds of creativity in Taiwan by encouraging innovation and design, providing ingenuity and talent needed for the upgrading and transition of Taiwan's industries. Through innovation, design and branding, TDC will increase the added value of Taiwan's industries and establish a 'Taiwan-based' globalized value network. The IDA's primary objectives for the congress are: (1) to promote the value of design-based collaboration between designers and non-design stakeholders; (2) to provide an engaging and educational experience for the memberships of the IDA Partners and to promote interaction among the memberships; (3) to position the IDA as the global voice of design and an enabler of innovation.

Taiwan economic development, based on Lin et al. [31] is a fusion of Dechnology (Design-Technology) and Humart (Humanity-Art), which can be represented as an interdisciplinary integration for design to fulfill the concept 'Collaboration'. Also, the results of Lin's study illustrated the interwoven experience of local design and global market in Taiwan's economy, industry and design development to provide a framework for looking at Taiwan's cross-cultural design development. The three stages also reflect the evolution of Taiwan design development: it evolves from 'use' to 'user' to realize 'Humanity', and transforms from 'function' to 'feeling' and from 'Hi-tech' to 'Hi-touch' to achieve 'Empathy'. In regards with the relationship between Dechnology and Humart, it can be merged into design thinking to explore 'Ecology'. Hence, the purpose of designing is to provide designers, companies, and organizations with an idea for how to direct their efforts to meet the requirements of a new proposed design strategy, which is a realization of 'Renaissance' in the domain of design. In summary, the words 'Collaboration', 'Humanity', 'Empathy', 'Ecology' and 'Renaissance' stand for CHEER, which is the globally important goal of design.

### 2.3   Build up the Bridge: From SAD to CHEER

Based on the concept of Shneiderman [29], we present a framework intended to combine Science, Arts and Design (SAD), which is able to produce a higher impact on cross-cultural communication in design process to reach the globally important goal of design – Collaboration, Humanity, Empathy, Ecology and Renaissance (CHEER). In a practical design process, four steps are used in product design, namely, (1) investigation – set a scenario, (2) interaction – tell a story, (3) development – write a script, and (4) implementation – design a product [32, 33]. These four steps are a reincarnation of the SAD principle, which calls for inter-course integration. With the fulfillment of the SAD principle, we can enable more successful application and basic research in design for CHEER. Given the interrelationship between SAD and CHEER, this study proposes a research framework as shown in Fig. 1. It may appear to be a 'new' concept that is a regrouping and re-categorizing of the previously known concepts of design as communication.

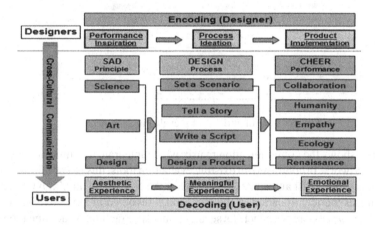

**Fig. 1.**   A framework of from SAD to CHEER

## 3   Cross-Cultural Communication Model

### 3.1   Communication Matrix

Thinking about design as a process of communication, this study intends to explore how the relationship between the designer and the user is potentially altered in cross-cultural communication. This process is able to respond by analyzing and interpreting the social communications of others, to derive and validate the cognitive factors that affect product design, and to propose a communication matrix for evaluating product design. For product design, Lin et al. [34] formulated a theory for examining how designers communicate with culture and users in the design process. For evaluating design, we need a better understanding of designer-user communication, not only for taking part in the social context, but also for developing the interactive experience between designer and user [9, 35]. A research framework has been proposed to study the cognition of emotional responses and visual scenes involved in turning poetry into painting [36, 37]. In addition, the research framework has been proven to be a better way for exploring the feeling of turning poetry into painting that is clearly worthy of further research [38]. Furthermore, Lin et al. [20] devised a theoretical skeleton combining communication theory with mental models to probe the application of communication matrix in evaluating artwork (Fig. 2).

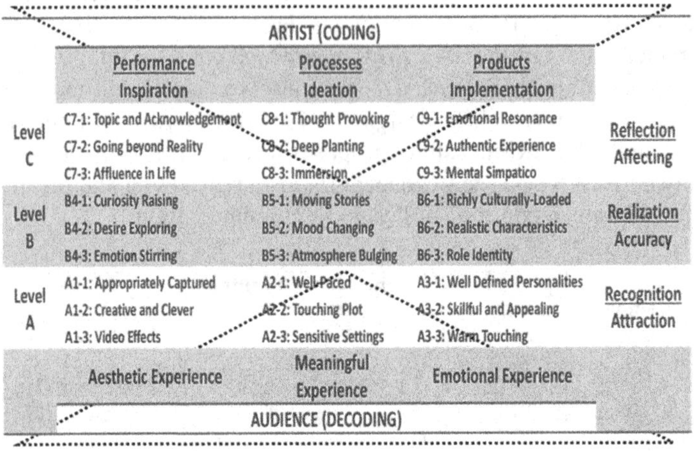

**Fig. 2.** A set of attributes for evaluating artwork [20]

Figure 2 shows the communication matrix which integrate the three dimensions for evaluating artwork. In contrast with existing evaluation tools, this is a multi-dimensional tool that places the artist and audience's values at the core of the matrix. Its first dimension facilitates the identification of the core values involved in any artwork, including performance, process and product. Its second dimension facilitates identification of the related theory that may need to be taken into account in assessing outcome and impact. These include communication theory, mental model and information processing. The third dimension is the flexibility, as the matrix can be adapted to the needs and priorities of the different context of the artist, viewer and artworks. It allows relevant measures and indicators of quality and impact to be identified [20].

## 3.2 Toward a Communication Perspective

Based on previous studies [20, 34, 39–41], a research framework combining communication theory with communication and mental models is put forth to explore the issue of cross-cultural communication in design, as shown in Fig. 3.

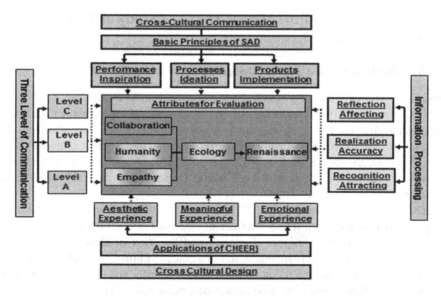

**Fig. 3.** Cross-cultural Communication model

In Fig. 3, cross-cultural communication is based on the principle of SAD (Science, Art and Design). For design as communication, the designer involves three key stages to express significance through his or her designs: performance (inspiration), process (ideation), and product (implementation). Performance is the inspiration to produce a kind of significance that the designer's intentions can be expressed through the designs. Process represents the designer's ideation that through the designs, the designer's imagination, thoughts, and feelings can be reproduced. Product is the implementation of signification and expression which can then be transmitted to the user while the designer's and the user's thoughts are identical [32–34, 46].

From the perspective of communication, a product design must have three functions in order to express its significance through the symbol system: signification, expression and communication. In the model of CHEER, the attributes are explored and identified as communication matrix for evaluating product design [20]. Norman [42] explicated three levels of design processing—visceral, behavioral, and reflective design that represents three kinds of user's experience as aesthetic, meaningful, and emotional experience, as shown in the bottom of Fig. 3 [33, 34]. These user's experience can be used for evaluating product design. As far as the communication theory is concerned, three levels of problems are identified in the study of communication: technical level, semantic level, and effectiveness level, as shown in the left of Fig. 3. Three key steps are identified as to understanding the meaning of a product design: recognition (attracting), realization (accuracy), and reflection (affecting), as shown in the right of Fig. 3 [36, 37].

# 4 An Instantiation of the Model: The Case Study of Taiwan Design Center

## 4.1 The Establishment of Taiwan Design Center: Goal and Missions

To promote the creative design industry, Taiwan's government established the Taiwan Design Center (TDC) (http://www.tdc.org.tw/) as a national design center in 2003 and officially started operations as an integrated service platform for creativity development in 2004. TDC's main missions are to elevate the originality of designers, promote international design exchanges and to strengthen market competitiveness. The global missions of TDC are the Development of Creative Design in Taiwan and Vital Link of Asian Design.

TDC successfully hosted the first '2011 IDA Congress, Taipei' and related 'Year of Design' activities, including IDA's International Design Forum, Taipei World Design Expo 2011, 2011 Young Designer Workshop and the Year of Design Certification Programs (http://www.icsid.org/events/events/calendar654.htm). Through these activities, more exchange and interaction between design industry and other domains have been achieved. Over 1.36 million people attended these activities and participators from around the world were greatly impressed. TDC was also a statement showing the world that the era of 'Design in Taiwan' has come.

The IDA congress is a great opportunity for Taiwan to show its design development from localization to globalization and share the 'Taiwan Design' experience with the international community. Moreover, Taipei has officially become the World Design Capital (WDC) 2016 by vote of the International Council of Societies of Industrial Design (ICSID: http://www.icsid.org/). The World Design Capital in 2016 has given Taipei the opportunity to show Taipei City to be a city of sustainable development with respect to life quality and health, ecological sustainability, smart living and urban regeneration. The slogan of Taipei City for WDC 2016 is 'Adaptive City – Design in Motion: By the People, For the People'. 'Adaptive City' is a process showing the evolution of Taipei city development. Moreover, Taipei will face the challenges of redefining itself by understanding the past, dealing with the present and facing the future through design thinking (http://www.taipeidesign.org.tw/) [43].

## 4.2 Make the Vision Come True – From Adaptive Design to Adaptive City

Adopting the concept of cross-cultural communication, Lin et al. [43] conducted a case study of 'Design in Motion for Taipei City' to explore not only for Taipei to meet the requirements of 'Adaptive City' for WDC 2016, but also for Taiwan to adopt this design development for the future. In order to achieve design in motion for Taipei City, we studied how to link 'Adaptive Design' to 'Adaptive City', and established a conceptual framework to provide companies, organizations, and designers with a valuable reference for using design thinking to build a design strategy. Based on design thinking [30], this framework combined 'from use to user', 'from function to feeling', and from hi-tech to hi-touch' with 'Environment', 'Authenticity' and 'Qualia' respectively as shown in Fig. 4 [44].

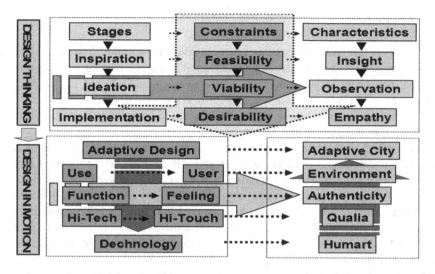

**Fig. 4.** The framework from 'Adaptive Design' to 'Adaptive City' [43]

With the reference to Fig. 4, let us proceed to explicate the realization of an Adaptive City through Adaptive Design. First, we shall address how the focus shift from 'use' to 'user' in design can help create a humanized environment. As establishing a sound man-environment relationship is a core mission of Taipei, 'Environment' is an important issue for the city as to how it can become a WDC 2016. This idea denotes the localization within a specific area, where the life style of the residents is taken for granted as a habitual and cultural activity. To be successful in localization, designers must pay particular attention to the technical specifications, sub-culture, and life style of the consumers, and to the nature of the product itself. There are numerous factors to consider for successful localization which must take into account the needs of the environment [44].

Now, let us spell out the evolving process from 'function' to 'feeling' and eventually to 'Authenticity' [45]. The notion 'Authenticity' is the core value of the user's emotional experience, which refers to the increasingly global relationships of residents, culture, and economic activity. Due to the fusion of cultures of similar nature, the consumer can become familiarized with a more diversified and wider local culture.

The last process that we need to specify is the transition pathway from 'Hi-Tech' to 'Hi-Touch', leading to the concept 'Qualia' [43]. 'Qualia' refers to entities that we cannot easily describe to one another or that we might each perceive slightly differently due to a variety of reasons. 'Qualia' and the similarly concept 'Glocal' are properties of 'Hi-Tech' and 'Hi-Touch', such as divisibility, comparability, connectivity, and satis-fiability. The portmanteau 'Glocalization' combines the influences of economic glob-alization and design localization. From the angle of design, 'Glocalization' is the trend of qualia in expressing a difference from similarity in local design under the concept of globalization and localization [32, 44, 46].

## 5   Conclusions

Thinking about design as a process of cross-cultural communication, how the designer's performances are conceived, developed, delivered and received, and how the user is attracted, accurately understanding the product design, and affected by the product design need to be pursued. Therefore, this study is intended to derive and validate the cognitive factors that affect artworks, and to propose a cross-cultural communication approach for evaluating product design.

In evaluating product design, understanding how the user evaluates the design is as complex as understanding the designer's perception itself. Because the cognitive factors that affect the appreciation of design have not been properly analyzed, the evaluation of artworks is typically ill-defined. For example, Shelley [19] asserted two key factors of character and role of principles in the evaluation of arts. Sullivan [47] argued that arts practice can be conceptualized as a form of research that can be directed towards a range of personal and public ends. In view of this knowledge gap, we took the initiative to use communication matrix as a technique for evaluating product design.

As clarified in the analysis of the case study, the three domains–science, arts and design– should be taken into account in the design process. Specifically, they should be viewed as inspiration for the performance, the design process from focusing on use to user, function to feeling, Hi-Tech to Hi-Touch, and finally to Dechnology (Design-Technology), which should be considered as the ideation of process. Furthermore, the notion of CHEER, which is proposed to the underpinning of 'Adaptive City', is identified to be the evaluation attributes for implementing design product. We advocate that Collaboration, Humanity, Empathy, Ecology and Renaissance (CHEER) should be the design principles or evaluation attributes for future design.

This research suggests that the communication matrix approach will be validated in more testing and evaluating of product design in further study to improve its completeness. Moreover, we hope that this study will encourage more researches to inspect the connection between design and cross-cultural communication in the near future.

## References

1. Gardner, G.H.: Cross cultural communication. J. Soc. Psychol. **58**(2), 241–256 (1962)
2. Rogers, E.M., Shoemaker, F.F.: Communication of Innovations; A Cross-Cultural Approach (1971)
3. Ting-Toomey, S., Chung, L.C.: Understanding Intercultural Communication. Oxford University Press, New York (2005)
4. Lenhart, A., Madden, M.: Social Networking Websites and Teens: An Overview, pp. 1–7. Pew/Internet (2007)
5. Dwyer, C., Hiltz, S., Passerini, K.: Trust and privacy concern within social networking sites: a comparison of Facebook and MySpace. In: AMCIS 2007 Proceedings, vol. 339 (2007)
6. Livingstone, S.: Taking risky opportunities in youthful content creation: teenagers' use of social networking sites for intimacy, privacy and self-expression. New media Soc. **10**(3), 393–411 (2008)
7. Pempek, T.A., Yermolayeva, Y.A., Calvert, S.L.: College students' social networking experiences on Facebook. J. Appl. Dev. Psychol. **30**(3), 227–238 (2009)

8. Trusov, M., Bucklin, R.E., Pauwels, K.: Effects of word-of-mouth versus traditional marketing: findings from an internet social networking site. J. Mark. **73**(5), 90–102 (2009)

9. Trivedi, S.: Artist-audience communication: tolstoy reclaimed. J. Aesthet. Educ. **38**(2), 38–52 (2004)

10. Aakhus, M.: Communication as design. Commun. Monogr. **74**(1), 112–117 (2007)

11. Porter, A., McMaken, J., Hwang, J., Yang, R.: Common core standards the new US intended curriculum. Educ. Res. **40**(3), 103–116 (2011)

12. De Vries, R.E., Bakker-Pieper, A., Konings, F.E., Schouten, B.: The communication styles inventory (CSI): a six-dimensional behavioral model of communication styles and its relation with personality. Commun. Res. **40**(4), 506–532 (2011). 0093650211413571

13. Gameren, K., Vlug, M.: The content and dimensionality of communication styles. Commun. Res. **36**(2), 178–206 (2009)

14. Rowland, C.: Using the communication matrix to assess expressive skills in early communicators. Commun. Disord. Q. **32**(3), 190–201 (2011). 1525740110394651

15. Allinson, C.W., Hayes, J.: The cognitive style index: a measure of intuition-analysis for organizational research. J. Manag. Stud. **33**(1), 119–135 (1996)

16. Cools, E., Van den Broeck, H.: Development and validation of the cognitive style indicator. J. Psychol. **141**(4), 359–387 (2007)

17. Peterson, R.A.: Sociology of the arts exploring fine and popular forms. Contemp. Sociol. J. Rev. **33**(4), 454–455 (2004)

18. Pratt, H.J.: Categories and comparisons of artworks. Br. J. Aesthet. **52**(1), 45–59 (2012)

19. Shelley, J.: The character and role of principles in the evaluation of art. Br. J. Aesthet. **42**(1), 37–51 (2002)

20. Lin, R., Qian, F., Wu, J., Fang, W.-T., Jin, Y.: A pilot study of communication matrix for evaluating artworks. In: Rau, P.-L.P. (ed.) CCD 2017. LNCS, vol. 10281, pp. 356–368. Springer, Cham (2017). https://doi.org/10.1007/978-3-319-57931-3_29

21. Archer, B.: Design as a discipline. Des. Stud. **1**(1), 17–20 (1979)

22. Cross, N.: Designerly ways of knowing. Des. Stud. **3**(4), 221–227 (1982)

23. Breiner, J.M., Harkness, S.S., Johnson, C.C., Koehler, C.M.: What is STEM? A discussion about conceptions of STEM in education and partnerships. Sch. Sci. Math. **112**(1), 3–11 (2012)

24. Kuenzi, J.J.: Science, Technology, Engineering, and Mathematics (STEM) Education: Background, Federal Policy, and Legislative Action (2008)

25. Yakman, G.: STEAM education: an overview of creating a model of integrative education. In: Pupils' Attitudes Towards Technology (PATT-19) Conference: Research on Technology, Innovation, Design & Engineering Teaching, Salt Lake City, Utah, USA (2008)

26. Norman, D.: Why design education must change. core77, 11, 26 (2010). http://jnd.org/dn.mss/why_design_education_must_change.html

27. Tsao, Y.C., Lin, R.: Reflections on the training and practice of industrial design in Taiwan. In: Proceedings of 2011 IDA Congress Education Conference, pp. 87–94. Taiwan Design Center, Taipei (2011)

28. Cross, N.: Designerly ways of knowing: design discipline versus design science. Des. Issues **17**(3), 49–55 (2001)

29. Shneiderman, B.: The New ABCs of Research: Achieving Breakthrough Collaborations. Oxford University Press, New York (2016)

30. Brown, T., Wyatt, J.: Design thinking for social innovation IDEO. Dev. Outreach **12**(1), 29–31 (2010)

31. Lin, C.L., Chen, J.L., Chen, S.J., Lin, R.: The cognition of turning poetry into painting. J. US-China Educ. Rev. B **5**(8), 471–487 (2015)

32. Hsu, C.H., Chang, S.H., Lin, R.: A design strategy for turning local culture into global market products. Int. J. Affect. Eng. **12**(2), 275–283 (2013)
33. Lin, R.: Transforming Taiwan aboriginal culture features into modern product design – a case study of cross cultural product design model. Int. J. Des. **1**(2), 47–55 (2007)
34. Lin, R., Lin, P.-H., Shiao, W.-S., Lin, S.-H.: Cultural aspect of interaction design beyond human-computer interaction. In: Aykin, N. (ed.) IDGD 2009. LNCS, vol. 5623, pp. 49–58. Springer, Heidelberg (2009). https://doi.org/10.1007/978-3-642-02767-3_6
35. Goldman, A.: Evaluating Art. The Blackwell guide to aesthetics, pp. 93–108 (2004)
36. Chen, S.J., Lin, C.L., Lin, R.: The study of match degree evaluation between poetry and paint. In: Proceedings of the 5th Asian Conference on the Arts and Humanities (ACAH2014), Osaka, Japan (2014)
37. Chen, S.J., Lin, C.L. Lin, R.: A cognition study of turning poetry into abstract painting. In: The Fifth Asian Conference on Cultural Studies (ACCS 2015), Kobe, Japan (2015)
38. Gao, Y.-J., Chen, L.-Y., Lee, S., Lin, R., Jin, Y.: A study of communication in turning "poetry" into "painting". In: Rau, P.L.P. (ed.) CCD 2017. LNCS, vol. 10281, pp. 37–48. Springer, Cham (2017). https://doi.org/10.1007/978-3-319-57931-3_4
39. Craig, R.T.: Communication theory as a field. Commun. Theory **9**(2), 119–161 (1999)
40. Fiske, J.: Introduction to Communication Studies. Routledge, London (2010)
41. Jakobson, R.: Language in literature. The Belknap Press of Harvard U. P, Cambridge (1987)
42. Norman, D.A.: Emotional Design: Why We Love (or Hate) Everyday Things. Basic books, New York (2005)
43. Lin, R., Yen, C.-C., Chen, R.: From adaptive design to adaptive city-design in motion for Taipei city. In: Rau, P.L.P. (ed.) CCD 2014. LNCS, vol. 8528, pp. 643–649. Springer, Cham (2014). https://doi.org/10.1007/978-3-319-07308-8_61
44. Yen, H.Y., Lin, P.H., Lin, R.: The effect of product qualia factors on brand image – using brand love as mediator. Bull. Jpn. Soc. Sci. Des. **62**(3), 3_67–3_76 (2015)
45. Gilmore, J.H., Pine II, B.J.: Authenticity: What Consumers Really Want. Harvard Business School Press, Boston (2007)
46. Lin, R., Kreifeldt, J., Hung, P.-H., Chen, J.-L.: From dechnology to humart – a case study of Taiwan design development. In: Rau, P.L.P. (ed.) CCD 2015. LNCS, vol. 9181, pp. 263–273. Springer, Cham (2015). https://doi.org/10.1007/978-3-319-20934-0_25
47. Sullivan, G.: Research acts in art practice. Stud. Art Educ. **48**(1), 19–35 (2006)

# Representation of Memory in Design for Humanity

Hsien-Fu Lo[1(✉)], I-Wen Wu[1], and Chien-Chih Ni[2]

[1] Graduate School of Creative Industry Design, College of Design,
National Taiwan University of Arts, New Taipei City, Taiwan
hsienfulo@gmail.com, service@even.tw
[2] Hsuan-Chung University, Hsinchu City, Taiwan
nancynil008@gmail.com

**Abstract.** Artists often visualize their inner feelings or spiritual levels through works of art. In this way, the concrete expression of inner feelings marks the process from abstraction to substantialization. The delivery and expression process of these works of art can be described in the saying of famous Scottish philosopher, David Hume that all the perceptions of human thought break down itself into two different things, which are so-called impressions and ideas. Hume's theory is used to verify how works of art are transformed by the transition of impressions and concepts to achieve emotional exchanges between artists and audiences. The mode of communication among an artist, a curator and an audience is that the artist transforms his idea into an authoring model through an inner transformation and presents works through the aesthetic external form. Through the curator's interpretation, the audience comes to know how to appreciate the artwork [3]. In this study, we used nine series of gazing paintings to explore the extent to which artists want to express their messages and audience receives the messages. A total of 291 subjects were asked to learn about the images and semantic meanings and the middle school students' art appreciation theory quality and effective art teaching are expected to be improved to achieve the social function of cultural and creative industry development policy through questionnaire of the matching degree of the work and the name of the work.

**Keywords:** Resemblance · Construction · Memory

## 1 Introduction

The greatest asset of an individual is the accumulation of self-traits and life experiences, which no one can replace and occupy. Kandinsky1 (Wassily Kandinsky, 1866–1944), mentions in Spirituality of Art that "every piece of art is a child of that age and every cultural period has its own art and cannot be repeated" [6]. Such spatial thinking has unique cultural symbols and spatial symbols. Therefore, by means of strong map ideas, attempts are made to present the meaning of objects in the interface of that space-time culture in their works. In his own creative experience, he decided to settle in the metropolis of Taipei City and commuted between the village and metropolis, but he had to adapt to the cultural differences and geospatial arrangements. This is an

© Springer International Publishing AG, part of Springer Nature 2018
P.-L. P. Rau (Ed.): CCD 2018, LNCS 10911, pp. 43–57, 2018.
https://doi.org/10.1007/978-3-319-92141-9_4

interesting topic, hoping to reappear the self-artistic life through the experience and feelings of the most real body. Due to the continuous conversion of the living space, the present experience also gives new experiences and feelings to the present culture. Today's living environment enjoys convenient transportation and the fast change of time, space suffocates people and dedication to artistic creation not only presents in form, but also actively seeks the value of self-existence. In the process of education and learning, we constantly expect to achieve the goal of "art is life, life is art".

The series of nine works of "Gazing" is to present his own experience of life through the installation artistic means and specifically present inner emotional or spiritual level, so that the specific inner emotional expression way is visualized to use the teaching field to try to study the students' intuitive feedback. The purpose of this creation is to find a stage where the work and audience can communicate. That is to say, it is an object arrangement that operates from a plane virtual space to a physical space. Growing up on the beautiful island of Taiwan, with different humanistic ideas, living habits, religious beliefs, etc., these multiple cultural faces have also redrawn our living space. In different spatial atmosphere, they have their own unique language, symbols and social structure. Based on Hume's theory, this paper discusses the similarities, causality and spatial proximity, explores the memory and imagination in artistic creation and explores the nine representative works selected from the self-created series "Gazing" through the style analysis, research. A questionnaire is developed to obtain the information and data needed for style analysis. Through such aesthetics education activities, art education appreciation or cognition related issues are imported into the campus. In 2007 general education reform program of Harvard University, the aesthetics education was listed as the first area of eight areas of core competencies. [2] What makes the import of aesthetics education into the campus so important?

Why does art impress students with vision that many fields of knowledge cannot give? I often ask high school students in the classroom: Will there be no art in life? What do you think in life doesn't require beauty? Of course, behind these questions, I am well aware that art education can stop at the technical level, but it can also be a cultivation of sense of beauty and an aesthetic training. On the contrary, in our world where industry and commerce and science and technology dominate the social life, everyone should need some skills or sense of beauty of art. Aesthetic perception should be put into practice in life and it should be one of the most important indicators for improving the quality of the people. It's an important way for everyone to self-develop and invest in the community [5].

In today's world, industry has grown to a plateau, and in the post-industrial period that followed, the most important industries are knowledge and aesthetically creative industries. Although there are still many people who doubt whether such a thing has happened, it is doubtless that the society is indeed moving toward the trend of development. Through this research project, statistical analysis of the name semantics of works and the images of works will be conducted in the hope to achieve more effective transmission way of art language and information.

## 2  Literature Review

"Beauty comes naturally from the experience of life. After appreciating more beautiful things and cultivating judgment of eyes, a power, national power will be formed gradually." [10]. In his series of works "Gazing", he mainly explores the space symbols and cultural symbols in self-creation from the current multi-dimensional artistic creation trend. "Life Experience," "Theoretical Exploration," and "Creative Work" are the processes that I practice in the creation. The three activities are mutually reinforcing and contain the ways in which art, such as memory, thinking, reflection and action, can be virtually presented.

It is just like the natural experience of breathing in air, trying to combine with contemporary digital image painting and collage experimental research to locate the artwork. Using modern computer tools and equipment, some of them are presented in digital computer graphics and trying to combine them with other media through a computer, which does not mean that it is completely limited by computer. Instead, it is trying to find another possibility and artistic performance accuracy. In the early stage of creation, it is completely invisible whether there is a system to follow or even most of the attempts are made on tools and media [8].

However, we gradually find that we can formulate issues and then experimentally produce a series of works until the state of independent creation is finally displayed, which is not just accidental creation. However, it is undeniable that the work style and development will still be affected by the computer media and the output materials. On the contrary, this is also a new thinking of a material civilization society. The use of ready-made objects and digital collage creation require the combination of experimenters, computers, and a variety of media to reflect the multi-media era in the works [9].

### 2.1  Collage Art Technique of Expression

Picasso's Still Life with the Caned Chair in 1912 creates a representative collage work of Cubism. Picasso leveraged on a wax cloth painted with caned chair, took rope as frame, and affixed the image with sketches of glasses and lemon slices. The upper left letter JOU represents journal or jouer, so that such thinking shows a diversity of creative changes that lead to another new milestone. The image of a work can be regarded as a meaningful language [4] (Fig. 1).

To find some creative elements from daily life is to use the keen observation that artists should have. Maybe the artwork is slow and quiet, but I believe it is a surreal feeling. After determining the creative direction and issues, the observed phenomenon of life is expected to be presented through the way of artistic creation.

The history of art development is like a large branch of a tree, and creation must be built on the complete branch before we can experience the wind and rain and flowering results. I also try to find some corresponding roots in the history of fine arts, and extend the objects I want to express in the real space. Through the process of self-creation and the fixed forms, I present the desired style and the ideal spatial structure. The most important thing about "creation" lies in the embodiment of life thinking and life experiences, as well as the historical trajectory of life presented [7].

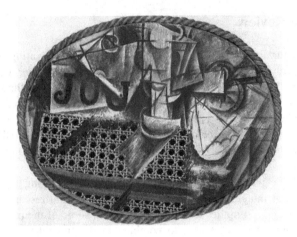

**Fig. 1.** Pablo picasso, still life with chair caning, 1912, oil on oil-cloth over canvas edged with rope, 29 × 37 cm (Musée Picasso)

Gestalt psychologist Rodulf Arnheim (1904–2007) argues that the human mind accepts and interprets the images of the external world in an individual conscious and unconscious interaction and the unconscious areas will not enter our experience without the reflection of perceivable things of mankind. [1] "Art is life, life is art", even if art stays close to life, it is sometimes overlooked, thus it is especially important to break through the previously established forms and restrictions of creation. Taking "gazing" series of works as example, the house of grandmother for childhood life is finally demolished as a shabby house for years. The action is not just building renovation, but a symbol of space, culture hidden behind it. It is fortunate that he projects his feeling on the art creation. The rubble of the remnant's house is not the end, but the beginning of another art creation life and the self-creation life thus starts. Demolition of the old house is not just the demolition of the house, but the demolition of home. The demolition of house is the demolition of entity space and emotional parts. There are some memories reconstructions while feeling the demolished object. The contradiction relationship appears between demolition and reconstruction [11].

"There is nothing in the world that craves for beauty and can be easily landscaped as beautiful as it originates from its inner needs; it is beautiful because it is inherently beautiful". [10] The feeling of artwork should come from the inner life, which is both the real expression and the hope of clarifying cultural symbols and spatial symbols in my creation through studying the corresponding roots of art history and related literatures.

## 2.2   Social Communication Theory

As far as communication theory is concerned, how does the artist convey the series of works "Gazing" to the audience and how does the audience convey the image information of the work completely? This is an interesting study. Therefore, the artist must have the process of coding at the very beginning when he creates the work, and the process of coding the process of materialization should convey the meaning of the image of the work. Naming is one of the pointers that materialize the image content.

You see a picture in the gallery with a couple of men and women dressed in European clothing from the early nineteenth century. You look a few more glances and have a deja vu feeling, finally recognize them as Napoleon and Josephine. So you come to such conclusion that this painting should portray the military genius and his first wife. However, when you look at the title of the painting, "Neighbor Couples before Masquerade", you immediately find that the original interpretation is incorrect. This painting shows the painter's neighbor, who looks very similar with Napoleon and Josephine in appearance after dressing up. The men in the painting are not Napoleon and Josephine and the scene is not in the nineteenth century. In the above example, one thing we can observe is that a title seems to be one of the elements that the audience notices in appreciation of a work of art. The American philosopher Jerrold Levinson calls this element "aesthetically relevant factor" or "appreciatively relevant factor".

In the case of the program school of communication theory (Fiske, 1990), in the communication process of an art work (message), from the creation of an artist (sender's) to the audience (receiver), there are three levels of communication that can be passed on to the audience: the first one is the technical aspect, so that the person who receives the message can see, hear, touch and even feel, that is, how the artist accurately convey the information through the artwork. [12] The second level is the semantic level, so that people who receive the message understand the meaning of the message, will not misunderstand or misinterpret the work, that is, how to let the audience understand the original intention of message. The third level is the effect level, that is how to let the people who receive the message take the correct action according to the original intention of the message, that is, how to effectively influence the expected behavior (Rungtai Lin, 1992).

Through Intuition experience, this study will analyze the extent of information transmitted through artwork by artists and readers based on the framework of communication theory (R. T., Lin & P. H., Lin, Personal Communication, 29/01/18), while "beauty" is more difficult to be divorced from concrete, sensible form. The artist or creator often transforms the image he sees, the inner or the imaginary image into the form of the work, and by means of which it conveys the emotional connotation of the self to resonate with the audience. The various forms and creation elements presented in the work are able to show their personal characteristics or personality, and reflect the impact of the spatiotemporal background, social environment and customs on the artist's spirit, thoughts, beliefs, life, events... and so on, and then to develop the artist's individual shaping of their unique style.

# 3   Research Methods

Appreciating artwork is like playing a new game. You may also need to know how to read the content of artwork in the first time of intuitive appreciation. To understand what art is, we cannot just look at the surface of the artwork, but rather understand the message conveyed by the art of viewing. In other words, we must continuously accumulate personal "artistic experiences" from the viewing and then discover the meaning through one appropriate "point of view". The so-called appreciation is a careful observation of an object and reflection on the observed things. After one learns how to view the artwork, one can even learn to see everything around life from an artistic point of view. Therefore, this study hopes to conduct a Chinese name matching study after the audience directly views the series of installation work of "Gazing".

## 3.1  Research Framework

There are seven basic relationships among thoughts in Hume's book Humanity, including (1) similarities (2) causal relations (3) spatial proximity (4) identity (5) contradiction (6) number proportion (7) degree of quality. [14] The first three of them are the factors that he assumes to be the most important. Through the visual experience of the audience, we can study and discuss them. In this study, we will take 2007 personal creations of "Gazing" as the object of study. The research will be divided into three phases. Phase I includes literature review and theoretical construction as mentioned above. Phase II is the matching name test of painting titled "Gazing". After the preliminary test and expert consultation, the formal matching questionnaire is conducted. Phase III will organize the questionnaire results into confusion matrix that matches work with name and explore related results with statistical analysis to obtain possible results and suggestions. The research framework is shown in figure (Table 1).

**Table 1.**  Structure of the memory and research architecture of reproduction

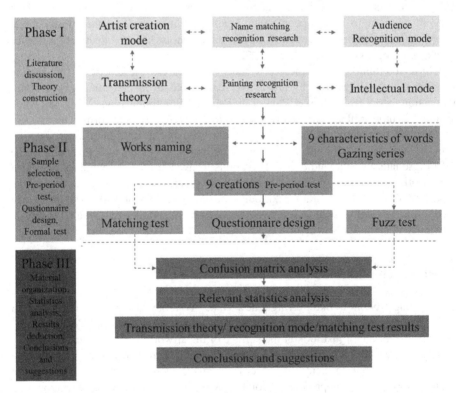

### 3.2    Sample Selection

In this study, nine of the personal "gazing" creation series are named with 9 words and sentences for name matching test. In the works, some Google map image symbols are used in combination with objects left over from time to space, so that the perception in the memory can be presented through the reconstruction of creation, hoping to explore emotionally the home and house in the memory through art creation and perceptual intuition of audience, including composite media decorative elements of red brick, Hakka cloth, ancient porcelain bowl, window grille, tile... and so on.

When artists combine the various visual elements of their work, they become another way of presenting feelings or ideas. Similarly, as a viewer, the impressions that we perceive in a work from one visual element are all influenced by the interrelationship among the visual elements of the picture. The most significant, enduring and easily recognizable symbol of urban space is constructed from buildings (Tables 2 and 3).

**Table 2.** "Gazing" works title options

| Work No. | Title options |
|----------|---------------|
| No. 01 | Trace of time |
| No. 02 | Dazzling world |
| No. 03 | Waves of time |
| No. 04 | Symbiosis |
| No. 05 | Confusing city |
| No. 06 | Inside and outside of window |
| No. 07 | Pure and rich |
| No. 08 | Awn, busy, confused, blind |
| No. 09 | Memory retention |

### 3.3    Questionnaire Design

The questionnaire content of this study is based on the communication theory discussed before and is divided into two groups. Group A only appreciates the work and the slide has no written explanation. Group B appreciates the work and reads the text below and then carries out name pairs. After the completion of the name options A1 to A9, students are invited to select their favorite piece of work, tick the 9 works listed by the researcher to benefit the follow-up analysis of researchers.

#### 3.3.1    Description for Group A Questionnaire

Here are 9 creations. Please read work for 1 min and determine the matching degree between the work and name; fill in the options and answer the matching degree of following questions based on the intuitive feeling given by the work.

**Table 3.** Works options (a total of 9 items)

| No.1 | No.2 | No.3 |
|---|---|---|
| | | |
| No.4 | No.5 | No.6 |
| | | |
| No.7 | No.8 | No.9 |
| | | |

### 3.3.2    Description for Group B Questionnaire

Here are 9 creations. Please read the works and painting text instructions for 1 min, determine the matching degree of the work and name; fill in the options and answer the matching degree of following questions based on the intuitive feeling given by the work.

### 3.3.3    Group B Questionnaire and Text Description

Group B questionnaire and text description (Table 4)

**Table 4.** "Gazing" works text description form

| No. | Image | Text description |
|---|---|---|
| 01 | | Diverse creative style is quite interesting, especially the beautiful elements left in life. It uses some abstract images to interpret the idea to be expressed in the hope to retain the simple self in gorgeous metropolitan color. Background map image (busy corner of Wanhua in Taipei) |
| 02 | | Perhaps the kid growing up in the city has never seen flocks of butterflies flying scene. Think carefully, the virtual world has been filled with the entire space -be real or sham, is it a kind of happiness? Deeply looking forward to flocks of butterflies flying to present the happiness inside again. Background map image (Riverside of Seine-Marne, Paris) |

*(continued)*

**Table 4.** (*continued*)

| No. | Image | Text description |
|-----|-------|------------------|
| 03 | | Our life course is often like a small river, from mountains to the ocean, where we have to overcome many obstacles in our lives and often try to ask ourselves what are we pursuing? What is clutched? What do we want exactly? Background map image is the growth place (Dajia River, Taichung, Taiwan) |
| 04 | | The convenience of transportation seems to have reduced the time and space and makes karst caves of the culture easier. However, it is not easy for people to live in different background cultures, and harmony is one of the necessary conditions for their own culture to be accepted. Background map image (South District, Taichung, Taiwan) |
| 05 | | The symbolic image of "ground glass" seems to have disappeared in life for a long time. "Fuzzy" images satisfy some of the people's desire. This is a special mystery. Is it prying into window from outside or prying out of window from inside? Background map image is the place where author grows up (Dajia Nonggong, Taiwan) |
| 06 | | In the dark corner, I saw the old woman still persist in putting up stalls for mid-night snack for nearly 40 years, which forms stark contrast with us, the university students having night life. Leveraging on this time-and-space-filled bowl of life to record different bits of life. Background map image (Readjustment Area, Taichung, Taiwan) |
| 07 | | The objects in the works are the window bricks removed from the old house in the hometown. When the house is demolished, the house in memory is also rebuilt so that the heart will remain the rustic and noble place forever. Background map image is the residence in the childhood (Chenggongling, Taichung, Taiwan) |
| 08 | | The chaotic city is full of thorns and the must-pass for wining the laureate. Busy cities and programs have not stopped. Busy? Confused? Blind? Stay vigilant as this is another battlefield that must first be overcome. Background map image is the residence for university life (New Taipei Banqiao City, Taiwan) |
| 09 | | Peony symbolizes prosperity and wealth. In Taiwan's Hakka culture, the mother gives a large cotton prints to her daughter who is about to get married and hopes to make it a sheet so that it will cover her with wealth for the whole life. Black and gray stripes are back towel for the author in the childhood. Background map image is the grandmother's house (Zhanghua Erlin, Taiwan) |

## 3.4   Subjects

A total of 291 participants were invited to assist in the study, including 174 first graders from high school, 117 third graders from high school, 74 male students and 217 female students who were from the six classes of three attributes of first-grade and the third-grade mathematics experimental class, Chinese experimental class and normal class. Researchers observe in the secondary education scene that the appreciation of modern art in Taiwan is lacked for secondary school students, trying to use the "Gazing" series as a research material to grow aesthetic education in the creative appreciation of modern art in the school worshiping credentialism.

In the face of the rapid social changes and the changing trends and challenges, the talents needed in the future must have both modern care and global citizenship. However, the cultivation of art and aesthetic sense of citizen literacy must be carried out through the improvement of the art and aesthetic education system, administrative support systems, teacher empowerment, curriculum and teaching material research and development, integration of social resources and shaping of good social mood for the appreciation of beauty and truly implement to meet the needs of all walks of life.

### 3.5 Questionnaire Process

This study is conducted in the classroom by projecting the artwork and simulating the gallery context. Students are invited to get involved and asked for permission. When a student enters the classroom, he or she first explains the purpose of the experiment and the mode of operation. After reading the image works, he or she fills in the questionnaire that matches the name of the painting. Questionnaire content contains personal basic data and paintings name matching options and one of the favorite works and the reason behind it. Subjects select the appropriate name for each painting and questionnaire content is arranged in an A4-size questionnaire.

The situation is built and the target is effectively answered. In Taiwan's art education, visual art is only one lesson in secondary school. In aesthetic experience, art-like teaching is easier for students to understandt modern art and abstract art are hard to be comprehended. The actual operation process is as follows: (1) The purpose of the study (2) Art appreciation situation shaping (3) The work name matching description (4) Filling in and answering. Each questionnaire contains open-ended questions which can be completed in about 15 min. I think that art is something that can challenge people's intellect and incite emotions. Appreciating the artistic creation of others can help one to enhance his creativity and thinking skills and find expressionist ways of expressing ideas of creators, and at the same time, help him to highlight the familiar tools and techniques of art and develop better ways of creating art.

After that, through practical creation practice, new artistic creation method is tested. By circular process of observing, experiencing and practicing, each of us can cultivate the ability to observe artistic works.

## 4  Research Discussion

The traditional matching test system is used to explore the visibility of public signs, and a confusion matrix is obtained through the pairing of graphic signs and written semantic meaning. The reasons for confusion between graphic signs and written semantics are further discussed. [13] The name and matching complexity of "Gazing Creation Series" far exceeds the recognition of graphic signs and written semantics. This paper uses the confusion matrix of matching test framework to explore subjective interpretations of subjects' acceptance of pictorial images and their semantic understanding, supplemented by objective data to try to study the possible causes of cognitive misunderstanding in the subject, and also try to develop a mode that is more suitable for middle school students in modern art appreciation in this study.

## 4.1    Test Results

Statistics of accuracy rate of name matching.

From Table 5, A8 is barely confused with A9. A8 uses "automatic writing" as the main creative technique. In addition, the background maps are densely populated cities and images convey the tension in urban life. In A9's work, with the traditional Taiwan Hakka ethnic cloth as the main decoration, peony flowers convey symbolic symbol of prosperity and wealth, so the recognition rate is high. In A4 and A5 works, because of the object and subject relationship, A4 works take roundness to highlight the only color area of the screen and modeling contrast is quite clear. A5 works use the entity former window objects and windows symbols can be clearly distinguished by tester. A5 and A6 are similar. The situation that A1 and A2 are confused is high, and the two works are confused with each other, affecting the recognition rate. A6 and A7 enjoy the lowest recognition rate. Straight figures indicate that the painting is mistaken for other titles, and horizontal figures indicate that the title is mistaken for other paintings.

**Table 5.**  Statistics of name matching accuracy rate of gazing works

| Votes (%) | A1 | A2 | A3 | A4 | A5 | A6 | A7 | A8 | A9 |
|---|---|---|---|---|---|---|---|---|---|
| Confusing city | **105 (0.36)** | 76 (0.26) | 9 (0.03) | 29 (0.10) | 3 (0.01) | 10 (0.03) | 16 (0.05) | 36 (0.12) | 5 (0.02) |
| Dazzling world | 55 (0.19) | **74 (0.25)** | 23 (0.08) | 16 (0.05) | 75 (0.26) | 6 (0.02) | 3 (0.01) | 19 (0.07) | 38 (0.13) |
| Waves of time | 17 (0.06) | 20 (0.07) | **128 (0.44)** | 14 (0.05) | 4 (0.01) | 22 (0.08) | 26 (0.09) | 28 (0.10) | 23 (0.08) |
| Symbiosis | 10 (0.03) | 5 (0.02) | 10 (0.03) | **126 (0.43)** | 10 (0.03) | 74 (0.25) | 14 (0.05) | 3 (0.01) | 32 (0.11) |
| Inside and outside of window | 40 (0.14) | 50 (0.17) | 12 (0.04) | 6 (0.02) | **154 (0.53)** | 9 (0.03) | 15 (0.05) | 4 (0.01) | 6 (0.02) |
| Memory retention | 11 (0.04) | 29 (0.10) | 33 (0.11) | 24 (0.08) | 13 (0.04) | **40 (0.14)** | 73 (0.25) | 18 (0.06) | 44 (0.15) |
| Trace of time | 21 (0.07) | 17 (0.06) | 46 (0.16) | 26 (0.09) | 7 (0.02) | 83 (0.29) | **37 (0.13)** | 16 (0.05) | 35 (0.12) |
| Awn, busy, confused, blind | 28 (0.10) | 10 (0.03) | 21 (0.07) | 9 (0.03) | 3 (0.01) | 15 (0.05) | 19 (0.07) | **161 (0.55)** | 15 (0.05) |
| Pure and rich | 4 (0.01) | 10 (0.03) | 9 (0.03) | 41 (0.14) | 22 (0.08) | 32 (0.11) | 88 (0.30) | 6 (0.02) | **93 (0.32)** |

## 4.1.1    The Same Name as the Artist

On the whole, in terms of A1 to A8 statistics, Group B has higher name matching degree than Group A. This Table 6 shows that the textual narration has a great influence on the extent to which the audience understands the work. Through text interpretation, artistic language conveyed by artists can be clarified. Only A9 enjoys extremely small difference in number and gap. The researchers analyze the reasons that the use of symbols in their works is quite significant in symbolic meaning, quite close to cognition of audience, especially the symbolic message conveyed by red print. In traditional art, flower images are always colorful, graceful and favored by general public. They are commonly used as the theme of literature and the arts with the Chinese cultural spirit and are often referred to as the symbol of personal style. Therefore, they have always been admired by the people. Peony is elegant with the reputation of the national fragrance. In Liu Yuxi's poem of "Peony Appreciation", "Only peonies are truly beautiful, which impress the capital with its bloom. In Song dynasty, Luoyang Peony is famous around the world with many varieties and documents… Peony flower features large size, rich fragrance, flowering in spring with red, white, yellow, green and other colors. They are elegant, extraordinary and auspicious and mark as a symbol of prosperity." Therefore, the red prints have a deep meaning of cultural significance and are easy to convey its meaning through the works.

**Table 6.** Statistical table for the matching number of the same name as author

|         |       | A1    | A2    | A3    | A4    | A5    | A6    | A7    | A8    | **A9** |
|---------|-------|-------|-------|-------|-------|-------|-------|-------|-------|-------|
| Group A | Votes | 25    | 9     | 48    | 21    | 44    | 9     | 27    | 62    | **47** |
|         | %     | 0.09% | 0.03% | 0.16% | 0.07% | 0.15% | 0.03% | 0.09% | 0.21% | 0.16% |
| Group B | Votes | 80    | 65    | 80    | 105   | 111   | 31    | 10    | 98    | **46** |
|         | %     | 0.27% | 0.22% | 0.27% | 0.36% | 0.38% | 0.11% | 0.03% | 0.34% | 0.16% |

In addition, A8 works are selected by 21% of the participants in group A, which ranks high in group A. The works techniques of expression are similar to abstract artist Pollock (Jackson Pollock 1887–1986). The images are mostly Automatism. The researchers speculate that the image delivers impatient messy psychological and visual images, so that the great pressure undertaken by subjects for higher school admission can be echoed, hence the high name matching degree.

### 4.1.2   Statistics of the Most Impressive Works

In this study, Question 10, "Which one of the 9 works above do you like most?", The top three works that were the most impressive are A8, A1 and A5, of which A8 is selected by 60 people, accounting for 20.6% of the total number. As mentioned in the previous section, the screen transmission allows the interviewer to feel more profound. The feedback part of the summary is as follows (Table 7):

**Table 7.** Statistical table for most impressive works on subjects

| Most                    | A1 | A2 | A3 | A4 | A5 | A6 | A7 | **A8** | A9 | Total |
|-------------------------|----|----|----|----|----|----|----|-------|----|-------|
| impressive<br>(votes)   | 37 | 27 | 36 | 36 | 37 | 26 | 13 | **60** | 19 | 291   |

A8 works gives upset visual impression and researchers speculate with the Taiwan government and experts and scholars that they attempt to alleviate the problem of examination-led teaching through the reform of high school education and further studies. However, high school students' anxiety about these factors is unlikely to be eliminated through high school education reform. As long as the working environment continues to be poor, the job market continues to highlight academic qualifications, student and parent's anxiety will not disappear. Therefore, the researchers speculate on the pressure source of high school students: (1) The pressure of course learning: learning is undoubtedly the main source of stress in high school students and poor test scores directly affect the students' college dreams, therefore, academic performance gives lots of pressure. (2) Pressure from peer competition: the excessive competitive pressure of students causes serious tension, which will affect the normal study and life. (3) Expectations from families and parents: every parent holds high expectation for their children. Under the high expectation and high pressure, the child will inevitably have anxiety. The strong pressure of high expectation on children and lack of inner harmony, concern, sincere feelings will inevitably lead to children's coercion and resistance; increase psychological pressure. One of the root causes of student horror is the simple repetition and brutality of parental education methods. (4) Pressure from schools: students have a heavy academic load and their physical activity and entertainment time are reduced to improve their enrollment rate. The current school lacks mental health education with life education as the core. Students psychological pressure cannot be excused and released and there is no time for self-regulation and mutual adjustment, resulting in piled psychological stress problems. In testing, the A8 work with messy structure image greatly impresses us.

## 5  Conclusions and Suggestions

After the improvement of the material life, the improvement of the spiritual life of sense of beauty will definitely help to develop all the spiritual and physical development of a person. It is especially important to enhance art appreciation through appreciation of art, understanding of art works. The way that art creators convey their message is an important part of the process for artists to write in artwork through code which is decoded by audience. The "creation" value lies in the reflection of life experience and life thinking as well as the historical path of life presented. "There is nothing in the world that craves for beauty and can be easily landscaped as beautiful as it originates from its inner needs; it is beautiful because it is inherently beautiful". The feelings of the artwork should come from real inner life presentation that artists can accurately convey their emotions. If we rely solely on the opinions of authority to "see", that is, to "see" through the eyes of a critic, we must absolutely not learn the experience that can satisfy ourselves. Only through the process of experiencing itself can we acquire useful experiences and knowledge that are useful to ourselves so that we can feel content in the world of visual images. It may be a good idea to educate through art appreciation. The conclusions of the study are as follows:

1. The works of art have narrative help, which helps the audience to accept the importance of the message sent by the creator; to peel off the established logic of life and the viewpoints of things out of the original view, reassemble and add to the author's perspective, and to have a greater understanding of the cultural representations represented by objects in the space in which we currently exist, and carry out further exploration.

2. In today's life, people enjoy the convenience brought by science and technology for the whole world and easily ignore the emotional transmission of people and things around us. We hope that by this study, we can promote the reflection on the self-creation environment and aesthetic education because something cannot be redeemed once it is lost. Art culture is required to retain it.

3. The small objects of life used in the creation are often the result of the exchange of perceptions between the human spirit and the objective environment. Therefore, not only the objects but the expressions of self-feelings in the heart are reproduced in creation with known and unknown facts combined.

4. Taking into account both the concrete and abstract forms, learning that object exists space and the cultural code that cannot be ignored are worth exploring for the teaching of the collage art which is more reserved for the future course of the researcher so as to make the life more artful, make art closer to life, so that each piece of art has become a meaningful story book.

5. In the daily communication, although the language is powerful, it is often too explicit. The writing is more moderate and indirect, but if the speech is not satisfactory, the effect will be greatly reduced. With artistic creation to show one's intention, the object serves as its material to interpret the symbolic meaning behind it. Even though the social culture has given some meaning, but with the interpretation of man, the cognitive space is more flexible and wide-ranging, creating subtle interactions and relationships with viewers to produce another communication language.

Living in this world, it is difficult to live happily by reason and sometimes a little more emotional artistic imagination will make life more harmonious and interesting. Many unknown things will become the taste of life. Therefore, the creation of works of art that resonates with viewers can also be an important driving force behind monotonous life. The imaginary and memory projection are projected in the artistic creation. It is like enjoying a wonderful essay, which is thought-provoking to read at any time. The study is surprised to find that the subject's favorite work, "A8", is messy and disordered for the general public. However, for middle school students, it is the most impressive and resonated and gives inspiration for the researchers that more art pressure release course will be introduced to the teaching curriculum to enrich their lives. Therefore, the research, combined with questionnaire feedback, statistical analysis, subjective speculation and comparative analysis, although not exhaustive, is only a preliminary research result and can provide reference for artists and teachers.

The participated test classes are concentrated and different learning groups are also the topic to be further explored by the researchers. In classes with more "science course" and "literature course", whether their content of art appreciation or depth presents difference? It is also worthwhile for researchers to study continuously. Moreover, such an art appreciation study in secondary education with academic advancement as the most important goal serves as is a novel and interesting art appreciation experience for the students. With the use of technology media, in the future, we can continue to develop artistic appreciation to join the voice of the emotional operation or lighting to stimulate the operation and creation of other situation. These are interesting topics of art education and can be researched in a sustainable manner.

# References

1. Alastair, D.: Art Deco. Yuan-Liou Press, Taipei City (1992). Weng, D. (Translator)
2. Chen, M.: Research on the Concept and Interpretation of Aesthetic Education. National Center for Humanistic Education and Aesthetic Education Interpretation and Dialogue, National Taiwan University of Arts, Taipei (1999)
3. Chen, X., Yan H., Li X., Lin Z.: Case study of curatorial design–a case study of the poetic picture–the beauty of immortal clouds painting exhibition. J. Des. **21**(4), 1–24 (2016)
4. Eddlewolfram: Collage Art History. Yuan-Liou Press, Taiwan (1992). Fu, J. (Translator)
5. Etétyedwards: Reflexive Thinking like an Artist. Shibao Press, Taipei (2005)
6. Gao, Q.: Phase of Contemporary Cultural Arts. Artist Press, Taiwan (1996). Astringent
7. Cassirer: Symbols Myths, Culture. Jiegouqun Press, Taipei City (1990). Luo, X. (Translator)
8. John, B.: Video Reading. Yuan-Liou Press, Taipei (2002). Liu, H. (Translator)
9. Nedloop Pontiac (Being Digital). Digital Revolution. Global Views – Commonwealth Publishing Group, Taiwan (1995)
10. Kandinsky: Spirituality of Art. Artist Press, Taipei City (1998). Wu, M. (Translator)
11. Kenneth, C.: Footprints of Civilization: Interpreting the Essence of Civilization from Western Art. Guiguan Book Company, Taipei City (1989). Yang, M. (Translator)
12. Lin, R.: Outsider Art, National Aesthetics–Enrichment of Retirement with Art. Humanit. Soc. Sci. Newsl. **18**(3), 13–26 (2017)
13. Lin, R.: Research on the Influence of Cultural Differences on Public Signs. Des. J. **3**(2), 81–87 (1998)
14. Tolstoy: Art Theory. Yuan-Liou Press, Taipei City (1989). Geng, J. (Translator)

# HCI Practices in Software-Development Environments in Saudi Arabia

Khalid Majrashi[1(✉)] and Areej Al-Wabil[2]

[1] Department of Information Technology, Institute of Public Administration,
Riyadh, Saudi Arabia
majrashik@ipa.edu.sa
[2] Center for Complex Engineering Systems, KACST and Massachusetts Institute
of Technology (MIT), Cambridge, USA
areej@mit.edu

**Abstract.** Within the human–computer interaction (HCI) community, there is a wide range of experience and approaches to integrating user research in the software-development life cycle. Independent HCI consulting and contracting is becoming a more prevalent mode of user research globally, but our understanding of the local context in some regions is limited. This paper reports the results of a survey of 65 practitioners working in software-development environments in Saudi Arabia. The survey was conducted in January 2018 and covered a range of aspects: profiles of respondents and their organizations, their perception of usability, user experience and user-centered design, assessment of current HCI activities, and motivation for and obstacles to adopting HCI practice in software-development environments. The results revealed recognition of HCI practices was greater than expected. The adoption of HCI practices in the industry and private sector was greater than in government organizations. The findings also suggested that the most-used HCI activities were prototyping and stakeholder meetings for requirements elicitation. The degree of importance of decision factors for adopting HCI practices and the frequency of obstacles to adoption of the practices varied slightly among government, private, and semi-government organizations. The study results also provided basic information for HCI practitioners and researchers who are interested in appropriating HCI methods to meet local needs. Here, we discuss the results and provide implications for advancing HCI practice in software-development environments in Saudi Arabia.

**Keywords:** Human–computer interaction · User experience · Usability
User-centered design · Saudi Arabia · Practice

## 1 Introduction

Interactive systems need to meet the users' needs, values, preferences, and expectations to be accepted. A number of human–computer interaction (HCI) fields have been growing steadily in the technology sectors, such as usability, user experience (UX), and user-centered design (UCD), which are concerned with how to design effective systems that are intended for human use. In the United States (US) and European countries, the

© Springer International Publishing AG, part of Springer Nature 2018
P.-L. P. Rau (Ed.): CCD 2018, LNCS 10911, pp. 58–77, 2018.
https://doi.org/10.1007/978-3-319-92141-9_5

role of UCD/usability became important in the 1980s and 1990s [1]. However, in many other countries where HCI has not been institutionalized, research suggests that HCI does not play a major role in the information technology (IT) industry and in the development life cycle [1, 2]. Although the topic of HCI in the Arab world has been explored in the academic context [3] and from a research and design perspective [4], HCI practices in professional domains have been inadequately explored in scientific and practitioner forums and infrequently discussed in the literature.

Saudi Arabia has a fast-developing information communication and technology (ICT) sector. Currently, it represents one of the largest telecom and IT markets in the Middle East. According to the Saudi Arabian Communications and Information Technology Commission (CITC), in 2016, spending on this sector reached around US $35 billion, with a growth rate of about 8.3% over 2015 as a result of digital-transformation initiatives adopted by several organizations across the country [5]. Digital services are rapidly growing due to the increase in Internet penetration rates and mobile phone usage. In Saudi Arabia, around 24.1 million people were using the Internet by the end of the second quarter of 2017, representing 76% of the total population, compared with 54.1% in 2012 [6]. There are also 43.63 million mobile phone subscribers, with a penetration rate of 137% [6]. As part of its National Transformation Program, the government has also been improving the IT industry to increase its contribution to the non-oil gross domestic product (GDP) [7].

In 2003, there were 1,650 IT companies in Saudi Arabia, including homegrown businesses, local subsidiaries, and multinationals; however, it is believed that the number of IT companies has increased substantially [8]. In 2003, only a few local IT companies were involved in system development [8], which might be due to organi-zations and individuals preferring offshore/outsourcing solutions. Currently, there are some signs that organizations have already moved from total reliance on outsourcing to being providers of some solutions and services. This could be due to businesses in Saudi Arabia preferring IT services customized to their local requirements, and this would be achieved by entities located inside the country [8]. In-house development of technology solutions has also been observed in public and private organizations. This could explain why "software developer" is currently one of the most common IT jobs, with the expectation of continued high demand for this specialty [9]. However, with these growth indicators of the software industry, it is still unclear if the human-centered approach is contributing to software product development in Saudi Arabia, as well as whether HCI practices are strengthening the capability of software-development enti-ties to provide competitive solutions to the local, regional, and global markets.

In the public sector, the Yesser e-Government Program was founded in 2005 to support establishing, developing, and managing e-government services in Saudi Arabia [10]. Recent research has highlighted the contributions of the Yesser program toward raising awareness of usability as an important factor for e-government services, and encouraging the development of better and more usable government services [11]. However, the scarcity of HCI research in the local context makes it difficult to understand whether usability practices are taken seriously and applied in software-development environments in the public sector.

Saudi Arabia is one of the countries in which HCI education has been getting increasing attention in the recent years. In Saudi higher education, HCI courses are offered at many universities. We conducted an informal analysis of a set of IT programs offered in the top 10 Saudi universities [12]. These programs included bachelor and master programs in computer science, software engineering, IT, and information systems. We found that 90% of the universities considered including at least one HCI course in their study plan. The different titles used for the courses included "Human-Computer Interaction," "User-Centered System Design," and "Human-Centered Design and Evaluation." However, not all IT programs seemed to have HCI courses as core courses in their study plans. It is still unclear if there are trends in increased adoption of usability/UX/UCD practices in software-development environments, or indicators of a growing culture of user-centric design methodologies aligned with contributions by IT graduates from the local academic programs.

This paper presents results from a survey of practitioners' perceptions of usability/UX/UCD, and current usability/UX/UCD practices, and decision factors in the adoption of usability/UX/UCD, and the obstacles that are hinder the adoption of usability/UX/UCD in software-development environments in Saudi Arabia.

## 2    Literature Review

### 2.1    Investigation of HCI Practice

Previous studies have been conducted to understand specific HCI practices in IT and software-development environments (e.g., Bak et al. [13], Bygstad et al. [14], Gunther et al. [15], Hudson [16], Hussein et al. [17], Ji and Yun [1], Rosenbaum et al. [18], Vredenburg et al. [19], Gulliksen et al. [20], Boivie et al. [21]). These studies had different foci and investigated different aspects, including the profile of HCI practitioners, UCD project profiles, the adoption and perception of specific HCI practices, the effectiveness of UCD/UX/usability methods, and obstacles to and decision factors in the adoption of UCD/UX/usability practices. Some of these prior studies investigated HCI practices in countries in which the field was established and strongly recognized in the software-development process (e.g., Vredenburg et al. [19]), while others inspected the practices in countries in which HCI was still playing a minor role (e.g., Ji and Yun [1]). However, to the best of our knowledge, none of these studies inspected HCI practices in Arab countries, where software-development environments may have different cultural and organizational standards, and societies have different cultural and local requirements of software products.

### 2.2    Perception of Usability and UCD

Practitioners' perceptions of HCI practices have also been investigated in prior works. Ji and Yun [1] found that both development and User Interface (UI)/usability practitioners generally recognize the importance of usability/UCD, but there is a higher degree of perception among UI/usability practitioners. Vredenburg et al. [19] found that a high percentage of the surveyed UCD practitioners agreed UCD methods had made a significant impact on product development, and improved the usefulness and usability of products developed in their company. Both Ji and Yun's [1] and

Vredenburg et al.'s [19] studies showed the perception that UCD methods are gaining popularity and they will be adopted widely in the future was rated highly by the surveyed UCD/usability practitioners. Similarly, respondents in a study that investigated the adoption of software-development methods and usability in the software industry in Norway believed usability was important for the success of projects in their company [14]. A recent study on current UX and usability practices in Malaysia also drew a similar conclusion, with many of the respondents agreeing that UX and usability are important; however, usability was perceived as more essential than UX [17].

Despite a growing body of literature on HCI design and UCD methodologies in research contexts in the Arab world, our understanding of the practitioners' perspective remains limited.

## 2.3 Usability and UCD Activities in Practice

Hudson [16] conducted a survey of professionals using HCI and usability e-mail lists. The respondents were asked to rate the frequencies within which a number of user-centered techniques, tools, and methods are employed in the practice. The study results indicated that the most commonly employed UCD techniques included informal usability testing, user analysis/profiling, evaluation of the existing system, low-fidelity prototyping, and expert (heuristic) usability evaluation. Another survey of 100 UCD practitioners about their successes and failures in implementing UCD in their organization confirmed Hudson's finding by showing that the most successful UCD techniques within different organization sizes included usability testing, prototyping, and heuristic evaluation [15]. Similarly, Vredenburg et al. [19] studied the most common UCD methods used in practice and identified iterative design, usability evaluation, task analysis, informal expert review, and field studies as the five most common UCD methods; four of these—iterative design, usability evaluation, task analysis, and field studies—were found to have the most significant impact in practice. The most recent study, conducted by Ji and Yun [1], investigated the frequencies of several UCD/usability techniques employed in projects in Korean IT-development environments. The results indicated that task analysis, evaluation of the existing system, user analysis/profiling, surveys, and heuristic evaluations to be the most commonly used methods.

Although there were some similarities in the findings of the reviewed studies (e.g., heuristic/expert evaluations appeared as used frequently in all studies), some differences still existed. For example, the most commonly used techniques were not always the same. This could be due to various factors such as differences in the profiles of surveyed practitioners and the IT-industry cultures in the different countries. As the studies were inconsistent, perhaps suggesting some differences according to country/culture, to better understand the HCI methods used in the development environments in Saudi Arabia, we sought to conduct a comprehensive survey.

## 2.4 Obstacles to and Problems with Adopting Usability and UCD

In the early 1990s, it was believed the UCD process was not often used in practice due organizational and technical factors [22], and usability engineering techniques were not employed because they were complex, time-consuming, and expensive [23]. In the

2000s, studies also identified a set of obstacles in the way of adopting UCD/UX practices. Rosenbaum et al. [18] surveyed 134 HCI professionals across three large HCI conferences to investigate organizational approaches and UCD/usability methods to increase the strategic impact of usability within companies. Their study highlighted a set of obstacles to strategic usability engineering/HCI. These obstacles included resource constraints, resistance to UCD/usability, lack of knowledge/understanding about usability, the unproven impact of work on usability, and lack of trained usability/HCI engineers. Ji and Yun [1] also identified a set of hindrances to UCD adoption, including lack of knowledge about usability/UCD, lack of practical usability/UCD methodologies, and concern about increase of development cost and time, and lack of trained usability/HCI engineers, confirming Rosenbaum et al.'s [18] findings. Gunther et al. [15] also showed that resistance to usability activities; unawareness of the value, methods, and processes of usability activities; and time constraints by management and development teams were frequent problems while engaging with development or management groups prior to usability activities. Similarly, Bak et al. [13] identified obstacles to the deployment of usability evaluation in software-development organizations, including the developers' mindset and the resource demands for conducting usability evaluation. Some of the reviewed obstacles (e.g., resource constraints) appeared in different studies; however, the findings were not always consistent and cannot be generalized as whole across different development environments. One aim of the study presented here was to identify the obstacles to adoption of user research (i.e., usability, UX, UCD methods and activities) that are prevalent in software-development environments in Saudi Arabia.

### 2.5   HCI Practices Outside the US and Europe

HCI practices face challenges across different countries, especially outside the US and Europe. Henry [2] discussed UCD practice in India and believed that HCI in the country is facing the same usability misconceptions that exist in some other parts of the world. However, he highlighted three main myths that he saw as responsible for the most damage to software development in India: "Pretty screens are all you need," "I can design on my own; just give me some guidelines," and "Usability is about testing." Ji and Yun [1] argued that Korea IT-development environments have also experienced similar misconceptions about usability, which led to resistance to adopting rigorous user research or considering UCD/usability studies in the design process.

In Saudi Arabia, the challenges are not clear. As such, the aim of this study was to uncover the challenges facing HCI practice to ensure better development in the field in the local context, with a view toward understanding how this can be generalized to the regional context.

## 3   Research Method

For the purpose of this study, we used a questionnaire consisting of 48 questions in six sections: respondent's profile, organization profile, perception of usability, UX and UCD; assessment of usability/UX/UCD practice; decision factors for adoption of usability, UX and UCD; and obstacles to adoption of usability, UX, and UCD. The questions were mostly adapted from related work [1, 15, 16, 19]. Different question formats—such as Likert-type scales and multiple choice—were employed.

In the questionnaire, we provided definitions of "usability," "UX," and "UCD," as shown following, to eliminate possible variances in interpreting these terms:

- Usability is "the extent to which a product can be used by specified users to achieve specified goals with effectiveness, efficiency and satisfaction in a specified context of use" [24].
- UX is "a person's perceptions and responses that result from the use and/or anticipated use of a product, system or service" [25].
- UCD is "a highly structured and comprehensive development methodology that takes account of user needs, limitations, and preferences for improving usability into the total user experience" (a definition adopted and modified by Ji and Yun [1]).
- User experience design (UXD) is a *process* that involves techniques and activities to improve the user's experience of a product.
- Usability versus UX: "usability" is an attribute of the system, while "UX" is the user perception that results from multiple factors, including system usability [26, 27]
- UXD versus UCD: "UCD" is a method to achieve ease of use in systems [1], while "UXD" covers traditional usability attributes and emotional, affective, experiential, hedonic, and aesthetic variables [27, 28].

The invitation and questionnaire were distributed in Arabic and English to target a larger population and increase the response rate—around half of the professionals working in the ICT sector in the country are not Saudi nationals [9], so they may not understand Arabic. Around 29% of the respondents used the English version. The questionnaire (both Arabic and English versions) was pre-tested by two HCI researchers and revised based on their feedback, and was further checked by two UX local consultants. No issues were identified by any of the reviewers.

The difficulty of identifying organizations that engage in software-development processes for sampling is one of the most cited challenges in this kind of research [29]. Generally, all organizations in Saudi Arabia involved in software development were defined as the study population, and this included private and public organizations, whether they were professional or non-professional IT organizations. The targeted respondents were IT practitioners with roles in software-development environments in these organizations.

No effort was previously made in establishing a population of organizations that engaged in software development, or that of IT practitioners working in the development environments of these organizations. Hence, we targeted respondents using different channels. The research department at Yesser e-Government Program e-mailed our invitation and questionnaire to 250 IT departments in public organizations through an e-mail list. The invitation and questionnaire were also posted on social media to target more IT practitioners, especially in private organizations that did not provide an accessible mailing list. In the invitation, we highlighted that the required condition for participation was being an IT practitioner with a role in a software-development environment. This description seemed to be effective, as 65 of the total 68 responses were from individuals working at organizations that engage in software development.

The three responses from individuals who were not working at organizations that engage in software development were not included in the analysis.

Besides highlighting the anonymity of responses, to encourage responses, we did not ask respondents to identify the name of their organization, as individuals may have had some concerns about releasing specific information about their organizations. Of the responses, 46.15% were generated in response to the invitation sent via the e-mail list (response rate: 12%), while 53.84% were generated in response to the invitation posted on social media.

To identify if there was more than one response from the same organization, we checked respondents' e-mail addresses for those who used their organization's e-mail servers, and compared respondents' answers to specific questions in the organization profile section. Overall, we were confident that respondents could be from at least 64 different organizations. We also could determine that some of the large organizations, especially in the public sector, were represented in the sample based on the organization e-mail address provided voluntarily by some respondents.

## 4   Findings and Analysis

### 4.1   Respondent Profiles

Most respondents were within the age categories 30–39 years old (63.07%) and 21–29 years old (30.76%). Around 27% of the respondents were female. Eighty-seven practitioners were Saudi nationals. All participants selected Arabic as their mother language. Most of practitioners had a bachelor's (53.84%) or master's degree (36.92%). The educational majors of the practitioners were computer science (37), engineering (8), information systems (3), design (3), business (3), user experience (2), computer engineering (2), software engineering (2), information science (1), HCI (1), and other (3). The countries in which respondents received their higher education were Saudi Arabia (50), Western countries (13), and other (8). Eighteen respondents were HCI practitioners. The primary roles for respondents were project manager/leader (23), developer (10), information architect (7), HCI/UX/user researcher (4), usability/UX consultant (2), UX designer (2), usability analyst (1), UI designer (1), web designer (1), and other (14). Practitioner experience was equated with the number of years they had worked in the field; 22 respondents had 5–9 years' experience, 19 had 2–4 years' experience, 15 had 10 or more years' experience, and nine had less than two years' experience.

Table 1 shows the HCI practitioners' and other IT practitioners' knowledge in HCI practices and their engagement in HCI-related activities. In terms of the level of practitioners' knowledge in usability engineering, UXD, and UCD practices, most respondents indicated 4 or more on a seven-point scale ranging from 1, "very poor," to 7, "very good"—76.92%, 87.69%, and 81.53%, respectively. However, not surprisingly, the HCI practitioners' level of knowledge was higher than that of the other IT practitioners. The differences between the two samples were significant for usability engineering practices ($p < 0.05$), as well as for UXD practices ($p < 0.05$) but not significant for UCD practices ($p = 0.09$). In regards to the differences within HCI practices (usability vs. UXD vs. UCD), practitioners seemed to have more statistically

**Table 1.** Knowledge in and work time on usability, UX, and UCD

| Statement | HCI practitioners (n = 18) | | | | IT practitioners (n = 47) | | | |
|---|---|---|---|---|---|---|---|---|
| | M. | Med. | Mode | SD | M. | Med. | Mode | SD |
| Level of knowledge in usability engineering practice* | 5.38 | 6 | 6 | 1.33 | 4.40 | 5 | 5 | 1.56 |
| Level of knowledge in UX design practice* | 5.50 | 6 | 6 | 1.29 | 4.72 | 5 | 5 | 1.34 |
| Level of knowledge with UCD practice* | 5.22 | 6 | 6 | 1.26 | 4.59 | 5 | 6 | 1.45 |
| Percentage of work time spent on usability or UX activities over the past 12 months | 55.00 | 50 | 50 | 29.55 | 27.31 | 23 | 40 | 21.63 |

*Rated on a seven-point scale, ranging from 1, "Very poor," to 7, "Very good."*

significant knowledge in UXD practices than UCD, which could be due to the recent global trend in considering UX in software design.

The HCI practitioners worked more on activities related to usability or UX over the past 12 months, and the *t*-test result showed a significant difference between the two samples ($p < 0.01$). However, most HCI practitioners spent only around half of their work time on HCI-related activities, which was less than the time spent on HCI-related activities by HCI practitioners surveyed in a related work [19].

In Table 1, the large standard-deviation (SD) scores for the percentage of work time spent on usability or UX activities could be explained by the variation observed in the sample (i.e., our respondents had different levels of engagement with HCI-related activities, and this could be an indication of the different HCI experiences of our respondents). In this paper, the medians (med.) and modes are sometimes reported beside the means (m.), as in Table 1, as they could help with interpreting the results in a more meaningful way.

In general, the results showed a good understanding of HCI practices and an acceptable degree of engagement with HCI-related activities among many of the HCI and IT practitioners. Hence, their assessment of the usability, UX, and UCD practices in their organizations could be considered.

## 4.2 Organization Profiles

The survey respondents' organization profiles are shown in Table 2. The diversity in the profiles (e.g., type and category) could be considered as a representation of the broad range of organizations in the country. As shown in Table 2, the organizations used different software-development methods, mostly agile, followed by others developed within the organizations and waterfall.

The results also indicated that most of the software projects conducted in the organizations were internal projects or projects for clients. This confirmed the shift to in-house development within public and private organizations from the large reliance on outsourcing solutions and adaptation of commercial software reported by the CITC

**Table 2.** Organization profiles*

| Type | Government (35), private (19), semi-government (11) |
|---|---|
| Size | Large: 250 + employees (46), medium: 50–249 (8), small: 10–49 (7), micro: 1–9 (4) |
| Location | Riyadh (36), other (29) |
| Category | Education/Training (17), computer/software (12), health/medicine (6), Internet/e-commerce (4), usability/UX (3), finance (3), military (2), other (18) |
| Development methodology | Agile (26), own method (15), waterfall (14), rapid application development (12), extreme programming (8), rational unified process (4), other (1) |
| Project types | Internal development (50), development for a client (33), adaptation of commercial software (14) |
| Product types | Web applications (54), websites (45), mobile applications (44), desktop applications (18), tablet applications (11) |

*Numbers in brackets refer to the number of organizations associated with each specific profile.

[8]. The results further showed different types of products were developed in the organizations, with web applications, websites, and mobile applications dominant.

Half of the HCI practitioners (nine out of 18) worked for private organizations, and the others worked for government and semi-government organizations. This result might indicate that organizations in both public and private sectors have started to recognize the importance of HCI practices.

At the HCI industry level, only three of the HCI practitioners worked at specialized usability/UX companies, suggesting that firms that are specialized in or consult on HCI have a limited presence in the country. In fact, the scarcity of specialized user-research firms—even though a growing trend is slowly emerging—is being observed at a regional context in the Arab world and the local observation is well aligned with this regional context.

### 4.3 Perception of Usability and UX

Our results on perception of usability and UX suggested that both HCI and IT practitioners recognize the importance of usability and UX (see Table 3). There were no statistically significant results for the degree of perception of usability and UX among HCI and IT practitioners except for one indictor. The degree of agreement with the statement that "UX design practice will have a significant positive impact on software product development within the next five years" was higher among HCI practitioners, and this was statistically significant ($p < 0.05$).

We also analyzed the perception of usability and UX among practitioners working in government (n = 35), private (n = 19), and semi-government (n = 11) organizations. We found that practitioners in private and semi-government organizations mostly recognized the importance of usability and UX in higher degrees compared with practitioners at government organizations, with some statistically significant differences in the results.

**Table 3.** Perception of usability and UX

| Statement | HCI practitioners (n = 18) | | | IT practitioners (n = 47) | | | Statistical difference | | |
|---|---|---|---|---|---|---|---|---|---|
| | M. | Mode | SD | M. | Mode | SD | t | df | p |
| Capability in usability is very important in strengthening the competitiveness | 5.8 | 7 | 1.33 | 5.7 | 7 | 1.41 | 0.17 | 33 | 0.85 |
| Adoption of more user experience activities and techniques to the current software-development methods is necessary | 6.11 | 7 | 1.40 | 5.78 | 6 | 1.28 | 0.84 | 28 | 0.40 |
| Methodology for improving user experience is required | 5.88 | 6 | 1.13 | 6.06 | 7 | 1.11 | −0.56 | 30 | 0.56 |
| Methodology for improving usability is required | 6 | 7 | 1.02 | 6.06 | 7 | 1.16 | −0.21 | 35 | 0.83 |
| Client requirement for user experience has increased in Saudi Arabia | 5.61 | 6 | 0.92 | 5.34 | 7 | 1.50 | 0.84 | 47 | 0.39 |
| Client requirement for usability has increased in Saudi Arabia | 5.27 | 6 | 0.75 | 5.19 | 7 | 1.46 | 0.31 | 58 | 0.75 |
| User experience design practice will have a significant positive impact on software product development within the next five years | 6.55 | 7 | 0.70 | 6.02 | 7 | 1.35 | 2.06 | 57 | 0.04 |
| User experience design activities, techniques, and tools will be adopted widely in software-development within the next five years | 5.88 | 6 | 1.02 | 5.44 | 6 | 1.33 | 1.42 | 40 | 0.16 |

*Statements were rated on a seven-point scale ranging from 1, "Strongly disagree," to 7, "Strongly agree."*

## 4.4 Practice of Usability, UX, and UCD

The results for overall assessment of HCI practices in software product development indicate that usability, UX, and UCD activities and methods had an average rate of employment in software product development (see Table 4). The degree of employment of UCD methods in organizations in Saudi Arabia seemed to be similar to that found by Vredenburg et al.'s 2002 study, which involved participants working primarily in the US and Europe [19].

Generally, HCI practitioners indicated that HCI activities and methods were applied in product development more than IT practitioners (see Table 4). This could be because the HCI practitioners who participated in our study were employed in organizations that already recognized the importance of HCI, resulting in the adoption of more user-centric activities and methods in the software-development life cycle.

**Table 4.** Overall assessment of usability, UX, and UCD practices

| Statement | HCI practitioners (n = 18) | | | IT practitioners (n = 47) | | | Statistical differences | | |
|---|---|---|---|---|---|---|---|---|---|
| | M. | Mode | SD | M. | Mode | SD | $t$ | $df$ | $p$ |
| User experience design activities and techniques are widely used in software product development | 5.27 | 6 | 1.48 | 4.44 | 5 | 1.48 | 2.01 | 31 | 0.05 |
| Usability evaluation methods are widely used in software product development | 5.00 | 5 | 1.32 | 4.55 | 6 | 1.62 | 1.13 | 38 | 0.26 |
| Usability requirements are often considered in software product development | 5.33 | 6 | 1.41 | 4.57 | 5 | 1.58 | 1.87 | 34 | 0.06 |
| User-centered design methods are widely used in software product development | 5.55 | 6 | 0.98 | 4.53 | 5 | 1.63 | 3.07 | 51 | 0.003 |

*Statements were rated on a seven-point scale ranging from 1, "Strongly disagree," to 7, "Strongly agree."*

The results also show that the employment of usability, UX, and UCD methods at private and semi-government organizations was higher than at government organizations. For example, responses to the statement "UCD methods are used widely in software product development" were higher among practitioners at private organizations than practitioners at government organizations. The difference between the two groups was statistically significant ($p < 0.05$).

Participants were asked to select the HCI activities/methods used in software-development environments in their organizations from a list of 46 usability, UX, and UCD activities. Definitions of these activities, which were mostly adopted from the literature (e.g., Hudson [16]), were provided to the participants. Participants also had the option of indicating activities not listed in the questionnaire. Table 5 shows the activities and their frequency of use as indicated by HCI and IT practitioners. Respondents from the HCI practitioners' group reported prototyping as the most frequently used method, whereas IT practitioners reported stakeholder meetings as the most common user-research method.

There were different sources of usability, UX, and UCD activities performed in software development. The most employed source mentioned by participants was internal personnel (76.92%), followed by a domestic company (20%), a foreign company (15.38%), a consultant (9.23%), and an academy (7.69%).

Participants who had been involved in activities related to HCI in software-development projects were asked to rate the effectiveness of the usability, UX, and UCD methods. Around 85% of respondents answered the effectiveness-related questions, which can be a good indication of the use of HCI methods in software-development environment. Practitioners mostly rated the methods as effective, in terms of three indictors:

**Table 5.** Usability, UX, and UCD activities/methods used in software-development environments as indicated by HCI and IT practitioners

| No. | Method | Frequency | | No. | Method | Frequency | |
|---|---|---|---|---|---|---|---|
| | | HCI prac. | IT prac. | | | HCI prac. | IT prac. |
| 1 | Stakeholder meetings | 10 | 35 | 24 | Metrics analysis | 2 | 8 |
| 2 | User analysis/profiling | 12 | 26 | 25 | Storyboards | 4 | 5 |
| 3 | Personas | 10 | 12 | 26 | Brainstorming | 9 | 22 |
| 4 | Task identification | 5 | 26 | 27 | Sketching | 9 | 20 |
| 5 | Task analysis | 6 | 22 | 28 | Wire frames | 7 | 9 |
| 6 | Set usability requirements | 6 | 13 | 29 | Remote usability/UX evaluation | 3 | 4 |
| 7 | Contextual analysis | 2 | 5 | 30 | Mood boards | 1 | 3 |
| 8 | Scenarios of use | 8 | 27 | 31 | Pattern libraries | 2 | 2 |
| 9 | Prototyping | 15 | 34 | 32 | Affinity diagrams | 3 | 2 |
| 10 | Visual interface design | 10 | 27 | 33 | Accessibility analysis | 1 | 3 |
| 11 | Navigation design | 5 | 13 | 34 | A/B testing | 5 | 6 |
| 12 | Heuristic evaluation/Expert evaluation | 2 | 5 | 35 | Service blueprints | 3 | 4 |
| 13 | Informal usability testing | 3 | 12 | 36 | Consumer journey maps | 4 | 7 |
| 14 | Formal (e.g., quantitative) usability testing | 4 | 5 | 37 | Ecosystem maps | 1 | 4 |
| 15 | Usability checklists | 3 | 6 | 38 | Empathy maps | 3 | 2 |
| 16 | Quantitative survey | 2 | 8 | 39 | Experience maps | 4 | 4 |
| 17 | Focus groups | 3 | 11 | 40 | Competitive analysis | 3 | 4 |
| 18 | User interviews | 8 | 25 | 41 | Key performance indicators | 3 | 13 |
| 19 | Participatory design | 2 | 6 | 42 | Inter-usability testing | 0 | 5 |
| 20 | Field studies (outside a lab) | 5 | 5 | 43 | User flow | 6 | 11 |
| 21 | Cognitive walkthrough | 3 | 4 | 44 | Content audits | 2 | 14 |
| 22 | Card sorting | 4 | 4 | 45 | Sitemaps | 4 | 15 |
| 23 | Eye tracking | 3 | 6 | 46 | Features roadmaps | 3 | 6 |

"made a significant positive impact on product development," "improved the usability," and "improved the UX" of the product developed (see Table 6). Generally, HCI practitioners gave the methods higher effectiveness ratings than IT practitioners, with the difference statistically significant for the "improved the UX" indicator.

**Table 6.** Effectiveness of usability, UX, and UCD methods as indicated by HCI and IT practitioners

| Statement | HCI practitioners (n = 18) | | | IT practitioners (n = 47) | | | Statistical differences | | |
|---|---|---|---|---|---|---|---|---|---|
| | M. | Mode | SD | M. | Mode | SD | $t$ | $df$ | $p$ |
| Usability/User experience/ User-centered design methods have made a significant positive impact on product development | 6.05 | 7 | 1.16 | 5.60 | 6 | 1.12 | 1.38 | 54 | 0.17 |
| Usability/user experience/ user-centered design methods have improved the usability of the product developed | 5.94 | 7 | 1.10 | 5.50 | 6 | 1.10 | 1.40 | 54 | 0.16 |
| Usability/user experience/ user-centered design methods have improved the user experience of the product developed | 6.16 | 7 | 0.92 | 5.47 | 6 | 1.10 | 2.29 | 54 | 0.02 |

*Statements were rated on a seven-point scale ranging from 1, "Strongly disagree," to 7, "Strongly agree."*

### 4.5   Decision Factors in Adoption of UX/UCD

Participants were asked to rate the importance of seven decision factors in the adoption of usability/UX/UCD practices on a seven-point scale. We analyzed the responses from practitioners working at government, private, and semi-government organizations (see Table 7). Based on the analysis, all seven factors seemed to be important to the adoption of HCI practices. "Improvement in client satisfaction," "improvement in user satisfaction," and "improvement in product usability/UX" were the three most important factors for government organizations. They were also highly important factors for private and semi-government organizations alongside the "impact on sales or profits" factor.

**Table 7.** Decision factors in adoption of usability/UX/UCD for three types of organizations

| Statement | Government (n = 35) | | | Private (n = 19) | | | Semi-government (n = 11) | | |
|---|---|---|---|---|---|---|---|---|---|
| | M. | Mode | SD | M. | Mode | SD | M. | Mode | SD |
| Improvement in client satisfaction | 6.11 | 7 | 0.96 | 5.89 | 6 | 1.24 | 5.81 | 6 | 1.16 |
| Improvement in user satisfaction | 6.28 | 7 | 0.85 | 6.31 | 7 | 1.45 | 5.72 | 6 | 0.90 |
| Improvement in product usability/UX | 6.02 | 6 | 0.95 | 6.15 | 7 | 1.30 | 5.72 | 5 | 1.009 |
| Impact on sales or profits | 5.34 | 7 | 1.55 | 6.00 | 7 | 1.15 | 5.90 | 7 | 1.13 |
| Savings in development time | 5.02 | 7 | 1.75 | 5.89 | 7 | 1.24 | 5.27 | 4 | 1.19 |
| Savings in development cost | 5.02 | 7 | 1.70 | 5.68 | 5 | 1.10 | 5.09 | 4 | 1.30 |
| Management support | 5.68 | 6 | 1.23 | 5.52 | 6 | 1.12 | 5.72 | 6 | 1.42 |

*Statements were rated on a seven-point scale from 1, "Not at all important," to 7, "Extremely important."*

The results shown in Table 7 also indicate that "savings in development time" was more important for private organizations than government organizations, while "management support" was perceived as a more important factor for government and semi-government organizations than private organizations. "Saving in development cost" seemed more important for private organizations than government or semi-government organizations.

## 4.6   Obstacles to Adoption

Respondents were asked identify the obstacles to or problems in the adoption of usability, UX, and UCD activities in the software-development life cycle in their organizations. The obstacles to adoption of usability, UX, and UCD and the frequency with which these were selected are shown in Table 8.

**Table 8.** Obstacles to adoption of usability/UX/UCD activities in government, private, and semi-government organizations

| Obstacle | Gov. (n = 35) | Private (n = 19) | Semi-gov. (n = 11) | Overall |
|---|---|---|---|---|
| Lack of understanding/knowledge about usability/user experience/ user-centered design | 29 (82.85%) | 8 (42.11%) | 6 (54.55%) | 48 (73.85%) |
| Lack of practical user experience design methodology | 17 (48.57%) | 5 (26.32%) | 9 (81.82%) | 29 (44.62%) |
| Concerns about updating current development environment or method | 15 (42.85%) | 9 (47.37%) | 3 (27.27%) | 25 (38.46%) |
| Concerns about increase of development cost | 18 (51.42%) | 13 (68.42%) | 9 (81.82%) | 38 (58.46%) |
| Concerns about increase of development time | 16 (45.71%) | 12 (63.16%) | 8 (72.73%) | 34 (52.31%) |
| Lack of trained human-computer interaction engineers or specialists | 19 (54.28%) | 10 (52.63%) | 7 (63.64%) | 34 (52.31%) |
| Lack of support from management | 15 (42.85%) | 9 (47.37%) | 6 (54.55%) | 28 (43.08%) |

The results suggest there are many issues in the way of the adoption of HCI activities in software development in public and private organizations in Saudi Arabia. Lack of understanding or knowledge about usability, UX, or UCD, and the lack of trained HCI professionals or specialists were the most two mentioned obstacles in government organizations. Concerns about increases in development cost and time were the most significant barriers to adopting HCI methods for private organizations, as well as for the majority of semi-government organizations. Lack of practical user experience design methodology did not seem to be a significant obstacle for private organizations but was a major problem for many semi-government and government organizations.

# 5  Discussion and Implications

This study aimed to reveal the current status of HCI practices in software-development environments in Saudi Arabia as the first survey of its kind in the country, as well is in the Arab world, as far as we are aware. One of the key findings of this study is that practitioners' knowledge of HCI practices is higher than expected. The study also reveals important information about the most commonly used software-development methods (e.g., agile, internally developed methods, and waterfall), and the most developed product types (web applications, websites and mobile applications) in software-development environments. This information can be used by HCI researchers who are interested in appropriating and integrating HCI practices into software-development methods in local contexts. Additionally, the results suggest it would be beneficial to investigate further the methods developed internally within the organizations so as to determine ways to adapt HCI techniques and activities to suit these software-development methods. Based on the findings, the local HCI community could also promote HCI practices at the different organizations with an aligned focus on web and mobile usability and UX.

In the public sector, although the Yesser e-Government Program has promoted usability as an important factor for e-government services [11], as mentioned previously, our study results show that practitioners at government organizations value the importance of usability and UX to a lesser degree than practitioners at private and semi-government organizations. Additionally, our results identify lack of understanding or knowledge about usability, UX, or UCD as the most significant obstacle to adopting HCI practices in government organizations, and we found that the adoption of usability, UX, and UCD practices was higher in private and semi-government organizations than in government organizations. Hence, the findings of this study suggest that Yesser needs to continue raising awareness of and promoting HCI practices in government organizations. It also needs to encourage IT managers in government organizations to support the adoption of HCI practices. This is because "management support" was identified as an important decision factor for HCI-practice adoption in software-development environments in government organizations. Our findings also highlight the need for programs such as Yesser to consider shifting paradigms from influencing individuals to influencing projects and products by establishing HCI best practices and requirements for government IT projects. Moreover, our results underscore the importance of encouraging IT managers in government sectors to integrate HCI methods into the development process to institutionalize HCI practices in software-development environments in government sectors.

The lack of trained HCI professionals or specialists was also mentioned as an obstacle to the adoption of HCI practices by survey respondents of more than half of all organizations, and across all types of organizations in the sample. Hence, HCI training programs would need to be considered for practitioners. For developers, as Seffah [30] suggested, the educational programs could be provided in their language and cultural context to help them understand and master human-centered design. In addition, these results emphasize the need to consider adding core HCI courses to academic curricula in Saudi universities to the existing IT programs or to develop specialized or advanced degree HCI programs to address the needs of technologists interested in HCI or UX design as a profession.

Concerns about increases in software-development cost and time were identified as main obstacles to the adoption of HCI practices across the different organization types, but mostly by private and semi-government organizations. This finding is aligned with the global context, as these two factors (cost and time) were also identified as obstacles to the adoption of HCI-related methods in related work [1, 19]. The cost–benefit trade-off also seemed to play a role in the adoption of usability, UX, and UCD methods (mostly in private and semi-government organizations), and this result is similar to findings by Vredenburg et al. [19]. Finally, lack of practical user experience design methodology was another problem in the way of HCI adoption in government and semi-government organizations. Together, these results suggest that the local HCI community should raise the awareness of the many low-cost and time-effective techniques (e.g., usability/UX heuristic evaluation) and practical HCI methods that can be used during software product development.

Table 9 is adapted from Ji and Lun [1] to show the top 10 usability, UX, and UCD methods identified in our study and other related work.

**Table 9.** Top 10 usability, UX, and UCD methods

| Rank | Our study results | Ji and Yun [1] | Vredenburg et al. [19] | Hudson [16] |
|---|---|---|---|---|
| | Saudi Arabia | Korea | US and Europe | US and other countries |
| 1 | Prototyping | Task analysis | Iterative design | Informal usability testing |
| 2 | Stakeholder meetings | Evaluation of existing system | Usability evaluation | User analysis/profiling |
| 3 | User analysis/ profiling | User analysis/ profiling | Task analysis | Evaluation of existing system |
| 4 | Visual interface design | Surveys | Informal expert review | Low-fidelity prototyping |
| 5 | Scenarios of use | Heuristic/Expert evaluation | Field studies (contextual inquiry) | Expert (heuristic) usability evaluation |
| 6 | User interviews | Scenarios of use | Focus groups | Task identification |
| 7 | Task identification | Navigation design | Formal heuristic evaluation | Navigation design |
| 8 | Brainstorming | Usability checklists | Prototype without user testing | Scenarios of use |
| 9 | Sketching | Focus-group interviews | User interviews | Set usability requirements |
| 10 | Task analysis | Lab usability testing | Surveys | Visual interface design |

In Table 9, seven of the top 10 methods used in the context of Saudi Arabia were identified within different contexts including the Korean IT-development environment [1], practitioners from US and Europe [19], and respondents from the US and 14 different countries [16]. However, an important observation from Table 9 is that evaluation methods such as usability testing and expert/heuristic evaluation were not among the top 10 methods used in the Saudi context. This suggests further investigation is needed of the reasons behind the limited use of HCI evaluation methods in the local context.

## 6   Advancing HCI in Software-Development Environments in Saudi Arabia

We highlight five elements that we believe should be considered in the way of advancing HCI in the software-development environments in Saudi Arabia (see Fig. 1). These elements were developed based on our results, discussion, and review of previous HCI development strategies in the IT industry (e.g., Smith et al. [31], Mayhew [32]). In practice, as Smith et al. [31] pointed out, all elements can occur in parallel; however, the main issue is ensuring there is enough feedback between the elements.

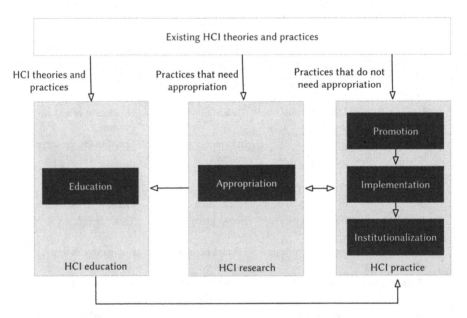

**Fig. 1.** Five elements in the development of HCI practices in Saudi Arabia

The five elements are explained in detail following:

- Education: a deep understanding of HCI will be the main player in adopting HCI in the development environment. This understanding will come only through formal education, which means the local HCI community should encourage educational institutions to take a major role in advancing HCI in the country.
- Appropriation: HCI methods developed in Western countries may not be appropriate to the local contexts (e.g., sociocultural and organizational structures) in Saudi Arabia, resulting in the need for localization of methods for local needs. Local HCI researchers should identify the local requirements and appropriate HCI methods to meet these requirements. Academics should consider efforts for appropriating HCI methods and embedding scientifically approved localized methods in HCI curricula.
- Promotion: the local HCI community should increase awareness of HCI practices, including of techniques that do not need appropriation and methods that have been adapted for local needs. Their task at this level is to influence the *individuals* (e.g., IT managers) at organizations that have not yet recognized the importance of HCI. In the public sector, the Yesser e-Government Program can play a role in increasing awareness of HCI practices.
- Implementation: the focus at this stage should be on influencing the *projects* at the organizations that have already recognized the importance of HCI by encouraging the use of HCI practices suitable to each specific project. At this stage, training programs should be provided if needed.
- Institutionalization: at this level, the focus should be on influencing the development *process* (e.g., by encouraging the integration of HCI practices with the standard development methodology in the organizations that have already seen the value of HCI practices in some projects). By this point, the local HCI community should have a good understanding of the local requirements, the methodologies used in development environments, and the organizations' cultures to enable it to provide insights into how HCI methods can be integrated into the organizations' development processes.

# 7 Conclusion

This paper has reported the results of a survey on usability, UX, and UCD practices in Saudi Arabia. Overall, the degree of awareness of HCI practices was found higher than anticipated. The results also show that the usage of HCI methods at private and semi-government organizations was more than at government organizations. Lack of understanding or knowledge about usability, UX, or UCD, and lack of trained HCI professionals or specialists were identified as the main obstacles to the adoption of HCI practices in government organizations, while concerns about an increase in development cost was the main obstacle to adoption in private and semi-government organizations. Most HCI methods used in software-development environments in Saudi Arabia were similar to those identified in previous surveys, but there seemed to be a limitation in the use of the HCI evaluation methods. Finally, five elements were suggested to advance HCI practices in software-development environments in Saudi Arabia: education, appropriation, promotion, implementation, and institutionalization. Further work is still required to confirm the results of our study and to reveal any other problems and practices of HCI in IT-development environments in Saudi Arabia.

# References

1. Ji, Y.G., Yun, M.H.: Enhancing the minority discipline in the IT industry: a survey of usability and user-centered design practice. Int. J. Hum. Comput. Interact. **20**(2), 117–134 (2006). https://doi.org/10.1207/s15327590ijhc2002_3
2. Henry, P.: Advancing UCD while facing challenges working from offshore. Interactions **10** (2), 38–47 (2003). https://doi.org/10.1145/637848.637861
3. Fardoun, H.M., Gallud, J., Alghazzawi, D.: HCI research and education in Arabic universities. In: CHI 2012: Extended Abstracts on Human Factors in Computing Systems, pp. 1201–1204. ACM, New York (2012)
4. Alabdulqader, E., Abokhodair, N., Lazem, S.: Designing for the Arab world. In: DIS 2017 Companion: Proceedings of the 2016 ACM Conference Companion Publication on Designing Interactive Systems, pp. 348–351. ACM, New York (2017)
5. Communications and Information Technology Commission (CITC): 2016 annual report of Communications and Information Technology Commission (2016). http://www.citc.gov.sa/en/MediaCenter/Annualreport/Pages/default.aspx. Accessed 10 Dec 2017
6. CITC: Indicators ICT KSA: end of Q2 2017 (2017). http://www.citc.gov.sa/en/Reportsandstudies/Indicators/Pages/CITCICTIndicators.aspx. Accessed 10 Dec 2017
7. Saudi Vision 2030: National transformation program 2020 (2016). http://vision2030.gov.sa/sites/default/files/NTP_En.pdf. Accessed 10 Dec 2017
8. CITC: IT report 2009 (2009). http://www.citc.gov.sa/en/mediacenter/annualreport/Documents/PR_REP_012Eng.pdf. Accessed 10 Dec 2017
9. CITC: ICT workforce report: 2015 (2015). http://www.citc.gov.sa/en/reportsandstudies/Reports/Documents/ICTWorkforce_en.pdf. Accessed 10 Dec 2017
10. Yesser e-Government Program (2005). Overview. https://www.yesser.gov.sa/en/programdefinition/pages/overview.aspx. Accessed 12 Nov 2017
11. Al-Khalifa, H.S.: Heuristic evaluation of the usability of e-government websites: a case from Saudi Arabia. In: ICEGOV 2010: Proceedings of the 4th International Conference on Theory and Practice of Electronic Governance, pp. 238–242. ACM, New York (2010)
12. QS Top Universities: QS university rankings: Arab region 2016 (2016). https://www.topuniversities.com/university-rankings/arab-region-university-rankings/2016. Accessed 29 Nov 2017
13. Bak, J.O., Nguyen, K., Risgaard, P., Stage, J.: Obstacles to usability evaluation in practice: a survey of software development organizations. In: NordiCHI 2008: Proceedings of the 5th Nordic Conference on Human-Computer Interaction: Building Bridges, pp. 23–32. ACM, New York (2008)
14. Bygstad, B., Ghinea, G., Brevik, E.: Software development methods and usability: perspectives from a survey in the software industry in Norway. Interact. Comput. **20**(3), 375–385 (2008). https://doi.org/10.1016/j.intcom.2007.12.001
15. Gunther, R., Janis, J., Butler, S.: The UCD decision matrix: how, when, and where to sell user-centered design into the development cycle (2001). http://www.ovostudios.com/upa2001/surf.htm. Accessed 10 Dec 2017

16. Hudson, W.: Toward unified models in user-centered and object-oriented design. In: Van Harmelen, M. (ed.) Object Modeling and User Interface Design: Designing Interactive Systems, pp. 313–362. Addison-Wesley Longman, Boston (2001)
17. Hussein, I., Mahmud, M., Tap AOM: A survey of user experience practice: a point of meet between academic and industry. In: Proceedings of the 2014 3rd International Conference on User Science and Engineering (i-USEr), pp. 62–67. IEEE, Piscataway (2014)
18. Rosenbaum, S., Rohn, J.A., Humburg, J.: A toolkit for strategic usability: results from workshops, panels, and surveys. In: CHI 2000: Proceedings of the SIGCHI Conference on Human Factors in Computing Systems, pp. 337–344. ACM, New York (2000)
19. Vredenburg, K., Mao, J-.Y., Smith, P.W., Carey, T.: A survey of user-centered design practice. In: CHI 2002: Proceedings of the SIGCHI Conference on Human Factors in Computing Systems, pp. 471–478. ACM, New York (2002)
20. Gulliksen, J., Boivie, I., Göransson, B.: Usability professionals: current practices and future development. Interact. Comput. **18**(4), 568–600 (2006). https://doi.org/10.1016/j.intcom.2005.10.005
21. Boivie, I., Åborg, C., Persson, J., Löfberg, M.: Why usability gets lost or usability in in-house software development. Interact. Comput. **15**(4), 623–639 (2003)
22. Gould, J.D., Boies, S.J., Lewis, C.: Making usable, useful, productivity-enhancing computer applications. Commun. ACM **34**(1), 74–85 (1991)
23. Nielsen, J.: Guerrilla HCI: using discount usability engineering to penetrate the intimidation barrier. In: Bias, R.G., Mayhew, D.J. (eds.) Cost-Justifying Usability. Academic Press, Orlando (1994)
24. International Organization for Standardization (ISO): ISO 9241-11: 1998—ergonomic requirements for office work with visual display terminals (VDTs), part 11: guidance on usability. ISO, Geneva (1998)
25. ISO: ISO 9241-210:2010: ergonomics of human-system interaction—part 210: human-centred design for interactive systems. ISO, Geneva (2010)
26. Majrashi, K.: Cross-platform user experience. Doctoral thesis, RMIT University (2016)
27. Hassenzahl, M., Tractinsky, N.: User experience: a research agenda. Behav. Inf. Technol. **25**(2), 91–97 (2006). https://doi.org/10.1080/01449290500330331
28. Hartson, R., Pyla, P.S.: The UX Book: Process and Guidelines for Ensuring a Quality User Experience. Elsevier, Waltham (2012)
29. Fitzgerald, B.: An empirical investigation into the adoption of systems development methodologies. Inform. Manag. **34**(6), 317–328 (1998). https://doi.org/10.1016/S0378-7206(98)00072-X
30. Seffah, A.: Learning the ropes: human-centered design skills and patterns for software engineers' education. Interactions **10**(5), 36–45 (2003)
31. Smith, A., Joshi, A., Liu, Z., Bannon, L., Gulliksen, J., Li, C.: Institutionalizing HCI in Asia. In: Baranauskas, C., Palanque, P., Abascal, J., Barbosa, S.D.J. (eds.) INTERACT 2007. LNCS, vol. 4663, pp. 85–99. Springer, Heidelberg (2007). https://doi.org/10.1007/978-3-540-74800-7_7
32. Mayhew, D.J.: Business: strategic development of the usability engineering function. Interactions **6**(5), 27–34 (1999)

# Mental Model Diagrams as a Design Tool for Improving Cross-cultural Dialogue Between the Service Providers and Customers: Case of the Chinese Restaurant Business in Milan

Margherita Pillan[(✉)], Milica Pavlović[(✉)], and Shushu He[(✉)]

Department of Design, Politecnico di Milano, Milan, Italy
{margherita.pillan, milica.pavlovic,
shushu.he}@polimi.it

**Abstract.** The globalization facilitated the spread of different ethnic cultures in the migratory flows, and enacted coexistence issues within local environments. The Chinese community is one of the most important foreign groups in Milan, with notable involvement of the community members in the restaurant business. The aim of the research is investigating design potentials for cross-cultural environments and scenarios. We focus on Chino-Italian services in Italy, and on the investigation of the value elements framed by different cultural points of view, so to extract design hints for the improvement of the offered services, within a design for experience approach. Specific focus of this paper is verifying the potentials of application of a tool, Mental Model Diagrams, used in the design for experience field, for framing the described main goal. While discussing the different perspectives between the service providers and customers, as well as diverse groups of the customers, we present also an enhanced structure of MMD supporting a triangulation between three mayor schemes of mental models. Such diagrams showed as helpful in underlining the mismatch of the three clusters, the Chinese catering business people and their customers, identified as Italian and Chinese cultural groups. The paper provides also a discussion on extracted design hints from the diagram, underlining its potential as a communication and design tool.

**Keywords:** Design for experience · Service design · Mental Model Diagrams
Cross-cultural dialogue · Design tools

## 1 Introduction

### 1.1 The Cross-cultural Context of the Chinese Restaurants in Milan

Milan is the city in Italy hosting the highest number of foreigners, and the Chinese community is the fourth largest foreign group [28]. Chinese people have reached a considerable business scale in Milan and developed a socioeconomic enclave [4]; at the same time, the situation calls for more intercultural communication between the

© Springer International Publishing AG, part of Springer Nature 2018
P.-L. P. Rau (Ed.): CCD 2018, LNCS 10911, pp. 78–96, 2018.
https://doi.org/10.1007/978-3-319-92141-9_6

Chinese community and the Italian locals. The catering business is one of the traditional strengths of the Chinese community in Milan, which accounted more than 1/4 of the Chinese enterprises [2]. During the last two years, we developed research aimed to investigate the situation of the Chinese food business in Milan [11]. The research revealed that most Chinese restaurateurs aim at improving their business. By performing observations in local contexts and preliminary case study, we observed that the Italians and Chinese are the majority customer groups. Both of them appreciate Chinese cuisine and service. However, these two groups showed some interesting differences in behaviors, motivations, and preferences. It appears that Italian and Chinese customers, in most cases, gain different values and experience from the Chinese cuisine and restaurant service, possibly due to different background knowledge and communication gaps. Meanwhile, the restaurateurs play a significant role in the catering business, as they offer dishes and service from the perspective of the service provider which is diverse from the customer's viewpoint.

The Chinese food business seems to have potentials of growth in Milan, and our research aims to investigate the cultural and practical obstacles that today reduce a full appreciation of Chinese cuisine and catering services, in order to outline some design strategies. In our research, more than on the growth of the economic business, we focus on the promotion and diffusion of a more profound knowledge of the Chinese culinary culture, as a mean for a better reciprocal understanding and acceptance of the two communities living in town. Several Chinese business people, permanently living in Milan and offering food products and services, are willing to improve the reputation of their business and the attraction they elicit in Italian customer; on the other hand, they are determined to maintain the cultural identity and the values of their root culture, while evolving from tradition toward contemporaneous values and paradigms. Our research starts from the assumption that cultural variety is much valuable for urban environments, and that designers can contribute to exploit differences in value proposition. To this purpose, one main task is the investigation of the user experience with respect to the food products and services, so to provide knowledge about expectations, motivation, pain points and all factors influencing the final evaluation of products and services. This analysis provides design hints and orients the definition of design strategies.

### 1.2    Design for Experience of the Chinese Restaurant Business in Milan

In this research, we carry on our investigation within a UX design approach. We regard the Chinese restaurant business not only as a business opportunity, but also as a rich and complex domain of experience [6], where knowledge, understanding, and appreciation are not only related to the intrinsic value of food and service, but also depend on culture and social influence.

**Investigating Different Perceived Values and Experience of Service Providers and Customers.** The aim of this paper is investigating and comparing the Chinese catering service experience perceived by both service providers and customers, so to extract the perceived values from different perspectives, and to outline opportunities and design strategies to support the Chinese catering business. We consider this research activity as a contribution to the intercultural dialogue in the current situation. Considering the specific field of an intercultural environment, and the need for comprehending an experience within a service, we draw the focus on the application of certain design tools, Mental Model Diagrams (MMDs), for meeting the described main goal.

**UX Tool Applied to User Group Triangulation for Extracting Design Opportunities.** We present the results of an investigation conducted on a Chinese restaurant taken as reference field to investigate the different perspectives and perceptions that characterize Italian customers, Chinese customers, and the restaurant owner. To inquire into these three roles, we adopt two sources of data, the interview of the restauranteur and the online observation of customers, and the MMDs play a crucial role to align these different two data source in a holistic perspective. We developed the dining experience MMDs of this Chinese restaurant which illustrate a triangulation analysis of the attitudes of Italian customers, Chinese customers, and the restaurant owner. The discussion of the result reveals the mismatched and aligned experience and perceived values that guide us to several design hints, and it is a contribution to the definition of a research strategy.

## 2  Method: Applying Mental Model Diagrams in Cross-cultural Dialogues

### 2.1  Introduction of Mental Models

**Mental Models.** Mental models, as a term in User Experience (UX) field, are referred to as more detailed understandings of how systems and institutions work [15, 17], as they are the conceptual frameworks consisting of generalizations and assumptions from which we understand the world and take action in it [26]. The term itself was established by Johnson-Laird in 1983 [13, 14], but the association of this notion to models appears much before. In 1943, Kenneth Craik [16] wrote about the 'small-scale model' of external reality linked to possible actions within an organism's head, which influences his behavior and choices of actions. Within this model, the knowledge of past events influences the attitude towards the future ones and becomes active in response to environmental stimuli that appear similar. Mental models, as cognitive structures, enable individuals to construct representations of knowledge towards objective aspects of an experience, object, situation, and/or person, and incorporate subjective aspects of that object as well [18, 19].

In the early 1980s, there were two approaches to mental models in academic writings [7], according to the distinction of main objectives [5]. The first one represents the theoretical approach to mental models focusing on cognitive phenomena, while the second one the instructional approach discussing the development of technological devices [7]. Even though mental models were considered as incomplete, unstable in their permanence of structure and thus unscientific (by reflecting the people's beliefs upon the represented system) [21], they show a value in creating 'mental simulations' of the real situation of a problem [7]. Problem in this context refers to a construction of a mechanism and physical system.

**Mental Models Applied in Design Field.** The idea that an organism may make use of an internal model of the world is not new but also being applied as concepts for human-computer interaction research [11, 27]. The use of mental models in this field was popularized by Norman [22] who defined them as 'system causality conveyance'. As such, he used them to describe how a user reasons about a system and anticipates its behavior, and to explain why the system reacts as it does. Norman's well-known statement is that the designer materializes his mental model of a given design, e.g. a computer system, which conveys his mental model to the user [22]. The difficulties appear in ensuring that the user's mental model corresponds to the designer's model, as their communication is happening only through the designed system [22]. Norman [21] also distinguishes between mental models and conceptual models. The conceptual model is thought through and implemented in the system, in order to ease the under-standing and teaching of physical systems for the users. Mental Models are used in the design field for diverse applications that concern the understanding of behaviors, motivations, social interactions, comprehension of a surrounding, as well as the pre-diction of same behaviors and reactions [8, 19, 25]. The prediction is attributed to an automatic unconscious behavior driven by 'mental models', which are observed as pragmatic solutions to the complexity of life [25]. Knowledge of such mental processes implemented in the design field is helpful in diverse modes of communication. The simplistic nature of mental models might be the key to their utility, as it is enabling faster intuitive decisions [25]. The simplicity of the cities' underground maps, for instance, represent the real network of tunnels and stations in an abstract enough way that makes them easy to read, while remaining very comprehensive in their complexity [30].

**Mental Models in Experience-Centered Design.** Mental Models are applied in design within the user-centric design approach, as they are associated to a deep understanding of people's motivations and thought-processes, along with the emotional and philosophical landscape in which they are operating [25]. Young observes it is a visual depiction of a particular audience's behavior, faithfully representing individual's root motivations and goals, and what procedure and philosophy the individual follows to accomplish.

The research of Mental Models can be carried out as a step in the design process that follows user data collection and precedes product and interaction design concepts [23, 30]. Considering the level of abstraction, the model holds, as well as the overview scale of the user studies, the same model can be applied for diverse projects and lead to diverse design outcomes. For this reason, measuring and representing mental models is a hard task, as there are multiple possible outcomes. Measuring, therefore, is guided by the final aim for the design application of the user research activity.

Developing design strategies in experience-centered design requires thorough understandings of the users, their goals, motivations and thought-processes, guided by emotional states and contexts. An experience can be observed as an episode, a story within a certain time length, that emerges from the dialogue of a person with the surrounding world through actions [9]. Designing for everyday activities from the perspective of perceived experience through emotions, rather than from the perspective of material output, opens up many possibilities for reflecting on meaningfulness in design scenarios [10]. When describing meaningful episodes of experiences, Forlizzi and Ford [6] consider "an experience" as a particular meaningful momentary construction, with a beginning and an end, that grows from the interaction between people and their environment.

This is where Mental Models take part in the design field, by supporting development of empathy towards potential users and their experiences. Understanding and getting to know the potential users in their lived and felt life implies understanding what it feels like to be those people, and this is calls for empathy [28]. The term 'design empathy' has been used in the field from 1990s for depicting the actual role of designers and user researchers [1].

## 2.2    Mental Model Diagrams (MMDs)

**Structuring the MMDs.** Understanding the other individuals in everyday life and in user research often involves an approach of empathy through dialogue, which brings to an empathic analytic response [28]. Pucillo et al., propose an extraction of psychological motives of the users through the narrative analysis of their stories with products [24]. It indicates that experiences can be observed as a sequence of events or actions, similar to a plot, which brings together different parts in the creation of a meaningful whole [4]. Michailidou et al. recognize a particular type of stories with UX related elements, referring to a narration about a specifically aimed interaction, developed between a subject and a system, emphasizing subject's needs, motives and goals that are shaped within a given physical and emotional context [20]. Such a narrative-oriented approach contributes to identifying the subject so to enable the empathy.

There are diverse channels, such as interviews and feedback surveys, available for gathering information as to extract empathic elements for analysis. Such channels, following a narrative manner of communicating information, are the first step towards a structural analysis for building Mental Models. It is possible to extract meaningful blocks for the construction of Mental Models from a narrative of an independent experience. Therefore, a structural analysis shows that Mental Models can support the segmentation of users' concerns.

A mental model is in essence based on cognitive mapping, that is presented through affinity diagrams [2]. Young, the author of the book 'Mental Models: Aligning Design Strategy with Human Behavior [25, 30] recognizes these diagrams as Mental Model Diagrams (MMDs), and we refer to them as such in this paper. Namely, Young points out the importance of providing an alignment between the service providers offerings and service customers' mental models, in order to define a design strategy. For this purpose, she provides a structure for building the MMDs, starting from the material gathered from user surveys. Analyzing the transcripts of the surveys requires a further interpretation to underline well the users' intentions, identify the patterns and group behaviors. Thus, coding is a significant step of transcript analysis. As elements for coding, Young proposes to follow some of the following: Task, Implied Task, Third-Party Task, Philosophy, Feeling, Preference, Desire, Expectation, Medium, Statement of Fact, Explanation, Circumstance, Complaint, Particular Task, High-Level Task. The grouping is represented in three scales of information in the diagram: Boxes, Towers and Mental Spaces (see Fig. 1).

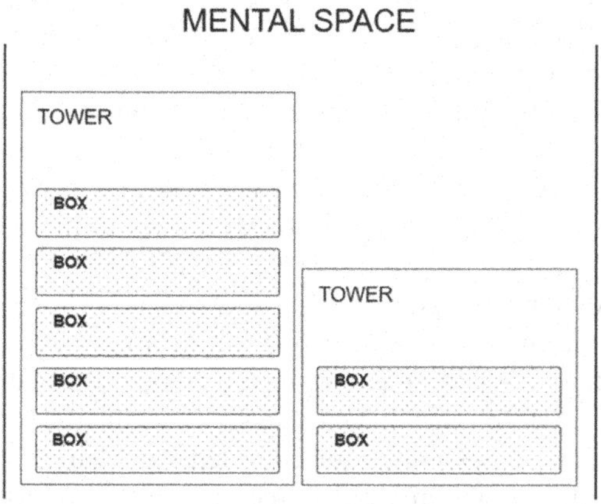

MENTAL SPACE

**Fig. 1.** Three scales within the structure of MMDs, according to Young (2008).

Boxes are the basic building blocks of the structure, and they reflect on subjects' thoughts, actions, feelings, and motivations. Further, the Boxes are being grouped into an upper level scale of reflection towards an experience, called the Towers. Finally, the Towers gather in order to build Mental Spaces. Connected Mental Spaces reflect to what is perceived as the "root" task, which would be the main goal a user sets for himself in a certain context. As an example of a Mental Space, Young refers to the diagram of a morning of a certain subject, by considering activities of waking up in the morning, getting dressed, eating, and getting on the train.

**Applying MMDs in a Cross-cultural Context.** Young points out that in her book she refers to models of a person's consistent behaviors, rather than the models that are seen as temporary representations of a situation [30], and we refer to the same in our analysis. To do so, we intend to deal with models that on the basis of an accumulation of entrenched reasons of why a person is acting in a certain way. These reasons were built over a long period of time of acting and experiencing, and represent a base for solid mental representations.

MMDs, as presented by Young, have as a backbone of their structure an alignment between the service providers and service customers [15]. Kalbach describes them as alignment diagrams that help understanding the feedback loop between the user and the system [15]. Namely, the upper aligned side is the one that is person-focused, while the lower side is the one that represents the elements of support deriving from service business aspects and offerings. Young suggests that in the part where there is a gap in the alignment, there are visible opportunities to redefine, combine, or augment existing aligned content [30]. Our research is rooted in a cross-cultural context, and we want to understand if MMDs are the suitable tool for extracting design hints for improving the Chinese restaurant business service in Milan, and possibly further support the inter-cultural dialogue. The alignment in our case is happening between the Chinese restaurant owners and the restaurant customers. However, the customers are classified in two groups, considering their cultural background, into Italian and Chinese customer groups.

In service design, the investigation for alignment is usually aimed at two main tasks: the detection of pain-points in the service process as it is perceived by customers, and the identification of potentials for innovation related to expectations, needs and motivation of customers. In other words, the issue of alignment is related to the effort of the service provider to become aware of what customers consider as valuable, so to evolve the service characteristics toward a more effective and efficient production of value. In our approach, alignment as a goal is not intended as the smoothing of cultural differences between the Chinese offer and the expectations of Italian and Chinese customers. On the contrary, our goal is the understanding of how to make differences acceptable and appreciated as value by customers. In our research, we focus on service providers offering Chinese food products of high quality, and capable to innovate their offer, while maintaining deep roots in the contemporary Chinese food culture. In order to produce a systematic representation of collected knowledge, we developed three mental models, according to the material extracted from user surveys. For the service provider part, we made a semi-structured interview with the restaurant owner. For the part of service customers, we gathered materials from online surveys for rating restaurant. The online surveys were chosen as a suitable source for building a model based on the opinion of a massive group, rather than making interviews with just a few selected visitors in the restaurant. The two diverse sources gave diverse outcomes that we manage to meet, according to the same coding principles, applied for building the structure of a mental model. Finally, after the analysis was made through the set coding, we provided a triangulation of the three mental model schemes through a developed MMD, that brought us to the extraction of the design hints. The points in whom the three models meet are recognized as the Mental Spaces, and are based on main actions that an individual is undertaking. The representation of the diagram is based on the structure defined by Young [30], explained previously. We observe MMDs as a design tool, therefore, all the research and analysis were guided by the final scope, which is the ability for extraction of design hints. MMDs lack of chronological flow, which according to Kalbach [15] is a lack. We, however, observe it as an advantage for the design application of the tool, considering that this is the tool to be used in the design process before development of the design concept [23]. Therefore, we want to take into account all the main points that brought to sense-making of an experience, observed through anticipation, interpretation and recounting of it [1, 28]. This does not require a chronological flow, but an opening of major field of consideration for possible design interventions. After MMDs, other tools should be applied within the process in order to define more in detail the steps to the realization of the final tangible outcomes, which also considers thorough reflection to detailed time sequences of interaction.

## 3    Understanding the Service Providers: Interview

### 3.1    Organization of the Interview

The restaurant locates in the neighborhood of Chinatown. It is one of the restaurants which first started to offer Chinese regional cuisine instead of Asian fusion in Milan.

After the owner changed the menu, the restaurant's reputation improved a lot, and there is an increase of Italian customers. The interviewee was the owner of the restaurant, and has been living in Italy for six years. He started the business since the third year in Italy. The interview aims to investigate the service provider's perceived value and the experience of the Chinese catering business, so to compare with the customers' perceptions latter. The restauranteur as a service provider holds his opinions about the customer expectations and evaluation criteria; thus, another aim is to understand the interviewee's viewpoints of Chinese and Italian customers. Also, the interview intends to investigate the service provider's current strategies regarding the service and product quality, cultural value and communication efficiency. The last question is dedicated to inquiring the service providers' awareness of the design contribution. Therefore, we set up 23 questions as shown in Table 1.

**Table 1.** Interview question list

| General view | Q1_ Could you introduce yourself and why did you start your business? |
|---|---|
| | Q2_ What do you expect to achieve? |
| Service process | Q3_ What service do you provide? |
| | Q4_ What is the service process in your restaurant? |
| | Q5_ What do you do for managing the service quality? |
| | Q6_ If we regard the restaurant operation and service as a system, what the customers can see and perceive is a part of this system. Can you introduce this part? |
| | Q7_ How about the 'backstage' part? |
| Ambient | Q8_ Why did you choose this neighborhood? |
| | Q9_ What were your concerns while setting the dining environment? |
| Service personnel | Q10_ Can you introduce your staff? |
| | Q11_ How do you train your staff? |
| Menu | Q12_ How did you decide the menu? What are the considerations? |
| Dishes | Q13_ How do you control the dishes' quality? |
| Social interaction | Q14_ How do you promote your restaurant? Which means of advertising have you adopted? Why? |
| | Q15_ Reasons for Italian customers to have picked your restaurant? And the Chinese customers? |
| Cultural differences | Q16_ What do you know about your customers? What are the differences and similarities between Italian and Chinese customers? Are there any gaps between you and your customers (both Chinese and Italian)? If it's possible, could you please tell me some examples? |
| | Q17_ How do you meet customers' needs for customers from different cultural backgrounds? |
| Value | Q18_ Do you see your restaurant as the 'traditional' cuisine or 'innovative' cuisine ones? |
| | Q19_ What are the values in your business? |
| | Q20_ What can customers get from your restaurant? |
| Future | Q21_ Are you satisfied with your business? Why? |
| | Q22_ What's your opinion of a successful/ideal catering service? What would it be like? |
| Design | Q23_ What can design do for your business? |

The interview lasted 80 min which was recorded on video. Besides, the researcher took notes of key points that might be the insights for capturing the interviewee's mental model. The interview was conducted in Chinese. The interviewee shared his thoughts and reflections in respect of the general view of his business, the brief understandings of the service he is providing, concerns of the significant touchpoints, the perceived value, and the feasible contribution of design. In order to stimulate the interviewee to share more and explain better, the conversation conducted a loose structure of deduction and the interviewee was encouraged to give some specific instances.

## 3.2 Analysis

To enable analysis, we transcribed all the original speeches from the video. Then, we refined the original transcript by taking away the stutters and grammar self-corrections. Since the interviewee answered the questions in loose structures, we also reformed the structure of the answers.

The criteria of coding are necessary for identifying meaningful information from interview and online comments, nevertheless, it can result in two kinds of data meet in the middle. Young [30] suggests focusing on what people are doing, thinking, and feeling and proposes five keywords (task, implied task, third-party task, philosophy, and feeling) to deal with the transcript. For the specific purpose of this research, we draw the focus on four questions: (1) what do they want; (2) what are the actions; (3) what do they think; (4) what do they feel? Table 2, in the following, shows the categories for coding.

**Table 2.** Categories for coding

| Type of insight | Code |
|---|---|
| T1: what do they want? | T1_1 goal |
| | T1_2 motivation |
| T2: what are the actions? | T2 action |
| T3: what do they think? | T3_1 stated opinion |
| | T3_2 other's opinion |
| | T3_3 implied opinion |
| T4: what do they feel? | T4_1 positive feeling |
| | T4_2 negative feeling |

Following the criteria, we selected quotes from the transcripts that refer to the four questions mentioned above. Furthermore, we labeled the quotes with the code while selecting, then we rephrased the labeled quotes to give them an overview. Table 3 lists several examples of such a transcribe-code-rephrase process.

# 4 Understanding the Customers: Online Surveys

## 4.1 Organization of Online Surveys

According to our preliminary research [11], most customer of the Chinese restaurants in Milan are the Italians and Chinese. They share some similarities and meanwhile hold divergences of the dining experience due to different cultural backgrounds. Nevertheless, the restaurateur's interview partly verified these findings.

We chose TripAdvisor as the first source of customers' online comments. As the second source, we chose Google Maps for Italian customers, and another Chinese website, DaZhongDianPing, as the second source of the Chinese customers' reviews due to the two clusters' different preferences of using restaurant recommendation sites. We considered all the customers' comments (33 Italian comments and 35 Chinese comments) from the year of 2017.

**Table 3.** Example of transcript and coding: interview

|  | Transcript | Code | Rephrase |
|---|---|---|---|
| Q1_ | so that I wanted to offer tasty Chinese food for an affordable price | T1_1 | offer good taste |
|  |  | T1_1 | offer affordable price |
| Q1_ | I wanted to operate the best Chinese restaurant in Milan | T1_2 | be the best |
| Q3_ | We kept some dishes of the old-fashioned Chinese restaurants, because many Italian customers believe this kind of dishes is the representation of real Chinese food | T3_3 | personal stereotype of current situation |
|  |  | T3_2 | Italian customers' stereotype |
| Q6_ | starts from when the customers arrive to the restaurant until they finish ordering | T3_1 | customers perceive the service from dining phase |
|  | I would recommend the dishes which was well-known by Italians so that it could be easy accepted by the Italian customers who didn't have Chinese food experience | T2 | follow the stereotype of beginners |
|  | For the 'advanced' Italian customers who already had some Chinese food experience, I would recommend the specialties of the restaurant and focus on explaining the cooking process to meet the customers' curiosities | T2 | meet customers' curiosities |
|  |  | T3_3 | change the stereotype of advancers |
| Q21_ | I was happy and 80% satisfied with my business | T4_1 | happy and satisfied |

## 4.2 Analysis

The analysis of the online comments follows the same coding criteria of the interview transcript, as the aim of the analysis is understanding customers' goals, motivations, actions, thoughts and feelings and comparing with the service provider's so to outline the mismatches and alignments. In order to lessen the language barrier between English and Chinese/Italian, two coders were involved in this session. The first coder speaks fluent Italian, and took charge of coding and rephrasing the Italian customers' comments. The second coder is a Chinese native speaker who interpreted the Chinese comments. The two coders cross-checked the results to ensure the reliability of the rephrases. Table 4 shows examples of the synthesis of the results.

**Table 4.** Examples of the transcript and coding: online survey

|  | Transcript | Code | Rephrase |
|---|---|---|---|
| IT_ | We often visit this restaurant and it is not the usual "Chinese restaurant". Excellent value for the payed amount. Friendly and pleasant staff. A proof of quality? Majority of the customers are Asian | T3_1 | Great quality-price ratio |
|  |  | T4_1 | Great |
|  |  | T3_1 | Friendly staff |
|  |  | T3_3 | The place is good when the majority are the Chinese customers |
|  |  | T1_1 | Frequent place for eating |
|  |  | T1_2 | Not a "usual Chinese" place |
| IT_ | Finally, a Chinese restaurant without the usual frills made of dragon pendants and Ming vases. Instead, there is an elegant furniture combined with excellent cuisine and impeccable service. Prices a bit higher than the average, but the quality-price ratio is good | T3_1 | Does not have a typical Chinese décor |
|  |  | T3_3 | It is appreciated the sophisticated appearance of the place, rather than a typical Chinese décor |
|  |  | T3_1 | Good dishes |
|  |  | T3_1 | Good service |
|  |  | T3_1 | Quality-price ratio is good |
| CH_ | I was here for dinner the day before yesterday. The taste for a Cantonese person like me was just so-so. However, it's already something for an uprooted Chinese (…) and that led me back here again. I wanted a typical dish of my home, the soup of fish and tofu, and I asked the chef to cook for us. That was so touching! We paid more, but it was worth. There is a huge gap between the taste here and home. The amazing thing was they offered me free fruits! We spent only 57 euros (we paid 30 euros for the soup), the rest dishes weren't expensive. Here attached the pictures we took from the other day | T1_1 | Revisit |
|  |  | T1_1 | A special dish |
|  |  | T1_2 | Ease nostalgia |
|  |  | T2 | Ask to cook a dish out of the menu |
|  |  | T2 | Take pics |
|  |  | T2 | Get free fruit |
|  |  | T3_1 | Taste is so-so |
|  |  | T3_1 | Worth |
|  |  | T3_1 | Not expensive |
|  |  | T4_1 | Touching |

# 5    Results and Discussion

## 5.1    The Triangulation Between the Mental Models

**Constructing Mental Model Diagrams for Chinese Customers, Italian Customers and the Restaurateur.** The coding of the transcripts contributes to extract meaningful quotes, as well as the further interpreted phrases from the original quotes, which provides the building blocks for constructing the MMDs. Thereafter, as shown from Figs. 2, 3, 4, 5 and 6, we construct the MMDs of the customers and the restaurant owner, based on the synthesis of the interview and online survey. The diagrams aim at facilitating a triangulation among the three key roles so to identify the matches and mismatches occurred in the Chinese restaurant business, by comparing the group and individual mental models. The diagram has been segmented into seven parts due to the limit of the margin of this paper. We sorted the phrases with similarities and grouped them as towers. In the MMDs, the Chinese and Italian customers are regarded as two clusters, and we illustrate the clusters' mental models by merging them in same mental spaces and comparing them between; meanwhile, the restaurant owner's mental model is identified as the view of the service provider. To enable such a triangulation, the customers' mental models are placed in the upper part of the diagrams which are colored in dark green, moreover, the boxes in white on the left part of the towers represent Chinese customers and the yellow ones on the right represent Italian customers. The service provider's mental model is put in the lower part and colored in red. Following the narrative flow of subsequent activities within the service, the similar towers are divided into 10 mental spaces: (1) reflecting on general beliefs, (2) becoming

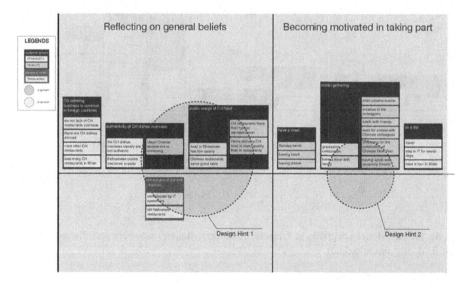

**Fig. 2.** Mental Model Diagrams of Chinese customers, Italian customers and the restaurateur (Part 1) (Color figure online)

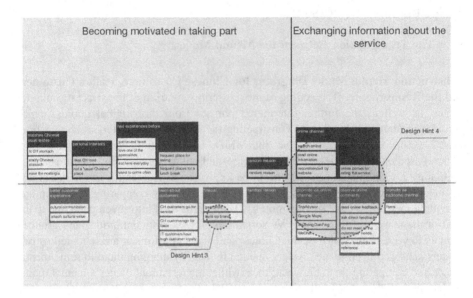

**Fig. 3.** Mental Model Diagrams of Chinese customers, Italian customers and the restaurateur (Part 2) (Color figure online)

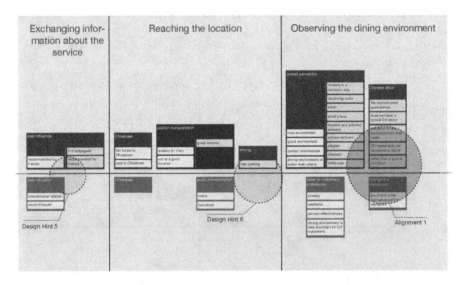

**Fig. 4.** Mental Model Diagrams of Chinese customers, Italian customers and the restaurateur (Part 3) (Color figure online)

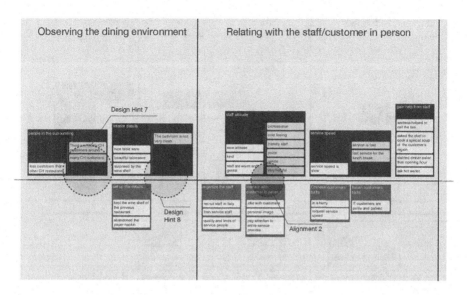

**Fig. 5.** Mental Model Diagrams of Chinese customers, Italian customers and the restaurateur (Part 4) (Color figure online)

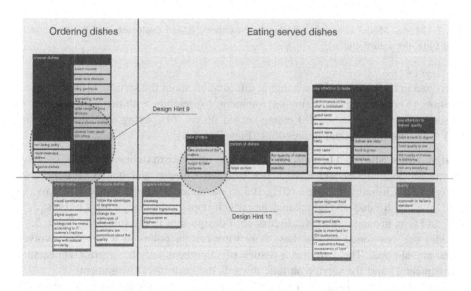

**Fig. 6.** Mental Model Diagrams of Chinese customers, Italian customers and the restaurateur (Part 5) (Color figure online)

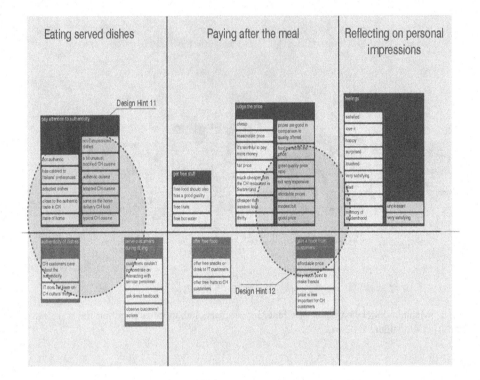

**Fig. 7.** Mental Model Diagrams of Chinese customers, Italian customers and the restaurateur (Part 6) (Color figure online)

motivated in taking part, (3) exchanging information about the service, (4) reaching the location, (5) observing the dining environment, (6) relating with the staff/customer in person, (7) ordering dishes, (8) eating served dishes, (9) paying after the meal, and (10) reflecting on personal impressions (Figs. 7 and 8).

**Design Hints Shown Through the Matches and Mismatches.** The MMDs have illustrated the matches and mismatches between Chinese and Italian clusters, also, between the Chinese customers (CH), Italian customers (IT) and the service provider (SP). We highlighted several mismatches which implied the design hints in Figs. 2, 3, 4, 5 and 6 as instances, and we discuss each design hint in the following Table 5:

Besides the mentioned mismatches, there were certain points in whom the involved sides are aligned. The two major issues of alignment are the interior appearance (Alignment 1) and the service attitude towards the customers (Alignment 2).

Some of the main issues derived from the application of the tool, are correspondent to the expectation we had at the beginning. Namely, the issues such as the considerations about the ratio between the prices and the quality of the food, as well as the reflection on the staff efficiency, were expected. These are the usual elements that are

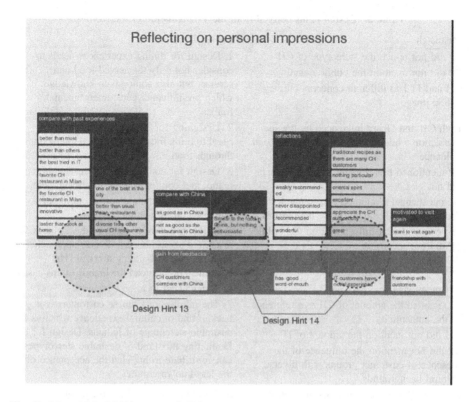

**Fig. 8.** Mental Model Diagrams of Chinese customers, Italian customers and the restaurateur (Part 7) (Color figure online)

proposed in the structures of online rating platforms, like TripAdvisor for e.g. However, we discovered that there are other considerations that are present in the mental models, that influence the experience of a service, but are not present in the online rating platforms. Here emerged the two main points we want to stress out – Authenticity and Stereotypes. These two considerations are present in the Mental Spaces, in regard to Chinese restaurant business, and have an influence on the holistic experience of the service. The two points provide a base for diverse design hints that can further be developed. Furthermore, the diagram itself showed that there are points in whom the coherence with stereotypes are desirable, and others in whom they are not. An example for a desirable stereotype is the believe that if the restaurant has a lot of Chinese customers, it serves good and authentic food. In this case, it is desirable as the customers support this belief, and practice it when choosing a restaurant. An example for a non-desirable stereotype is the belief that Chinese restaurants should have Chinese decor in the dinning environment. This is not desirable from the side of the customers, as they perceive it as bad taste, and they do not want their experience of a Chinese cuisine to be augmented by an obvious fake trivial surrounding.

**Table 5.** Design Hints derived from the Triangulation of the MMDs

| Mismatch | Design Hints |
|---|---|
| SP did not notice the stereotype of CH | 1. Design for dining experiences needs to consider not only the served food and service, but also some given knowledge which pre-influences customers' mental frames |
| SP did not mention the public image | |
| CH and IT had different concerns on the public image | |
| Both CH and IT are influenced by the social interaction while SP did not notice the social influence | 2. Designing for dining experiences as a ritual to bring more interpersonal interactions through food |
| SP mentioned brand value while customers did not | 3. Design for constructing the restaurant brand, and communicating the brand value |
| Online channel is an important source for CH and IT, while SP did not make the most of it | 4. Coordinating the suggested outline of online recommendation |
| IT perceived peer influence from CH, while SP did not specify it | 5. Building a public image of the Chinese restaurant should have a diverse approach from the one of building a brand. The customers do not read the brands in this case |
| CH mentioned free parking | 6. A neglected location advantage |
| IT regarded the amount of CH as a reference of the authenticity | 7. The number of Chinese customers is a background of cultural experience which is a desirable stereotype of Italians. Design for facilitating this kind of desirable stereotypes can contribute to broaden the acceptance of the less-known culture |
| CH did not mention the amount of IT | |
| SP did not mention the influence of the presence of customer groups with diverse cultural backgrounds | |
| SP and CH reach a consensus of interior décor while neglected IT's perspective | 8. An opportunity to improve dining environment by refining the interior design |
| CH and IT held divergent viewpoints about the menu | 9. Cultural value can be better-communicated through the menu design |
| SP's applied strategies did not match with the customers' viewpoints | |
| Only CH mentioned taking photos during dinner | 10. Design for triggering customers to share more pictures on social network |
| SP thought IT were not interested in the cultural value which was the opposite of the real situation | 11. The design focus can fall on illustrating the authenticity and cultural values which is undifferentiated between Chinese and Italian clusters |
| SP mentioned that price was less important for CH while CH recommended the fair cost many times | 12. Price benefits can be another desirable stereotype, however, the cheapness is not the only attraction. Improving the quality of dishes and service is helpful, as the customers also consider the quality-price ratio |
| IT discussed the quality-price ratio | |
| CH and IT both made comparisons with their past dining experiences, while SP did not make a similar reflection | 13. Service provider needs to better understand customers' past experience, thus, coordinating the suggested outline of online recommendation |
| SP thought IT were looking for novelty from Chinese cuisine, however IT also expected the authenticity | 14. Do not focus on designing a 'novel' experience, but an experience as much authentic as possible |

## 6 Conclusion

The results reported in this paper are part of a wider research aimed at investigating design methods for the design of services and products in multicultural environments. We focus on the analysis of the mismatch between the perception of value between the different stakeholders of the Chinese food business in Milan and we employed a tool, MMDs, to frame the different perspectives of the service provider and customers. As we deal with different groups of customers, we adapted the MMDs to the purpose of envisioning the triangulation of information. The approach produced design hints orienting re-design of existing services, and it revealed suitable to support service design in multi-cultural environments; we consider this result as a contribution to the development of a shared language for the project of intangible sources of value.

## References

1. Battarbee, K., Koskinen, I.: Co-experience: user experience as interaction. CoDesign **1**(1), 5–18 (2005)
2. Camera di Commercio di Milano. http://www.mi.camcom.it/indici-statistici. Accessed 20 Feb 2018
3. Coopamootoo, P.L.K., Groß, T.: Mental models: an approach to identify privacy concern and behavior. In: Symposium on Usable Privacy and Security (SOUPS), 9–11 July, Menlo Park, CA (2014)
4. Cologna, D., Mauri, L.: Oltre l'ethnic business. Nuovi scenari d'integrazione nell'area milanese. La Riv. Politiche Soc. **3**, 93 (2004)
5. Feldman, M.S., Sköldberg, K., Brown, R.N., Horner, D.: Making sense of stories: a rhetorical approach to narrative analysis. J. Public Adm. Res. Theory **14**(2), 147–170 (2004)
6. Forlizzi, J., Ford, S.: The building blocks of experience. An early framework for interaction designers. In: Proceedings of DIS 2000 (Designing Interactive Systems), pp. 419–423 (2000)
7. Greca, I.M., Moreira, M.A.: Mental models, conceptual models, and modeling. Int. J. Sci. Educ. **22**(1), 1–11 (2000)
8. Halevy, N., Cohen, T.R., Chou, E.Y., Katz, J.J., Panter, A.T.: Mental models at work: cognitive causes and consequences of conflict in organizations. Pers. Soc. Psychol. Bull. **40** (1), 92–110 (2014)
9. Hassenzahl, M.: Experience Design: Technology for All the Right Reasons. Morgan & Claypool, San Rafael (2010)
10. Hassenzahl, M., Eckoldt, K., Diefenbach, S., Lenz, E., Laschke, M., Kim, J.: Designing moments of meaning and pleasure. Experience design and happiness. Int. J. Des. **7**(3), 21–31 (2013)
11. He, S., Pillan, M.: Design for changing the stereotypes: the Chinese food business as a breakthrough point. In: Valušytė, R., Biamonti, A., Cautela, C. (eds.) 4D-Designing Development Developing Design, pp. 326–336. KTU Design Centre, Lithuania (2017)
12. Johnson-Laird, P.N.: Mental models in cognitive science. Cogn. Sci. **4**, 71–115 (1980)
13. Johnson-Laird, P.N.: Mental Models: Towards a Cognitive Science of Language, Inference, and Consciousness. Harvard University Press, Cambridge (1983)
14. Johnson-Laird, P.N.: Mental Models. Harvard University Press, Cambridge (1986)
15. Kalbach, J.: Mapping Experiences: A Complete Guide to Creating Value Through Journeys, Blueprints, and Diagrams. O'Reilly Media, Inc., Sebastopol (2016)

16. Kenneth Craik, J.W.: The Nature of Explanation. Cambridge University Press, Cambridge (1943)
17. Kuniavsky, M.: Observing the User Experience. Morgan Kaufmann, San Francisco (2010)
18. Mastro, D.: Effects of racial and ethnic stereotyping. In: Bryant, J., Oliver, M.B. (eds.) Media Effects: Advances in Theory and Research, pp. 325–341 (2009)
19. McGloin, R., Farrar, K.M., Krcmar, M., Park, S., Fishlock, J.: Modeling outcomes of violent video game play: applying mental models and model matching to explain the relationship between user differences, game characteristics, enjoyment, and aggressive intentions. Comput. Hum. Behav. **62**, 442–451 (2016)
20. Michailidou, I., von Saucken, C., Lindemann, U.: Extending the product specification with emotional aspects: introducing user experience stories. In: Proceedings of the 19th International Conference on Engineering Design (ICED13), Design for Harmonies. Human Behaviour in Design, vol. 7, Seoul, Korea (2013)
21. Norman, D.: Some observations on mental models. In: Gentner, D., Stevens, A. (eds.) Mental Models, pp. 6–14. Lawrence Erlbaum Associates, Hillsdale (1983)
22. Norman, D.A.: The Design of Everyday Things. Doubleday, New York (1990)
23. Pavlovic, M., Pillan, M.: Mapping hybrid physical/digital ambient experiences: towards a shared language for the design of complex systems. In: Proceedings of the Cumulus Conference, To Get There: Designing Together. Manuscript submitted for publication (2018, forthcoming)
24. Pucillo, F., Michailidou, I., Cascini, G., Lindemann, U.: Storytelling and a narrative. In: Analysis Based Method for Extracting Users' Motives in UX Design Processes. DS 81: Proceedings of NordDesign (2014)
25. Sax, H., Clack, L.: Mental models: a basic concept for human factors design in infection prevention. J. Hosp. Infect. **89**(4), 335–339 (2015)
26. Senge, P.M.: Mental models. Plann. Rev. **20**(2), 4–44 (1992)
27. Staggers, N., Norcio, A.F.: Mental models: concepts for human-computer interaction research. Int. J. Man Mach. Stud. **38**, 587–605 (1993)
28. The Italian National Institute of Statistics (ISTAT). http://demo.istat.it/str2016/index.html. Accessed 20 Feb 2018
29. Wright, P., McCarthy, J.: Empathy and experience. In: HCI Proceedings of the SIGCHI Conference on Human Factors in Computing Systems, pp. 637–646. ACM, New York (2008)
30. Young, I.: Mental models: aligning design strategy with human behavior. Ubiquity **2008**(2), 1 (2008)

# Integration of Communication Matrix for Evaluating Microfilm

Jun Wu[1,2(✉)], Yang Gao[2], and Sandy Lee[3]

[1] School of Journalism and Communication,
Anhui Normal University, Wuhu, People's Republic of China
junwu2006@hotmail.com
[2] Graduate School of Creative Industry Design,
National Taiwan University of Arts, New Taipei City, Taiwan
Lukegao1991@gmail.com
[3] Sandy Art Studio, Taishan 24351, New Taipei City, Taiwan
sleel95600@gmail.com

**Abstract.** With the development of the global economy, the cultural and creative industries have become more and more important. The development of the
film and television industry has witnessed a steady growth in recent years. The
past pure visual entertainment of film and television works has been transformed
into the current spiritual consumption and its core attraction to the audience is its
creative ideas. With the increasing popularity of video equipment and availability of video equipment for everybody, the ways for artists' works to stand
out lie in the audience's correct cognition of their ideas, which is exactly the
topic discussed in this study. This study is one of the film and television art
series studies which construct the research framework of film and television
animation. It focuses on viewers and tests cognitive differences of film and
television professionals in Taiwan and Chinese Mainland and the general
audience for the film. Results: (1) The cognition of microfilm by professionals
from Taiwan and Chinese Mainland is obviously different. (2) There are some
differences among different genders and occupations in the recognition of
microfilm. (3) The research framework can be better applied to the audience's
evaluation of video works.

**Keywords:** Microfilm · Cognition evaluation

## 1 Introduction

In nowadays, the arts are the media which provide powerful and essential means of
communication. For every artist was first an amateur [1], thus, artistically literate
citizens apply a variety of artistic media, symbols and metaphors to independently
create and perform work that expresses their own ideas and communicates their life
experience. Social Communication is a relatively new term that has emerged over the
last decade. It may appear to be a "new" concept that is a regrouping and
re-categorizing of the previously known concepts of social interaction, communication
and language. This process is able to respond by analyzing and interpreting the social
communications of others. Thinking about art as a process of social communication,

© Springer International Publishing AG, part of Springer Nature 2018
P.-L. P. Rau (Ed.): CCD 2018, LNCS 10911, pp. 97–107, 2018.
https://doi.org/10.1007/978-3-319-92141-9_7

this article intends to understand how the relationship between the artist and the audience is potentially altered in social communication. Therefore, this study proposed a research framework.

The research was designed to take into account the changing nature of social communication, resistance to artwork evaluation and the context for evaluation and impact assessment. It involved the following steps.

(a) A review of current claims for artistically literate citizens in relation to arts practice and social communication.
(b) Exploration of the purpose and nature of evaluation and impact assessment.
(c) Development of an evaluation framework and tools for assessing the impact of artwork.
(d) Recommendations for development of the framework and evaluation of communication matrix.
(e) Validation of the communication matrix for evaluating microfilm.

## 2 Literature Review

Lin pointed out that "any perception on design or product must undergo three basic processes of seeing, understanding and touching." [2] Yang divides the evaluation of design works into technical layers, meaning layers and strategic layers according to the semiotic principle. The technical layers mainly include media (creative materials) and aesthetic forms (the composition principle of beauty); meaning layers are stories composed of words, sentences; strategic layers consist of persuading position and strategy [3]. Five elements for the success of low-middle budget film success include: get close to life, trigger emotional resonance; strengthen the audio-visual language, create the overall effect; emphasize screenwriter quality, tell good story; cleverly use black humor, highlight the humanistic care; combined with their current situation, implement multiple marketing [4]. In addition, the film's style tone, character and plot selection, the regional characteristics of the scene, characteristics of the era, the action fulcrum and scene color are also the main factors in the creation of video clips [5]. Story close to life, exaggerated and simple performance style and the rational use of theme song are also important factors in the success of video clips [6]. Video synthesis is to realize the ideal picture and strive to get close to reality as much as possible [7].

Paper concept in the film linguistics does not refer to the work, but refer to the language symbol that constitutes the work and its coding process. The analysis of the film is different from the general work analysis. Instead of exploring the film's aesthetic characteristics from essentialism or studying the artistic style of a film, it explores the interaction of the image coding and the structural style of this paper [8, 9]. As for a film, the so-called reading and explaining this article means the analysis of the film's internal system and study the meanings of all the courseware or their potential meaning and find the precise structure in the various intertwined symbols and signs. To read and explain this article, it is necessary to study the composition of a film, learn ideational function of lens group, image structure, sound element, etc. and carry out the detailed correlation study [10].

Film art work is also a kind of aesthetic entertainment or cathartic product, which provides the audience with physical and psychological enjoyment in vision and audition, so that the audience can feel the same way and losing themselves in the work. By providing a virtual scene to arouse the feelings to please the audience, and make the audience's emotions release and met the aesthetic needs, then the audience finally can obtain spiritual enjoyment and aesthetic pleasure [11]. Film art can give the audience physical enjoyment in audio vision, giving a physical and psychological pleasure through pure form feature. Film art can also play compensatory and catharsis role, that is, the audience's wish can get compensatory satisfaction under screen influence, while their repressed emotion can get released.

Schmitt suggests that firms can use "aesthetics" and "satisfaction degree" as brand awareness and recognition elements, and also use "aesthetics" to plan and execute strategies as a part of marketing [12]. Cultural creativity contains two elements: culture and creativity. The concept of cultural creativity attempts to incorporate "culture" into commodity. In the commercialization process, "creativity" is regarded as a prerequisite to enhance the value of the commodity. Meanwhile, this can also help create brand recognition [13]. Cai believes that consumer's taste and aesthetic claims are implied in brand life style and consumer trends [14].

## 3   Research Method

### 3.1   Research Framework

In contrast with existing evaluation tools, this is a multi-dimensional tool that places the artist and artistically literate citizen's values at the core of the matrix. Figure 1 shows the communication matrix which integrated the three dimensions for evaluating microfilm.

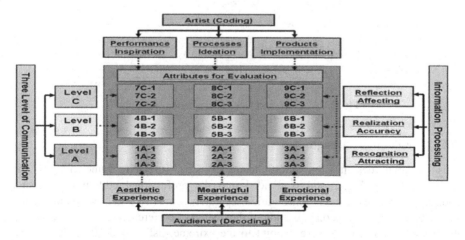

**Fig. 1.** Communication matrix for evaluating microfilm.

Its first dimension facilitates the identification of the core values involved in any artworks, including performance, process and product. Its second dimension facilitates identification of the related theory that may need to be taken into account in assessing outcome and impact. These include communication theory, mental model and information processing. The third dimension is the flexibility, as the matrix can be adapted to the needs and priorities of the different context of the artist, viewer and artworks. It allows relevant measures and indicators of quality and impact to be identified.

Based on the Fig. 1, how the artist's performances are conceived, developed, delivered and received, and how the viewer is attracted, accurately understanding the artwork, and affected by the artwork which all need to be studied. Results of this study proposed a set of attributes of communication for evaluating artworks in practices as shown in Fig. 2. For future studies, we need a better understanding of performance, process and product not only for the artist and artworks, but also for the viewer and social communication. While artistically literate citizens have become important issues in the interactive experience between artist and audience, it becomes a key issue in social communication and is worthy for further in-depth study. However, effectiveness of using the proposed communication matrix is still needed to be further enhanced. This can be done by incorporating with more information of best practice in artist's performance, process and product.

| ARTIST (CODING) | | | |
|---|---|---|---|
| | **Performance** Inspiration | **Processes** Ideation | **Products** Implementation | |
| Level C | C7-1: Topic and Acknowledgement<br>C7-2: Going beyond Reality<br>C7-3: Affluence in Life | C8-1: Thought Provoking<br>C8-2: Deep Planting<br>C8-3: Immersion | C9-1: Emotional Resonance<br>C9-2: Authentic Experience<br>C9-3: Mental Simpatico | **Reflection** Affecting |
| Level B | B4-1: Curiosity Raising<br>B4-2: Desire Exploring<br>B4-3: Emotion Stirring | B5-1: Moving Stories<br>B5-2: Mood Changing<br>B5-3: Atmosphere Bulging | B6-1: Richly Culturally-Loaded<br>B6-2: Realistic Characteristics<br>B6-3: Role Identity | **Realization** Accuracy |
| Level A | A1-1: Appropriately Captured<br>A1-2: Creative and Clever<br>A1-3: Video Effects | A2-1: Well-Paced<br>A2-2: Touching Plot<br>A2-3: Sensitive Settings | A3-1: Well Defined Personalities<br>A3-2: Skillful and Appealing<br>A3-3: Warm Touching | **Recognition** Attraction |
| | Aesthetic Experience | Meaningful Experience | Emotional Experience | |
| AUDIENCE (DECODING) | | | |

Fig. 2. A set of attributes for evaluating microfilm.

## 3.2 Questionnaire Design

This research designs the questionnaire by the research framework of the above-mentioned Fig. 2 and is divided into the professional edition and general audience edition. The professional edition separately scores 18 questions to the left and the right separately, plus one question of the degree of preference for the work, adopts the percentage system to give 1 point to the extreme dislike and 100 points to the favorite; the audience give hundred-mark system on the nine questions on the right side and the most impressive item in the nine questions on the left side will be listed. Questionnaire is filled online. Before filling, the examinee is detailed on the filling instruction of questionnaire. The time for answering the questionnaire is limited for 15 min.

General audience version: https://goo.gl/forms/Xg4s0KfkhhP4MyuB2

Professional version: https://goo.gl/forms/3mwB0q2x4dhrgJPf2

### 3.3    Audience

A total of 204 professionals and 146 audiences are invited to participate in the test. Among them, a total of 204 professionals are included with 100 persons from Taiwan and 104 from Chinese Mainland, 99 males and 105 females; 59 persons below 20 years of age and 107 persons between 20 to 40 years old, 38 persons above 40; 37 film and television producers, 169 general audience; 15 persons with the degree of junior college, 66 with the degree of bachelor, 123 with the degree of master; 118 persons with professional art background, 86 with other professionals. A total of 146 audience include 70 from Taiwan and 76 from Chinese Mainland; 47 males and 99 females; 71 persons under the age of 20, 38 persons between 20 to 40 years old, 37 persons over the age of 40; 12 film and television producers, 134 general audience; 25 persons with the degree of junior college, 91 with the degree of bachelor, 30 with the degree of master; 69 persons with professional art background, 77 with other professionals.

## 4    The Results and Discussion

### 4.1    Analysis of Validity

The reliability analysis of the questionnaire is to discuss the internal consistency of all dimensions of this scale and the impairment of the Cronbach's $\alpha$ coefficient from all dimensions after the deletion of the single item, which is the reference standard for the reliability of the scale. The questionnaire analysis finds that: the Cronbach $\alpha$ coefficient is .956. The total corrections of the assessment dimensions and the content of the single question range from .744–.873, .949–.956 after "deletion of $\alpha$ coefficient". It can be learned that the internal consistency among questions is higher and the setting is reasonable. Through the validity analysis, the KMO coefficient is .923, which has higher value, Sig value is .000 with significant strength and the eigenvalue is 6.728, which can explain the default use of 74.753% variation. The load of each question ranges from .707–.907, commonalty ranges from .792–.905.

### 4.2    Cognitive Differences Between Taiwan and Chinese Mainland

Comparing the cognition of microfilm between professionals and the general audience from Taiwan and Chinese Mainland, taking the two different regions as the dependent variable and the scores as the independent variable, the independent sample t test is conducted. The results are shown in Table 1. It can be seen that both Taiwan and mainland professionals have notable differences in the perception of microfilm and all the scores are presented as Taiwan more than Chinese Mainland. For sound creation, lens language, visual effects, plotting, and immersion, the two places present significant difference. For rhythm, spatial environment, emotional expression, real experience, mood creation, empathy, spiritual fit, emotional resonance, they present moderately significant differences. The audiences in both places show a significant negative correlation only with the lens language awareness, the scores of which are presented as Taiwan less than Chinese Mainland and the remaining items are not significant.

**Table 1.** Summary of rating data and comparison with two areas.

| | Subjects | N | Total image | | | | Key factors of performance | | | |
|---|---|---|---|---|---|---|---|---|---|---|
| | | | Q | Mean | sd | t value | Q | Mean | sd | t value |
| Expert | Taiwan | 100 | A1-1 | 82.35 | 12.37 | 3.35*** | A3-1 | 81.53 | 14.31 | 2.54* |
| | Mainland | 104 | | 75.36 | 16.90 | | | 74.64 | 16.22 | |
| | Taiwan | 100 | A1-2 | 84.81 | 10.71 | 3.80*** | A3-2 | 82.85 | 12.60 | 2.63** |
| | Mainland | 104 | | 78.65 | 12.35 | | | 77.90 | 14.22 | |
| | Taiwan | 100 | A1-3 | 84.32 | 10.22 | 3.41*** | A3-3 | 81.44 | 15.15 | 3.21** |
| | Mainland | 104 | | 78.21 | 15.00 | | | 75.81 | 16.52 | |
| | Taiwan | 100 | B4-1 | 84.68 | 10.65 | 2.92** | B6-1 | 83.62 | 12.21 | 2.97** |
| | Mainland | 104 | | 79.73 | 13.32 | | | 77.52 | 15.49 | |
| | Taiwan | 100 | B4-2 | 85.06 | 10.71 | 3.03** | B6-2 | 83.18 | 11.06 | 3.57*** |
| | Mainland | 104 | | 80.06 | 12.76 | | | 76.36 | 15.91 | |
| | Taiwan | 100 | B4-3 | 83.86 | 11.25 | 3.67*** | B6-3 | 83.46 | 11.24 | 3.12** |
| | Mainland | 104 | | 77.47 | 13.44 | | | 78.06 | 14.50 | |
| | Taiwan | 100 | C7-1 | 82.35 | 12.37 | 2.79** | C9-1 | 81.38 | 11.98 | 2.98** |
| | Mainland | 104 | | 75.38 | 16.91 | | | 76.95 | 17.99 | |
| | Taiwan | 100 | C7-2 | 77.71 | 15.23 | 1.96* | C9-2 | 81.99 | 14.62 | 3.19** |
| | Mainland | 104 | | 74.90 | 16.01 | | | 75.45 | 14.68 | |
| | Taiwan | 100 | C7-3 | 82.55 | 12.47 | 2.94* | C9-3 | 81.34 | 82.61 | 2.06* |
| | Mainland | 104 | | 80.20 | 13.84 | | | 76.87 | 76.64 | |
| Ordinary | Taiwan | 70 | A1-2 | 79.37 | 11.78 | −2.02* | | | | |
| | Mainland | 76 | | 83.72 | 14.06 | | | | | |

*p<.05, **p<.01, ***p<.001

## 4.3    Differences in the Recognition of Microfilm Due to Gender Difference

Taking gender as an independent variable, various evaluation items of film serves as dependent variables for independent sample t test and the results refer to Table 2. It can be seen that in the professional evaluation, the emotion expression (t = 2.08 **) and performance skills in the technical layer shows a significant difference (t = 1.03 *) and men more than women. There is no significant difference in ratings scores of various factors among the general audiences. It can be seen that in the microfilm cognition, general audience across the strait have less cognitive differences in the genders.

**Table 2.** Summary of rating data and comparison of different genders.

| | Subjects | N | Total image | | | | Key factors of performance | | | |
|---|---|---|---|---|---|---|---|---|---|---|
| | | | Q | Mean | sd | t value | Q | Mean | sd | t value |
| Expert | Male | 99 | C7-1 | 81.38 | 11.98 | 2.08** | C7-2 | 79.77 | 12.68 | 1.03* |
| | Female | 106 | | 76.95 | 17.99 | | | 77.63 | 16.77 | |

*p<.05,**p<.01

### 4.4 Differences in the Recognition of Microfilm Due to Occupation Difference

As there is no significant difference in the cognition of microfilm due to different age and academic qualifications, further exploration on the differences in the cognition of the microfilm due to different occupations is conducted. Film and television workers and the general audience serve as an independent variable, various evaluation items of film serves as dependent variables for independent sample t test and the result is shown in Table 3. It can be seen that there are significant differences in the average scores between the performance skills (t = .64 *) and the immersion (t = .45 *), and the film and television workers more than general audiences. The image design of the micro-movie (t = 2.85 *) from audience shows significant differences, and film and television workers more than general audience. There is no significant difference in cognition of other item of microfilm due to occupation differences.

**Table 3.** Summary of rating data and comparison of different occupations.

| | Subjects | N | Total image | | | | Key factors of performance | | | |
|---|---|---|---|---|---|---|---|---|---|---|
| | | | Q | Mean | sd | t value | Q | Mean | sd | t value |
| Expert | Film workers | 34 | C7-2 | 77.15 | 17.91 | .64* | C9-3 | 80.38 | 16.06 | .45* |
| | Ordinary audience | 170 | | 78.96 | 14.36 | | | 81.50 | 12.66 | |
| Ordinary | Film workers | 12 | C7-3 | 88.00 | 7.68 | 2.85** | | | | |
| | Ordinary audience | 134 | | 80.67 | 15.04 | | | | | |

*p<.05, **p<.01

### 4.5 Impacts of Factors on the Degree of Preference of the Work

To explore the influence of various elements of microfilm on audience's preference on the work, the technical layer, semantic layer and effect layer serve as predictive variables and work preference serves as dependent variable for multiple regression and the results are shown in Table 4. It can be seen that the general audience's cognition is not significant and the three items of professionals are all significant. The correlation(R) of overall predictive variables and dependent variables is .94, predictive variables and dependent variables ($R^2$) is 89%. The correlation coefficients of technical level,

**Table 4.** Impacts of technical layer, semantic layer, effect layer on the degree of preference on the work.

| | Dependent variables | Predictive variables | B | β | t value |
|---|---|---|---|---|---|
| Expert | Work preferences | A1: Technical layer | .355 | .379 | 8.27*** |
| | | B4: Semantic layer | .327 | .302 | 4.93*** |
| | | C7: Effect layer | .317 | .313 | 5.74*** |
| R = .942 Rsq = .888 F = 532.566*** | | | | | |

***p<.001.

semantic level, effect level and overall preference are 8.27, 4.93 and 5.74, respectively, which are all positively correlated and reach a significant level of .001.

To further explore the impacts of nine factors on the degree of preference of the work, nine factors including sound creation, lens language and visual effects are used as predictive variables, the degree of preference of the works serve as dependent variables for multiple regression and the results are shown in Table 5. It can be seen that in the comparison of items score and overall preference of professionals, five items are significant. The correlation(R) of overall predictive variables and dependent variable is .94 and the explanatory variance ($R^2$) of predictive variables and dependent variables is 89%. The correlation coefficients of visual effects, plotting, performance skills and overall preference are 4.97, 4.46 and 5.52 respectively, which are all positive correlation, reaching significant correlation level of .001. The correlation coefficients of sound creation, rhythm and preference are 3.17 and 1.98 respectively with .01 and .05 significant positive correlation. Lens language and the overall preference reach –2.51 negative significant correlation.

**Table 5.** Impacts of various dimensions on the degree of preference on the work.

| | Dependent variables | Predictive variables | B | β | t value |
|---|---|---|---|---|---|
| Expert | Work preferences | Video effects | .221 | .230 | 4.97*** |
| | | Creative and clever | –.155 | –.146 | –2.51* |
| | | Appropriately captured | .134 | .160 | 3.17** |
| | | Emotion stirring | .259 | .261 | 4.46*** |
| | | Curiosity raising | .091 | .088 | 1.98* |
| | | Going beyond reality | .261 | .323 | 5.52*** |
| R = .942 Rsq = .888 F = 170.754*** | | | | | |

*p<.05, **p<.01, ***p<.001

## 4.6    Impacts Difference of Factors on the Overall Rating of the Work

To explore the difference of influence of technical layer, semantic layer and effect layer on the overall rating of works, the technical layer, semantic layer and effect layer serve as predictive variables, the three overall ratings of the works serve as dependent variables for multiple regression and the results are shown in Table 6. It can be seen that the comparison of each item score and overall score of subjects is significant. The overall predictive variables and dependent variable reach .001 strong significant correlation, which can well explain the relationship. Under comparison, it can be seen that the effect layer (t = 14.295 ***) is significantly and strongly correlated with the effect overall rating. The semantic layer (t = 7.951 ***) and the effect layer (t = 6.066 ***) are significantly and strongly correlated with semantic overall rating and the technical layer (t = 4.957 ***) and the semantic layer (t = 5.784 ***) are significantly and strongly correlated with the technical overall rating.

**Table 6.** The impacts of technical layer, semantic layer, effect layer on the overall rating of the three items.

| Dependent variables | Predictive variables | B | β | t value |
|---|---|---|---|---|
| C9: Overall effect evaluation | C7: Effect layer | .835 | .840 | 14.295*** |
| R = .915 Rsq = .838 F = 343.291*** | | | | |
| B6: Overall semantic evaluation | B4: Semantic layer | .510 | .577 | 7.951*** |
| | C7: Effect layer | .313 | .378 | 6.066*** |
| R = .904 Rsq = .818 F = 298.347*** | | | | |
| A1: Overall Technical evaluation | A1: Technical layer | .299 | .328 | 4.957*** |
| | B4: Semantic layer | .461 | .477 | 5.784*** |
| R = .875 Rsq = .765 F = 215.968*** | | | | |

***p<.001.

## 5   Conclusions

Due to its dynamic nature, the film and TV works have become the fast-consuming industries. The driving force behind the development of the industry lies in the creativity of new ideas. The film and television artists create the final works by constantly coding and compiling the various elements such as ingenuity and skill and creativity. However, the expression of creativity in film and television works is inseparable from the audiences' experience of consumption of movies. Only when the audience admits the ideas contained in watching and listening, the value emerges, so the way the film and television artists convey their ideas and the way the audience agrees with the ideas are worth discussing and exploring. In this study, the artist's creative communication is set as the process of continuous coding. In the process of viewing the works, the audience decodes the elements continuously and discusses the audience's cognition of the works and attributes of the film and television so as to help the film and television artists to be creative. The results of this study are organized as follows:

(1)  The cognition of film and television works by professionals in different geographical and cultural backgrounds is quite different, while the general audiences' cognition of works is less obvious.

(2)  There is no obvious difference in cognition among subjects with different qualifications and ages. There are differences between "emotion expression" and "performance skills" among professionals of different genders and male surpasses female. There is no significant difference among general audiences. For professionals

of different professions, the "performance skills" and "immersion" of film and television workers are more significant than that of ordinary profession. For general audiences, the "image design" of film ad television workers is more significant than that of ordinary profession.

(3) The technical layer, semantic layer and effect layer of the research framework have a strong and significant impact on the preference of the film and television works. The score of the three subjects directly affects their preference of the film and television works. Among the nine evaluation elements on the left side of Fig. 2, the six elements of "visual effects", "plotting", "lens language", "performance skills", "sound creation" and "rhythm" have a significant impact on a subject's preference.

(4) Through the subjects' assessment of the general rating, it can be seen that the technical layer, semantic layer and effect layer in Fig. 1 respectively have a significant impact on the technical overall rating, semantic overall rating and effect overall rating, indicating that the architecture is reasonable and can be verified. At the same time, the scores of technical layer and semantic layer also have a significant impact on the score of technical and semantic overall rating. This also shows that in the cognitive process of film and television works, the subjects interpret the work as a whole and it is difficult to distinguish each one of the element. There is the phenomenon of cross-mixing, which is in line with the features that film and television work sets video, sound, sports and many other elements in one.

The cognition of film and television works is a relatively complicated issue. The influence of the effect layer in Fig. 1 on the overall rating has not been mixed yet and needs to be further verified. In Fig. 2, the specific differences and correlations among the various elements of communication and psychology involved in the process of interpreting video and TV programs and the overall cognition need to be further explored.

# References

1. Emerson, R.W.: Poetry and imagination. Lett. Soc. Aims **8**, 3–4 (1883)
2. Yen, H.-Y., Lin, P.H., Lin, R.: Emotional product design and perceived brand emotion. Int. J. Adv. Psychol. (IJAP) **3**(2), 59–66 (2014)
3. Lv, Z.-H., He, M.-Q.: Product design using cultural symbols. Des. Res. **121**(6), 140–146 (2006)
4. Qiu, L.: Analysis of the five elements of the success of small and medium cost movies. Media **231**(9), 67–68 (2016)
5. Ji, G.-G.: On the basic elements of the design of film and television art scene. Hundred Sch. in Arts **146**(S2), 111–112 (2013)
6. Li, K.: Features of chopsticks brothers series microfilms. Movie Lit. **612**(15), 111–112 (2013)
7. Zhou, Y.: Realism and lens sensation of synthetic elements of film and TV special effects production of special effects lens in "Taiwan 1895". J. Beijing Film Acad. **195**(145), 72–75 (2009)

8. Jia, L.-L.: Film Linguistics, 1st edn. China Film Press, Beijing (1996)
9. Brown, N.: History of Film Theory, 1st edn. China Film Press, Beijing (1994)
10. Peng, J.-X.: Film Aesthetics, 2nd edn. Peking University Press, Beijing (2016)
11. Collingwood, R.G.: The Principle of Art, 1st edn. China Social Sciences Publishing House, Beijing (1985)
12. Simonson, A., Schmitt, B.H.: Marketing Aesthetics: The Strategic Management of Brands, Identity, and Image. Simon and Schuster, New York (1997)
13. Zheng, Z.-L.: Cultural and Creative Marketing, 1st edn. Five South, Taipei (2013)
14. Cai, S.-L.: Aesthetic Business Profit Model, 1st edn. Far-Flowing, Taipei (2015)

# Story Board Tools and Methods for User-Knowledge-Based Automotive Human-Machine Interface Design

Qingshu Zeng[1]([✉]) and Mingxiang Shi[2]

[1] School of Design Arts and Media, Nanjing University of Science and Technology, 200, Xiaolingwei Street, Nanjing 210094, Jiangsu, China
45157331@qq.com
[2] School of Fine Arts, Hunan Normal University, 36, Lushan Street Changsha 410081, Hunan, China

**Abstract.** Conceptual design is a creative activity in the early phase of the design process, during which designers usually stimulate their inspiration with related tools and methods. Therefore, methods of conceptual innovation are important issues of concern in the area of design research. This study is oriented towards automotive human-machine interface (HMI) design objects and user knowledge, and explores the tools and methods for supplementing conceptual innovation. By combining theoretical and empirical analysis, this research obtains user knowledge related to automotive HMI, and constructs and presents a new storyboard framework using the axes of vision, scenario, and process to contribute to automotive HMI design innovation. The work presented in this paper examines the case of interactive design for an electric automobile navigation interface, and addresses two key problems in the design process: (1) the framework of navigation functions; and (2) the conceptual design of human-machine navigation interfaces. This research further constructs a navigation interface design storyboard based on user knowledge, thereby aiding designers in the creation of a design interface that integrates software with hardware. The effectiveness and feasibility of the method are preliminarily validated.

**Keywords:** User knowledge · Automotive Human-Machine Interface
Automotive styling design · Storyboard

## 1 Introduction

The automotive human-machine interface (HMI) has gradually become one of the critical issues in the automotive design field [1]. Tan and Zhao [2] studied the changes in human-automobile interaction modalities with respect to the automobile interior space, human-machine interface, and processes of operation and interaction. Other researchers [3, 4] focused on the design objects and modalities in automotive HMI, and concluded that the traditional priorities of industrial design, with interior layout and in-vehicle information systems (IVIS) as separated parts, are giving way to a trend of increasing integration, with car styling designers, UI designers, and third party developers (e.g., makers) working more closely and becoming increasingly involved in the design

© Springer International Publishing AG, part of Springer Nature 2018
P.-L. P. Rau (Ed.): CCD 2018, LNCS 10911, pp. 108–119, 2018.
https://doi.org/10.1007/978-3-319-92141-9_8

process. Against this backdrop, aiding design teams by using integrated tools for innovative conceptual design has taken on great importance [5]. On the one hand, design tools enable designers to quickly respond to user needs, thus reducing the costs of data collection. On the other hand, with the change from a modality relying on a single individual expert to those centering on self-organizing, which facilitates nimble and flexible adaptation to changing design environments, these tools are foreseen to further enable communication and sharing of concepts among designers [6]. Therefore, this research begins with the storyboard tool, which is widely used in automotive HMI design as the starting point from which to develop a small-scale design tool that can be used across users of automotive HMI and user knowledge.

Design is essentially a process of collecting, storing, and applying knowledge [7]. Viewed from the theoretical standpoint of the semantics of information encoding and decoding, knowledge related to design can be classified into two categories: design knowledge and user knowledge [8]. In 2001, Sato and Sakol argued that the design process is a knowledge implementation process through which a designer engages in design behavior to transform internal knowledge into external product attributes and physical manifestations [9]. Sakol further advanced the idea by arguing that the design process is a continuous cycle of user knowledge becoming design knowledge and vice versa [10]. Furthermore, when designers apply internal knowledge during the problem-solving process, the knowledge itself takes on the functions of tools [11].

Automotive HMI design knowledge includes car styling knowledge, human-computer interface knowledge, automotive human factors engineering, knowledge of the psychology of driving, and other descriptive knowledge related to the design domain [12]. User knowledge is the experience of solving problems, and is gained when using the product(s); it is linked with the user's needs, behaviors, and mental model. User knowledge pertaining to automotive HMI design is a kind of procedural knowledge of how users accomplish driving tasks, which is intimately related to driver behavior and operational procedures, and organized as a task flow through the arrangement of key tasks in a logical, time sequenced manner. The vehicle information systems that are presently being introduced have led to the functional enhancement of the automotive HMI such that in addition to driving, users are also required to engage in numerous other activities unrelated to driving such as interacting with the navigation, social communication, and entertainment systems. This has increased the complexity of driving [13]. Therefore, the acquisition and description of procedural knowledge related to users' driving is the key factor aiding the conceptual design of automotive HMI. This knowledge has the attributes of methods, plans, and resources; design tools derived from and inspired by user knowledge aids designers in understanding users' driving behavior and their interaction context. This approach improves the design efficiency of inter-group collaboration between car styling designers and UI designers. Figure 1 shows the knowledge related to automotive HMI design.

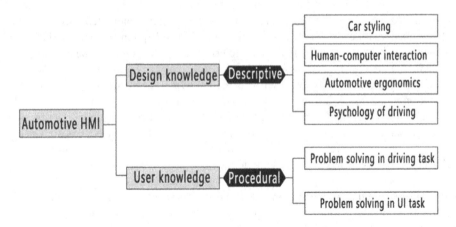

**Fig. 1.** Knowledge relevant to automotive HMI

## 2  Storyboard Tool

Storyboards were widely used in the early stage of movie filming as a tool for assisting in screenplay and scene visualization. Storyboards use conceptual diagramming to visualize individual shots thus allowing the entire production team to visualize camera angles, scene and location changes, spatial arrangements, lighting, movement, and other elements before actual shooting. Sherman pointed out that the creation of movie storyboards involves diagramming a series of rough sketches and providing an explanation for every scene and each position within scenes. Storyboards are a visual record of the entire film prior to shooting. Hart considered the storyboard to be an effective tool that offers a way to set up every shot and scene during filming [14]. Metz refers to camera shots, which is the basic element of the storyboard, as "the basic unit of communication through film." Typically, the organization of shots and scenes is based on a logical narrative sequence with the storyboard explaining each action of each scene. Visualization by means of storyboard expression permits the production team members to improve their understanding of complex movements and positions in a scene. Therefore, the storyboard is also known as the "visual script" [15].

As a very expressive creative tool, storyboards have also been used in the field of design. (1) The storyboards gives rise to improved communication between different roles. During the design process, the designers' concepts can be transmitted via storyboards to the entire design team, clients, and potential users. This frame-by-frame method assists designers in describing issues and communicating solutions. The use of accessible, visual language enables people of different backgrounds to comprehend the creative concepts. (2) Similar to a rough sketch, the storyboard creating process is also a visual thought process. Garner asserted that the form and function of storyboards would change as the product development process evolves [16]. (3) From the standpoint of finding solutions to design demands, storyboards reflect the divergence in design thinking, that is, the evolution of the solutions and deduction process of designers. The function of the storyboard evolves with each stage of creative design of the product; it is an effective way of activating conceptual ideas throughout the design process.

In the automotive HMI conceptual design process, storyboards can "sequentialize" the observable features of user knowledge with a series of driver behaviors and operations, thus forming a process flow that creates a comprehensive design solution that integrates system functions, interactive process flow, and interface design.

## 3 Method

### 3.1 Storyboard Framework Based on the Axes of Vision, Scenario, and Process

In movie and animation production, the storyboard, with a subtitle script, is usually divided into four axes: picture, action, dialog, and time. Each axis separately describes different aspects of a character, a scene, time, or other elements, thereby fully presenting each kind of information [17]. This paper draws on the multi-dimensional axes model used in movie storyboard making to gain user knowledge, by using axes of vision, scenario, and process, to build a storyboard for the automotive HMI. This storyboard is expected to help realize the goals of rapidly comprehending user behavior and transforming them into design solution concepts. The framework of the storyboard presented in this paper is shown in Fig. 2.

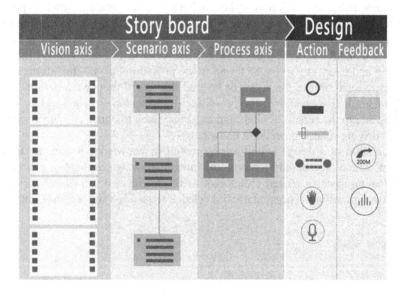

**Fig. 2.** Storyboard framework

The vision axis describes user knowledge from the perspective of user groups and their needs; it consists of characters, events, interfaces, and other elements. The visual axis features the visual communication and event-based narrative flow of traditional storyboards, all of which help designers to understand designated users and design tasks.

The scenario axis describes the procedural knowledge of users in the operational state of interactive tasks and is composed of the environment, behavioral, and other elements. It is the procedural and knowledge transformation of people and events in the visual axis. It offers conceptual assistance to designers in dealing with interactive behavior and interactive semantics.

The process axis describes the sequence of interactive tasks from the operational point of view and is composed of operational processes. It is the transformation of procedural knowledge into the design, and the transformation of auxiliary interface information, interaction flow, interaction mode, and usage cases into the design.

The axes of vision, scenario, and process constitute a new interactive interface design storyboard for the automotive HMI; it is based on the traditional visual narrative storyboard to describe and communicate the procedural knowledge of drivers, thereby sequentially and logically promoting the transformation of the interactive process, interface styling, and visualization into design.

### 3.2    Interactive Design of Automotive HMI Based on Storyboard

According to the Theory of Design Processes proposed by Tovey in 2005 [18], storyboard-based design activities can be abstracted into two categories: analytics-user knowledge acquisition, and synthesis-design program generation.

1. User knowledge acquisition: Storyboards function as intermediary tools to promote the transformation of user knowledge into design. The storyboard transforms user knowledge into three types of useful design information: in the vision axis – the needs and intentions of the user (driver), in the scenario axis - the status of the user's solving and executing in the task, and in the procedural axis – the information on the operational time of the task. The layered storyboard framework permits extraction of implicit user knowledge for explicit representation to aid auxiliary HMI styling and to the benefit of UI designers as they seek to obtain and incorporate the user's driving-related procedural knowledge.
2. The creation of a design solution is the result of knowledge processing to drive design, which here mainly refers to the integrated design of display, control, and information systems related to automotive HMI. Figure 3 shows the storyboard-based design solving process of user knowledge acquisition and proposal generation.

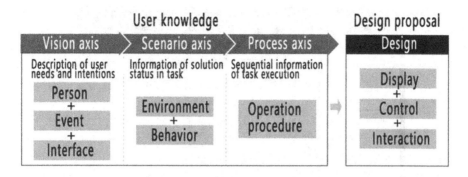

**Fig. 3.** Design solving process based on storyboard construction

# 4   Case Study of Navigation Interface UI Design

In this work, the case analysis method was used to verify the theoretical framework of the above research. The studied case is based on the UI design of a navigation interface for an independently developed electric vehicle. Navigation is an important function of the interactive system of electric vehicles. The key issues in this design are: (1) the functional framework of navigation and (2) the conceptual UI design of the navigation interface.

## 4.1   Constructing an Interactive Navigation Storyboard Based on User Knowledge

1. Building the vision axis: Based on field research in the car and its environment, this work analyzed the behavior in relation to driving tasks and interaction with the navigation system, and extracted procedural knowledge related to the operations from it, and then formulated it as a storyboard to create a script, which is displayed in seven frames. The vision axis shows the entire process from the moment the user starts until they finish a navigation task. This visualization of procedural knowledge helps designers rapidly understand user needs and intentions, and paves the way for cognitive transformation on the scenario axis. Figure 4 shows the vision axis.

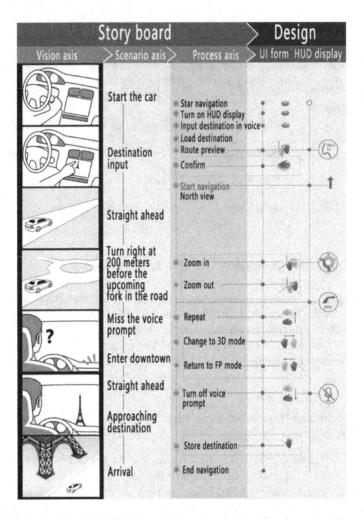

**Fig. 4.** Storyboard for UI design of the navigation interface in an electric car

2. Building the scenario axis: Based on the vision axis, and as shown on the scenario axis of Fig. 4, the overall procedure is: start the car - input destination - ... - end navigation. The message conveyed by the vision axis shows that the interactive tasks of navigation route planning are dynamically associated with the driving environment. For example, prompts such as "turn right 200 m before the upcoming fork in the road" uses changes in the road environment to trigger the user's anticipation of the task. The extraction of task objectives from the scenario axis of the task helps designers understand the characteristics of real-time interactive tasks according to the dynamic driving conditions, as to promote the subsequent knowledge transformation of the means of interaction and procedures. Figure 4 shows the scenario axis.

3. Building the process axis: Based on the set of the vision axis, the basic process is: initiate navigation - turn on the head-up display (HUD) - voice input of destination - load destination - route preview - route confirmation - end navigation. The details are as shown in the process axis in Fig. 4. Depending on real-time traffic conditions, there may be incremental interactive tasks in the navigation process, such as switching views and repeating voice announcements. The designer's understanding and design optimization of the operational process in these tasks can enhance the user's emotional experience. Therefore, the process axis not only establishes the chronological sequence of the interactive tasks but also coordinates the interaction between the car and environment through the scenario axis, thus helping designers to improve their understanding of the dynamic navigation decision-making process and supporting the display and control interface design in later stages.

## 4.2   Concept UI Design of the Navigation Interface with the Use of Storyboards

The functional framework and the concept design of interactions are as follows:

1. The functional framework design is shown in Fig. 5. Based on the user knowledge transformation in the storyboard tool axes of vision, scenario, and process, it can be observed that there are different levels of interactive tasks. Basic tasks correspond to route planning functions (destination input, route selection, preview, etc.); incremental tasks correspond to decision-supporting functions (view switching, zooming, etc.). The next step involves designing the form of interaction corresponding to the functional framework and tasks.

| Function architecture | Form of interaction |
|---|---|
| Star navigation | Button/touch screen |
| Input destination | Voice/touch input |
| Route selection | Gesture |
| Route preview | Gesture |
| Zoom view | Gesture |
| Shift view | Gesture |
| Adjust volume | Gesture |
| Repeat voice prompt | Gesture |
| Store destination | Gesture |
| Turn on HUD display | Button on steering wheel |

**Fig. 5.** Navigation functional framework and form of interaction

2.  The conceptual UI design of navigation is shown in Fig. 4. In the early research and development stage, designers working on the interactive aspects would have developed a general set of gestures and information frameworks for the information systems functions of the electric vehicle such as those for music playback and answering the phone. In this context, navigation decision-supporting functions that are controlled imprecisely (i.e., view switching, volume control, and so forth), and route planning functions (destination input) will be operated using a combination of interaction through a touch-screen in the center console and the voice channel. The general design cue is to reduce the cognitive load during the driving process via the multi-channel integration of voice commands and gestures and create a functional framework for navigation with more natural man-machine interactions. In line with the functional framework, interface styling designers work on the number of function keys and the interface layout, as shown in Fig. 6, based on the concept sketches of the navigation control interface on the steering wheel.

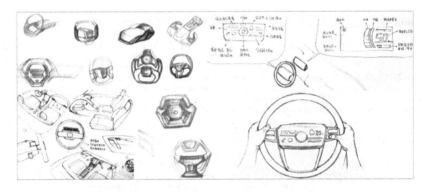

**Fig. 6.** Concept sketches of multi-functional steering wheel navigation control interface

Navigation HMI design: With the help of the storyboard showing the interactions with the navigation system, the designers subsequently designed the display and control interface. The hardware part of the navigation interface includes the shapes, layout, color, and materials. In accordance with the principle of functional importance, the designers positioned the navigation activation key on the upper right side of the central spoke of the steering wheel to facilitate operation with the push of a thumb by the driver. According to the principle of functional similarity, the navigation eye-level display button is positioned above the navigation start button, and the button is designed to feature a textured matte material, which is distinct from the glossy material of the navigation keys. This approach would enable the driver to find the position on the control interface according to different functional needs without having to lower their head and looking away from the road. With regard to the interactive gesture interface of the navigation system, the UI designers integrated the functional framework, interaction procedure, and gesture set (shown in Fig. 7) and utilized experienced user testing and design iteration. The interface design of the heads-up display (HUD) in the navigation system includes information architecture and visual design. In terms of its content, the navigational information is organized according to the principle of cognitive economy. To reduce interference, in accordance with visual design strategy, the sizes, proportions, and colors of the arrow symbols, numbers, and characters in the visual interface were repeatedly scrutinized. Figure 8 shows the design rendering of the control interface integrated navigation HUD with the multi-function steering wheel.

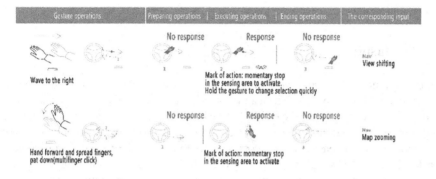

**Fig. 7.** Interactive gesture design for navigational functions (team solutions)

**Fig. 8.** Rendering of the interactive navigation interface

## 5    Discussion

This study used the case analysis method for the interactive storyboard design of electric vehicles to investigate the use of the storyboard tool and method in designing automotive HMI based on user knowledge. The research shows that the storyboard can play the role of an intermediate tool of conceptual thinking integration during the process of solution development. This research proposed a storyboard framework based on the axes of vision, scenario, and process. The vision axis is a visual description of the user's intention and behavior. The scenario axis describes the user's procedural knowledge pertaining to the execution of the interactive task. The process axis describes the sequence of interactive tasks from the operational point of view and is the concrete manifestation of the procedural knowledge present in the scenario axis. The storyboard tool proposed in this research is based on the traditional narrative storyboard used in visual media; the tool facilitates the use of procedural, temporal, and logical driver knowledge in the transformation into the design of interactive processes, interface styling, and visuals.

## 6   Conclusion

The development of automotive HMI is headed towards software and hardware integration and intelligent systems. In an agile, open, and collaborative design environment, the exploration of design tools capable of assisting cross-domain teams to seek out user needs and create solutions quickly is worth studying. This paper presented a new form of the storyboard tool based on the incorporation of user knowledge with design solution transformation in the solution-seeking process, thus driving innovations in HMI, interactive processes, and the form of interaction. The paper also presented a case study of the design of an interactive navigation interface in an electric automobile. The results were verified by applying the tool and method in the design process; thus, it can be concluded that this research enabled the development of automotive HMI design tools with a vital theoretical and practical foundation.

**Acknowledgement.** This research is supported by National Social Science Fund of China program (17BG149) and Nanjing University of Science and Technology Independent Research program(30917013111). We also gratefully acknowledge their financial support.

## References

1. Schmidt, A., Spiess, W., Kern, D.: Driving automotive user interface research. IEEE Pervasive Comput. **9**(1), 85–88 (2010)
2. Tan, H., Zhao, J., Wang, W.: Vehicle human machine interface design research. Chin. J. Automot. Eng. **9**(12), 315–320 (2012)
3. Krum, D.M., Faenger, J., Lathrop, B., et al.: All roads lead to CHI interaction in the automobile. In: Proceeding of ACM CHI Conference on Human Factors in Computing Systems, Florence, Italy, pp. 2387–2390 (2008)
4. Zeng, Q.: A Integrated Design Study of Automotive Soft and Hard Human-Machine Interface. Ph.D. Thesis, p. 126. Hunan University, Hunan (2016)
5. Cross, N.C.: Creativity in design: not leaping but bridging. creativity and cognition. In: Proceedings of the Second International Symposium, Loughborough, pp. 115–120 (1996)
6. Sanders, E.B.N., Stappers, P.N.: Co-creation and the new of design. CoDesign **4**, 5–18 (2008)
7. Wallace, K.: Capturing, storing and retrieving design knowledge in a distributed environment. In: Proceedings of The 9th International Conference on Computer Supported Cooperative Work in Design, pp. 10–15. IEEE Press (2005)
8. Wang, W.: Description and application of domain knowledge in automotive styling. Ph.D. thesis, p. 36. Hunan University, Hunan (2007)

9. Sato, K., Sakol, T.: Object-mediated user knowledge elicitation method. In: The 5th Asian International Design Research Conference, Seoul Korea, pp. 21–27 (2001)
10. Sakol, T.: A approach to user knowledge and product architecture for knowledge lifecycle. Ph.D. Dissertation, pp. 21–76. Illinois Institute of Technology, USA (2002)
11. Zhao, J., Tan, H., Tan, Z.: Car Styling: Theory, Research and Application, p. 47. Beijing Institute of Technology Press, Beijing (2011)
12. Julian, W.: Automotive Development Process: Process for Successful Customer Oriented Vehicle Development, p. 29. Springer, Heidelberg (2009). https://doi.org/10.1007/978-3-642-01253-2
13. Hankey, J.M.T.A., Dingus, R.J., Hanowski, C.: Invehicle information systems behavioral model and design support. Virginia Tech Transportation Institute, Blacksburg, VA, pp. 145–150 (2001)
14. Sherman, E.: Directing the Film: Film Directors on Their Art, p. 59. Guangxi Normal University Press (2006)
15. Hart, J.: The Art of the Storyboard: A Filmmaker's Introduction. Focal Press, p. 45 (2007)
16. Garner, S., McDonagh-Philp, D.: Problem interpretation and resolution via visual stimuli: the use of mood boards in design education. J. Art Des. Educ. **20**, 57–64 (2001)
17. Brajnik, G., Giachin, C.: J.: Using sketches and storyboards to assess impact of age difference in user experience. Int. J. Hum Comput Stud. **72**(6), 552–566 (2014)
18. John, C., Claudia, E.: Design process improvement: a review of current practice, pp. 57–58. Springer, London (2005)

# Cross-Cultural Product Design

# Research on Selection Differences Between Parent and Child on Toys

Yang Gao[1(⊠)], Jun Wu[1,2], and Po-Hsien Lin[1]

[1] Graduate School of Creative Industry Design,
National Taiwan University of Arts, New Taipei City, Taiwan
Lukegao1991@gmail.com, junwu2006@hotmail.com,
t0131@mail.ntua.edu.tw
[2] School of Journalism and Communication,
Anhui Normal University, Wuhu, People's Republic of China

**Abstract.** As the living standard is significantly improved due to economic development, more and more parents have reached the consensus on giving children happy childhood. Toys have become an important growth partner for children nowadays. Can the children be satisfied from the selective purchase behavior led by parents? Whether the parents' selection is consistent with the children's expectation becomes a topic for discussion. This research is one of the series of researches on the toy interest. This paper collects the preference information of parents and children on toys by the questionnaire, compares, quantitatively analyzes and learns about reasons resulted in the differences between parents and children in the toy selection. It is found in the research that: (1) there are differences between parents and children in the toy selection; (2) parents with different education backgrounds have different requirements on toys; (3) boys and girls have different selection on toys due to the genders; (4) parents will select different toys for children with different genders; (5) parents' acuity on new and old toys is low. The research result can provide toy manufacturers with preference information of parents and children on toys and provide parents with suggestions on the toy selection.

**Keywords:** Parent-child · Toy · Selection

## 1 Introduction

As the living standard is significantly improved due to economic development, it has been the wish of all parents to give children happy childhood. Parents endeavor to create the children with a carefree environment and atmosphere and provide them with the best conditions in learning and entertainment, while the purchase of toys is an important link to reach the target. As shown by Report for Toys and Baby Supplies Industry Development in China 2017 published at the 9th Toys and Baby Supplies Industry in China by Liang Mei: In 2016, the national gross imports of toys was USD 1.069 billion, witnessing a growth rate by 22.96% compared that of 2015 [1]. It can be seen that the increase of market demand on toys increases quickly. The toy has abundant connotations, transmits the value and exception of the last generation to the younger generation

© Springer International Publishing AG, part of Springer Nature 2018
P.-L. P. Rau (Ed.): CCD 2018, LNCS 10911, pp. 123–133, 2018.
https://doi.org/10.1007/978-3-319-92141-9_9

and tells the acknowledgement and freedom of the young generation to the last generation [2]. When selecting tools, because the child age is young, parents' selection will lead up. However, the child is actually the host and user of toys, more attention should be paid to the preference of children. Although children often require parents to buy tools, the requirement is unreliable under most conditions [3]. They know how to watch parents' mood and usually choose toys acceptable for parents, therefore, the independent judgment of parents is especially important. Do parents and children have the same selection and need? What is the difference in standards considered by parents and children when selecting toys? These are topics worth discussing.

Most current researches on the toy selection discuss the scientific selection of toys taking parents as the subject or discuss separating parents and children, only a few conduct the comparative study taking children as the subject. This research focuses on children at 7–9 years old and their parents, obtains the preference of parents and children on toys by the questionnaire and factoring influencing their selections, and expects that the result can provide toy manufacturers with current preference information of parents and children on toys and provide parents with suggestions on the toy selection.

(1) What is the reason resulting in differences between parents and children in the toy selection?
(2) What is the influence to the toy selection of education background of parents?
(3) What are the differences between boys and girls in the toy selection?
(4) What is the attitude difference of parents when selecting toys for children of different genders?

## 2 Literature Review

### 2.1 Factors Affecting the Toy Selection

There are a lot of factors affecting parents' selection on toys. Bian Yufang divided these factors into four grades from high to low as per the importance in this paper Factors Influencing Children's Selection and Purchase of Toys, among which the most important factor is: security of toys and cultivation to children's skills and creativeness. The attraction and originality of toys rank the second. The child gender ranks the third [4]. As for children, the physiological hormone will influence children's selection tendency [5]. As for children over 7 years old, because they have completed the sound gender constancy development and established a complete and stable set of gender frame. When selecting toys, the gender stereotype will greatly influence them [6]. In other words, children will tend to choose toys with the gender tendency same to themselves and affirm that a certain type of toys belong to the opposite gender [7]. It is pointed out by other researches that when selecting toys, games and playmates, children tend to behave as per social norms [8].

As shown by the research, the most popular toys among boys are the model toy, electronic toy and pop-up toy; while plush and cloth toys are popular among girls, as well as balls and chesses [9]. As shown by the research, although many parents encourage girls and boys engage in cross-sex activities, they are still limited by traditional norms when selecting toys for children, toys with masculinity for boys and toys with femininity for girls [3].

## 2.2  Four Different Pleasures

Lionel Tiger has been proposed four different pleasures: Physio-pleasure, Psycho-pleasure, Socio-pleasure and Ideo-pleasure. He explained these four pleasures as follows:

| | |
|---|---|
| Physio-pleasure: | Bodily pleasures derived from sensory (touch, taste, smell, etc.) organs. |
| Socio-pleasure: | Socio-pleasures arise from relationships with other people or society as a whole. Social need pleasures avoid discomfort of not being socially accepted. |
| Psycho-pleasure: | People's cognitive and emotional reactions. Jordan groups usability as a product property that is connected to psycho-pleasure.Poor usability can cause annoyance, frustration and stress. |
| Ideo-pleasure: | Pleasures that are connected to people's values, pleasures that are derived from such as books, music and art. Pleasures that relate to personal aspirations and moral values. (closely related to be/do goals) [10] |

# 3  Research Method

## 3.1  Research Object and Selection Method

This research takes 18 toys popular in Chinese Mainland as a research object. The selection process of toy samples is divided into 3 steps:

(1) Select top 30 best-sold toys on the online shopping platform in Chinese Mainland.
(2) Classify them according to four different pleasures proposed by Lionel Tiger.
(3) Invite 10 different experts to select 16 most representative toys per person, separately 4 for each pleasure, account the final result and select 16 most representative toys, 4 for each pleasure (considering the gender tendency ratio of toys). The sample selection and grouping results are as follows: Remote control car(male), Big teddy Bear(female), clockwork toy(male), Transformers(male) for Psycho-pleasure; Screaming chicken(male), Silicone toys(female), Fidget spinner(all), Music Box(female) for Physio-pleasure; electric ride on(male), Playhouse(all), Gun(male), Barbie(female) for Socio-pleasure; cosplay clothes(all), Sparkles(female), LEGO(all), Snow globe(female) for Ideo-pleasure.
(4) Based on the investigation of 5 6–8 years old children, the social pleasure toy - RichMan board game (all) is added, and the cosplay costume is divided into hero costume (male) and princess costume (female), and finally determine 18 toy samples in the questionnaire. Among all toy samples, the gender tendency of 7 are the male, 7 are the female, and 4 are without obvious gender tendency. (As shown in Fig. 1 and Table 1).

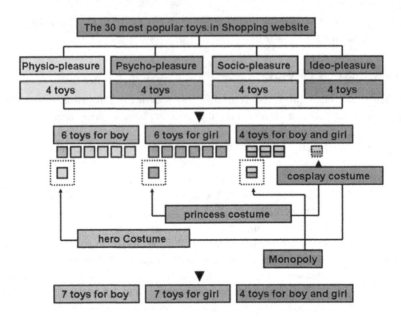

**Fig. 1.** Process for sample selection

## 3.2 Research Object and Selection Method

Between two versions, separately for parents and children, A-side is printed with clear and colorful pictures of 18 toy samples mentioned above, B-side is printed with specific questions. The part for parents is set with two basic information questions, separately education background and age, and four major topics: I. Select four favorite toys among all samples that you want to send to your children; II. Give a mark to every toy as per the beautiful shape, comfortable hand feeling, sense of humor, available for playing alone, development of imagination, artistry and suitable for playing together; III. Importance of three additive factors, separately economy, safety and edutainment; IV. the coincidence of meeting child's vision, helping child's growth, cultivating child's independent playing ability and sharing your favorite toy with the child. Choose the score the most suitable for you as per 5-points scale. 1 is the lowest and 5 is the highest.

The questionnaire for children is set with one basic information question, separately education background and age, and two major topics: I. select you favorite 4 toys, and rank them as per your preference degree II. the same to it of the second question in parents' questionnaire, while the word and tone are changed correspondingly for children, words suitable for low-grade children to read and understand are selected. The paper questionnaire is adopted, in order to avoid mutual influence between children and parents, questionnaires for parents and children are printed are separately printed on both sides of A3 paper, which will be filled in separately after being folded. There is no time limit for the filling, and this investigation will not record the name.

**Table 1.** Corresponding table of toy sample and its gender tendency

| Fidget spinner | Music Box | Screaming chicken | Silicone toys |
|---|---|---|---|
| For all | For girl | For boy | For girl |
| Physio-pleasure | | | |

| Transformers | Big teddy Bear | Clockwork toy | Remote control car |
|---|---|---|---|
| For boy | For girl | For boy | For boy |
| Psycho-pleasure | | | |

| Gun | Barbie | Monopoly | Electric ride on | Playhouse |
|---|---|---|---|---|
| For boy | For girl | For all | For boy | For all |
| Socio-pleasure | | | | |

| Sparkles | LEGO | Snow globe | Hero Costume | Princess Costume |
|---|---|---|---|---|
| For girl | For all | For girl | For boy | For girl |
| Ideo-pleasure | | | | |

## 3.3  Subjects

The subjects are 120 students and one of their parents from Grade II (6) and (7) of Wuyishan Experimental School. Total 120 questionnaires are released, and 115 are recovered. Among all recovered questionnaires, 108 questionnaires from children are effective, 52 (48%) from boys, and 56 (52%) from girls; 60 questionnaires from parents are effective, 30 (50%) from boys' parents, and 30 (50%) from girls' parents. The effective questionnaire both from parents and children are just 57.

# 4  Analysis and Discussion of the Results

## 4.1  Reliability and Validity Test

The reliability analysis of the questionnaire is to discuss the internal consistency of each surface of the scale and the impairment of the Cronbach $\alpha$ coefficient of each dimension after single deletion, which is as the reference standard of the topic selection and the reliability of the scale. The analysis of the questionnaire found that: the Cronbach $\alpha$ coefficient is . 748. The corrected total correlation of each element: 654–870, [the $\alpha$ coefficient after deletion] case: 312–659. It is clear that the internal consistency between the topics is higher, and the topic settings are reasonable. The validity analysis shows that the KMO coefficient is. 605, which means high value, and the Sig value is. 000, meeting the great significance. The characteristic value is 1.342, which can explain 69.49% variance of the preset uses. The factor load quantity of each question from .638–.816, intercommunity from .532–.824.

## 4.2  Influence of Different Parental Education Background on the Different Selection of Toys

To explore the influence of parental education differences on the selection of toys, the parents' academic qualifications are taken as an independent variable, and the elements to be considered during the selection of toys are taken as a dependent variable. The variance analysis is conducted, and the results are shown in Table 2. It can be seen that the artistic($f = 3.523*$) selection of toys of children's parents of different educational degrees have a significant difference, which is up to .05. After the Scheffe comparison, the score of artistic sense of the parents with undergraduate degree below is significantly larger than that of the parents with undergraduate education. It is visible that parents with the undergraduate degree below have the stronger expectations of the artistic sense of the toys, who also hope that their children accept the edification of art.

**Table 2.** Influence of parental education differences on the selection of toys

| Sex | | SS | DF | MS | F | Scheffe |
|---|---|---|---|---|---|---|
| Artistic | SSb | 9.922 | 2 | 4.961 | 3.523* | 1>2 |
| | SSw | 80.261 | 57 | 1.408 | | |
| | n | 90.183 | 59 | | | |

P* < .05

## 4.3  Influence of Children's Gender Differences on the Toy Selection of Parents and Children

To explore the influence of gender differences on the toy selection of parents and children (the used data are the child's gender, parents' best selection and the child's best selection, excluding the selection 2, 3 and 4), the child's gender is taken as an independent variable, and the results of the child's selection of toys are shown in

Table 3. The selection of boys and girls in the Fidget spinner (t = 4.636***), Gun (t = 6.552***), Transformers (t = 3.638***), Electric ride on (t = 2.732**), Remote-Control Car (t = 6.372***), Hero Clothing (t = 4.344***) have significant differences, showing positive correlation, and the boys have significant preference to these toys compared to girls. In the selection of Music Box (–5.256***), Barbie (–5.373***), Sparkles (–2.331*), Big Teddy Bear (–2.305*), PlayHouse (–2.985**), Snow Globe (–3.190**), Silicone Toys (–5.704***), Princess Costume (–4.518***), there is a significant difference, showing the negative correlation, and the girls have significant preference to these toys compared to boys. From the above results, the sex characteristics of the selection of toys with significant differences of boy and girls are more obvious, which is consistent with the preferences of boy and girls.

Parents' selection of toys did not show significant differences in children's sex. The sexual orientation of a toy is not a decisive factor when parents choose toys for their children.

## 4.4    Ranking Results for Toy Selection of Parents and Children

The toy's preference degree is converted into the integral form (the first selection is 4 points, the second selection is 3, the third selection is 2, and the fourth selection is 1.) to make the ranking table, and the excerpt data is shown in Table 4. The top three toys that boys like best are Guns, and Remote-Control Cars and Fidget Spinner, which are all the toys with significant male characteristics as shown in "Table 3". The selection of Toy Guns and Remote-Control Cars is consistent with the results of Sang and Wang [3], which belong to models, electric or ejection toys. In the top 3 of the parent-child selection, the boy and his parents had 2 of the same selection, and in the difference item, boys chose the Fidget Spinner and the parents chose LEGO. In the selection of parents, the Gun is followed by the "Fidget Spinner", and the score gap is only 2 points, which is obvious that selection of parents and boys have a higher consistency.

The top three toys that girls like the best are Snow Ball, Silicone Toys and Barbie, which are all toys having significant female characteristics according to "Table 3". However, the results are biased with the study of Sang and Wang [3], in which the Big Teddy Bear which should be popular with girls ranked only the seventh, while Snow Ball contrary to the texture of the soft and warm plush or cloth toys is the most loved by girls. In the top 3 of the selection, there is no common toy selected both by the girls and the parents, which shows that the selection of parents and girls are less consistent. The girls' favorite 3 toys appeared in 4, 5 and 6 of the parents' selection rank list, indicating that parents had a certain understanding of girls' preferences, while they did not show enough inclusion when buying toys for them compared with boys.

The 3 toys that parents want to buy for the girls most are LEGO, Monopoly and PlayHouses. Although data in "Table 3" show that LEGO and Monopoly do not have a significant gender orientation, the data in "Table 4" show that the points of LEGO (children's selection) are: Boys 56 points, girls 35 points. The points of Monopoly (children's selection) are: Boys 41 points, girls 27 points. The points of boys are 50% more than those of girls, showing more obvious male characteristics, indicating that parents want girls to do a number of transgender attempts in the selection of toys. This is a little bit different from the research done by Chen [9]. Regardless of boys and girls,

**Table 3.** Effects of gender differences on toy selection

| Toy | Sex | N | M | SD | T value | Comparative coefficient |
|---|---|---|---|---|---|---|
| Fidget spinner | Male | 52 | 1.15 | 1.601 | 4.636*** | Male>Female |
|  | Female | 56 | .09 | .438 |  |  |
| Music box | Male | 52 | .13 | .627 | −5.256*** | Female>Male |
|  | Female | 56 | 1.18 | 1.336 |  |  |
| Gun | Male | 52 | 1.50 | 1.651 | 6.552*** | Male>Female |
|  | Female | 56 | .00 | .000 |  |  |
| Barbie | Male | 52 | .00 | .000 | −5.373*** | Female>Male |
|  | Female | 56 | 1.18 | 1.642 |  |  |
| Transformers | Male | 52 | .58 | 1.144 | 3.638*** | Male>Female |
|  | Female | 56 | .00 | .000 |  |  |
| Sparkles | Male | 52 | .10 | .495 | −2.331* | Female>Male |
|  | Female | 56 | .41 | .869 |  |  |
| Electric ride on | Male | 52 | .37 | .908 | 2.732** | Male>Female |
|  | Female | 56 | .02 | .134 |  |  |
| Big teddy bear | Male | 52 | .31 | .829 | −2.305* | Female>Male |
|  | Female | 56 | .77 | 1.221 |  |  |
| Play house | Male | 52 | .25 | .837 | −2.985** | Female>Male |
|  | Female | 56 | .89 | 1.358 |  |  |
| Snow globe | Male | 52 | 1.02 | 1.421 | −3.190** | Female>Male |
|  | Female | 56 | 1.98 | 1.711 |  |  |
| Remote control car | Male | 52 | 1.42 | 1.486 | 6.372*** | Male>Female |
|  | Female | 56 | .07 | .375 |  |  |
| Silicone toys | Male | 52 | .15 | .500 | −5.704*** | Female>Male |
|  | Female | 56 | 1.36 | 1.432 |  |  |
| Hero costume | Male | 52 | .90 | 1.418 | 4.344*** | Male>Female |
|  | Female | 56 | .00 | .000 |  |  |
| Princess costume | Male | 52 | .00 | .000 | −4.518*** | Female>Male |
|  | Female | 56 | .86 | 1.420 |  |  |

P* < .05, P** < .01, P*** < .001

LEGO are the toys preferred by the parents, which embodies the parents' high attention to the toy education, which is consistent with research results of Sang and Wang [3].

## 4.5 The Results Comparison of Parents and Children

In the 57 parent-child correspondence questionnaires, the parent-child coincidence number of 4 toys is 128 times without considering the toy preference ranking, and the average coincidence rate is 56.14%. For the favorite toys, the number of questionnaires in which parent-child selection was the same is 16, accounting for 28.07% of the total. And the number of questionnaires in which child's favorite toys did not appear in the parents' 4 selections is 20, accounting for 35.09% of the total (As shown in Fig. 2).

**Table 4.** The score rankings of toys selected by parents

| The score rankings of toys (Boy) | | | | | | |
|---|---|---|---|---|---|---|
| 1 | 2 | 3 | 4 | 5 | 7 | 8 |
| Gun | Remote control car | Fidget spinner | Snow globe | LEGO | Monopoly | Transformers |
| 79 | 74 | 64 | 59 | 56 | 41 | 28 |
| The score rankings of toys (For Son) | | | | | | |
| 1 | 2 | 3 | 3 | 5 | 6 | 9 |
| LEGO | Remote control car | Transformers | Gun | Fidget spinner | Monopoly | Snow globe |
| 64 | 33 | 31 | 31 | 29 | 26 | 14 |
| The score rankings of toys (girl) | | | | | | |
| 1 | 2 | 3 | 4 | 5 | 8 | 9 |
| Snow globe | Silicone toys | Barbie | Music box | Play house | LEGO | Monopoly |
| 111 | 86 | 66 | 65 | 52 | 35 | 27 |
| The score rankings of toys (For Daughter) | | | | | | |
| 1 | 2 | 3 | 4 | 5 | 6 | 9 |
| LEGO | Monopoly | Play house | Barbie | Snow globe | Silicone toys | Music box |
| 59 | 44 | 39 | 37 | 32 | 26 | 8 |

The toys that were not selected by the parents and selection times were: LEGO x2, Gun x2, Snow Globe x4, Fidget Spinner x4, Barbie x1, Silicone Toys x2, Monopoly x2, PlayHouse x2, Music Box x1, Princess Costume x1.

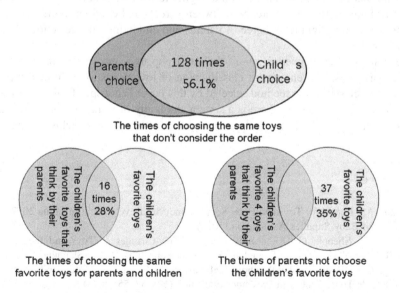

**Fig. 2.** A schematic diagram of the selection coincidence degree of 57 parent-child correspondence questionnaires

This shows that almost half of the toys selected by parents are not children's favorite, and only less than 30% of them can get their favorite toys from their parents, and nearly 40% of children have trouble getting their favorite toys. After finishing the toys, it is known that the most neglected toys are the Snow Ball and Fidget Spinner. Among them, the Snow Globe reached its mass production in 1905, and the Fidget Spinner was popular in the beginning of the spring of 2017. The one of the two pieces of toys is a classically traditional toy, while the other is the currently popular toy. It can be seen that parents lack of confidence in traditional toys, and lack of sharp insight on the popular toys.

## 5  Conclusions and Recommendations

Toys are fascinating and everyone enjoys the joy of toys. Children want to simply enjoy happiness, while parents want to use the toy to bring the child the meaning of fun. Whether a parent's selection of toys makes the child happy depends on the degree of consistency between the parent's and the child's selection. This study investigated the selection of toys by questionnaire. This study shows that:

(1) The parents with undergraduate degree below have more expectation to the artistic sense of the toy than the parents with bachelor degree or above.
(2) The selection of toys of children has significant gender orientation, while the selection of toys of parents for their children does not have a significant gender orientation.
(3) Differences exist in the selection of parent and child. The boys' selection of toys is of higher consistency with that of parent, and the girls' selection is less consistent with that of parent. Parents encourage girls to try transgender attempts on toys.
(4) There are significant differences between parents and children in the selection of toys, and misalignment degree of parents and children on the selection of toys is about 44%.
(5) Parents are not concerned about the latest pop toys and lack confidence in traditional toys. The enjoyment classification of toys needs to be further explored, and the classification method selected by this paper is not specifically for toys, but for all products, so that there is a certain ambiguity of some toys in the definition of interest, which did not reflect the expected value in the conclusion analysis.

## References

1. Liang, M.: Report for Toys and Baby Supplies Industry Development in China 2017. China Toys and Baby Supplies Association (2017)
2. Cross, G., Shengli, G.: Kids' Stuff Gadgets: The Changes of Toys and the American Childhood World, 1st edn. Shanghai Translation Publishing House, Shanghai (2010)
3. Sang, Q.S., Wang, W.T.: Psychological Factors of Parents' Selection and Purchase of Children's Toys. Studies in Preschool Education (12), 52–55 (2008)

4. Bian, Y.F.: Investigation on the affecting factors of the selection and purchase of children toys. Psychol. Sci. Newslett. (05), 57-58 (1990)
5. Berenbaum, S.A., Hines, M.: Early androgens are related to childhood sex-typed toy preferences. Psychol. Sci. **3**(3), 203–206 (1992)
6. Du, D., Su, Y.J.: Effects of gender stereotypes and stereotypes information on the selection of toys for children aged 3–9. Psychol. Explor. **25**(4), 56–61 (2005)
7. Caldera, Y.M., Huston, A.C., O'Brien, M.: Social interactions and play patterns of parents and toddlers with feminine, masculine and neutral toys. Child Dev. **60**(1), 70–76 (1989)
8. Bussey, K., Bandura, A.: Self-regulatory mechanisms governing gender development. Child Dev. (63), 1236–1250 (1992)
9. Chen, Y.J.: Study on the Development of Gender Cognition of Preschool Children. Master's thesis of Institute of Gender Education, National Kaohsiung Normal University (2004)
10. Tiger, L.: The Pursuit of Pleasure. Transaction Publishers, New Brunswick (1992)

# Study on the Application of Peak-End Rule in the Design of App Blank Pages

Canqun He[(⊠)] and Zhangyu Ji

College of Mechanical and Electrical Engineering, Hohai University,
Changzhou, China
hecq@163.com, 113925724@qq.com

**Abstract.** This paper studies the effect of application of Peak-End Rule on user experience in the design of App blank pages, taking the mobile App loading process for case study. It simulates the waiting scenes caused by system response when users use mobile applications. Participants are asked to estimate the waiting time-distances for loading page time in the waiting process. Simultaneously, five-point scale is used to mark the network abnormal page for users by the questionnaire. It is found that, compared with circle loading and progress bar loading, fun loading can shorten user's judgment of waiting time through the rich and interesting animation form. Graphic design has more influence on user experience than text expression in the design of network abnormal page.

**Keywords:** User experience · Peak-End Rule · App blank pages
Loading page · Network abnormal page

## 1 Introduction

With the rapid development of mobile products, application interfaces such as product home page, detail page, list page and other key interfaces are continuously innovated and improved under the trend of design to better meet user's experience requirements. In the design of App's numerous interfaces, blank pages tend to be arranged by designers to the end of design schedule or even ignored. As one of the details that can easily be overlooked in mobile products, it is full of unlimited potential and possibilities. The potential value of blank pages requires designers to improve their user experience in a reasonable and interesting way.

App blank pages can be divided into two categories based on static and dynamic state: no data page and data loading page. The former contains Null page, network abnormal page and server abnormal page. Data loading page and network abnormal page constitute the loading and waiting process. Using fluency is the basic expectation of most users, just like eating without a long queue. However, the instability of mobile network and different configuration of mobile hardware can cause page load waiting to become an inevitable factor that affects user experience of mobile terminal products for users.

The related research of waiting time has been a research topic in the field of cognitive psychology and social psychology, and even consumer psychology. Waiting time is a key factor affecting user experience. It is difficult to change due to some

© Springer International Publishing AG, part of Springer Nature 2018
P.-L. P. Rau (Ed.): CCD 2018, LNCS 10911, pp. 134–147, 2018.
https://doi.org/10.1007/978-3-319-92141-9_10

objective reasons. Therefore, how to improve user experience in the loading process becomes one of the important issues in waiting research.

## 2  Peak-End Rule

Peak-End Rule was first proposed by psychologist Danny Kahneman. He found that people's memory of an experience is determined by two factors: the feeling of the peak (whether positive or negative) and the end. In other words, people can only remember the experience of "peak" and "end" after experiencing one thing. The overall feeling of users can be improved by enhancing the experience of these two critical moments.

Peak-End Rule also has some applications in the field of design. Chen yan, Xin Xiangyang, Hu Weifeng applied Peak-End Rule to the design of bus ticket machine interface improved design. They confirmed and improved the key interface of "peak" and "end" experience of bus ticket machine and tested the results, which verified that the improvement of product interface based on Peak-End Rule is an effective way to improve the product operation experience [1]. Zhang analyzed the design of 404 error page through eye movement experiment and proposed the design principle that 404 error page should follow on the basis of Peak-End Rule [2].

In the user experience of App page loading process, the browsing of data loading page belongs to the "peak" moment of loading process, and the loading result page which may be a network abnormal page or a normal result page belongs to the "end" moment of loading process. User satisfaction of these two critical moments needs to be improved to enhance the user experience of App loading process.

## 3  App Loading Process

When designing App, designers will focus more on the appearance of interface, and often ignore an important part, namely, the jump between interfaces and the operation feedback given to users. In the App loading process, users will face a long waiting time for data loading when the network is not smooth and the data loading will be in a failed state when there is no network. The experience in these situations determines user's impression of the product. Therefore, it is important to improve user experience on data loading page and network abnormal page.

### 3.1  Data Loading Page

Data loading page is a blank page generated in the page jump process. The waiting time of this page is subject to actual network problem, and "Do not let me wait" is a luxury for users when the network is in poor condition. The main influencing factors that affect user's waiting time-distances estimated are actual waiting time and feeling waiting time. Actual waiting time can not be changed because it is affected by some objective conditions such as network conditions and hardware configuration of the mobile device. Therefore, user's waiting time-distances estimated can only be reduced through the later loading design to improve user satisfaction in the waiting process.

User's subjective feeling waiting time is called "perception of waiting time" in psychological cognition. It refers to people's subjective feelings and psychological experience of waiting time in the process of waiting, which will affect people's behavior [3, 4]. There are many factors influencing perception of waiting time: network connection status, loading form, visibility of loading progress, personal cognition level and personality characteristics. At present, common loading forms include concept loading model, fun loading, non-modal loading and hidden-type loading [5]. He and Fu found that non-modal loading and hidden-type loading have a better effect on shortening user's perception of waiting time through study [6]. In view of the fact that not all mobile products are suitable for both loading modes and lack of progress bar loading with visibility of loading progress, this paper will experiment with several loading models except non-modal loading and hidden-type loading, enriching research results of data loading page. The loading methods of study are shown in Table 1.

**Table 1.** Loading methods of data loading pages.

| Loading method | Concept | Feature |
| --- | --- | --- |
| Circle loading | The rotation of circle graph shows loading process | The form is monotonous and loading schedule is not visible |
| Progress bar loading | A rectangular bar shows loading speed and schedule | The form is monotonous and loading schedule is visible |
| Fun loading | A fun icon or animation shows loading process | The form is rich and interesting and loading schedule is not visible |

1. Circle loading. Circle loading is a common method in concept loading models. It is through repetitive rotation animation to inform users that data is being loaded and the form is simple. This loading method appears in the loading of mobile device system page. For example, the "theme beautification" application of Meizu mobile phone adopts the form of circle loading, as shown in Fig. 1(a).
2. Progress bar loading. Progress bar loading is another common method in concept loading models. In addition to informing users what is going on, it also gives users a clear, informed view of loading schedule. Part of Pocket Office mobile terminal pages adopt this kind of loading method. Forward blue rectangle prompts users the current loading schedule which affects user's judgment of time to a certain extent, shown in Fig. 1(b).
3. Fun loading. Fun loading transfers user's attention through some interesting elements such as creative writing, color, dynamic effect and sound, so as to satisfy the "pleasure" of upper needs of users [5]. Meaningful things can attract people's attention faster [7]. Faced with something of interest, individuals tend to underestimate time-distances [8]. Page loading method of Where to Travel Mobile client simulates camel walking and disperses user's perception of time in an interesting form, shown in Fig. 1(c).

**(a)** Circle Loading  page  **(b)** Progress Bar Loading  page   **(c)** Fun Loading page

**Fig. 1.**  Classification of data loading pages.

### 3.2  Network Abnormal Page

Network abnormal pages generally appear in two cases. One is the network interruption when network is switched from WiFi state to 3G/4G. The other is the network interruption when data is transferred between App and server. Network interruption terminates user's browsing action, directly influencing user's current experience. Good network abnormal pages can effectively appease users' emotions, guide users to perform next steps, and improve the experience of network abnormality.

Network abnormal page is usually composed of graphics and text.

(1)  Graphic design

The graphic design of network abnormal page is currently divided into two types. One is the icon, as shown in Fig. 2(a). A simple gray icon indicates the current network anomaly. The other is fun picture, as shown in Fig. 2(b). It creates artistic patterns through rich colors and expression forms, increases user's visual pleasure, and improves the effect of information communication. It has remarkable effect.

(2)  Text expression

The same meaning expressed in different words can give a completely different psychological feeling. In Fig. 2(a), designers convey the state of network interruption with a plain text without any embellishment. Figure 2(b) compares the network to a waiter with the figurative rhetoric, and conveys the situation of network abnormality humorously.

(a)                              (b)

**Fig. 2.** Network abnormal page.

## 4 Experiment 1: Study on Time-Distances Estimated of Data Loading Pages

### 4.1 Experiment Purpose

Based on the previous studies, this experiment complements progress bar loading with visibility of loading schedule. This paper aims to find out which loading method can shorten user's perception of waiting time and improve user experience of loading process with basic principles and experiment methods of cognitive psychology.

### 4.2 Experiment Method

The experiment was designed by two factors: 2 (Page loading time: 5.0 s, 10.0 s) * 3 (Page loading method: fun loading, circle loading, progress bar loading). In order to avoid the impact of test sequence on participants, experiment samples were presented to them in a random manner.

### 4.3 Experiment Sample

In order to ensure the accuracy of experiment results, experiment equipment chose the same mobile phone with the same hardware configuration as test platform. Search is one function that is used more often in mobile application software. This experiment chose search results list loading page of ticketing mobile products as experiment scene to simulate user's waiting process of purchasing tickets. According to the blank page loading types mentioned in this paper, a practice sample Demo and two groups of experiment samples were made, shown in Fig. 3.

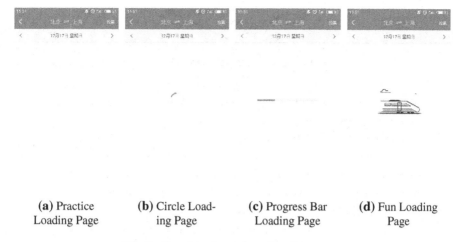

| (a) Practice Loading Page | (b) Circle Loading Page | (c) Progress Bar Loading Page | (d) Fun Loading Page |

**Fig. 3.** Experiment samples of loading pages.

### 4.4 Participants

The report data of CNNIC 40th China Internet Statistics shows that in the age distribution of Chinese netizens, users aged 20–29 years old are the mainstream users, with 29.7% of the total users in this age group [9]. Therefore, this experiment selected similar age group of students as participants. Sixty subjects were recruited on campus, including 32 men and 28 women. There were 55 valid data, including 30 men and 25 women, with an average age of 23.5 years old and a standard deviation of 1.835.

### 4.5 Experiment Task

In Experiment 1, participants are required to click the search icon of search page first and proceed to the next operation when the page jumps to result page, which represents the completion of an experiment task. Each time an experiment task is completed, the participant is required to estimate the waiting time-distance (unit:/s, to be accurate to one decimal point) and record at the corresponding position on the experiment paper. Before the experiment, each participant is given an table about waiting time-distances estimated of samples and informed the purpose and requirements of experiment. Before the formal experiment begins, each participant is familiar with the experimental flow and perceives the loading time through practice sample. In order to avoid the influence of test sequence of experiment samples on participants, the experiment samples in this experiment are presented to participants in a random manner. The experimental flow is shown in Fig. 4.

### 4.6 Analysis of Experiment Results

55 valid data are obtained for each experiment sample after the end of the experiment. All valid data are statistically analyzed by SPSS software.

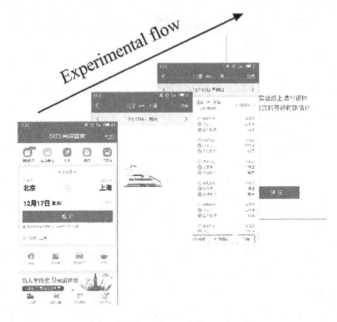

**Fig. 4.**  Experimental flow sketch.

When the page loading time is 5.0 s, the loading methods of waiting time-distances estimated mean from short to long loading time are respectively fun loading, circle loading and progress bar loading, as shown in Fig. 5. According to the experiment results of single factor variance analysis, it is found that there is a significant difference ($P < 0.05$) in the estimation of waiting time-distance between fun loading and progress bar loading, while there is no significant difference($P > 0.05$) between fun loading and circle loading and circle loading and progress bar loading, as shown in Table 2.

When the page loading time is 10.0 s, the loading methods of waiting time-distances estimated mean from short to long loading time are respectively fun loading, progress bar loading and circle loading, as shown in Fig. 6. According to the experiment results of single factor variance analysis, it is found that there is a significant difference ($P < 0.05$) in the estimation of waiting time-distance between fun loading and circle loading, while there is no significant difference($P > 0.05$) between fun loading and progress bar loading and circle loading and progress bar loading, as shown in Table 3.

According to the results of experiment 1, it can be seen that different loading methods and different loading times have different effects on waiting time-distances estimated. However, whether the loading time is 5.0 s or 10.0 s, the mean of waiting time-distances estimated of fun loading is the shortest. This experiment uses a lovely little train styling and realistic state of motion to indicate the loading process instead of the traditional concept loading model, which makes waiting progress enjoyable and allows users to feel fresh and interesting without sense of anxiety, thereby reducing the perception of change of time. Therefore, its mean of waiting time-distances estimated is shortest. Progress bar loading has the visibility of loading schedule compared to the

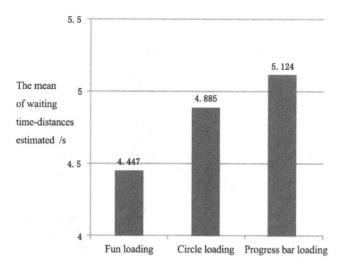

**Fig. 5.** Waiting time-distances estimated mean (Page loading time: 5.0 s).

**Table 2.** The significant difference analysis of experiment 1 (Page loading time: 5.0 s).

| Page loading model | Page loading Time/s | Mean (M) | Standard deviation (SD) | Compared samples (J) | Average difference (I–J) | Sig. (P) |
|---|---|---|---|---|---|---|
| Fun loading | 5.0 | 4.447 | 1.1130 | Circle loading | –0.4382 | 0.094 |
| | | | | Progress bar loading | –0.6764 | 0.010* |
| Circle loading | 5.0 | 4.885 | 1.6226 | Fun loading | 0.4382 | 0.094 |
| | | | | Progress bar loading | –0.2382 | 0.361 |
| Progress bar loading | 5.0 | 5.124 | 1.3094 | Fun loading | 0.6764 | 0.010* |
| | | | | Circle loading | 0.2382 | 0.361 |

Note: * represents P < 0.05

other two loading methods. When the loading time is 5.0 s, the mean of waiting time-distances estimated of progress bar loading is 5.124 s which is longer than the actual loading time, tending to be negative. When the loading time is 10.0 s, the mean of waiting time-distances estimated of progress bar loading is 8.527 s which is shorter than the actual loading time, tending to be positive. Tencent "mobile page user behavior report" shows that when loading time is more than 5 s, 74% of users will leave the page [10]. 5 s is the boundary value of most user load tolerance. The visibility of progress bar loading schedule may increase the level of anxiety for part of users. The loading time of 10.0 s has exceeded most users' tolerance range. Progress bar loading lets users see the completion of loading, which appeases user's waiting psychology to some extent. Circle loading is the most common loading method in daily life. It has neither the fun of fun loading nor the schedule visibility of progress bar loading. When the loading time is 5.0 s, the invisibility of its loading schedule does not

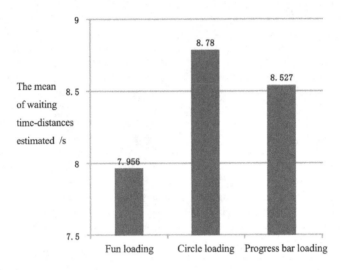

**Fig. 6.** Waiting time-distances estimated mean (Page loading time: 10.0 s).

**Table 3.** The significant difference analysis of experiment 1 (Page loading time: 10.0 s).

| Page loading model | Page loading Time/s | Mean (M) | Standard deviation (SD) | Compared samples (J) | Average difference (I–J) | Sig. (P) |
|---|---|---|---|---|---|---|
| Fun loading | 10.0 | 7.956 | 1.9439 | Circle loading | 0.8236 | 0.047* |
| | | | | Progress bar loading | –0.5709 | 0.168 |
| Circle loading | 10.0 | 8.780 | 2.3076 | Fun loading | 0.8236 | 0.047* |
| | | | | Progress bar loading | 0.2527 | 0.540 |
| Progress bar loading | 10.0 | 8.527 | 2.2111 | Fun loading | 0.5709 | 0.168 |
| | | | | Circle loading | –0.2527 | 0.540 |

Note: * represents $P < 0.05$

bring too much pressure to user psychology, so the mean of waiting time-distances estimated of circle loading is shorter than that of progress bar loading. When the loading time is 10.0 s, the simple and boring loading method becomes its biggest disadvantage, resulting in the longest mean of waiting time-distances estimated.

In general, fun loading effectively shortens user's perception of waiting time and makes the load waiting no longer boring, improving the "peak" experience during loading with its vivid animation.

# 5   Experiment 2: Study on Design Experience of Network Abnormal Page

## 5.1   Experiment Purpose

The purpose of this experiment is to study the influence of text and graphics on the user experience of network abnormal page, and the influence of gender difference on the experience of both text and graphics.

## 5.2   Experiment Method

In this experiment, we collected and produced 20 network abnormal pages (see Fig. 7) in the early stage and distributed them in the form of questionnaires. The five-point scale method was used to rate the graphic design, text expression and the overall of 20 pages. (1-experience is not good, 2-experience is not very good, 3-neutral, 4-experience is not bad, 5-experience is very good).

## 5.3   Analysis of Experiment Results

The participants of this experiment were consistent with experiment 1, with a total of 60. There were 57 valid data, including 31 men and 26 women, with an average age of 23.4 years old and a standard deviation of 1.753.

The 20 pages were grouped by ABCD from two angles of graphic design and text expression, and each group had five pages, as shown in Table 4.

Table 5 shows the score mean of 20 network abnormal pages from three angles. It can be seen that the overall score mean of 9 pages is more than 3. The experience tends to be positive. Eight of them belong to the design of colorful interesting pictures. The means of each group are calculated according to grouping (see Table 6). It can be seen that the score means of group A and group C are lower than 3 and the experience tends to be negative. The score means of group B and group D are higher than 3 and the experience tends to be positive. From the score mean of group B and group C, it can be seen that colorful and interesting graphic designs can make up for lack of expression, making the overall experience of network abnormal pages tend to be positive (overall score mean >3). However, good text expression does not make up for simple and tasteless graphic design, and the overall experience of network abnormal pages tends to be negative (overall score mean <3). Words and pictures are recognized through human visual system, and words need to be understood. Everyone may have a different understanding on words because of individual differences. Pictures present a more intuitive and informative content. The reasonable collocation of color can improve the overall appeal of pictures, so users are more sensitive to pictures. It can be seen that the quality of graphic design has a greater impact on user experience.

Tables 7 and 8 show the mean of network abnormal page scores in text expression and graphic design, respectively. The mean of women's scores are higher than that of men in various aspects, but there is no significant difference. Therefore, gender difference has little influence on the experience of graphic design and text expression.

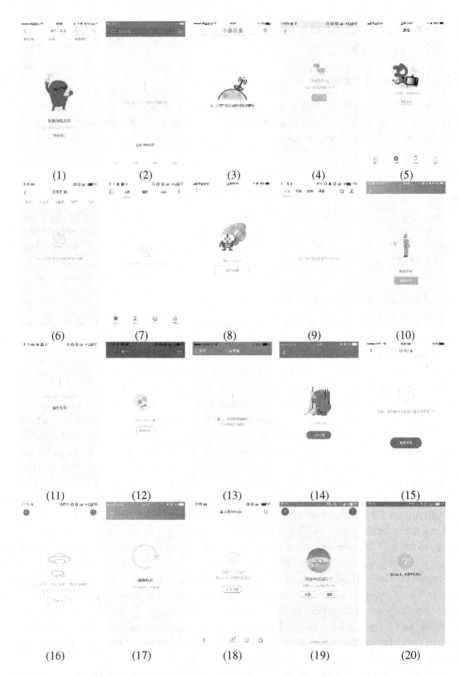

**Fig. 7.** Questionnaire samples of network abnormal pages.

**Table 4.** Network abnormal page classification.

| | Icons with monotonous color | Colorful interesting pictures |
|---|---|---|
| Plain text expression | (A) | (B) |
| Special text expression | (C) | (D) |

**Table 5.** Results statistics of network abnormal page scores.

| Number-group | Overall score mean | Text expression score mean | Graphic design score mean | Number-group | Overall score mean | Text expression score mean | Graphic design score mean |
|---|---|---|---|---|---|---|---|
| 1-B | 2.93 | 3.04* | 2.86 | 11-A | 2.19 | 2.23 | 2.04 |
| 2-A | 2.35 | 2.58 | 2.25 | 12-D | 3.89* | 3.72* | 4.05* |
| 3-D | 3.89* | 3.93* | 3.95* | 13-C | 2.74 | 3.25* | 2.30 |
| 4-B | 3.25* | 3.02* | 3.40* | 14-B | 3.65* | 3.26* | 3.98* |
| 5-D | 3.42* | 3.44* | 3.47* | 15-C | 3.44* | 3.70 | 2.86 |
| 6-C | 2.77 | 3.14* | 2.61 | 16-D | 3.81* | 3.77* | 4.00* |
| 7-A | 2.28 | 2.40 | 2.19 | 17-A | 2.12 | 2.16 | 2.05 |
| 8-B | 3.21* | 2.95 | 3.49* | 18-C | 2.35 | 2.56 | 2.12 |
| 9-C | 2.54 | 2.88 | 2.18 | 19-D | 2.89 | 2.96 | 2.82 |
| 10-B | 3.18* | 2.68 | 3.49* | 20-A | 1.91 | 2.00 | 1.89 |

Note: * represents score mean>3

**Table 6.** Overall score mean of network abnormal pages of each group.

| Group | A | B | C | D |
|---|---|---|---|---|
| Overall score mean | 2.17 | 3.244 | 2.768 | 3.58 |
| Text expression score mean | 2.274 | 2.99 | 3.06 | 3.564 |
| Graphic design score mean | 2.084 | 3.444 | 2.414 | 3.648 |

**Table 7.** Text expression score mean of network abnormal pages of each group.

| Group | A | B | C | D |
|---|---|---|---|---|
| Score mean (Men) | 2.176 | 2.922 | 2.944 | 3.406 |
| Score mean (Women) | 2.392 | 3.07 | 3.3 | 3.752 |

**Table 8.** Graphic design score mean of network abnormal pages of each group.

| Group | A | B | C | D |
|---|---|---|---|---|
| Score mean (Men) | 2.078 | 3.362 | 2.324 | 3.638 |
| Score mean (Women) | 2.128 | 3.508 | 2.552 | 3.642 |

## 6   Conclusion and Prospect

Based on the above analysis, it can be concluded that fun loading can shorten user's estimation of waiting time more than circle loading and progress bar loading, reduce the anxiety in the waiting process, and thereby improve the experience of "peak" moment. In the design of network abnormal page, graphic design is more important than text expression. Reasonable color matching and interesting and cute design can placate users when they face the abnormal state of network, and thereby improve the experience of "end" moment.

Although this paper studies how to improve user experience of "peak" and "end" moment in loading waiting from the perspective of Peak-End Rule, data loading page and network abnormal page are just two types of App's blank pages. Therefore, future research will consider selecting other App blank pages as objects to study, and enrich the application of Peak-End Rule in the design of App blank page.

## References

1. Chen, Y., Xiangyang, X., Hu, W.: Improvement design of the car ticket dispenser interface on the basis of peak-end rule. Packag. Eng. (6), 57–61 (2016)
2. Zhang, L., Zhang, Y.: The improvement of 404 error page based on "peak-end rule". Packag. Eng. (24), (2012)
3. Chien, S.Y., Lin, Y.T.: The effects of the service environment on perceived waiting time and emotions. Hum. Factors Ergon. Manuf. Serv. Ind. **25**(3), 319–328 (2015)

4. Baker, J., Cameron, M.: The effects of the service environment on affect and consumer perception of waiting time: an integrative review and research propositions. J. Acad. Mark. Sci. **24**(4), 338–349 (1996)
5. Zheng, J.: The waiting experience design research of loading page. Art Des. (1) (2016)
6. He, R., Fu, Y.: Mobile APP page loading methods based on time perception. Packag. Eng. (18) (2017)
7. Thomas, E.A.C., Weaver, W.B.: Cognitive processing and time perception. Atten. Percept. Psychophys. **17**(4), 363–367 (1975)
8. Chu, Y., Feng, C., Ji, W.: The impact of length of duration and change in velocity on duration perception of progress bars. Psychol. Sci. (2) (2014)
9. CNNIC: The 40th Statistical Report on the Internet Development in China in 2017. http://www.199it.com/archives/619827.html. Accessed 04 Aug 2017
10. Tencent "mobile page user behavior report". https://socialone.com.cn/tencent-mobile-page-user-behavior-report-2016/. Accessed 29 Mar 2016

# Influence of Different Types of Auxiliary Sensors on the Behaviors of Right Turn and Right Changes of Lane

Jitao Li[1], Hua Qin[1], and Linghua Ran[2(✉)]

[1] Beijing University of Civil Engineering and Architecture, Beijing, China
[2] AQSIQ Key Laboratory of Human Factors and Ergonomics, China National Institute of Standardization(CNIS), Beijing, China
ranlh@cnis.gov.cn

**Abstract.** There is a visual blind spot when a driver tries to change his direction to right. If the driver ignores the blind spot, the vehicle accident may be occurred. Therefore, many drivers install sensor devices which can help them to know the blind spots on the right of the road. The paper conducted the online questionnaire to acquire the degree of driver's subjective acceptance of for different external tips. And later a simulation experiment was conducted to compare the performances of three different modes of human-computer interaction for the auxiliary devices during the turning right and changes of lane process, including the sound tips, flash tips and vibration tips. Nine non-professional drivers aged between 21 and 24 with one to five years of driving age conducted the experiments. The times of action and response time were recorded and analyzed. The result shows that in the three kinds of tips in the sound tips is more effective.

**Keywords:** Auxiliary sensors turn right · Sound tips · Flash tips
Vibration tips

## 1 Introduction

There are more and more cars on the road and the traffic become more and more worse. The more the traffic volume is, the more obvious of the conflict between pedestrians and vehicles [1].

There is a visual blind spot when a driver try to change his direction to right or change his lane to right. Visual blind spots make drivers not see pedestrians clearly. Many auxiliary sensors have been sold on the market. Sensors can give the drivers the tips if there is any obstacle in the blind spot. The sensors as the tips can improve the efficiency of converting information, but when the driver catch the traffic tips, he will lose about 30% of the attention. And nearly 36.4% of all traffic accidents caused by distracted [2]. So the different ways of tip will affect driving safety. It is necessary to discuss the effect of different tips on drivers' behaviors.

At present, a lot of researches have been conducted on the vehicle driving. Pei [3] proposed the relationship between reaction time and interactive security. By sending tips to the driver can effectively reduce the possibility of accidents. It is possible to improve driving safety by improving the way of tips. When a driver made a decision on the road, he will only make decision relied on the information currently available to him, not the information provider. [4] Young drivers are more likely to drive at risk than older one [5]. Therefore, for the male drivers, the similar period of driving as the main aspects would be considered in the choice of subjects.

Most of the researches adopt the method of constructing the models. Bao [6] proposed the movement model of right-turn vehicle and pedestrian crossing at signalized intersection. Zhang [7] studied on the conflict characteristics of right-turn vehicles and pedestrians ahead of time. He established the time distribution model of right-turn ahead vehicles with right-right mixed mode and right-turn dedicated right-turn mode. Yang [8] putted forward the factors that may influence the merging decision-making and established a decision-making model of right-turning vehicles merging. Through these models, it can be considered that in the process of driving motor vehicles, drivers mainly derive information from visual, auditory and tactile. Among them, sub-tasks of vision and hearing will make the driver's mental workload increase significantly [9], affecting the driver's normal driving. So we choose flash, sound, and vibration as independent variables.

It can be seen from the above research results that most researches on the performance of right-turn vehicles are from the perspectives of signalized intersection, traffic delay and other aspects. There are not many researches focus on the connection between the way of tips and driver behavior in driving process. Therefore, based on the driver's response to different tips, the different behavior of drivers in response to different tips and the time for response are analyzed.

## 2   Experimental Design

In order to clearly understand the subjects' acceptance of external tips during driving, an online questionnaire was designed to acquire the degree of driver's subjective acceptance of for different external tips. And later a simulation experiment was conducted, and the objective data was analyzed to acquire which tip was optimal.

### 2.1   Questionnaire Survey

By consulting the literature, we summarize three main types of tips for the right turn and right changes of lane. They are sound, flash and vibration.

The online survey was used to explore drivers' perception of right-turn behavior. The questionnaire includes three questions: the factors that could cause accidents when turning right or changing to the right lane, the most acceptable way of prompting and the reasons.

The questionnaire surveyed 41 Chinese drivers with more than a year of driving experience. The Table 1 shows the proportion for the factors that could cause accidents when drivers turn right or change to the right lane.

As we can see from Table 1, most pilots think the speed and blind spots are the main causes of driving accidents. Among them, about 65.80% pilots regard the blind spots are the main factors. The Table 2 gives the degree of acceptance of the three tips

**Table 1.** The proportion of the factors that could cause driving accidents

| The factors | Proportion |
|---|---|
| Speed | 75.60% |
| Blind spots | 65.80% |
| Driving habit | 53.70% |
| The number of cars | 46.30% |
| Reasons of other vehicles | 34.20% |
| Other | 17.00% |

for the blind spots when turning right or changing to the right lane, and Table 3 gives the reasons for the degree of acceptance of the three tips.

**Table 2.** Driver's acceptance of different tips

| Tip ways | Proportion |
|---|---|
| Sound | 58.50% |
| Flash | 2.50% |
| Vibration | 2.40% |
| Sound+flash | 36.60% |

From Table 2, we can see that most drivers think that sound tip is more effective. The reason is the sound has less distraction during driving than the flash and vibration. About 44% persons think it is a distraction during driving, the proportion is lower than the flash and vibration tips, which are 61% and 51% respectively. So from the online subjective questionnaire, we can see that the sound tips has the highest acceptance when drivers turn right or change to the right lane.

## 2.2 Simulation Experiment

### 2.2.1 Research Goal
Later, we conducted a quantitative study by means of simulated driving. The experiment compares the performance of the drivers under the three different modes.

The experiment takes three different interaction modes as independent variables, and the response time of the driver as the dependent variable. In addition, for the sake of comparison, the behavior of the subject is also recorded.

### 2.2.2 Test Subject
The subjects were nine non-professional drivers aged between 21 and 24 with one to five years of driving age, all of whom were college students.

### 2.2.3 Experiment Preparation
This experiment was carried out in the vehicle laboratory of Beijing University of Architecture and the experiment environment was quiet. There is a car parked in the middle of the laboratory, and at the top of the car there's the projector. The projector's

**Table 3.** The reasons for the degree of acceptance of the three tips.

| Reasons | Proportion |
|---|---|
| The sound is a distraction during driving | 44% |
| The flash is a distraction during driving | 61% |
| The vibration is a distraction during driving | 51% |

screen is adjusted to the white wall in front of the car. The Torcs driving system is used as the simulated software. A LED light connected with a thin wire is placed on the right side of the car's glass to achieve flash tips. A small motor is placed on the steering wheel to achieve the vibration prompt mode. The LED light and small motor are both connected with the battery box to ensure they are under control (Fig. 1).

**Fig. 1.** Experiment scene

Three driving scenarios with different speeds and different speed limits were modeled, which are the highway, the city road and the mountain road. All of three scenes are two lanes with no speed requirements. The driving scenarios are shown in Fig. 2 and the detailed settings for the three experimental scenes are shown in Table 4.

### 2.2.4 Experimental Process
First, the contents of the experiment and experimental tasks were introduced to the subjects to ensure they can successfully complete the experiment. In order to avoid the error caused by the subjects' incompatibility with the experimental environment, they are required to make a practice for 5 min before the formal experiment.

The formal experiment process lasts about 20 min. The subjects are required to overtake the vehicle right in front of their own vehicle and reduce the speed, then observe the right rearview mirror to change the lanes. Once the subject attempts to turn

**Fig. 2.** Three driving scenarios

**Table 4.** Experimental scene

| Simulated road | Number of lanes | Speed limit | Traffic | Terrain |
|---|---|---|---|---|
| Highway | 3 | 120 | Smooth | Straight |
| City road | 3 | / | Complex | Curved |
| Mountain road | 2 | / | Smooth | Uphill and curved |

right, a warning is given. At this time, subjects may face four different situations: no prompt, sound tips, flash tips and vibration tips. Two speeds of 60 km/h and 100 km/h are set during the experiment. The subjects were observed whether they were taking the experiment seriously by setting experimental scene, such as setting pedestrians and obstacles on the roadside. Once the participant was found that they had a random driving behavior, the experiment was stopped immediately and the experimental data of the subject was considered invalid. The response of subject will be recorded by a video camera.

## 3   Experimental Results and Analysis

### 3.1   Basic Data

Two data were recorded during the experiment. The response time, that is the time from the instruction to the response of the subject. The shorter the time, the better the effect. The times of action of the subjects, that is what is the behavior of the subject after they receiving the prompt instructions, such as turning back, and the length of time. The time of turning right, that is the numbers for the subjects to conduct the behaviors.

The response time and the times of action in Speed of 60 kg/h are given in Table 5. From the data in Table 5 we can see that the sound tip has less response time than the other two tip ways (Table 7).

The response time and the times of action in Speed of 100 kg/h are given in Table 6. From the data in Table 6 we can see that the sound tip has less response time than the other two tip ways.

Similar with the Table 6. The data in Table 8 also indicate that the flash will cause fewer respond, while the sound tip will cause a faster react.

**Table 5.** Action and response time in speed of 60 kg/h

| Subjects | Sound tip | | Flash tip | | Vibration tip | |
|---|---|---|---|---|---|---|
| | Times of action | Response time | Times of action | Response time | Times of action | Response time |
| 1 | 2 | 2 | 2 | 1.5 | 2 | 2 |
| 2 | 4 | 1.5 | 2 | 2 | 2 | 2 |
| 3 | 2 | 2 | 2 | 1.5 | 2 | 2 |
| 4 | 4 | 1.5 | 2 | 2 | 2 | 2 |
| 5 | 2 | 2 | 2 | 2 | 2 | 2 |
| 6 | 2 | 2 | 2 | 2 | 4 | 2.5 |
| 7 | 2 | 1.5 | 2 | 2 | 2 | 2 |
| 8 | 2 | 2 | 2 | 1.5 | 4 | 2.5 |
| 9 | 2 | 1 | 2 | 2 | 2 | 2 |

**Table 6.** Action and response time in speed of 60

| Tip method | Mean value | |
|---|---|---|
| | Times of action | Response time |
| Sound | 2.44 | 1.72 |
| Flash | 2.22 | 1.83 |
| Vibration | 2.56 | 2.11 |
| Total | 2.41 | 1.89 |

**Table 7.** Action and response time in speed of 100 kg/h

| Subjects | Sound tip | | Flash tip | | Vibration tip | |
|---|---|---|---|---|---|---|
| | Times of actions | Response time | Times of action | Response time | Times of action | Response time |
| 1 | 4 | 1 | 2 | 1.5 | 2 | 2 |
| 2 | 2 | 1 | 2 | 2 | 2 | 2 |
| 3 | 3 | 1.5 | 3 | 2 | 3 | 2.5 |
| 4 | 6 | 1.5 | 2 | 3 | 4 | 1.5 |
| 5 | 3 | 1.5 | 3 | 2.5 | 2 | 1.5 |
| 6 | 2 | 2 | 2 | 2 | 3 | 2 |
| 7 | 2 | 2.5 | 3 | 1.5 | 3 | 2.5 |
| 8 | 2 | 2 | 2 | 1.5 | 4 | 2 |
| 9 | 2 | 1.5 | 2 | 2 | 2 | 2 |

By comparing Tables 6 and 8, we can see that they have a similar trend. With the increase of speed, both the number of actions and reaction time have increased. A correlation analysis is performed to determine which one is more effective.

**Table 8.** Mean value in speed of 100

| Tip method | Mean value | |
|---|---|---|
| | Times of action | Response time |
| Sound | 2.89 | 1.61 |
| Flash | 2.33 | 2 |
| Vibration | 2.78 | 2 |
| Total | 2.67 | 1.87 |

## 3.2  Statistical Data

Single factors of ANOVA

If the $\alpha$ value is more than 0.05, there is no significant difference. If it is less than 0.05, there is a significant difference. As can be seen from Table 9, only the $\alpha$ value of response time in 60 km/h was less than 0.05, and the other three $\alpha$ value are more than 0.05. The times of action for the three tip ways in 60 km/h and 100 km/h have no significant difference. It shows that the total times of action has no significant influence on the ways of tip, and it can not be judged more effective.

**Table 9.** Comparison of significance level

| | $\alpha$ value of times of action | $\alpha$ value of response time |
|---|---|---|
| 60 km/h | 0.646 | 0.023 |
| 100 km/h | 0.447 | 0.13 |

At the same level of risk, the amount and manner of behavior mainly depend on individual experience, including the different ways of getting current information And how to deal with the results of the information. The research on risk perceptions has found that driver's emotions can influence their perception of risk and lead to different behaviors [10]. And the driver's own factors, such as age, driving experience, education, safety consciousness are also the direct factors to effect the driving behaviors [11].

## 4  Conclusion

According to the result of questionnaire survey, there are 58% of drivers who can accept the sound tip. The results of the quantitative simulation experiment are consistent with the results of the questionnaire. The sound tip interaction has less response time and it is more effective.

However, it can be seen from the analysis data of the significant difference that there is no difference in the number of actions for the three tip ways, indicating that the actions during the driving can not be used as a measure criterion of the validity of tips and the relative response time can be used as a measure criterion. The average response time of the sound tip is superior to the other two tips at both 60 km/h and 100 km/h. It is concluded that sound as a reminder is better than vibrations and flashes and it is more acceptable to the driver because the sound tips are more direct to make the driver aware of the current road and to make response.

**Acknowledgement.** The research project presented in this paper is a part of the Project "Research on the Technology and Standard of Ergonomics Design for Information Display Interface", which was supported by the Beijing Natural Fund. The authors would like to acknowledge the support of the Beijing Natural Fund for this project (9172008).

# References

1. Chen, Y., Zhang, H., Qu, Z., Cao, N.: Signal intersection ahead of right turn vehicles and pedestrian conflict characteristics. J. Southwest Jiaotong Univ. **49**(5), 897–903 (2014)
2. Xian, H.: Sub-task driving safety evaluation index and evaluation model research. Jilin University, Ph.D. thesis, August 2014
3. Pei, W.: The impact of information and communication on unsafe driving behavior. Tsinghua University, Ph.D. thesis, April 2011
4. Guan, W.: Experimental study on visual process of traffic signs by drivers. Beijing University of Technology, Ph.D. thesis, June 2014
5. Xia, X.: Study on the impact of overconfidence on risk driving behavior. Southwest Traffic University, Master thesis, November 2015
6. Bao, Y.: Signal intersection right turn motor vehicle and pedestrian movement process modeling and simulation. Nanjing University of Science and Technology, Master thesis, January 2017
7. Chen, Y.-H., Mingli, W.E.I., Qu, Z.-W., Zhang, H., Cao, N.: Parking characteristics of pedestrian crossing with left-hand car jamming at signalized intersection. J. Jilin Univ. **2015**(1), 62–67 (2015)
8. Yang, X.: Study on decision-making model of turn-by-turn vehicles at signalized intersection. Beijing Traffic University, Master thesis (2012)
9. Wang, Q., Zhu, T., Zhu, K.N., Wu, L.: Visual and auditory sub-tasks on the driver's visual impact and differences. Saf. Environ. **14**(4), 49–51 (2014)
10. Chen, H.-H., Chen, S.-C.: The empirical study of automotive telematics acceptance in Taiwan: comparing three technology acceptance models. Int. J. Mobile Commun. **1**(7), 53–56 (2009)
11. Yuan, W.: Experimental study on dynamic visual characteristics of car drivers in urban road environment. Chang'an University, Xi'an, China, Ph.D. thesis, June 2008

# Three Dimensional Head Modeling
# Based on Direct Free Form Deformation

Haixiao Liu[1], Yanling Zheng[1], Xiai Wang[1], Taijie Liu[2], Linghua Ran[2],
and Jianwei Niu[1(✉)]

[1] School of Mechanical Engineering, University of Science and Technology Beijing,
Beijing, China
niujw@ustb.edu.cn
[2] China National Institute of Standardization, Beijing, China

**Abstract.** Three dimensional (3D) head models are the fundamental basis for ergonomic design of head and face wearable products. This paper presents a novel intuitive modeling approach of human head from the unorganized point cloud. The approach comprises two main phases. In the first phase, a standard head was constructed from laser scanned 3D unorganized points. At the beginning, we adopted pattern recognition algorithm to automatically identify the locations of key landmarks on the head. Then we conducted interpolation and approximation of points lying on the curves in the horizontal planes passing through the mentioned above key landmarks of the head. These curves are called feature wireframe. In this way, we obtained a complete mesh model, called standard head. In the second phase, free form deformation (FFD) was applied to the standard head to perform customization of head size and shape. We used an efficient FFD method based on Non-Uniform Rational B-Splines (NURBS) for this objective. One hundred 3D human head models (all males), from the latest and largest anthropometry survey of Chinese minors conducted by Chinese National Institute of Standardization in the last decade, were used as the sample data to calculate the standard head. The proposed approach can synthesize the standard head to any customized head according to user input head dimensions. This approach can be extended to other human body segment and will benefit the ergonomic design of quite a lot of wearable products.

**Keywords:** Ergonomic design · Head model · Free form deformation (FFD)
Non-Uniform Rational B-Splines (NURBS) · Product customization

## 1 Introduction

Ergonomic design of wearable products, e.g., helmet, respirator, mask, have increasingly be a focus in the area of anthropometry. There have been a lot of efforts to find out an efficient and robust digital head modeling method for this purpose. However, the previous researches are derived mainly from the computer graphics and animation areas. The researchers from those areas usually have a preference for visual fidelity and vivid image, and have no interest and also no attempts to fitting design of human wearable products. Consequently, a general method for human head modeling is highly anticipated.

© Springer International Publishing AG, part of Springer Nature 2018
P.-L. P. Rau (Ed.): CCD 2018, LNCS 10911, pp. 156–165, 2018.
https://doi.org/10.1007/978-3-319-92141-9_12

There have been a lot of methods for body shape modeling in the literature, categorized into four different categories, i.e., direct model creation, template model-based scaling, image-based reconstruction, and statistics-based model synthesis [1]. The direct model creation methods include the 3D scanning methods [2] and the anatomy-based model construction methods [3]. 3D scanning methods are the most accurate of obtaining the human body shape, but the extremely high cost often prevents their wide application. Additionally, the original points cloud is not suitable for product design, and it still needs a great deal of effort for post-processing work. The anatomy-based modeling methods derive the outer skin mesh point cloud from the underlying body structures. But they require great amounts of knowledge on human anatomical structures, and they are usually used in medical imageology for pathological diagnosis, or as the pre-process for finite element analysis in biomechanics. The template model-based methods create different body shapes by deforming and scaling a pre-defined template, usually prepared by other modeling methods [4]. These methods are becoming popular in the past due to its simplicity, and this merit especially attracts attention from on-line games. However, it is still a challenge to answer how to conserve the semantic meaning of different human parts during template fitting. The image-based methods reconstruct 3D human body shape from a set of images [5], so far as to using low-cost cameras such as equipped in mobile phones. However, it is still a long way for these methods to deal with the annoying noise and the dependency on the background. Statistics-based methods are believed inspired from the work of Blanz and Vetter [6], and also other research groups extend the original method [7, 8]. These methods generate a consistent mesh structure for every scan data, and construct a homogeneous face model database from those examples. These methods are based on identical topologies and mesh connectivity of the example models, but it is difficult for them to satisfy the input constraints and thus fail to evolve into an interactive parametric body shape modeler.

Inspired by the concept of free form deformation (FFD), a powerful digital sculpture tool in Computer Aided Design (CAD), we proposed a novel modeling approach of human head from the unorganized point cloud. First, we constructed a standard head from laser scanned 3D unorganized points. Second, we applied FFD to the standard head to perform customization of head size and shape according to the user-specified head dimensions.

The remainder of this paper is organized as follows: in Sect. 1, the samples of our research were introduced. The methodology of how to construct the standard head model and conduct FFD on the model was described in Sect. 2. The results of our research are introduced in Sect. 3. In Sect. 4, our paper was summarized and gives some discussions. Our conclusion and future work were presented in Sect. 4 as well.

## 2   Method

### 2.1   Sample Data

The 100 (all males) sample data used for our research is from the latest and largest 3D human body survey of Chinese minors. This survey was conducted by Chinese National Institute of Standardization in the last decade. In this survey, about 20,000 subjects (9,666 males and 9,699 females) participated and 19 anthropometric dimensions were measured. Human Solutions Vitus 3D scanner was primarily used, except weight, stature and some other measurements were measured manually.

The population database has ages ranging from four to seventeen years old. The children were classified into five age groups: preschool (4–6 ages), junior primary school (7–10 ages), senior primary school (11–12 ages), junior high school (13–15 ages), and senior high school (16–17 ages). The criterion of age stratification is based on ISO15535: 2003 General requirements for establishing anthropometric databases. The population database includes 2,117 pre-school students, 4,263 junior primary school students, 3,930 senior primary school students, 5,527 junior high school students, and 3,527 senior high school students. The subjects were recruited from six geographical areas in China: the northeast-north China, the central and western China, the lower reach of Yangtze River, the middle reach of Yangtze River, the south-east and the south-west China. The sample size in each area was determined based on the distribution of children's population reported by China National Bureau of Statistics.

## 2.2   Pre-processing

To get the standard head, we calculated the mean values of traditional dimensions, e.g., head length, head width, of the 100 head samples, and then calculated the Euclidean distance between the mean dimensions and the dimensions of the 100 samples. We chose the head whose dimension distance is the closest to the mean dimensions as standard head candidate, which still needs further pre-process.

There are holes and noise in the original scanned head, because of the light absorption and occlusions. We used Geomagic (3DSystems Inc.), a re-engineering soft package, to fill the holes, cut off the spikes, and remove the outliers of the scanned head data.

Moreover, because the original head scan data are scattered points, we re-sampled the point cloud on the head surface in order to make the surface point in a regular arrangement. We first define several feature wireframes parallel to the horizontal plane. These wireframes are important for fitting of head and face wearable products. Based on our previous research [9, 10], we used geometric characteristics and pattern recognition algorithm to automatically identify the landmarks on the head. Eleven anthropometric landmarks, i.e., left entocanthion left eye (LEL), right entocanthion left eye (REL), left entocanthion right eye (LER), right entocanthion right eye (RER), left alare (LAL), apex nasi (AN), right alare (RAL), subnasale (SU), left cheilion (LCH), right cheilion (RCH), and gnathion (GN), were identified.

These facial landmarks points are lying on the curves in the horizontal planes of the head. We call the landmarks as the facial features, and the curves as the feature wireframe. Based on the eleven facial landmarks, we defined five feature wireframe. They are, from top to bottom, eye wireframe passing through the four canthi, pronasale wireframe passing through the pronasale parallel to the horizontal plane, subnasale wireframe passing through the two subnasales, cheilion wireframe passing through the two cheilions, and gnathion wireframe passing through the gnathion parallel to the horizontal plane. We conducted interpolation and approximation of points lying on the feature wireframes to get re-sampled points arranged in a regular way, other than un-organized scatter points. To get a good trade-off between model quality and computational efficiency, we resampled the head mesh into 5901 points. In this way, we obtained a complete and has well-shaped mesh model, called standard head.

### 2.3    Traditional Free Form Deformation

FFD, proposed by Sederberg and Parry [11] and based on tri-variate Bernstein polynomials, is used to deform 3D models in a free-form manner. In this method, the objects to be deformed are embedded into a plastic parallelepiped. If the parallelepiped is deformed, the embedded objects are deformed along with it as well. The parallelepiped consists of one Non-uniform rational basis spline (NURBS) hyperpatch. Each hyperpatch is a $4 \times 4 \times 3$ space, where 4/3 stands for 4/3 control points; in other words, there exist 48 control points for each hyperpatch. The hyperpatch is specified by a three-dimensional grid of 48 control points $P_{ijk}$ and defines a volume of space parametrized by the three parameters $s$, $t$, and $u$ where $s$, $t$, $u \in [0, 1]$. The original FFD block before deformation consists of a rectangular lattice of control points arranged along three mutually perpendicular axes.

First we determine the positions of the vertices on the head surface in the FFD lattice space. We set up a local parametric coordinate system of the FFD block (Fig. 1),

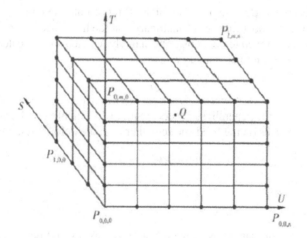

**Fig. 1.** Local parametric coordinate system of the FFD block

Then the local coordinates of any given point $Q$ lying in the FFD block can be defined as:

$$Q(s, t, u) = \sum_{i=0}^{4} \sum_{j=0}^{4} \sum_{k=0}^{3} P_{ijk} B_i(s) B_j(t) B_k(u) \tag{1}$$

where $P_{ijk}$ represents a control point, and $B_i(s)$, $B_j(t)$, and $B_k(u)$ are Bernstein polynomial of degree 3,

$$B_i(s) = \frac{4!}{i!(4-i)!} s^i(1-s)^{4-i}, B_j(t) = \frac{4!}{j!(4-j)!} t^j(1-t)^{4-j}, B_k(u) = \frac{3!}{k!(3-k)!} u^k(1-u)^{3-k} \tag{2}$$

When one or a number of control points are moved, then the vertices on the head surface in the lattice block will be deformed along with the control points. The new position of each affected vertex due to the change of lattice space can be obtained by replace the $P_{ijk}$ by its new position, namely $P_{ijk}'$, and calculate Eq. (1) again.

### 2.4  Direct Free Form Deformation

Even though traditional FFD provides the freedom to transform any 3D object into another new shape, the complex principle and tenebrous mathematical fundamental behind this method prevents its spread to non-mathematicians or non-CAD-experts. Users prefer direct manipulation of the vertices lying on the model surface other than the control points. In other word, the control point has no meaning for them because it is not intuitive. In this study, we extended the traditional FFD to Direct FFD.

Given

$$X = BP \tag{3}$$

where $B$ represents the Bernstein polynomials, $P$ represents the control points, and $X$ represents the original positions of the landmarks on the head face before deformation. If the landmarks are moved to new positions, namely $X'$, then we can calculate the new positions of the control points, namely $P'$ as

$$P' = B^{-1}X' \tag{4}$$

where $B^{-1}$ represents the generalized inverse matrix of $B$. Finally, we calculate the new positions of the vertices on the head surface other than the deformed landmarks $X''$ as

$$X'' = BP' \tag{5}$$

## 3  Results

The original head scan data contain plenty of holes, spikes and outliers, as shown in Fig. 2.

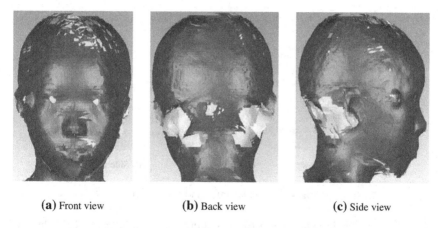

(a) Front view          (b) Back view          (c) Side view

**Fig. 2.** An example of original scanned head data

The head data after hole filled, spike cut-off and outlier removed, is as shown in Fig. 3.

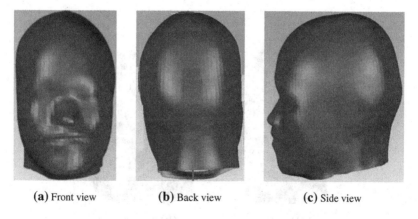

(a) Front view          (b) Back view          (c) Side view

**Fig. 3.** An example of head data after pre-processing

The eleven facial landmarks resulted from automatic identification are as shown in Fig. 4.

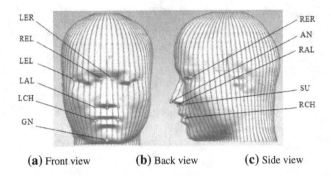

(a) Front view        (b) Back view        (c) Side view

**Fig. 4.** Facial landmarks identification

Tips: left entocanthion left eye (LEL), right entocanthion left eye (REL), left entocanthion right eye (LER), right entocanthion right eye (RER), left alare (LAL), apex nasi (AN), right alare (RAL), subnasale (SU), left cheilion (LCH), right cheilion (RCH), and gnathion (GN)

The complete well-shaped standard head model after pre-processing is as shown in Fig. 5.

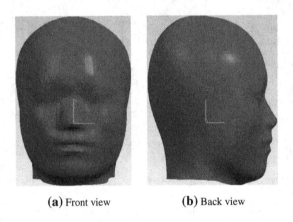

(a) Front view              (b) Back view

**Fig. 5.** The standard head model

The comparison of head model before and after deformation is as shown in Fig. 6. In the upper-left, there is the head model before deformation, whose head width is 156.1 mm, while in the upper-right, there shows the head model after deformation, whose head width is 145.0 mm. It can be seen the deformation is intuitive and high visual fidelity is kept for the deformed head model. The head width deformation takes the centroid of the head model as the reference point. The coordinates of the first and second points on the end of the line of head width before deformation are $(-1.1, 81.6, 39.3)$ and $(-0.7, -74.5, 41.8)$, respectively. In contrast, the coordinates of the first and second points on the end of the line of head width after deformation are changed to be $(-1.1, 76.1, 39.4)$ and $(-0.7, -68.9, 41.7)$, respectively. From what we have explained about the fundamental of Direct FFD in previous section, we can see the two end points of the line of the head length also changed their positions around the centroid of the head model. In details, the coordinates of the two points before deformation are $(-99.7, -2.7, 30.2)$ and $(100.9, 0.9, 0.2)$, respectively. While after deformation, they changed their positions to $(-93.4, -2.6, 29.2)$ and $(94.5, 0.7, 1.1)$, respectively.

**(a)** Head model before deformation (wide)     **(b)** Head model after deformation (narrow)

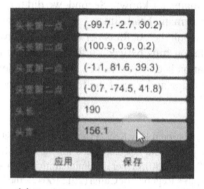

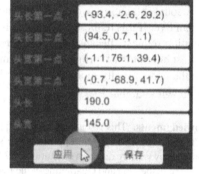

| 头长第一点 | (-99.7, -2.7, 30.2) |
| 头长第二点 | (100.9, 0.9, 0.2) |
| 头宽第一点 | (-1.1, 81.6, 39.3) |
| 头宽第二点 | (-0.7, -74.5, 41.8) |
| 头长 | 190 |
| 头宽 | 156.1 |

| 应用 | 保存 |

| 头长第一点 | (-93.4, -2.6, 29.2) |
| 头长第二点 | (94.5, 0.7, 1.1) |
| 头宽第一点 | (-1.1, 76.1, 39.4) |
| 头宽第二点 | (-0.7, -68.9, 41.7) |
| 头长 | 190.0 |
| 头宽 | 145.0 |

| 应用 | 保存 |

**(c)** Head dimensions before deformation     **(d)** Head dimensions after deformation

**Fig. 6.** The comparison of head models (before vs. after deformation)

## 4   Discussion and Conclusion

Free Form Deformation has been a research focus since its birth in last eighties. Even though researchers from ergonomics also noticed this kind of method and applied it to ergonomic design [12], there is no further deeper investigation on this topic from that time. For example, in the work conducted by Mochimaru et al. [12], they put the normal foot form in a $9 \times 5 \times 5$ lattice and manipulated the control points to deform the normal foot into different foot. By applying the same deformation of the control points, they deformed the last shape for normal foot to new last shape for different foot. However, they set up the local coordinate system in the FFD lattice based on traditional Cartesian coordinate system. This will lead to high computation load and lower degree of freedom of manipulating the control points. Another thing is their method is not intuitive, because the users should manipulate the control points of the FFD lattice, other than the points on the model surface. Usually the users have no idea of the meaning of control points, and also they cannot predict the displacement of the control points to move the points on the model surface to their anticipated new positions. In our study, we adopted FFD based on NURBS, which is more efficient and flexible. NURBS is a mathematical model commonly used in computer graphics for generating and representing models. It offers great flexibility and precision for handling modeled shapes. NURBS are commonly used in computer-aided design (CAD) and are part of numerous industry wide standards. NURBS are useful for constructing many types of organic 3D forms because of the smooth and minimal nature of the curves they use to construct surfaces. NURBS tools are also found in various 3D modeling and animation software packages. They can be efficiently handled by the computer programs and yet allow for easy interaction. It's highly intuitive and predictable to edit NURBS models. Besides based on NURBS, we also extend the traditional FFD to direct FFD, which means the users can directly manipulated the points on the model surface to new positions wherever they would like.

There are also some limitations for our method. First, we only verified the method on the head linear dimensions, e.g., head length, head width. Whether this method still applies to head dimensions with curvature remains un-known. Second, we did not take it into account if the users would like to change many head dimensions, as an example, more than five. If this request happens, there would be conflicts between the dimension deformation requests because there exist relationships between different head dimensions. Last but not least, progressive deformation is expected, since during form deformation the users usually modify the general shape and size of the form and re-edit the detailed geometry step-by-step.

**Acknowledgments.** This research is supported by National Key R&D Program of China (2017) YFF0206602. The authors also appreciate the support from Special funds for the basic R&D undertakings by welfare research institutions (522016Y-4680), General Administration of Quality Supervision, Inspection and Quarantine of the People's Republic of China (201510042), the State Scholarship Fund from China Scholarship Council (201208110144), the National Natural Science Foundation of China (51005016), and Fundamental Research Funds for the Central Universities, China (FRF-TP-14-026A2).

# References

1. Baek, S.Y., Lee, K.: Parametric human body shape modeling framework for human-centered product design. Comput.-Aided Des. **44**, 56–67 (2012)
2. Trieb, R., Seidl, A., Hansen, G., Pruett, C.: 3-D body scanning - systems, methods and applications for automatic interpretation of 3D surface anthropometrical data. In: Proceedings of the Human Factors and Ergonomics Society Annual Meeting, pp. 844–847 (2000)
3. Kahler, K., Haber, J., Yamauchi, H., Seidel, H.P.: Head shop: generating animated head models with anatomical structure. In: Proceedings of the ACM SIGGRAPH Symposium on Computer Animation, pp. 55–64 (2002)

4. Kasap, M., Magnenat-Thalmann, N.: Parameterized human body model for realtime applications. In: Proceedings of the 2007 International Conference on Cyberworlds, pp. 160–167 (2007)
5. Wang, C.C.L., Cheng, T.K.K., Yuen, M.M.F.: From laser-scanned data to feature human model: a system based on fuzzy logic concept. Comput.-Aided Des. **35**(3), 241–253 (2003)
6. Blanz, V., Vetter, T.: A morphable model for the synthesis of 3D faces. In: Computer Graphics Proceedings, SIGGRAPH 1999, pp. 187–194. ACM, New York (1999)
7. Allen, B., Curless, B., Popovic, Z.: The space of human body shapes: reconstruction and parameterization from range scans. ACM Trans. Graph. **22**(3), 587–594 (2003)
8. Wang, C., Hui, K.-C., Tong, K.: Volume parameterization for design automation of customized free-form products. IEEE Trans. Autom. Sci. Eng. **4**(1), 11–21 (2007)
9. Niu, J.W., Wu, Y.M., Hou, F., Feng, A.L., Chen, X.: Automatic landmark identification from three dimensional (3D) human body data using geometric characteristics. In: 4th International Conference on Applied Human Factors and Ergonomics (AHFE 2012), San Francisco, USA, July 21–25 (2012)
10. Liu, J.C., Zhang, L., Chen, X., Niu, J.W.: Facial landmark automatic identification from three dimensional (3D) data by using Hidden Markov Model (HMM). Int. J. Ind. Ergon. **57**, 10–22 (2017)
11. Sederberg, T.W., Parry, S.R.: Free-form deformation of solid geometric models. SIGGRAPH Comput. Graph. ACM **20**(4), 151–160 (1986)
12. Mochimaru, M., Kouchi, M., Dohi, M.: Analysis of 3-D human foot forms using the free form deformation method and its application in grading shoe lasts. Ergonomics **43**(9), 1301–1313 (2000)

# Influence of Song Porcelain Aesthetics on Modern Product Design

Xiao Song[1(✉)], Zhaoqi Wu[1], Li Ouyang[2], and Jei Ling[3]

[1] Beijing Technology Institute, Zhuhai, People's Republic of China
842766039@qq.com, 58013048@qq.com
[2] Guangzhou Fine Art Academy, Guangzhou, People's Republic of China
Oylee@163.com
[3] Zhongkai University of Agriculture and Engineering,
Guangzhou, People's Republic of China
kiddoo@163.com

**Abstract.** Based on the aesthetic conclusions from works on Ding white porcelain of Song dynasty, this paper is intended to illustrate the relationship between design and culture symbols by studying a case on the design of a culturally creative product combining cultural icons derived from both the aesthetic perfection of white porcelain and modern products. Ding white porcelain of Song dynasty is one of the most prominent products in the history of Chinese porcelain craft. The purpose of this study is to expound that the design styles of modern culturally creative products in China should be based on the heritage of China porcelain aesthetics, and uniquely integrate both fascination of ancient culture and the charisma of modern times, and that the design of porcelain products should be stemmed from culture. Therefore, the purpose of this paper is to build up a theoretical frame for designers to follow in their design of culturally creative porcelain products, and to explicitly discuss on cross-cultural communication and propagation and the Chinese porcelain culture as the foundation of modern porcelain products design.

**Keywords:** Ding white porcelain · White porcelain aesthetics
Culturally creative products · Technological design

## 1 Introduction

The ceramic art in China reaches its first summit in Song dynasty. The porcelains in this period have always been admired and adored for its 'born beauty' [1] and graceful elegance, which embodies the amazing creativity of ancient Chinese and demonstrates the high level of science and technology as well as the Chinese people's pursuit of beauty, art and happiness in the past thousand years. The study of the ceramic art in Song period, therefore, is of great historical value. Ding, one of the five famous kilns in Song dynasty, mostly produced white porcelains which were selected as royal porcelain for its fine craft, its simple color and elegant luster, and beautiful decorative patterns (see Figs. 1, 2 and 3). Its unique monochrome glaze decoration, the connotation of

© Springer International Publishing AG, part of Springer Nature 2018
P.-L. P. Rau (Ed.): CCD 2018, LNCS 10911, pp. 166–174, 2018.
https://doi.org/10.1007/978-3-319-92141-9_13

Confucianism, Buddhism and Taoism culture and the aesthetic value of zen influenced magnificently on the development of ceramics design in the later world.

**Fig. 1.** A large vase white glazed with lotus pattern and a dragon head

**Fig. 2.** A five-foot censer white glazed

**Fig. 3.** A handed ewer white glazed with peony pattern and a dragon head

## 2 Research Value of Ding White Porcelain in Song Dynasty

Ding kiln, was located in Ding Zhou in Song dynasty, which is nowadays Quyang County of Hebei Province. Ding began to produce white porcelains as early as in the late Tang Dynasty, and became one of the five famous kilns in Song dynasty. Song period witnessed lot of creation and improvement in ceramics production, and the enormous production scale of a wide varieties of Ding porcelains including bowls, dishes, bottles, discs and pillows made Ding one of the five famous kilns in Song dynasty along with Ru, Jun, Guan and Ge (as was called in later ages). Deeply influenced by the politics, religion and economy at that time, Ding developed an aesthetic perception of simplicity, naturalness and harmony. Unfortunately, compared to other kilns, study on Ding aesthetic and its influence on ceramic design in later ages can hardly be traced due to lack of history and literature record as a result of various restrictions. Therefore, the author believes that analysis on aesthetic features of Ding kiln should be of certain academic value and practical guiding significance to the study of the development of ceramic design. In the late Tang dynasty, Ding kiln had begun to produce white porcelain, imitating Xing kiln in the early days. In Song dynasty, Ding had already surpassed Xing kiln in the technology of sintering, and gradually replaced the latter as a main kiln [2]. For its exquisiteness, fine glaze color and beautiful patterns (as shown in Figs. 4, 5 and 6), Ding had gradually outstood from a common commercial kiln at the beginning to become the imperial porcelain kiln for rulers of Song dynasty and the paragon of the time. On the other hand, thanks to the open foreign trade policy of Song dynasty, export of ceramics boomed amazingly, In Pingzhou Ketan, a book recording anecdotes, businessman in the Northern Song dynasty carried countless ceramic articles to southeast Asia by various ships [3]. More than 30 countries maintained trade relationship with the Southern Song dynasty, over 20 of which were frequented by traders shipping ceramics from the Southern Song dynasty [4]. The Song porcelain salvaged from the shipwreck "South China Sea No.1" showed that the Ding aesthetic perception had been accepted and widely spread, which promoted the development of ceramic design in the world, especially in Southeast Asia.

# 3   The Main Aesthetic Features of Ding in Song Dynasty

## 3.1   An Aesthetic of Refinement and Naturalness

Song, a dynasty advocating literature or fine art but despising military and physical labor, is awash with literati and scientists. While rulers of Song dynasty adopted a strategy of emphasizing civil administration at the expense of national defense, the aggressiveness and powerfulness as well as the warship of military achievements were replaced by literature and art and an aesthetic of refinement, meditation and metaphysics [5]. Song dynasty implemented Confucian political thought in civil administration, while Buddhism and Taoism are the main religions at that time. The new Confucianism emerged after its absorption of Buddhism and Taoist thoughts [6]. The reflection on aesthetics intrigued by the integration of Confucianism, Buddhism and Taoism made it a trend for literati of Song dynasty to pursue the spiritual realm, and all kinds of ceramic and porcelain wares had become something to express feelings and aesthetics in their hands, which greatly influenced the shaping and patterning.

**Fig. 4.** White glaze clean bottle

**Fig. 5.** White glaze loop-handled teapot

**Fig. 6.** White glaze engraved lotus matrass

Lao Tse and Chuang-Tzu, the representatives of Taoism say that the nature of human beings lies in being natural, and what Taoism emphasizes is "essence", and what they pursuit is "being" and "simplicity". "Simplicity" is to keep the essence of things and eliminate artificial factors to achieve a beauty of simplicity, naturalness, and silence. Zen, which has always been the main Chinese Buddhist sect, is a mixture of the Indian Buddhism and the traditional Chinese Taoism, flourishing most in Song dynasty, influencing on the then aesthetic with a profound life outlook and social ideologies [7]. Being indifferent and natural, white porcelains are quite in consistence with Taoism and zen in their pursuit of a mental state and temperament of nothingness. The ceramic art style and Chinese aesthetics have been influenced by the mixed Confucianism, Buddhism and Taoism ever since Song dynasty, with a different dominating philosophy in a different era.

## 3.2  Animal and Plant Modeling and Decoration Aesthetics

In Song dynasty, imagery modeling and decoration were adopted for the design of white porcelain, which is to imitate the biological form in nature in the design to achieve the goal of aesthetic originality. The aesthetic of Song dynasty is mainly attributed to the Taoist culture advocating a doctrine of "natural beauty", i.e. anything that is beautiful is of nature. Ceramic and porcelain wares, inseparable from daily life, such as pottery pots, pomegranate shaped boxes, human-shaped pots, etc., naturally follow the "life-copy" policy, and are usually decorated with flowers and landscapes and fancy animal images. Figure 7 The design of the baby pillow is mimicking the naive posture of a sleeping baby. Figure 8 Delicate, light, and handy, the five pointed petal plate produced by Ding kiln was made out of exquisite workmanship.

**Fig. 7.** White glaze baby pillow

**Fig. 8.** 5-Petaled plate

**Fig. 9.** White glaze lotus pattern round waist pillow

Professor Li-xin Li said: "The integration and transformation of Buddhist artifacts into China ceramic and porcelain wares is the sinicization of Buddhist artifacts design, which almost changed the history of art development of China ceramic and porcelain wares after Han dynasty [8]." From the imagery ceramic artifacts of Song dynasty, we can see the impact of Buddhism-zen thought on white porcelain design, which is directly embodied in the shape and decorative patterns, as shown in Fig. 9, a waist pillow with carved patterns of lotus flower, whose character and moral are regarded as to be in conformity with the Buddhist doctrine and is treated as the symbol of Buddhism. The love of nature and the influence of religion in Song dynasty can be seen in the existence of a large number of carved flower patterns.

## 3.3  An Aesthetic Integrating Simplicity, Beautifulness and Practicability

The urban prosperity of Song dynasty led to the most prosperous industry in the city, the catering and entertainment services. The streets were full of restaurants, tea shops, and restaurants, Vacherie, the earliest entertainment place in Song Dynasty, and brothels all over the cities. In the northern Song dynasty, there were more than 3,000 "Zhengdian" (the authorized wine dealer) and "Jiaodian"(the retail wine dealers) in Bianjing, the capital city, whose main business was to offer catering services.

According to the statistics of "Meng Liang Lu" by Wu Zimu of the southern Song dynasty, there were as many as 335 types of dishes on the market in the city of Hangzhou [9]. The development of the catering industry brought by urban prosperity required a large number of household utensils, which naturally promoted the rapid development of ceramics in Song dynasty. Ding kiln produced large quantities of ceramic ware in many varieties in a big scale, greatly satisfying the life needs. Meanwhile it set up its own image during its rapid development and formed its own

**Fig. 10.** White glaze flower plate

**Fig. 11.** White glaze engraved teacup with saucer

**Fig. 12.** White glaze engraved tea-cup with saucer

unique shaping and molding norm (see Figs. 10, 11 and 12).

In general, the understanding of art often demands an unpractical emphasis on the appreciation of artistry, while Song porcelain relates the artistry to the practical function, showing the symbolic connotation of Song dynasty culture by its shaping and patterns. Before Tang and Song dynasties, the ancients were seated on the ground, usually kneeling on the grass mats. The invention of chair liberated human body and mind [10]. Song dynasty is a period for the transition of Chinese sitting position. The matching of table and chairs released the mental productivity, and the dimensions of household furniture also subsequently became bigger and higher. Indoor layout also changed correspondingly with the coming of light and small daily house wares easily movable and suitable to put on the furniture. Then came the era for ceramics and porcelains to accommodate the modern life habit, which perfectly explained why daily life articles accounted for most part of Ding white porcelain.

Although Ding porcelain is of high cultural value, it is not too noble to keep common people away. On the contrary, it is the most common articles for daily use, which embodies its aesthetic of simplicity, beautifulness and practicability.

## 4   The Influence of Ding White Porcelain on the Design of Modern Ceramics

The design of ceramic creative products is a new concept of ceramic products along with cultural creation. The promotion of culturally creative industry has currently become a trend for many countries in drafting their economic development strategies. The traditional culture of each nation and its lifestyle has its unique identification. To meet global market competition, a design with cultural features can demonstrate the uniqueness of the product and bring a special consumption experience [11]. With a higher life level, an economy era has come when the consumer market began to emphasize on experience and aesthetic. A unique regional culture and creative ideas have become the key to the development of ceramic products [12]. With an extremely high aesthetic norm and exquisite ceramics technique, Ding porcelain has become the source of modern ceramic culture and product design, constantly inspiring designers to reflect on culture, creativity, technology innovation.

## 4.1 Heritage of Simple Beauty and Simulation Modeling

Confucianism, Buddhism and Taoism are the three thoughts that have been influencing Chinese culture and art and the Chinese society, life and mentality. The aesthetic tastes of the three schools are also similar in some ways, which is why white porcelain has been held in high regard for its simple elegance and ethereal decorative style. With this aesthetic, white porcelain influences greatly on the design of modern creative ceramics, helping the evolvement of modern design philosophy which covers today's humanity, conciseness, and practicability. It is a very important guide for modern designers, which helps them to remove trivial adornment and retain precise workmanship. An aesthetic tendency in product design can be formed through innovation of culture symbols and keep the balance between the culture and design.

From the 1980s, designers began to concentrate on product semantics-to regard a product as a symbol system. By studying its operation and application, designers created symbols out of product shapes, which were applied to product design [13]. The design of lid in Figs. 14 and 15 shows the influence of the traditional white glazed pottery jar (see Fig. 13) of Song dynasty. The originality lies in combination of the rock in traditional landscape gardening with the design of the pot lid. The combination of two different kinds of ceramic materials adds to the decorousness in addition to its simplicity and elegance and ethereal beauty of a traditional white porcelain glaze. This well explains the designers 'research on culture symbols.

**Fig. 13.** White glazed earthenware with button lid

**Fig. 14.** White glaze can with a rockery lid

**Fig. 15.** White glaze can with a rockery lid

## 4.2    Heritage of Practicability and Ethereal Glaze

The design of modern white porcelain mainly inherits practicability as daily products in people's life. In Song dynasty, among many colored glaze daily utensils, Ding white porcelain is unadorned but in good taste, showing off a unique temperament aloof and proud. This clean glaze color and the simple modeling proportion have a far-reaching influence on the later generations. Throughout the modern ceramic market, with stricter inspections on internationally traded goods and more requirements on products related to human health, porcelain tableware has seen an overnight change from colored ones into plain white porcelain, which has now become an irreversible trend [14] (see Fig. 16).

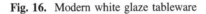

**Fig. 16.**  Modern white glaze tableware          **Fig. 17.**  Modern white glaze teapot

With changing consumers' demands, their cognition must also be taken into account in current product design in addition to product function and practical usage [15]. On the vigorous development of global creative industry, the consumer market is becoming more and more concerned with its cultural characteristics and aesthetic perception. Therefore ceramic products with culture symbols may lead to resonance of the consumers. In the design of white porcelain teapot, for example, the designer will try to find inspiration from the traditional modeling which has been publicly accepted for satisfying consumer's perception of products and cultural appeal, and design more models to meet the aesthetic needs of consumers (see Fig. 17).

## 4.3    Inheriting Skills and Exquisite Workmanship

Ding eggshell porcelain is a craft that has a profound influence on modern creative products. The crafts include gilding "mankou"(a defect on the porcelain being calcined) with gold or copper, and three main decoration tactics of engraved design, incised design and printing design. Ding initiated "Fushao" method to produce a fine quality product described as being thin as a piece of paper, with a sound like that of chime stone, and a glaze of a jade". The technical invention greatly increased the yield and improved the quality, and is still used in today's production. On the other hand,the new method according to which the vessel mouth is put upside down while being fired has a defect that the mouth of the vessel is not glazed. The unfired pottery has no color and appears rough. This is what we commonly know as "Mangkou". In order to cover up the flaws, skilled craftsmen wrapped "Mangkou" with silver, gold or copper to hide it when they made utensils for the palace. Now it has become a characteristic of Ding kiln [16] (see Fig. 18). Although better solutions have been found for the faults, this kind of adornment characteristic, a splendid show of fine workmanship and ornamental technique, has been inherited, which we often see on the white porcelain decoration (see Fig. 19).

**Fig. 18.** White glaze lotus matrass

**Fig. 19.** White porcelain teacup set

**Fig. 20.** White porcelain printed single teacup

The common decoration techniques of Ding porcelain are engraved flowers, incised flowers and printing. Engraving flowers is to carve on the surface of the utensil into a bevel so that the pattern can suggest volume with different shade and depth. With concise and fashionable composition and firm lines in symmetry, these patterns are usually lotus, peony, and other natural flowers. Printing refers to the method of copying the pattern on the surface of the utensil with a patterned mold. In Song dynasty, the printing of Ding kiln is the most superb. In addition to the common flowers, there are also animals such as mandarin ducks, lions, fish and so on. These patterns are usually combined with flowers and plants to present a harmonious nature picture of great complexity [17]. These decoration method is well applied in modern creative ceramic products. White eggshell porcelains with distinct printing decoration show how exquisite Ding white porcelain craft is, and how popular it is in the market (see Fig. 20).

## 5   Conclusion

The evolution of Ding white porcelain aesthetic thoughts is closely connected with Song dynasty's political culture, religion, science, and ways of life. From the modeling and decorations of white porcelain in Song dynasty, we can see how ceramic designers in Song dynasty had been influenced by culture in creating such highly reputable ceramic products. Professor Rongtai Lin said: " The design of culturally creative products is a taste or lifestyle which is to be realized through the industrialization of culture. [18]." Ceramics, as a traditional art material, enjoys a treasure of cultural heritage. Ding porcelain of Song dynasty is what we can learn from to create a product of such taste and lifestyle.

# References

1. Feng, X.: Chinese Ceramics, p. 435. Shanghai Ancient Books Publishing House, Shanghai (2006)
2. The Economic History of the Song Dynasty, p. 63. China Publishing House, Beijing (2009)
3. Feng, X.: Research on Ancient Export Porcelain, p. 51. Imperial Palace Press, Beijing (2013)
4. Chen, W.: Research on Dingyao, p. 5. Huayin Press, Beijing (2003)
5. Fang, L.: The aesthetic trend of Song dynasty ceramics. Group Statements Cent. Comm. China Democr. Alliance (4), 32 (2009)
6. Mei, Y.: On the influence of literati consciousness of Song dynasty on ceramic art, Chinese ceramics. China Inst. Light Ind. Ceram. (44), 73 (2008)
7. Zhang, H.-M.: Zen Aesthetics Realm of Theory of the Song Dynasty Ceramics, China Excellent Full-Text Data 2011, The First S1 Master Degree Theses of Master of Philosophy and the Humanities Series of Chinese Master 'S Theses Full - Text Database, No. S1 Philosophy and Humanities Sciences F088-323-1 (2011)
8. Li, L.: The penetration of Buddhism and its design history. Nat. Art Guangxi Cult. Art Res. (2), 79 (2003)
9. Yi, Z.: Great Song Innovation, p. 22. Zhejiang Literature and Art Publishing House, Hangzhou (2016)
10. TanTian: Research on aesthetic orientation and aesthetic characteristics of ceramics in Song dynasty. Xi 'an Engineering University, Xi 'an (2012)
11. Xu, Q., Lin, R.: Design program for cultural products. J. Des. 16(4), 1 (2011)
12. Handa, R.: Against arbitrariness: architectural significance in the age of globalization. Des. Stud. 20(4), 363–380 (1999)
13. Xu, Q., Lin, R.: Design program for cultural products. J. Des. 16(4), 5 (2011)
14. Chen, W.: Research on Dingyao, p. 214. Huayin Press, Beijing (2003)
15. Norman, D.A.: Emotional Design: Why We Love (or Hate) Everyday Things. Basic, New York (2004)
16. Zhong, H.: The History of Chinese Arts and Crafts, p. 69. People's Fine Arts Publishing House, Beijing (2007)
17. Shulan, Zhou: Chinese Ceramic Decoration, p. 196. Beijing Gongmei Press, Beijing (2009)
18. Lin, R.T.: Transforming Taiwan aboriginal cultural features into modern product design: a case study of cross-cultural product design model. Int. J. Des. 1(2), 45–53 (2007)

# User-Oriented Research on Perceivable Indicators of Smartphone Interactive Operation Performance

Zhengyu Tan[1(✉)] and Xiao Tan[2]

[1] State Key Laboratory of Advanced Design and Manufacturing
for Vehicle Body, Hunan University, Changsha, China
Tanzy2004@126.com
[2] School of Design, Hunan University, Changsha, China
xiaotan@hnu.edu.cn

**Abstract.** Smartphone interactive operation performance perception refers to the user experience when they operate the smartphone. Studying the specific perception needs of users on the interactive operation performance can provide a theoretical user-centered guidance for the mobile R&D agency. This paper discusses perceivable indicators of smartphone interactive operation performance and the typical Chinese apps and the relationship between them, which provides a basis for the study for the user's perceivable difference of smartphone interactive operation performance in different apps. First, we use the method of literature research to obtain the overall perceivable indicators of smartphone interactive operation performance: Coherence, Responsiveness, and Smoothness. Furthermore, the set of perceivable indicators is achieved by combining operation tasks and gestures. Second, sensitive users are screened by questionnaire. In order to draw the relationship between the perceivable indicators and the typical apps, we organized sensitive users into the focus group. The study found that the typical apps of Coherence are: Album, Meitu, Baidu Map; the typical apps of Responsiveness are: Weibo, Wechat, Camera; the typical apps of Smoothness are: Weibo, Zhihu, Taobao. This relationship provides typical apps for the following research on the modeling for each indicator and the overall model of three overall indicators.

**Keywords:** Smartphone interactive operation performance · User perception
User experience · Typical applications

## 1 Introduction

With the popularization of touchscreen smartphones and the development of multi-touch technologies, interactive gestures which conforming to the daily habits of users can directly interact with touchscreen smartphones and interaction between users and touchscreen phones become more natural and convenient [1]. The mounting number of smartphone R&D institutions begin to study the relationship between the touchscreen phone interactive operation and the user experience. How to make the user experience better while operating the touchscreen phone is a hot research topic [2].

© Springer International Publishing AG, part of Springer Nature 2018
P.-L. P. Rau (Ed.): CCD 2018, LNCS 10911, pp. 175–186, 2018.
https://doi.org/10.1007/978-3-319-92141-9_14

In fact, which perceivable indicators of interactive operation performance can be directly perceived by users, how the effect of different tasks and different gestures on user perception, and what kind of perceivable preferences do users have for different types of apps are the foci of this research.

These studies help developers optimize the apps by exploring the user's preference of perceivable indicators in different types of apps, which improve the user experience when they using a smartphone.

## 2 Related Research

### 2.1 Smartphone Interactive Operation Performance

The interactive operation performance of smartphone refers to the performance of users feeling when they operate a smartphone. The performance is affected by the hardware and software of the smartphone. There is a certain gap between interactive operation performance and preset performance. The better the hardware and software, the smaller the gap.

### 2.2 User Perception

Interactive perception refers to user expectations for interactivity and their subjective satisfaction with interactivity [3]. The interactive process of the user with the smartphone is the process of control and feedback [4]. Users control screen by using gestures, and give instructions to the smartphone, and then, smartphone give feedback to the user. After the user receives the feedback, the user can experience the interactive operation performance of the smartphone. This experience is called the smartphone interactive operation performance perception.

The research of this paper is aimed at sensitive users who have more demand for smartphone interactive operation performance and they are adept at expressing their needs. If a certain indicator can satisfy the sensitive user, can satisfy the needs of quite a few users.

### 2.3 The Overall Perceivable Indicators of Smartphone Interactive Operation Performance

Li explored that a good user experience is achieved with things such as user perceivable Coherence, Responsiveness, Smoothness, and Accuracy [5]. Coherence shows the ability of smartphone continuously feedback when the user continuously controls the phone. Coherence has a wide range of evaluation, includes assessing the lag distance between the fingertips and the dragged object (not only an icon but also any objects that can be dragged) in the screen. It also evaluates whether the user operation is consistent with the controlled objects, such as the angle difference between the tilting controlled water flow and the device inclination angle [5]. Nevertheless, the research of this paper is based on the interactive operation of the touchscreen phone. It only studies the performance of the dragged object can be synchronously moved with fingertip [6].

Li Proposed that the responsiveness can evaluate the time between an input being delivered to the device and device showing visible response [7]. Chu proposed that the smoothness evaluates how smooth graphics transition on the screen [8].

Nowadays, due to advanced technology, making the accuracy of smartphones greatly improved, and the accuracy has little impact on user experience [9]. Therefore, the research of this paper focuses on the user perceivable Coherence, Responsiveness, Smoothness, and we call these 3 indicators are the overall perceivable indicators of smartphone interactive operation performance (see Fig. 1).

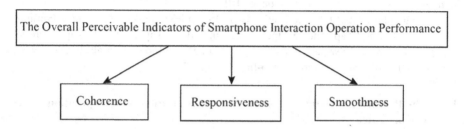

**Fig. 1.** The overall perceivable indicators of smartphone interactive operation performance.

Although these three indicators represent the user's overall perception for smartphone interactive operation performance, they are not linked with specific interaction scenarios in the interaction chain. The interaction scenario means that the process of users operate smartphone to achieve the specific task by using gestures. In the process of interaction, the same task can be mapped to a variety of gestures, and the same gesture can also be mapped to different tasks. Therefore, when we use different gestures to fulfill different tasks, the perception of the user on the mobile operation performance is different. For instance, for responsiveness, there is a perceivable difference between the response time of opening the application and closing the application. When the user taps the icon to open the app, hoping the phone to quickly enter the main page, and have enough time for other operations. Therefore, users have less patience under such circumstances. However, after the task is accomplished, the user intends to exit the application. At this time, the user has no specific operation target in the app, so they have more patience under the response time of closing the application. Therefore, it is necessary to combine tasks and gestures to get the set of perceivable indicators based on the overall perceivable indicators.

This paper is organized as follows: Sects. 3 and 4 provide an overview of our study and Sect. 5 discusses the results of our study and provides useful suggestions for the soft developer; finally, Sect. 6 presents the conclusion and future work.

## 3    Study1: The Perceivable Indicators Set of Smartphone Interactive Operation Performance

### 3.1    Smartphone Interactive Operation Tasks and Smartphone Interactive Gestures

Based on the application of the smartphone's own and download, there are 10 common tasks: open the application, enter the child page, popup, switch among sibling pages, feedback on input, return to the parent page, exit the application, move the picture or icon, zoom in/out and rotate, view page [10].

On four platforms, iOS, Android, Palm OS, and Windows, there are 7 common gestures, including "Tap" and "Swipe". "Tap" includes: "Tap", "Double-Tap", "Press". "Swipe" includes: "Swipe" and "Drag". "Drag" includes "Single-finger Drag", "Two-finger Pinch/Spread" and "Two-finger Rotate" [11, 12].

### 3.2    The Perceivable Indicators Set of Smartphone Interactive Operation Performance

Based on 3 overall perceivable indicators, combining with 10 tasks and 7 gestures. We initially obtained 26 initial perceivable indicators. The following Table 1 is about the process of how we get the 26 initial perceivable indicators: "A" shows the perceivable indicators of Coherence. "B" shows perceivable indicators of Responsiveness. "C" shows the perceivable indicators of Smoothness. Under the overall perceivable indicators, not every gesture and task can be combined to derive a specific perceivable indicator, on account of the user's operating habits and the definition of the three overall perceivable indicators. For example, in "1. Tap–1. Open the application", there is no specific perceivable indicator can be obtained with coherence, because based on the definition of coherence, we find that coherence is associated with drag, nothing to do with tap, and the user does not open the application by dragging.

Since there are repeated indicators in the 26 initial perceivable indicators, the Delphi Method was used to integrate and screen perceivable indicators [13]. By several rounds of consultation and feedback, 15 smartphone interaction experts integrated the 26 initial perceivable indicators into 21. Finally, the following Table 2 shows the set of perceivable indicators of smartphone interactive operation performance.

## 4    Study2: The Typical Apps of Perceivable Indicators in Smartphone Interactive Operation Performance

According to study1, we got 21 perceivable indicators, but we found that users have perceivable difference of smartphone interactive performance in different apps when they using apps. And some users have more demand for smartphone interactive operation performance and are adept to expressing their needs. Therefore, we designed questionnaire to screen sensitive users and organized sensitive users into the focus group to explore the relationship between the perceivable indicators and the typical apps.

**Table 1.** The initial perceivable indicators of smartphone interactive operation performance.

| | 1. Open the application | 2. Enter the child page | 3. Popup | 4. Switch among sibling pages | 5. Feedback on input |
|---|---|---|---|---|---|
| 1. Tap | A: —<br>B: The response time of entering the app main page after tapping the icon<br>C: The animation smoothness of entering the main page after tapping the icon | A: —<br>B: The response time of jumping to the child page after tapping<br>C: The animation smoothness of jumping to the child page after tapping | A: —<br>B: The response time of popup after tapping<br>C: The animation smoothness of popup after tapping | A: —<br>B: The response time of switching among sibling pages<br>C: — | A: —<br>B: The response time of typing feedback<br>C: — |
| 2. Double tap | — | — | — | — | — |
| 3. Press | — | — | — | — | — |
| 4. Swipe | — | — | A: —<br>B: The response time of swiping the taskbar<br>C: The animation smoothness of swiping the taskbar | A: —<br>B: The response time of swiping left or right among sibling pages<br>C: The animation smoothness of swiping left or right among sibling pages | — |
| 5. Single-finger drag | — | — | — | — | A: When using Hand-written Input Method, the coherence between the finger dragging and the trace displaying, etc.<br>B: —<br>C: — |
| 6. Two-finger Pinch/Spread | — | — | — | — | — |

*(continued)*

**Table 1.** (*continued*)

|  | 1. Open the application | 2. Enter the child page | 3. Popup | 4. Switch among sibling pages | 5. Feedback on input |
|---|---|---|---|---|---|
| 7. Two-finger rotate | — | — | — | – | — |
|  | 6. Return to the parent page | 7. Exit the application | 8. Move the picture or icon | 9. Zoom in/out and Rotate | 10. View page |
| 1. Tap | A: —<br>B: The response time of returning to the parent page after tapping<br>C: The animation smoothness of returning to the parent page after tapping | A: —<br>B: The response time of exiting the app after tapping<br>C: The animation smoothness of exiting the app after tapping | — | — | — |
| 2. Double tap | — | — | — | A: —<br>B: The response time of zooming in/out after double tapping<br>C: The animation smoothness of zooming in/out after double tapping | — |
| 3. Press | — | — | A: —<br>B: —(In user perception, the responsiveness is weakened by the feature of press)<br>C: — | — | — |

(*continued*)

**Table 1.** (*continued*)

|  | 6. Return to the parent page | 7. Exit the application | 8. Move the picture or icon | 9. Zoom in/out and Rotate | 10. View page |
|---|---|---|---|---|---|
| 4. Swipe | A: — B: The response time of returning to the parent page, after swiping right on the current page C: The animation smoothness of returning to the parent page, after swiping right on the current page | — | — | — | A: The response time of swiping up and down to scroll pages B: — C: The animation smoothness of swiping up and down to scroll pages |
| 5. Single-finger drag | — | — | A: The coherence between the single-finger dragging and the controlled objects B: — C: — | — | — |
| 6. Two-finger Pinch/spread | — | — | — | A: The coherence between fingers pinching/spreading and the photo zoomed B: — C: — | — |
| 7. Two-finger rotate | — | — | — | A: The coherence between fingers rotating and the photo rotated B: — C: — | — |

**Table 2.** The set of perceivable indicators of smartphone interactive operation performance

| Coherence | Responsiveness | Smoothness |
|---|---|---|
| Drag coherence | The response time of opening | The smoothness of opening |
| Zoom coherence | The response time of exiting | The smoothness of exiting |
| Rotate coherence | The response time of entering, | The smoothness of entering |
| Input coherence | The response time of returning | The smoothness of returning |
| | The response time of popup | The smoothness of popup |
| | The response time of Inputting | The smoothness of swiping left or right |
| | The response time of switching | The smoothness of swiping up or down |
| | The response time of swiping | The smoothness of zooming page by double taps |
| | The response time of zooming page by double taps | |

## 4.1   Sensitive Users

"The user experience evaluation questionnaire of smartphone interactive operation performance" includes "basic information" and "sensitive user screening scale". "The sensitive user screening scale" comprises 1. "The attention ranking of smartphone interactive operation performance" 2. "The satisfaction ranking of the smartphone". Users were asked to rate the approval ranking of each question. The approval ranking is divided into five levels: strongly disagree, disagree, neither agree nor disagree, agree, strongly agree, which correspond to the 1,2,3,4,5 points. Two scales contain 16 topics, with a total of 65 points, and the users who have scored in the top 20% are regarded as sensitive users.

368 online questionnaires were obtained, including 344 valid questionnaires and 24 invalid ones. There are 168 men and 176 women, and the proportion of men and women is nearly the same. According to market positioning (the models and price of the smartphone), 9 users who use lower-end phones were excluded among 69 sensitive users. Other 60 users are sensitive users, accounting for 17.4% of the total number of users (see Fig. 2).

These sensitive users' average age is 23 years old, 85% of them use the iOS system. They spend more than 4 h on smartphone every day, and they buy a new mobile phone once 6 months to once one year. Sensitive users often use the higher-end smartphone. They are familiar with the operation of the smartphone and often take the initiative to seek more convenient interactive operation mode. They are concerned about whether the smartphone interaction performance is satisfactory.

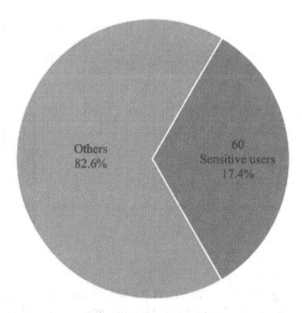

**Fig. 2.** The proportion of sensitive users accounted for the total users.

## 4.2 Typical Apps

Twenty-four sensitive users (12 Males, 12 Females) participated in the focus group. Users were divided into 4 groups to fulfill the following two tasks: 1. For each perceivable indicator, choose the most important 1–3 apps from your smartphone (both the system apps or the downloaded ones) 2. Describe the reason for your choice. In the course of the experiment, each group with a camera to record their oral expression. The data as shown (see Fig. 3).

The number of choices from yellow (less) to green (more). Colors are normalized by row, with green indicating each application's maximum number of indicators, and white indicating each app's minimum.

Twenty-nine apps are selected by users. In accordance with the Android market and the iPhone app store, 29 apps are grouped into 11 categories: Social, Reading, Photography, Map, Shopping, Note, Music, Brower, App Management, Education, Finance. Social apps are the most plentiful, which have 5 apps, including WeChat, Weibo, QQ, Zhihu, Address book. The total number of perceivable indicators in Social app is the most, followed by Photography, Shopping, etc. It can be seen that users are sensitive to the interactive operation performance of Social apps.

In Music and App Management, the number of app choices of each perceivable indicator is basically below 3, indicating that sensitive users have low attention to the perceivable indicators of these two types of apps.

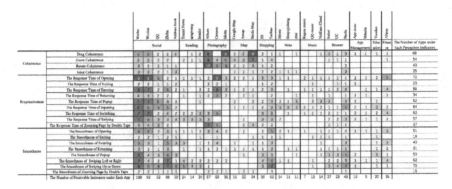

**Fig. 3.** The choices condition of applications under each perceivable indicator. (Color figure online)

## 5 Discussion

Coherence. For Drag Coherence, Meitu and Baidu Map have the maximum number of choices. Users usually use Meitu to retouch pictures. For instance, they use the dragging of gesture to pat off black eyes and thin face, etc. On the Baidu Map, users drag the map to find a location. For Zoom Coherence, Photography and Map are crucial, because users usually pinch/spread the picture and map by two fingers. However, Social and Taobao are also significant, because there are many pictures in these apps. Users often zoom in/out pictures and drag the list of pages for viewing. Input Coherence has the minimum number of apps, only 25, but the number of apps reached 64 for The Response Time of Inputting. Through user interview, it is found that the number of apps in Input Coherence is less because sensitive users rarely use the hand-written input method, and they use the keyboard input method instead. Keyboard input is more important for the Responsiveness. Sensitive users are mostly young, while people who use the hand-written input method are middle-aged and elderly people. If developing a smartphone or apps for the elderly, the importance of Input Coherence will increase.

In general, Albums, Meitu, Baidu Map are important to the Coherence.

Responsiveness. The Response Time of Opening is the most important, following the Response Time of Entering and the Response Time of Inputting, etc. Sensitive users said they often pay attention to the response time. If there are many apps running and the smartphone is used for a long time, the response time would be increased. The number of apps of four indicators in Responsiveness is above 60, illustrating that users have strong awareness for the Responsiveness. The apps of Responsiveness are mostly distributed in Social, Photography, Shopping. In Weibo, Wechat, Camera, sensitive users are most concerned about the Response Time of Opening.

Weibo, Wechat, and Camera are important to the responsiveness.

Smoothness. The indicator that have the maximum number of the apps is the Smoothness of Swiping Up or Down, following the Smoothness of Swiping Left or Right and the Smoothness of Popup. On the Smoothness of Swiping Up or Down,

Social, Reading, and Taobao are important because they have long pages, and users require swiping pages to view content. As for The Smoothness of Swiping Left or Right, it is applicable to the apps which have lots of sibling pages. On the Smoothness of Popup, Social and Browser are important, for the reason that users often use searching, typing and other functions, which will pop search box and keyboard.

Weibo, Zhihu, Taobao are important to the smoothness.

## 6   Conclusion and Future Work

This paper explores the specific perceivable needs of users for the smartphone inter-active operation performance, and get 21 perceivable indicators. Coherence: Drag Coherence, Zoom Coherence, Rotate Coherence, Input Coherence. Responsiveness: The Response Time of Opening, The Response Time of Exiting, The Response Time of Entering, The Response Time of Returning, The Response Time of Popup, The Response Time of Inputting, The Response Time of Switching, The Response Time of Swiping, The Response Time of Zooming Page by Double Taps. Smoothness: The Smoothness of Opening, The Smoothness of Exiting, The Smoothness of Entering, The Smoothness of Returning, The Smoothness of Popup, The Smoothness of Swiping Left or Right, The Smoothness of Swiping Up or Down, The Smoothness of Zooming Page by Double Taps.

The typical apps of the Overall Perceivable Indicators. Coherence: Albums, Meitu, Baidu Map. Responsiveness: Weibo, Wechat, and Camera. Smoothness: Weibo, Zhihu, Taobao. These typical apps provide a basis for the study of the user's perception of smartphone interactive operation performance in different Apps.

For future studies of this research, there are numerous works we need to do on the smartphone interactive operation performance with user perception.

- We will use the perceivable indicators and typical apps derived from this paper. Using electrophysiological equipment and eye tracker to finish the Coherence, Responsiveness, and Smoothness of the experiments.
- In combination with the change of physiology and eye movement, the reliability of the user's MOS scores for will be verified. The data model and equation of each perceivable indicator will be established by SPSS. Finally, the overall model of the smartphone interactive operation performance perception will be obtained by cal-culating the weight of Coherence, Responsiveness, and Smoothness.

**Acknowledgments.** The research was supported by National Natural Science Foundation of China (61402159, 51605154), the State Key Laboratory of Advanced Design and Manufacturing for Vehicle Body Funded Projects. We also would like to express our gratitude to Xiaohui Zhang who helped us during the research.

# References

1. Zhang, F.J.: Research on three-dimensional interaction technique for smartphone. J. Comput. Aided Des. Comput. Graph. **25**(1), 16–25 (2013)
2. Zhu, J.C.: Interaction design of touch-screen phone based on the user analysis. Packag. Eng. **38**(12), 239–243 (2017)
3. Miao, X., Han, D.N., Wang, T.: Application strategy analysis of interactivity in promoting e-commerce website user loyalty. Packag. Eng. **37**(12), 143–148 (2016)
4. Huang, B.L.: Design relationships between sight flow and operation flow in touch screen cell phone interface. Packag. Eng. **38**(4), 66–69 (2017)
5. Li, X.F., Wang, Y., Wu, J., et al.: The trend of mobile operation system architecture. Technol. J. **4**(16), 1–18 (2012)
6. Zuo, Y.M.: Design and Research of Desktop Document Operation Interaction Based on Multi-touch technology. Kunming University of Science and Technology, Kunming (2014)
7. Li, J.W.: Evaluation System Research and Implementation of the Smartphone User Experience. Beijing University of Posts and Telecommunications, Beijing (2014)
8. Chu, C.H., Wang, F., Tian, F., et al.: Usability of Finger Sliding Direction Based on Touching Device. In: Harmonious Man-machine Environment Joint Academic Conference, Guangzhou (2012)
9. Wang, L.: Touch sensing circuit printing in phone touch pane. Screen Print. **7**(7), 12–20 (2017)
10. Wu, J.D., Li, H.T., Wang, H.C., et al.: Usability of touch-based gestures for middle-aged and elderly people on touch screen mobile devices. Chin. J. Ergon. **22**(2), 12–20 (2016)
11. Wang, H.: Touching Screen Gesture Design Based on User Experience. Wuhan University of Technology, Hubei (2012)
12. Liang, L.L.: Analysis of single hand gesture interaction design based on touch screen mobile phone. Ind. Des. 95–96 (2017)
13. Chang, C.S.: Multi-level grey relation comprehensive evaluation method for universal design. J. Grey Syst. **17**, 229–238 (2014)

# Applications of Metaphors in Jewelry Design

I. Ting Wang[1(✉)], Chien-Chih Ni[2], and I-Wen Wu[1]

[1] Graduate School of Creative Industry Design,
National Taiwan University of Arts, New Taipei City, Taiwan
etinw@ms43.hinet.net, service@even.tw
[2] Hsuan-Chung University, Hsinshu, Taiwan
nancyni1008@gmail.com

**Abstract.** According to Michael Porter's concept of building a competitive advantage on culture, what Taiwan lacks in its current economic development is a social value that encourages creativity and innovation, that is, a "economic culture" that supports an aesthetic economy. In the contemporary development of jewelry design, the role of jewelry design is directly or indirectly interpreted by the forms of jewelry. Jewelry is one of the best means to define characteristics, signify status, and deliver thoughts and culture. Jewelry gives consumers a sense of identity and carries ideas of a thinking design. Based on Chinese literature criticism, this study attempts to apply a specific model presented in the "Bi Xing" chapter of Liu Xie's *Wen-Xing-Diao-Long* to develop a metaphorical design model. Through case study of jewelry works, this study explores use of metaphors in each work and discusses use of metaphors in a literary framework. In addition to investigating the forms and meanings of metaphors, this study also extends the jewelry design thinking model and conducts a quantitative evaluation of the proposed model. The results can not only offer guidance to metalworking instructions but also promote awakening of the aesthetic awareness in our culture, deepening of the power of jewelry design in our society, cross-domain cultural exchanges, and creation of a consciousness that speaks for the contemporary or the future society.

**Keywords:** Jewelry design · Thinking design · Metaphor design model

## 1 Introduction

### 1.1 Background and Motivation

In the researcher's observation of classroom instructions of metalworking, techniques are always the focus, and how to integrate creativity in metalworking is seldom addressed. Students often ask the instructor with a confused look "Sir, how should I convert my ideas into creative vocabulary?". The researcher deeply believes that in addition to the thinking design curriculum, how to read art works, how to interpret artists' thoughts and creative styles, and how to analyze the connections between design ideas and jewelry works in a theoretical framework of metaphors should all be incorporated into the current metalworking education.

In contemporary jewelry design, using various forms and techniques to deliver the creator's thoughts has become an increasingly dominant approach. The value of a

© Springer International Publishing AG, part of Springer Nature 2018
P.-L. P. Rau (Ed.): CCD 2018, LNCS 10911, pp. 187–202, 2018.
https://doi.org/10.1007/978-3-319-92141-9_15

jewelry design needs to be interpreted through in-depth observation from multiple perspectives. This study will analyze applications of metaphors in contemporary jewelry designs using the case study approach. The spiritual meanings, conversion of symbols, cultural value, and perspective reflections in the selected jewelry works will be explored. This study is intended to awaken the pursuit of aesthetic awareness in people, promote the application of metaphors in the thinking and creation of art works, and encourage more rational analyses of the associations between object, affect, and words. The ultimate goal is to create a consciousness that is particular to the contemporary or the future society through deepening of the influence of design, improvement of aesthetic knowledge, and promotion of the cultural and creative industry.

## 1.2   Objectives

In addition to formulating a design thinking process through analysis of applications of metaphors in jewelry designs, this study aims to achieve the following goals:

(a) Explore the Eastern and Western theoretical frameworks of metaphors;
(b) Construct the contemporary jewelry design model and conduct a case analysis.
(c) Examine whether the traditional literary criticism theory supports the analysis result to verify the feasibility of the theory.

## 1.3   Scope and Limitation

In this study, the subjects are students and experts in the art, design, and metalworking areas. From these subjects, this study will explore the importance of the structure of design process in the learning and cognition of metalworking knowledge. Besides, through a review of related theories and data, this study will investigate the applications of metaphors in design and further discuss the approach and thinking process of using metaphors in literature and poetry as described in the "Bi Xing" chapter of *Wen-Xing-Diao-Long*.

## 2   Literature Review

### 2.1   Metaphor as a Means of Interpreting Designs

In Chinese literature, Liu Xie's *Wen-Xing-Diao-Long* is a critical and theoretical work that offers a method of devising metaphors. Compared to contemporary design methodologies, this work provides a fairly specific operational model, and this model is also commonly used in design. In the "Bi Xing" chapter, Liu Xie states "metaphors can be applied to various kinds of subjects, including a sound, an appearance, feelings or an event" [7] . "Bi" is the method of describing one thing by comparing it to another thing with similar features. There is no particular rule of using it. It can be used to describe anything from a sound to an appearance, feelings or an event. "Xing" is to devise metaphors. Metaphors promote extended thinking, leading people to consider the deeper meaning or the value of the subject being described. To devise a metaphor, one has to be discerning and describe the subject in an intuitive and implicit manner. In terms of format, the subject and the object of the metaphor are both equal and opposite in certain aspects. Herbert Read explains Aristotle's definition of metaphor as follows: "metaphor is the swift illumination of an equivalence. Two images, or an idea and an image, stand equal and opposite; clash together and respond significantly, surprising the reader with a sudden light" [11]. Chou [1] states in the Chinese translation of *Metaphors We Live By* (by Lakoff and Johnson) that metaphor is a thinking model, and from the perspective of cognition, it is not just a rhetoric device. It is a thinking model where we comprehend a concept based on cognitive experience of another. In the cognition of a metaphor, we identify similarities between two concepts and then transfer one's image to another. This process also establishes the significance of cognitive linguistics research. In literature, metaphors are linguistic decorations. Reducing use of metaphors in our daily lives will probably make no significant difference. However, it cannot be denied that metaphors force people to think and infer a deeper and extended meaning of the subject described.

In the creation of art, artists create a work intuitively based on an impression of the senses or through imagination, to subjectively express a perspective. This process applies not only to art but also to literature. Literature, especially the form of poetry, is created to convey human feelings too. According to Francis Bacon, poetry is mainly based on imagination, and imagination is free and not bound by any principle. Through imagination, what is naturally divided can be combined, and what is naturally integrated can be divided [12]. Richard mentions in *The Philosophy of Rhetoric* that it is recognized in the contemporary research of metaphors that there is a reciprocal relationship between the tenor (subject) and the vehicle (object) of a metaphor. Essentially, through language, text induces philosophical discussion, where the perception of one thing is transferred to another in the comprehension of a metaphor. Lin and Yeh [8] mention that when designing conversion of signs, one has to consider the original meaning of the subject and, more importantly, get hold of the extended meaning of the vehicle. As to the application of rhetoric in creative design of cultural products, they also propose a metaphorical design model as show in Fig. 1.

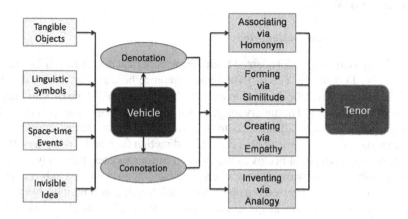

**Fig. 1.** The metaphorical design model for cultural products ([8], p. 447)

## 2.2  When Jewelry Becomes a New Concept

In a broad sense, jewelry refers to any decorative item worn on human body. Since the ancient times, people have used various ways to wear or attach decorative items, including animal bones, iron, gold, stone, flowers, tree leaves, and other natural materials on the body or clothes. These decorative items are pleasing to the eye. Moreover, because of rarity or uniqueness, these items have gradually become a signifier of value and social status. For example, the use of precious metals, such as gold and gemstones, in Egypt can be dated back to 3000 BC. Precious metals were used to make exclusive decorative items for pharaoh and funeral goods for aristocrats. Application of gold and gemstones in jewelry making was also prevalent in ancient China too. At that time, jewelry was also considered a symbol of status and power.

In the 1970s, there was a trend of reflecting on art creations among artists in Europe. Jewelry designers were no exception. They began to contemplate beyond common conceptions of jewelry, doubt the decorative meaning of jewelry, and discuss jewelry wearing issues from broader perspectives. Viewing jewelry as a means of social communication, they applied different forms, compositions, material vocabularies or wearing styles to convert an intangible disposition into a three-dimensional jewelry work. Neither aesthetics nor jewelry value was their primary consideration in the creation of a jewelry work. During the 1970s and 1980s, many bold and innovative jewelry works were created because most designers were very skillful. Although these designers sought to create a design beyond the face value and focused on discussion and visualization of the mind, most jewelry works were created in an illustrative or abstract form or in an experimental manner in pursuit of a breakthrough in jewelry design.

In contemporary jewelry design, jewelry artists play a special role. They integrate individual experience, status consideration, background of the times, and perceptions about life into their designs. As a result, most contemporary jewelry works carry multiple meanings for wearers to define themselves.

## 3  Research Method

### 3.1  The Metaphorical Design Model

This study is based on a model adapted from the metaphorical design model for cultural products (Fig. 1) (Lin and Yeh [8]).The main difference between the modified model and original model lies in the integration with the theory presented in the Bi Xing chapter of *Wen-Xing-Diao-Long*. This theory suggests that we rely on images to explain a feeling or make analogies. This study attempts to find a new thinking model as show in Fig. 2 hope can make the design process that can offer a direction for jewelry designers. Based on the vertical thinking that occurs in the creation of four themes, this study classifies the design subjects into two groups, namely tangible and abstract. For subjects in the tangible group, the focus is placed on observation and description "tangible objects" and "time events". For subjects in the abstract group, the goal is to give meanings to "communicative signs" or "invisible concepts". For jewelry designers, there are a variety of subjects to choose from in each group. They can apply a different form or technique to express a perception or opinion. Metaphors are prevalent and exist in various forms. Designers need to determine the material and form for their work first and then create the implicit meaning of the design that can induce spiritual interactions with viewers. The use of metaphors in depicting an appearance, an event, a sound or feelings will trigger association in viewers' mind and add beauty to the design.

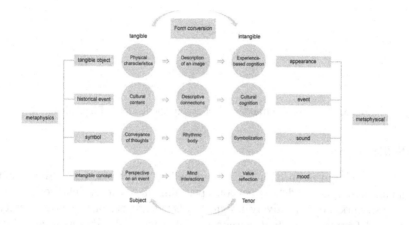

**Fig. 2.**  The metaphorical model for jewelry design (Revised from [8])

## 3.2  Case Analysis and Questionnaire Survey

In order to develop a metaphorical model for jewelry design, this study adopts a qualitative approach. Based on literature, this study develops a two-axis model as shown in Fig. 3. One axis denotes the "development of a metaphorical model", and the other shows the "development of a jewelry design model". The former is also the main framework of this research. The latter is intended to support the development of this framework. In this study, case analysis will also be conducted to analyze the background, thinking, and the metaphorical method of each selected work. To determine the form, genre, and meaning of each work, this study further conducts a questionnaire survey. The survey provides data for analysis of the differences between viewers' perceptions and the classification of the proposed model. Finally, this study also conducts a multidimensional scaling (MDS) factor analysis and style analysis to evaluate the feasibility of the proposed model.

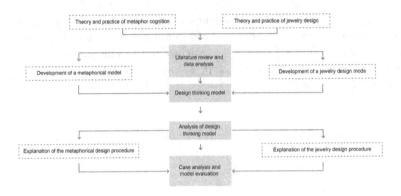

**Fig. 3.** The research framework of design applications of metaphors

## 3.3  Subjects

Based on the above-mentioned four themes, including "tangible objects", "time events", "communicative signs", and "abstract concepts", this study selects eight works for case study. These works are respectively designed by Dutch artists Felieke van der Leest and Lucy Sarneel, German artists Franze Bette and Otto Kunzli, Slovakia artist Jana Machatova, French artist Nathalie Perret, Spanish artist Ramon Puig Cuyàs, and the researcher I-Ting Wang. Survey participants were mainly recruited from sophomore and junior-year college students studying arts, design or metalworking. Before the survey, these students were introduced to the artists' works and experiences during classroom instructions. In addition to these students, participants of the survey also include experts in art.

## 4    Case Analysis of Applications of Metaphors in Jewelry Design

Jewelry is pleasing to the eye. When worn as a decorative item, it signifies status and reflects the identity of the wearer; it also induces deeper thoughts on the materials used, value, as well as the relationship between the culture and the body. The focus of discussions about jewelry has transcended its face value or functions to cover art, technology, aesthetics, design, sociology, politics, economics, environment, and humanity. In the researcher's observation of creative thinking among contemporary jewelry designers, there are three creative styles of jewelry designs, including "expression of personal feelings", "representation of craftsmanship", and "depiction of a social phenomenon". Starting from the top of the central axis, one can express an inspiration from nature or a personal feeling and then take the left path to revisit or seek a breakthrough in craftsmanship or take the right one to reflect on the humanistic value in a social phenomenon. As shown in Fig. 4, this is roughly the model of contemporary jewelry design. In this study, eight jewelry designs that conform to this model are selected. In addition to creative thinking which is presented along the vertical axis, this study will also discuss the structure, representation, and meaning of metaphors used in jewelry design. The category of messages carried by the metaphor, the similarities, and differences between these designs will all be analyzed from the perspective of a viewer and a designer.

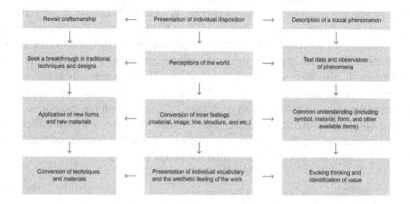

**Fig. 4.** The rough model of contemporary jewelry design

## 4.1 Case Analysis

### Case 1: Anti-war Warrior

Dutch artist Felieke van de Leest is good at using knitting, crotch, and beading techniques in jewelry design. In the choice of materials, he uses the image of a terrier dog to represent a warrior. At the center of visual attention to this work, the dog holds in its hand a broken arrow as an anti-war symbol. The target at which the arrow is aimed consists of numerous colors, which conform to the colors used in the rainbow flag of gay rights. Due to limited space, the missing purple color in the target is used on the hair of the dog. This anti-war warrior is also intended to highlight the controversy over an anti-homosexual regulation passed by Russia in Jun 2013 ahead of the 2013 Sochi Olympic Games. This artist cleverly uses an animal model to initiate more public discussions about the issue. This unique, interesting and humorous work shows the designer's concern about environmental, sociological and social issues. It evokes people's reflection on problems in the realistic world as well as the lifestyle of modern people (Fig. 5).

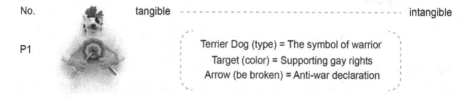

**Fig. 5.** The metaphorical structure of Anti-war Warrior [4]

## Case 2: Flower Power

Dutch artist Lucy Sarneel creates works to highlight the disappearing traditions and culture in the Netherlands. This work is a medal-style pendant. Its surface material is texture containing traditional Dutch symbols. From the perspective of historical signif-icance, it represents an article that mothers pass on to their daughters, from generation to generation. For the designer, jewelry signifies individual territory and characteristics and also defines the perceptions of its wearer. This designer is devoted to searching for subject matters that need attention in Dutch culture and history. This work is named Flower Power. It also has an anti-war implication. The designer advocates peaceful resistance to war. Hippies are believers of symbolism. They wear embroidered and colorful clothes and attach flowers to their head. This tradition has become a way of expressing opinions in the hippie movement. Created with the designer's attention to traditions and spirituality, this design shows that jewelry has the function of highlighting cultural phenomena and conveying spiritual meanings (Fig. 6).

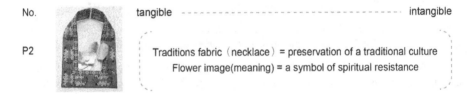

**Fig. 6.** The metaphorical structure of Flower Power [6]

## Case 3: Connection Series

Spanish artist Ramon Puig Cuyàs uses symbolic elements as the basic components of this design. Through intuitive dialogues with materials, he tries to use abstract signs to express human perceptions and opposite/parallel alignments of signs to interpret the operation of the universe. Like the beats in a rhythm, the points, lines, planes, and body in his works are delicately aligned to create a harmonious or contracting relation. The tempo and music come from a natural and simple metaphor (Fig. 7).

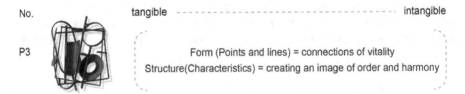

**Fig. 7.** The metaphorical structure of Connection Series [10]

## Case 4: Necklace Form

The work of French artist Nathalie Perret is heavily influenced by the Latino American culture of mourning, rituals, and ancient codes. Her research focuses on the link between birth and death. In creating this necklace work, she uses plaster to represent death. The plaster necklace will leave a mark on anyone who wears it. It reminds that we are all made of time and will leave a memorable mark but also a fleeting memory of our own death. Designers' material choice is usually associated with the symbolic meaning of the material. This work is intended to stimulate reflections on ways of dying. Using plaster as a symbol of death and performance art as a presentation style, she tries to express the fleeting symbolic meaning and the load of death (Fig. 8).

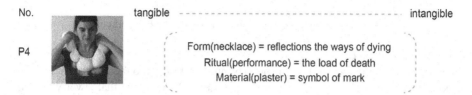

No.          tangible ---------------------------------------- intangible

P4          Form(necklace) = reflections the ways of dying
            Ritual(performance) = the load of death
            Material(plaster) = symbol of mark

**Fig. 8.** The metaphorical structure of Necklace Form [9]

### Case 5: Bloom Series

Taiwanese artist I-Ting Wang often uses "colors" as a medium to express emotions and also as a means of communication. In this work, she uses aluminum as the material. As an industrial material, aluminum is seldom used to show craftsmanship. This choice of material therefore denotes a revisit to metalworking techniques. In this work, the subject is a butterfly hidden in the flowers. This design creates a double contrast for discussion about the fading of life. When the butterfly dies, the beauty of its appearance remains; when the flowers wither, they dry up and lose color. The appearance of the butterfly implies that the spiritual existence of the butterfly is hidden in the flower body, whereas the status of the flowers implies that the symbolic existence of the flowers remains in the flower body. This suggests that the will to live in every living thing will eventually diminish and there will always be new lives. The aluminum material is colored through anodic treatment to represent the flower color that never fades and its blooming state (Fig. 9).

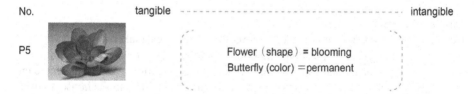

No.          tangible ---------------------------------------- intangible

P5          Flower（shape）= blooming
            Butterfly (color) =permanent

**Fig. 9.** The metaphorical structure of Bloom Series (I ting Wang 2004)

### Case 6: Love for the Brotherhood

Jana Machatova from Slovakia creates her works based on memories. She describes the political system and social phenomena she went through when she was young. She expresses her political perspective in her works. Based on the well-known historical event about the strategic cooperation between former Soviet Union and East Germany, she has also developed a series of works that touch upon political issues (Fig. 10).

**Fig. 10.** The metaphorical structure of Love for the Brotherhood [5]

### Case 7: Poetic Space

German artist Franz Bette has been inspired by an early fascination for materials. Jewelry making has been a part of his life for half a century. The meaning that jewelry makers give to materials is above and beyond their market value. His application of non-precious metals, including stainless steel and iron, requires more sophisticated craftsmanship. The design is simple. It consists of numerous units that are rhythmically aligned in the space. In his design, lines and circles are design words. Using combinations of basic elements, he tries to express inner feelings and personal observations of life. The feeling of action added to the structure manifests the difference of jewelry from other art forms. Through the wearing behavior, wearers have a dynamic relation with the hand and the body, which can also be considered a dialogue between the material and the mind (Fig. 11).

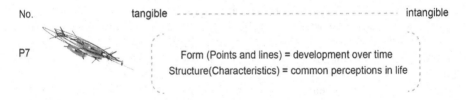

**Fig. 11.** The metaphorical structure of Poetic Space [3]

### Case 8: Wallpaper Series

German artist Otto Kunzli is considered one of the most critical makers in jewelry design. In his works, he expresses personal reflections and doubts about values using minimalistic symbols. He is good at using metaphors and images to convey ideas and challenge viewers. This selected work uses wallpaper, a decorative element in the house, to ironically highlight the gap between the rich and the poor. The work is intended to depict a society where only households with a higher social rank are able to decorate their house with wallpaper. Wallpaper is converted into a piece of jewelry to symbolize wealth. The wearing style of the jewelry is designed based on the clothing characteristics of anti-establishment punk. Punk originally refers to a musical style characterized by dissatisfaction with social classes and the social system. Punk is in the class opposite to the wealthy class. The decorative elements they use are undoubtedly the focus of artists' attention. Using materials to create a sarcastic metaphor is one of the best ways of making analogies (Fig. 12).

No.      tangible - - - - - - - - - - - - - - - - - - - - - - - - - - - - - - - - - - - - - intangible

P8

Form(necklace) = symbol of the punk spirit
Material(wallpaper) = interpretation of the meanings of decoration
Irony (concept) = ironically criticizing the gap between social classes

**Fig. 12.**  The metaphorical structure of Wallpaper Series [2]

## 4.2   Verification of Attributes

### 4.2.1   Descriptive Statistics of the Participants

According to the research objective, this study recruited survey participants from four areas, including metalworking, design, art, and others. The questionnaire was administered online. A total of 83 valid responses were collected. The sample comprised 19 males and 64 females. In this sample, 60 participants are aged below 25, 16 between 26–35, 4 between 35–45, and 3 above 45; 48 participants have an academic background in metalworking, 18 have an academic background in design, 16 have an academic background in arts, and 1 has an academic background in other areas. Participants aged below 25 were given a brief introduction of each artist's background and works before the formal survey. This procedure was intended to understand whether students were able to comprehend or appreciate the meanings underlying each work and to validate the proposed theoretical framework.

### 4.2.2   Analysis of the Theme Attribute

To explore the thinking and meanings behind what is perceived in each work, the participants were asked to evaluate each work's theme based on the four categories of analogies stated in the Bi Xing chapter of *Wen-Xing-Diao-Long*. As shown Fig. 13, P1 is most conforming to the category of depicting symbolic meanings, followed by P6 and P5. As shown in Fig. 14, P6 ranks top in the category of expressing an event-based theme, and P2 ranks second. As shown in Fig. 15, P3 is rated as most qualified for a work using semiotic expressions and is followed by P7. As shown in Fig. 16, in terms of clear expression of a concept, P1 wins the most votes, and P8 and P6 take second and third respectively.

| Work No. | P1 | P6 | P5 | P2 | P4 | P8 | P3 | P7 |
|---|---|---|---|---|---|---|---|---|
| Research Object | | | | | | | | |
| Votes | 57 | 45 | 44 | 31 | 19 | 17 | 12 | 7 |

**Fig. 13.**  The order of jewelry designs by describing a subject matter

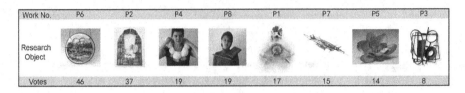

**Fig. 14.** The order of jewelry designs by having an emotional connection with a past event

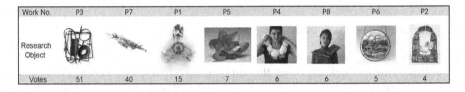

**Fig. 15.** The order of jewelry designs by carrying a sound message

**Fig. 16.** The order of jewelry design by evoking reflection or a sympathetic response to an issue

### 4.2.3    Analysis of the Style Attribute

Based on the proposed model, this study identifies four design styles, including "tangible and physical articles", "time events", "communicative signs", and "abstract concepts" and then determines the category of each work. The multidimensional scaling analysis (MDS) shows that stress is .135, which is smaller than 2, and R squared correlation (RSQ) is .929, which is close to 1, suggesting a high level of consistency between the data and the model. The relationship among the eight works and three major themes is plotted on a two-dimensional figure as shown in Fig. 17. Through factor analysis, these eight works can be further classified into three groups, as shown in Table 1. The MDS figure shows that P4, P8, P3, and P7 have a simple form and use the most concrete approach of expression conversion; P2 and P5 are created following strict rules of form and with a characteristic symbol; P6 and P1 have an easy-to-identify form and are intended to describe an event. These works are basically intended to stimulate our visual and hearing perceptions. From their classification results and statistics, two findings can be obtained. The former is to convey an idea or perspective through the image of an event or object as the works plotted on the right side of the graph; the latter is to recreate a mental image for an event or object as the works plotted on the left side of the graph. Both are the ways that creative content resides in a jewelry work.

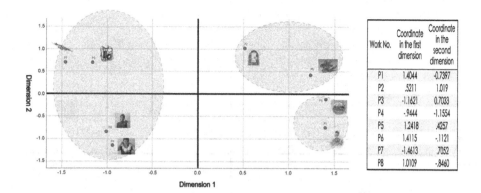

| Work No. | Coordinate in the first dimension | Coordinate in the second dimension |
|---|---|---|
| P1 | 1.4044 | -0.7397 |
| P2 | .5211 | 1.019 |
| P3 | -1.1621 | 0.7033 |
| P4 | -.9444 | -1.1554 |
| P5 | 1.2418 | .4257 |
| P6 | 1.4115 | -.1121 |
| P7 | -1.4613 | .7052 |
| P8 | 1.0109 | -.8460 |

**Fig. 17.** Distribution of the style attributes of jewelry works

**Table 1.** The distance of the point on which the attribute vector is plotted from the base point

| Style attribute | Adjective of the style | P1 | P2 | P3 | P4 | P5 | P6 | P7 | P8 |
|---|---|---|---|---|---|---|---|---|---|
| F1 FORM | Interesting-Strict | 0.31 | 1.12 | −0.18 | −1.49 | 1.11 | 0.80 | −0.37 | −1.29 |
| F2 Meaning | Abstract-Tangible | 1.50 | 0.35 | −1.26 | −0.75 | 1.16 | 1.41 | −1.55 | −0.86 |
| F3 Naming | Clear-Obscure | 1.57 | 0.14 | −1.33 | −0.49 | 1.02 | 1.36 | −1.62 | −0.65 |
| F4 Material | Novel-Traditional | −0.33 | 1.12 | 0.36 | −1.37 | 0.75 | 0.28 | 0.28 | −1.09 |
| F5 Appearance | Complicated-Simple | 0.51 | 1.08 | −0.36 | −1.48 | 1.19 | 0.95 | −1.58 | −1.32 |
| F6 Expression | Straightforward-Converted | 1.55 | 0.24 | −1.31 | −0.61 | 1.09 | 1.39 | −1.59 | −0.76 |
| F7 Senses | Visual-Hearing | 1.58 | −0.08 | −1.36 | −0.21 | 0.84 | 1.27 | −1.62 | −0.43 |
| F8 Approach | Static-Dynamic | 0.73 | 1.01 | −0.55 | −1.43 | 1.26 | 1.10 | −0.80 | −1.31 |

### 4.2.4 Analysis of the Form Attributes

The form attributes of these works are further analyzed. In the MDS analysis, opposite adjectives are employed, and each score on a five-point scale is converted into an angle relative to the axis. Therefore, a three-dimensional spatial graph can be obtained as shown in Fig. 18. The attributes analysis is shown in Table 2. Among works whose attributes conform to the expected classification of this study, "P7 Poetic Space" and "P4 Necklace Form" are two leading works. P7 is intended to stimulate hearing perceptions. Its designer creates a unique semiotic system to make the design a record of an event and also a carrier of a metaphor. P4 has a strong visual appeal and conveys a message through performance art.

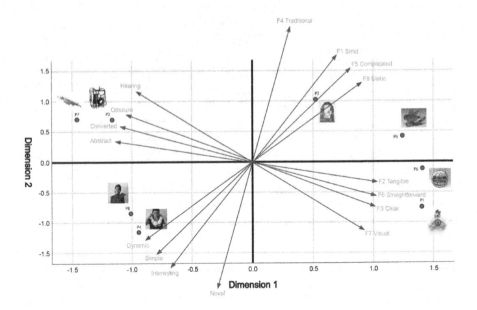

**Fig. 18.** Multidimensional distribution of the form attributes

**Table 2.** Factor analysis and attributes of work forms

| Style attribute | Component | | | Representative work | Explanation of the meaning of the form |
|---|---|---|---|---|---|
| | Component1 | Component2 | Component3 | | |
| F6 Expression | .978 | −.149 | .087 | P7 Poetic Space | F7 > F3 > F6 > F2 Senses > Naming > Expression > Meaning |
| F3 Naming | .954 | −.123 | −.026 | | |
| F2 Meaning | .796 | .349 | .479 | | |
| F7 Senses | −.941 | .175 | −.275 | | |
| F4 Material | .121 | .905 | −.255 | P4 Necklace Form | F1 > F5 > F8 > F4 Form > Appearance > Approach > Material |
| F5 Appearance | .370 | −.882 | .045 | | |
| F8 Approach | .164 | −.136 | .950 | P4 Necklace Form | |
| F1 FORM | −.146 | .596 | −.740 | | |

In the prediction of the theme attribute, only the ranking of the items in the category of evoking reflection or a sympathetic response to an issue is not the same as expected by the researcher as shown in Fig. 16. The ranking is P1 > P8 > P6 > P2. These works convey a strong message about an event or issue in a humorous manner. Despite cultural differences, these works can visually and perceptually arouse an awareness and create a higher level of resonance among viewers. To a certain extent, they also facilitate cultural exchange. The analysis of the Table 2 attribute shows that P4 has an interesting form and presentation style, which can often attract viewer attention more easily. This explains why there has been a continuous effort in contemporary jewelry design to look for a creative perception-stimulating form that can be used as a communication medium. In terms of form and content, P7 is the most typical among these works. An abstract presentation method is used to evoke perceptions at the spiritual level. Despite the absence of concrete associations, this work shows the representation of a meaningful text. The organized structure leads viewers to explore the essence of the embedded metaphor and the relationship between elements. The connections between points are not created following any specific formula. This creates questions in viewers' mind, allowing the designer to more specific.

# 5   Suggestions and Conclusions

Human perception and thinking is multidimensional. This study discusses metaphor as a carrier of thoughts and analyzes use of metaphors in jewelry works created based on personal opinions, an event, nature or certain issues. As in poetry, empathy can also be employed in jewelry making. In jewelry making, imagination is essentially empathy and also one of the fundamentals. However, imagination is a useful instrument that has been increasingly ignored by modern students. Poets use metaphor-loaded descriptions and borrow meanings from another object to visualize a space, a movement or a tranquil state of the subject. Many forms and principles used in poetry can also be applied in jewelry design.

This study attempts to explore the links and correlations between literature and jewelry design. In qualitative and quantitative analyses, this study propose a model, explore the forms, and induce the attributes. Between literature and jewelry design, there are common principles. Through use of metaphors, designers convey their perspective and force viewers to think. In a deeper sense, metaphors allow viewers to be exposed to certain culture, learn history, and reflect on issues. Jewelry reflects the significance of the times and designers' perceptions of life. When worn on the body, it becomes a means of social communication and cross-domain cultural exchange.

It is hoped that the proposed metaphorical design model can be applied in future metalworking instructions. However, there is no absolute definition of the art of jewelry or absolute outcome of any particular design. Depending on designer's personal experience, cognition, and culture, the design result will vary. The debate over aesthetics is the process where the value of aesthetics is created.

# References

1. Chou, S.Z.: Metaphors We Live By (by Lakoff and Johnson). Linking Publishing, Taipei (2006)
2. Das, B.: Otto Kunzli, p. 216. Arnoldsche, Stuttgart (2013)
3. Franz Bette (2014). (Online image). http://www.franz-bette.de/eng/schmuck/Raum1/gallery.html. Accessed 25 Nov 2017
4. Felieke van der Leest (2012). (Online image). http://www.arterritory.com/print.php?lang=en&id=3586. Accessed 28 Nov 2017
5. Jana Machatova (2014). (Online image). http://www.machmach.sk/index.php?/jana/where-are-you-from/. Accessed 28 Nov 2017
6. Lucy Sarneel (2003). (Online image). http://artjewelry-forum.org/lucy-sarneel-in-conversation. Accessed 28 Nov 2017

7. Lu, K.R., Mo, S.J.: Liu Xie and Wen-Xing-Diao-Long. Shanghai Guji Publisher, Shanghai (1978)

8. Lin, P.H., Yeh, M.L.: Representing traditional culture—applying Ho Lo culture elements on creative product design. In: Ho Lo Culture and Taiwanese Culture, 10th Conference of Ho Lo Culture, pp. 579–588 (2011)

9. Nathalie Perret (2007). (Online image). http://www.van-deragallery.be/artists/nathalie-perret/indexen.php. Accessed 10 Dec 2017

10. Ramon Puig Cuyàs (2011). (Online image). http://puigc-uyas2.blogspot.tw. Accessed 20 Dec 2017

11. Shen, C.: Weng-Xing-Diao-Long and Modern Rhetoric, p. 54. The Liberal Arts Press, Taipei (1992)

12. Zuo, H.L.: On Poetry, p. 56. The Commercial Press, Taipei (2003)

# A 3D Head Model Fitting Method Using Chinese Head Anthropometric Data

Haining Wang[1(✉)], Wanrong Chen[1], Yi Li[1], Yang Yu[1],
Wenxiu Yang[1], and Roger Ball[2]

[1] School of Design, Hunan University, Changsha, China
{wanghn, chenwanrong, liyiyi, yuyangyang,
yangwenxiu}@hnu.edu.cn
[2] School of Industrial Design, Georgia Institute of Technology, Atlanta, USA
roger.ball@coa.gatech.edu

**Abstract.** The rapid growth of the Chinese consumer market has created a demand for new Chinese fit wearable products. The industry requires accurate digital data on Chinese head and facial shapes to develop new consumer products. 3D head models that express the dimension of Chinese head anthropometry are of great importance in various product design processes. Previous 3D statistical models were fitted mostly using dimensional frames made by head and facial landmarks that cannot adequately demonstrate the complex facial geometry. This paper proposed a 3D head fitting method for the 5th, 25th, 50th, 75th and 95th percentiles using a progressive scanning algorithm based on differential approximation. The high-precision point cloud data obtained were transformed into mesh models, and the facial details were integrated and improved by 3D facial feature frameworks and artistic digital sculpting. The 3D digital models and 3D printing models with different percentiles constructed in this research can be utilized as design-aided tools for physiological comfort optimization in wearable products design and other ergonomic evaluation procedures.

**Keywords:** Chinese head and face · Anthropometry · Ergonomics design
3D head fitting · Progressive scanning algorithm

## 1 Introduction

Traditional 1D anthropometric data have been the primary source of the information adopted by ergonomists for the dimensioning of head and facial tools [1, 2]. Features such as head-breadth, head-length and head-circumference are commonly utilized during the product lifecycle from product design to ergonomic evaluation procedures [3–5]. Although these data are easy to understand and use, they only provide univariate analysis of key dimensions that cannot accurately capture the complex parts of human face shapes. Therefore, traditional data collection methods cannot fulfill the demand of current wearable product design that highly emphasizes the importance of the head and facial structures. For example, the design of virtual reality (VR) headsets requires not only features such as head-circumference, but also information about the head-shapes

© Springer International Publishing AG, part of Springer Nature 2018
P.-L. P. Rau (Ed.): CCD 2018, LNCS 10911, pp. 203–215, 2018.
https://doi.org/10.1007/978-3-319-92141-9_16

and complex structures including eyes, noses and ears to perfectly fit the human head and face to provide better user experiences.

The application of 3D scanning technology in product design has contributed to creating more user-friendly products, which provide a better fit, satisfaction, and safety for users. To design a headgear for Australian cyclists, a hair thickness offset method was introduced to describe the true head shape more accurately [6]. Some researchers used a machine learning-based method to design customizable 3D respiratory masks [2]. The sizing system and representative models were generated based on the Civilian American and European Surface Anthropometry Resource (CAESAR) database to design various head-products [7–9]. A framework model was applied to the database of facial motion data for anthropometric measurements related to the design of face masks [10]. Marketing products depend mostly on the standard of existing Western human-body datasets (such as CAESAR data), which are the same products used by Chinese users. However, researchers demonstrated that the Chinese head shapes are significantly different from those of other races [11–13]. It is widely assumed that some famous VR products such as the Oculus rift and Google Daydream are not designed for the Chinese population. The ergonomic designs are not suitable for Chinese heads and noses, which lead to terrible immersive experiences. Therefore, up to date, accurate and usable Chinese head and facial data are the key for wearable products designed for the Chinese market.

The current market demand in China is absolutely huge. The design progress needs to consider Chinese anthropometric data to make the products more suitable for Chinese consumers. The Chinese national standard of head-and-face dimensions for adults was first published in 1986, and it was slightly modified in 2009. However, no head forms were fitted based on these data for product design and testing [14]. Ball et al. [15, 16] created 10 head forms from 2000 subjects in the SizeChina project using 3D scanned data and principal component analysis to design helmets for Chinese people. However, these head forms are primarily intended to only describe the head shape. The low accuracy and resolution of face-shape fitting cannot express the complicated facial details in designing head-related products, such as masks, goggles, and head-mounted displays. Zhuang et al. [17, 18] collected 2D dimensions and 3D models on 3000 Chinese civilian workers in 2006. After editing, landmarking, and measurement, 5 head models were fitted based on the clustering analysis of 350 3D scans, and the differences between Chinese head shapes in the last 30 years were compared. However, most of these methods were not aimed to fit a certain template or generic model for anthropometric purposes. The models are comparatively simple, and their accuracy and resolution were not specified in those studies. In addition, most of these studies were based on few human scans and did not provide convincing statistical results which considered Chinese population variations.

The 3D anthropometric data describe the complete shape characteristics of the head surface but are complicated to interpret due to the abundance of information they contain. Compared to traditional measurements, fitting heads obtained by scan models can provide more comprehensive morphological diversity in a target population for designers. Such fitting heads would facilitate the optimal design of products and improve the development of related standards and protocols for better ergonomic evaluations.

Chinese national standard GB/T 12985-91 [19] stipulates the general rules of using percentiles of body dimensions for product design progress. The percentile of a specific dimension means all the dimensional values of that percentile for a certain population are below that level. In the industrial design process, various products require different percentiles of human body dimensions as the upper and lower limits. Therefore, to facilitate Chinese population-oriented wearable products, this research adopted the dataset of 1900 Chinese head models to extract 33 head and facial feature points for each model, then built 3D head frameworks from different percentiles of these features. Furthermore, high-precision 3D head fitting was accomplished for each percentile by a progressive scanning algorithm integrated with these head frameworks. Finally, artistic digital sculpting was appropriately performed to create more facial details on each 3D model for appearance improvement (refer to Fig. 1).

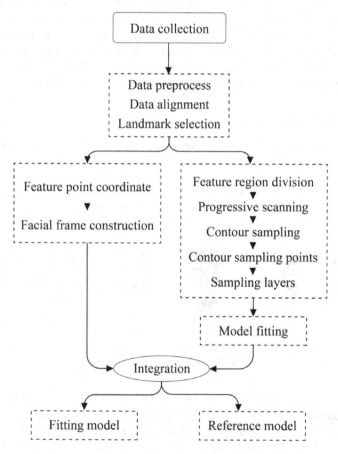

**Fig. 1.** The system flow of the 3D head fitting method

## 2    Methods

### 2.1    Data Collection

The 3D head dataset adopted in this research was from the anthropometric survey accomplished by Hunan University in 2017. The major goal of that project was to construct a scalable, interactive and minable repository of high-resolution Chinese facial data available to designers and researchers. As such, 1900 male and female adult subjects between the ages of 18 and 45 were surveyed from 7 representative cities in China, including Harbin, Beijing, Xi'an, Chengdu, Guangzhou, Hangzhou and Changsha.

During the survey process, participants filled out a questionnaire that recorded basic information including age, gender, family background, and the location where they grew up. Traditional anthropometric measurements were also recorded, which included height, weight and 3 head measurements. A wig cap was fitted to obtain a better scan quality of the hair during the 3D scanning. Fourteen selected manually marked landmarks were directly labeled on each participant's face to identify the critical bone structures [15]. Participants were scanned using the Artec EVA$^{TM}$ 3D scanner, and high-resolution data were automatically captured as point cloud data.

### 2.2    Data Processing

Then, 1900 raw scans were collected during the scanning. The scans required extensive post-processing before they were suitable for use in the development of design tools. Each scan data file was processed according to the steps shown in Fig. 2, which includes (a) data alignment, (b) irrelevant features removal, (c) global registration, (d) sharp fusion, (e) feature smoothing, and (f) texture mapping.

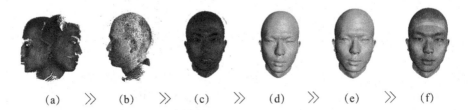

(a)    ≫    (b)    ≫    (c)    ≫    (d)    ≫    (e)    ≫    (f)

**Fig. 2.** Data processing steps

During the data processing procedure, 30 models were abandoned due to irreparable damage such as missing textures, unfixable holes, closed eye(s), or a disordered model. Finally, a total of 1870 head models were adopted for the 3D head fitting. Given all the 3D head models, $S$ stands for the set of head and facial surfaces, and $H_S$ denotes the set of all points on a specific surface. This gives us $H_S \subset S$. The elements in $H_S$ can be represented as $P_{Si} = \{(X_{Si}, Y_{Si}, Z_{Si}) | i = 1, 2, \cdots, N_P\}$.

**Data Alignment.** In the 3D scanning process, different scan angles, offsets or rotations of participants would cause the coordinates to deviate among various models. The statistical analysis in this research was based on the coordinates of all feature points extracted from each scan to finish the 3D head and facial fitting. This requires the feature extraction to be performed within the same space coordinate system where data alignment was conducted. First, the *Frankfurt plane* was defined according to the coordinates of the 3 reference points on each head model, which include the left tragion, the right tragion and the left infraorbitale (or right infraorbitale). This plane was denoted as the $XOY$ plane for the coordinate system. The positive direction of the $X$ axis is set to the direction of the apex nasi, while the positive direction of the $Y$ axis is set to the same direction of the right tragion. By letting $H_A$ represent the set of all points on the head and facial models, we can get $H_A \subset S$. After the data alignment, each element $Psi$ from $H_S$ was transformed to $P_{Ai} = \{(X_{Ai}, Y_{Ai}, Z_{Ai}) | i = 1, 2, \cdots, N_P\}$.

**Landmark Selection.** Landmarking is a common method for data representation among individual human features. It was necessary for anthropometry experts to mark anatomical features that required palpation to be located on the invisible skull. To create consistent head and face models, in this research, 14 anatomical landmarks were manually marked on each participant's face before 3D scanning. They are *Chin, Glabella, Frontotemporale (left and right), Infraorbital (left and right), Pronasale, Sellion, Tragion (left and right), Zygofrontale (left and right)* and *Lat. Zygomatic (left and right)*. The selection approach of the landmarks was mainly based on the anthropometric analysis in [20]. Due to complicated head and facial structures, those anatomical landmarks could not obtain more detailed data for analyzing the human face. Then, 19 more landmarks indicating identifiable facial features were located and extracted in Geomagic Wrap 2017. The name and location of the final 33 landmarks for all subjects are shown in Fig. 3 (No. 2, 3, 4, 6, 7, 8, 9, 10, 21, 22, 23, 24, 29 and 30 are manually marked landmarks, and the rest are physical landmarks). The feature set can be defined as $H_{AL}$, while $P_{AL} = \{(X_{ALi}, Y_{ALi}, Z_{ALi}) | i = 1, 2, \cdots, 33\}$ denotes all the elements.

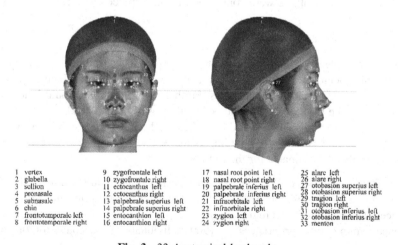

| | | | |
|---|---|---|---|
| 1 vertex | 9 zygofrontale left | 17 nasal root point left | 25 alarc left |
| 2 glabella | 10 zygofrontale right | 18 nasal root point right | 26 alare right |
| 3 sellion | 11 ectocanthus left | 19 palpebrale inferius left | 27 otobasion superius left |
| 4 pronasale | 12 ectocanthus right | 20 palpebrale inferius right | 28 otobasion superius right |
| 5 submasale | 13 palpebrale superius left | 21 infraorbitale left | 29 tragion left |
| 6 chin | 14 palpebrale superius right | 22 infraorbitale right | 30 tragion right |
| 7 frontotemporale left | 15 entocanthion left | 23 zygion left | 31 otobasion inferius left |
| 8 frontotemporale right | 16 entocanthion right | 24 zygion right | 32 otobasion inferius right |
| | | | 33 menton |

**Fig. 3.** 33 Anatomical landmarks

## 2.3    Anthropometric Face Frame Construction

**Percentile Computing of Feature Points Coordinate.** The definition of human head dimensions requires the locations and distances among all sampling points in space. Once the coordinate system is unified, the Euclidean distances between each sampling point to the center of the system can be obtained by $d = \sqrt{X^2 + Y^2 + Z^2}$. Therefore, the computing of the percentiles of head dimensions can be transformed into the percentiles of the absolute value of feature point coordinates along the $X$, $Y$ and $Z$ directions.

For example, given a certain feature point $P_{AL}$, the $p$ percentile along the $X$ axis can be computed as follows. First, the absolute values of $P_{AL}$'s x-coordinates for $n$ scan models were sorted in ascending order to get the sorted distances $B_i = [X_1, X_2, \cdots, X_n]$. Then, let $l$ and $m$ represent the integral and decimal parts of the calculation results of $n \times p$, respectively. Lastly, the $p$ percentile of the feature point $P_{AL}$ along the $X$ axis is obtained by $B_{AL} = (1 - m) \times B_{l-1} + m \times B_l$.

In the computing process, due to inevitable coordinate deviations caused by data alignment and feature extraction, the coordinate values along the $X$ and $Y$ axes could be positive or negative for feature points such as the *vertex, glabella, sellion, pronasale, subnasale, chin, menton, otobasion superius (left and right), tragion (left and right)* and *otobasion inferius (left and right)* that can be mapped to the $Z$ axis. The means of the coordinate values for these feature points were taken in this research to balance the error. Meanwhile, the feature point vertex was computed by percentiles only on the $Z$ axis because it was the peak of all 33 feature points, and its coordinate errors along the $X$ and $Y$ axes cannot be ignored.

**Face Frame Construction.** The 5th, 25th, 50th, 75th and 95th percentiles of the 33 feature points were separately computed, and all the points were marked based on their spatial locations and connected by lines according to the facial morphology in Rhinoceros™ 5.14 for each percentile. Anthropometric facial frames embodying the characteristics of all features were constructed for each percentile (refer to Fig. 4).

## 2.4    Head and Facial Model Fitting

Due to the complexity and irregular nature of human heads, the facial frame can represent only facial information approximately 33 feature points, which cannot adequately express the surface characteristics. Furthermore, the frame would ignore most of the details of the frontal, parietal and occipital areas of human heads. In this paper, a progressive scanning algorithm based on differential approximation was proposed to subdivide scan models, and the sampling points set was obtained by the percentiles computed by their coordinates for the 3D head fitting.

**Feature Region Division.** Wearable product design often requires dimensions from various regions of the human head (such as the *Glabella-Infraorbitale distance*) as references. The height of each region on the face significantly varies thanks to the great differences among the appearances of 1900 individuals. To account for the facial

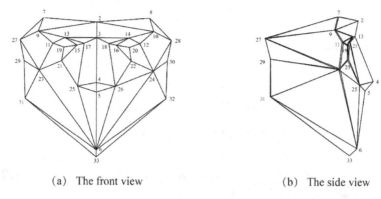

(a)  The front view                    (b)  The side view

**Fig. 4.** The anthropometric facial frame of the 95$^{th}$ percentile

features of every individual, this paper vertically divided the head and face into several regions and made the 3D fitting based on feature mapping for related regions from all head models.

**Progressive Scanning.** According to 4 facial organs (including the forehead, eyes, nose and mouth) and the common areas for wearable product design, the head and face were vertically divided into 4 regions by the $Z$ axis coordinates of the *vertex, glabella, Frankfurt plane, subnasale* and *menton*. Then, each region was scanned with the corresponding layers that were determined according to the demanded accuracy and the height proportions of different regions in the head. In this paper, each scan model was divided into 528, 192, 144 and 384 layers separately from top to bottom, which totals 1248 layers, and let $L_j, j \in [-528, 720)$ represent all layers on head and facial surface. Let $d_1, d_2, d_3$ and $d_4$ represent the furthest distance between each facial region to the *Frankfurt plane* on the $Z$ axis. Therefore, each layer's $Z$ axis coordinate can be denoted in Eq. (1) and the facial region division was shown in Fig. 5.

$$
Z_j = \left\{
\begin{array}{ll}
d_2 + \frac{d_1 - d_2}{528}(j - 192), & 192 \leq j < 720 \\
\frac{d_2}{192} j, & 0 \leq j < 192 \\
-\frac{d_3}{144} j, & -144 < j < 0 \\
-d_3 + \frac{d_4 - d_3}{384}(j + 144), & -528 \geq j \leq -144
\end{array}
\right\}
\tag{1}
$$

**Contour Sampling.** In the progressive scanning process, a closed and continuous contour was obtained for each layer. We took the intersection between the $Z$ axis with one specific layer as the center, started from the positive direction of the $X$ axis and rotated clockwise with an angular increment of $\frac{\Pi}{864}$ (refer to Fig. 6). For each rotation, the intersection point between the line and the contour was sampled, and $H_F$ denotes the set of all sampling points on head and facial surface, $H_F \subset H_S$. $H_{FL}$ represents the intersection point set on Layer $L$, and the number of the sampling points for each layer

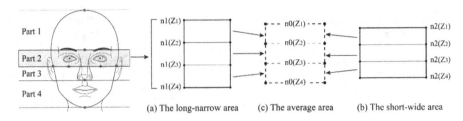

Part 1
Part 2
Part 3
Part 4

(a) The long-narrow area    (c) The average area    (b) The short-wide area

**Fig. 5.** Facial feature region division

was $N_{FL} = \frac{\Pi}{864} \cdot \frac{1}{2\Pi} = 1728$ and elements are $P_{FLi} = \{(r_{FLi}, \theta_{FLi}, Z_j) | i = 1, 2, \cdots,$ 1728\}, the distance $r_{FLi}$ can be denoted as below.

$$\begin{cases} r_{FLi} = \sqrt{X_{FLi}^2 + Y_{FLi}^2} \\ \theta_{FLi} = \frac{\Pi}{864} i \end{cases} \tag{2}$$

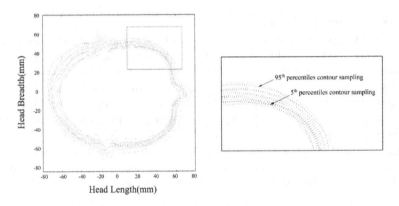

**Fig. 6.** Contour sampling process for each scanning layer (20 subjects)

**Percentile Computing of Contour Sampling Points.** During the contour sampling for all head scans, the $p$ percentile of the distance $r_{j\alpha k}$ was computed for layer $j$ with angle $\alpha$. The method is shown as follows. The $r_{j\alpha k}$ of $n$ scans were sorted in ascending order to obtain $C_n = [r_{j\alpha 1}, r_{j\alpha 2}, \cdots, r_{j\alpha n}]$. Then, let $l$ and $m$, respectively, represent the integral and decimal parts of the calculation results of $n \times p$. Therefore, the $p$ percentile of $r_{j\alpha k}$ can be denoted by $C_k = (1 - m) \times C_{l-1} + m \times C_l$. $H_T$ represents the point set obtained by 3D fitting and elements can be written as $P_T = \{(X_{j\alpha}, Y_{j\alpha}, Z_j) | j \in [-528, 720), \alpha \in [0, 2\Pi)\}$,

where

$$\begin{cases} X_{j\alpha} = C_K \cos \alpha \\ Y_{j\alpha} = C_K \sin \alpha \end{cases} \tag{3}$$

**Height Computing of Sampling Layers.** The 3D head fitting requires the $Z$ coordinate for each sampling layer that was determined by the division of various feature regions. Therefore, the $Z$ coordinate for each layer can be computed by dividing the percentiles of $d_a$, $a = 1, 2, 3, 4$ equally according to the number of the sampling layers. The $d_{ai}$ of $n$ scans were sorted in ascending order to obtain $D_n = [d_{a1}, d_{a2}, \cdots, d_{an}]$. Then, let $l$ and $m$, respectively, represent the integral and decimal parts of the calculation results of $n \times p$. Therefore, the $p$ percentile of $d_{ai}$ can be denoted by $D_a = (1 - m) \times D_{l-1} + m \times D_l$. Thus, the $p$ percentiles of the further distance along the $Z$ axis between each region to the *Frankfurt plane* can be obtained as $D_1, D_2, D_3$ and $D_4$. The elements of $H_T$ can be written as $P_T = \{(X_{j\alpha}, Y_{j\alpha}, Z_j) | j \in [-528, 720), \alpha \in [0, 2\Pi)\}$, where

$$Z_j = \begin{cases} D_2 + \frac{D_1 - D_2}{528}(j - 192), & 192 \le j < 720 \\ \frac{D_2}{192} j, & 0 \le j < 192 \\ -\frac{D_3}{144} j, & -144 < j < 0 \\ -D_3 + \frac{D_4 - D_3}{384}(j + 144), & -528 \ge j \le -144 \end{cases} \tag{4}$$

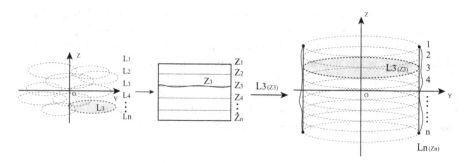

**Fig. 7.** Height computing process for sampling layers

The whole computing process is shown in Fig. 7.

**Head and Facial Model Fitting.** Let $H_T$ be the point set of the head and facial fitting results. Thus, the number of its elements is $N_P = 528 + 720 \times 1728 = 2156544$. The C ++ program based on the 3D head and facial fitting methods was implemented on Microsoft Visual Studio 2015. It was run in the National Super Computing Center in Changsha, considering the huge memory consumption of 1900 3D models. Users can input parameters (including the sample size and scan layers for each feature region, the sample numbers for each layer and the specific percentiles) to get the fitting result as a *.txt format file with coordinates of all sampling points. The coordinates of all points were imported into Geomagic Wrap 2017 to get the surface model for each percentile using the wrap function. The results include fitting models of all sampling points and the mesh model transformed from them, which are shown in Fig. 8.

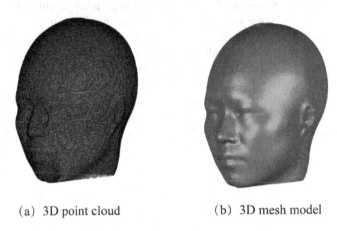

(a)  3D point cloud          (b)  3D mesh model

**Fig. 8.** The result of the 3D fitting models

## 2.5   Head and Facial Model Fitting

The sampling point coordinates of the surface model obtained by 3D fitting were in accordance with the percentile value across all subjects on corresponding positions. However, the fitting model emphasized the extraction of percentiles for the entire head and face, which would contain inevitable errors on facial details caused by individual differences during the feature mapping process. Therefore, adjustments were made to the fitting model according to the coordinates of 33 feature points from the face frame. Due to the noise caused by the huge volume of data in the point cloud of the fitting model, artistic digital sculpting was appropriately performed during the model fusion,

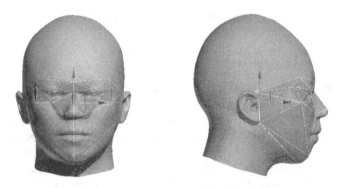

**Fig. 9.** Adjustments between the fitting model and the facial frame

and more facial details were created on each 3D model to improve the appearance. At last, the ear model was joined with the head fitting model according to the coordinates of *otobasion superius, tragion* and *otobasion inferius* on each side (refer to Fig. 9).

## 3    Result

This paper presents two types of Chinese head and facial models, the high-resolution fitting model and the 3D printing reference model. The former can be imported into 3D modeling software to accomplish dynamic ergonomics analysis and testing, while the reference model could be utilized for product design references and product fitting evaluations. 3D Models with different percentiles can be obtained according to specific design scenarios in the future. All fitting models and 3D printing reference models were verified with original statistical data to ensure the accuracy and reliability of the data (refer to Fig. 10).

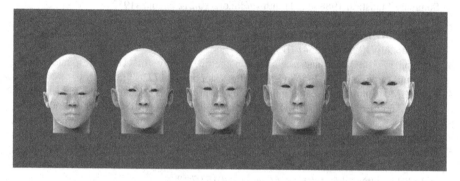

**Fig. 10.** The final fitting models after digital sculpting

## 4    Conclusion

Traditional 3D anthropometric head models were constructed by frames composed of feature points and straight lines between them, which cannot adequately express the complicated surface details of human heads and faces. This paper proposed a 3D fitting algorithm based on progressive scanning for different facial feature regions and contour sampling on each scanning layer. The fitting meshes were reconstructed on the sampling points through 3D software and integrated with 3D facial frames built by percentiles of 33 feature point coordinates to improve the accuracy. Lastly, artistic digital sculpting was appropriately performed to create more facial details on each 3D model to improve the appearance.

The 3D head and facial fitting algorithm proposed in this paper is of important significance in the research on contemporary Chinese head sizes and Chinese market-oriented wearable product designs (such as smart glasses, VR&AR headsets, face masks, etc.). Product designers only need to set the 3D model with the specific percentiles they require to define the design boundary in the corresponding scenarios. It does not require professional statistical knowledge or time to analyze mass anthropometric data. In addition, 3D printing models with different percentiles can also be utilized for the design-aided tools for product comfort analysis and other ergonomics evaluation. So far, the methods and models proposed in this research have been applied in several companies for the design of the next generation of wearable devices.

In the future, the algorithm can also be generalized to other anthropometric issues, and the fitting models can be extended to other body parts to guide the product design in that area. Furthermore, our algorithm can be modified to support the Chinese head size research for different age groups, genders and cities.

# References

1. Donelson, S.M., Gordon, C.C.: Anthropometric Survey of U.S. Army Personnel: Pilot Summary Statistics, 1988 (1991). https://doi.org/10.21236/ada241952
2. Chu, C.H., Huang, S.H., Yang, C.K., Tseng, C.Y.: Design customization of respiratory mask based on 3D face anthropometric data. Int. J. Precis. Eng. Manuf. **16**, 487–494 (2015). https://doi.org/10.1007/s12541-015-0066-5
3. Bradtmiller, B.: Head-and-face anthropometric survey of U.S. Respirator users. J. Occup. Environ. Hyg. **2**, 567 (2005). https://doi.org/10.17226/11815
4. Kolich, M.: Automobile seat comfort: occupant preferences vs. anthropometric accommodation. Appl. Ergon. **34**, 177–184 (2003). https://doi.org/10.1016/s0003-6870(02)00142-4
5. Robinette, K.M., Daanen, H.A.: Precision of the caesar scan-extracted measurements. Appl. Ergon. **37**, 259 (2006). https://doi.org/10.1016/j.apergo.2005.07.009
6. Perret-Ellena, T., Skals, S.L., Subic, A., Mustafa, H., Pang, T.Y.: 3D anthropometric investigation of head and face characteristics of Australian cyclists. Procedia Eng. **112**, 98–103 (2015). https://doi.org/10.1016/j.proeng.2015.07.182
7. Lee, W., Yang, X., Jung, H., You, H., Goto, L., Molenbroek, J.F.M., Goossens, R.H.M.: Application of massive 3D head and facial scan datasets in ergonomic head-product design. **1**, 344 (2016). https://doi.org/10.1504/ijdh.2016.10005368
8. Lee, W., Lee, B., Kim, S., Jung, H., Bok, I., Kim, C., Kwon, O., Choi, T., You, H.: Development of headforms and an anthropometric sizing analysis system for head-related product designs. **59** (2015). https://doi.org/10.1177/1541931215591308
9. Lee, W., Goto, L., Molenbroek, J.F.M., Goossens, R.H.M., Wang, C.C.C.: A shape-based sizing system for facial wearable product design. In: International Digital Human Modeling Symposium (2017)
10. Bolkart, T., Bose, P., Shu, C., Wuhrer, S.: A general framework to generate sizing systems from 3D motion data applied to face mask design. In: Second International Conference on 3D Vision, pp 425–431. IEEE, Tokyo (2014). https://doi.org/10.1109/3dv.2014.43
11. Ball, R., Shu, C., Xi, P., Rioux, M., Luximon, Y., Molenbroek, J.: A comparison between Chinese and Caucasian head shapes. Appl. Ergon. **41**, 832–839 (2010). https://doi.org/10.1016/j.apergo.2010.02.002
12. Yang, L., Shen, H., Wu, G.: Racial differences in respirator fit testing: a pilot study of whether American fit panels are representative of Chinese faces. Ann. Occup. Hyg. **51**, 415 (2007). https://doi.org/10.1093/annhyg/mem005

13. Niezgoda, G., Zhuang, Z.: Development of headforms for ISO eye and face protection standards. Procedia Manuf. **3**, 5761–5768 (2015). https://doi.org/10.1016/j.promfg.2015.07.822
14. Standards Administration of the People Republic of China, GB/T 5703-2010: Basic human body measurements for technological design. Standard Press of China, Beijing (2011). (in chinese)
15. Ball, R., Molenbroek, J.F.M.: Measuring Chinese heads and faces (2008)
16. Ball, R.: 3-D design tools from the SizeChina project. Ergon. Des. Mag. Hum. Factors Appl. **17**, 8–13 (2009). https://doi.org/10.1518/106480409X12487281219931
17. Yu, Y., Benson, S., Cheng, W., Hsiao, J., Liu, Y., Zhuang, Z., Chen, W.: Digital 3-D headforms representative of Chinese workers. Ann. Occup. Hyg. **56**, 113–122 (2012). https://doi.org/10.1093/annhyg/mer074
18. Du, L., Zhuang, Z., Guan, H., Xing, J., Tang, X., Wang, L., Wang, Z., Wang, H., Liu, Y., Su, W.: Head-and-face anthropometric survey of Chinese workers. Ann. Occup. Hyg. **52**, 773–782 (2008). https://doi.org/10.1093/annhyg/men056
19. Standards Administration of the People Republic of China, GB/T 12985-91: General rules of using percentiles of the body dimensions for products design. Standard Press of China, Beijing (1991)
20. Yan, L., Ball, R., Justice, L.: The Chinese face: a 3D anthropometric analysis. In: Proceeding of the TMCE, Italy (2010)

# Responsive Web Design for Chinese Head and Facial Database

Haining Wang[1(✉)], Yang Yu[1], Wanrong Chen[1], Wenxiu Yang[1], and Roger Ball[2]

[1] School of Design, Hunan University, Changsha, China
{wanghn,yuyangyang,chenwanrong,yangwenxiu}@hnu.edu.cn
[2] School of Industrial Design, Georgia Institute of Technology, Atlanta, USA
roger.ball@coa.gatech.edu

**Abstract.** The complex geometry of the human head's facial surface presents a challenge for designers and engineers seeking to create properly fitting wearable products. The rapid growth of the Chinese consumer market has created a demand for new Chinese fit wearable products. The head and facial information of the Chinese population differs significantly from that of their western counterparts. The industry requires accurate digital data on Chinese head and facial shapes to develop new consumer products, such as virtual reality (VR) goggles or protective safety glasses. The industry has not had adequate time or expertise to create their own digital databases of Chinese human head surfaces. Therefore, they must rely on head and facial scan databases from 3D scan surveys. Collecting 3D head and facial scan data is the first step in creating a database, and the second step is communicating the results through user-friendly interfaces. A major challenge with 3D scan databases is to make them available online with real-time interactive tools and an effective interface. Industry users require demographic details, searchable database statistics and high-resolution 3D scans that can be delivered to a variety of digital devices. This research has developed an interactive and responsive web-based database of Chinese 3D head and facial models and measurements using a 1900-person head scan survey completed in 2017. It can be used as a reference for the design and testing of head and facial equipment and can facilitate the use and spread of anthropometric databases among designers and researchers.

**Keywords:** Chinese head and face · Anthropometric database · Responsive web
Interface design · Ergonomics

## 1 Introduction

The rapid growth of the Chinese consumer market has created a significant demand for new Chinese fit wearable products. The industry requires accurate digital data on Chinese head and facial shapes to develop new consumer products such as virtual reality (VR) goggles and protective safety glasses. The head and facial information of the Chinese population varies significantly from that of their western counterparts. For example, Chinese heads are generally characterized as rounder than western heads and as having a flatter back and forehead [1]. Likewise, Chinese civilian adults have a shorter facial length and nose protrusion and larger facial width and lip length compared with

© Springer International Publishing AG, part of Springer Nature 2018
P.-L. P. Rau (Ed.): CCD 2018, LNCS 10911, pp. 216–231, 2018.
https://doi.org/10.1007/978-3-319-92141-9_17

the facial dimensions of US subjects [2]. Consequently, it is essential for the industry to have 3D head and facial anthropometric databases to rely on due to the lack of the time or expertise to conduct anthropometric studies.

For decades in China, a few 3D anthropometric surveys on heads and faces have been undertaken. A head-and-face anthropometric study of Chinese civilian workers was conducted by Zhuang et al. [3, 4]. Overall, 3000 subjects were measured using traditional techniques (tapes and calipers), but only 350 of them were selected to acquire their 3D head scans. The data from this survey were limited in terms of demographic coverage. SizeChina [5, 6] captured the 3D digital shapes of the Chinese heads in mainland China. It surveyed 1620 adult civilian subjects aged 18 to over 70 years and provided summary-level data files, digital 3D scans and a set of physical Chinese head forms that were developed from measurements. Nevertheless, the 3D scanning technologies used in SizeChina are not sufficiently developed to collect accurate scan data compared to the latest 3D scanning technologies. Furthermore, the head and facial features extracted a dozen years ago may have a significant difference with the latest data which could affect the product design. More importantly, the database could not be accessed officially since 2014. China National Institute of Standardization collect full-body data (including heads) from 3000 Chinese adults using 3D anthropometric devices in 2009 [7], aiming to revise the survey in 1988 [8]. It provided new data on Chinese adult human body dimensions for more effective and comfortable ergonomic products, machines and work environments. However, these data from the whole-body scan survey cannot be applied in Chinese head and face studies not only because the 3D full body scanner had low accuracy and resolution, but the numbers of facial measurements and statistics values derived from this survey were also relatively insufficient to serve such studies. In summary, these existing Chinese 3D anthropometric surveys are insufficiently qualified to be used as the recourse for the development and enhancement of new Chinese fit wearable products. Therefore, the industry has lacked an up-to-date and accurate Chinese head and facial database for many years. Most of the dimensions for existing wearable products design in China depend on industry experience or modification based on western anthropometric data, which leaves no accurate data to design wearable products such as VR headsets and AR glasses.

Even though 3D anthropometric surveys have been available for years, surprisingly little research and design have been reported concerning the use of 3D data to improve consumer products. Typically, the principal deliverables from previous studies have been 3D scan files, a document with summary-level statistics for the population, including means, standard deviations and percentiles [9], which is an inappropriate way for data use. First, even though these deliverables are well documented, very few of previous surveys provide a process for the industry to interact with them in a meaningful way. For example, they are not available online, and they cannot be effectively interacted with or downloaded. More importantly, these deliverables—the raw individual-level data—are normally not accessible by outside researchers and designers. They are collected to be used by only a small group of investigators [10]. The 3D Facial Norms Database [11] is a large, web-based, interactive craniofacial normative database that allows access to and interaction with the large-scale, individual-level head and facial anthropometric data, including raw 3D facial surfaces. iSize [12] is an international body dimension portal that offers access to body dimensions, size tables and market shares for Germany and France. No Chinese anthropometric survey creates any online database that can be interacted with or downloaded.

In conclusion, the development and enhancement of new Chinese fit wearable products require the creation of an interactive and responsive web-based database containing the latest Chinese 3D head and facial models and measurements, presenting it in a comprehensive way to the industry. The website should contain summary-level statistics, individual-level data and 3D scan models.

## 2   3D Scan Survey

A full-scale 3D anthropometric measurement was conducted at seven sites in mainland China to collect the anthropometric data of Chinese adults' heads and faces. We surveyed 1900 male and female adult subjects between the ages of 18 and 45.

During the survey process, participants filled out a questionnaire that recorded basic information including age, gender, family background, and the location where they grew up. Traditional anthropometric measurements were record afterwards, which included

**Table 1.** Traditional measurements and 3D facial measurements

| Head and facial measurements | Region | Landmarks involved | Category |
|---|---|---|---|
| *Traditional measurements* | | | |
| Head circumference | Head | Glabella, opisthocranion, euryon left, euryon right | Perimeter |
| Head length | Head | Glabella - opisthocranion | Length |
| Head breadth | Head | Euryon left - euryon right | Breadth |
| *3D facial measurements* | | | |
| Frontotemporale distance | Face | Frontotemporale left - frontotemporale right | Breadth |
| Glabella - pronasale distance | Face | Glabella - pronasale | Depth |
| Infraorbitale - pronasale distance | Face | Infraorbitale - pronasale | Depth |
| Tragion distance | Face | Tragion left - tragion right | Breadth |
| Zygofrontale distance | Face | Zygofrontale left - zygofrontale right | Breadth |
| Otobasion superius distance | Face | Otobasion superius left - otobasion superius right | Breadth |
| Glabella - otobasion superius distance | Face | Glabella - otobasion superius | Length |
| Vertex - glabella distance | Face | Vertex - glabella | Depth |
| Vertex - tragion distance | Face | Vertex - tragion | Depth |
| Infraorbitale distance | Eye | Infraorbitale left - infraorbitale right | Breadth |
| Glabella - infraorbitale distance | Eye | Glabella - infraorbitale | Depth |
| Biocular distance | Eye | Ectocanthus left - ectocanthus right | Breadth |
| Interocular distance | Eye | Entocanthion left - entocanthion right | Breadth |
| Interpupillary distance | Eye | Pupil left - pupil right | Breadth |
| Otobasion superius-pupil distance | Eye | Otobasion superius - pupil | Length |
| Sellion - pronasale distance | Nose | Sellion - pronasale | Depth |
| Sellion - subnasale distance | Nose | Sellion - subnasale | Depth |
| Pronasale - subnasale distance | Nose | Pronasale - subnasale | Depth |
| Nasal distance | Nose | Alare left - alare right | Breadth |
| Otobasion superius - otobasion inferius distance | Ear | Otobasion superius - otobasion inferius | Depth |

height, weight and 3 head measurements (refer to Table 1). A wig cap was fitted to obtain a better scan quality of the hair during the 3D scanning. Fourteen selected manually marked landmarks were directly labeled on the participants' faces to identify the critical bone structures [13]. Participants were scanned using the Artec Eva® 3D scanner, and high-resolution data was automatically captured as point cloud data.

## 3   Data Processing

The raw scans collected during the field survey required extensive post-scanning processing before they were suitable for use in the development of a database. All scan files were processed through data alignment, noise elimination, mesh simplification, hole filling and texture mapping, then statistical analysis could proceed subsequently.

Apart from the 14 manually marked landmarks, there were 19 landmarks based on identifiable facial features that were obtained by the trained post-scanning operators. Those 14 manually marked landmarks were the Chin, Glabella, Pronasale, Sellion, Frontotemporale (left and right), Tragion (left and right), Infraorbitale (left and right), Zygion (left and right) and Zygofrontale (left and right) (refer to Fig. 1). The selection of these 33 landmarks (refer to Fig. 1) was based on the head-and-face research in [13]. The coordinates of 33 landmarks were captured because we aimed to obtain more detailed data for analyzing the human face. For facial measurements using completed 3D modeling data, 20 items were measured according to SizeChina [14] and 'China national standard head-face dimensions of adults' [15], as shown in Table 1.

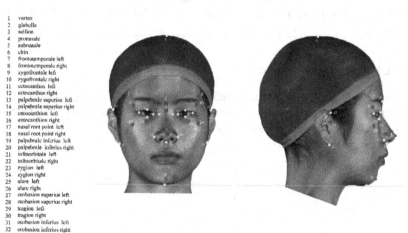

| | |
|---|---|
| 1 | vertex |
| 2 | glabella |
| 3 | sellion |
| 4 | pronasale |
| 5 | subnasale |
| 6 | chin |
| 7 | frontotemporale left |
| 8 | frontotemporale right |
| 9 | zygofrontale left |
| 10 | zygofrontale right |
| 11 | ectocanthus left |
| 12 | ectocanthus right |
| 13 | palpebrale superius left |
| 14 | palpebrale superius right |
| 15 | entocanthion left |
| 16 | entocanthion right |
| 17 | nasal root point left |
| 18 | nasal root point right |
| 19 | palpebrale inferius left |
| 20 | palpebrale inferius right |
| 21 | infraorbitale left |
| 22 | infraorbitale right |
| 23 | zygion left |
| 24 | zygion right |
| 25 | alare left |
| 26 | alare right |
| 27 | otobasion superius left |
| 28 | otobasion superius right |
| 29 | tragion left |
| 30 | tragion right |
| 31 | otobasion inferius left |
| 32 | otobasion inferius right |
| 33 | menton |

**Fig. 1.**  Head scan example with 33 landmarks

The statistical analysis of the anthropometric data was performed using IBM® SPSS® Statistics 24 software. The percentiles (5, 10, 25, 50, 75, 90, and 95), mean, median, variance, SD, maximum, minimum, skewness and kurtosis for every group of measures were calculated.

# 4   Html5-Based Responsive Database Design

Although previous anthropometry has a long history and has accumulated a vast amount of data, little research or design has been reported concerning using human data to improve design models. It is limited by the publication form of its principal results, such as 3D scan files and documents with summary statistics for the population. Any anthropometric studies that aim to make its information available to designers must address the communication methods that best suit designers' needs.

An online database website offers many solutions to the communication problem between users and the dataset. First, since the information exists as computer data, it can be readily displayed in the form of a pictorial image, so users can intuitively and easily understand the complex information being described. Second, the web provides varied interactions between users and data instead of only data listed in a spreadsheet. Third, an online dataset could be spread more widely among the public, experts and designers. However, as noted earlier, except for the few databases available on the web, almost all existing anthropometric survey groups saved, delivered and used their results in the form of conventional files, and neither has occurred in China. Therefore, it is essential and ground-breaking for this research to display the overall human head and facial data on the website in a comprehensive and meaningful way.

Crucially, this database's website is being developed using Html5-based responsive web technology that can adapt to multiple browsers in devices such as mobile phones, PADs and personal computers, which makes the database website respond and adjust to different device environments. A website compatible with various devices satisfies the user's needs for use in a variety of scenarios, which ensures the continuity of the user experience.

## 4.1   Database Website Structure

The Chinese head and facial database website (Chinese Headbase) is composed of six modules: (1) home, (2) percentiles, (3) search, (4) models, (5) summary, and (6) about. The structure of this website is shown in Fig. 2.

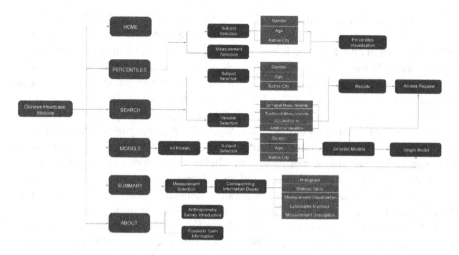

**Fig. 2.** The structure of the database website

**Home.** There is a human head facial image outlined with lines and grids at the core of the home page, and different kinds of smart glasses' images alternately emerge over the face. This reveals that the website contains an ample amount of human data for wearable products design. (see Fig. 3 below).

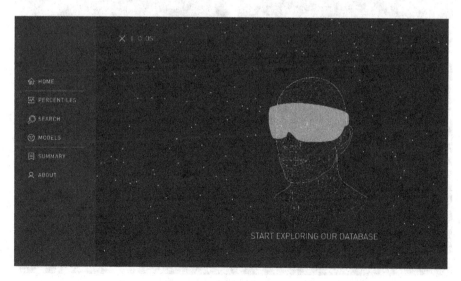

**Fig. 3.** The home page of the database website

**Percentiles.** As a measurement visualization tool for every traditional measurement (head circumference, head length and head breadth) and 3D facial measurements (extracted from 3D models), the line drawing human head facial image changes in real time according to the measurement the user chose, showing the specific location and the shape of the feature selected. Additionally, a percentile visualization tool for all measurements is offered in this module, which is a slider right below the line that draws the human head facial image. The numbers on the left and right sides represent the respective minimum and maximum of measurements. Moreover, the group of subjects for percentiles is customizable. The default percentile is based on the total number of subjects, but users can choose specific target groups by clicking the options in the left area. The percentile would switch in real time based on different groups.

When a user clicks "Frontotemporale Distance" with females, all ages, Guangzhou and Hangzhou checked, the corresponding image appears on the forehead of the head facial image to visually describe the "Frontotemporale Distance". Its minimum and maximum are 92.179 and 138.559, respectively. Sliding the slider to 25%, the corresponding value is 103.77 mm, and the line drawing feature in the head facial image changes in accordance with the percentile value (refer to Fig. 4). The visualization and customization tools in this database greatly accelerate the understanding of all measurements.

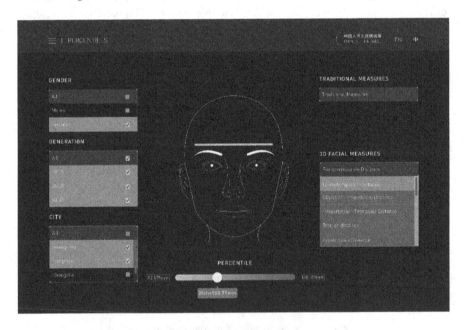

**Fig. 4.** The percentiles page of the database website

**Search.** Users can query and retrieve individual-level raw data in this module. Currently most available databases present only summary-level data, which means that only age- and sex-specific means and standard deviations for all anthropometric measures are available. The lack of raw source materials, such as individual-level data, seriously limits the additional analyses. One of the superiorities of the web-based database is that users are not limited to the summary statistics provided.

Available individual-level raw data include the whole set of 33 3D facial landmarks, including their associated $x$, $y$, and $z$ coordinate values, all 3D facial measurements, all traditional measurements, the basic human characteristics (height, weight) and basic demographic information (gender, age, and native city).

In this *search* page, the search parameters can be defined to query the individual-level data. For example, users can limit queries to only one gender, a specific range of ages, or a specific native city for the subjects. Further, users can limit searches to specific variables of interest, such as landmarks, 3D facial measurements, traditional measurements, and basic human characteristics (refer to Fig. 5). Through this search, the number of participants in the database that are in accordance with the condition(s) of interest would be demonstrated. For example, a user could construct a very narrow search to query how many men between the ages of 18 and 25 have a certain feature in the database. Alternatively, a user can select all measurements in both genders across all ages of all 7 cities. Once the query is determined and submitted, a results page (refer to Fig. 6) will display the items and numbers of the variables selected by users and the number of specific target subjects in that group. The retrieval process can be repeated by revising the criteria each time.

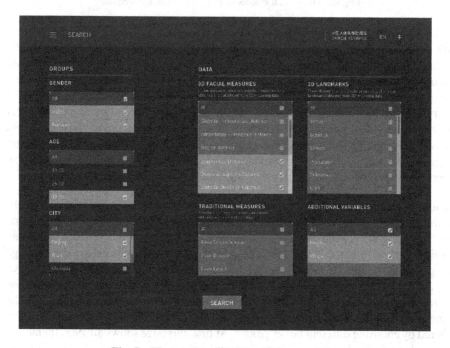

**Fig. 5.** The search page of the database website

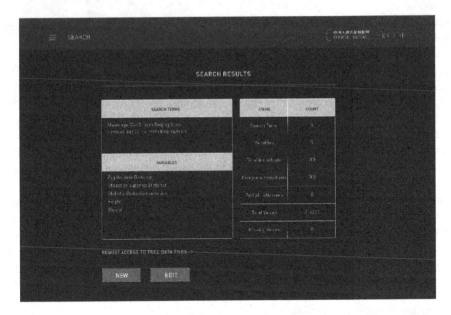

**Fig. 6.** The search results page of the database website

In the *search results* page, there is also the option to access detailed results from the full individual-level raw data. The full access to the individual-level raw data in the Chinese Headbase is controlled. Users must apply for access through the research team according to the guidelines in the access introduction dialog box. Once access is granted, users can locally work with the full dataset, and the individual-level raw data would be sent by the project team as a standard flat file that can be opened by any spreadsheet program. Individual measurement data and demographic information allow designers to customize the information for their specific needs. For example, a designer might focus on the needs of specific individuals or a demographic group. Designers can approach their own analyses with these raw data.

**Models.** This is a module for visualizing and interacting with 3D head facial models. In the past, 3D scan data obtained in anthropometric studies were published as folders, leading to a gap between 3D models and users. However, on this website, users can intuitively browse all the 3D models. They can click on the thumbnails to view the large images online, where the models can be rotated and zoomed in/out on for a better view.

The 3D models' thumbnail images are tiled on the page in bulk and are accompanied by the subjects' numbers. All 1900 models' thumbnails can be seen by accessing the page. Like the searchable individual-level data above, the 3D head facial models can be filtered by choosing different target groups. At first, this page shows all 1900 thumbnail images by default. However, users can customize the genders, ages and native cities of the subjects at the top of the page, and the 3D models' thumbnail images displayed on the page would be switched in real time with the selected demographic features. For example, a researcher interested in 3D models of men in Xi'an can click on "males" in the "gender" drop-down box and on "Xi'an" in the "city" box. The remaining ages are in their default setting. Then, the thumbnail images are filtered, and 135 eligible 3D models are shown on the page (see Fig. 7 below).

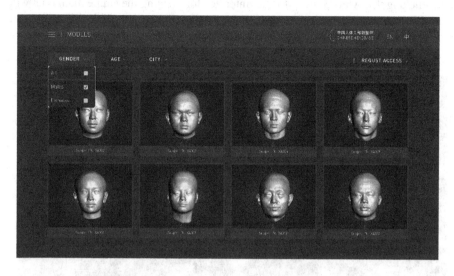

**Fig. 7.** The model's page of the database website

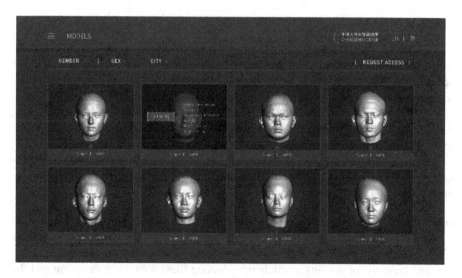

**Fig. 8.** The model's page of the database website showing the subject's basic information

The subject's basic information will be displayed with subject ID, native place, age, height and weight (refer to Fig. 8) when the mouse cursor hovers over a thumbnail image. After clicking the "view 3D" button, an interface for viewing the single 3D model will pop out where users can rotate and scale the head model by left-clicks, dragging and scrolling mouse action to check more surface details (see Fig. 9 below).

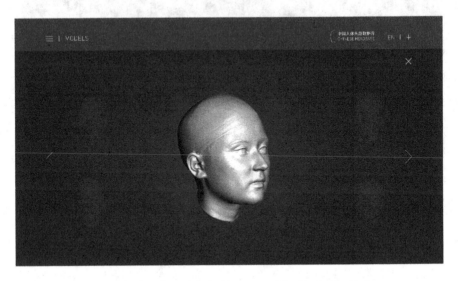

**Fig. 9.** The single model viewing page of the database website

As with the search module, the access is required to locally gain the 3D models. Users can apply for permission from the research team according to the guides in the access introduction dialog box. Once access is granted, 3D models that meet users' requirements will be sent as standard 3D files that can be opened by any mainstream 3D software. These models have been stripped of identifying colors and textural maps, leaving the surface geometry bare so researchers can directly discover the locations of their interested feature points.

With individual-level raw data and these 3D scan data, researchers can use the landmarks and 3D facial measures to perform analyses, derive additional facial measurements as often as they need.

**Summary.** In this module, users can view and download the summary data tables and histograms of all measurements (refer to Fig. 10). Each statistic table lists 8 statistics including the mean, median, variance, standard deviation, maximum, minimum, skewness, and kurtosis for all 1900 participants. Among these data, only the mean and the standard deviation are supplied in the previous methods of data publication [9]. Based on this situation, the median, maximum and other measures were added to directly offer more effective information. The histogram of each feature shows the distribution of this measure data for the 1900 subjects with percentiles marked on the corresponding locations below the $x$-axis. The bar is highlighted for the user's easier recognition.

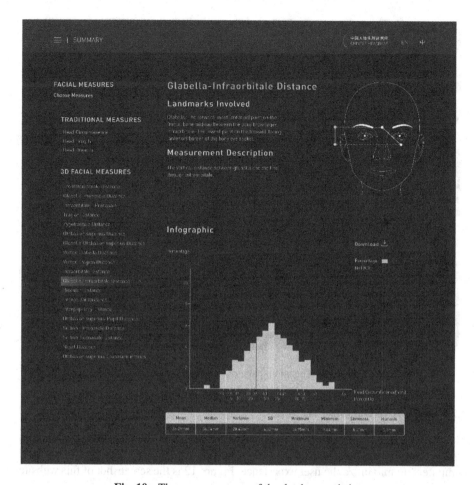

**Fig. 10.** The summary page of the database website

There is a list of 3 traditional measurements and 20 3D facial measurements on the left of this module. Clicking on each option, the table and a histogram of the corresponding feature are shown along with the descriptive image and text. All users have unlimited access to all tables and histograms in this database.

**About.** The objective of this module is to introduce the whole 3D anthropometry briefly with a Chinese map set on the right of the page highlighting all 7 mainland cities. We also offer information about the research team including contact information and the address (refer to Fig. 11).

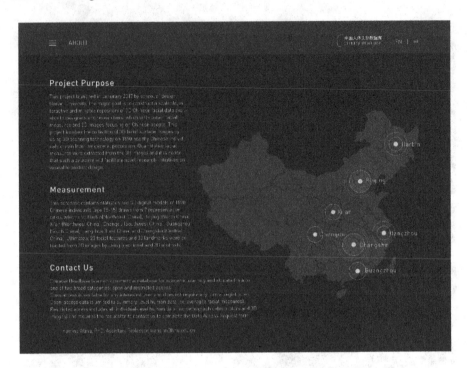

**Fig. 11.** The about page of the database website

## 4.2  Responsive Database Website

The Chinese Headbase website is a responsive website that can automatically adapt to whatever device the users are using to view the site, such as mobile phones, PADs and computers, to maximize the user experience. Figure 12 is the screenshot of this website on mobile phone browsers.

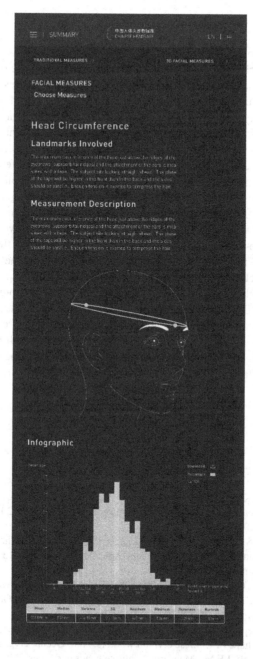

**Fig. 12.** The summary page of the database website shown on a mobile phone

# 5   Conclusion

This research developed a responsive Html5-based database based on a full-scale Chinese head and facial 3D anthropometry dataset built using state of art 3D scanning technology on 1900 healthy Chinese individuals drawn from 7 representative cities. On this website, users can access summary-level statistics for 23 head and facial features extracted traditionally and from 3D scanning data, as well as individual-level data including facial landmark coordinates, anthropometric measurements, 3D head models and demographics for every individual. Users could perform further statistics or ergonomics analyses based on the information acquired from this website. Furthermore, this database offers customizable searches, data visualization and responsive layouts of the database website across different platforms for researchers and designers to interact with complicated anthropometric information easily and smoothly. In summary, this database is the first H5-based website in known studies to provide an effective and intuitive way to demonstrate the up-to-date adult head and facial data drawn from the general Chinese population. This will facilitate the use and spread of the anthropometric dataset among the industry and accelerate novel research on Chinese fit wearable product designs.

However, although current research constructed a scalable, comprehensive and easy-to-use repository of 3D Chinese head and facial data, it's limited to the sample of Chinese adults between ages of 18 and 45. The lack of adolescent and elder individuals may narrow its usage in the future. Further anthropometric measures of different populations will be implemented, and more design-driven measurements will be added to the database to enrich the data.

**Acknowledgements.** This work was supported by the National Key Technology R&D Program of the Ministry of S&T of China 2015BAH22F00.

# References

1. Ball, R., Shu, C., Xi, P., Rioux, M., Luximon, Y., Molenbroek, J.: A comparison between Chinese and Caucasian head shapes. Appl. Ergon. **41**, 832–839 (2010). https://doi.org/10.1016/j.apergo.2010.02.002
2. Yu, Y., Benson, S., Cheng, W., Hsiao, J., Liu, Y., Zhuang, Z., Chen, W.: Digital 3-D headforms representative of Chinese workers. Ann. Occup. Hyg. **56**, 113–122 (2012). https://doi.org/10.1093/annhyg/mer074
3. Du, L., Zhuang, Z., Guan, H., Xing, J., Tang, X., Wang, L., Wang, Z., Wang, H., Liu, Y., Su, W.: Head-and-face anthropometric survey of Chinese workers. Ann. Occup. Hyg. **52**, 773–782 (2008). https://doi.org/10.1093/annhyg/men056
4. Liu, Y., Xi, P., Joseph, M., Zhuang, Z., Shu, C., Jiang, L., Bergman, M., Chen, W.: Variations in head-and-face shape of Chinese civilian workers. Ann. Occup. Hyg. **59**, 932–944 (2015)
5. Ball, R., Molenbroek, J.F.M.: Measuring Chinese heads and faces (2008)
6. Ball, R.: 3-D design tools from the SizeChina project. Ergon. Des. Mag. Hum. Factors Appl. **17**, 8–13 (2009). https://doi.org/10.1518/106480409X12487281219931
7. Standards administration of the People Republic of China, GB/T5703-2010: Basic human body measurements for technological design. Standard Press of China, Beijing (2011). (in Chinese)

8. Standards administration of the People Republic of china, GB10000-88: Human dimensions of Chinese adults. Standard Press of China, Beijing (1989). (in Chinese)
9. Robinette, K.M., Blackwell, S., Daanen, H., Boehmer, M., Fleming, S.: Civilian American and European surface anthropometry resource (CAESAR), final report, vol. 1. Summary. United States Air Force Research Laboratory (2002). https://doi.org/10.21236/ada406704
10. Weinberg, S.M., Raffensperger, Z.D., Kesterke, M.J., Heike, C.L., Cunningham, M.L., Hecht, J.T., Kau, C.H., Murray, J.C., Wehby, G.L., Moreno, L.M.: The 3D facial norms database: Part 1. A web-based craniofacial anthropometric and image repository for the clinical and research community. The Cleft Palate-Craniofacial Journal: Official Publication of the American Cleft Palate-Craniofacial Association (2015). https://doi.org/10.1597/15-199
11. 3D Facial Norms Database|Facebase. https://www.facebase.org/facial_norms/
12. iSize-start. http://portal.i-size.net/
13. Luximon, Y., Ball, R., Justice, L.: The 3D Chinese head and face modeling. Comput. Aided Des. **44**, 40–47 (2012). https://doi.org/10.1016/j.cad.2011.01.011
14. Ball, R.M.: SizeChina: a 3D anthropometric survey of the Chinese head, p. 54 (2011)
15. Standards administration of the People Republic of China, GB/T2428-1998: Head-face dimensions of adults. Standard Press of China, Beijing (1998). (in Chinese)

# Modeling and Analyzing Information Preparation Behaviors in Cross-Device Search

Dan Wu[✉], Jing Dong, and Yuan Tang

School of Information Management, Wuhan University, Wuhan, China
woodan@whu.edu.cn

**Abstract.** The cross-device search usually happens when the tasks are complex and spanning multiple sessions. It takes time to switch devices in the cross-device search, which interrupts the search task and leads to the repeated search. In this paper, we presented a study on the search behaviors of a pre-switch device if there is repeated search occurring in the cross-device search. We attributed these search behaviors as information preparation and trained a model of information preparation behavior by three supervised classification methods: Binary Logistic Regression, C5.0 Decision Tree and Support Vector Machine. Our results showed that C5.0 Decision Tree performed the best. It is found that five features of dissatisfied click rate, valid click rate, first valid click time, satisfied click rate and Jaccard distance of queries are important to describe the information preparation behavior. An in-depth analysis of these five features was conducted to understand the information preparation behavior, which can support the personalized cross-device search.

**Keywords:** Information preparation behavior · Cross-device search
Repeated search · Modeling information behavior

## 1 Introduction

The popularity of smart phones makes the computer not the only choice when people need to search on web. Cross-device searches become prevalent. The device transition, which means the behavior of changing devices when searching, is an indispensable feature of the cross-device search. A tourist who is planning the trip may search introductions of places of interests by a laptop before she sets out. Then the mobile phone is used to search the introduction again for the address information to help her get there. Alternatively, a GoT (Game of Thrones) fan is told about the plot leak when outside for dinner and he searches the news on the mobile phone. He may search the news in detail through the computer after arriving at home. In both cases, the device transition due to the context change interrupts the search task and the user has to resume the search by repeated searches. If the post-switch session is regarded as the resumption, the pre-switch session can be seen as the preparation. In this paper, we discuss about search behaviors in the session of preparation.

Although the discussion of information preparation behavior is witnessed quite a few, the re-finding behavior on web search is well-studied. Previous research has shown that queries at the beginning of a session are likely to search results found at the end of a previous session [1]. As can be seen, behaviors of repeated searches are studied from a perspective of resumption. Little is known about how users of repeated search activity perform from the angle of preparation, which this paper researches through a cross-device search experiment. Via the analysis of logs, we investigated features of the information preparation behavior and developed a model of it. The model can be used as a basis for clustering search log results of cross-device search. This paper can extend the researches about cross-device search behaviors and support the personalized cross-device search.

## 2  Related Work

What is studied in this paper are features of the search behavior on pre-switch device, if a user repeats the search after converting the device. Related work falls in the following areas: (1) cross-device search behavior, (2) cross-session search behavior and (3) behavior of the repeated search.

### 2.1  Cross-Device Search Behavior

Multiple Information Seeking Episodes (MISE), a conceptual model proposed by Lin and Belkin [2], can be applied to explain why and how people engage in a cross-device search. It is common for people to have multiple search devices, providing the cross-device search with a good personal device ecosystem [3]. The cross-device search has been researched intensively in recent years. Large scale logs from search engines are applied to study the cross-device search [4–6]. For example, Montañez et al. [4] characterized the cross-device search in terms of topic distributions and device transitions. It is found that search interests varied across different devices and time of a day and the most frequent transition is self-transition, which means continuing the search through the same device. Understanding the cross-device search behavior helps to predict whether the task of pre-switch session is continued [5]. To support the cross-device web search, social navigation-based mobile touch interactions were investigated, which showed the effectiveness of search performance improvement [7]. Besides, synchronizing web history among different devices is also useful for cross-device interaction [8].

### 2.2  Cross-Session Search Behavior

Researches on cross-session search are also relevant to this paper, since the cross-device search consists of pre- and post-switch sessions. Cross-session search behavior was modeled by Kotov et al. [9] through machine learning. This behavior was decomposed into identifying queries on the same task and predicting task continuation. Han et al. [10] compared user behaviors between the cross-device search and the same device, cross-session search. It was noticed that more queries were issued and more web pages were visited and saved in the anterior session in cross-session search than in cross-device search, while the landing page dwell time was significantly longer in the anterior session of cross-device search than that of cross-session search. In addition, behaviors of cross-session search have been actively studied to identify cross-session search tasks. Wang et al. [11] developed a semi-supervised clustering model based on the latent structural SVM framework to extract cross-session search tasks from users' search activities.

### 2.3  Behavior of the Repeated Search

There are various concepts associated with repeated search, such as re-finding, re-search, re-retrieval, re-access and revisit [10, 12–14]. The concepts of re-finding, re-access and revisit mean seeking the URL previously visited, while re-search and re-retrieval indicate re-issuing queries to revisit a web page or to find new websites. The fact that search engine users often re-find viewed resources was revealed in the previous study [15]. From a one-year web query log, it was demonstrated that 40% of all queries were re-finding queries [12]. Repeated queries and revisited landing pages were more at the beginning than in the middle and ending of a session [10]. Tyler et al. [13] classified types of re-search into the same query, minimal change query and term overlap query. The intentions of re-search were concluded as "re-finding", "new finding", "new content seeking" and "result list change". Re-finding prediction can be used to re-rank search results, which improves retrieval performance of personalized search. Experiment showed ranking relevant URLs with higher re-finding probability helped improve NDCG (Normalized Discounted Cumulative Gain) than just re-ranking URLs by relevance [14].

In summary, research work in this paper extents the previous related work in the following ways. First, differing from existing studies of cross-device search, we focus on the cross-device search occurring repeated search behaviors. This is gaining importance because repeated search reveals users' continuing interests which can trigger the cross-device search. Second, no matter revisiting web pages or re-issuing queries focuses on the perspective of resumption. However, what we discuss about the information preparation is concerning the perspective of preparation.

## 3  Definitions

### 3.1  Session

The concept of a search session is employed to segment queries and associated search behaviors into short-time units for analysis. A threshold time is used to segment sessions in previous log analysis. However, in this paper, we define a session using the device. Every cross-search consists of two sessions which are the pre-switch session (Session 1) and the post-switch session (Session 2).

### 3.2  Cross-Device Search

A cross-device search is defined by Wang et al. [5]. as a combination of an anterior device, a posterior device, a pre-switch session, a post-switch session and queries in both sessions. Based on this, in this paper, the cross-device search is defined as searching on different devices for the same topic.

### 3.3    Information Preparation

Since cross-device search users tend to repeat their task in a post-switch session, we consider how they perform in a pre-switch session is the preparation for the task. Thus, given a cross-device search which repeated search occurs, information preparation refers to search behaviors before switching the device.

## 4    Research Design

### 4.1    Motivation and Research Questions

The idea of studying information preparation behaviors derives from the task resumption behavior in the cross-session search. Previous studies confirm a common phenomenon of repeated searches in the cross-session search and repeated searches are regarded as task resumption behaviors [1, 12, 13]. A cross-device search can be considered as a special example of cross-session search, therefore, we think there is the information resumption behavior of post-switch session when repeated searches occur in a cross-device search. Correspondingly, search behaviors of pre-switch session are regarded as preparing information for resuming the task.

This information preparation behavior can be both conscious and unconscious due to whether the cross-device search is intended from the beginning. For example, a person is recommended a movie when having dinner outside. She searches the online video of movie on her mobile phone and decides to search it again by a laptop after home. In this conscious cross-device search case, the user searches on mobile phone to make sure there is online video available so that she can watch the movie on laptop. In other words, she prepares the resumption of online video search by searching on mobile phone first. Even when users are involved in a cross-device search without planning in advance, activities of information preparation still exist when users resume the search, because what users search before the device transition lets an impression produce in their mind and influences the post-switch search.

Overall, this paper aims to explore features of information preparation behaviors. Specifically, two research questions will be answered: (1) What are important features that describe the information preparation behavior? (2) How do the features characterize the information preparation behavior? In order to find the features, we collected behavior data of information preparation by a within-subject designed experiment.

### 4.2    Experiment Environment and Search System

As it found in cross-session search studies that users tend to resume their task by repeated searches when the task is interrupted. During the cross-device search, the interval of device transition can be considered as an interruption. Enlightened by this, we designed a user experiment with cross-device search tasks. The way of device transition was preset and an interval was used to interrupt the task artificially, which inspired users to repeat the search.

The user experiment was conducted in a laboratory which was a controlled environment. The cross-device search that we discuss focuses on transiting the search between the desktop and mobile devices. Therefore, two transition ways of *desktop-mobile* and *desktop-mobile* were included in the experiment. We provided a laptop in the experiment and users were expected to use their own smart phones for the mobile search.

Cross-device Access and Fusion Engine (CAFÉ)[1], a self-developed search system, was used to conduct the desktop and mobile search. Referring to the cross-device search system developed by Han et al. [7], the context-sensitive retrieval model is adopted in CAFÉ. The system provides users with search results by re-ranking results of Bing based on context information of Mobile Touch Interaction (MTI) and viewing time. In addition, the system can remind users of URLs clicked previously by showing information of the previous device, search time, and queries.

### 4.3    Cross-Device Search Tasks

Complex information need cannot be satisfied by a single session and device, which makes complex information search common in cross-device search. Thus, we considered complex search tasks in the experiment. Since the task type and subtask amount have effect on the complexity of task [16], we designed informational search tasks with four subtasks of each task in the experiment. To determine the task topics, we asked the frequent categories searched across devices in every-day life by the participant recruitment survey. Details of the survey are explained in Sect. 4.4. We selected the top four, which were *Movie, Drama, Music* and *Language*. For two transition ways, the reason why we selected four topics rather than two was to prevent the effect of topics on search behaviors. We rotated the orders of tasks based on topics using Latin Squares and asked users to search the first task by *desktop-mobile* and the second task by *mobile-desktop*, which let every topic be searched on both desktop and mobile. In order to be sure every task could not be fulfilled by a few queries in a single session, we did a pilot search and the result showed the tasks were too complex to be completed in a session.

An example of four search tasks is shown in Fig. 1. Users were provided with printed tasks, avoiding the fact that viewing the task on screen influences the behavior data collection. In the description of each task, four subtasks were written in bold and several instructions were given in italic. The instructions were designed to help users generate clear information need. Users were asked to submit a report for each task, including information that was useful for the instructions.

> Task Topic: Movie
>
> Imagine you have seen the movie Leon in class and you are told to write an essay about the **photography** and **lines** of the movie (*collect related information for the essay*). After class, you want to review **class fragments of the movie** (*describe the content of a fragment*). Social media comments the actress of leading role is an outstanding person and you want to know **the reasons** (*list at least 5 reasons*).

**Fig. 1.** Task example

---

[1] http://crosssearch.whu.edu.cn/login.html.

## 4.4  Participants

The participants of experiment were recruited among university students. Electronic questionnaires were sent to students via e-mail to investigate their backgrounds and cross-search experience, seeing questions in Fig. 2. The fourth question helps to determine the topics of experiment tasks and the last question helps to confirm the participant's cross-device experience is authentic. The choices of categories were adopted from Wang et al. [5] with a little change. 47 people replied and were willing to participate the experiment. We only recruited 36 participants who were not familiar with the task topics of experiment. Even though the pilot search of four tasks showed it was difficult to complete the task by one session, there were two participants claimed that they finished the task within one session and thus they did not search across different devices. We had to exclude the data of them. Finally, we collected the cross-device search behavior data of 34 participants (22 females and 12 males), among which there were 18 undergraduates and 16 postgraduate students from 22 different majors. A third of the them self-estimated their search ability as over 4 and their cross-device search frequency as over 3 (based on the 5-level Likert scales). We reached an agreement on privacy protection with all of participants. We paid them unequally from 100 to 150 yuan to encourage them search seriously.

| Participant Recruitment Survey |
| --- |
| 1.   Background including sexuality, major and graduation degree. |
| 2.   How well do you think your search ability is? (5-level Likert scale) |
| 3.   How often do you conduct cross-device search in daily life? (5-level Likert scale) |
| 4.   What are the categories do you search across devices frequently? (Multi-choice question) |
| 5.   Describe the latest experience of cross-device search. |

**Fig. 2.**  Questions of the participant recruitment survey

## 4.5  Experiment Procedure

Every participant had to complete two tasks by two device transition ways. For each task, both desktop and mobile devices were used and participants were allowed to spend at most 20 min on each device. Search sessions of a task are divided based on devices, therefore, every task consists of two sessions. In order to stimulate the interruption of cross-device search activity in real context, we designed an interval between two sessions of a task to interrupt the search artificially. We required participants to complete the first sessions (Session 1) of two tasks firstly and then the second sessions (Session 2). Participants were allowed to rest for 20 min after finishing all the Session 1 of two tasks, avoiding fatigue influences search behaviors. Therefore, the interval between two sessions of a task was 40 min. During the 20 min of each session, participants needed not only to search information but also to save useful information for organizing the report. Moreover, after every session, the participant had to fill in a questionnaire, the outline of which is presented in Fig. 7.

We take User 1 for example to explain the entire procedure of experiment, as seen in Fig. 3. At the beginning, we asked User 1 to try the CAFÉ system and explained the entire procedure. We also told User 1 his task order was *Movie-Drama* and corresponding device transition ways. Next, User 1 searched *Movie* task on desktop and *Drama* task on mobile in sequences. When User 1 claimed he finished the task or the 20 min was out, he had to stop searching and answered the *Questionnaire of Session 1*. Then, User 1 were asked to take a break for 20 min. After that, User 1 resumed *Movie* task on mobile and *Drama* task on desktop in sequences. The stopping rule was the same as mentioned above and the *Questionnaire of Session 2* was required to complete.

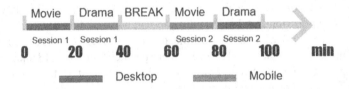

**Fig. 3.** Experiment procedure: an example of User 1

## 4.6  Data Collection

**System Logs**

The search system of both desktop and mobile search was CAFÉ System, the SERP of which can be seen in Figs. 4 and 5. Different areas of the SERP are labelled.

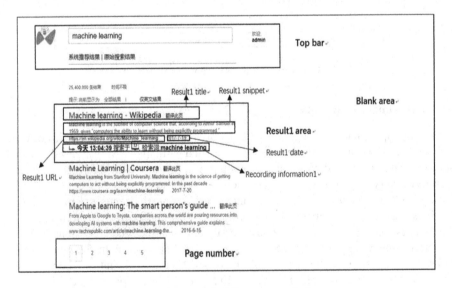

**Fig. 4.** SERP of CAFE system on desktop

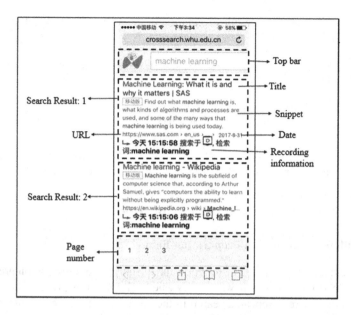

**Fig. 5.** SERP of CAFE system on mobile

The CAFÉ system can log SERP load time, SERP URL (including coded queries), search device, interaction types, timestamps of starting and stopping the interaction, and areas of interactions. The interactions on desktop indicate the movement of mouse, including move, dwell and click, while the MTIs include drag up/down/left/right, tap and press. An example is shown in Fig. 6.

| username | loadtime | currenttimestamp | pageUrl | eventType | startTime | stopTime | Area | platform |
|---|---|---|---|---|---|---|---|---|
| admin02 | 1496649523964 | 1496649527420 | http://www.bing.com/search?&q=%E7%BA%B8%E7%89%8C%E5%B1%8B%E7%AC%AC%E5%9B%9B%E5%AD%A3&first=0 | dwell | 1496649525644 | 1496649527420 | | Desktop |
| admin02 | 1496649523964 | 1496649551819 | http://www.bing.com/search?&q=%E7%BA%B8%E7%89%8C%E5%B1%8B%E7%AC%AC%E5%9B%9B%E5%AD%A3&first=0 | click | | | result2 title | Desktop |

**Fig. 6.** An example of CAFE system logs.

Over the entire procedure, every participant searched 2 tasks and 4 sessions. In total, we collected search behavior data of 136 sessions, of which 68 Session 1 and 68 Session 2. Since what discusses in this paper is information preparation behaviors, we only develop the model by the behavior data of 68 Session 1. The rest data of 68 Session 2 will be used in another study of information resumption behaviors.

**Questionnaire**

In order to know whether the participant repeat the search, we used the *Questionnaire of Session 1 and Session 2* to record the subtasks that the participant searched. We also asked about the participant's subjective evaluation of the search task, to understand the influence of previous device and the search experience on the current searches. The outline of these questionnaires is shown in Fig. 7. Totally 136 questionnaires were collected.

| Questionnaire of Session 1/Session 2 |
|---|
| 1.  User ID and task number. |
| 2.  What subtasks did you search. (multi-choice question) |
| 3.  How familiar do you feel with each subtask? (5-level Likert scale) |
| 4.  How satisfied do you feel about the current session? (5-level Likert scale) |

**Fig. 7.** The outline of questionnaire of Session 1 and Session 2

# 5    Information Preparation Behavior Model

## 5.1    Identifying Information Preparation Behaviors

Since repeated searches indicate resumption and the purpose of information preparation behaviors is to resume the search, we identify whether information preparation behaviors exist by whether there is repeated search in the cross-device search. Results of *Questionnaire of Session 1 and Session 2* tell what subtasks the participant searched. We consider the participant perform information preparation if there is any subtask repeatedly searched. Table 1 shows the distribution of repeated searches. Over 90% participants had information preparation behaviors, specifically 30 participants repeated the search of the first task and 32 participants repeated the second task.

**Table 1.** The number of users performing repeated searches

| Repeated subtask number | 0 | 1 | 2 | 3 | 4 |
|---|---|---|---|---|---|
| The first task | 4 | 13 | 8 | 3 | 6 |
| The second task | 2 | 13 | 8 | 7 | 4 |
| Percentage | 8.8% | 38.2% | 23.5% | 14.7% | 14.7% |

## 5.2    Features

We extracted features of query-based, click-based, time-based and subjective evaluation groups from logs and questionnaire results, described in more detail below and shown in Table 2. These features are used to train the model.

**Table 2.** Features for modeling the information preparation behavior

| Query-based features | |
| --- | --- |
| Query number | The number of queries |
| Unique query number | The number of unique queries |
| Query char | The number of characters in the query |
| Unique query char | The number of characters of unique queries in the query |
| Query term | The number of terms in the query |
| Ave ED | The average length of Levenshtein edit distance of queries of a session |
| Jaccard distance | The length of Jaccard distance between sessions of a task |
| **Click-based features** | |
| Valid click rate | The proportion of clicks within result areas in a session |
| valid query rate | The proportion of clicks within result areas per query in a session |
| Satisfied click rate | The proportion of clicks with landing page time of at least 30 s in a session |
| Dissatisfied click rate | The proportion of clicks with landing page time of at most 15 s in a session |
| **Time-based features** | |
| First click time | The interval of the first action and the first click in a session |
| First valid click time | The interval of the first action and the first click within result areas in a session |
| SERP time | The total dwell time on SERPs in a session |
| Landing page time | The total dwell time on landing pages in a session |
| Session time | The total time that a session lasts |
| **Subjective evaluation features** | |
| Satisfaction scores | The average scores to evaluate the satisfaction of the search |
| Familiarity scores | The average scores to evaluate the familiarity of the task |

Query-based features describe the characteristics of characters and terms in queries of the information preparation behavior. Features associated with queries are used to predict the re-finding behavior [14], and the information preparation behavior is associated with re-finding. Thus query-based features are important to model the information preparation behavior.

Click-based features aim to capture the clicking behavior of information preparation. The concept of valid click derives from the result click [17], referring clicks within the result area, like title, snippet, URL et al. Clicking the result area means the user makes a use of the result information. The concepts of satisfied click and dissatisfied click are defined by the dwell time on the landing page. 30 and 15 s have been used as thresholds in previous researches [17, 18]. Through these click-based features, it is revealed that how much effort is required for the information preparation.

Time-based features characterize the information preparation behavior from the perspective of time length. Time can reflect the efficiency of information preparation. The experiment offers users 20 min to search, however effective participants spent less than it. A user clicks when he/she thinks the result is useful to the task, therefore the time it takes to act a click illustrates the speed of acquiring useful information. Users stay on SERPs to scan results, while they remain on landing pages to acquire the knowl-edge. The dwell time of SERPs and landing pages indicates the efficiency of information selection and information utilization.

The above groups of features are extracted from logs, while subjective evaluation features are from the questionnaires. Scores of satisfaction and familiarity aim to capture the subjective feeling of information preparation.

### 5.3   Classifiers

Three classifiers experimented to model the information preparation behavior were Binary Logistic Regression (BLR), C5.0 Decision Tree (C5.0) and Support Vector Machine (SVM). Logistic Regression is applied to predict the task resumption by Kotov et al. [9]. Since the information preparation is associated with resuming the task, the Binary Logistic Regression can be used to train the information preparation behavior model. We referred to this classifier as a baseline, which was used the same way in ref. [19]. Decision trees are effective for search behavior modeling, which is shown in ref. [14]. It is easy to see what makes up the information preparation behavior by the structure of tree. The Support Vector Machine shows its advantage on binary classification prob-lems, although it is difficult for a model learnt from it to explain the behavior. We ran these machine learning algorithms by IBM SPSS Modeler 18.

### 5.4   Dataset

It is mentioned in Sect. 5.1 that the number of participants who performed information preparation behaviors is far more than that of those who did not. Therefore, we balanced the positive and negative samples of all 68 sessions by the way of random over-sampling. The size of negative samples was increased to three times and finally we got 80 sessions for modeling. Among the sessions, 70% of them were used to train the model and the rest 30% were used as the testing dataset. In order to overcome the overfitting problem of small sample size, the five-fold cross validation was applied when training the model. The results of modeling are discussed in Sect. 5.5.

### 5.5   Results of Model Evaluation

The performance of three machine learning methods is compared using classic evalua-tion metrics of precision, recall, accuracy and F1-score. Modeling results for whether the user performs the information preparation in the cross-device search on training and testing datasets are presented in Table 3. It can be seen from the training dataset that C5.0 Decision Tree predicts as well as the baseline, but Support Vector Machine performs a little poor. From the testing dataset, both C5.0 Decision Tree and Support Vector Machine outperformed the baseline and C5.0 Decision Tree presents the best performance. Meanwhile, results show the prediction of null by both the baseline and Support Vector Machine, but not by C5.0 Decision Tree, which indicates better perform-ance of C5.0 Decision Tree. Considering the evaluation results and the interpretability, we gain insight into the information preparation behavior model by examining the structure of the C5.0 Decision Tree model.

**Table 3.** Evaluation results for model training by three classifiers

| | Training | | | Testing | | |
|---|---|---|---|---|---|---|
| | Baseline | C5.0 | SVM | Baseline | C5.0 | SVM |
| TP | 41 | 42 | 33 | 15 | 17 | 14 |
| FP | 0 | 0 | 5 | 0 | 0 | 1 |
| TN | 13 | 13 | 8 | 5 | 5 | 4 |
| FN | 0 | 0 | 2 | 4 | 3 | 3 |
| Null | 1 | 0 | 7 | 1 | 0 | 3 |
| Precision | 100.0% | 100.0% | 86.8% | 100.0% | 100.0% | 93.3% |
| Recall | 100.0% | 100.0% | 94.3% | 79.0% | 85.0% | 82.4% |
| Accuracy | 100.0% | 100.0% | 85.4% | 83.3% | 88.0% | 81.8% |
| F1 | 100.0% | 100.0% | 90.4% | 88.2% | 91.9% | 87.5% |

# 6   Understanding the Information Preparation Behavior Model

### 6.1   Overview of the Model

Figure 8 shows the tree structure of information preparation behavior model. We labeled the session by *yes* and *no* based on whether the participant performed information preparation behaviors. Three rules based on C5.0 Decision Tree and regarding the information preparation behavior are presented. First, the dissatisfied click rate of information preparation is no more than 0.636. Second, when the dissatisfied click rate is over 0.636, then the valid click rate is no more than 0.467 and the first valid click time is over 13610 ms. Last, when the dissatisfied click rate is over 0.636, the valid click rate is no more than 0.467 and the first valid click time is no more than 13610 ms, then the Jaccard distance is no more than 0.778 and the satisfied click rate is no more than 0.114.

The high dissatisfied click rate (<=0.636) and the low satisfied click rate (<=0.114) indicate users' information need cannot be easily fulfilled during the information preparation phase of cross-device search. Clicks within result areas are witnessed a low frequency (<=0.467), meaning users of information preparation cannot easily find results relevant to the search task. The interval between the beginning of search and the first valid click during the information preparation is at least 14 s. In other words, users of information preparation spend over 14 s determining the result relevance. The Jaccard distance of queries between pre- and post-switch sessions is quite high (<=0.778), which illustrates the distinctive queries of information preparation.

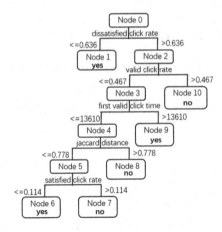

**Fig. 8.** Information preparation behavior model

## 6.2 Feature Analysis

There are five features included in the information preparation behavior model. The importance of features is calculated by the Eq. (1), in which $p$ refers to the *p-value* of F-Test. The higher *p-value* is, the more likely the feature is correlated with the information preparation behavior. Figure 9 compares the importance of features. The most important feature is dissatisfied click rate, followed by first valid click time. Features of valid click rate, satisfied click rate and Jaccard distance contribute less to the information preparation behavior model. We explore the five features in depth as following based on data of those who performed information preparation.

$$importance_i = \frac{1 - p_i}{\sum_i (1 - p_i)} \tag{1}$$

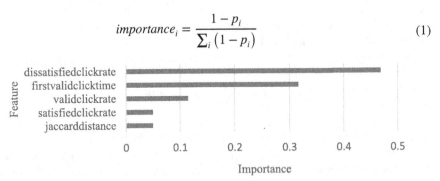

**Fig. 9.** Importance of features in information preparation behavior model

**Dissatisfied Click Rate and Satisfied Click Rate**

Distribution of the dissatisfied and satisfied click rate is shown in Table 4. Dissatisfied click rate is a little higher than satisfied click rate by comparing the average and median, however the standard deviations of those two features are similar. The result of Levene's Test illustrates the equal variances of two features and the T-test result indicates a significant difference. The number of dissatisfied clicks is significantly more than that of satisfied clicks, which induces users search the same task again on another device.

**Table 4.** Distribution of satisfied and dissatisfied click rate

| Feature | Satisfied click rate | Dissatisfied click rate |
|---------|---------------------|------------------------|
| AVE | 0.36 | 0.49 |
| MED | 0.32 | 0.51 |
| SD | 0.25 | 0.26 |
| F(sig.) | 0.46 | |
| t(sig.) | 0.00 | |

### First Valid Click Time

The length of time taken to conduct the first click within result areas varies a lot, with about 2 s the shortest and 19 min the longest. We compare the distribution of first valid click time and first click as presented in Fig. 10. Both types of the click mainly occur within 1 min from the beginning of search, and the frequency drops as the time increases. The frequency of first valid click is less than that of first click within the time of 1 min, then exceeding the first click when the time is over 1 min. Significant difference of distributions of first valid click time and first click time is concluded by sig. = 0.01 of Levene's Test and sig. = 0.03 of T-test.

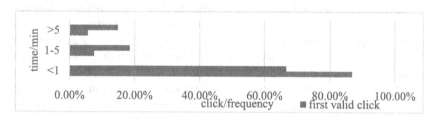

**Fig. 10.** Contrast of first valid click time and first click time

### Valid Click Rate

Clicking within result areas can be considered as a useful and effective search behavior. The average of valid click rate is 0.55 with the standard deviation of 0.27, implying a better than general level of search performance. We further investigated the distribution of valid clicks in the session of 20 min, showing in Fig. 11. It is found that valid clicks focus on three periods of the session, which are the very beginning, middle back and near ending of the session. K-means clustering method is applied to find the specific time of three focusing periods and results show three cluster centers are 2, 9 and 16 min respectively (see Table 5).

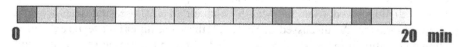

**Fig. 11.** Distribution of valid click rate in the session

**Table 5.** Clustering valid clicks in a session

| Cluster | Center/time | Item number |
|---------|-------------|-------------|
| 1       | 2.46        | 153         |
| 2       | 16.17       | 164         |
| 3       | 9.41        | 132         |

**Jaccard Distance**

This feature describes the similarity of queries between the pre- and post-switch sessions. The feature of Levenshtein edit distance illustrates the query similarity from a character perspective, while Jaccard distance is from the perspective of query terms. However, what is included in the information preparation behavior model is Jaccard distance not Levenshtein edit distance. Hence, we assume that the characteristic of query term plays more essential part in information preparation behavior. The average of Jaccard distance is 0.71 and the number of participants with Jaccard distance over 0.5 accounts for 89%. A conclusion can be drawn that queries of information preparation distinguish greatly from queries used to resume the search.

## 7 Discussion and Implication

In this paper, it is found that 5 features of dissatisfied click rate, satisfied click rate, first valid click time, valid click rate and Jaccard distance are important to characterize information preparation behaviors. An in-depth analysis of these features shows that users of information preparation are often dissatisfied with search results, leading to a continuous search on a post-switch device. Further, valid clicks are focus on three periods of the session, meaning effective searches not only occur at the beginning of information preparation. The averaged Jaccard distance of queries indicates users of information preparation tend to explore the search by different queries.

To discuss the relationship of the information preparation behavior and search behaviors of pre-switch session in a cross-device search, it is considered that not all search behaviors of pre-switch session has an effect on information preparation, though the information preparation behavior is performed before the device transition. We captured 18 features from the search behavior data on pre-switch device, however only 5 features are proved of importance to train the information preparation behavior model.

Speaking of the information preparation and cross-session search, on the one hand, the information preparation behavior of cross-device search has something in common with the search behavior of cross-session search. It is shown that queries of information preparation are of variety, shown by the wide Jaccard distance. Similarly, this variation characteristic of queries was observed in cross-session search by the ref. [9]. On the other hand, the information preparation behavior of cross-device search is distinguished from the search behavior of cross-session search by the feature importance. As discussed in Sect. 6.2, the most important feature of information preparation is dissatisfied click rate and 4 of all 5 features are associated with clicking. However, in previous studies, important features of modeling cross-session search are corresponding to querying [9, 11].

The concept of information preparation and the way of modeling information preparation behavior can provide personalized supports to cross-device search. Cross-device searchers who perform information preparation behaviors are likely to repeat the search on post-switch device. Therefore, detecting the information preparation behavior is useful to identify potential cross-device search users in advance. As it shown in feature analysis, features related to clicking are important to the information preparation behavior. It is suggested that search engines providing cross-device supporting service should attach importance to users' clicking behavior data. Due to the wide Jaccard distance of queries of information preparation, queries recommended to support cross-device search should be different from queries issued previously.

## 8 Conclusion

Interruption caused by the device transition leads to a common phenomenon of repeated searches in cross-device search. In this paper, the concept of information preparation is defined by search behaviors on pre-switch device if the search task is resumed on post-switch device. We conducted a cross-device search experiment and collected behavior data of information preparation by logs and the questionnaire. Four groups of features were extracted and we trained the information preparation behavior model by three machine learning methods. Evaluation results of Binary Logistic Regression, C5.0 Decision Tree and Support Vector Machine were compared and finally we selected the model trained by C5.0 Decision Tree. It is shown that dissatisfied click rate, satisfied click rate, first valid click time, valid click rate and Jaccard distance are included in the model. In order to build a better understanding of the information preparation behavior model, each feature was discussed in depth. This research is novel because studies of repeated search usually focus on behaviors from the angle of resumption rather than preparation. Also, cross-device search has been well-studied but the repeated search occurring in cross-device search tasks has been rarely explored.

We acknowledge the small sample size is the limitation of this paper. The future work will focus on extending the sample size. Further, we studied the information resumption behavior based on the same experiment in another paper. The further work will integrate both preparation and resumption behaviors to frame behaviors of a complete cross-device search procedure.

**Acknowledgement.** This work was supported by National Natural Science Foundation of China (Grant No. 71673204).

# References

1. Tyler, S.K., Teevan, J.: Large scale query log analysis of re-finding. In: The Third ACM International Conference on Web Search and Data Mining, pp. 191–200. ACM, NY, USA (2010)
2. Lin, S., Belkin, N.: Validation of a model of information seeking over multiple search sessions. J. Assoc. Inf. Sci. Technol. **56**(4), 393–415 (2005)
3. Geronimo, L.D., Husmann, M., Norrie, M.C.: Surveying personal device ecosystems with cross-device applications in mind. In: The 5th ACM International Symposium on Pervasive Displays, pp. 220–227. ACM, NY, USA (2016)
4. Montanez, G.D., White, R.W., Huang, X.: Cross-device search. In: The 23rd ACM International Conference on Conference on Information and Knowledge Management, pp. 1669–1678. ACM, NY, USA (2014)
5. Wang, Y., Huang, X., White, R.W.: Characterizing and supporting cross-device search tasks. In: The Sixth ACM International Conference on Web Search and Data Mining, pp. 707–716. ACM, NY, USA (2013)
6. Kim, S., Kini, N., Koh, E., et al.: Probabilistic visitor stitching on cross-device web logs. In: The 26th International Conference on World Wide Web, pp. 1581–1589. ACM, NY, USA (2017)
7. Han, S., He, D., Yue, Z., Brusilovsky, P.: Supporting cross-device web search with social navigation-based mobile touch interactions. In: Ricci, F., Bontcheva, K., Conlan, O. (eds.) UMAP 2015. LNCS, vol. 9146, pp. 143–155. Springer, Cham (2015). https://doi.org/10.1007/978-3-319-20267-9_12
8. Sohn, T., Mori, K., Setlur, V.: Enabling cross-device interaction with web history. In: International Conference on Human Factors in Computing Systems, CHI, Extended Abstracts, pp. 3883–3888. ACM, NY, USA (2010)
9. Kotov, A., Bennett, P.N., White, R.W., et al.: Modeling and analysis of cross-session search tasks. In: The 34th International ACM SIGIR Conference on Research and Development in Information Retrieval, pp. 5–14. ACM, NY, USA (2011)
10. Han, S., Zhen, Y., He, D.: Understanding and supporting cross-device web search for exploratory tasks with mobile touch interactions. ACM Trans. Inf. Syst. **33**(4), 1–34 (2015)
11. Wang, H., Song, Y., Chang, M.W., et al.: Learning to extract cross-session search tasks. In: The 22nd International Conference on World Wide Web, pp. 1353–1364. ACM, NY, USA (2013)
12. Teevan, J., Adar, E., Jones, R., et al.: Information re-retrieval: repeat queries in Yahoo's logs. In: The 30th Annual International ACM SIGIR Conference on Research and Development in Information Retrieval, pp. 151–158. ACM, NY, USA (2007)
13. Tyler, S.K., Zhang, Y.: Multi-session re-search: in pursuit of repetition and diversification. In: 21st ACM International Conference on Information and Knowledge Management, pp. 2055–2059. ACM, NY, USA (2012)
14. Tyler, S.K., Wang, J., Zhang, Y.: Utilizing re-finding for personalized information retrieval. In: The 19th ACM International Conference on Information and Knowledge Management, pp. 1469–1472. ACM, NY, USA (2010)
15. Teevan, J., Liebling, D. J., Geetha, G. R.: Understanding and predicting personal navigation. In: The Fourth ACM International Conference on Web search and Data Mining, pp. 85–94. ACM, NY, USA (2011)
16. Liu, P., Li, Z.: Task complexity: a review and conceptualization framework. Int. J. Indus. Ergonomics **42**(6), 553–568 (2012)

17. Guo, Q., Agichtein, E.: Ready to buy or just browsing?: detecting web searcher goals from interaction data. In: The 33rd International ACM SIGIR Conference on Research and Development in Information Retrieval, pp. 130–137. ACM, NY, USA (2010)
18. Sculley, D., Malkin, R.G., Basu, S., et al.: Predicting bounce rates in sponsored search advertisements. In: The 15th ACM SIGKDD International Conference on Knowledge Discovery and Data Mining, pp. 1325–1334. ACM, NY, USA (2009)
19. Agichtein, E., White, R.W., Dumais, S.T., et al.: Search, interrupted: understanding and predicting search task continuation. In: The 35th International ACM SIGIR Conference on Research and Development in Information Retrieval, pp. 315–324. ACM, NY, USA (2012)

# From Traditional Culture to Lifestyle - A Case Study on Local Specialties in the Lingnan Area

Zhaoqi Wu[1]([✉]), Xiao Song[1], Jie Shen[2], and Jie Tang[3]

[1] Beijing Institute of Technology,
6# Jinfeng Road, Xiangzhou District, Zhuhai, China
58013048@qq.com, 842766039@qq.com
[2] Primary School of Xiangzhou District,
No. 17 East Cuiqian Road, Xiangzhou District, Zhuhai, China
504058697@qq.com
[3] Macau University of Science and Technology,
Avenida Wai Long, Taipa, Macau, China
13612557@qq.com

**Abstract.** Local specialties or souvenirs are called 'shouxin' in the Lingnan area. Through market research on a number of shouxin enterprises in Zhuhai, this thesis contrasts different products of the same type investigated with multi-dimensional analysis, and summarizes the features and benefits of the various products. Referring to theories and experience of cultural innovation in Taiwan especially the design context "building a brand on the basis of culture and using it in daily life in the form of a specific product", it proposes that souvenir enterprises in Zhuhai could take humanity as the core of its creative design and culture as the basis. It constructs a development strategy and framework of creative design for local shouxin enterprises in Zhuhai.

**Keywords:** Cultural creative industry · Shouxin in Lingnan · Local specialties
Product design

## 1 Introduction

From Taiwan, shouxin can be a small gift and doesn't have to be expensive. And it is mostly used in occasions when you meet someone for the first time or see a relative, a friend, a colleague or a teacher again after a long separation. The word shouxin is widely used throughout Lingnan in areas such as Guangdong, Guangxi, Hainan, Hong Kong and Macau, and it represent culture and lifestyle in the region. Shouxin becomes one of the important carriers of the local lifestyle with high endemicity, strong cultural features, ease of use, accessibility and affordable.

It's quite clear that an essential difference exists between shouxin and souvenirs. On one hand, a souvenir is set commemorating as its core concept, its product categories are usually crafts and daily necessities. Bought on journey, souvenirs definitely represent certain aspects of the tourist spot and serve its value in a specific limited of time. The word "cultural and creative product" can also explain it. If only from literally, it is designed based on culture combined with originality as its core concept. It covers a

© Springer International Publishing AG, part of Springer Nature 2018
P.-L. P. Rau (Ed.): CCD 2018, LNCS 10911, pp. 250–258, 2018.
https://doi.org/10.1007/978-3-319-92141-9_19

wider range involving more content centering on any crafts and daily necessities which can be redesigned and sold depending on local culture. On the other hand, shouxin refers mostly to food products, but includes more than local specialties. While in this thesis, shouxin refers to an extended scope of objects including many souvenirs and cultural creative products.

## 2  Classification and Characteristics of Shouxin Products in Zhuhai

Being endowed with a broader meaning in modern society, shouxin products have grown to include crafts as well as more and more other products besides food items. From 2015 to 2017, in order to boost tourism, promote local culture and make the local characteristics prominent, Zhuhai selected a total of 22 products as the representative shouxin for the city, including four food items, four crafts and fourteen daily commodities. Most of the selected products are easy to carry and affordable, but not all of them are highly endemic with strong cultural characteristics, some of them don't even have such characteristics at all. Therefore, some of these products have been "shouxinized". Great design plays a vital role in making them local representative shouxin products by focusing on cultural creativity development to effectively improve the shouxin characteristics and its cultural value.

Nine pieces of the products were selected for our market research to gain further insight into shouxin enterprises, their representative products and design features for organizing targeted design thoughts. Including three of food, three of crafts and three of daily commodities, the nine pieces' characteristics, selling points and design feature of the nine pieces were analyzed and concluded as Table 1 below.

As a coastal city, Zhuhai is known as "City of a Hundred Islands", seafood is the main aquatic product of Zhuhai where seafood souvenir is also a market that many food enterprises actively explore. The products provided by the three enterprises include ready-to-eat seafood (Fig. 1), frozen seafood (Fig. 2) and Duck Feet Wraps which are included into intangible heritage (Fig. 3). These three items are highly endemic with favorable market prospect and good reputation score, well accepted by retailers and consumers. However, disadvantages are also obvious especially poor design. The package forms and design are still following those from more than ten years ago, the graphics and texts of the packages are not seriously designed but casually processed with grafting of photos. Besides, the attributes of the food are not well considered in package color selection, and the unappealing colors can't bring strong visual identity.

Crafts are one of the essential shouxin categories. One of the selected crafts is a Craved Glass Plate (Fig. 4), which features special multi-layer glass carving craft and the graphic design of the plate. The second is Tin Tea Canister (Fig. 5), of which the main selling point is physical attributes of the metal such as good sealing and sterilizing functions, as well as the graphic design and carving of the body. The third is a miniature metal model of Amussium Theater, a new landmark building of Zhuhai (Fig. 6), mainly for display with major selling point of local representative shape. All the three products are easy to carry and affordable, but weak in representing culture of

**Table 1.** Advantages and disadvantages of different products

| Product name | Food | | | Crafts | | | Daily commodities | | |
|---|---|---|---|---|---|---|---|---|---|
| | Conghai aquatic product | Zhenzhi local specialty pack | Zhao's duck Feet wraps | Tin tea canister | Glass carving plate | Miniature model of the theater | Swan bottle opener | Pocket umbrella | Ceramic telescope |
| Characteristics & selling points | Fresh, special processing | Instant food, popular flavor | Great taste & local culture | Tin material | Special craft and design of multi-layer glass carving | Miniature model of the landmark building of zhuhai | Attractive appearance, electric, wine culture | Special design that free your hands | Easy to carry, convenient |
| Shouxin characteristics | Accessibility affordable, high endemicity | Ease of use, accessibility affordable, high endemicity | Accessibility affordable | Accessibility affordable | Accessibility affordable | Accessibility affordable | Ease of use, accessibility affordable | Accessibility affordable | Accessibility affordable |
| Disadvantages | Weak brand influence, package design, lack of cultural characteristics | Weak brand influence, package design, lack of cultural characteristics | Lack of cultural characteristics and low endemicity | Lack of cultural characteristics and low local endemicity, weak design | Lack of cultural characteristics and low endemicity | Lack of cultural characteristics and weak package design | Lack of cultural characteristics and low endemicity | Lack of cultural characteristics and low endemicity | Lack of cultural characteristics and low endemicity |

**Fig. 1.** Conghai    aquatic    **Fig. 2.** Zhenzhi seafood    **Fig. 3.** Duck feet wraps
product

**Fig. 4.** Carved    glass    **Fig. 5.** Tin tea canister    **Fig. 6.** Miniature model
plate

Chinese traditional crafts. What's more, they can't represent the characteristics and heritage of the local endemic crafts.

Compared with the two categories above, daily commodities cover a wider range and involve more products. All the three selected products, a wine bottle opener (Fig. 7), a pocket umbrella (Fig. 8) and a ceramic telescope (Fig. 9) are easy to carry and affordable. The wine bottle opener is one of a product series based on wine culture. Under the design and development idea of products related to wine tasting, this product series has relatively integrated logic of design with distinct design appearance and features. The pocket umbrella is designed and marketed around the selling point of its hand-freeing handle design, but it's rather weak in cultural representativeness and endemicity. Featured by its body of ceramic material, the ceramic telescope bears cultural value in the form of "ink painting outlined in gold".

The different products above have different characteristic in package, product and technology design, and design concept. How to construct idea and models of creative design products for a certain category is the key question for the following discussion.

**Fig. 7.** Bottle opener

**Fig. 8.** Pocket umbrella

**Fig. 9.** Ceramic telescope (Color figure online)

## 3  Analysis on Shouxin Products Under the Idea of "Building a Brand on the Basis of Culture and Using it in Daily Life in the Form of a Specific Product"

Professor Rung-Tai Lin of National Taiwan University of Arts proposed the business model "building a brand on the basis of culture and using it in daily life in the form of a specific product" [1] for the cultural creative industry of Taiwan. This model guides well the development of products, design, packaging and brand building analyzed in this thesis. The three products of the daily commodity category are selected and analyzed for establishing design idea and a model for this category.

"On the basis of culture" means that the product design (shape, pattern, color, structure, use, etc.) shall be originated from culture instead of pure imagination or casual transplantation. "In the form of a specific product" means various forms and shapes originated from culture should be used for product design. "Using in daily life" means the products experienced the previous two processes should be used and accepted in various life styles. "Building a brand" means the product design rooted in culture will certainly be accepted by market and build great brand image. The four processes are closely related to each other step by step in logic and can well guide shouxin products design.

Being one of numerous product lines, the Swan Bottle Opener (Figs. 10 and 11) catches one's eye by its appearance. Based on the outline of two swans face to face, it reserves lines which can best describe as having a swan appearance with high visual tension by segmenting the original lines. However, no cultural origin can be found in such aspects as its color, structure and use method when exploring the cultural source. Consumers won't feel or experience endemicity and cultural characteristics when they buy and use these products, which in turn can barely be regarded as shouxin, but rather as an average commodity. The manufacturer of these products cannot be seen as a shouxin enterprise with brand benefit or firm corporate culture and market recognition.

The most attractive feature of the pocket umbrella is the modification of the normal umbrella handle (Figs. 12 and 13). The handle is the only sector of the umbrella in contact with people's hand when an umbrella is opened. [2] Fully understanding umbrella's restriction of people's hands during use, the designer considers it necessary to redesign the handle to relieve fatigue from holding umbrella during long use.

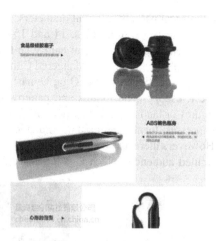

**Fig. 10.** Swan bottle opener

**Fig. 11.** Details of the bottle opener

However, only the handle, not the entire umbrella, is redesigned, and no trace of cultural origin or ergonomics has been added. The clamping of the handle with clothes does help when hands are not free, but the size of the handle is clearly not enough when held by hand. The design catches one but loses another in the lack of further optimization of the shape and material, resulting in an uncomfortable holding experience. As to the umbrella cover which takes up the largest area, it doesn't represent the local culture or endemicity of Zhuhai because of no further design or conception on the color, pattern and material. Thus, there is still much left for improvement on the way of enhancing culture transmission through shouxin, which we can call it 'souvenirizing'.

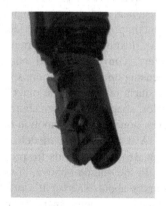

**Fig. 12.** Handle design details 1

**Fig. 13.** Handle design details 2

Compared with the umbrella, the Ceramic Telescope has an even narrower application range and more limitation for users. It's classified as artware by its material and daily commodity by its usability. The telescope has a simple shape consisting of several cylindrical parts in different diameters. Its two ends are made of metal material and the body part of ceramic (Figs. 14 and 15). In respect of "on the basis of culture", traditional cultural elements can hardly be found from its shape but can be found some in the graphic pattern. An endangered Chinese traditional technique "ink painting outlined in gold" originated in the Qing Dynasty is adopted on the body surface and pattern of the telescope. The figures and patterns include iconic subjects of Zhuhai, traditional figures or landscape, or reproductions of famous Chinese painting works. This product expresses local culture and endemicity to some extent with an affordable price. However, there isn't much value added through "using in daily life" because of its limited audience, which also limits its ability in "building a brand".

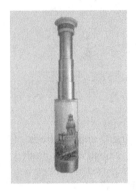 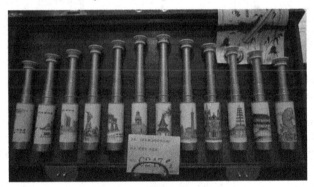

**Fig. 14.** Ceramic tele-scope (Color figure online)    **Fig. 15.** Ceramic telescope set (Color figure online)

Culture is a complex combination of value, taste and life style [1]. From design of the three shouxin products above, we see an inability to deliver cultural identity to consumers and designs which stay on a rather primary level. The creative design of shouxin products can be divided into three levels: outer (appearance) level focusing on color, texture, shape, pattern and etc., middle (behavior) level focusing on operability, safety, convenience and constitutive property, and the inner (psychology) level focusing on story, emotion, special meaning and culture [3]. It is evident that the three products remain on the outer level, as it pays much attention on primary design of color, shape and pattern, but little attention on constitutive property and operability, even none on story, emotion or culture.

A 3-dimensional model of consumer, market and provider is shown as below (Fig. 16) for the needs for product design.

In the diagram above, "functionality" refers to the most primary demand of consumers about whether it's practical. "Appearance" refers to shape, form and so on, reflecting further demand from consumers and market. Meaning personalization and differentiation, "model" is the demand at an even higher level. And "emotion" means being designed in emotional and experience-oriented way. Design reflects life taste, creativity represents acceptance based on affection, [3] which are the highest of consumers and the market. Building a brand will be well-reasoned if a provider or the designer can pay close attention to these demands.

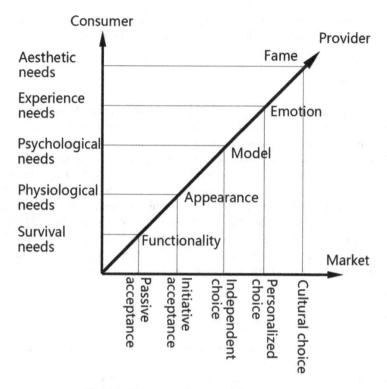

**Fig. 16.** Schematic diagram of the 3D model

It can be seen from the graph above that needs of consumers and market change gradually. The consumers develop their wants from survival needs at the primary level to experiencing and aesthetic needs at the top, while the market's needs change from passive acceptance to initiative choice of cultural consumption. Accordingly, the provider is supposed to attach importance on creative design and develop from the primary stage of focusing on functionality and appearance to the higher levels of differentiation and emotion. The core value of design is the integration of art, culture and technology to solve social problems and redefine life style. [1] The function diagram shows the market, consumers and enterprises' wants and choices at different stages considering. If enterprise is unable to keep pace with the two other factors, it is up against unfavorable situation of being replaced by an alternative provider at the whims of either the market or consumers.

Designers are supposed to consistently think about all the matters in the consideration of enterprises, market and consumption factors. The model in the diagram guides significantly both cultural creative products and the generalized conception of shouxin mentioned above. Not only crafts and daily necessities, but also food package designs are expected to highlight aesthetic demand and cultural selection, supply products and package with emotional sense of belonging for consumers in addition to catching their eyes and arousing a psychological response. Therefore, this model is ideal as a framework for designing shouxin. The detailed thoughts and application method within the framework will be analyzed and discussed more.

## 4    Conclusion

Shouxin represents reminiscence, endemicity and local culture. Shouxin is not supposed to be created because it should be native-born and rooted in the culture. We don't deny that more and more enterprises have realized the market demand and "shouxinized" their products, or that governments put shouxin labels on some products for the development of local tourism and creative industries. However, in an age in which economy has evolved gradually from agricultural, to industrial, to a service dominated economy and now finally to the current experiential economy, consumers' pursuit for "high technology" has transitioned to the taste for "superior experience". [1] It's time for our enterprises and designers to in turn transition their practice from designing for OEM and manufacture to independent brand and aesthetic experience creation, complying with the times and market development [4].

## References

1. Lin, R.-T.: Cultural Creativity, New Taipei City: Creative Industry Institute, National Taiwan University of Arts. October 2014
2. Li, L.: Chinese Ancient Arts, Peking University Press, November 2017, 045
3. Lin, R.-T.: Probe into Cultural Creative Design from Angles of Perceptual Science & Technology, User-friendly Design and Cultural Creativity, Culture and Social Sciences, Issue 1, Volume 11
4. Lin, R.-T.: Cultural Creative Experience of Taiwan

# Augmenting Food Experience While Traveling Abroad by Using Mobile Augmented Reality Application

Yue Yuan[✉]

Department of Interaction Design, School of Visual Arts,
136 West 21st Street, New York City, USA
yuelilianyuan@gmail.com

**Abstract.** Local cuisine is an essential part of a travel experience. Food is not only nourishment and entertainment but also helps travelers understand the people, traditions, and culture of a particular country. However, communication gaps and lack of information make it very challenging for travelers to experience truly local cuisine and the restaurants that serve it.

In this paper, I present a solution which makes travelers' food experience manageable and engaging by combining augmented reality with location-based functions, translation for both language and currency, and food-focused social networks on smartphones.

**Keywords:** Augmented reality · Mobile devices · Food · Experience design
Travel · User-centered design · Human-computer interaction

## 1 Problems

### 1.1 Background

According to an article from the International Trade Administration [7], "Of the more than 25 subsectors that make up the travel and tourism industry, three sectors – food services, air travel, and accommodations – account for over 45% of total output." In 2016, travelers spent nearly $174 billion on food and drinks, supporting nearly 1.9 million U.S. jobs. When people travel abroad [5], tasting local cuisine is an essential part of travel experience. Beyond energy and nutrition, food also links them with entertainment and culture. Therefore, improving the travelers' experience around food while traveling abroad is significant, which can either boost or degrade local business and economic development.

© Springer International Publishing AG, part of Springer Nature 2018
P.-L. P. Rau (Ed.): CCD 2018, LNCS 10911, pp. 259–268, 2018.
https://doi.org/10.1007/978-3-319-92141-9_20

## 1.2   Research and Problems

Out of 143 travelers surveyed, over 90% were concerned about where good local restaurants were located, what true a local cuisine was, and how to best engage with a local food culture.[1]

A later set of interviews[2] helped identify two major problems:

**Language Barrier.** Language is a major barrier to understanding and communication while traveling abroad. Most American interviewees only spoke English. When they were in countries where people did not speak English, they could not communicate well with locals. For the same reason, travelers had difficulty to fully understand the regional menus and to order dishes that required them to talk with local people.

Some interviewees said that they used translation tools to translate local languages into English one word at a time to understand a local menu. Or, they translated English into the local language and then showed the translated result to a waitress while ordering food. Both activities were time-consuming and inconvenient.

**Limited Knowledge and Information About Local Restaurants and Foods.** Almost all interviewees stated they wanted to know which restaurants were favored by local people and what foods local people liked to eat, but they had little information. Therefore, some interviewees had to use online resources in advance, which was time consuming and difficult.

When asked how they chose food in a local restaurant, interviewees responded that they normally asked servers' recommendations if the servers could speak English. Or they observed what other people were eating and then evaluated whether they also were interested in that food. Some mentioned that they used Yelp or Trip Advisor to seek information for reference. However, they could not always find information, or results were too broad and there were many unrelated comments that were not about the dishes.

## 2   Solution

### 2.1   Objectives

In order to make the entire food experience easier and simpler, including helping with decisions of where to eat, what to eat, how to order, and what to do while waiting for food, I designed objectives in different stages to enhance the overall experience that solves the main problems identified in user research.

- Stage 1: Learning about a local restaurant: Showing primary information about a local restaurant is necessary, including its food, price, service, and reviews, with a special emphasis on comments from people who have eaten there several times.

---

[1] Online survey about traveling abroad conducted by the author in 2017.
[2] Remote user interviews with twenty American travelers whose ages are from 22 to 55 years old and who had previous experience traveling to foreign countries.

- Stage 2: Recommending dishes from a local menu: Aggregating related comments from different user-generated content applications and efficient on–the-fly translation will be crucial for the application, the digital translation includes both language and currency.
- Stage 3: Ordering food: Help ease communication issues with the server and make travelers easily know if the total-order price matches their budget.
- Stage 4: Waiting for food preparation: The time waiting for food could be utilized for accessing supporting editorial content about food, culture and other engaging content for a person who expressed interest and initiative in finding the best the host country has to offer.

New digital technologies make implementation and use of advance mixed reality (MR) technology easy to build and easy to use [2]. I anchor ideas in that space, as the potential is vast and adaptation is likely to become exponentially positive in years to come. I expect to use augmented reality (AR) [1] for real–time translation, user generated reviews and other supporting content. The user experience (UX) paradigm will layer digital information on top of physical local menus to bring the travelers high convenience.

## 2.2  Persona

Based on research findings from the user interviews, I have created a user profile named Steven who is 27 years old and lives in New York City. He is a travel enthusiast and a food lover, but he only speaks English. He believes that food not only means great taste but also it is a good way to learn local culture. He likes walking around to explore local restaurants and local food without a precise travel plan when traveling abroad.

However, it is not easy for Steven to get information about a local restaurant if it is good before he directly walks into or uses search engines for comments. Due to the language barrier, it is also hard for him to fully understand a local physical menu and decide what to order. Furthermore, it is time-consuming for Steven to identify helpful and relevant reviews while making a food decision among a large volume of user-generated reviews, such as on applications like Yelp, Foursquare or Trip Advisor. He hopes travelers like him discover and experience local food in an easier and simpler way.

## 2.3  Use Senario

Steven travels to Shanghai, China for one week. It is his first time to China. Based on his friends' recommendation, he installs an AR mobile app named Foodies, which can help him choose good local restaurants and good local foods with ease.

He walks around and wants to have lunch. When he passes by a local restaurant, he sees some local people go into a restaurant. He is curious and wonders if it is a good local restaurant. So, he uses Foodies to scan the name of the restaurant for information.

The screen shows rating, specialties, average price, number of returning customers. These data look good to Steven. Therefore, he walks in.

A waitress brings him a menu after he sits down. Steven uses Foodies to scan the physical menu. Instantly, a digital translated menu shows on his mobile screen. He well understands the Chinese food menu and easily knows how much a dish costs in US dollars. He is happy to see the most popular dishes highlighted on the digital menu.

He taps the non-spicy items within the most popular dishes on the filter function. Based on these filtered results, he is interested in stewed pork in brown sauce. Therefore, he taps the dish on the digital menu for more details.

A summary indicates that 90% comments from a local food application, Yelp, and Foursquare about the current dish are positive. Steven quickly scans snippets of comments that are highly relevant to this dish. Then he decides to choose it.

The screen shows dishes he has selected and the total price, which meets his budget. It is also helpful for Steven to learn how to pronounce the selected food in Chinese. Steven follows the instructions and reads them to the waitress.

When Steven is waiting for his food, Foodies suggests to him to play food games that are related to the Shanghai cuisine and the local culture to kill time. He is happy to try. Through the games, he learns some interesting information about the Shanghai food culture.

Soon, the dishes are placed on the table. He enjoys the Shanghainese food. Foodies helps make food experience more convenient for travelers like Steven while traveling abroad.

### 2.4   User Interface

I put designs and flows in traditional windows and screen-based interfaces within digital and spatial contexts (see Figures).

**Learning About a Local Restaurant.** Tourists can use Foodies to scan the name of the restaurant for primary information. Based on GPS detection, computer vision, and text recognition, the mobile phone screen shows the important information about the current restaurant, such as rating, specialties, and average cost, which are of concern to most tourists while choosing a restaurant (See Fig. 1).

**Fig. 1.** Learning about a local restaurant

**Reading and Understanding a Local Menu.** The tourists can use Foodies to scan a physical local menu for a digital translated menu shown on their mobile screen by utilizing computer vision and text recognition technologies. Therefore, tourists will understand the local food menu and easily know how much a dish costs in US dollars by real-time translation for language and currency. They also can see the most popular dishes highlighted on the digital menu by data being extracted from the Internet (See Fig. 2).

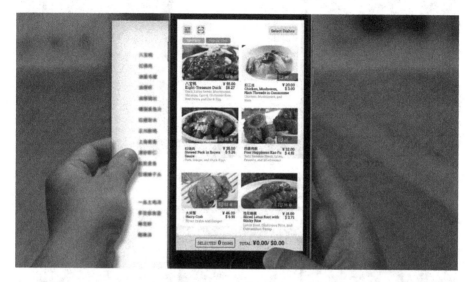

**Fig. 2.** Reading and understanding a local menu

**Filtering Dishes.** The tourists can tap filter function to further look for what to order in the digital menu. They can filter the dishes by multiple criteria, like price range, category and taste to best match the individual's preference (See Fig. 3).

**Viewing Highly Relevant Reviews About a Dish.** The tourists can see a summary of other customers' opinions about the current dish by using data mining and extracting technologies [3]. The customer reviews include positive and negative [4]. The comments aggregating in the detail page mainly are from the Dianping app, which is a local food app, Yelp, and Foursquare. Thus, the users are able to scan with ease what previous customers thought with a snippet that is highly relevant to the dish [6] (See Fig. 4).

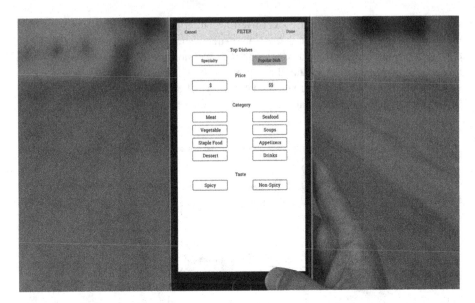

**Fig. 3.** Filtering dishes

**Fig. 4.** Viewing highly relevant reviews about a dish

**Ordering Food.** The screen shows dishes the users have selected and total price. As a result, users can know if the total price meets their personal budget. Foodies also displays how to pronounce the selected dishes and frequent phrases used in ordering the dishes in the local language. Thus, the users can follow the instructions, read, or directly show the screen to a waiter/waitress while ordering the food (See Fig. 5).

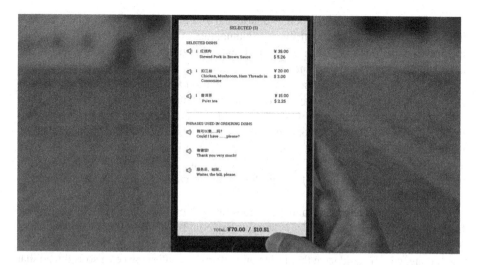

**Fig. 5.**  Ordering food.

**Learning Local Food Culture by Playing Games.**  When the tourists are waiting for food preparation, the app suggests food games that are about the local food culture. Hence, the tourists can learn the local food and culture through an engaging way (See Fig. 6).

**Fig. 6.**  Learning local food culture by playing games

## 3   Evaluation

In order to learn if the solution can enhance food experience for travelers when they travel abroad, that is if information contributes to making easily a decision about choosing restaurants and local foods. I conducted user testing with twenty-six American travelers, 22 to 49 years old, with average annual income of $74,000. Every interviewee had travel experience in countries where locals did not speak English or spoke other languages that travelers were unable to speak and understand.

Most of the interviewees thought key information about a local restaurant such as average price, special dishes, rating and service were helpful for them to make a decision for choosing a local restaurant while they stood in the front of the restaurant and used Foodies to scan the restaurant for overall impression. Some of them mentioned that they wanted to see the full menu in order to better decide if walking into or not. Because specialties were recommended by the local restaurant. They might not be interested in that. If they could view the full menu, they would have better ideas if they wanted to choose the local restaurant.

Scanning the local menu and auto-translating local language into English were favorable to all interviewees. They thought they could well understand the local menu without other's help or they did not need to input local language to Google Translator one by one, which could save them time and effort. The interviewees also believed that two prices displayed along with each dish were a creative good idea. Since the local price for a dish has been translated into US dollar based on current rate of exchange and the translated currency was displayed on the individual mobile phone screen. They did not need to spend time in doing the math on their own in order to see if the price of a dish was too high or acceptable.

When viewing details of a specific dish for more information, most interviewees stated that aggregating reviews from different applications that are about user-generated reviews were an easy and useful way for them to obtain important feedback from other customers about the quality of the food provided. Therefore, they did not need to separately open different food applications such as Yelp or Foursquare to look for reviews. It saved their time. From the perspective of the tourists, consumer experiences shared by other customers could facilitate their decision-making for food choices.

After reviewing the prototype of showing total price for selected dishes that included local price and US dollar, and phrases used in ordering the local dishes, interviewees thought the functions were pretty helpful. Most of the interviewees wanted to order the food by using local language because it was a learning process for the local food to them. Few of them wanted to know extra phrases, like how to say delicious or grateful in the local language. Since they wanted to praise if the ordered food was really great. Some interviewees said if they could not pronounce the local language clearly, they would like to directly show what they have chosen on the mobile phone to the waitress. They also suggested showing how much to tip in a foreign country. Therefore, they could better control budget.

However, it was debatable if using food games was good for the travelers to learn local food and relevant food culture. Because most interviewees stated that they did not want to play a game even if they were waiting for food. Some interviewees thought if they were children, they would be more likely to play a food game. Some of them said they preferred to directly read the simple paragraph about the introduction of local food and culture, because the paragraph was straightforward. Therefore, I redesigned the experience about how to make travelers easily discover iconic local food and good restaurants where they can eat that food and related food culture.

## 4   Conclusion

Based on the feedback from the interviewees, I updated the design for learning local food and culture while waiting for ordered dishes. Instead of the games, Foodies shows information about other traditional local foods and which best local restaurants to eat them. The users can tap "Add Food to Notes" to add to their mobile phone as a to-do list and try entries later (See Fig. 7).

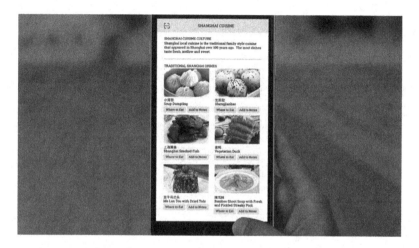

**Fig. 7.** Learning local foods by auto recommendation

Overall, I have received positive feedback from the travelers during user testing. Over 85% interviewees said they would download Foodies to assist them to more easily choose good local restaurants and local foods while traveling abroad. They believed that Foodies could simplify the process of from choosing where to eat, what to order to learn how to order and what to try on their next tours.

**Acknowledgement.** The author thanks Aaron Marcus, who is principal of Aaron Marcus and Associates, and Nitzan Hermon, a designer and researcher for their advice.

## References

1. Carmigniani, J., Furht, B., Anisetti, M., Ceravolo, P., Damiani, E., Ivkovic, M.: Augmented Reality Technologies, systems and applications. Multimed. Tools Appl. **51**(1), 341 (2010)
2. Etienne, A.: Augmented Reality in 10 Lines of HTML. https://medium.com/arjs/augmented-reality-in-10-lines-of-html-4e193ea9fdbf
3. Hu, M., Liu, B.: Mining and Summarizing Customer Reviews. University of Illinois at Chicago

4. Malik, M.S.I., Hussain, A.: Helpfulness of product reviews as a function of discrete positive and negative emotions. Comput. Hum. Behav. **73**, 290–302 (2017)
5. Marcus, A.: Mobile Persuasion Design. Springer, London, UK (2015). http://www.springer.com/gb/book/9781447143239
6. Reschke, K., Vogel, A., Jurafsky, D.: Generating Recommendation Dialogs by Extracting Information from User Reviews. Stanford University
7. Travel, Tourism & Hospitality Spotlight: The Travel, Tourism and Hospitality Industry in the United States. https://www.selectusa.gov/travel-tourism-and-hospitality-industry-united-states. Accessed 1 Sept 2017

# An Exploratory Study on Design and Implement an Emotional Karaoke Robot (EKR)

Yi-Lun Zheng[1,2,3(✉)], Pei-Luen Patrick Rau[1,2,3(✉)],
Hsiu-Ping Yueh[1,2,3(✉)], Pin-Hsuan Chen[1,2,3(✉)],
and Ding-Long Huang[1,2,3]

[1] Department of Industrial Engineering, Tsinghua University, Beijing, China
{zhengyl17, cpxl7}@mails.tsinghua.edu.cn,
rpl@mail.tsinghua.edu.cn
[2] Department of Bio-Industry Communication and Development,
National Taiwan University, Taipei, Taiwan
yueh@ntu.edu.tw
[3] Shenzhen Malong Artificial Intelligence Research Center, Shenzhen, China
dlong@malong.com

**Abstract.** The objective of this study is to design and evaluate an Emotional Karaoke Robot system (EKR) which improves user experience. An exploratory study was conducted to discover the changes of participants' emotion toward the EKR system during the experiment. 16 Chinese participants who had been to karaoke TV in the past 6 months were invited to use the EKR system. Four interactive conditions (simple interaction task, diverse neutral emotional interaction task, diverse positive emotional interaction task, diverse negative emotional interaction task) with a within-subject design were conducted. The results indicated that participants' emotional reaction were enhanced a lot during the study. The average level of arousal, hedonic value, and user satisfaction under diverse positive/negative emotional interaction condition is greater than under the neutral one. Participants in diverse positive/negative emotional interaction task felt more positive than in diverse neutral emotional interaction task. Emotional Karaoke Robot system successfully elicited participants' emotion and improved users' experience.

**Keywords:** Human-robot interaction · Interaction design · Emotional robot
Social robot · Karaoke TV

## 1 Introduction

Robot nowadays becomes involved in Human's life. Robot has been applied in various industries and bring people's daily lives more convenience and efficiency. Previous studies have revealed that social robots can be used as museum guides (Gehle et al. 2017), as information-providers at shopping malls (Kanda et al. 2009), as teaching assistants (Ferrarelli et al. 2018), mental-care for elderly people (Broadbent et al. 2014), in autism therapy (Rudovic et al. 2017). User's interactive experience is an important issue as people interact with technological artifacts. Emotional experience has recently aroused wide attention in the field of human-robot interaction (Breazeal 2003; Jokinen 2015).

Karaoke is one of the most popular recreational activities in China. The statistics from 2017 Music Industry Development Report, introduced by Music Industry Promotion Industry, showed that the total revenue of karaoke industry in China was estimated to 86.9 billion RMB. However, the number of traditional karaoke has decreased with the development of technology. Many people no longer satisfy with the physiological needs in Maslow's Hierarchy of Needs, they are seeking for love, belonging and other higher needs instead. Previous research shows that karaoke singing reflects human being's psycho-social needs (Ruismäki et al. 2013). Thus, traditional karaoke cannot meet these kinds of needs and has been gradually replaced by mini KTV, a new type of karaoke. Some mini KTVs adopt new technology as novel entertaining devices in karaoke, such as augmented reality (AR) and virtual reality (VR), in order to attract more consumers. Besides, as mini KTV popping up on the street, people can approach to karaoke more easily. According to the 2017 China Mini KTV Market Research Report, released by the AskCI Consulting, the scale of mini KTV in China is expected to hit more than 200,000 in 2022 and the market size will reach 31 billion RMB. Based on the trend of mini KTV, we explored the application of robot in karaoke environment and designed an Emotional Karaoke Robot (EKR) system in this study. The purpose of EKR system was to improve user's satisfaction and emotional experience in KTV. There were four different conditions (simple interaction task, diverse neutral emotional interaction task, diverse positive emotional interaction task, diverse negative emotional interaction task) designed to help researchers explore how participants interact with, perceive and react toward Emotional Karaoke Robot under four kinds of condition.

## 2 Literature Review

### 2.1 Emotion in Human-Robot Interaction

Emotions play a significant role in human-robot interaction and emotional behaviors are commonly used in the design of social robots. Previous studies have explored design factors which cause human empathy toward robots (Kwak et al. 2013). Kim et al. (2009) designed a robot which expressed emotional state by displaying with its bruising and complexion color. The robot could recognize humans' emotion in a conversation. A blue bruise was emerged when the robot perceived the negative emotional state of the human. Choi et al. (2014) tested the effect of robot types on emotional communication and indicated people felt more embarrassed when they interacted with tele-operated robots than autonomous robots. Wei et al. (2016) examined the effects of robots' emotional motion patterns on the user's perception of the robot. In addition, emotion recognition system was established by Devillers et al. (2015) and the system could further drive the expressive behavior of the robot.

Affection is a specific set involving emotions, moods, or attitude, among which the intensity of emotion is the most significant. Emotion is a dynamic process between organism and environment (Lazarus 1982). In psychology research, there are two primary approaches used to describe emotions: One is "dimensional approach" (continuous), which describes the full and continuous spectrum of human emotions into three independent, bipolar dimensions: Pleasure (the one perceived positively or negatively), Arousal (one's sense of energy, ranging from sleepy to excited) and Dominance (PAD) (Mehrabian and Russell 1974). The Self Assessment Manikin (SAM) is a widely adopted visual self-report tool to measure subjective feelings. The other one is "discrete emotion approach" (categorical), which describes the spectrum of human emotions as a mixture of a limited number of different basic emotions. Those basic emotions are considered to be universal and possess distinct adaptive values (Ekman 1992).

## 2.2   Human-Social Robot Interaction

It has become increasingly apparent that social robots play a crucial role in the world, collaborating with humans and engaging in people's lives. The social robot is different from an industrial robot. The core element of social robot is its interactivity with a human. Breazeal (2004) defined sociable robot as "socially intelligent in a human-like way, interacting with it is like interacting with another person". It means a sociable robot is designed to interact with human as if human being. Humanoid social robots were divided into utilitarian humanoid social robots and affective humanoid social robots (Zhao 2006). The former one was designed for instrumental purposes, whereas the latter one was used to interact with humans on an emotional level.

The term "socially interactive robot" was proposed by Fong et al. (2003) and it focused on peer-to-peer human-robot interaction. The concept of the socially interactive robot is largely different from "master-slave" command ways of conventional human-robot interaction. Therefore, "socially interactive robot" referencing "human social" characteristics such as express and perceive emotion, learn/recognize models of other agents, communicate with high level dialogue, establish and maintain social relationships, use natural cues (gaze, gestures etc.), exhibit distinctive personality and character, and learn/develop social competencies (p. 145.).

In addition, previous research indicated that usefulness, adaptability, enjoyment, sociability, companionship and perceived behavioral control are key variables for the acceptance of social robots (De Graaf and Allouch 2013). Successful human-social robot interaction requires the robot engage in properly. The most common interactive modalities in current in human-robot interaction could be inducted as follows:

1. Appearance: Mori (1970) proposed the well-known uncanny valley hypothesis, which suggested the relationship between the degree of a human-like object and emotional response to the object. The more humanoid object, the more likable people perceive. However, an object in real human being appearance would elicit uncannily and make people feel revulsion. Nevertheless, Goetz et al. (2003) suggested that a robot's appearance and behavior should match the situation which people expect the robot's role in. Hence, participants did not always choose the more humanlike one in their experiment but preferred the robot's appearance matched the sociability required.

2. Gestures: Sidner et al. (2005) indicated the engagement gestural abilities of robots attract humans' attention directly. Riek et al. (2010) showed that gesture type and gesture style of a robot significantly affected overall reaction and cooperation time when interacting with a robot.

3. Speech: Conversation is a basic way of social interaction. Kanda et al. (2002) indicated that subjects interacted with the robot in the similar way of communicate with humans. In the experiment, they observed subjects performed interpersonal behaviors such as giving responses to the robot and voluntarily spoke to it. Hence, a conversational robot may be designed to communicate with humans seamlessly and effectively with the human voice.

4. Emotion: Emotional interaction is a key issue in HRI. An emotional interactive social robot can benefit from its natural and human manner interaction. Emotion expression through multimodal communication channels. For instance, some studies focused on face-based emotion expressions (Kirby et al. 2010; Kishi et al. 2012), gesturing (wei et al. 2016), and emotional speech (Devillers et al. 2015). Hence, in the design of the emotional social robot, emotional expression, including facial expression, body movement and gesture, and speech and vocalization, should be taken into consideration.

### Hypotheses

We expect the interaction with Emotional Karaoke Robot will improve participants' psychological well-being in all four experimental conditions. Due to manipulation of the level of emotional enhancement and fulfillment by the robot, we predict each task will have a different effect. Based on the overview above, we draw the following hypotheses:

- Participants' emotional reactions will be enhanced during the experiment.
- Participants under positive/negative emotional interaction condition will have stronger emotional reactions than under neutral condition.
- Participants under positive/negative emotional interaction condition will rate higher user satisfaction scores than under neutral condition.

## 3   Concept Design

An overview of the system architecture is shown in Fig. 1. There are three main parts of EKR system that create human-robot interaction: sensor, dialogue, and motion. The speech and visual input signals are detected by sensors embedded in the NAO robot. The sensor is capable of detecting the presence of a person. Nao can detect human faces and track users. The face detection module enables better non-verbal human-robot interaction. Moreover, Nao has four directional microphones and loud-speakers. The speech dialogue interactive system comprises user's input speech reception and speech response delivery. The robot identifies the user and has eye contact with the user to make the interaction more natural. The speech recognition module makes NAO recognize users' voice and provide adequate feedback. It generates the movement corresponding to the speech content simultaneously.

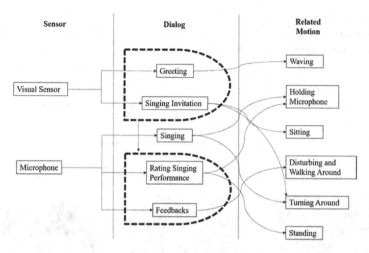

**Fig. 1.** Concept of the EKR system design

# 4  Method

## 4.1  Participants

16 subjects, including 8 men and 8 women (mean age M = 23), were recruited from Tsinghua University. Besides, participants have been to karaoke in the past 6 month (mean times M = 3). Informed consents were written by all subjects prior to the experiment. At the end of experiment, each of them was paid 20 RMB for participation.

## 4.2  Apparatus

We employed NAO robot in our experiment for three reasons. Firstly, NAO robot is an interactive medium-sized humanoid robot. Previous research showed that human-like appearance facilitates an intuitive style and familiarity (Oztop et al. 2005). Secondly, the appearance of NAO robot is lifelike. Moreover, with 25 degree of freedom and a suite of joint sensors, NAO can move smoothly and flexibly. (SoftBank Robotics 2017).

## 4.3  Scenarios

The NAO robot was pre-programmed to interact with the participants, and each participant interacted alone with NAO in a room lasted on average for 40 to 50 min. The procedure for the simple interaction task session was as follows:

1. NAO greeted the participant with a hand wave and gave a brief self-introduction.
2. NAO sang the song "Actor" written by Xue Zhiqian
3. The participant sang a song
4. NAO sang the song "She Says" written by Lin Junjie
5. The participant sang a song

6. The participant sang a song
7. The session was finished by the robot saying, "Nice meeting you and thanks for having a great karaoke experience"

In our experiment, we programmed three main motions in different situations. They were waving, holding microphone and sitting respectively. Table 1 showed how NAO performed in the real scenes. In addition, the experiment set-up was shown in Fig. 2.

**Table 1.** NAO's three main motions

| Waving | Holding microphone | Sitting |
|---|---|---|
| | | |
| 1.NAO greeted the participant with a hand wave and gave a brief self-introduction. 7. NAO said, " Nice to meet you and thanks for having a great karaoke experience " | 2.NAO sang the song "Actor" written by Xue Zhiqian 4.NAO sang the song "She Says" written by Lin Junjie | 3.The participant sang the first song 5.The participant sang the second song 6.The participant sang the third song |

## 4.4 Task and Procedure

We designed four conditions, which were associated with certain feeling that could be triggered within participants. A within-subject design was adopted to each subject and we explored important factors that affect users' satisfaction with Emotional Karaoke Robot. The details in four tasks were described as follow:

**Task 1** is a basic set, called Simple interaction task. The NAO robot and the participant sang song by turns. The experiment design of human-robot interaction was less. And it would not provoke negative or positive feelings within the participant.

**Task 2** is a diverse neutral emotional interaction task, which is the set that the robot had more interactions with the human, such as imitating another singer, bringing a dance show.

**Task 3** is called diverse positive emotional interaction task, which is the set of eliciting positive emotion. Namely, NAO robot tend to give the participant positive feedback and the lucky money will be sent as reward via WeChat after his/her singing.

**Fig. 2.** Experiment set-up: participants sang songs with the robot

In addition, participants also sent lucky money to robot, and the amount of lucky money depends on the performance of robot. It is also an alternative way to grade the robot's singing performance.

While **Task 4** is diverse negative emotional interaction task, which is the set of eliciting negative emotion. In other words, NAO robot will interrupt the participant directly during the singing and give the participant negative feedback.

Speaking of the experiment procedure, participants were given a brief description of the experiment's procedure and the consent form after arriving the laboratory. Then, they were provided with a pre-test questionnaire, which is about the perception of robot. After listening to the "Weightless" music, participants assessed their affective state with the SAM (Self-Assessment Manikin) scales and DES (Differential Emotion Scale).

In the period of the experiment, they interacted with NAO and followed NAO's instructions. At the end of the task, participants had to fill out the post-test questionnaire, including SAM scales, DES, hedonic value and satisfaction. Afterwards, each participant was asked for a brief interview and was paid a 20 RMB participation fee.

### 4.5   Measures and Analysis

In order to assess participants' affective state, the Self-Assessment Manikin (SAM) and Differential Emotion Scale (DES) (5-point Likert scale) were used. And the four-item hedonic value questionnaire (5-point Likert scale) from Wu et al. (2015) was adopted. (e.g., 'I had a good time singing here because I felt a sense of freedom', 'I enjoyed being immersed in singing songs here', 'Compared to other things, the experience was truly enjoyable', 'Compared to other things, the experience was truly enjoyable'). Furthermore, we evaluated the design of Emotional Karaoke Robot system via the fourteen-item satisfaction questionnaire, which was proposed by Cook (1991).

## 5   Results and Discussion

### 5.1   Quantitative Data (Questionnaire Results)

*How do the participants perceive and their affect toward Emotional Karaoke Robot in the four different conditions?*

The results of participants' emotions toward robot interaction from the Self-Assessment Manikin (SAM) questionnaire were shown in Figs. 3 and 4. Participants in task 1, task 3 and task 4 had the same average arousal level ($M = 4.25$), which was higher than task 2 ($M = 4.00$) (Fig. 3). An analysis of the ratings of the robot's valence indicated that participants in task 3 had a highest average score ($M = 4.75$) (Fig. 4). In a sequence were task 4 ($M = 4.5$), task 1 ($M = 4.25$), and task 2 ($M = 4.00$). Among all the four tasks, average rating of the robot's valence lay between 4 to 4.75 on the five-point scale. Therefore, the results showed that participants had positive attitudes toward Emotional Karaoke Robot.

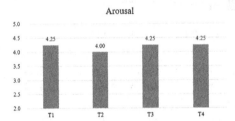

**Fig. 3.** Average ratings of the robot's arousal of all tasks from questionnaire

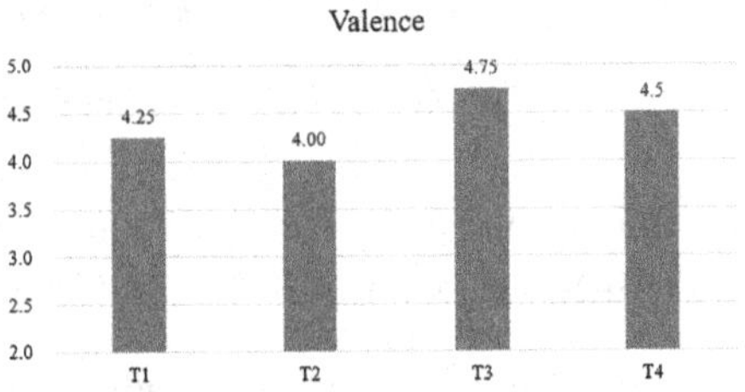

**Fig. 4.** Average ratings of the robot's valence of all tasks from questionnaire

For the analysis of hedonic value, the mean hedonic value score of task 3 was the highest (4.63) while the followings were task 1 (4.31), task 4 (4.06), and task 2 (3.56) (Fig. 5). Thus, the results suggested that participants in task 1, task 3, and task 4 had great hedonic experiences.

In terms of the analysis of satisfaction, the mean satisfaction score was 4.64 in task 1 group, 4.52 in task 2 group, 5.3 in task 3 group, and 5.38 in task 4 group (Fig. 6). Hence, participants in diverse **positive/negative** emotional interaction task rated higher satisfaction scores than in diverse **neutral** emotional interaction task.

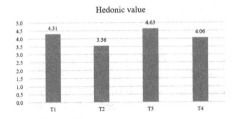

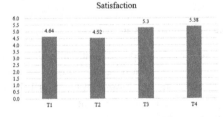

**Fig. 5.** Average ratings of the robot's hedonic value of all tasks from questionnaire

**Fig. 6.** Average ratings of the robot's satisfaction of all tasks from questionnaire

According to the analysis of pre and post emotion, we found that no matter what task it was, all participants were aroused and had positive emotional reactions in the period of the experiment (Figs. 7 and 8).

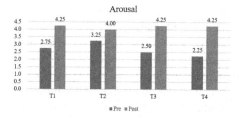

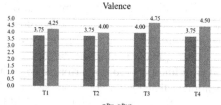

**Fig. 7.** Average ratings of the robot's arousal of all tasks from pre-post questionnaire

**Fig. 8.** Average ratings of the robot's valence of all tasks from pre-post questionnaire

Figure 9 showed the overall differential emotion scale (DES) scores of participants before and after the experiment under four tasks. Based on the DES analysis, participants felt more interested, joyful and surprised after the experiment stimulus.

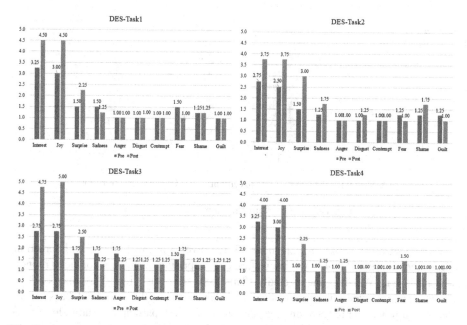

**Fig. 9.** Average ratings of the robot's differential emotion of all tasks from pre-post questionnaire

## 5.2   Qualitative Data (Observations of Interactions with ERK)

*How do the participants interact with Emotional Karaoke Robot?*

We observed participants' interaction from three perspectives during the experiment, including sing with the robot, movement and respond to the robot (Fig. 10). In the dimension of singing with the robot, there were 11 participants (11 out of 16) singing with the robot. As for the movement of robot, participants felt surprised and awesome while watching the dancing robot. Furthermore, most participants (8 out of 12) gave full marks to the performance of the robot. In the interview, many participants mentioned that they were impressed a lot when they saw the robot performing the Gangnam Style dance. From the aspect of responding to the robot, only five-sixteenths participants greeted the robot with hand waving. But more than half participants (10 out of 16) responded or talked to the robot. For instance, one participant asked the robot, "Can you sing Cantonese song?"

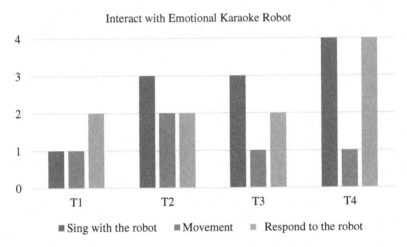

**Fig. 10.**   Interact with Emotional Karaoke Robot

Moreover, those who took part in task 3, the diverse positive emotional interaction task, further expressed that it was interesting and surprising when they got lucky money from robot via WeChat unexpectedly. This behavior was viewed as one kind of encouragement to their performance and it also motivate them to send back lucky money as a reward to robot's singing performance. Also, participants' attitude toward sending lucky money was optimistic (Table 2).

**Table 2.** Interact scenes

| Sing with the robot | Movement (greet) | Reaction to the danc-ing robot | WeChat's Lucky Money reward |
|---|---|---|---|

# 6   Conclusion

This study applied the robot to karaoke and explored the design and the implementation by conducting experiments. The experiment results showed that the participants were successfully aroused and affected by Emotional Karaoke Robot during the experiment time. The participants felt interested, joyful and surprised while interacting with the robot in the period of the experiment. Hence, designers can refer the design system of Emotional Karaoke Robot. The average level of arousal, hedonic value, and user satisfaction under diverse positive/negative emotional interaction condition is greater than under the neutral one. Moreover, participants in diverse positive/negative emotional interaction task felt more positive than in diverse neutral emotional interaction task.

However, this study has several limitations. First, the sample size was small. Only 16 participants were recruited in the experiment and only 4 participants were tested for each condition. Second, participants had positive attitudes toward the Emotional Karaoke Robot on the whole. It was a new thing for all participants to sing with the robot. Therefore, long-term interaction should be take into consideration. Finally, participants' personality and attitude toward robot would influence their behavior. According to previous studies, people with gender, age, cultural background, and region difference have an impact on their acceptance toward social robot (Kaplan 2004; Rau et al. 2009). As a result, these variables should be taken into account in designing the social robots.

In conclusion, people's attitude is positive toward the application of robot in karaoke. And appropriate feedbacks will lead more hedonic and satisfied for people, which tend to arouse people's emotions and also elevate the circumstance of karaoke environment. With the combination to some social media, for example, the lucky money in WeChat, also a good way to enhance people's motivation to use robot as their partner in karaoke.

**Acknowledgement.** This research was supported by Shenzhen Malong Artificial Intelligence Research Center.

# References

AskCI Consulting. http://www.askci.com/reports/20161104/1423415293732347.shtml

Breazeal, C.: Emotion and sociable humanoid robots. Int. J. Hum Comput Stud. **59**(1), 119–155 (2003). https://doi.org/10.1016/S1071-5819(03)00018-1

Breazeal, C.L.: Designing Sociable Robots. The MIT Press, Cambridge (2004)

Broadbent, E., Peri, K., Kerse, N., Jayawardena, C., Kuo, I., Datta, C., MacDonald, B.: Robots in older people's homes to improve medication adherence and quality of life: a randomised cross-over trial. In: Beetz, M., Johnston, B. (eds.) ICSR 2014. LNCS (LNAI), vol. 8755, pp. 64–73. Springer, Cham (2014). https://doi.org/10.1007/978-3-319-11973-1_7

Choi, J.J., Kim, Y., Kwak, S.S.: Are you embarrassed? The impact of robot types on emotional engagement with a robot. In: 2014 ACM/IEEE International Conference on Human-robot Interaction, pp. 138–139. ACM, Bielefeld (2014). https://doi.org/10.1145/2559636.2559798

Cook, J.R.: Cognitive and social factors in the design of computerized jobs. Doctoral Dissertation, Purdue University, West Lafayette, Indiana (1991)

De Graaf, M.M., Allouch, S.B.: Exploring influencing variables for the acceptance of social robots. Robot. Auton. Syst. **61**(12), 1476–1486 (2013). https://doi.org/10.1016/j.robot.2013.07.007

Devillers, L., Tahon, M., Sehili, M.A., Delaborde, A.: Inference of human beings' emotional states from speech in human–robot interactions. Int. J. Soc. Robot. **7**(4), 451–463 (2015). https://doi.org/10.1007/s12369-015-0297-8

Ekman, P.: An argument for basic emotions. Cogn. Emot. **6**(3–4), 169–200 (1992). https://doi.org/10.1080/02699939208411068

Ferrarelli, P., Lázaro, María T., Iocchi, L.: Design of robot teaching assistants through multi-modal human-robot interactions. In: Lepuschitz, W., Merdan, M., Koppensteiner, G., Balogh, R. (eds.) RiE 2017. AISC, vol. 630, pp. 274–286. Springer, Cham (2018). https://doi.org/10.1007/978-3-319-62875-2_25

Fong, T., Nourbakhsh, I., Dautenhahn, K.: A survey of socially interactive robots. Robot. Auton. Syst. **42**(3–4), 143–166 (2003). https://doi.org/10.1016/S0921-8890(02)00372-X

Gehle, R., Pitsch, K., Dankert, T., Wrede, S.: How to open an interaction between robot and museum visitor? Strategies to establish a focused encounter in HRI. In: 2017 ACM/IEEE International Conference on Human-Robot Interaction, pp. 187–195. ACM, Vienna (2017). https://doi.org/10.1145/2909824.3020219

Goetz, J., Kiesler, S., Powers, A.: Matching robot appearance and behavior to tasks to improve human–robot cooperation. In: 12th IEEE International Workshop on Robot and Human Interactive Communication (Roman 2003), pp. 55–60. IEEE, Millbrae (2003). https://doi.org/10.1109/roman.2003.1251796

Jokinen, J.P.: Emotional user experience: traits, events, and states. Int. J. Hum Comput Stud. **76**, 67–77 (2015). https://doi.org/10.1016/j.ijhcs.2014.12.006

Kanda, T., Ishiguro, H., Ono, T., Imai, M., Nakatsu, R.: Development and evaluation of an interactive humanoid robot "Robovie". In: Proceedings of IEEE International Conference on Robotics and Automation (ICRA 2002), pp. 1848–1855. IEEE, Washington (2002). https://doi.org/10.1109/robot.2002.1014810

Kanda, T., Shiomi, M., Miyashita, Z., Ishiguro, H., Hagita, N.: An affective guide robot in a shopping mall. In: 4th ACM/IEEE International Conference on Human Robot Interaction, pp. 173–180. ACM, New York (2009). https://doi.org/10.1145/1514095.1514127

Kaplan, F.: Who is afraid of the humanoid? Investigating cultural differences in the acceptance of robots. Int. J. Humanoid Rob. **1**(03), 465–480 (2004). https://doi.org/10.1142/S0219843604000289

Kim, E.H., Kwak, S.S., Kwak, Y.K.: Can robotic emotional expressions induce a human to empathize with a robot? In: 18th IEEE International Symposium on Robot and Human Interactive Communication (ROMAN), pp. 358–362. IEEE, Toyama (2009). https://doi.org/10.1109/roman.2009.5326282

Kim, E.H., Kwak, S.S., Hyun, K.H., Kim, S.H., Kwak, Y.K.: Design and development of an emotional interaction robot, mung. Adv. Robot. **23**(6), 767–784 (2009). https://doi.org/10.1163/156855309X431712

Kirby, R., Forlizzi, J., Simmons, R.: Affective social robots. Robot. Auton. Syst. **58**(3), 322–332 (2010). https://doi.org/10.1016/j.robot.2009.09.015

Kishi, T., Otani, T., Endo, N., Kryczka, P., Hashimoto, K., Nakata, K., Takanishi, A.: Development of expressive robotic head for bipedal humanoid robot. In: Intelligent Robots and Systems (IROS), pp. 4584–4589. IEEE, Portugal (2012). https://doi.org/10.1109/iros.2012.6386050

Kwak, S.S., Kim, Y., Kim, E., Shin, C., Cho, K.: What makes people empathize with an emotional robot? The impact of agency and physical embodiment on human empathy for a robot. In: 22nd IEEE International Symposium on Robot and Human Interactive Communication, pp. 180–185. IEEE, Gyeongju (2013). https://doi.org/10.1109/roman.2013.6628441

Lazarus, R.S.: Thoughts on the relations between emotion and cognition. Am. Psychol. **37**(9), 1019–1024 (1982). https://doi.org/10.1037/0003-066X.37.9.1019

Mehrabian, A., Russell, J.A.: An Approach to Environmental Psychology. The MIT Press, Cambridge (1974)

Mori, M.: The uncanny valley. Energy **7**(4), 33–35 (1970)

Oztop, E., Franklin, D.W., Chaminade, T., Cheng, G.: Human–humanoid interaction: is a humanoid robot perceived as a human? Int. J. Humanoid Rob. **2**(04), 537–559 (2005). https://doi.org/10.1142/S0219843605000582

Rau, P.P., Li, Y., Li, D.: Effects of communication style and culture on ability to accept recommendations from robots. Comput. Hum. Behav. **25**(2), 587–595 (2009). https://doi.org/10.1016/j.chb.2008.12.025

Riek, L.D., Rabinowitch, T.C., Bremner, P., Pipe, A.G., Fraser, M., Robinson, P.: Cooperative gestures: effective signaling for humanoid robots. In: 5th ACM/IEEE International Conference on Human-robot Interaction, pp. 61–68. IEEE, Osaka (2010). https://doi.org/10.1109/hri.2010.5453266

Rudovic, O., Lee, J., Mascarell-Maricic, L., Schuller, B.W., Picard, R.W.: Measuring engagement in robot-assisted autism therapy: a cross-cultural study. Front. Robot. AI **4**, 36 (2017). https://doi.org/10.3389/frobt.2017.00036

Ruismäki, H., Antti, J., Lehtonen, K.: Karaoke – the chance to be a star. Eur. J. Soc. Behav. Sci. **7**(4), 1222–1233 (2013). https://doi.org/10.15405/ejsbs.102

Sidner, C.L., Lee, C., Kidd, C.D., Lesh, N., Rich, C.: Explorations in engagement for humans and robots. Artif. Intell. **166**(1–2), 140–164 (2005). https://doi.org/10.1016/j.artint.2005.03.005

SoftBank Robotics: Find out more about NAO. https://www.ald.softbankrobotics.com/en/robots/nao/find-out-more-about-nao

Wei, Y., Wei, Y., Zhao, J., Zhao, J.: Designing robot behavior in human robot interaction based on emotion expression. Ind. Robot Int. J. **43**(4), 380–389 (2016). https://doi.org/10.1108/IR-08-2015-0164

Wu, S.H., Huang, C.T., Chen, Y.F.: Leisure-service quality and hedonic experiences: Singing at a karaoke house as a form of theatre. Total Qual. Manag. Bus. Excell. **26**(3–4), 298–311 (2015). https://doi.org/10.1080/14783363.2013.814290

Zhao, S.: Humanoid social robots as a medium of communication. New Media Soc. **8**(3), 401–419 (2006). https://doi.org/10.1177/1461444806061951

# Cultural Differences

# Automatic Assessment of Personality Traits Using Non-verbal Cues in a Saudi Sample

Sharifa Alghowinem[✉] and Basmah AlKadhi

College of Computer and Information Sciences,
Prince Sultan University, Riyadh, Saudi Arabia
sghowinem@psu.edu.sa, basmah.a.k@hotmail.com

**Abstract.** Different factors shape individuals' personality, where their interaction with others in certain situations could reveal their personal characteristics. Studies have explored the influence of culture in forming personalties, where differences in behaviours are observed. The advancement in communication technologies has opened the world and increased the cultural diversity. Therefore, understanding individual personalities is crucial for the enhancing the effectiveness in communication and for the development of an interconnected world. Such an understanding not only would guarantee smooth group interaction in workplace, education, and social environments, but also would allow for better resource utilization and role allocation for group members. Moreover, with the emergence of HCI technologies and affective computing, automation of personality assessment using non-verbal cues seems feasible. Acknowledging the differences in personality traits between cultures, several studies have analysed such traits clusters in different countries. However, given the unique culture of Arabs in general and Saudi Arabian in particular, personality traits distribution is yet to be investigated. This research investigates two aspects: (1) the distribution of personality types of individuals living in Saudi Arabia compared to other countries, and (2) the feasibility of automatically classifying personality types by analysing non-verbal cues during an interaction setting. To accomplish the first part of the this work, we used the big-five personality assessment survey, where a total of 232 individuals have responded. The results showed a slight difference in the personality assessment of individuals living in Saudi Arabia compare to other cultures. For the second part, we conduced physical interviews with eight subjects where their body actions are recorded. Several non-verbal features were extracted from the body movement (e.g. touching face) and used for automatic classification. The results are generally reasonable, where the accuracy on average was 67% using Support Vector Machines. The slight differences in the personality types from this study results compared suggest the uniqueness of Arab culture in general and Saudi culture in particular. Moreover, the automatic assessment of personality types using body language demonstrate a potential success. Linking the two aspects of personality distribution and automatic assessment of personality, could increase the reliability and accuracy of the results.

© Springer International Publishing AG, part of Springer Nature 2018
P.-L. P. Rau (Ed.): CCD 2018, LNCS 10911, pp. 285–299, 2018.
https://doi.org/10.1007/978-3-319-92141-9_22

**Keywords:** Personality assessment · Non-verbal cues · Body action
HCI

## 1    Introduction

The process of forming and shaping a human's behaviour emerges throughout a
lifetime. This evolution describes how an individual acts and interacts, which is
exposed through their attitudes and values. It refers to emotions and actions that
are observable and are driven by a human's thoughts and feelings. Understanding the way an individual behaves has been carried out through many studies
that are aiming at a deeper comprehension of human behaviours. Based on these
studies, an emphasis on cultural role in forming an individual's personal characteristics and behavioural patterns was given [1]. It has been found that these
personal traits are affected by several factors including genetics, social norms
and culture [1].

Thus, to understand an individual's personality, it is important to correlate
their behaviour with their culture. As humans, we are constantly follow certain
rules and act in ways that are only acceptable by society, which therefore habit-
uates the way we behave. Culture can be defined as a combination of shared
traits, values, beliefs, and expected behaviours [1]. Moreover, the behaviour of
individuals, groups, institutions and societies is constituted by culture (i.e. the
rituals, practices, and symbolic and physical artefacts). Recognizing the huge
diversity in people's way of thinking, feeling, and acting is crucial for the development of a better interconnected world, especially with the increase interaction
with diverse cultures.

With the advancement of HCI and affective computing research and their
applications, several studies showed potential success in the automatic detection
of non-verbal cues using body actions, as surveyed in [2]. Other studies focused
on linking the detected non-verbal cues with behaviours and personality [3–7].

Even though the personality traits have generalizability across cultures, a
study showed that certain personality traits clusters differently depending in
cultures [8]. Of the cultures investigated in the study, only a few countries of the
Arab world are included. Given the unique and diverse cultures within the Arab
world, including and comparing personality traits distribution in more Arab
countries is necessary not only for understanding personality traits, but also for
automating the process.

Our ultimate aim is to develop a system that automatically assess personality
traits from non-verbal cues, which not only could assist group and team leaders
in smoothing communication, but also could assist in allocating the members'
roles according to their behavioural characteristics. To reach this future goal,
this study focuses on initiating the understanding of personalties within cross-
cultural context and their associated non-verbal cues. The contributions of this
research are as follows:

– Investigating the distribution of personality types of individuals living in
  Saudi Arabia.

- Studying the feasibility of automatically classifying personality types by analysing body language cues during an interaction setting.
- Linking personal traits with non-verbal characteristics.

## 2  Related Work

### 2.1  Big-Five Personality Types Around the World

Several personality assessments exist, where their purpose is to increase the accuracy of behavioural prediction. One of which is the Big-Five Model, which is considered the leading model of personality structure in trait psychology [9, 10]. Moreover, the Big-Five organizes personality characteristics into five core personality domains: Extroversion, Openness, Agreeableness, Conscientiousness and Neuroticism [11]. The Big-Five model has been validated in a cross-cultural context, where the findings suggest its generalizability across cultures [12].

Moreover, studies have compared the personality traits of the Big-Five model in different nations [8,13,14]. Results of an initial study on 26 cultures showed differences in the Big-Five personality traits that confirms with the perception of the nation [13]. A later study expanded to 56 nations suggested a regular, systematic geographic patterns in the distribution of personality traits [8]. The latest study updated the investigation by covering 62 cultures, where the results showed a clear clustering into distinctive groups of countries or cultures [14]. However, only a few countries from the Arab world were included: Lebanon and Jordan in [8] and Algeria in [14]. Saudi Arabia has a unique culture, where covering the personality traits to be compared to other nations is important for understanding the personality distribution.

### 2.2  Non-verbal Cues for Personality Types

In the light of typical human interaction, non-verbal cues are considered the meta-message that provides implications on receiving and interpreting verbal messages. These cues, such as head nods, hand gestures and body posture, complement verbal cues and thus improve communication. For example, classes of complex mental states were analysed from head movement and facial expression [15]. Then these non-verbal actions were abstracted into displays and mental states such as thinking and agreeing. Some of the hand gestures have been reported along with their indicators, such as palms turned toward the floor suggest dominance and the open-palm-up hand-shrug indication of helpless uncertainty and confusion [16]. The arm-cross could present suggestive of arrogance, disliking, or disagreement behaviour. Moreover, upright body lean include familiarity, inclusiveness, and emotionality, whereas backward body lean indicates detachment, disinterest, and relaxation [17].

A previous psychological study [18] reported that people unconsciously touch parts of their bodies when emotions run high to comfort, relieve, or release stress. Self-stimulating behaviours include holding an arm or wrist, massaging a hand

and scratching or pinching the skin, which have been found to increase with anxiety and indicate deception, disagreement, fear, or uncertainty. Furthermore, disbelief and scepticism indicators include unconscious face-touching gestures such as touching or masking the mouth with fingers or hand.

As it can be noticed, non-verbal behaviours are in fact communicative and these concurrent cues are then considered in combination, based on the meanings associated with these cues individually [17].

Despite the fact that non-verbal communication is a universal phenomenon, interpretations of non-verbal cues are not universal. Moreover, the differences on non-verbal cues can reveal different attitudes and behavioural patterns. For instance, gestures and eye contact are two major fields of non-verbal communication that are interpreted differently across cultures, and can be characterized using behaviour analysis [19]. A case in point is the comprehension of the difference between Arab, Western and East Asian communication styles [19]. As a matter of fact, there is a tremendous variance of these cues across cultures, and they are often obscure. Hence, it is important to have a primitive understanding of how these non-verbal cues are linked to personality traits within different cultures.

### 2.3   Automatic Assessment of Personality

Automatic body action detection including non-verbal (body language) cues using pattern recognition has been investigated in several studies as surveyed in [2]. For example, [20] investigated automatically detecting spontaneous laughter from nonverbal full body movement such as: head side movement, head-front/backmovement, weight shift, and knee bending, where the average accuracy was 75%. Moreover, in the specific context of gesture recognition in healthcare, a study automatically identified medically recognized body gestures related to pain in various diseases, where an accuracy of 94.29% was yielded [21].

Based on the general body action recognition studies, a few studies focused on linking the detected non-verbal cues with behaviours and personality. As part of the hiring decision, personality was assessed using the Big Five Model traits in [3]. In the context of personality impressions in social media, video-blogs (vlogs) was collected for audio-visual behavioural analysis [5]. Automatic detection of the Big Five personality traits by analysing non-verbal cues from short videos of self-presentation was investigated in [4].

Automatic detection of the Big Five personality traits in the context of group meetings was investigated in [6,7]. Findings of this work support the idea that social interaction is a good context to conduct automatic personality assessment. However, only one personality dimension (Extroversion) was considered from the Big Five traits, while a more comprehensive personality assessment could be achieved by considering the full set of Big Five's scales.

As it can be noticed, previous mentioned work have targeted the issue of automatic recognition and analysis of behaviours using non-verbal communication which included audio, visual and audio-visual cues. The majority of these studies have extracted non-verbal features from facial expressions and focused on gestures of the head and hands rather than gross body language. Also, they used different types of assessments for different purposes, as not every study was focused on personality.

# 3    Methodology

To answer the two folds of our study, we divide our methodology into two sub-section, as follows.

## 3.1    Survey Collection for Saudi Arabians' Personality Traits

The first part of this research is to investigate the Saudi Arabia distribution of personality types compared to other countries. We approach this by employing the widely used Big-Five personality traits in order to determine the subject's personality dimensions. For this purpose, the big-five personality assessment survey was distributed upon different social media platforms including WhatsApp, Twitter and LinkedIn, where participation is voluntary and anonymous. Moreover, given the fact that personalities are influenced by many factors, we collect demographic information. Data about gender can have an effect on the person's personality, thus majorly affecting the result of the test. As personalities change slightly with age, we also collect information about age groups in order to learn more about respondents' different personality types. Since our target audience is Saudi Arabians, a respondent's nationality and primary language are critical for our survey analysis, as personality interpretation differs from one culture and spoken language to another.

The Mini-IPIP assessment is used in this study as a benchmark for the automatic recognition of an individual's personal characteristics. It is a self-report scale, where it measures five domains of an individual's personality, where each domain is measured by four questions. The questions are statements that describe the participant. These statements are to be rated on a scale from 1 (Strongly Agree) to 5 (Strongly Disagree). Questions related to each domain are then calculated by summing up the number of points.

A total of 232 individuals responded to the personality assessment survey. Majority of the respondents were females (85%), 41% are between 21 to 25 years old, and 90% were Saudi (n = 208 Saudi).

## 3.2    Automatic Detection of Personality

The second part of this work investigates the feasibility of automatically assess personality using non-verbal cues. To accomplish this, body language cues are captured during interview setting. By recording and tracking body movements and gestures using a sensor, several non-verbal cues could be extracted. Detailed of the data collection procedure and classification process are described below.

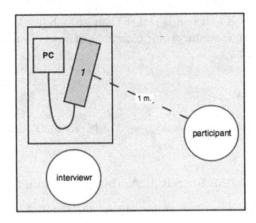

**Fig. 1.** Interaction Setting: (1) Kinect sensor device

**Interview Procedure.** Recruitment of participants is done by advertising a volunteering opportunity to participate in a research. A consent form is signed by both the interviewer and participants upon arrival at the interview room, followed by Mini-IPIP questionnaire, as explained in Sect. 3.1.

To create a structured behavioural interview, the interaction is designed to strictly follow the same sequence of a fixed set of questions and to capture a wide diversity of behavioural responses. The interview duration takes about 10 to 15 min, where it follows standard job interview questions, behavioural questions (e.g. How do you work under pressure), and personal questions (e.g. What motivates you). Eight female subjects were interviewed in this research, age between 20–23. The interview average duration was 10.8 min.

**Recording Settings.** Interaction recording is held at a quite room, where all interviews are conducted in the same room by the same interviewer to avoid any variations. The interviewer is seated at one end of a table, and the participant is seated approximately one meter across from the table in order to capture the full body movement using the sensor without obstructing the participant body (see Fig. 1). As a recording sensor, we utilize Kinect SDK, which enables tracking the skeletal of users facing it. Kinect sensor tracks 21 body joints including their position and orientation.

**Classification Process.** As the objectives of this work is to investigate the automatic personality classification, the collected dataset will be analysed following the feature extraction, and classification phases.

Skeleton output tracked by the sensor is used to extract body language cues. The extracted features are the duration percentage of: Head Nods (i.e. Head Up, Head Down), Arm Cross (e.g. Right hand near left elbow), Body Lean (i.e. Lean Forward and backward), Legs Cross (e.g. Right knee on top of left knee),

Touch Face (i.e. Right/left hand near head). To extract these features Ecludian distances between certain tracked joints are calculated, and a threshold was estimated. The duration percentage is then calculated based on the number of frames where the feature is present compared to the total interview duration. This process will also assure normalisation that would reduce the variability in interview duration differences.

For classification, we use Support Vector Machine (SVM) using Radial Basis Function (RBF) kernel. LibSVM is used for SVM implementation, where *Cost (C)* and *Gamma (G)* are set to default parameters. Statistical measures are calculated to measure the performance of classifiers, such as accuracy and F-score. We use Leave-one-out cross-validation in order to avoid over-fitting especially in small datasets. Each personality dimension is classified in a binary manner. Since each of the five dimensions results in continuous values (i.e. sum of the scores from the questions), we define a threshold value of 50% to convert the dimension into one of two classes (e.g. Agreeableness or Disagreeableness).

# 4 Results

## 4.1 Analysis of Survey Results

A total of 232 individuals participated in the personality assessment survey, of which 90% were Saudi (n = 208) and the remaining lives in Saudi Arabia. Among all participants, the results showed high similarity and clustering in each domain scores, as the majority were above 50% in all five dimensions. Table 1 shows the detailed survey results, and Figs. 2, 3 and 4 show the differences in personalities in term of gender, age group and nationality, respectively.

**Table 1.** Survey results

| | | | Extraversion | | Agreeableness | | Conscientiousness | | Neuroticism | | Openness | |
|---|---|---|---|---|---|---|---|---|---|---|---|---|
| | | | <10 | >=10 | <10 | >=10 | <10 | >=10 | <10 | >=10 | <10 | >=10 |
| GENDER | Male | 15% | 14% | 86% | 11% | 89% | 34% | 66% | 17% | 83% | 0% | 100% |
| | Female | 85% | 4% | 96% | 18% | 82% | 16% | 84% | 23% | 77% | 4% | 96% |
| AGE | -16 | 1% | 0% | 100% | 0% | 100% | 0% | 100% | 50% | 50% | 0% | 100% |
| | 17-20 | 24% | 7% | 93% | 32% | 68% | 14% | 86% | 29% | 71% | 2% | 98% |
| | 21-25 | 41% | 5% | 95% | 14% | 86% | 27% | 73% | 27% | 73% | 4% | 96% |
| | 26-30 | 13% | 3% | 97% | 13% | 87% | 13% | 87% | 16% | 84% | 0% | 100% |
| | 31-35 | 7% | 6% | 94% | 6% | 94% | 0% | 100% | 0% | 100% | 0% | 100% |
| | 36+ | 12% | 4% | 96% | 15% | 85% | 19% | 81% | 19% | 81% | 7% | 93% |
| NATIONALITY | Saudi | 90% | 5% | 95% | 17% | 83% | 19% | 81% | 21% | 79% | 2% | 98% |
| | Non-Saudi | 10% | 8% | 92% | 21% | 79% | 17% | 83% | 29% | 71% | 8% | 92% |

*(a) Extroversion vs. Introversion.* Mainly, this domain includes traits such as being energetic, talkative, and assertive. Extroverts get their energy from interacting with others, while introverts get their energy from within themselves. Of the Saudi respondents, 95% of them scored high in this domain. Moreover, 96% of the females and 86% of the males scored as extroverts. 95% of people of age from 21 to 25 years old scored as extroverts, as well as most of those of age from 17 to 20 years old (93%).

*(b) Agreeableness vs. Disagreeableness.* Major traits include being kind, affectionate, and sympathetic. Agreeable people are mostly friendly, cooperative, and compassionate, where disagreeable individuals may be more distant. A significant percentage of female respondents (82%) had high scores in this domain, and hence they are classified as agreeable individuals. Similarly, 89% of male respondents scored high in this area. Only 32% of people aging 17 to 20 years old were found to be disagreeable, as opposed to the group aging 21 to 25 years old, who where 86%, and scored high in agreeableness.

*(c) Conscientiousness vs. Un-Conscientiousness.* Most traits include being organized, methodic, and thorough. People with a high degree in conscientiousness are reliable and prompt, while people with a low degree in conscientiousness dislike structure and schedules. An estimated 84% of female and 66% of male respondents scored high in this domain. Most members of age group 17 to 20 (86%) as well as 73% of age group 21 to 25 were found to be conscientious. On the other hand, 19% of age group 36+ resulted as un-conscientious.

*(d) Neuroticism vs. Emotional Stability.* This relates to one's emotional stability and degree of negative emotions, where traits include being moody and tense. People that score high on neuroticism experience a lot of stress and dramatic shifts in mood, while people that score low in this domain are emotionally stable and very relaxed most of the time. Only 21% of the 208 Saudis resulted as emotionally stable individuals. A relatively small proportion of the 197 female respondents (23%) scored low in this domain, which means they are emotionally stable. On the other hand, 83% of the 35 male respondents were high in neuroticism. Three quarters of age group 21 to 25 (73%) and 71% of age group 17 to 20 also scored as neurotic individuals.

*(e) Openness vs. Creativity.* Generally, traits include being insightful, imaginative and having a wide variety of interests. People who like to learn new things and enjoy new experiences usually score high in openness. Whereas people who dislike change and abstract or theoretical concepts mostly score low in this domain. Only 2% of Saudis scored low in this domain. A majority of the female respondents (96%) scored high in openness, as well as all 35 male respondents. Almost the whole age group 17 to 20 (98%) and age group 21 to 25 (96%) were found to be open to experience.

Life events and a person's history do not necessarily construct personality traits, instead, they collaborate and interact in forming an individual's characteristic adaptations [22]. Moreover, with the expanding development in human society, gender differences in personality traits have been proven to become more extreme [23], as it can be noticed in Fig. 2 that illustrates our study results. For instance, previous studies found that typically, females have higher anxiety levels than males, as males lean more towards assertiveness and risk-taking [23]. This can be noticed in our results, where males tend to be more agreeable than females. Moreover, females seem to have lower neuroticism scores (higher

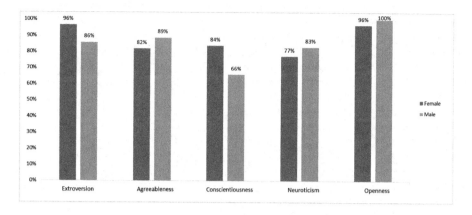

**Fig. 2.** Personality assessment results by gender

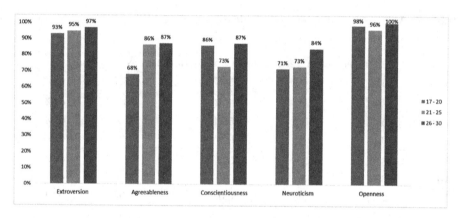

**Fig. 3.** Personality assessment results by age

emotional stability) than males. We can also see the difference in both extroversion and conscientiousness domains, where males are having lower scores than females.

Also, age difference effects on personality traits development have been determined in previous studies, where age-related shifts were found in the mean levels of personality traits in adolescence and adulthood [24]. Figure 3 shows that mature people (age 26–30) are more structured and conscientious than the younger group (age 21–25). Another variance can be seen in the agreeableness domain between age groups (17–20) and (26–30), where adults appear to be more cooperative and acceptable. Also, people of age (26–30) appear to be more stressed and less stable emotionally than the younger group of age (17–20).

Furthermore, culture and history have been found to actually affect attitudes, beliefs, and habits [22]. So, culture can be considered one of many factors that influence an individual's character or personality; as diversity in personality

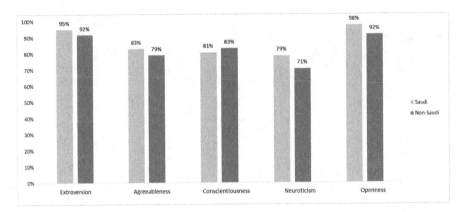

**Fig. 4.** Personality assessment results by nationality

**Table 2.** Average score for each personality domain with the comparison of age and gender

|  | Extraversion | Agreeableness | Conscientiousness | Neuroticism | Openness |
|---|---|---|---|---|---|
| All | 61% | 54% | 56% | 57% | 64% |
| Female | 62% | 54% | 57% | 56% | 64% |
| Male | 58% | 55% | 55% | 59% | 65% |
| t-test | 0.01 | 0.38 | 0.25 | 0.26 | 0.50 |
| College age | 61% | 53% | 59% | 53% | 64% |
| Adult | 62% | 55% | 55% | 58% | 64% |
| t-test | 0.52 | 0.08 | 0.02 | 0.01 | 0.81 |

throughout the lifespan show similar patterns across cultures. With regard to culture, our results (Fig. 4) show a notable distinction between Saudis and Non-Saudis who lives in Saudi Arabia in neuroticism. The chart also illustrates difference in the openness domain, where Non-Saudis have lower scores than Saudis.

With regards to the Big-Five cross-culture validation studies [8,13,14], our study results present a slight difference in the personality assessment of individuals living in Saudi Arabia (see Table 2). For example, [13] indicated that adults (22+) score low in 3 domains but in Agreeableness and Conscientiousness in cross-cultures context. However, our results indicates that adults scores similar to younger participants in Extroversion, Agreeableness, and Openness domains, and significantly higher in Neuroticism ($p < 0.05$) and significantly lower in Conscientiousness than younger participants.

Moreover, across-culture the studies reported that gender differences were most pronounced in European and American cultures [13]. Our results are in line with the study finding, where there was no significant differences between gender in most domains, except for Extroversion domain, where women scored higher. Nevertheless, due differences in Big-five test used in our study and the other studies, direct score comparisons are not feasible. Moreover, even experts reported difficulty in judging cross-cultural differences in personality traits [13]. Nevertheless, conducting a comparable study with objective measures would facilitate such comparison.

## 4.2  Automatic Assessment of Personality Traits

Moreover, interviews were conducted and body motion was recorded for eight subjects. With respect to the analysis of non-verbal cues, we notice that head nods, arms-cross, legs-cross, body-lean and face-touch could be utilized for the automatic classification of personality characteristics.

**Table 3.** Subjects' extracted duration features and personality dimensions

| | Subject ID | 1 | 2 | 3 | 4 | 5 | 6 | 7 | 8 |
|---|---|---|---|---|---|---|---|---|---|
| **Extracted Features** | HeadUp | 0.08% | 14.43% | 15.12% | 13.30% | 11.37% | 15.79% | 15.46% | 14.03% |
| | HeadDown | 13.08% | 14.46% | 10.79% | 15.62% | 11.04% | 14.64% | 22.04% | 14.07% |
| | ArmCross | 47.75% | 71.02% | 89.18% | 29.38% | 55.04% | 56.57% | 54.01% | 89.12% |
| | BodyLeanY | 20.80% | 14.51% | 15.92% | 18.12% | 11.98% | 16.75% | 14.97% | 14.27% |
| | BodyLeanN | 16.89% | 14.87% | 19.80% | 15.60% | 13.06% | 16.60% | 13.16% | 16.66% |
| | LegsCross | 0.24% | 0.03% | 0.05% | 0% | 43.87% | 6.56% | 65.31% | 0.29% |
| | TouchFace | 67.74% | 81.81% | 67.94% | 80.96% | 77.11% | 78.95% | 81.11% | 99.34% |
| **Personality Dimensions** | Extroversion vs. Introversion | Extroversion | Extroversion | Extroversion | Extroversion | Extroversion | Introversion | Extroversion | Extroversion |
| | Agreeableness vs. Disagreeableness | Disagreeable | Disagreeable | Agreeable | Agreeable | Agreeable | Agreeable | Agreeable | Disagreeable |
| | Conscientiousness vs. Un-conscientiousness | Conscientious | Conscientious | Conscientious | Conscientious | Un-conscientious | Conscientious | Un-conscientious | Conscientious |
| | Neuroticism vs. Emotional Stability | Neurotic | Emotionally Stable | Emotionally Stable | Neurotic | Neurotic | Neurotic | Neurotic | Neurotic |
| | Openness vs. Creativity | Open | Open | Open | Open | Open | Open | Open | Open |
| **Interview Duration** | | 20 mins | 15 mins | 10 mins | 11 mins | 10 mins | 11 mins | 5 mins | 5 mins |

After preprocessing skeleton output of each subject, features are extracted. Table 3 links subjects' non-verbal cues using the extracted features to their Big-Five personality dimensions. With regards to the Big-Five personality dimensions' description and the feature extraction approach, we can describe and link subjects' non-verbal cues with their personality dimensions as follows.

Looking at subject (1), we notice that she is moving her head downwards about 13% of the interview duration (20 min) and also crossing her arms 48% of the time. She is leaning forward 21% of the time and touching her face about 68% of the time. Her personality results show that she is a person who tends to be involved in activities and has a potential to lead a work group (extrovert), more focused on her own self-interests (disagreeable), dependable and a compulsive perfectionist (conscientious), lacks a positive psychological adjustment (neurotic) and is open to new experiences and ideas (open).

Another observation is found in subject (3), as her interview duration is shorter that the first one (10 min). Her arms appear to be crossed about 89% of the time, she is touching her face almost 68% of the time and moving her head upwards 15% of the time. She is sitting upright most of the time and her head is moving downwards for only about 11% of the time. Her personality scores describe how she has the tendency to dominate conversations and hence lacks listening skills (extrovert), she is optimistic and tends to go-with-the-flow (agreeable), achieves high levels of success through good planning (conscientious), free from persistent negative feelings (emotionally stable) and is intellectually curious (open).

Furthermore, an even shorter interview duration than the one before is noted with subject (7). She is crossing her legs 65% of the time, her arms are crossed about 54% of the time, and she is touching her face 81% of the time. She is leaning forward about 15% of the time and her head is moving downwards more than it is upwards, that is 22% of the time. Her personality results indicate that she can be comfortable with lots of sensory stimulation (extrovert), builds strong relationships with her team members (agreeable), lacks ambition and could be unreliable (un-conscientious), vulnerable to situations that demand high social skills (neurotic) and prefers novelty over familiarity (open).

Nevertheless, analysing and associating these non-verbal patterns to automatically assess personality are one of the main investigation of this paper. All interview subjects had similar high scores in Extroversion and Openness dimensions, which is expected as the survey results show that most Saudis are highly similar in these two dimensions. Hence, Extroversion and Openness classification are excluded, and the three remaining dimensions (Agreeableness, Conscientiousness and Neuroticism) are considered for the automatic classification.

A balanced dataset is needed in order to get reliable classification results, and to reduce classification bias toward the class with higher number of observations. Thus, four subjects are chosen to form a dataset for each of the three selected dimensions. Two of these four subjects belong to the opposite dimension (i.e. two subjects are agreeable, whereas the other two are disagreeable). Then, each subject's observation is labelled by assigning a binary value (0/1) for each of the three dimensions. This results in five subjects formed the complete dataset.

**Table 4.** Basic classification results

|  |  | Agreeableness | Conscientiousness | Neuroticism |
|---|---|---|---|---|
| SVM (RBF kernal) | Accuracy | 0% | 100% | 100% |
| LOO cross validation | F-score | 0% | 100% | 100% |

Table 4 shows the classification results of the SVM classifier based on the selected and explained set of features. Since our training set is very small, models' performance may be sensitive to which samples end up in the training set. Thus, resulting in a larger variance.

With reference to the calculated accuracies and F-scores, the table shows that on average, SVM with RBF classifier was able to correctly classify all the subjects in conscientiousness and neuroticism personality dimensions, but no subjects were correctly classified in agreeableness domain. This might be caused by the small number of sample set and extracted non-verbal features. Nonetheless, this indicates a promising results. Capturing a wider range of body movements as features and increasing the sample size could improve the recognition process of other personality dimensions in terms of classification performance.

## 5  Conclusion and Future Directions

Aiming at utilizing HCI technologies and affective computing with the consideration of cross-cultural differences, this study investigates automatic personality assessment in Saudi sample from non-verbal cues. As people from different cultural backgrounds usually work in groups for many different purposes, providing an insight of an individual behaviour could be central to the construction, maintenance and progression of these groups. For cross-cultural personality assessment, the big-five personality assessment survey was used to analyse the distribution of personality types of individuals living in Saudi Arabia compared to other countries. A total of 232 individuals have responded, where the results showed The results showed a slight difference in the personality assessment of individuals living in Saudi Arabia compare to other cultures. This could indicate a uniqueness of Arab culture in general and Saudi culture in particular. More investigation is needed in bigger sample to validate this initial results.

Moreover, it is important to understand cross-cultural personality traits through an objective observation of how an individual communicate, and perceive others and the world around them. Therefore, interviews were conduced with eight subjects, where several non-verbal features were extracted from the body movement for the purpose of automatically classifying personality types. The classification results are generally reasonable, where the accuracy on average was 67% using Support Vector Machines. Even though the results are moderate, they demonstrate a potential success of the automatic assessment of personality types using body language.

Future work should expand in the number of subjects, personality domains, as well as extracted non-verbal features. Moreover, toward a cultural aware systems, using personality distribution statistics in a given culture in association with the automatic assessment of personality, could enhance not only the accuracy, but also the reliability of the classification.

## References

1. Hayton, J.C., George, G., Zahra, S.A.: National culture and entrepreneurship: a review of behavioral research. Entrep. Theory Pract. **26**(4), 33 (2002)
2. Kleinsmith, A., Bianchi-Berthouze, N.: Affective body expression perception and recognition: a survey. IEEE Trans. Affect. Comput. **4**(1), 15–33 (2013)
3. Nguyen, L.S., Frauendorfer, D., Mast, M.S., Gatica-Perez, D.: Hire me: computational inference of hirability in employment interviews based on nonverbal behavior. IEEE Trans. Multimed. **16**(4), 1018–1031 (2014)

4. Batrinca, L.M., Mana, N., Lepri, B., Pianesi, F., Sebe, N.: Please, tell me about yourself: automatic personality assessment using short self-presentations. In: Proceedings of the 13th International Conference on Multimodal Interfaces, pp. 255–262. ACM (2011)
5. Biel, J.I., Gatica-Perez, D.: The youtube lens: Crowdsourced personality impressions and audiovisual analysis of vlogs. IEEE Trans. Multimed. **15**(1), 41–55 (2013)
6. Jayagopi, D., Sanchez-Cortes, D., Otsuka, K., Yamato, J., Gatica-Perez, D.: Linking speaking and looking behavior patterns with group composition, perception, and performance. In: Proceedings of the 14th ACM International Conference on Multimodal Interaction, pp. 433–440. ACM (2012)
7. Pianesi, F., Mana, N., Cappelletti, A., Lepri, B., Zancanaro, M.: Multimodal recognition of personality traits in social interactions. In: Proceedings of the 10th International Conference on Multimodal Interfaces, pp. 53–60. ACM (2008)
8. Schmitt, D.P., Allik, J., McCrae, R.R., Benet-Martínez, V.: The geographic distribution of big five personality traits: patterns and profiles of human self-description across 56 nations. J. Cross Cult. Psychol. **38**(2), 173–212 (2007)
9. Donnellan, M.B., Oswald, F.L., Baird, B.M., Lucas, R.E.: The mini-IPIP scales: tiny-yet-effective measures of the big five factors of personality. Psychol. Assess. **18**(2), 192 (2006)
10. Chittaranjan, G., Blom, J., Gatica-Perez, D.: Who's who with big-five: analyzing and classifying personality traits with smartphones. In: 2011 15th Annual International Symposium on Wearable Computers (ISWC), pp. 29–36. IEEE (2011)
11. Soto, C.J., John, O.P.: Ten facet scales for the big five inventory: convergence with NEO PI-R facets, self-peer agreement, and discriminant validity. J. Res. Pers. **43**(1), 84–90 (2009)
12. McCrae, R.R., Costa Jr., P.T., Del Pilar, G.H., Rolland, J.P., Parker, W.D.: Cross-cultural assessment of the five-factor model: the revised neo personality inventory. J. Cross Cult. Psychol. **29**(1), 171–188 (1998)
13. McCrae, R.R.: Trait psychology and culture: exploring intercultural comparisons. J. Pers. **69**(6), 819–846 (2001)
14. Allik, J., Church, A.T., Ortiz, F.A., Rossier, J., Hřebíčková, M., De Fruyt, F., Realo, A., McCrae, R.R.: Mean profiles of the NEO personality inventory. J. Cross Cult. Psychol. **48**(3), 402–420 (2017)
15. Kaliouby, R.E., Robinson, P.: Real-time inference of complex mental states from facial expressions and head gestures (2005)
16. McNeill: Guide to Gesture Classification, Transcription and Distribution (1992)
17. Burgoon, J., Buller, D., David, B., Hale, J., Turck, M.: Relational messages associated with nonverbal behaviors. Hum. Commun. Res. **10**(3), 351–378 (1984)
18. Ekman, P., Friesen, W.V.: The repertoire of nonverbal behavior: categories, origins, usage, and coding (1969)
19. Alotaibi, A., Underwood, G., Smith, A.D.: Cultural differences in attention: eye movement evidence from a comparative visual search task. Conscious. Cogn. **55**, 254–265 (2017)
20. Niewiadomski, R., Mancini, M., Varni, G., Volpe, G., Camurri, A.: Automated laughter detection from full-body movements. IEEE Trans. Hum. Mach. Syst. **46**(1), 113–123 (2016)
21. Pal, M., Saha, S., Konar, A.: Distance matching based gesture recognition for healthcare using microsoft's kinect sensor, pp. 1–5 (2016)
22. Yang, J., McCrae, R.R., Costa, P.T.: Adult age differences in personality traits in the United States and the People's Republic of China. J. Gerontol. **53**(6), 375–383 (1998)

23. Schmitt, D.P., Realo, A., Voracek, M., Allik, J.: Why can't a man be more like a woman? Sex differences in big five personality traits across 55 cultures: Correction to Schmitt et al. (2008). J. Pers. Soc. Psychol. **96**(1), 118 (2009)
24. Lehmann, R., Denissen, J.J.A., Allemand, M., Penke, L.: Age and gender differences in motivational manifestations of the Big Five from age 16 to 60. Dev. Psychol. **49**(2), 365–383 (2013)

# Determinants of E-Commerce Websites' User Interface: A Cross-Cultural Investigation Between Saudi Arabia and Philippines

Regina Garcia Almonte[✉]

City College of Calamba (CCC), Calamba City, Laguna, Philippines
reginagalmonte@gmail.com

**Abstract.** It is an argument that the cultural background plays a significant role in the web design of different kinds of websites. Since e-commerce websites are progressing in every country due to the convenience it brings to different web users around the world, it is vital to examine the e-commerce websites as a support to the argument mentioned previously. This paper utilized ISO/IEC 9126-1 quality model criteria to assess and investigates the quality of e-commerce websites and its user interface components of two different cultures: Saudi Arabia and the Philippines. The two countries were chosen since Saudi Arabia has become one the countries where many Filipinos are required for employment due to the latter's professional work ethics and dedication to work that made them recognized as instrumental in the growth of Saudi Arabia. A tested and validated questionnaire was used for the evaluation of the quality of e-commerce websites of the two cultures. It is found out that across the two cultures, there are significant differences in terms of the user interface components in some features of functionality, usability, and reliability but not found in efficiency component. The findings of the study should be taken into consideration for future research and for the web developers to design websites that are culturally appropriate.

**Keywords:** E-commerce · Cross-cultural · Website · User interface

## 1 Introduction

For over the years, online commerce has tremendously grown and continues to improve their way of serving to a great extent their target consumers. Electronic commerce (e-commerce) is one of the successful online commerce, which allows exchange information and transactions through the use of electronic communication. The globalization is what makes e-commerce. With globalization, the buyer and seller come together to make transactions using electronic medium, they sign a written agreement in terms of the price and delivery options of a specific goods and services, and complete the transactions through different types of payments and have the goods and services delivered as agreed (Zhang et al. 2006). It is simply defined as selling and buying of goods and services via internet which happens between the transactions of business and consumers, businesses and businesses, consumers and consumers, and intra-companies. The higher competition among business through e-commerce has been very stiff, thus

© Springer International Publishing AG, part of Springer Nature 2018
P.-L. P. Rau (Ed.): CCD 2018, LNCS 10911, pp. 300–313, 2018.
https://doi.org/10.1007/978-3-319-92141-9_23

global firms engage themselves more than just having a website and offered the products and services worldwide, but realizing the fact that the virtual world of commerce must be supported with physical, financial and information processes which local companies cannot offer to consumers with convenience and economy (Totonchi and Manshady 2011; Meyer 2008). There are numerous benefits that e-commerce has to offer to businesses targeting consumers globally. First, transaction costs, which are reduced costs when consumers are dealing with e-commerce, such as: search costs that consumers do not require to go through several stores or intermediaries to search for the supplies, products and compared prices; costs of processing transactions which is an automated transactions with efficient and quicker results, and; the online transactions improves inventory management and logistics. Second, disintermediation benefit wherein suppliers can directly deal with their buyers and do not need the interference of distributors or intermediaries. Lastly, there is an increase in price transparency where buyers are able to compare the prices of one product to another before making a decision in purchasing of goods and services (Khurana et al. 2011). Since the goal of each e-commerce website is to serve the consumers worldwide at their best, it is important to note that these websites should be designed objectively by its designers and not based on their personal perceptions. Worldwide, consumers consist of users with different cultures with different preferences. Thus, it is recommended to conduct a cross cultural analysis on e-commerce websites of different cultures in website development.

Generally, the objective of this paper is to assess the quality of e-commerce websites of Saudi Arabia and the Philippines through the use of the revised ISO/IEC 9126-1 quality criteria. Specifically, (1) to identify the user interface components that exists in e-commerce websites of Saudi Arabia and the Philippines; (2) to evaluate and analyze if the e-commerce websites of Saudi Arabia and the Philippines are designed based on cultures; (3) to determine if there is a significant correlation between the e-commerce websites of two cultures, and (4) to serve as a justification of the findings of number of researches that it is vital for the websites to be culturally appropriate.

This paper is organized as follows: Sect. 2 explains the user interface components of e-commerce websites; Sect. 3 provides the hypotheses that have been tested if a particular component or features have differences between the two cultures; Sect. 4 give the importance of the study; Sect. 5 presented the method of research and the research instrument that have been utilized in the study; Sect. 6 discusses the findings of the study, and; Sect. 7 provides the conclusions based on the evaluation of the results.

## 2   E-commerce Website's User Interface Components

Web site development is one of the challenging tasks of every website designers most especially in the field of e-commerce were websites will accommodate users around the world. It is important that the websites that the users would like to explore and utilize to develop in a high quality graphical user interfaces are essential factors for website designers because it allows users to carry out their daily tasks by interacting with e-commerce applications via menu-driven user interface components, such as toolbars and dialog windows (Zhang et al. 2006). There is a need to accommodate the increasing requirements of the business, as a result e-commerce applications and capabilities changes in order to provide the user interfaces that are suited to their needs. On the other hand, the interface design success is beyond the pleasant appearance of the website, it is the most important phase for its success (Bodker 1991). Its role is the key factor in user satisfaction (Burns and Madey 2001). Hence, the knowledge of the users as well as their cognitive skills and their limitations should be taken into consideration in the website design process to ensure its success.

There are a number of research conducted regarding the features that should be included in e-commerce websites. According to Coopee et al. (2000), website designers should consider the inclusions of the essential features into a commercial website that they used to design and created, namely, catalog development, users tracking, payment processing, online fulfillment, web site security, privacy, business-business sales models, and business-customer sales models. In addition, Cell (2000) enumerated some guidelines to be able to create a customer friendly website. The guidelines are for the websites to make company easy to find online, keep site navigation simple and clear, give customers a reason to visit the site, make the site visually appealing, offer a menu of communications options, and answer e-mail promptly and professionally. Indeed, designing the e-commerce websites' interface is a challenging task (Najjar 2001). The overall page format, navigation, catalog, registration, personalization, checkout, and customer service should be the inclusions of the major sections. Format download speed, the use of graphics, scrolling, and highlighted that a web designer should format the page to make it easy for users to interact with the web site by put user interface elements in familiar locations are the considerations under the web page format. In addition, search, contact us, and shopping carts are noted as an important feature of the e-commerce websites. To be able to deliver "breadcrumb" navigation page, website must show the page titles users came through to get the current page. Across cultures, the differences in the preferences and perceptions toward he design of the website really exists (Cyr and Trevor-Smith 2004). The design of the menu layout can consider the access to product info, professional design, logical info presentation, screen design, navigation, sequencing, product attributes, and product availability as an important web site features. Numerous researches revealed that the are variety of characteristics to describe websites (Tarafdar and Zhang 2006). There were five features involved: the content of information on the website, navigation characteristics, usability, personalization characteristics and the capability to cater to customized information requirements of the specific groups of customers, and the technical properties of the websites.

The revised ISO/IEC 9126-1 (2001) quality model made an end with the several arguments pertaining to the components or characteristics of e-commerce website. The model standardized the list of characteristics that must be included in every kind of software. The ISO/IEC 9126-1 model includes website quality characteristics and sub-characteristics and this will serve as a guide for software development which definitely includes e-commerce websites. The following are the characteristics defined by the model:

1. Functionality. It is an arrangement of qualities that bear on the presence of an arrangement of capacities and their predefined properties; the capacities are those that fulfill expressed or suggested needs (ISO/IEC 9126-1 2001; Al-Safadi and Garcia 2012). It is the significant component of an e-commerce website because it covers the user interaction with the websites.

2. Reliability. It is an arrangement of characteristics that bear on the capacity of programming to keep up its level of execution under expressed conditions for an expressed timeframe (ISO/IEC 9126-1 2001; Al-Safadi and Garcia 2012). It affects customer satisfaction which will lead to customer decision to purchase the goods and services that an e- commerce website has offered.

3. Usability. It is a collection of properties that bear on the effort essential to utilize, and on the individual evaluation of such use, by a stated or implicit set of users. (ISO/IEC 9126-1 2001; Al-Safadi and Garcia 2012). It is the ease of use that e-commerce website is provided to users which will make the websites' success.

4. Efficiency. It is a collection of properties that bear on the association between the degree of performance of the software and the amount of resources utilized, under expressed conditions (ISO/IEC 9126-1 2001; Al-Safadi and Garcia 2012). It covers the performance of the e-commerce websites and the promptness of the website when the user is trying to access a particular section of the website.

5. Maintainability. It is an arrangement of properties to bear the effort required to build particular modifications (ISO/IEC 9126-1 2001; Al-Safadi and Garcia 2012). It is the way of the website in dealing with the errors that users might encounter.

6. Portability. It is a collection of properties that bear on the capability of software to transfer from one environment to another (ISO/IEC 9126-1 2001; Al-Safadi and Garcia 2012). It is the ability of the e-commerce website when the users decided to access in different kinds of browsers, whether it would have a compatibility issue or not.

## 3 Hypotheses of the Study

The following are the hypotheses of the study:

- $H_1$: There is a variance in e-commerce website features concerning its functionality component between Saudi Arabia and the Philippines.
- $H_2$: There is a variance in e-commerce website features concerning its usability component between Saudi Arabia and the Philippines.
- $H_3$: There is a variance in e-commerce website features concerning its reliability component between Saudi Arabia and the Philippines.
- $H_4$: There is a variance in e-commerce website features concerning its efficiency component between Saudi Arabia and the Philippines.
- $H_5$: There is a variance in e-commerce website features concerning its maintainability component between Saudi Arabia and the Philippines.
- $H_6$: There is a variance in e-commerce website features concerning its portability component between Saudi Arabia and the Philippines.

## 4 Significance of the Study

The study is beneficial to the following:

- Web site designers to be able to develop a quality e-commerce websites across cultures. To develop a website that is not based on personal preferences of web designers is a significant factor of website development. This study will assist the designers to develop and design a website which will be effective for all kinds of people from all walks of life.

- Government sectors and private companies or institutions to be able to provide their target users worldwide, an e-commerce website that is culturally appropriate.
- Future researchers to be able to have a foundation or initial investigation in more in-depth analysis of e-commerce website development.

## 5  Research Methodology

Saudi Arabia and the Philippines were selected because the two countries possess distinctly different cultural features which were clearly revealed in Hofstede's (2005) cultural dimensions: power distance, individualism, masculinity, uncertainty avoidance, and long-term orientation. Ever since e-commerce has been introduced worldwide, the users from Saudi Arabia and the Philippines have seen the values and conveniences that e-commerce has provided for them. The adoption of e-commerce is progressing for the two countries. Aside from these facts, the two countries were chosen because they have bilateral relations of which clearly seen in Saudi Arabia allows millions of Filipinos are able to work in different companies in Saudi Arabia.

As shown in Table 1, twenty e-commerce websites which include the top and most commonly used e-commerce websites in the two countries and they were selected for evaluation of the components of a standard quality model. There are three procedures involved in this study. First is to identify the characteristics of each component of the websites which is based on the revised ISO/IEC 9126-1 model. Second is to evaluate each websites characteristics or features through the use of tested and validated questionnaire (Al-Safadi and Garcia 2012). Last procedure was the invitation of the two design experts on e-commerce websites from Saudi Arabia and Philippines who evaluated each feature of the websites. In their evaluation using the tested questionnaire, the evaluator indicated 0 if the feature is not present in the e-commerce website and 1 if it is present in the website.

After gathering the information needed for the study, analysis of the results has been taking place. In the study descriptive method of research was utilized to identify the features of the e-commerce websites involved in the study. And to test the significant differences between the two cultures, an inferential statistic was employed through the use of chi-square (x2) test. The following formulas were used:

1.

$$x^2 = \sum (\text{Actual Count} - \text{Expected Count})^2 / \text{Expected Count}$$

2.

$$\text{degrees of freedom(df)} = (\#\_\text{of\_rows} - 1)(\#\_\text{of\_columns} - 1)$$

**Table 1.** Online shopping websites in Saudi Arabia and the Philippines

| Saudi Arabia | | Philippines | |
|---|---|---|---|
| Company | Website/URL | Company | Website/URL |
| Awal-net | http://portal.awalnet.com | Metrobank | http://metrobank.com.ph |
| Nashirnet | http://www.nashirnet.net/ | Dynaquest PC | http://dynaquestpc.com/ |
| Dell | http://www.dell.com | Sulit | http://www.sulit.com.ph/ |
| Samba | http://www.samba.com | Metrodeal | http://www.metrodeal.com/ |
| Naseej | http://www.naseej.com/ | Shopinas | http://www.shopinas.com/ |
| Nesma | http://nesma.com/ | PhilRegalo | http://philregalo.com/ |
| Alahli | https://www.alahlionline.com | Filters Exchange | http://filters-exchange.net/ |
| Saudi Arabian Airlines | http://www.saudiairlines.com/ | Philippine Airlines | http://www1.philippineairlines.com/ |
| ABB | http://www.abb.com/ | Flowers Express | http://www.flowersexpress.com.ph |
| Souq | http://saudi.souq.com/ | Chicify | http://chicify.com/ |
| Danube | http://danubeco.com/ | Remal Sale | http://www.remalsales.com/ |
| Carrefour | http://www.carrefourksa.com | Beeconomic | http://www.beeconomic.com.ph/ |
| Lulu Hypermarket | http://saudi.luluhypermarket.com/ | BDO | https://www.bdo.com.ph/ |
| Panda | http://www.panda.com.sa/ | Dealgrocer | https://dealgrocer.com/ |
| Cobone | http://www.cobone.com/ | CashCashPinoy | http://www.cashcashpinoy.com/ |
| Namshi | http://en-sa.namshi.com/ | Ensogo | http://www.ensogo.com.ph/ |
| Sukar | http://www.sukar.com/ | Zalora | http://www.zalora.com.ph/ |
| MarkaVIP | http://markavip.com/ | Island Rose | http://www.islandrose.net/ |
| iZone | http://www.izone-stores.com/ | Taste Central | https://tastecentral.com/ |
| 3laModak | http://www.3lamodak.com/ | Dealgrocer | https://dealgrocer.com |

It was expected that the two cultures will reveal that there is significant differences with e-commerce website quality characteristics between two cultures.

# 6    Results and Discussion

The results of the e-commerce website quality characteristics are shown in Tables 2, 3, 4, 5, 6, 7, 8, 9 and 10.

**Table 2.** Functionality

| Variables | Actual count | | Expected count | $X^2$ | df | Sig. Level |
|---|---|---|---|---|---|---|
| | Saudi Arabia | Philippines | | | | |
| *Searching and Retrieving* | | | | | | |
| Quick search | 12 | 13 | 12.5 | 0.040 | 1 | 0.841 |
| Advanced search | 6 | 4 | 5.0 | 0.400 | 1 | 0.527 |
| Average level of retrieving customization | 20 | 20 | 20.0 | 0.000 | 1 | 1.000 |
| *Navigation and Browsing* | | | | | | |
| Orientation | 20 | 20 | 20.0 | 0.000 | 1 | 1.000 |
| Average links per page | 19 | 20 | 19.5 | 0.026 | 1 | 0.873 |
| Presentation permanence | 20 | 20 | 20.0 | 0.000 | 1 | 1.000 |
| Stability of sub-sites controls | 20 | 20 | 20.0 | 0.000 | 1 | 1.000 |
| Vertical level of scrolling | 20 | 20 | 20.0 | 0.000 | 1 | 1.000 |
| Horizontal level of scrolling | 0 | 1 | 0.5 | 0.000 | 1 | 1.000 |
| Links title with explanatory help | 0 | 0 | 0.0 | 0.000 | 1 | 1.000 |

* Sig. Level <0.05, there is significant difference

In terms of functionality component of e-commerce website and in support for H1, there were six significant differences under this component among the two cultures. These findings indicate a support for H1. There are 73% of Saudi Arabia's e-commerce websites have searching and retrieving category while 71% in the Philippines. Under navigation and browsing category, 67% of the Saudi Arabia's e-commerce website has this, while 68% in the Philippines. There is only one e-commerce website that uses "horizontal level of scrolling" feature, but none of the e-commerce websites of Saudi Arabia. With regards to "link title with explanatory help" and "links comment or descriptions" are not utilized by most of the e-commerce websites of both cultures. Under products category, 26% of the Saudi Arabia's e-commerce website contains this while 35% in the Philippines. The "product rating" category is not being utilized by the e-commerce websites of Saudi Arabia and only 5 e-commerce websites have this feature in the Philippines. In purchase category, 37% of the e-commerce websites in Saudi Arabia includes this while a higher percentage of 71% in the Philippines. The

**Table 3.** Functionality

| Variables | Actual count | | Expected count | $X^2$ | df | Sig. Level |
|---|---|---|---|---|---|---|
| | Saudi Arabia | Philippines | | | | |
| *Navigation and Browsing* | | | | | | |
| Links comment or description | 0 | 0 | 0.0 | 0.000 | 1 | 1.000 |
| Quick browse | 19 | 19 | 19.0 | 0.000 | 1 | 1.000 |
| *Products* | | | | | | |
| Textual description | 20 | 20 | 20.0 | 0.000 | 1 | 1.000 |
| Contents and structure | 20 | 19 | 19.5 | 0.026 | 1 | 0.873 |
| Image | 20 | 0 | 10.0 | 20.000 | 1 | 0.000* |
| Evaluation and comparison | 2 | 1 | 1.5 | 0.000 | 1 | 1.000 |
| Rating | 0 | 5 | 2.5 | 3.200 | 1 | 0.074 |
| Related product recommendation | 8 | 1 | 4.5 | 4.000 | 1 | 0.046 |
| Catalog download facility | 4 | 2 | 3.0 | 0.167 | 1 | 0.683 |
| Product personalization | 0 | 20 | 10.0 | 20.000 | 1 | 0.000* |
| Top products | 2 | 7 | 4.5 | 4.000 | 1 | 0.046* |
| Best seller products | 2 | 8 | 5.0 | 3.600 | 1 | 0.058 |
| *Purchase* | | | | | | |
| Shopping basket | 10 | 14 | 12.0 | 0.667 | 1 | 0.414 |
| Continues buying feedback | 0 | 0 | 0.0 | 0.000 | 1 | 1.000 |
| Edit/recalculate feature | 10 | 12 | 11.0 | 0.182 | 1 | 0.670 |
| Full integration of payment provider | 10 | 16 | 13.0 | 1.385 | 1 | 0.239 |
| Forms of payment via credit card | 10 | 16 | 13.0 | 1.385 | 1 | 0.239 |
| Forms of payment via bank transfer | 10 | 17 | 13.5 | 1.815 | 1 | 0.178 |
| Forms of payment via PayPal | 6 | 13 | 9.5 | 2.579 | 1 | 0.108 |
| Forms of payment via Google checkout | 0 | 3 | 1.5 | 0.000 | 1 | 1.000 |
| Other forms of payment | 9 | 16 | 12.5 | 1.960 | 1 | 0.162 |

* Sig. Level <0.05, there is a significant difference

form of payment through Google checkout is not being used by e-commerce websites in Saudi Arabia, but 3 e-commerce websites have this in e-commerce websites in the Philippines. There is no e-commerce websites in Saudi Arabia have used "recent purchase (gift service)" feature, but 9 e-commerce websites in the Philippines. And the

**Table 4.** Functionality

| Variables | Actual count | | Expected count | $X^2$ | df | Sig. Level |
|---|---|---|---|---|---|---|
| | Saudi Arabia | Philippines | | | | |
| Printable check-out form for offline transaction | 13 | 10 | 11.5 | 0.391 | 1 | 0.532 |
| Fax/Telephone/Email purchase | 8 | 9 | 8.5 | 0.059 | 1 | 0.808 |
| Quick purchase | 10 | 13 | 11.5 | 0.391 | 1 | 0.532 |
| Checkout security | 9 | 14 | 11.5 | 0.391 | 1 | 0.532 |
| Cancelling feedback | 9 | 14 | 11.5 | 0.391 | 1 | 0.532 |
| Purchase cancellation policy | 7 | 14 | 10.5 | 2.333 | 1 | 0.127 |
| Return policy | 7 | 15 | 11.0 | 2.909 | 1 | 0.088 |
| Shipping and handling policies | 7 | 17 | 12.0 | 4.167 | 1 | 0.041* |
| Payment policy | 7 | 16 | 11.5 | 0.391 | 1 | 0.532 |
| Recent purchase (gift service) | 0 | 9 | 4.5 | 4.000 | 1 | 0.046* |
| Multiple delivery options | 1 | 17 | 9.0 | 14.222 | 1 | 0.000* |
| Customer | | | | | | |
| e-subscriptions | 7 | 7 | 7.0 | 0.000 | 1 | 1.000 |
| Account availability | 14 | 20 | 17.0 | 1.059 | 1 | 0.303 |
| Account security | 14 | 20 | 17.0 | 1.059 | 1 | 0.303 |
| Account settings | 14 | 20 | 17.0 | 1.059 | 1 | 0.303 |
| Wish list | 4 | 3 | 3.5 | 0.000 | 1 | 1.000 |
| *Promotion* | | | | | | |
| With-sale | 11 | 6 | 8.5 | 1.471 | 1 | 0.225 |
| Appetizer promotions (e.g. contests, miles, etc.) | 14 | 9 | 11.5 | 0.391 | 1 | 0.532 |

* Sig. Level <0.05, there is a significant difference

"multiple delivery options" is being used by only one e-commerce websites in Saudi Arabia, but there are quite higher score of 17 e-commerce websites have utilized this in the Philippines. The form of payment that is widely used in Saudi Arabia is through SADAD payment system. In customer category, 42% in Saudi Arabia's e-commerce website and half of the number of websites in the Philippines that are evaluated in this study have this feature. Inclusion of "wish list" feature is not commonly used in e-commerce website of two cultures having 4 websites in Saudi Arabia and 3 websites in the Philippines. In promotion category, 63% of the Saudi Arabia's e-commerce websites includes this, but only 38% of the websites in the Philippines. In order management category, 80% of the e-commerce websites in the Philippines contains this, but only 35% in Saudi Arabia. There is only 1 e-commerce website in Saudi Arabia uses "order tracking" feature while a quite higher score of 16 e-commerce

**Table 5.** Functionality

| Variables | Actual count | | Expected count | $X^2$ | df | Sig. Level |
|---|---|---|---|---|---|---|
| | Saudi Arabia | Philippines | | | | |
| *Order Management* | | | | | | |
| Order history | 13 | 16 | 14.5 | 0.310 | 1 | 0.577 |
| Order tracking | 1 | 16 | 8.5 | 1.471 | 1 | 0.225 |
| Services | | | | | | |
| Discussion forums | 2 | 11 | 6.5 | 6.231 | 1 | 0.013 |
| Surveys/Polls | 1 | 0 | 0.5 | 0.000 | 1 | 1.000 |
| Newsletter | 5 | 11 | 8.0 | 2.250 | 1 | 0.134 |

* Sig. Level <0.05, there is a significant difference

websites in the Philippines. And in services category, both e-commerce website of the two cultures have quite lower percentage: 13% of Saudi Arabia's and 37% in the Philippines. The use of "survey/polls" feature is not popular in both cultures.

In terms of usability component of e-commerce website and in support for H2, there is one significant difference under this component among the two cultures. This finding indicates a support for H2. The global site understandability category is moderately used in e-commerce websites of Saudi Arabia and the Philippines. The use "table of contents" feature is not popular in e-commerce websites both cultures. The utilization of "alphabetical/subject index" feature is not widely used in e-commerce websites of both cultures having only 1 website in Saudi Arabia and 3 websites in the Philippines. The inclusions of "guided tour for first time visitor" can be found in just 2 e-commerce websites in Saudi Arabia and 2 websites in the Philippines. In help category, 82% of the e-commerce websites in Saudi Arabia includes this feature and a higher percentage of 91% in the Philippines. In interface and aesthetic category that covers presentation permanence and stability of controls, 82% of the e-commerce websites in Saudi Arabia has this feature and 71% in the Philippines. The miscellaneous category includes "foreign language support" and "What's new", 75% of Saudi Arabia's e-commerce websites has this feature but a lower percentage of 385 in the Philippines. The "foreign language support" is widely used in e-commerce websites in Saudi Arabia, but contrary with websites in the Philippines.

In terms of maintainability component of e-commerce website, there is no variance between the two cultures. On the other hand, there is one significant difference under reliability component between the two cultures. This finding indicates a support for H3. A very remarkable higher percentage was gained by the response of the e-commerce websites of Saudi Arabia and the Philippines when it comes to link errors, miscellaneous errors and drawbacks features. Most of the e-commerce websites of the two cultures handles such errors in a controlled manner providing display messages to users. While in accuracy and relevance of information, a lower percentage was given to the e-commerce websites of both cultures having a percentage of 38% in Saudi Arabia and 40% in the Philippines. The utilization of "references or links" feature is not popular in most of e-commerce websites of both cultures.

**Table 6.** Usability

| Variables | Actual count | | Expected count | $X^2$ | df | Sig. Level |
|---|---|---|---|---|---|---|
| | Saudi Arabia | Philippines | | | | |
| *Global Site Understandability* | | | | | | |
| Table of contents | 0 | 0 | 0.0 | 0.000 | 1 | 1.000 |
| Sitemap | 5 | 1 | 3.0 | 1.500 | 1 | 0.221 |
| Alphabetical/subject index | 1 | 3 | 2.0 | 0.250 | 1 | 0.617 |
| Text labels | 20 | 19 | 19.5 | 0.026 | 1 | 0.873 |
| Picture labels | 20 | 20 | 20.0 | 0.000 | 1 | 1.000 |
| Images | 20 | 19 | 19.5 | 0.026 | 1 | 0.873 |
| Guide tour for first time visitors | 2 | 2 | 2.0 | 0.250 | 1 | 0.617 |
| *Help Features* | | | | | | |
| Global help | 20 | 20 | 20.0 | 0.000 | 1 | 1.000 |
| Search help | 19 | 20 | 19.5 | 0.026 | 1 | 0.873 |
| Purchase help | 7 | 16 | 11.5 | 0.391 | 1 | 0.532 |
| Checkout help | 7 | 14 | 10.5 | 2.333 | 1 | 0.127 |
| Email directory | 20 | 20 | 20.0 | 0.000 | 1 | 1.000 |
| Telephone/Fax directory | 20 | 20 | 20.0 | 0.000 | 1 | 1.000 |
| Post Mail list | 20 | 20 | 20.0 | 0.000 | 1 | 1.000 |
| FAQ feature | 9 | 14 | 11.5 | 0.391 | 1 | 0.532 |
| Real-time customer service | 18 | 19 | 18.5 | 0.027 | 1 | 0.869 |
| Comments/suggestions | 20 | 20 | 20.0 | 0.000 | 1 | 1.000 |
| *Interface and Aesthetic Features (include presentation permanence and stability of controls)* | | | | | | |
| Main control | 20 | 20 | 20.0 | 0.000 | 1 | 1.000 |
| Search control | 20 | 20 | 20.0 | 0.000 | 1 | 1.000 |
| Browse control | 20 | 20 | 20.0 | 0.000 | 1 | 1.000 |
| Account control | 14 | 20 | 17.0 | 1.059 | 1 | 0.303 |
| Shopping basket control | 12 | 15 | 13.5 | 0.333 | 1 | 0.564 |
| Indirect controls | 6 | 8 | 7.0 | 0.000 | 1 | 1.000 |
| Control's stability | 20 | 19 | 19.5 | 0.026 | 1 | 0.873 |
| Link color style consistency | 20 | 20 | 20.0 | 0.000 | 1 | 1.000 |

* Sig. Level <0.05, there is a significant difference

There is no significant difference between the two cultures in terms of efficiency and portability components of an e-commerce website. However, the results shown in Table 10 revealed that under performance feature, Saudi Arabia's e-commerce websites gained 70% and 83% in the Philippines. The accessibility feature has been

**Table 7.** Usability

| Variables | Actual count | | Expected count | $X^2$ | df | Sig. Level |
| | Saudi Arabia | Philippines | | | | |
|---|---|---|---|---|---|---|
| Aesthetic designs | 20 | 19 | 19.5 | 0.026 | 1 | 0.873 |
| *Miscellaneous* | | | | | | |
| Foreign language support | 20 | 1 | 10.5 | 17.190 | 1 | 0.000* |
| What's new feature | 10 | 14 | 12.0 | 0.667 | 1 | 0.414 |

* Sig. Level <0.05, there is a significant difference

**Table 8.** Maintainability

| Variables | Actual count | | Expected count | $X^2$ | df | Sig. Level |
| | Saudi Arabia | Philippines | | | | |
|---|---|---|---|---|---|---|
| Maintainability | | | | | | |
| *Link errors* | | | | | | |
| Broken links | 20 | 20 | 20.0 | 0.000 | 1 | 1.000 |
| Invalid links | 20 | 20 | 20.0 | 0.000 | 1 | 1.000 |
| Unimplemented links | 20 | 20 | 20.0 | 0.000 | 1 | 1.000 |

* Sig. Level <0.05, there is a significant difference

**Table 9.** Maintainability and Reliability

| Variables | Actual count | | Expected count | $X^2$ | df | Sig. Level |
| | Saudi Arabia | Philippines | | | | |
|---|---|---|---|---|---|---|
| Maintainability | | | | | | |
| *Miscellaneous errors and drawbacks* | | | | | | |
| Different browsers | 20 | 20 | 20.0 | 0.000 | 1 | 1.000 |
| Browser independent | 20 | 20 | 20.0 | 0.000 | 1 | 1.000 |
| Dead-end web nodes | 20 | 20 | 20.0 | 0.000 | 1 | 1.000 |
| Destination nodes under construction | 20 | 20 | 20.0 | 0.000 | 1 | 1.000 |
| Reliability | | | | | | |
| Accuracy and relevance of information | | | | | | |
| Testimonials display | 3 | 6 | 4.5 | 4.000 | 1 | 0.046* |
| References or links pro-vision | 1 | 0 | 0.5 | 0.000 | 1 | 1.000 |
| List of physical address of the office | 9 | 16 | 12.5 | 1.960 | 1 | 0.162 |

* Sig. Level <0.05, there is a significant difference

**Table 10.** Efficiency

| Variables | Actual count | | Expected count | $X^2$ | df | Sig. Level |
|---|---|---|---|---|---|---|
| | Saudi Arabia | Philippines | | | | |
| *Efficiency* | | | | | | |
| Quick pages | 20 | 19 | 19.5 | 0.026 | 1 | 0.873 |
| Quick checkout and payment | 8 | 14 | 11.0 | 2.909 | 1 | 0.088 |
| *Portability* | | | | | | |
| Support for text-only version | 0 | 0 | 0.0 | 0.000 | 1 | 1.000 |
| Image title | 20 | 20 | 20.0 | 0.000 | 1 | 1.000 |
| Global readability | 20 | 20 | 20.0 | 0.000 | 1 | 1.000 |
| Browsers' version who do not support frames | 0 | 2 | 1.0 | 0.500 | 1 | 0.480 |
| Mobile device accessibility | 20 | 20 | 20.0 | 0.000 | 1 | 1.000 |

* Sig. Level <0.05, there is a significant difference

moderately used by the e-commerce websites of both cultures having 50% in Saudi Arabia and 53% in the Philippines. No e-commerce website in both cultures utilized the "support for text-only" version.

In general, the results of the study indicate that in terms of functionality, usability, and reliability component of e-commerce website variance in some of its features exist between the two cultures. The two countries have common characteristics pertaining to high-context cultures (Hall and Hall 1990) which support the claim of Hofstede's (2005) cultural dimensions that the two cultures both have higher power distance, collectivist and masculine society. People from high-context cultures emphasize interpersonal relationships and they are relational, collectivist, intuitive, and contemplative type of people (Hall and Hall 1990).

# 7 Conclusion

The study supports the argument that there is a significant difference exists on e-commerce websites of different cultures. With the findings of the study, it is important for the web developers to consider the features that have significant differences when improving an existing website or designing a new one. It is essential for the websites to be culturally appropriate most especially that the e-commerce websites' target users are users across different cultures.

This study has limitations that should be taken into consideration for future research related to cross-analysis of e-commerce websites. First, the study covers only twenty e-commerce websites of Saudi Arabia and of the Philippines; a higher number of websites that will be included in the study will further justify that there are differences in web design of e-commerce websites of different cultures. And second, both of the countries included in the study are both from Asia; if the two countries are from different continents then it could possibly provide major differences in the design of e-commerce websites.

# References

Al-Safadi, L.A., Garcia, R.A.: ISO9126 based quality model for evaluating B2C e-Commerce applications – Saudi market perspective. IJCIT 3(2), 8–15 (2012)

Bodker, S.: Through the Interface: A Human Activity Approach to User Interface Design. Lawrence Erlbaum, Hillsdale (1991)

Burns, J., Madey, G.R.: A framework for effective user interface design for web-based electronic commerce applications. Informing Sci. 4(2), 67–75 (2001). (Special Issue: Expanding the Focus)

Cell, B.: Web site design: what do i need to know? Pennsylvania CPA J. 71(1),15 –19 (2000)

Coopee, T., Mitchell, L., MacDonald, T., Steinacher, S.: Catching net customers. Info World 22 (14), 54–55 (2000)

Cyr, D., Trevor-Smith, H.: Localization of web design: an empirical comparison of German, Japanese, and US web site characteristics. J. Am. Soc. Inf. Sci. Technol. 55(13), 1199–1208 (2004)

Hall, E., Hall, M.: Understanding Cultural Differences. Intercultural Press, London (1990)

Hofstede, G.: Cultures and Organizations: Software of the Mind. McGraw-Hill, London (2005)

ISO/IEC 9126-1: Software engineering – Product Quality – Part 1: Quality Model, 1st ed. (2001)

Khurana, H., Goel, M.K., Singh, H., Bhutani, L.: E-Commerce: role of E-Commerce in today's business. VSRD Int. J. Bus. Manag. Res. 1(7) (2011)

Meyer, N.: E-Commerce Interface Design Parameters and their Relation to Website Popularity (2008). Accessed 28 Jan 2014

Najjar, L.J.: E-commerce user interface design for the Web (2001). http://www.lawrence-ajjar. com/papers/Ecommerce_user_interface_designfor_the_Web.html. Accessed 8 May 2008

Tarafdar, M., Zhang, J.: Analysis of critical website characteristics: a cross category study of successful websites. J. Comput. Inf. Syst. 46(2), 14–24 (2006)

Totonchi, J., Manshady, K.: Relationship between globalization and e-Commerce. Int. J. e-Education, e-Business, e-Management e-Learning 2(1), 83–87 (2011)

Zhang, Q., Chen, R., Zoe, Y.: reengineering user interfaces of E-Commerce applications using business processes. In: Proceedings of the 22nd IEEE International Conference on Software Maintenance (ICSM 2006) (2006)

# Cross-Cultural Design for Employability: Mobile Support for Healthcare Professionals

Nataliya Berbyuk Lindström[✉]

Department of Applied Information Technology, University of Gothenburg,
PO Box 115 405 30 Gothenburg, Sweden
nataliya.berbyuk.lindstrom@ait.gu.se

**Abstract.** Supporting migrants in entering host societies is a challenge. In Sweden, influx of migrants resulted in problems with access to in-classroom Swedish language courses for migrants in general, and for health care professionals (HCPs) in particular. Due to its accessibility, mobile technology can be a bridging tool between migrants and host societies, providing an alternative/complement to classroom teaching.

This study reports on the non-European HCPs' employability needs, and how these needs can be met by a mobile application. A qualitative methodology based on semi-structured focus group interviews and interactive workshops with HCPs, mentors and language teachers is used to (a) investigate the HPCs' needs; (b) discuss the content and the design of a mobile prototype application (app) for supporting labour market integration of HCPs. Further, based on the findings, a prototype is created for user testing. Thematic content analysis is used for analysis of the data from the focus groups and workshops. Descriptive statistics is used for the analysis of questionnaires for prototype testing.

The results show that the HCPs need a targeted language and culture training as well as opportunities to develop contacts with Swedish HCPs. Further, a roadmap for the main steps needed to get a medical license is requested. The users are in general positive about the prototype. The results suggest a possibility of cultural impact on design preferences.

The study gives suggestions for developing a mobile app for enhancing integration of HCPs in the Swedish labor market, which can potentially be further developed for other professional groups.

**Keywords:** Migrants · Healthcare professionals · Mobile technology
Application design · Employability

## 1 Introduction

### 1.1 European Migrant Crisis 2015–2016

In 2015–2016, over 1.2 million first time asylum seekers were registered in Europe, the majority coming from Syria, Afghanistan and Iraq [1]. Host societies meet many challenges in supporting migrants' integration [2]. Providing equal opportunities for all members, regardless of their background, and to enable and motivate newly arrived

© Springer International Publishing AG, part of Springer Nature 2018
P.-L. P. Rau (Ed.): CCD 2018, LNCS 10911, pp. 314–326, 2018.
https://doi.org/10.1007/978-3-319-92141-9_24

migrants to participate in the life of host society is essential for preventing social exclusion [3].

Early language training in combination with labour market entry are the cornerstones of successful integration [4]. Due to the large number of newly arrived migrants in Sweden, providing access to in-classroom courses has been challenging, which resulted in an increase in development of online language courses and mobile apps to meet the needs [5]. However, though a variety of apps are available for both language learning and societal information [6], few provide a targeted language training for highly skilled migrant professionals in general, and for health care professionals (HCPs) in particular [7].

### 1.2  Healthcare Professionals (HCPs) in Sweden

Though in Sweden "Swedish language for immigrants" courses are provided free of charge, little attention has been paid to migrant diversity in terms of educational and professional background [8]. Targeted training courses for highly skilled professionals, which include both professional and language training, are few. Some examples are *Korta vägen programme* ("Short way") for doctors, nurses, pharmacists, biomedical analysts, teachers, and engineers, *Korsvägen* ("Crossroad") for teachers, and supplementary education for HCPs (primarily doctors) in Sahlgrenska Academy, Gothenburg, Lund University, Lund, and Karolinska Institute, Stockholm. Today, it takes 4 to 6 years for doctors coming from outside the European Union to enter the labour market in Sweden [9]. Validating education, passing Swedish language test, medical licensing examination and managing internship to fulfil the requirements for Swedish medical license is a lengthy process, which results in frustration and losing professional skills [10]. Further, those HCPs who get the license and start working report communication problems in interactions with patients and colleagues, which often result in patient complains, stress, discrimination, and exclusion from decision making, etc. [11].

## 2  The Aim of the Study

The study investigates the needs in terms of employability and integration into the labor market of HCPs with a medical degree outside the European union and how these can be met in a mobile application. Research questions include:

1. What professional needs in terms of integration into the labor market do the newly arrived HCPs have?
2. How can a mobile app be designed taking into account cross-cultural design aspects to support the transition to employability in the new country?

## 3   Background

### 3.1   Integration and Mobile-Assisted Learning

Integration is the acculturation strategy when migrants have an interest in both maintaining one's original culture and learning the culture of host society [12]. Integration can only be "freely" chosen and successfully pursued by non-dominant groups when the dominant society "is open and inclusive in its orientation towards cultural diversity" [12]. Getting employment together with education, housing and access to healthcare are essential markers and means of integration, which can be facilitated by language proficiency and cultural knowledge [13] as well as contacts with the members of host society [14].

Many immigrants have smartphones and use them for keeping in contact with families back home and geographical navigation [15, 16]. Mobile technologies enable portable, networked and new contexts of learning [17, 18] promoting progressive, authentic, interactive and social learning environments [19].

A number of mobile applications (apps) have been developed in the countries that accepted large numbers of migrants, e.g. Germany, the UK, and Sweden to supply migrants with different kinds of information. In Germany, *Ankommen* app [20] contains a basic German language course, societal information (food, labour market, housing), overview of the asylum procedure, transportation, child care, and other relevant information for newly arrived migrants. In Sweden, *Welcome* app was created by volunteers in 2015 to enable contacts and networking between locals and migrants via chat and social events [21]. In the UK, within MASELTOV (Mobile Assistance for Social Inclusion & Empowerment of Immigrants with Persuasive Learning Technologies & Social Network Services) project, smartphone services to support geographical navigation and development of communication skills to enable a situated incidental language and culture learning integrated in a prototype app (*MApp*) for immigrants were developed [22]. In another British project, SALSA (Smart cities and language learning), the city's network infrastructure and language learning solutions for immigrants through smartphones were developed [23, 24].

Few studies offer a systematic review of the mobile applications for immigrants. Berbyuk Lindström et al. [7] and Sofkova Hashemi et al. [5] show that there are distinct discrepancies in relation to the available resources on the market, their use and the newly arrived migrants' needs. Most of the mobile resources in the Swedish market are language training apps, e.g. *Duolingo, Lingio, Hej svenska* (Hello Swedish), which are weakly related to the migrants' social and economic integration needs, i.e. managing employment, education and accommodation. It results in lack of motivation for learners to use them regularly [19]. Further, little attention has been paid to the targeted mobile assisted support for migrants from different educational and professional backgrounds as well as to cultural aspects both in terms of app content and design.

### 3.2  Cross-Cultural Design and Development of Mobile Applications for Migrants

Since the world is becoming more globalized, paying attention to cultural differences (and similarities) among people is essential. To design mobile applications successfully for people with different cultural backgrounds, sensitivity to cultural nuances is needed [25, 26]. Awareness of cultural differences can especially be important in designing mobile apps for newly arrived migrants, many of which suffer from stress and anxiety, in order to support their interest and motivation to integrate and to ensure product usability.

Culture can be defined as "the collective programming of the mind that distinguishes the members of one group or category of people from another" [27]. Kroeber and Kluckhohn consider even "distinctive achievements of human groups, including their embodiments in artefacts" as elements of culture [28]. Though often criticized [29], Hofstede's framework, composed of six main dimensions, is broadly accepted and used in relation to user-interface design [30, 31]. The dimensions include *power distance* (acceptance and expectance of unequal power distribution), *uncertainty avoidance* (tolerance for ambiguity), *individualism versus collectivism* (expectations of connections between people), *masculinity versus femininity* (preference for achievement vs cooperation), *long- versus short-term orientation* (relation to past and future) and *indulgence versus restraint* (free versus suppressed gratification).

Hall theory of High- and Low context cultures [32] is also used in relation to design, e.g. in the use of visuals [33]. According to Hall, cultures differ in the extent to which the environment, more specifically, social context (i.e., the network of social expectations that determine a person's behavior) is meaningful for communication. Hall divides cultures into high-context (HC), represented by the Japanese, Arab, and Mediterranean cultures. The low-context (LC) are the Swiss, German, Scandinavian (except Finland, which is an HC culture [34]) and North American cultures. Compared to LC, HC communication is less verbally explicit, little is the coded, transmitted part of the message. LC communication, on the contrary, is characterized by more reliance on verbal communication.

## 4  Methodology

First, to address the research question 1 (RQ1) concerning the integration needs, the 1st interactive workshop (3.5 h) was organized. Working groups consisting of 17 participants (10 newly arrived HCPs, doctors and nurses, 2 coaches, 2 course managers, 2 Swedish language teachers and an employment agency agent) explored the needs and concerns the non-European HCPs had in various stages of the process towards employment. The research question 2 (RQ2) concerning the app design was addressed in the 2nd interactive workshop (3 h), when the participants from the 1st workshop could discuss and visualize their ideas (Fig. 1).

**Fig. 1.** Workshop 2: Brainstorming about visualization of the way to the Swedish medical license

Further, nine focus group interviews with HCPs (6.7 h) were conducted focusing on both RQ1 and 2. Apart from the newly arrived participants from the workshops, 11 participants from the *Korta vägen*-courses were involved. In total 21 Arabic-speaking HCPs (12 males and 9 females), primarily doctors, pharmacists and dentists, enrolled in preparatory courses, participated in the study. The majority of them were between 26–45 years old, came from Syria (17), Iraq (3), and Algeria (1) and spent between 1,5-3 years in Sweden.

Both workshops were based on participatory design principles [35], where participants used tangible materials and co-creative practices to explore possible future supports [36]. The focus group interviews and the workshops were carried out in Swedish and English. The focus group interviews were audio-recorded and transcribed. The workshops were documented using field notes, video-recordings and photos.

Thematic Content analysis [37] was used for the analysis of focus groups and interviews from the workshops. Each project member read two transcripts and identified the themes related to use of the app and integration needs to develop a preliminary coding scheme. It was then applied to two more transcripts. A working coding scheme was developed and applied to all transcripts. Differences in coding were resolved during the team meetings, and the themes were identified.

Based on the analysis of data, a prototype was created using React programming language [38] and tested three weeks after the workshops. After a brief introduction of the prototype, 22 HCPs (including five participants from the interactive workshops and the interviews) were asked to freely explore the prototype and answer the questionnaire related to design and content. In conclusion, a brief collective discussion was held about the participants' impressions.

The project was approved by the Ethical Review Board, Gothenburg, Sweden. Prior to conducting the study, all participants got information from the project group in both oral and written form. All involved participants gave their written consent for participation. Anonymity was emphasized as well as the possibility for the participants to withdraw from the project at any point. The participants' names and other material facts, such as place names, identification numbers, etc., were altered to preserve their anonymity. As the project is related to the Swedish Migration Agency, the participants were ensured that their participation would not affect their status in any way, e.g. residence permit, benefits, etc.

## 5    Results

### 5.1    RQ 1. Integration Needs in Relation to Employability of Newly Arrived Migrants

In regard to integration needs in relation to employability, three main themes emerge in the data:

(1)  getting a clear picture of career steps to get a Swedish license to practice;
(2)  developing contacts with Swedish HCPs and
(3)  learning the language and culture codes in relation to the Swedish healthcare context.

**Theme 1. Getting a Clear Picture of Career Steps to Get a Swedish License to Practice.** Getting a picture of what steps to take in order to get a Swedish license to practice is one of the central needs mentioned by both the HCPs, their mentors and teachers. The entire process is perceived as quite difficult and confusing to keep track of. Though much information is available online in text form, it can be complicated to find and to understand it due to language problems. Information about validation of medical education, the structure of the Swedish healthcare system, the information useful for passing the medical licensing examination and getting internship is essential.

**Theme 2. Contact with Fellow HCPs from Sweden.** The majority of HCPs feel isolated. Many report little or no contact with the Swedes in general, and with the Swedish HCPs in particular. Some reasons for getting more contact with the locals are: (a) getting the information and support concerning to the aspects mentioned in Theme 1; (b) learning the Swedish language and cultural codes in general, and in relation to healthcare context in particular (Theme 3 below); and (d) finding an internship. Many HCPs believe that "referral is important here in Sweden, you need a reference, it can help you to solve your problems," e.g. to get an internship.

**Theme 3. Learning the Swedish Language and the Cultural Codes.** The participants emphasize that, apart from learning the Swedish language in classrooms, additional training is needed in relation to the Swedish cultural values. Many respondents report having no/little insight in the Swedish healthcare communication and expressed anxiety about managing cultural differences when they get an internship.

Hierarchy, doctor and patient roles, decision making, trust, gender, family role, expression and recognition of emotions, conflict management and ethical challenges are mentioned as especially challenging by the HCPs.

## 5.2  RQ 2. Prototype Designing and Prototype Testing

**Prototype Designing.** On the question about designing the app, the HCPs report a strong need to visualize the career steps (related to Theme 1). An interactive roadmap is suggested to contain different paths which can lead to license and a short information about each step. For instance, providing sample tests for the users "to be able to study after the courses" is mentioned by the participants.

Developing a contact making function to support getting in touch with Swedish HCPs (Theme 2) is also requested. The respondents consider initial contacts via chat being the easiest way, requesting voice messaging and video-chat functions for developing further contacts. Many perceive written chats as impersonal and "childish."

Concerning Theme 3, the respondents believe that video-recorded dialogues, embedded in the app can be used for both language and cultural training. Consultation structure, communication in different stages of consultation, illustrations of bodily communication are suggested to be included in the app.

Analysis of the data resulted in a prototype. To meet the needs of Theme 1, a" roadmap" to support the HCPs on their way to license, based on the requirements from National Board for Health and Welfare (see Figs. 2, 3, 4 and 5 below) was designed. Three main "paths to license" are distinguished, presented below. The prototype contains 4 tabs with a roadmap for the three different paths to medical license, including knowledge test (Fig. 2), getting an additional education (Fig. 3) or the Swedish medical education (Fig. 4). The fourth tab (Fig. 5, All Roadmaps) is a merging of the three different paths with the purpose of providing a holistic picture for the users which options exist and how the three different paths differ.

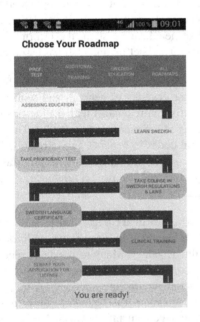

**Fig. 2.** "Medical knowledge test"

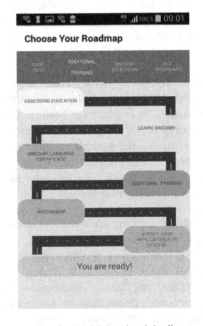

**Fig. 3.** "Additional training"

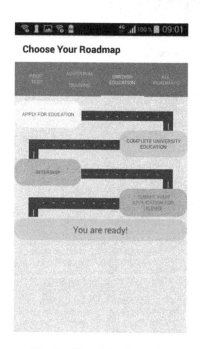

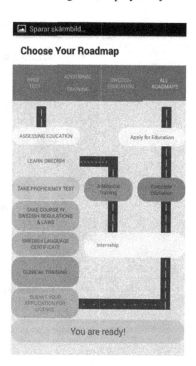

**Fig. 4.** "Swedish education"          **Fig. 5.** "All roads"

For more information, the user can click on the steps in the map (see Fig. 6). This will show a new page with a short description of the step, other relevant information, tips, and the links to other web resources.

To address the Themes 2 and 3, the links to video-recordings are made in the step "Learn Swedish." A short video-recording of interaction with a transcript, vocabulary section, a word list with medical terms (Swedish-Arabic) and a space for comments about the cultural aspects, e.g. eye contact and touch, with links to a discussion forum are designed.

**Prototype Testing.** During the testing, the majority of the respondents (72%) report a better understanding of the process for getting a medical license after using the prototype, while 9% answered "maybe". Regarding the information that the participants lacked, many comment on providing more information about medical licensing examination and internship.

More pictures and increased font size to ensure readability are also mentioned by some HCPs (23%). Some respondents suggest that the colours can be improved to reinforce the connection between different steps. Medical language quizzes, sample medical tests with a forum for discussions are suggested to be further developed.

**Fig. 6.** Information about additional training

## 6 Discussion

Today's migration is characterized by the vital role technology plays for millions of migrants. About 86% of Syrian young people in refugee camps have smartphones [39]. Upon coming to the host countries, smartphones can be used for supporting migrants in learning a new language, acquiring a new culture, getting employment/education, managing housing, as well as contacts with locals.

The results of the study show that getting employment is the primary concern for the migrant HCPs. One of the main obstacles is lack of knowledge what steps to take in order to fulfil the requirements for medical license. Sweden is a highly technological society, and much information is available online, from different sources, which can be complicated to search for and to understand by newly arrived migrants with limited Swedish language competence. It might partially explain the HCPs' need of providing a simplified visual "roadmap" of the process.

Making contacts with fellow Swedish HCPs is emphasized by the HCPs as well. Sweden is characterized by individualistic cultural values [27], favouring independence, loneliness and solitude [40], while the HCPs in this study come from more collectivistic countries (e.g. Syria and Iraq [27]), in which making contacts is somewhat easier. This cultural difference, together with language problems, might be a possible reason for the problems related to making contacts and requesting mobile support to solve them.

Learning the language and culture codes in relation to the Swedish healthcare context, e.g. videos, pictures, quizzes, were also mentioned by the participants. As the respondents report limited opportunities to work/practice in Sweden and little/no contact with the Swedes, a mobile app is perceived as a possible source of information about the Swedish healthcare context.

Concerning the prototype design, the Arabic HCPs expressing wishes for video and voice chat might be related to cultural factors, such as preferences for face-to-face communication and developing relationships common for HC societies [32, 41]. Further, it can also be related to language competence, as possibility to see an interlocutor can contribute to better understanding in communication. As the application is aimed to be used for communication between Swedes and non-Swedes, attention should be paid to the preferences of Swedish users as well. Taking into account that Sweden is a relatively LC culture, the Swedish users might (though not necessarily) show preferences for written distance communication. Thus, designing mobile applications, understanding of users' characteristics and their immediate needs are essential to ensure usability [42] which might become increasingly complex when the users are from different cultural backgrounds.

## 7 Conclusions

This study explores the needs of the non-European HCPs and design of mobile application for supporting their integration in the Swedish labor market. Results indicate that the designers should take into account the users' design preferences, some of which can be related to their cultural backgrounds. Further studies can be done to get a better picture of the HCPs needs, develop the design and test the usability of the application.

**Acknowledgments.** The study was conducted as part of the MInclusion research project: Integration with mobiles, minclusion.org. The author wishes to acknowledge the support of the Asylum, Migration and Integration Fund (AMIF), Chalmers Innovation and Rise Interactive. The author is particularly grateful to the respondents for their participation and to the project members for providing their advice in the research.

## References

1. Eurostat. Record number of over 1.2 million first time asylum seekers registered in 2015, http://ec.europa.eu/eurostat/web/products-press-releases/-/3-04032016-AP.    Accessed 17/11/28
2. Metcalfe-Hough, V.: The migration crisis? Facts, challenges and possible solutions. A policy brief. http://www.odi.org. Accessed 17/09/16
3. Silver, H.: Social exclusion and social solidarity: three paradigms. Int. Labour Rev. **133**(5–6), 531 (1994)

4. Degler, E., Liebig, T.: Finding their way. Labour market integration of refugees in Germany, OECD. http://www.oecd.org/migration. Accessed 17/11/ 28

5. Olsson, G., Brundin, K.: Drygt 14 000 nyanlända får onlinekurser i svenska (About 14000 newly arrived migrants get online Swedish courses). https://www.uhr.se/erasmusplus. Accessed 17/11/17

6. Sofkova Hashemi, S., Berbyuk Lindström, N., Bartram, L., Bradley, L.: Investigating mobile technology resources for integration: the Technology-Pedagogy-Language-Culture (TPLC) model. In: Loizides, F., Papadopoulos, G., Souleles, N. (eds.) Proceedings of the 16th World Conference on Mobile and Contextual Learning, mLearn 2017, Larnaca, Cyprus, 30 October–1 November, 2017, pp. 20:1–20:8. ACM (2017)

7. Berbyuk Lindström, N., Sofkova Hashemi, S., Bartram, L., Bradley, L.: Mobile resources for integration: how availability meets the needs of newly arrived Arabic-speaking migrants in Sweden. In: Borthwick, K., Bradley, L., Thouësny, S. (eds.) CALL in a Climate of Change: Adapting to Turbulent Global Conditions – Short Papers from EUROCALL 2017, pp. 40–45. Research-publishing.net (2017)

8. Lundgren, B., Rosén, J.: 15 års forskning om sfi - en överblick (15 years research about sfi – an overview). http://www.ifous.se/forstudie-15-ars-forskning-om-sfi-en-overblick/. Accessed 17/11/28

9. Jelmini, M.: Lång väntetid för utländsk vårdpersonal (Long waiting time for foreign healthcare staff). https://www.svd.se/lang-vantetid-for-utlandsk-vardpersonal. Accessed 17/10/28

10. Andersson, M.: Lång kamp för att få svensk läkarlegitimation (A long struggle to get the Swedish medical license), Fria tidningar. http://www.fria.nu/artikel/118018. Accessed 17/10/11

11. Berbyuk Lindström, N.: Intercultural communication in health care – Non-Swedish physicians in Sweden, Ph.D. thesis. Gothenburg Papers in Theoretical Lingustics, Gothenburg (2008)

12. Berry, J.: Immigration, acculturation, and adaptation. Appl. Psychol. 46(1), 5–34 (1997)

13. Rooth, D., Åslund, O.: Utbildning och kunskaper i svenska: Framgångsfaktorer för invandrade? (Education and Knowledge in Swedish: Success factors for Immigrants?). SNS, Stockholm (2006)

14. Ager, A., Strang, A.: Understanding integration: a conceptual framework. J. Refugee Stud. 21(2), 166–191 (2008)

15. Bradley, L., Berbyuk Lindström, N., Sofkova Hashemi, S.: Integration and language learning of newly arrived migrants using mobile technology. J. Interact. Media Educ. 1(3), 1–9 (2017)

16. Ram, A.: Smartphones bring solace and aid to desperate refugees. https://www.wired.com/2015/12/smartphone-syrian-refugee-crisis/. Accessed 17/02/22

17. Pachler, N., Bachmair, B., Cook, J., Kress, G.: Mobile Learning: Structures, Agency, Practices. Springer, US, Boston, MA (2009)

18. Viberg, O., Grönlund, Å.: Mobile assisted language learning: a literature review. In: Mlearn 2012 - Mobile and Contextual Learning, pp. 9–16 (2012)

19. Kukulska-Hulme, A., Shield, L.: An overview of mobile assisted language learning: from content delivery to supported collaboration and interaction. ReCALL 20(3), 271–289 (2008)

20. Toor, A.: Germany launches smartphone app to help refugees integrate. https://www.theverge.com/2016/1/13/10761150/germany-refugee-smartphone-app-ankommen. Accessed 16/2/22

21. Lutero, L.: Refugees now find it easier to make friends in Sweden. https://www.psfk.com/2016/03/welcome-app-helps-refugees-friends-in-sweden.html. Accessed 17/06/28

22. Paletta, L., Dunwell, I., Gaved, M., Bobeth, J., Efremidis, S., Luley, P., Kukulska-Hulme, A., de Freitas, S., Lameras, P., Deutsch, S.: Advances in the MASELTOV game – mobile assistance for social inclusion and empowerment of immigrants with persuasive learning technologies and social network services. In: Katayose, H., Reidsma, D., Nijholt, A. (eds.) Proceedings of the 10th International Conference on Advances in Computer Entertainment, pp. 440–455. ACE (2013)

23. Demmans Epp, C.: Migrants and mobile technology use: gaps in the support provided by current tools. J. Interact. Media Educ. **2017**(1), 1–13 (2017)

24. Gaved, M., Peasgood, A.: Fitting in versus learning: a challenge for migrants learning languages using smartphones. J. Interact. Media Educ. **2017**(1), 1–13 (2017)

25. Lee, D.Y., Waller, M.: Cross-cultural design learning tool: Cross-Cultural Design (CCD) approach: a study of south korean student projects in collaboration with Goldsmiths, University of London, UK. In: Rau, P.-L.P. (ed.) CCD 2016. LNCS, vol. 9741, pp. 89–97. Springer, Cham (2016). https://doi.org/10.1007/978-3-319-40093-8_10

26. Chen, C.-H., Tsai, C.-Y.: Designing user interfaces for mobile entertaining devices with cross-cultural considerations. In: Aykin, N. (ed.) UI-HCII 2007. LNCS, vol. 4559, pp. 37–46. Springer, Heidelberg (2007). https://doi.org/10.1007/978-3-540-73287-7_6

27. Hofstede, G.: Culture's Consequences: Comparing Values, Behaviors, Institutions, and Organizations Across Nations, 2nd edn. Sage, Thousand Oaks (2001)

28. Kroeber, A.L., Kluckhohn, C.: Culture: A Critical Review of Concepts and Definitions. Harvard University Press, Cambridge (1952)

29. McSweeney, B.: The essentials of scholarship: a reply to Geert Hofstede. Hum. Relat. **55**(11), 1363–1372 (2002)

30. Marcus, A., Gould, E.: Crosscurrents: cultural dimensions and global Web user-interface design. Interactions **7**(4), 32–46 (2000)

31. Burgmann, I., Kitchen, P., Williams, R.: Does culture matter on the web? Mark. Intell. Plan. **24**(1), 62–76 (2006)

32. Hall, E.T.: Beyond Culture. Anchor P, Garden City (1981)

33. Würtz, E.: Intercultural communication on web sites: a cross-cultural analysis of Web sites from High-Context Cultures and Low-Context Cultures. J. Comput. Mediat. Commun. **11**(1), 274–299 (2005)

34. Lehtonen, J., Sajavaara, K.: The silent Finn. In: Tannen, D., Saville-Troike, M. (eds.) Perspectives on Silence, pp. 193–201. Ablex Publishing Corporation, Norwood (1985)

35. Sanders, E.B.-N.: From user-centered to participatory design approaches. In: Frascara, J. (ed.) Design and the Social Sciences: Making Connections, vol. 1. Taylor and Francis, London (2003)

36. Holmlid, S., Mattelmäki, T., Visser, F.S., Vaajakallio, K.: Co-creative practices in service innovation. In: Agarwal, R., Selen, W., Roos, G. (eds.) The Handbook of Service Innovation, pp. 545–574. Springer, London (2015). https://doi.org/10.1007/978-1-4471-6590-3_25

37. Braun, V., Clarke, V.: Using thematic analysis in psychology. Qual. Res. Psychol. **3**(2), 77–101 (2006)

38. React homepage. https://reactjs.org/. Accessed 18/01/12

39. Maitland, C., Tomaszewski, B., Fisher, K., et al.: Youth mobile phone and Internet use, January 2015, Za'atari Camp, Mafraq, Jordan. Penn State College of Information Sciences and Technology (2015)

40. Barinaga, E.: Swedishness through lagom: Can words tell us anything about a culture? Research Paper Series 6. Stockholm School of Economics, Center for Advanced Studies in Leadership, Stockholm (1999)

41. Zaharna, R.: Understanding cultural preferences of Arab communication patterns. Public Relations Rev. **21**(3), 241–255 (1995)
42. Bobeth, J., Schreitter, S., Schmehl, S., Deutsch, S., Tscheligi, M.: User-centered design between cultures: designing for and with immigrants. In: Kotzé, P., Marsden, G., Lindgaard, G., Wesson, J. (eds.) INTERACT 2013. LNCS, vol. 8120, pp. 713–720. Springer, Heidelberg (2013). https://doi.org/10.1007/978-3-642-40498-6_65

# Sociability from the Perspective of Cultural Diversity in Virtual Communities of Practice

Tatiany Xavier de Godoi[1]([⊠]), Breno Guerra Zancan[2],
Daniela Freitas Guilhermino[2], Eduardo Filgueiras Damasceno[1],
Jose Reinaldo Merlin[2], Thiago Adriano Coleti[2], André Menolli[2],
and Ederson Marcos Sgarbi[2]

[1] Universidade Tecnológica Federal do Paraná, Cornélio Procópio, PR, Brazil
tatigodoi_ll@hotmail.com, damasceno@utfpr.edu.br
[2] Universidade Estadual do Norte de Paraná, Bandeirantes, PR, Brazil
brenozancan@gmail.com, {danielaf,merlin,
thiago.coleti,menolli,sgarbi}@uenp.edu.br

**Abstract.** Virtual Communities of Practice (VCoPs) create spaces for collaboration that provide communication and interaction between individuals, so that knowledge and experiences are shared. Collaboration is a significant tool for building knowledge around a domain. In this sense, a significant effort has been expended to discover guidelines that it allows to facilitate the collaboration. A significant aspect of collaboration is the sociability, since it refers to how people interact in an environment. In VCoPs the aspects of sociability and interactivity are significant for achieving the objectives of the collaboration. However, we must consider that people have cultural differences, and it sometimes impose conditions that prevent the access and inclusion of some people in virtual environments of collaboration. Thus, in this work, is proposed a heuristic to evaluate how sociability is treated in VCops, with emphasis on cultural diversity aspects. The proposed heuristic was applied in the evaluation of some VCoPs. The results support the proposal of guidelines for the treatment of cultural diversity, seeking to assist specialists to plan and create environment interfaces that allow to promote sociability effectively and satisfactorily.

**Keywords:** Cultural differences · Sociability · Cultural diversity
Virtual Communities of Practice · Heuristic

## 1 Introduction

Virtual Communities of Practice (VCoPs) are developed in order to allow the users to discussing about subject and sharing experiences through the Web. Benbunan and Hiltz (1999) affirm that "working in group brings motivation to the individual, because their work will be observed, commented and evaluated by people from a community of which they are a part". Corroborating, Fuks et al. (2002) describe that "collaborating the abilities, knowledge and the individual efforts complement each other".

A significant aspect of Virtual Communities of Practice (VCoPs) is the sociability issue, that, according to Baechler (1995) "is the human capacity to create and maintain

© Springer International Publishing AG, part of Springer Nature 2018
P.-L. P. Rau (Ed.): CCD 2018, LNCS 10911, pp. 327–340, 2018.
https://doi.org/10.1007/978-3-319-92141-9_25

social ties, using units of individual or collective activities and makes circulate information representing the interests and opinions".

Sociability allows the interaction among people who present cultural diversity, which could include: religious, economic, gender, among others.

In order to understand the cultural diversity, it is necessary to understand the concept of culture. According to Candau (2000), the culture refers to meanings historically transmitted, formed by symbols. Thus, as the actor mentions, the big challenge on the cultural issue is dealing with diversity, multiplicity of trends in relation to the culture issue.

In this paper is proposed a heuristic to assist in the research of the main difficulties caused by cultural diversity during the socialization in VCoPs.

This research was performed in three stages: (1) Diagnosis of difficulties related to cultural diversity; (2) Proposed heuristic for the evaluation of cultural diversity; (3) Application of the proposed heuristic.

## 2    Virtual Communities of Practice

The expression "Community of Practice" (CoP), was coined by Lave and Wenger (1991), it is defined as a group of people informally and contextually connected, with responsibilities in the process, who share a concern or passion about a topic, and who deepen their knowledge and expertise in this area by interacting on an ongoing basis in order to improve their knowledge on the same topic.

According to Wenger et al. (2002) three structural components characterize the CoP: domain, community and practice:

- The *domain* is the essential element of a community of practice, and it corresponds to an area of knowledge, interest or human activity. It defines its identity and the key issues that members need to address (Wenger 2004). It is the focus of the CoP and evolves over its life span in response to new, emerging challenges and issues (Henri 2006).
- The *community* is the central element of a CoP, it is composed by members, their interactions and by the building of relationships. From the communities it is that the CoP are characterized, thus forming the identity of the individuals in the group (Wenger et al. 2002).
- *Practice* can be understood as the knowledge shared by members. Sharing knowledge and experiences with the others users is one of the usual ways of interaction and socialization in CoP, these relationships include a set of structures, tools, information, styles, language, documents and understanding, shared by members (Wenger et al. 2002).

Thus, to create a CoP it is necessary that a group of people (community) interact each other, collaborate, share knowledge and perform a common activity (practice) in the same context (domain) (Trindade 2013).

Mengalli (2014) states that CoPs tend to have their own identity and, if well-developed, they can develop their own language allowing members to have a better communication and affirmation in identifying, as a result, each member in a community contributes with some important aspect to its characterization, one of these contributions is related to a specific language. According to Mengali (2014), these expressions help communities to work in communion, they differentiate from the other communities and strengthen themselves as they fell part of a solid group.

The CoP involves a series of elements (actors, resources, competencies, activists, among others) and their interrelationship, necessary to achieve the purposes. In a robust work, Tifous et al. (2007a, 2007b) presents the main elements and semantic annotations for the learning in CoP. The concepts related to members, resources and knowledge were defined from an investigation into 12 CoPs from Palette4 project (Henri 2006). Table 1 presents a synthesis, made by Trindade (2013) from the research of Tifous et al. (2007a, 2007b).

**Table 1.** Main concepts inherent in CoPs.

Source: Trindade (2013) adapted from Tifous et al. (2007a, 2007b)

| CoP – main concepts | | Autores |
|---|---|---|
| Community | Motivation, Domain, Practice | Wenger (2001) |
| | Area; Purpose; Structure; Composition | Tifous et al. (2007a, 2007b) |
| | Cultural Diversity | Langelier and Wenger (2005) |
| Members | Personal Characteristics; Type of involvement; Role in the CoP; Peripheral Role | Miller (1995), Tifous et al. (2007a, 2007b) |
| Competence | Type of Competence | Tifous et al. (2007a, 2007b) |
| Collaboration | Collaboration objective; Collaboration Activities; Actors Involved (Roles); Geographic Dimension; Temporal Dimension; Collaboration Resources; Media and Modes of communication; Type of interaction, | Vidou et al. (2006) |
| | Engagement, Coordination | Deaudelin et al. (2003), Weiseth et al. (2006) |
| Decision-Making | Actors Involved (Roles); Resources for decision making | Tifous et al. (2007a, 2007b) |
| CoP Resources | Interactions registration; Tools CoP | |

Related to CoP, the term Virtual Community of Practice (VCoP), is defined by Souza (2000) as a group of people sharing the same interests through the Internet.

According to Teigland and Wasko (2004) VCoPs can present some different functions in relation to CoPs, they are: the sent messages are automatically recorded, allowing you to interact at any time, in addition to being able to consult past information; the interactions may be instantaneous, however, in most cases they do not happen in real time; most of the time people are not aware of the people they are interacting with, in this case it is not necessary to know the other person as an individual, the interest is to know about the person's knowledge.

Considering some of the main differences between CoP and VCoP, it is verified that the VCoP incorporates some functions related to the technological aspect, which allows, among other things, the storage of information for the future recovery. Nevertheless, the information storage has also been predicted on the ontology of Tifous et al. (2007a, 2007b), which describes the CoP Resources as tools that can support the Interaction Registration (as presented in Table 1).

Thus, in this research, it was considered that the work of Tifous et al. (2007a, 2007b), which details the main elements and interrelationships of a CoP (characteristics, objectives, possible roles, skills that actors can presente), can also be related to VCoPs.

## 3 Sociability and Cultural Diversity

Sociability refers to the joining of people, which generates purposes and practices in which individuals share the same idea, and also have different relationships (harmonic or conflicting), thus, they always acquire knowledge of the competences and contributions of each other. Each person usually has prior knowledge about the subject being treated, and for this reason the information is transmitted with greater speed, going straight to the point (Recuero 2009).

Preece (2001) cites three components that contribute to have a good sociability:

(i) Purpose - A community's shared focus on an interest, need, information, service, or support, that provides a reason for individual members to belong to the community; (ii) People - Some of these people may take different roles in the community, such as leaders, protagonists, comedians, moderators, etc.; (iii) Policies - The language and protocols that guide people's interactions within the community. More formal policies may also be needed, such as registration policies, and codes of behaviour for moderators.

According to Marcotte (2003), the members of the community are involved in a culture, a value system and a symbolic universe, of the members that constitute it and helps them to create an identity. This identification and cultural development of communities finds the maximum expression in the CoPs, in which the individual comes from different cultures and, consequently, there is great diversity in various aspects, thus sharing their culture, history, goals and meanings.

Wenger (1998) considers that diversity in a CoP arises from the interaction among participants in their practices and it is related to the competencies of each participant, resulting in organized and coherent practices. The author estimates that this diversity present in the CoPs is responsible for the organization and the coherence of the community to the extent that it makes possible the complementation of functions and individual skills within the CoP. This interdependence among the elements of CoP can become a limit when it comes to a component that is resistant to interaction.

A diversity of people, from adolescents to adults, students or not, professionals, retirees, elderly are increasingly using interaction tools. The cultural aspect can cause differences in behavior among people, such as differences in work planning, decision-making, style of argument, conversation flow, among others (Olson and Olson 2003).

Cultural diversity can take many forms, such as: Physical Distance; Temporal Distance; Language; Social Interation Rules and Legislation.

## 4 Heuristic of Support for the Evaluation of Sociability from the Perspective of Cultural Diversity in VCoPs

This research aims to complement the heuristic aspects of sociability proposed by Lopes et al. (2015), considering that cultural diversity is also a fator that influences social interactions. The heuristic proposed by Lopes et al. (2015), named SVCoP, addressed different aspects inherent to VCoPs. However, considering the breadth and complexity of each aspect, it did not addressed the aspects of cultural diversity, which seeks this research in order to contribute with this model of evaluation.

Figure 1 presents the conceptual model of the heuristic of Lopes et al. (2015) with the inclusion of the evaluation of cultural diversity, proposed in this article highlighted in blue.

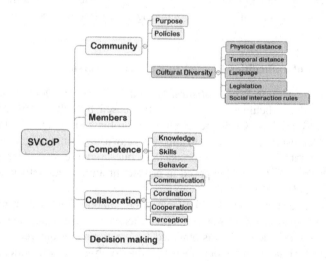

**Fig. 1.** - Conceptual model of Heuristics – SVCoP with aspects of Cultural Diversity (Color figure online)

SVCoP (Lopes et al. 2015) was organized in the following order:

- "Community" refers to the domain, objective, composition and cultural diversity of CoP, it is aligned to the concepts of Preece (2001) highlighted in green on the second level, "Purpose" is a reason why a member would belong to VCoP and "policies" are records and codes that guide interpersonal interactions in VCoP.

- "Members" are people from CoP with your given roles and personal features, referring to the features of people from VCoP, to their different roles and positions.
- "Competency" is defined as a set of resources provided to be acquired by an actor, highlighted in blue on the second level of the tree. The resources to acquire the expected competency are "knowledge", which refers to acquiring theoretical information of a determined subject, "skills", which is the capacity of an actor to perform tasks in practice and "behavior", which is summarized by the way in which actor behaves in a group or in a particular situation.
- "Collaboration" groups concepts of "communication", "coordination", "cooperation" and "perception" as cited by Fuks et al. (2002) in Collaboration Model 3C. This model is based on the premise of in order to have collaboration, not only communication junction, but also coordination, cooperation and perception is required.
- "Decision Making" refers to available resources for such, to the individuals involved and to the strategies utilized in the process.

Langelier and Wenger (2005) (as presented in Table 1), relates in his work the cultural diversity to the "Community" aspect, considering that a community can be homogeneous or heterogeneous (nationality, organizational culture, among others). Thus, the aspects related to cultural diversity were included in the community axis: physical distance; temporal distance; language; legislation and rules of social interaction.

### 4.1 Diagnosis of Difficulties Related to Cultural Diversity

To support the development of heuristics, an initial survey was done, based on literature, to verify the difficulties found in VCoPs caused by cultural diversity. Nevertheless, not many papers were found about these problems in practice communities.

In these circumstances, a questionnaire was drawn up, containing 7 questions, in order to investigate better these aspects. The questionnaire was developed using google's form creation tool and exposed in private through social networks (facebook and whatsapp) and by e-mail.

This questionnaire was sent to 25 VCoPs users, among them, undergraduates and graduates of Information Systems and Computer Science courses from the Universidade Estadual do Norte do Paraná. It was obtained 18 questionnaires answered.

Therefore, from the questionnaire, was possible to observe some difficulties related to cultural diversity in social interactions in VCoPs:

- Time-based separation affects interaction when it occurs between people from different countries, due to differences in time zones. Because VCoPs can involve people of all nationalities, language differences can also be found, which could be solved with the help of some online translators, but using some dialects and slang may complicate communication.
- Problems related to the difference in religion were observed. Some have reported that they have witnessed some discussion related to the type of belief and its inherent customs. A reported custom is that of Sabbath, in which people "keep the

Sabbath." Thus, Sabbath-keepers from the sunset from Friday to sundown do not engage in activities, do not work, dedicating themselves only to rest.

- The internet allows us to contact people from all over the world in a VCoP, so participants are free to exchange information and experiences with people they have never seen in life and even with people who pretend to be what they are notIn the questions raised on this subject, 8 of the respondents reported that there is a certain mistrust about the profile of the participants, which makes trust and relationship difficult. The others state that there is no problem because people in this environment share a common interest which, in a way, characterizes the participant's profile.

- Some respondents have argued that Brazilian international forums are highly criticized, since the vast majority of Brazilians tend to be informal and even jokers, which creates fears among participants who are more formal.

Based on the research conducted, both in the literature review and in the questionnaire applied to VCoPs users, the main difficulties related to cultural diversity in VCoPs are presented in Table 2, the main difficulties related to cultural diversity in VcoPs. It also sought to establish the guidelines for minimizing these difficulties. The guidelines presented were based on a literature review of Cibotto et al. (2009), Olson and Olson (2003) and the other works present in the theoretical basis of this research.

The main problems of physical distance are related to the fact that users access communities from anywhere and at any time, becoming subject to local physical transmission problems, such as, storms, earthquake. These problems may make VCoP inaccessible for a given time, in this way, the availability of historical data is required.

As members are interacting with people from different places, there is a certain uncertainty about the personality and the real intentions of each member. This can lead, in some users, to the fear of interacting. In this case, it would be interesting for the community to have an active moderator to control actions that diverge from the real interest of the community, contributing to its enrichment.

The difference of calendars is another problem related to the physical distance, because, the different places have different commemorative dates or holidays. Therefore, it is necessary to have good agenda planning for the important events, in order to minimize these differences.

Time-based separation also implies the time difference, which makes it difficult to exchange synchronous information. Thus, it is necessary to devise strategies to find times more accessible to all for the events. An alternative could be the alternation of schedules, so as not to always harm the same members.

The time zone may also involve the willingness of participants to interact. There is a chance that people tend to be more productive earlier in the day.

Information overload and delay in decision-making are also consequences of temporal separation, given the differences in timetables, schedules, rhythms, and disposition. In this case, a tool for creating polls could help in decision making, contributing to polls more efficiently and without the dependence of synchronous communication.

Another relevant role in this case could be that of a facilitator who could provide a summary table containing the most important topics that were treated in the VCoP on a

**Table 2.** Problems related to cultural diversity

| Type | Problems Identified | Diretrizes para VCoPs relativas à diversidade cultural |
|---|---|---|
| Physical Distance | – Diffusion in the transmission of information <br> – Difficulty in informal communication <br> – Insecurity due to lack of confidence <br> – Difference of calendars | – Provide an easy search tool by subject <br> – Register and make available old topics for the consultation <br> – Define a moderator to assist in the organization and control of VCoP <br> – Define a facilitator to compile the issues at the end of each day <br> – Use a graphic facilitator in the events in real time to visually synthesize the topics covered <br> – Follow the interactions in order to verify if the participants actually have the profile registered in the VCoP (when applicable) <br> – Use calendar scheduling to organize virtual events (calendar) |
| Temporal Distance | – Difficulty in exchanging synchronous information <br> – Difficulty in face-to-face meetings <br> – Differences in participants' willigness to communicate <br> – Delays in making decisions <br> – Information overload <br> – Wealth of affected context | – Provide an easy search tool by subject <br> – Register and make available old topics for the consultation <br> – Check an appropriate time in common for most members to make the main decisions <br> – Set a time limit for each decision to be made. <br> – Dispose a questionnaire's own tool <br> – Divide the topics into different topics or forums |
| Language | – Conflicts of errors of interpretations due to the use of dialects and slangs <br> – Loss of important topics | – Define a default language for a particular VCoP <br> – Create a protocol to avoid the use of slang <br> – Provide an instant translation tool |
| Social Interation Rules | – Difficulty of demonstrating nonverbal emotions <br> – Misinterpretation of actions <br> – Difficulty in environmental governance <br> – Difference of beliefs and customs related to religion | – Pre-establish rules in the VCoP so that each respects the custom and belief of others <br> – Disseminate the meanings of the emoticons and symbols available for use in VCoP <br> – Prohibit discrimination and disrespect to members |
| Legislation | – Difference in legislation <br> – Government restrictions on Internet access | – Take advantage of Legislation <br> – Make visible the governmental restrictions of each country for all the members |

given day or period. One feature that has been widely used in meetings, conferences, and other events and that could be useful in VCoP is the graphic facilitator. The graphic facilitator could, for example, graphically represent, through comics or other type of drawing, the topics covered in a videoconference.

The difference in language is a very recurrent problem in VCoPs, which makes communication difficult due to the numerous conflicts of interpretations errors due to the use of dialects and slangs. These conflicts can compromise the interaction by the loss of important content. To avoid upsets and disorganization it is necessary to set a default language for the community or, if some members have a problem with the default language, it would be viable to divide subgroups into common languages. The availability of instant translation tools can also facilitate VCoP communication.

The difficulty of expressing oneself through writing can be overcome by the use of images, emoticons and some abbreviations, nevertheless, it is necessary to avoid distortions and ambiguities. One solution would be the availability of a manual of meanings, in several languages, for the pre-determined symbols for use in VCoP.

Establishing a communication protocol is an interesting way to avoid discussions and misunderstandings in VCoP. The protocol may explain some rules and also penalties for members who disregard such rules. The descriptions of the rules must be clear, without excess or lack of elements, and without semantic ambiguity. The absence of protocol with the rules of "conduct" could drastically affect governance and lead the environment to chaos.

Another significant issue is that members of VCoPs are subject to different civil, commercial and labor laws. Therefore, it is necessary to have knowledge and care before making certain publications. Government restrictions on Internet access are a clear example of the difference in legislation between countries. Thus, it is important to make these government restrictions visible and to have the user read these restrictions before accessing the community so that they are aware of the actions that will be taken.

### 4.2  Heuristic for the Evaluation of Cultural Diversity

Based on the aspects of cultural diversity raised and their relationships (Table 2), the heuristic was developed to evaluate cultural diversity in VCoPs, containing 15 questions. Table 3 presents the questions and aspects of cultural diversity related to each of them.

The questions were described through an online form and for each question three alternatives were presented in order to analyze the occurrence of these aspects.

At the beginning of the online form some terminologies relevant to the heuristics were described, such as the meaning of VCoP and an event. An event in the context of a VCoP refers to activities such as a forum, a poll, a videoconference, among others, possibly scheduled, that encourage interaction among the participants by providing opportunities for collaboration, which may be asynchronous (e.g.: forum discussions) or synchronous (e.g.: videoconference).

Two questions of identification were also elaborated to know the profile of the evaluator (IT student or HCI specialist), and which VCoP would be evaluated.

**Table 3.** Analysis of Heuristic Questions

| Diversity | Question | Aspect Evaluated |
|---|---|---|
| Temporal Distance | 1. Is it possible to perceive in VCoP an overload of information for the contents made available? | Information overload |
| | 2. Is synchronous event time setting done respecting time zone differences? | Schedule definition of synchronous events |
| | 3. Is there a time limit for running events? | Time limit for running events |
| Physical Distance | 4. Does the VCoP develop the group spirit in the members, so that they are willing to share information, knowledge and experiences? | Team spirit |
| | 5. Is there a VCoP content history (news, forums, polls, etc.) available for the consultation? | Context Information |
| | 6. Are there any moderators active in the community who can convey trust and confidence to members? | Difficulty of interaction |
| | 7. Is scheduling planned for the organization of virtual events due to calendar difference? | Planning of calendars |
| Language | 8. Are the differences in languages respected? | Language difference |
| | 9. Is there any tool in the instant translation community itself? | Instant translation tool |
| | 10. Is there a rule in the community prohibiting the use of slang? | Prohibition of use slang |
| Social Interaction Rules | 11. Does VCoP allow communication in the use of symbols that represent facial expressions, posture, gestures, voice intonations, and so on (called emoticons)? | Means of communication |
| | 12. Is there a manual of meanings of the symbols (emoticons) available for communication that can be used in the community? | Symbols meaning manual |
| Legislation | 13. Does VCoP guide the rules of good use of the virtual community in order to guarantee the overall compliance of the legislation (e.g. information secrecy, content guarding, offensive use)? | Rules of good use |
| | 14. Are government restrictions on members spread? | Government Restrictions |
| | 15. Is there a more severe punishment for cases of a lack of respect for religion, beliefs, customs, among others? | Penalty for lack of respect |

For each question, the same verification parameters presented in Lopes et al. (2015), they are: (i) No – when there is no occurrence, the aspect is not identified in the VCoP; (ii) Partially – partial occurrence, aspect and unsatisfactorily identified in VCoP; (iii) Yes, when the occurrence is complete, the aspect of satisfactory in the VCoP; (iv) It is not possible to evaluate when it is not possible to evaluate the question.

It should be noted that the verification parameters were adapted for each question, as can be seen in the example given in Fig. 2:

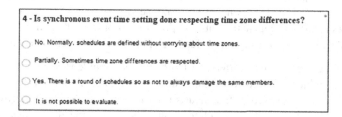

**4 - Is synchronous event time setting done respecting time zone differences?**

○ No. Normally, schedules are defined without worrying about time zones.

○ Partially. Sometimes time zone differences are respected.

○ Yes. There is a round of schedules so as not to always damage the same members.

○ It is not possible to evaluate.

**Fig. 2.** Example of parameters used in heuristics

For almost all questions, the "No" response parameter represents that the evaluated aspect has a negative impact, the "Yes" represents a positive impact, but only in question 1 the inverse occurs, the "No" answer has an aspect and the "Yes" response has a negative aspect to the evaluation.

Thus, it was possible to analyze the occurrence of each aspect in a VCoP and it was also possible to identify the VCoPs that present aspects that promote and favor sociability from the perspective of cultural diversity.

### 4.3  Application of the Proposed Heuristic

The heuristic was applied to two classes of students of the courses of Systems of information and Computer Science of the State University of the North of Paraná at previously defined schedules.

The students could choose the VCoPs for the evaluation, in order to evaluate the communities with which they had more familiarity, thus guaranteeing a more faithful result, since they could identify the evaluated aspects more easily. In the application, 52 students participated, responding in full to the questionnaire, by which we can observe:

Regarding temporal separation axis questions, it is noticed that in most cases time zone and synchronous events are not dealt with, and that in most VCoPs, there are not many problems related to content overload.

- The data are more positive when it comes to physical distance, that is, it means that the analyzed VCoPs present tools to avoid problems related to this axis, for example, they have a history of contents, they have a moderator active and develop in the group spirit. Only in the matter of planning of agendas did we get more negative responses. But despite this, this was the axis that presented the most positive evaluations.
- Data related to the language axis shows that most communities do not address language-related problems, not imposing a default language or rules on it, and also not offering instant translation tools. Although this aspect is the most important, since it is the form of communication, this was the axis that presented the most negative aspects.

- Regarding the rules of social interaction, it can be observed that most VCoPs have tools that allow the use of facial expressions, posture, gestures, voice intonations, among others (called emoticons), facts that facilitate understanding, however, do not present a manual of meanings of the symbols, which may be different depending on the region, which brings negative responses to the axis of social interaction.
- On issues related to legislation, it was possible to observe that most VCoPs have some rules, but they do not go so far as to present laws based on such rules.

Through the evaluation of different VCoPs, it was possible to verify the viability of the heuristics, which allowed to evaluate how the cultural diversity is treated by the VCoPs. It is hoped, therefore, that heuristics can contribute to the improvement of VCoPs, which, following the guidelines, may alleviate some difficulties caused by cultural diversity.

## 5 Final Considerations

This work proposes the complementation of the proposed heuristic in Lopes et al. (2015) regarding the dimension of cultural diversity. The heuristic called SVCoP contained 46 questions, organized into five main axes (1-Community, 2-Member, 3-Competency, 4-Collaboration and 5-Decision Making). Thus, a new dimension was considered in the Community axis - Cultural Diversity - adding another 15 questions to the heuristic.

To identify the problems related to sociability and cultural diversity, we studied some factors, such as physical distance, temporal separation, language difference, social interaction and legislation. In order to complement the literature review, a questionnaire was developed and applied to a group of users of VCoPs, to help identify the aspects that have the greatest impact on the use of these communities.

Then, from this survey was proposed the heuristic related to cultural diversity that complements the sociability heuristic proposed by Lopes et al. (2015).

The proposed heuristic was applied to selected VCoPs users. From the answers, the analyzes were made from the point of view of the most critical aspects and also of the analyzed VCoPs. Nevertheless, other evaluations of the instrument are already being prepared by other IHC specialists. From the application of the new heuristic evaluations it will also be possible to verify, in a more complete way, how VCoPs treat and promote sociability among its members.

As a contribution of this work, it was identified that the proposed instrument allowed to evaluate some of the main aspects of sociability related to cultural diversity in VCoPs.

## References

Benbunan, F.R., Hiltz, S.R.: Impacts of asynchronous learning networks on individual and group problem solving: a field experiment. Group Decis. Negot. **8**, 409–426 (1999)

Baechler, J.: Grupos e sociabilidade. In: Boudon, R., et al. (eds.) Tratado de sociologia. Rio de Janeiro, Zahar (1995)

Baldanza, R.F.: A comunicação no ciberespaço: reflexões sobre a relação do corpo na interação e sociabilidade em espaço virtual. In: Congresso Brasileiro de Ciências da Comunicação, 29. Brasilia, São Paulo, CD-ROM (2006)

Candau, V.M. (Org): Reinventar a escola. Vozes, Petrópolis, RJ (2000)

Cibotto, R.A.G., Pagno, R.T., Tait, T.F.C., Huzita, E.H.M.: Uma Análise da Dimensão Sociocultural no Desenvolvimento Distribuído de Software. Workshop Olhar Sociotécnico sobre a engenharia de software - Woses 2009. In: VIII Simpósio Brasileiro de Qualidade de Software. Ouro Preto (2009)

Costa, C.S.: As Implicações na Engenharia de Requisitos em Ambiente de Desenvolvimento Distribuído de Software. 2008. 37 f. Monografia (Especialização) - Curso de Ciência da Computação, Universidade Federal de Pernambuco, Recife (2008)

Deaudelin, C., Nault, T.: Collaborer pour apprendre et faire apprendre – La place des outils technologiques, Presses de l'Université du Québec (2003)

Fuks, H., Raposo, A.B., Gerosa, M.A.: Engenharia de Groupware: Desenvolvimento de Aplicações Colaborativas. In: XXI Jornada de Atualização em Informática, Anais do XXII Congresso da Sociedade Brasileira de Computação, V2, Cap.3 (2002). ISBN 85-88442-24-8

Henri, F.: Communities of Practice: Social Structures for the Development of Knowledge. Palette Kick off Meeting, Lausanne (2006)

Langelier, L., Wenger, E. (eds.): Work, Learning and Networked, Québec, CEFRIO (2005)

Lave J., Wenger, E.: Situated Learning: Legitimate Peripheral Participation. Cambridge University Press, Cambridge (1991)

Lopes, L.A., Guilhermino, D.F., Coleti, T.A., Sgarbi, E.M., de Oliveira, T.F.: Heuristic to support the sociability evaluation in virtual communities of practices. In: Kurosu, M. (ed.) HCI 2015. LNCS, vol. 9171, pp. 3–14. Springer, Cham (2015). https://doi.org/10.1007/978-3-319-21006-3_1

Marcotte, J-F.: Communautés virtuelles et sociabilité en réseaux: pour une redéfinition du lien social dans les environnements virtuels. Espirit Critic, 5(4). Acedido em 22/02/2004, disponível em (2003). http://vcampus.univperp.fr/espritcritique/0504/esp0504article04.html

Mengalli, N.M.: Conceitualização de comunidade de prática(CoP). Projeto, Org/E-mapbook (2014)

Miller, G.A.: WordNet: a lexical database for English. Commun. ACM 38(11), 39–41 (1995)

Olson, J.S., Olson, G.M.: Culture surprise in remote software development teams. Queue Focus Distrib. Dev. 1(9), 52–59 (2003)

Preece, J.: Sociability and usability in online communities: Determining and measuring success (2001)

Recuero, R.: Facebook x Orkut no Brasil: alguns apontamentos. Social Media, 24 Ago. (2009)

de Souza, Y.S.: Conversação e aprendizagem organizacional: perspectivas para a investigação. In: XXIII Encontro da Associação Nacional dos Programas de Pós-Graduação - ENANPAD, 24, Florianópolis. Anais. ANPAD, Florianópolis (2000)

Teigland, R., Wasko, M.M.: Extending richness with reach: participation and knowledge exchange in electronic networks of practice. In: Kimble, C., Hildreth, P. (eds.) Knowledge Networks: Innovation Through Communities of Practice, pp. 230–242. Idea Group, London (2004)

Tifous, A., Ghali, A.E., Dieng-Kuntz, R., Giboin, A., Evangelou, C., Vidou, G.: An ontology for supporting communities of practice. In: K-CAP 39-4 (2007a)

Tifous, A., Dieng-Kuntz, R., Durville, P., El Ghali, A., Evangeli, C., Giboin, A., Vidou, G.: CoP-dependent ontologies. Palette IST-FP6-028038 Deliverable D.KNO.02 (2007b)

Trindade, D.: InCoP: Um framework conceitual para o design de ambientes colaborativos inclusivos para surdos e não surdos de cultivo a comunidade de prática (2013)

Vidou, G., Dieng-Kuntz, R., El Ghali, A., Evangelou, C., Giboin, A., Tifous, A., Jacquemart, S.: Towards an ontology for knowledge management in communities of practice. In: Reimer, U. (ed.) PAKM 2006. LNCS (LNAI), vol. 4333, pp. 303–314. Springer, Heidelberg (2006). https://doi.org/10.1007/11944935_27

Weiseth, P.E., Munkvold, B.E., Tvedte, B., Larsen, S.: The wheel of collaboration tools: a typology for analysis within a holistic framework. In: CSCW 2006, Banff, Canada, pp. 239–248 (2006)

Wenger, E.: Communities of Practice: Learning, Meaning and Identity. Cambridge University Press, Cambridge (1998)

Wenger, E.: Supporting communities of practice - survey of community oriented technologies. Technical report 1.3, Etienne Wenger Research and Consulting (2001)

Wenger, E., Mcdermott, R., Snyder, W.M.: Cultivating Communities of Practice. Harvard Business School Press, Boston (2002)

Wenger, E.: Knowledge management as a doughnut: Shaping your knowledge strategy through communities of practice. Ivey Bus. J. **68**(3), 1–8 (2004)

# International Users' Experience of Social Media: A Comparison Between Facebook and WeChat

Hanjing Huang, Hengameh Akbaria, Nina Alef, Phairoj Liukitithara, Monica Marazzi, Bastian Verhaelen, Gina Chi-Lan Yang, and Pei-Luen Patrick Rau[✉]

Department of Industrial Engineering, Tsinghua University, Beijing, China
rpl@tsinghua.edu.cn

**Abstract.** Social media are becoming more and more popular all around the world, but it remains unclear whether people have different user behaviors in different social media. WeChat and Facebook assist international users in China to communicate with their families and friends from different countries. We conducted the comparative study that examined international users' behaviors in WeChat and Facebook. The data were collected from 98 international users who used both WeChat and Facebook through questionnaire surveys. We mainly compared the satisfaction, trust and usage in different social media. The comparative analysis showed that Facebook was more like a news application, while WeChat was more like a communication tool for international users living in China. The results revealed that international users had higher satisfaction levels of voice call, video call, voice message, and emoji/sticker in WeChat, while they had higher satisfaction levels of posting and accessing news in Facebook. International users relied more on WeChat during their stay in China. Although international users used Facebook and WeChat frequently, they did not fully trust them. We also gathered some information about their reasons to use or not to use functions of social media. These findings would help designers have a deeper understanding of international users and help social media companies to globalize their products.

**Keywords:** Social media · Usage · Satisfaction · Trust · Globalization

## 1 Introduction

Social media are Internet-oriented forms of communication, which can be accessed whenever people have an Internet connection. In social media, people are able to have conversations, upload photos, share information, get access to information, and write blogs. There are various social media platforms in nowadays life including blogs, wikis, photo-sharing platforms, podcasts, instant messaging and many more. Examples include Facebook, WeChat, Twitter and WhatApp, each of which is used by hundreds of millions of people. Social media are fast changing people's ways of communication and entertainment. Billions of people all around the world use social media in their everyday life. Especially, the younger generation is fully integrated in the world of social media. Moreover, social media are becoming inerasable parts of modern people and their

© Springer International Publishing AG, part of Springer Nature 2018
P.-L. P. Rau (Ed.): CCD 2018, LNCS 10911, pp. 341–349, 2018.
https://doi.org/10.1007/978-3-319-92141-9_26

tentacles have extended beyond communication. Social media are further used in various aspects of people's life including business, advertising, education, news, entertainment and research.

It should be pointed out that different social media have different unique character-istics. For example, WeChat is an all-in-one messaging app, which is different from western social media apps. WeChat adds various functions such as online-to-offline services, advertising, e-commerce, booking, social game, and finance. In 2016, there existed over 800 million monthly active users in WeChat [1]. About a third of WeChat users used WeChat payments to make regular online purchases [2]. Moreover, a majority of Chinese organizations or companies can make an "official account" on WeChat. Almost all media companies, banks, celebrities, brands, and startups already have their own WeChat official accounts. Although Facebook tried to add more functions, WeChat still leads in terms of popularity of offering various services to its users [3]. There are trends to suggest that different social media have their own biases in terms of different types of communication that bring different social consequences for users [4]. Mean-while, users may not completely replace one form of social media with another because each form supports the unique communication needs that the other cannot completely fulfill.

Moreover, social media with different features are targeted to different user bases. WeChat is developed by the Chinese company Tencent. WeChat users are mainly living in China. Now, WeChat sees a shift in the demographics of the user base and sets its sights on globalization. A quarter of WeChat users are already non-Chinese [1]. WeChat faces the challenges that whether Asia-inspired functions will be acceptable to its inter-national users. Facebook also faces the challenges in exploring larger global markets. Understanding user behaviors in different social media has become increasingly impor-tant. However, research on people's user behaviors in eastern social media and western social media has not been sufficiently conducted.

Therefore, the goal of this study was to examine whether there existed differences between users' behaviors, satisfaction and trust in different social media. To achieve this goal, we compared user behaviors of international users who used both WeChat and Facebook to gain a deeper understanding of user behaviors in different social media.

## 2   Literature Review

Culture affects everything from people's attitudes to motivations. Culture also affects people's needs and their behaviors to fulfill needs, as well as people's behaviors in social media [5, 6]. In Correa et al.'s definition, social media is "a mechanism for the audience to connect, communicate, and interact with each other and their mutual friends through instant messaging or social networking sites." [7]. Previous research has supported the opinion that online cultures are mirrors of the offline cultures of which they are products [8, 9].

Recent research has further investigated effects of culture on user behaviors in social media. It has been reported that Chinese users compared to US users tended to create and share content more: 40% of Chinese users were contributing content, compared to 20% in US [10]. Additionally, Chinese tended to live much more in the Internet than westerners, perceiving their online-life as more real than their offline-life. Some research also compared user behaviors in Renren and Facebook as examples of the East–West distinction. [11]. As a result, Facebook culture was perceived as more individualistic than Renren culture. For example, Facebook users were more self-talk and self-interested, while Renren users were more benevolent in in-group sharing. Other research also found that users from different countries used social media differently. Chen et al. [12] compared social media usage of Chinese users and that of German users. They found that Chinese users had more online friends than German users, but German users met their friends more frequently in real life. Some research on WeChat also examined effects of different motives and attitudes toward using WeChat [13–15]. They found that entertainment acted as a dominant role in influencing WeChat users' attitudes [13]. Meanwhile, seeking information was another important motive of Chinese users to adopt WeChat [13–15]. Additionally, social interaction was also a major motivation of Chinese users to use WeChat [13, 14].

## 3 Research Framework and Hypotheses

Facebook is the dominant social network site in all over the world, while Chinese rely more on WeChat. In this research, we mainly compared international users' use behaviors of social media. Participants were living in China. They were using Facebook and WeChat to keep in touch with their friends in the host and home country. They could use Facebook for bridging, bonding, maintaining home country social capital, whereas they could use WeChat for entertainment, sociality, seeking information during their stay in China.

We mainly focused on three dimensions of social media usage, including satisfaction, perceived trust and privacy, and extent of use. We also explored the reasons to use or not to use functions in social media. Regarding these dimensions, our hypotheses are listed below:

**Hypothesis 1: The satisfaction level of Facebook is higher than that of WeChat.**
Facebook and WeChat are targeted at different populations. WeChat is designed especially for Chinese users. WeChat's concept model and functions within it can be less accepted by International users. Therefore, it is hypothesized that international users will have lower satisfaction level of WeChat.

**Hypothesis 2: International users trust Facebook more than WeChat.**
Perceived trust and privacy can be influenced by the familiarity and by how much control users have regarding privacy settings. International users are more familiar with Facebook compared to WeChat. Therefore, it is hypothesized that international users trust Facebook more than WeChat.

**Hypothesis 3: International users use WeChat more than Facebook in China.**
Since Facebook is blocked in China, and international users' new social circle will mainly use WeChat. Therefore, it is hypothesized that international users will use WeChat more frequently than Facebook while they are living in China.

# 4    Methodology

The goal of this study was to investigate international users' user behaviors and user experience in different social media. To achieve this goal, we compared the user behaviors of international users who belonged to both WeChat and Facebook. We used questionnaire surveys to gain information about international users' user behaviors and user experience in different social media.

## 4.1    Participants

Participants were recruited via an advertisement posted on both WeChat and Facebook. Participants answered the questionnaire through the online link. In all, 98 international users (Female: 51, Male: 47) took the questionnaire survey. They used both WeChat and Facebook in everyday life. The age distribution of these international users was represented in Fig. 1. Their nationalities included the United States, German, Italy, Australia, French, Thai, Iran, Mexico and other countries.

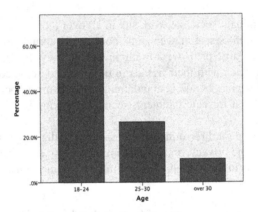

**Fig. 1.** Participants' age distribution

## 4.2    Questionnaire Designs

The questionnaire included items from satisfaction, perceived trust and privacy, extent of use, and reasons to use or not to use functions.

### Satisfaction

We used the System Usability Scale (SUS) to evaluate how international users were satisfied with different social media. We used the Single Ease Question (SEQ) to evaluate the ease of use perceived by participants. We used a 5-point Likert scale for the questions following these models.

**Perceived Trust and Privacy**

We were interested in how they perceived trust and privacy when using WeChat and Facebook. We designed question items based on previous research [16]. We applied a 5-point Likert scale for the questions.

**Extent of Use**

We were also interested in how frequently international users used Facebook and WeChat differently. Therefore, we developed survey items to ask them how much time they spent on Facebook/WeChat per day.

**Reasons to Use or not Use Functions**

We included fill-in-the-blank questions in the survey to explore the international users' reasons of using or not using functions in social media.

# 5  Results

We analyzed the results from questionnaires into several aspects: satisfaction, perceived trust and privacy, extent of use, and reasons to use or not to use functions of social media.

**Satisfaction**

To test Hypothesis 1, we compared the satisfaction of voice call, video call, voice messages, emoji/sticker, posting, and access of news in WeChat and in Facebook. We conducted t-tests to investigate the difference between Facebook and WeChat in users' satisfaction.

The results (see Table 1) showed that WeChat got the higher satisfaction with the following functions: voice call, video call, voice messages and emoji/sticker. But Facebook achieved higher satisfaction in the posting and accessing of news.

Table 1.  Users' satisfaction of social media

|  | Facebook | | WeChat | | | |
|---|---|---|---|---|---|---|
|  | M | SD | M | SD | t | p |
| Voice call | 2.93 | 1.21 | 4.15 | 0.97 | −7.82 | <.001 |
| Video call | 2.81 | 1.23 | 3.88 | 0.97 | −6.77 | <.001 |
| Voice messages | 2.78 | 1.16 | 4.18 | 1.04 | −8.94 | <.001 |
| Emoji/Sticker | 3.26 | 1.15 | 4.16 | 1.13 | −5.58 | <.001 |
| Posting | 3.87 | 1.17 | 3.37 | 1.23 | 2.91 | .004 |
| Access of news | 3.57 | 1.32 | 2.50 | 1.35 | 5.61 | <.001 |

**Perceived Trust and Privacy**

To test Hypothesis 2, we considered 5 dimensions of trust of Facebook and WeChat: trust of data security, reliability of data, influence of data, trust of personal data security and fraud concern. We conducted t-tests to investigate the difference between Facebook and WeChat in users' trust.

The results from t-tests (see Table 2) showed that there was no significant difference in perceived trust and privacy between Facebook and WeChat based on the 5 dimensions. However, from data analysis, we concluded the trusting levels in 5 dimensions.

**Table 2.** Users' trust of social media

|  | Facebook | | WeChat | | | |
| --- | --- | --- | --- | --- | --- | --- |
|  | M | SD | M | SD | t | p |
| Trust of data security | 2.46 | 1.15 | 2.47 | 1.20 | −0.61 | .952 |
| Reliability of data | 2.35 | 1.08 | 2.31 | 1.07 | .27 | .790 |
| Influence of data | 2.30 | 1.20 | 2.07 | 1.20 | 1.31 | .192 |
| Trust of personal data security | 2.26 | 1.09 | 2.18 | 1.07 | .46 | .643 |
| Fraud concern | 2.96 | 1.05 | 3.16 | 1.18 | −1.28 | .204 |

1. Trust of data security: participants had low levels of trust in both Facebook and WeChat's data security.
2. Reliability of data: participants rated low levels of data reliability in both Facebook and WeChat.
3. Influence of data: participants rated low levels of influence of data from both Facebook and WeChat.
4. Trust of personal data security: participants had low levels of trust in both Facebook and WeChat's personal data security.
5. Fraud concern: participants showed medium levels of fraud concern in both Facebook and WeChat.

From all 5 dimensions, the results indicated that people still did not trust the security of WeChat and Facebook entirely.

**Extent of Use**

To test Hypothesis 3 on extent of use, we compared the distribution charts for usage time of each application (see Fig. 2). We found that about 32% of participants spent more than 3 h on WeChat every day, while only 7% of them spent more than 3 h on Facebook every day. Therefore, participants used WeChat more than Facebook when they were living in China.

From the survey, we also explored the reasons that participants used or not used WeChat functions and Facebook functions. Participants' answers were listed in Tables 3 and 4. It was noteworthy that participants pointed out the convenience of functions was a key factor affecting their use of functions in WeChat and Facebook. Entertainment was another crucial factor affected participants' use of functions. Moreover, participants believed that Facebook and WeChat could help them keep in touch with their families and friends, which made them use the communication function in these applications. Participants also mentioned that the ease of use affected their use of the social media. For example, participants mentioned that they would face the problem that they could not know some functions or were not sure how to use it, which stopped them from using these functions. Particularly, some WeChat functions did not include English interface. International users could not understand the use of these functions. In design of global social media,

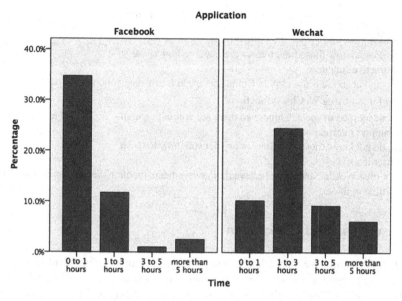

**Fig. 2.** Users' usage of social media

designers should care more about users' cultural background and language ability. It was interesting that participants also liked the payment, video call, voice call, and news function in WeChat. But participants did not fully trust WeChat and some believed that governments would monitor WeChat, so it was not free to express their opinions. Meanwhile, participants pointed out that it was difficult for them to get access to Facebook, which made them to rely more on WeChat when they were staying in China.

**Table 3.** Reasons for using the social media functions

| Reasons for using Facebook's functions |
| --- |
| – Facebook is very convenience |
| – Up to date |
| – Entertainment and killing time |
| – Easy to make event or appointment |
| – Contact with family |
| – To keep in touch with old friends, see friend updates and see what friend are doing |
| – Effective platform to communicate with friend |

| Reasons for using WeChat's functions |
| --- |
| – It is the most convenient communication platform in China |
| – To keep in touch with friends and school communities |
| – Use WeChat instead of phone call |
| – It is the only way to contact with family by video call or voice call |
| – WeChat pay is very convenient |
| – It is a channel to read news |
| – Have no choice |

**Table 4.** Reasons for not using the social media functions

| Reasons for not using Facebook's functions |
|---|
| – Users do not know those functions or are not sure how to use it |
| – Not attractive function |
| – Access to Facebook is not easy in China and speed is not very good when you use VPN |

| Reasons for not using WeChat's functions |
|---|
| – User cannot read or speak Chinese so there are communication problems when the functions do not support international user |
| – Users do not know those functions or are not sure how to use it |
| – Bad user interface |
| – Do not trust WeChat and some believe that governments monitor WeChat, so it is not free to express their opinion |

## 6 Discussion and Conclusion

Based on the results, we found that international participants in China had different user behaviors in Facebook and WeChat. The results revealed international users had higher satisfaction of WeChat in voice call, video call, emoji/sticker and voice message functions and higher satisfaction of Facebook in posting and accessing of news functions. We also found that both social media inspired a low level of trust. International users felt unsafe to give their personal information, and did not trust information on Facebook and WeChat that much. This suggests more efforts should be taken to enhance users' perception of security in social media. For instance, social media should make users know how their personal data will be used. However, the low trust did not seem to affect the popularity: one third of the participants claimed that they used WeChat more than three hours a day. International users tended to rely more on WeChat in everyday life. Moreover, we explored the reasons for using and not using functions of WeChat and Facebook. These findings would help companies and designers develop and improve the global social media.

**Acknowledgement.** This research was supported by Shenzhen Malong Artificial Intelligence Research Center.

## References

1. Statista: Number of active WeChat messenger accounts 2010–2016 (2016). https://www.statista.com/statistics/255778/number-of-active-wechat-messenger-accounts/
2. Jaivin., L.: WeChat: A new Chinese empire? http://www.sbs.com.au/news/feature/wechat-new-chinese-empire
3. Wang, H.H.: It's time for Facebook to copy WeChat. http://www.forbes.com/sites/helenwang/2016/08/11/its-time-for-facebook-to-copy-wechat/?yptr=yahoo-79dcefba27a4
4. McLuhan, M., Powers, B.R.: The Global Village: Transformations in World Life and Media in the 21st Century. Communication and Society, Oxford (1989)
5. Gudykunst, W.B.: Bridging Differences: Effective Intergroup Communication. Sage, Thousand Oaks (2004)

6. Van Dijck, J.: The Culture of Connectivity: A Critical History of Social Media. Oxford University Press, Oxford (2013)

7. Correa, T., Hinsley, A.W., De Zuniga, H.G.: Who interacts on the Web?: The intersection of users' personality and social media use. Comput. Hum. Behav. **26**(2), 247–253 (2010)

8. Morling, B., Lamoreaux, M.: Measuring culture outside the head: A meta-analysis of individualism—collectivism in cultural products. Pers. Soc. Psychol. Rev. **12**(3), 199–221 (2008)

9. Marcus, A., Krishnamurthi, N.: Cross-cultural analysis of social network services in Japan, Korea, and the USA. In: Aykin, N. (ed.) IDGD 2009. LNCS, vol. 5623, pp. 59–68. Springer, Heidelberg (2009). https://doi.org/10.1007/978-3-642-02767-3_7

10. Li, X., Chen, W.: Facebook or Renren? A comparative study of social networking site use and social capital among Chinese international students in the United States. Comput. Hum. Behav. **35**, 116–123 (2014)

11. Qiu, L., et al.: Putting their best foot forward: Emotional disclosure on Facebook. Cyberpsychol. Behav. Soc. Netw. **15**(10), 569–572 (2012)

12. Chen, Z., Rau, P.-L.P., Frank, B., Ignazio, F., Zhou, J., Sajed, S., Xiang, Y.: How to make friends in social network service? A comparison between Chinese and German. In: Rau, P.L.Patrick (ed.) CCD 2013. LNCS, vol. 8024, pp. 373–382. Springer, Heidelberg (2013). https://doi.org/10.1007/978-3-642-39137-8_42

13. Lien, C.H., Cao, Y.: Examining WeChat users' motivations, trust, attitudes, and positive word-of-mouth: Evidence from China. Comput. Hum. Behav. **41**, 104–111 (2014)

14. Chu, S.-C., Choi, S.M.: Electronic word-of-mouth in social networking sites: a cross-cultural study of the United States and China. J. Glob. Mark. **24**(3), 263–281 (2011)

15. Sun, Y., et al.: Understanding Chinese users' continuance intention toward online social networks: an integrative theoretical model. Electron. Mark. **24**(1), 57–66 (2014)

16. Yang, H.: Young American consumers' online privacy concerns, trust, risk, social media use, and regulatory support. J. New Commun. Res. **5**, 1–30 (2013)

# Status Effects on Attributions for Online Knowledge Sharing Failures: A Comparison Between Chinese and Korean Cultures

Nan Qie, Pei-Luen Patrick Rau[(⊠)], and Jun Liu

Institute of Human Factors and Ergonomics, Department of Industrial Engineering, Tsinghua University, Beijing, China
rpl@mail.tsinghua.edu.cn

**Abstract.** Social status and culture can affect attributions. In this study, the authors utilized a knowledge-sharing failure scenario to test the effects of status and culture on attributions with a survey conducted among 127 Chinese and 120 Koreans. The results showed that both Chinese and Koreans felt significantly more disappointed when the failure occurred because of the senior's rather than the junior's ability-related issues. Chinese participants tended to ascribe the failure significantly more to contexts than ability, while Korean participants had the opposite tendency. Although both Chinese and Korean participants gave lower ratings on motivation attribution when the one who failed to share knowledge was a peer, the gap was markedly larger for Korean participants. Further testing on self-construal revealed that Korean participants rated individualism significantly higher than their Chinese counterparts did. The results indicated that even in two similar cultures the status effects on attribution can differ. Managers of international companies should respond accordingly to group affairs regarding status issue.

**Keywords:** Attribution · Status hierarchy · Chinese culture · Korean culture
Self-construal

## 1 Introduction

Social status can affect attributions. For example, people of high status are considered to be more competitive and less warm (Fiske et al. 2002), and this stereotype can cause attribution biases. In some studies, low-status group members make in-group favoring attributions more than their high-status counterparts (Hunter et al. 1993; Stringer and Hunter 1999). Yet, sometimes high-status group members make stronger in-group favoring attributions (Hewstone and Ward 1985, Study 1). Still in other studies, both high and low status group members have shown in-group favoring attributions (Bond et al. 1985) or, neither the high nor low status group members make such attributions (Hewstone and Ward 1985, Study 2; Khan and Liu 2008, Study 1). Sometimes, low-status groups make outgroup favoring attributions (Hewstone et al. 1989), and sometimes high-status groups do so (Mann and Taylor 1974).

Social status is perceived differently among cultures. People holding an independent view towards themselves can treat social status in a very different way from those

© Springer International Publishing AG, part of Springer Nature 2018
P.-L. P. Rau (Ed.): CCD 2018, LNCS 10911, pp. 350–361, 2018.
https://doi.org/10.1007/978-3-319-92141-9_27

holding an interdependent view. People holding an interdependent view emphasize more on relationships and the sense of belonging, thus they pay more attention to social status. People in East Asia usually hold an interdependent view towards themselves and East Asian cultures are regarded as collectivism. In Japanese culture, high and low status members of a group are stratified into a special hierarchical social system. High-status members often gain a higher status, level, or rank because of their age, experience or qualification. On the contrary, low-status members are those who are younger, join the organization later, or earn the qualification later. It is required to call senior members by their honorific social titles (the Senpai) instead of their names; otherwise the juniors will be judged negatively by other people (Enyo 2013; Sano 2014).

Besides social status, culture can also affect attributions. Morris and Peng (1994) provided a demonstration of cultural divergence in causal attribution for Chinese and Americans. They focused on two parallel tragedies that recently occurred in the U.S. In both events, the criminals were angry with their supervisors and killed them. Morris and Peng found that the English newspapers speculated heavily about the mental instability and other negative dispositions of the perpetrators as possible causes (e.g., "the man was mentally unstable," "darkly disturbed man who drove himself to success and destruction," and "he had a short fuse"). In contrast, the Chinese newspapers emphasized contextual, situational, and even societal factors (e.g., "did not get along with his advisor," "tragedy reflects the lack of religion in Chinese culture," and "followed the example of a recent mass slaying in Texas"). Morris and Peng showed in their study that when Chinese and American university students explained the events, they had different attributional patterns: Chinese participants preferred contextual explanations while American participants preferred dispositional ones. Choi and Markus (1998), in a conceptual replication of the Morris and Peng study, discovered a similar divergence in causal attribution between Koreans and Americans. Menon et al. (1999) conducted a series of experiments to demonstrate that North American and East Asian cultures differed in implicit theories of individuals and groups. In these experiments, participants read an event in which both individuals and groups were involved and an unusual bad outcome had occurred. Participants from both North America (the U.S.) and East Asia (Japan and Hong Kong) rated the attributions of individual, group and situation factors. It was found that North Americans were more likely to attribute causality to individuals and dispositions, while the East Asians preferred to attribute the outcome to dispositions of collective-level agents. It was consistent with the findings that East Asian culture was collectivism while American culture was individualism.

Considering the factors that influence attributions, the effects of culture and status can interact with each other. However, there existed no such experimental study. According to Social Identity Theory (Tajfel and Turner 1979, 2004) and research (Bettencourt et al. 2001), status effects are often qualified by the perceived legitimacy of status discrimination. Collectivism culture regards status discrimination as more acceptable. Therefore, the effects of status on attribution can vary across cultures. In East Asian cultures such as China and Korea, status plays an important role, and seniors in the group are highly respected. In these cultures, attributions can highly depend on the target person's social status.

Even in the same cultural group, the status hierarchy may endow with different meanings, consequently influencing casual attributions. Previous studies compared Confucian values in East Asian cultures, and found that China placed the most emphasis on interpersonal harmony and relational hierarchy (Zhang et al. 2005). To regard all East Asian cultures as the same is too arbitrary, and cultures have been changing over time. In this study, we would like to explore the effects of status on attributions in Chinese and Korean cultures. In Hofstede's research (1983), responses in four cultural dimensions from 54 nations and regions were summarized, including data from Hong Kong and Korea. Pitifully, there was no direct comparison between mainland China and Korea in this study. However, as Hong Kong was close to mainland China from the cultural perspective, the results can still be a credible reference. Korea ranked higher than Hong Kong in the individualism dimension (Korea IDV = 25, Hong Kong IDV = 18). At the time when Hofstede's research was carried out, China had just started its reform and opening-up policies while Hong Kong was already an international city. It is reasonable to infer that China should rank even lower in individualism than Hong Kong.

Usually, a deviance was chosen as the scenario to test attribution, because negative outcomes were easier to evoke attributions. Meanwhile, the scenario should involve both individuals and groups. Knowledge-sharing failure can be a good choice. Knowledge sharing is an important issue in teamwork. Any failure in knowledge sharing on either individual or group level can do harm to the team performance. Status distinction has been a barrier to sharing knowledge. Jones et al. (2006) found that eliminating seniority and functional distinctions among team members can initially enhance knowledge sharing, but the success deteriorated to limited knowledge sharing over time. This happened when the senior team members began to resent the lower-level members so that the lower-level employees no longer felt free to provide input. As a result, knowledge sharing is a suitable scenario to study the effects of both culture and status on attributions.

Following previous attribution research and the above line of reasoning, we would use the scenario of knowledge sharing failure to test the status effects on attribution between Chinese and Korean cultures. In these two East Asian cultures, the seniors are often held in high regard, and their experience and ability greatly valued. Thus, it is reasonable to have the following hypotheses.

**H1:** Participants would attribute more to ability failure when the target person is a peer; While they would attribute more to motivation or context failure when the target person is a senior.

The disappointment levels of different attributions can differ. When the failure is due to the senior's ability or motivation failure, Chinese and Korean participants should be more disappointed, because these kinds of failure go against their expectations of the senior.

**H2:** Participants feel more disappointed when the failure is the result of the senior's motivation or ability.

Culture can also affect attributions. Inferred from previous research, Chinese participants can be more interdependent than Korean participants. Thus, Chinese participants may make more contextual attributions.

**H3:** Chinese participants would rate higher on relational self-construal and group self-construal; While Korean participants would rate higher on individual self-construal.

**H4:** Chinese participants would attribute a failure more to context, while Korean participants would attribute a failure more to ability and motivation.

## 2 Methodology

### 2.1 Participants

One hundred and twenty-seven Chinese students (36 women) were recruited from six universities in Beijing. One hundred and twenty Korean students (50 women) were recruited from nine universities in Seoul. Chinese participants were from 18 to 34 years old ($M = 25$, $SD = 2.93$), and Korean participants were from 18 to 29 years old ($M = 22$, $SD = 2.59$). Each participant received a monetary reward equal to five US dollars.

### 2.2 Procedure

In each culture, the participants were randomly assigned to two conditions. One was a senior condition and the other was a peer condition. For the senior condition, the participants first read about an online knowledge-sharing scenario, in which a senior member failed to share knowledge with the group. Then, the participants rated different attributions for the senior member's failure. For the peer condition, the process was almost identical except that the target person changed to a peer.

The scenario was adapted from Menon et al. (1999), which described a failed collaboration between a group and one of its member. In the current study, the situation narrowed down to a member's failure of sharing knowledge with other members. In addition, in the senior member condition, the actor is a senior member in the group. In both conditions, half participants read about a male actor, and the other half a female actor.

**Senior Condition**

In a company, a group of coworkers from interdisciplinary backgrounds was responsible for a very important project. A key factor, which determined the success of the project, was knowledge sharing within the team. The team used many online communication tools to facilitate sharing knowledge, including email, instant messaging software, group chatting applications, online bulletin forum, and blogs.

There were not many difficulties in the project itself, but one problem constantly plagued the group. One senior team member, who we will call "Z", was consistently irresponsive to sharing his knowledge. For example, in one case a junior member, who was working in a different place, asked Z a question through email. The question was in Z's reign of expertise and he was the most senior people to ask for reference from. However, Z replied very late after 2 weeks without any answers but only with an excuse for his late reply. In another case, a newcomer asked a question another team member tagged Z about some professional knowledge through the online forum, and said he was the best people to answer. However, Z never replied.

In the final analysis, owing to his failure to share knowledge, the group were not satisfied with Z's work, and had to burden with the responsibilities that should have been Z's. Group relations suffered, and the members of the group often lost their trust in Z and sidetracked from the project. Consequently, the final product did not meet the quality expectation.

**Peer Condition**
In a company, a group of coworkers from interdisciplinary backgrounds was responsible for a very important project. A key factor, which determined the success of the project, was knowledge sharing within the team. The team used many online communication tools to facilitate sharing knowledge, including email, instant messaging softwires, group chatting applications, online bulletin forum, and blogs.

There were not many difficulties in the project itself, but one problem constantly plagued the group. One team member, who we will call "Z", was consistently irresponsive to sharing his knowledge. For example, in one case a coworker, who was working in a different place, asked Z a question through email. The question was in Z's reign of expertise. However, Z replied very late after 2 weeks without any answers but only with an excuse for his late reply. In another case, a newcomer asked a question another team member tagged Z about some professional knowledge through the online forum, and said he was the best people to answer. However, Z never replied.

In the final analysis, owing to his failure to share knowledge, the group were not satisfied with Z's work, and had to burden with the responsibilities that should have been Z's. Group relations suffered, and the members of the group often lost their trust in Z and sidetracked from the project. Consequently, the final product did not meet the quality expectation.

## 2.3 Measures

**Attributes**
Modified from Menon et al. (1999)'s scenario, we asked the participants to evaluate "reasons as to why Z didn't play as successfully as he could have done." We presented a list of possibly relevant factors, including motivational and ability-related dispositions and contextual reasons. The participants were asked to rate the items on a 7-point Likert scale with 1 = very impossible 7 = very possible (see Table 1).

**Disappointment**
The participants were then asked to fill in another section about disappointment. The descriptions were the same as in Table 1. This time the participants evaluated "if these reasons were the fact, would you be disappointed with Z?" Participants were asked to rate how disappointed they would be, from 1 = not disappointed at all to 7 = very disappointed.

**Table 1.** Attribution lists in the experiment

| Motivation dispositions |
|---|
| The success of the project was not Z's concern, and he didn't care |
| Z lacked teamwork spirit |
| Z didn't like to help juniors/other members |
| Z didn't care about juniors/other members' needs |
| Z was afraid that sharing his knowledge would make him lose his unique value in the team |
| Z wanted to harm juniors/other members' performance so that he could be more competitive |
| **Ability dispositions** |
| Z didn't have enough knowledge to answer the questions |
| Z didn't have the professional skills juniors/other members expected him to have |
| Z couldn't talk about his knowledge clearly |
| Z couldn't write out a meaningful answer related to his knowledge |
| Z didn't know how to post a message on the forum |
| **Contextual reasons** |
| Z didn't see the question on time |
| Z was too busy to answer the question |
| Z preferred to communicate face to face rather than answer questions online |
| Junior/other members were not polite enough when asking questions |
| The whole group was not friendly in the process of communication |
| Z thought that other people were more suitable for answering this question |

**Self-construal**

This section included 13 descriptions about individual, relation and group self-construal. The participants were asked to rate how much they agree with these descriptions, from 1 = totally disagree to 7 = totally agree (see Table 2).

## 3   Results

### 3.1   Descriptive Statistics

Descriptive statistics of how Chinese and Korean participants rated attributes and disappointment is calculated and summarized in Table 3. When considering the failure in knowledge sharing within the group, Chinese participants attribute it less to the lack of ability and more to the context than their Korean counterparts do. How Chinese and Korean participants attributed to knowledge sharing, and why they felt disappointed was dependent on status of the target person.

To compare self-construal between Chinese and Korean participants, the descriptive statistics on self-construal for the two cultures was calculated and summarized in Table 4. Korean participants gave higher ratings on individual self-construal and slightly higher ratings on relational self-construal, while Chinese participants rated group self-construal higher.

**Table 2.** Self-construal questionnaire

| Individual self-construal |
| --- |
| I like to be special in many aspects |
| I'm always doing "my own business" |
| I am a unique person |
| **Relational self-construal** |
| My happiness depends on the happiness of people around me |
| I always feel that the relationship between others and me is more important than my own achievements |
| If people who work together with me get rewards, I will feel proud |
| To me, happiness means spending time with others |
| The happiness of people who work together with me is very important |
| I feel good when working together with others |
| **Group self-construal** |
| In general, my identity as a group member has nothing to do with how I look at myself |
| Which social groups I belong to is an important aspect of "who I am" |
| In general, the social group I belong to is a very important part of my self-identity |
| What kind of person I regard myself as is not determined by which social group I belong to |

**Table 3.** Descriptive statistics on attributions and disappointment

| Culture | Status | Attribution | M | SD | Disappoint | M | SD |
| --- | --- | --- | --- | --- | --- | --- | --- |
| CH | Peer | Ability | 3.78 | 0.94 | Ability | 3.63 | 1.22 |
| | | Motivation | 3.92 | 0.96 | Motivation | 5.91 | 0.94 |
| | | Context | 3.84 | 0.87 | Context | 3.73 | 0.94 |
| | Senior | Ability | 3.59 | 1.32 | Ability | 4.13 | 1.29 |
| | | Motivation | 3.89 | 1.04 | Motivation | 5.86 | 1.27 |
| | | Context | 3.84 | 1.94 | Context | 3.49 | 1.15 |
| KR | Peer | Ability | 4.07 | 1.03 | Ability | 3.37 | 1.07 |
| | | Motivation | 4.16 | 1.07 | Motivation | 5.70 | 0.97 |
| | | Context | 3.29 | 1.06 | Context | 3.41 | 0.89 |
| | Senior | Ability | 4.13 | 0.89 | Ability | 3.95 | 1.25 |
| | | Motivation | 3.62 | 0.86 | Motivation | 5.56 | 1.22 |
| | | Context | 3.44 | 0.80 | Context | 3.72 | 1.03 |

**Table 4.** Descriptive statistics on self-construal

| Culture | | Individual self-construal | Relational self-construal | Group self-construal |
| --- | --- | --- | --- | --- |
| CH | M | 4.62 | 4.79 | 5.14 |
| | SD | 0.97 | 0.71 | 0.86 |
| KR | M | 4.94 | 4.84 | 4.76 |
| | SD | 1.00 | 0.67 | 0.88 |

## 3.2    The Effects of Culture and Status

Two-way ANOVA models were established to study the effects of culture and status on three different causes of attribution and disappointment. The results were summarized in Table 5.

**Table 5.** Results of two-way ANOVA

|  |  | Attribution | | | Disappoint | | |
|---|---|---|---|---|---|---|---|
|  |  | Ability | Motivation | Context | Ability | Motivation | Context |
| Culture | F(1,243) | 9.28 | <0.01 | 16.55 | 1.97 | 3.24 | 0.19 |
|  | P | **0.003** | 0.928 | **<0.001** | 0.161 | 0.073 | 0.661 |
|  | Ges | 0.04 | <0.01 | 0.06 | <0.01 | 0.01 | <0.01 |
| Status | F(1,243) | 0.22 | 4.95 | 0.45 | 12.09 | 0.44 | 0.04 |
|  | P | 0.638 | **0.027** | 0.505 | **<0.001** | 0.510 | 0.833 |
|  | Ges | <0.01 | 0.02 | <0.01 | 0.05 | <0.01 | <0.01 |
| Culture*Status | F(1,243) | 0.89 | 4.31 | 0.42 | 0.06 | 0.10 | 4.51 |
|  | P | 0.346 | **0.039** | 0.518 | 0.804 | 0.753 | **0.035** |
|  | Ges | <0.01 | 0.02 | <0.01 | <0.01 | <0.01 | 0.02 |

The effect of culture*status was significant on motivational attribution (F(1,243) = 4.31, p = 0.039, ges = 0.02) and contextual disappoint (F(1,243) = 4.51, p = 0.035, ges = 0.02). The effect of culture was significant on ability attribution (F(1,243) = 9.28, p = 0.003, ges = 0.04) and contextual attribution (F(1,243) = 16.55, p < 0.001, ges = 0.06). The effect of status was significant on ability disappoint (F(1,243) = 12.09, p < 0.001, ges = 0.05).

Chinese and Korean participants attributed knowledge sharing failure to different reasons, because of the status effect. Chinese participants attributed it significantly more to lack of motivation than Korean participants when the senior caused knowledge sharing failure, while they attributed it significantly less to lack of motivation than Korean participants when the peer caused knowledge sharing failure. Chinese participants attributed it remarkably more to contextual but significantly less to lack of ability than Korean participants did.

Failure to share knowledge causes disappointment. Chinese and Korean participants felt disappointed by different reasons. Chinese participants felt a lot more disappointed with contextual issues than Korean participants did when the peer caused the failure, while they felt significantly less disappointed with contextual issues than Korean participants did when the senior caused the failure. Status also had an effect. Both Chinese and Korean participants felt significantly more disappointed with ability issues when the senior caused the failure than when the peer caused the failure.

## 3.3    The Influence of Self-construal

To test whether Chinese and Korean participants differed in self-construal, three t-tests were conducted. The results of cultural effect on individual self-construal, relational self-construal, and group self-construal were summarized in Table 6. Chinese participants gave significantly higher ratings than Korean participants did on group self-construal (t = 3.45, p < 0.001, d = 0.44). Korean participants rated individual self-construal (t = −2.52, p = 0.012, d = 0.32) significantly higher than Chinese participants.

**Table 6.** T-test result of culture effect on self-construal

| Type of self-construal | T | P | Cohen's d |
|---|---|---|---|
| Individual | −2.52 | **0.012** | 0.32 |
| Relational | −0.52 | 0.604 | 0.07 |
| Group | 3.45 | **<0.001** | 0.44 |

Correlation tests were conducted to study the relationship between self-construal and attributions. Ability attribution and group self-construal was found negatively correlated (r = −0.14, p = 0.032).

## 4   Discussion

The scenarios were almost the same except for the team member's status (peer or senior), and this small change led to different levels of disappointment. When considering the team member's ability, both Chinese and Korean participants were significantly more disappointed with the ability failure when the team member was described as a senior in the group. It was reasonable because in these two cultures the senior or the Senpai was highly respected for their rich knowledge and experience. It would be more unacceptable if a senior made an ability failure rather than an unexperienced peer. As for the disappointment to motivation failure, no significant difference was discovered between peers and seniors. No matter it was a peer or a senior that made a mistake due to motivation failure, the disappointment levels remained very high.

Chinese participants attributed the failure more to contextual causes, while Korean participants attributed it more to ability-related causes. It was in accordance with the fact that Chinese culture was more collectivism (Hofstede 1983). Data collected in this study also supported this explanation. Korean participants rated individual self-construal significantly higher, and group self-construal significantly lower than Chinese participants did. Thus, in our experiment, Chinese participants ascribed the failure more to contextual issues, while Korean participants more to individual issues (personal ability). Negative correlation between group self-construal and ability attribution also supported the results.

Hofstede (1983) also ranked Korea higher than Hong Kong in the power-distance dimension, meaning that a higher percentage of Koreans agreed that their bosses made decisions in an autocratic or paternalistic way, that a higher percentage of Koreans disliked the consultative management style and were more afraid to disagree with superiors. This can explain the interaction effects of culture and status on motivational attribution. Although both Chinese and Korean participants rated motivational attribution lower when the team member was described as a peer, the gap was significantly larger for Korean participants. In a culture with larger power distance, people emphasize more on hierarchy and status issues, so the effect of status was larger for Korean participants.

Previous cross-cultural researches usually focused on cultures that were distinctive in geographic and historical characters. This research involved two nations, China and Korea, both belonged to the East Asian cultural group. Previous researches studied the differences among countries from different cultural groups, providing meaningful guidance for cross-cultural interaction and management and drawing valuable conclusions. In that sense, it is equally important to study the differences among countries within the same cultural group. According to our daily experience and cases, Chinese and Korean cultures have a lot in common; however, they are also different in many ways. Koreans attach more importance to status and hierarchical relationship. Korean juniors must address the seniors with honorific titles. If not, they would get blame. However, this practice is not necessary in China. Learning about these facts and differences will bring huge benefits to the international companies that wish to seek opportunities in East Asian markets.

This research also has some limitations. As there is a lack of previous empirical studies on the differences between China and Korea, we had to adopt Hofstede's analysis as the theoretical framework and made no direct comparison between China and Korea. Hong Kong is like China; however, it cannot represent China completely due to its special location and history. In fact, this research is more like an exploratory study.

This research has its contributions despite limitations. Failures are inevitable in team work. To learn how team members attribute and treat the person who makes a mistake is very useful in dealing with the consequences of a failure. The status of the person who makes a mistake influences people's attributions and levels of disappointment. Managers should learn about this fact and come up with appropriate solutions and explanations accordingly. Culture affects the way people treat status so it is related to attributions. Managers of international companies should recognize the importance of cultural diversities which exist in two similar cultural groups like China and Korea and give it their due respect.

# 5 Conclusion

Towards the same event each person attributed in his or her own way. Through the survey conducted among Chinese and Koreans, it concluded that culture could influence how status affected attributions. Facing a knowledge-sharing failure scenario caused by ability-related issues, both Koreans and Chinese felt more disappointed if the target person was a senior rather than a peer. Chinese participants attributed the failure more to context, while Korean participants attributed it more to ability. The status effect was more obvious in Korea than in China. Cultural context variables like collectivism-individualism and power distance can explain those findings. In addition, the findings in this study are objective facts that managers of international companies should attach importance to.

**Acknowledgement.** This study was funded by a National Natural Science Foundation China grant 71661167006.

# References

Bettencourt, B., Charlton, K., Dorr, N., Hume, D.L.: Status differences and in-group bias: a meta-analytic examination of the effects of status stability, status legitimacy, and group permeability. Psychol. Bull. **127**(4), 520 (2001)

Bond, M.H., Hewstone, M., Wan, K.-C., Chiu, C.-K.: Group-serving attributions across intergroup contexts: cultural differences in the explanation of sex-typed behaviours. Eur. J. Soc. Psychol. **15**(4), 435–451 (1985)

Choi, I., Markus, H.R.: Implicit theories and causal attribution East and West, University of Michigan (1998). Unpublished Manuscript

Enyo, Y.: Exploring Senpai-Koohai Relationships in Club Meetings in a Japanese University. University of Hawai'i at Manoa (2013). http://www.ling.hawaii.edu/graduate/Dissertations/YumikoEnyoFinal.pdf

Fiske, S.T., Cuddy, A.J., Glick, P., Xu, J.: A model of (often mixed) stereotype content: competence and warmth respectively follow from perceived status and competition. J. Pers. Soc. Psychol. **82**(6), 878 (2002)

Hewstone, M., Wagner, U., Machleit, U.: Self-, ingroup, and outgroup achievement attributions of German and Turkish pupils. J. Soc. Psychol. **129**(4), 459–470 (1989)

Hewstone, M., Ward, C.: Ethnocentrism and causal attribution in Southeast Asia. J. Pers. Soc. Psychol. **48**(3), 614 (1985)

Hofstede, G.: National cultures in four dimensions: a research-based theory of cultural differences among nations. Int. Stud. Manag. Organ. **13**(1/2), 46–74 (1983)

Hunter, J.A., Stringer, M., Coleman, J.T.: Social explanations and self-esteem in Northern Ireland. J. Soc. Psychol. **133**(5), 643–650 (1993)

Jones, E.E., Davis, K.E.: From acts to dispositions the attribution process in person perception. Adv. Exp. Soc. Psychol. **2**, 219–266 (1965)

Jones, M.C., Cline, M., Ryan, S.: Exploring knowledge sharing in ERP implementation: an organizational culture framework. Decis. Support Syst. **41**(2), 411–434 (2006)

Khan, S.S., Liu, J.H.: Intergroup attributions and ethnocentrism in the indian subcontinent the ultimate attribution error revisited. J. Cross Cult. Psychol. **39**(1), 16–36 (2008)

Mann, J.F., Taylor, D.M.: Attribution of causality. Role of ethnicity and social class. J. Soc. Psychol. **94**(1), 3–13 (1974)

Menon, T., Morris, M.W., Chiu, C., Hong, Y.: Culture and the construal of agency: attribution to individual versus group dispositions. J. Pers. Soc. Psychol. **76**(5), 701 (1999)

Miller, J.G.: Culture and the development of everyday social explanation. J. Pers. Soc. Psychol. **46**(5), 961 (1984)

Morris, M.W., Peng, K.: Culture and cause: American and Chinese attributions for social and physical events. J. Pers. Soc. Psychol. **67**(6), 949 (1994)

Reeder, G.D., Brewer, M.B.: A schematic model of dispositional attribution in interpersonal perception. Psychol. Rev. **86**(1), 61 (1979)

Sano, K.: The study of the Senpai-Kouhai culture in junior high schools in Japan. Sociol. Insight **6**, 59 (2014)

Stringer, M., Hunter, J.: Attributional bias and identity in a conflict region: the mediating effects of status. Curr. Res. Soc. Psychology **4**(9), 160–175 (1999)

Tajfel, H., Turner, J.C.: An integrative theory of intergroup conflict. Soc. Psychol. Intergroup Relat. **33**(47), 74 (1979)

Tajfel, H., Turner, J.C.: The Social Identity Theory of Intergroup Behavior (2004). http://psycnet. apa.org/psycinfo/2004-13697-016

Zhang, Y.B., Lin, M.-C., Nonaka, A., Beom, K.: Harmony, hierarchy and conservatism: a cross-cultural comparison of confucian values in China, Korea, Japan, and Taiwan. Commun. Res. Rep. **22**(2), 107–115 (2005)

# "Which Country Are You from?" A Cross-Cultural Study on Greeting Interaction Design for Social Robots

Mohammad Shidujaman[✉] and Haipeng Mi[✉]

X-Studio, Department of Information Art and Design, Academy of Arts and Design, Tsinghua University, Beijing, China
shangt15@mails.tsinghua.edu.cn, haipeng.mi@acm.org

**Abstract.** Greeting gestures are one of the most important aspects of social robot behavior design. Existing research has shown different greeting gesture design methods for social robots when they interact with humans. However, cultural difference, which is an important factor between human greetings, is less explored for robot greeting gesture design. In this paper, we present our effort on understanding how different robot greeting behaviors will affect human perception in a cross-cultural context. We designed four different greeting gestures for NAO robot based on human greeting customs from different Asian countries. We also conducted a user experiment, in which participants from the different countries interact with the robot after it performs a designated robot greeting gesture. In the experiment, we investigated: (1) Whether a user could perceive a robot coming from a specific country or region when the robot has a specific greeting gesture; and (2) If the user demonstrates higher valence when the robot has the same greeting gesture with his/her country. We recruited 20 participants from four different countries in the experiment. The result of the experiment suggests a cross-cultural design method for humanoid social robots interacting with users from different cultural backgrounds.

**Keywords:** Social robots · Social presence · Engagement · Greetings
Cross-cultural differences

## 1 Introduction

Greeting gestures are one of the most important aspects of social robot behavior design. Existing research has shown different greeting gesture design methods [1, 7] for social robots when they interact with humans [2]. However, although recognized as an important factor between human greetings, cultural difference [13] in robot greeting gesture design is less explored [4, 18]. For any social relationship, greeting is one of the common universal actions people follow to be close to each other [3, 6, 26]. Greeting study has been extensively explored in the social sciences in an effort to analyze the parameters that arbitrate and configure the nature of interactions between humans. Greeting is a principle component of daily intercommunication and is considered necessary for building and maintaining social relationships. It is nearly impossible for human beings to be present physically near each other and indicate that they are "conscious" and

© Springer International Publishing AG, part of Springer Nature 2018
P.-L. P. Rau (Ed.): CCD 2018, LNCS 10911, pp. 362–374, 2018.
https://doi.org/10.1007/978-3-319-92141-9_28

"properly engaged" without physical or emotional subsistence [26–28]. The dimension of greeting can be easily welcoming and assuring to others. In this way, humans use greetings as a means for making apart the other side of the interaction, and to signal approval and rejection [26].

Social interactions are a leading framework in Human-Computer Interaction [HCI], Human-Machine Interaction [HMI], Human-Robot Interaction [HRI] and Robot-Robot Interaction [RRI] research. The nature of popular greetings in a special engagement may have a wide range of influence on the management of social interaction [27]. "Social robots" are specifically designed to add a social aspect to HRI and RRI [5, 6, 39]. Figure 2 show a human-human greeting approach.

Social robots have also been developed for diverse contexts [41] including child education and development [20, 36, 37, 40], such as boosting children's creativity through robot storytelling [29, 31–33], as well as physiotherapy and medical treatment [15, 35]; care-giving company for the elderly and lonely in affective state [3, 8–10]; learning systems for human communication and speech perfection [14, 21, 28]; education and social development [22, 33], wireless power charging robots and networking [39], virtual reality, augmented reality, mixed reality, human-robot teaming and cognition [30], smart robot homes and restaurants [2, 23, 25], intelligent robot systems [12], and so on. Robots are about to become commonplace in our personal and professional lives and in common working spaces [6], and human-robot teamwork approaches [24] for long term interaction are being developed accordingly [11, 17]. As such, it is important to design the HRI carefully [9, 19], and specifically the first "encounter" between humans and robots, i.e. greeting. The social importance of greeting provides an opportunity for social robot researchers to influence people's interaction and engagement with the robot [23]. Findings from these studies draw an interesting picture and confirm the possibility of creating a meaningful greeting experience in a HRI [13, 16].

## 2  Related Work

### 2.1  Cross-Culture Technology

The use of mobile and computing devices, e.g., personal computers, mobile phones, smart watches, glasses, and wearable devices has become common in our daily life [39, 42]. These devices can be significant in influencing the quality of our conversations and social attention [52]. For example, when talking with partners, we may occasionally search for information on our smart devices. In these scenarios, our partners may notice such attention shifts, and react accordingly, e.g., by raising their voice, or pausing until our attention returns back, to prevent possible intercommunication breakdowns. Similar situations, whereby humans shift their attention to peripheral computing devices, could happen in HRI and RRI [2].

### 2.2  HRI Greetings

The idea of robot greeting gesture design comes from human-human gestures, which are an essential part of human introductions. Figure 2 shows a common human-human greeting gesture, while Fig. 3 shows greeting gestures in Japan and Thailand. Greeting has been shown to take different forms in different cultures, including verbal and nonverbal aspects of the interaction. Researchers have also argued that robots should adapt to cultural differences in order to communicate effectively. In one study, a humanoid robot performed physical gestures including bowing, raising a hand, moving it to the heart and nodding. Results showed that participants felt more comfortable when interacting with a robot that greets using language and gestures that matched the participants' culture [4].

Human-robot greeting is important toward connecting human-robot intimacy, and could be important in contexts such as personal robot assistance. For example, a robot could act as a shopkeeper that recommends the best product selections. In this scenario, the robot greeting gesture could play a significant role in influencing the customer's affective state [34, 44–46]. Performing a greeting gesture that matches that of the customer's culture could be important in establishing trust, reliability, and affecting the customer's decision-making [38, 48–50].

## 2.3  Robot Greeting Gesture Design

Robot greeting gesture design so far is less explored in the cross-cultural context as greeting gesture design is a challenge for robotic researchers. Related research on robot greeting gesture is mainly focused on bowing, waving, handshakes and nodding [43–47, 51].

Figure 4 shows the common greeting gesture between a NAO humanoid robot and a human. In the next section we will introduce four robot gesture designs. For example, Fig. 1 shows the common hand gestures in China and Thailand for representing Chinese and Thai greeting culture, respectively. We decided to design greeting gestures by NAO robot for four countries greeting culture, namely China, Bangladesh, Thailand and Japan.

**Fig. 1.** Common greeting hand gesture in China and Thailand.

**Fig. 2.** Human-human greeting approach.

**Fig. 3.** Greeting gesture in Japan and Thailand.

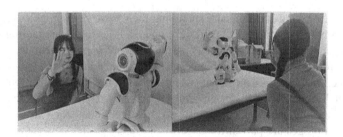

**Fig. 4.** Common greeting gesture in HRI.

## 3  Evaluation Experiments

We design four interactive greeting processes using the NAO robot platform based on our research questions.

Research question 1: Whether a user could perceive a robot coming from a specific country or region if the robot has a specific greeting gesture; and
Research question 2: If the user demonstrates higher valence when the robot has the same greeting gesture with his/her country.

## 3.1   Experiment Design

This section describes the four interactive greeting processes using the NAO robot. We designed four greeting interactions according to culture-based greetings in China, Bangladesh, Thailand, and Japan. Figure 5 shows our greeting design for these four countries. For China, the robot is bowing with both hands together in front of the torso, and the head faces downwards; Bangladesh, the robot is raising one hand up, and the head is facing directly forward; Thailand, the robot is holding both hands together near the chest, with the head is facing directly forward; Japan, the robot is bowing with both hands at each side of the body, and head facing downwards.

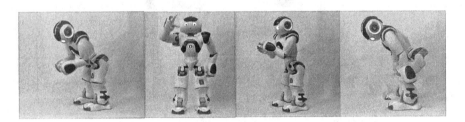

**Fig. 5.**   Native robot greeting design, (1) China, (2) Bangladesh, (3) Thailand and (4) Japan.

## 3.2   Experiment Protocol

Participants filled out a questionnaire surveying their basic demographics (e.g. gender, age, major, robot experience, etc.), and were given a brief tutorial regarding the basics of the NAO robot interaction before they participated in the experiment. In the first part, the robot performs a common greeting gesture once, and then a native greeting gesture once, and the participant is asked to answer the question of "where the robot is coming from?" after looking at the robot gesture. Participants from four different countries participants had the chance to participate in this experiment for two rounds. In the common greeting gesture part of the experiment, many participants answered that the robot performed a common or standard greeting gesture, whereas for the native greeting gesture part, most participants answered that the robot is coming from their native countries. This is explained in the data analysis section of this paper in Sect. 4.

For the second part of the experiment, we observed whether the user demonstrated higher valence if the robot has the same greeting gesture with his/her country. This was measured via a Likert chart. Figure 6 shows the native human-human greeting gesture (upper row) and native human-robot greeting gesture design (lower row), for (1) China, (2) Bangladesh, (3) Thailand and (4) Japan.

**Fig. 6.** Native human-human greeting (upper row) and native human-robot greeting design (lower row), (1) China, (2) Bangladesh, (3) Thailand and (4) Japan.

### 3.3 Procedure and Measurement

Evaluation items are scored using self-report questionnaires. The questionnaire includes evaluation items for both common and native gesture conditions. There are two parts to the evaluation. The first is to measure participants' ability to perceive where the robot comes from (the country) by understanding the robot gesture; the second part is for understanding likeability and valence toward the robot. Figure 7 shows the Self-Assessment Manikin used to rate the affective dimension of valence, i.e. to gauge participants' emotional response towards the robot (Table 1).

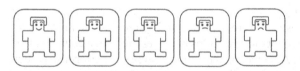

**Fig. 7.** The Self-Assessment Manikin (SAM) used to rate the affective dimension of Valence.

**Table 1.** Qualitative description list for study 1.

| Category | Description | Participants answer ratio |
|---|---|---|
| Positive feeling during greeting gesture | Happy to see, look at me, good morning, good afternoon, welcome and laughing | 70% |
| Negative feeling during greeting gesture | Scared of robot greeting behavior, avoiding eye contact with robot, careless | 10% |
| Normal feeling during greeting gesture | Resting, good eye contact, normal movement | 20% |

### 3.4  Participants

Participants consisted of four nationalities including China, Bangladesh, Thailand and Japan. For Experiment 1 and 2, a total number of 20 participants (10 males, 10 females, average age: 24.7; min age: 18: max age: 32) were recruited from different universities in Beijing. The same participants were recruited for experiment 1 and 2.

### 3.5  Assessment

We used a 7-point scale to measure different emotional responses of participants towards the robot, after the robot greeting was performed.

| Unsafe | 1 2 3 4 5 6 7 | Safe |
| Anxious | 1 2 3 4 5 6 7 | Relaxed |
| Excited | 1 2 3 4 5 6 7 | Calm |
| Quiescent | 1 2 3 4 5 6 7 | Surprised |

## 4  Data Analysis

Two experimental studies have been done during the experimental process. Study 1 findings show the calculation of the percentage ratio of participants' preferred choice of the answered countries. Study 2 findings carry out the ANOVA analysis results.

**Study 1- Findings**

Four greeting gestures were demonstrated by our designed NAO robot to each participant, where the robot only performs body gesture with a counterbalancing technique to offset order bias. After the robot greeting gesture was performed, participants were asked whether the robot performed a common greeting gesture, or a greeting gesture native to his/her country. Among 20 participants from different countries, the ratio of answers identifying the robot greeting gesture was 70%, 10% and 20% for Native, Common and Others, respectively (Fig. 8). This indicates that users often correctly identified where the robot greeting gesture came from. Participants who answered "Others" mostly confused the greeting behavior of Thailand with India or other countries in south Asia, and the greeting behavior of China with Japan, while the greeting behavior of Bangladesh was sometimes regarded as a western greeting by participants.

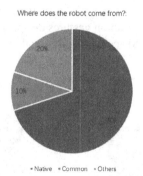

**Fig. 8.** Ratio of calculating native, common and others in terms of evaluating where the robot coming from.

Qualitative description list: We used some frequent descriptions written by the participants in study 1 (as answered to the open ended questions) and created a measurement list for NAO robot greeting. These included: Happy to see, look at me, good morning, good afternoon, welcome and laughing, scared of robot greeting behavior, avoiding eye contact with the robot, careless, resting, good eye contact, normal movement (See Table 1).

**Study 2- Findings**
We conducted a 1-way-ANOVA with the following independent variables: Greeting acceptance rate for valence (Common vs Native). A single factor ANOVA (Common vs Native) on the valence scale reveled a main effect: native feeling significantly affected valence $F = 7.43$, $p < .05$, $p = .009$. Participants rated native gestures as more close compared to the common gestures designed by the NAO robot greeting. Figure 9 shows the mean and SD comparison for calculating valence.

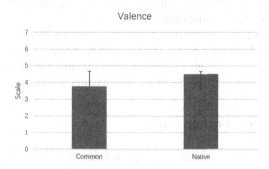

**Fig. 9.** Mean and SD comparison for calculating valence.

We conducted a 1-way-ANOVA with the following independent variables: greeting acceptance rate for likeability (Common vs Native). A single factor ANOVA (Common vs Native) on the Likeability scale revealed a main effect: native feeling significantly affected the likeability F = 5.22, p < .05, p = .028. Participants rated native gestures as more likeable compared to the common gestures designed by the NAO robot greeting. Figure 10 shows the mean and SD comparison for calculating likeability.

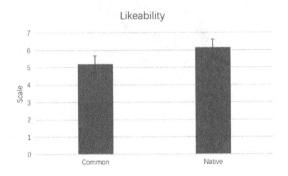

**Fig. 10.** Mean and SD comparison for calculating likeability.

## 5    Discussion

In this work we presented the NAO greeting design, implementation and user evaluation. In the design and implementation section we showed the NAO greeting design process for four Asian countries: China, Bangladesh, Thailand and Japan. We then reported two studies in which we used qualitative and quantitative methods to evaluate whether participants perceived the NAO robot greeting gesture as a greeting experience, and how the movement features of the gestures influence greeting expressivity.

In study 1, participants watched a common greeting gesture and native greeting gesture, then described the greeting feeling by using the Self-Assessment Manikin (SAM) and 7-point Likert scale. Qualitative analysis also showed that participants perceived the gestures as either a Positive Greeting or a Negative Greeting or a Normal Greeting using different emotional state descriptions.

In study 2, participants experience the native greeting interaction with the NAO robot. This was found to have a profound impact on participant's perception. The native gesture was perceived as a Positive Greeting, reflecting that the user has higher valence if the robot has the same greeting gesture with his/her country.

## 6    Conclusion and Future Work

In this work we presented a greeting design process during HRI that performs body gesture to welcome people from different nationalities. The design evaluation method has been verified by a cross-cultural user experiment to investigate the research question. In the future we aim to develop greeting technology by designing expressive social robots with more functionality. We would also like to develop emotion-based social robots, given their importance during the human-robot greeting interaction process.

**Acknowledgement.** The authors would like to thank Xiaowei Lu, Yuting Diao and Chung Wui Kang, three graduate student members from X-Studio, Information Art and Design department at Tsinghua University for help during the user experience experiment. This work is supported by National Key Research & Development Plan of China under Grant No. 2016YFB1001402.

# References

1. Trovato, G., Ramos, J.G., Azevedo, H., Moroni, A., Magossi, S., Simmons, R., Ishii, H., Takanishi, A.: A receptionist robot for Brazilian people: study on interaction involving illiterates. Paladyn J. Behav. Robot. **8**(1), 1–17 (2017)
2. Luria, M., Hoffman, G., Zuckerman, O.: Comparing social robot, screen and voice interfaces for smart-home control. In: Proceedings of the 2017 CHI Conference on Human Factors in Computing Systems, pp. 580–628. ACM, May 2017
3. Bradley, M.M., Lang, P.J.: Measuring emotion: the Self-Assessment Manikin and the semantic differential. J. Behav. Ther. Exp. Psychiatr. **25**(1), 49–59 (1994)
4. Trovato, G., Zecca, M., Sessa, S., Jamone, L., Ham, J., Hashimoto, K., Takanishi, A.: Cross-cultural study on human-robot greeting interaction: acceptance and discomfort by Egyptians and Japanese. Paladyn J. Behav. Robot. **4**(2), 83–93 (2013)
5. Schiffer, S.: Integrating qualitative reasoning and human-robot interaction in domestic service robotics. KI-Künstliche Intelligenz **30**(3–4), 257–265 (2016)
6. de Graaf, M.M., Allouch, S.B., van Dijk, J.A.: Long-term acceptance of social robots in domestic environments: insights from a user's perspective. In: AAAI 2016 Spring symposium on "Enabling Computing Research in Socially Intelligent Human–Robot Interaction: A Community-Driven Modular Research Platform", Palo Alto, March 2016
7. Glas, D.F., Wada, K., Shiomi, M., Kanda, T., Ishiguro, H., Hagita, N.: Personal greetings: personalizing robot utterances based on novelty of observed behavior. Int. J. Soc. Robot. **9**(2), 181–198 (2017)
8. Dautenhahn, K., Campbell, A., Syrdal, D.S.: Does anyone want to talk to me? Reflections on the use of assistance and companion robots in care homes. In: Salem, M., Weiss, A., Baxter, P., Dautenhahn, K. (eds.) Proceedings of the 4th International Symposium on New Frontiers in Human-Robot Interaction. The Society for the Study of Artificial Intelligence and the Simulation of Behaviour (AISB), Canterbury, pp. 17–20, 21–22 April 2015
9. Faridi, F., Breazeal, C., JIBO, Inc.: Multi-segment social robot. U.S. Patent Application 15/014,963 (2016)
10. Samani, H., Samani, H.: The evaluation of affection in human-robot interaction. Kybernetes **45**(8), 1257–1272 (2016)
11. Leite, I., Martinho, C., Paiva, A.: Social robots for long-term interaction: a survey. Int. J. Soc. Robot. **5**(2), 291–308 (2013)
12. Shih, Y.S., Samani, H., Yang, C.Y.: Internet of Things for human—pet interaction. In: International Conference on System Science and Engineering (ICSSE), pp. 1–4. IEEE, July 2016
13. Samani, H., Saadatian, E., Pang, N., Polydorou, D., Fernando, O.N.N., Nakatsu, R., Koh, J.T.K.V.: Cultural robotics: the culture of robotics and robotics in culture. Int. J. Adv. Robot. Syst. **10**(12), 400 (2013)
14. Liu, J., Rau, P.L.P., Wendler, N.: Trust and online information-sharing in close relationships: a cross-cultural perspective. Behav. Inf. Technol. **34**(4), 363–374 (2015)

15. Moosaei, M., Das, S.K., Popa, D.O., Riek, L.D.: Using facially expressive robots to calibrate clinical pain perception. In: Proceedings of the 2017 ACM/IEEE International Conference on Human-Robot Interaction, pp. 32–41. ACM, March 2017

16. Bisio, A., Sciutti, A., Nori, F., Metta, G., Fadiga, L., Sandini, G., Pozzo, T.: Motor contagion during human-human and human-robot interaction. PLoS ONE 9(8), e106172 (2014)

17. Leite, I., Castellano, G., Pereira, A., Martinho, C., Paiva, A.: Empathic robots for long-term interaction. Int. J. Soc. Robot. 6(3), 329–341 (2014)

18. Haring, K.S., Silvera-Tawil, D., Watanabe, K., Velonaki, M.: The influence of robot appearance and interactive ability in HRI: a cross-cultural study. In: Agah, A., Cabibihan, J.-J., Howard, A.M., Salichs, M.A., He, H. (eds.) ICSR 2016. LNCS (LNAI), vol. 9979, pp. 392–401. Springer, Cham (2016). https://doi.org/10.1007/978-3-319-47437-3_38

19. Li, D., Rau, P.P., Li, Y.: A cross-cultural study: effect of robot appearance and task. Int. J. Soc. Robot. 2(2), 175–186 (2010)

20. Zaga, C., de Vries, R.A., Li, J., Truong, K.P., Evers, V.: A simple nod of the head: the effect of minimal robot movements on children's perception of a low-anthropomorphic robot. In: Proceedings of the 2017 CHI Conference on Human Factors in Computing Systems, pp. 336–341. ACM, May 2017

21. Shinozawa, K., Naya, F., Yamato, J., Kogure, K.: Differences in effect of robot and screen agent recommendations on human decision-making. Int. J. Hum. Comput. Stud. 62(2), 267–279 (2005)

22. Heenan, B., Greenberg, S., Aghel-Manesh, S., Sharlin, E.: Designing social greetings in human robot interaction. In: Proceedings of the 2014 Conference on Designing Interactive Systems, pp. 855–864. ACM, June 2014

23. Dautenhahn, K., Walters, M., Woods, S., Koay, K.L., Nehaniv, C.L., Sisbot, A., Alami, R., Siméon, T.: How may i serve you? A robot companion approaching a seated person in a helping context. In: Proceedings of the 1st ACM SIGCHI/SIGART Conference on Human-Robot Interaction, pp. 172–179. ACM, March 2006

24. Satake, S., Kanda, T., Glas, D.F., Imai, M., Ishiguro, H., Hagita, N.: How to approach humans? Strategies for social robots to initiate interaction. In: Proceedings of the 4th ACM/IEEE International Conference on Human Robot Interaction, pp. 109–116. ACM, March 2009

25. Acosta, L., González, E., Rodríguez, J.N., Hamilton, A.F.: Design and implementation of a service robot for a restaurant. Int. J. Robot. Autom. 21(4), 273 (2006)

26. Firth, R.: Verbal and bodily rituals of greeting and parting. In: The Interpretation of Ritual, pp. 1–38 (1972)

27. Kendon, A.: Conducting interaction: patterns of behavior in focused encounters, vol. 7. CUP Archive (1990)

28. Goffman, E.: Behavior in Public Place. The Free Press, New York (1963)

29. Alves-Oliveira, P., Arriaga, P., Hoffman, G., Paiva, A.: Boosting children's creativity through creative interactions with social robots. In: 11th ACM/IEEE International Conference on Human-Robot Interaction (HRI), pp. 591–592. IEEE, March 2016

30. Park, H.W., Rosenberg-Kima, R., Rosenberg, M., Gordon, G., Breazeal, C.: Growing growth mindset with a social robot peer. In: Proceedings of the 2017 ACM/IEEE International Conference on Human-Robot Interaction, pp. 137–145. ACM, March 2017

31. Druga, S., Williams, R., Breazeal, C., Resnick, M.: Hey Google is it OK if i eat you? Initial explorations in child-agent interaction. In: Proceedings of the 2017 Conference on Interaction Design and Children, pp. 595–600. ACM, June 2017

32. Park, H.W., Gelsomini, M., Lee, J.J., Breazeal, C.: Telling stories to robots: the effect of back channeling on a child's storytelling. In: Proceedings of the 2017 ACM/IEEE International Conference on Human-Robot Interaction, pp. 100–108. ACM, March 2017

33. Striepe, H., Lugrin, B.: There once was a robot storyteller: measuring the effects of emotion and non-verbal behaviour. In: Kheddar, A., et al. (eds.) ICSR 2017. LNCS, vol. 10652. Springer, Cham (2017). https://doi.org/10.1007/978-3-319-70022-9_13

34. Woiceshyn, L., Wang, Y., Nejat, G., Benhabib, B.: Personalized clothing recommendation by a social robot. In: 2017 IEEE International Symposium on Robotics and Intelligent Sensors (IRIS), pp. 179–185. IEEE, October 2017

35. Riek, L.D.: Robotics technology in mental health care. In: Artificial Intelligence in Behavioral and Mental Health Care, pp. 185–203 (2016)

36. Lupetti, M.L., Yao, Y., Mi, H., Germak, C.: Design for children's playful learning with robots. Futur. Internet 9(3), 52 (2017)

37. Lupetti, M.L.: Shybo. An open-source low-anthropomorphic robot for children. HardwareX 2, 50–60 (2017)

38. Winkler, J., Bozcuoğlu, A.K., Pomarlan, M., Beetz, M.: Task parametrization through multi-modal analysis of robot experiences. In: Proceedings of the 16th Conference on Autonomous Agents and MultiAgent Systems, pp. 1754–1756, May 2017

39. Shidujaman, M., Rodriguez, L.T., Samani, H.: Design and navigation prospective for wireless power transmission robot. In: International Conference on Informatics, Electronics & Vision (ICIEV), pp. 1–6. IEEE, June 2015

40. Lupetti, M.L., Gao, J., Yao, Y., Mi, H.: A scenario-driven design method for Chinese children edutainment. In Proceedings of the Fifth International Symposium of Chinese CHI, pp. 22–29. ACM, June 2017

41. Breazeal, C.L.: Sociable machines: expressive social exchange between humans and robots. Doctoral dissertation, Massachusetts Institute of Technology (2000)

42. Baddoura, R., Venture, G.: Social vs. useful HRI: experiencing the familiar, perceiving the robot as a sociable partner and responding to its actions. Int. J. Soc. Robot. 5(4), 529–547 (2013)

43. Salem, M., Eyssel, F., Rohlfing, K., Kopp, S., Joublin, F.: To err is human (-like): effects of robot gesture on perceived anthropomorphism and likability. Int. J. Soc. Robot. 5(3), 313–323 (2013)

44. Nomura, T., Suzuki, T., Kanda, T., Han, J., Shin, N., Burke, J., Kato, K.: What people assume about humanoid and animal-type robots: cross-cultural analysis between Japan, Korea, and the United States. Int. J. Humanoid Robot. 5(01), 25–46 (2008)

45. Kaplan, F.: Who is afraid of the humanoid? Investigating cultural differences in the acceptance of robots. Int. J. Humanoid Robot. 1(03), 465–480 (2004)

46. Suzuki, S., Fujimoto, Y., Yamaguchi, T.: Can differences of nationalities be induced and measured by robot gesture communication? In: 4th International Conference on Human System Interactions (HSI), pp. 357–362. IEEE, May 2011

47. Riek, L.D., Mavridis, N., Antali, S., Darmaki, N., Ahmed, Z., Al-Neyadi, M., Alketheri, A.: Ibn sina steps out: exploring arabic attitudes toward humanoid robots. In: Proceedings of the 2nd International Symposium on New Frontiers in Human–Robot Interaction, AISB, Leicester, vol. 1, April 2010

48. Groen, F.C., Pavlin, G., Winterboer, A., Evers, V.: A hybrid approach to decision making and information fusion: combining humans and artificial agents. Robot. Auton. Syst. 90, 71–85 (2017)

49. Heerink, M., Kröse, B., Evers, V., Wielinga, B.: Influence of social presence on acceptance of an assistive social robot and screen agent by elderly users. Adv. Robot. 23(14), 1909–1923 (2009)

50. Cramer, H., Evers, V., Ramlal, S., Van Someren, M., Rutledge, L., Stash, N., Aroyo, L., Wielinga, B.: The effects of transparency on trust in and acceptance of a content-based art recommender. User Model. User Adapted Interact. **18**(5), 455 (2008)
51. Lohse, M., Rothuis, R., Gallego-Pérez, J., Karreman, D.E., Evers, V.: Robot gestures make difficult tasks easier: the impact of gestures on perceived workload and task performance. In: Proceedings of the SIGCHI Conference on Human Factors in Computing Systems, pp. 1459–1466. ACM, April 2014
52. Gans, G., Jarke, M., Kethers, S., Lakemeyer, G., Ellrich, L., Funken, C., Meister, M.: Towards (dis)trust-based simulations of agent networks. In: Proceedings of the 4th Workshop on Deception, Fraud, and Trust in Agent Societies, pp. 49–60, May 2001

# The Literature Review of Human Factors Research on Unmanned Aerial Vehicle – What Chinese Researcher Need to Do Next?

Xin Zhang, Guozhu Jia, and Zhe Chen[✉]

School of Economics and Management, Beihang University,
Xueyuan Road No. 37, Haidian District, Beijing 100191, China
zhechen@buaa.edu.cn

**Abstract.** This study reviewed the literature on human factors issues in unmanned aerial vehicles. Cultural differences on human factor in unmanned aerial vehicles were considered in this study between China and the United States to find the future research directions for human factor specialists in China. After a screening and selection process in the literature search, eighty papers were included in full paper reading and discussed in this study. According to the results, there was still a gap between research development of human factors in unmanned vehicles in China and that in the United States, no matter considering the quantity or quality of papers in two countries. Five topics, human factors identification, display and interface, automation and system, crew performance, and election and training, may be Chinese researchers' future research directions.

**Keywords:** Literature review · UAV · Human factor

## 1 Introduction

The UAV (Unmanned Aerial Vehicle) is operated remotely by pilot on ground-based controller with communication system. As a typical human-computer interaction system, human factors issues are critical to reliability of UAVs.

Human factor problems have been encountered since uninhabited aerial vehicles were used for military and civilian missions. Data links broken down while operators hardly realized readily. It was also difficult for human to keep vigilance for long periods of time and exploit imagery on multiple stream at a time [1].

Tvaryanas et al. (2006) found that 60.2% of 221 mishaps associated with causal causes of operators' errors at the organizational, supervision, preconditions, and operator levels [2]. Oncu and Yildiz (2014) revealed that among 68 accidents due to casual factors, 65% of the factors were relevant to humans [3]. Identification of human factors as different categories is particular concern to improve the UAV flight safety, such as Displays and Controls, Automation and System Failures, and Crew Composition, Selection and Training [4]. Williams's (2004) investigation showed that the effect of human factor issues was related to particular UAV systems, the type of automation incorporated, and the user interface employed, based on the data from Army Navy and Air Force [5].

© Springer International Publishing AG, part of Springer Nature 2018
P.-L. P. Rau (Ed.): CCD 2018, LNCS 10911, pp. 375–384, 2018.
https://doi.org/10.1007/978-3-319-92141-9_29

With worldwide concerned in aviation accident analysis, human factors study is an important theme to research.

Besides, the uniqueness of Chinese culture may have a potential influence on the human factors issues in UAVs. On the one hand, human factors issues are often misunderstood and ignored with predilection toward technological solutions. Domestic human factor researches on UAV are comprehensive, but a gap exists as compared with those in the United States. On the other hand, the culture of a country has impact on crew performance in Unmanned Aircraft Systems. There are five dimensions of national culture differences identified in Hostede's culture model [6]. Power distance tend to be higher for China than the USA. Individualism is prevalent in Western countries, while collectivism prevails in China. Uncertainty avoidance is one uniquely Western dimension and a long-term orientation is mostly found in China [7]. All these characteristics make Western thinking analytical and Eastern thinking synthetic [8] and may result in unique behavior potentially. UAV pilots with various national cultural backgrounds do different analysis facing the same condition, consequently causing diverse human factor errors. Accordingly, developers can design specific interfaces and automation system based on different mind to adapt to human using habits. In addition, improving efficiency of pilot selection and training can help to enhance human reliability of UAV with consideration of dimensions of national culture.

Thus, it is necessary to review human factors research of UAV in China. Human Factors Analysis and Classification System (HFACS) is a reductionist tool for analyzing human performance failures within a mishap database and widely used in aviation accident analysis to identify recurrent human factors error. Moreover, the completeness of HFACS analysis was improved by the AcciTree model with reliable graphic part and logical taxonomic part enhancing [9]. In terms of relations among accident factors, Edwards and Hawkins regarded accident causes as inappropriate interactions among human, aircraft and environment in software–hardware–environment–liveware–liveware (SHELL) model [10].

Although the above methodology has been adopted by domestic researchers, their analysis is mainly on the basis of American military accident data. There is rarely relevant study on Chinese UAV applications in the existing literature published. Existing literatures provide varieties of human factors issues in UAVs and suggest directions of future research for Chinese scholars.

## 2    Method

This study conducted a literature review in terms of human factors research on UAV from 1998 to 2007. The literature search process was detailed in Fig. 1.

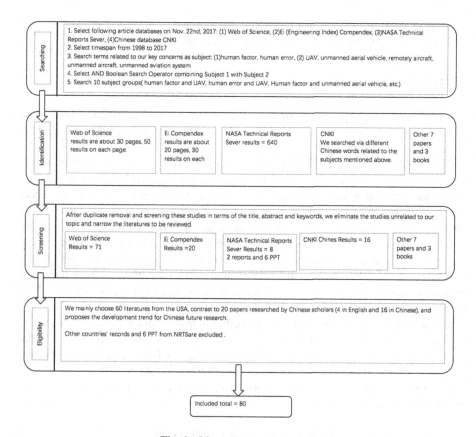

**Fig. 1.** Literature search process

## 2.1 Literature Sources

In order to make a comprehensive review, the literature sources derive from academic publications, public reports, conference papers and books. Our databases cover "Web of Science", "Ei (Engineering Index) Compendex", NASA Technical Reports Sever and Chinese database "China Knowledge Resource Integrated Database".

## 2.2 Search

Use "AND" Boolean search operators to narrow the search field. Search with the keywords "human factor", "human error" and "UAV", "unmanned aerial vehicle", "remotely aircraft", "unmanned aircraft", "unmanned aviation system".

## 2.3 Eligibility Criteria

There is a mass of relevant literatures on the field of human factors or UAV. We need to combine both two subjects and narrow the list of literatures. By screening these studies in terms of the title, abstract and keywords, we eliminate the studies unrelated to our topic and narrow the literatures to be reviewed to 80 articles.

# 3   Results

This study reviewed 80 papers, 60 from the United States and 20 from China. In Chinese papers, 4 papers were written in Chinese and 16 were written in English by researchers from China.

Since the military in the USA has a relatively rich experience of UA utilization and mass of data accurately recorded about incidents (Williams 2004) [5], American scholars have conducted much more researches on human factor issues in last 20 years. There are more than 50% of literatures published by American scholars, especially from 1998-2007. Obviously, the USA is in a dominant position in human factors field compared to any other countries. Although some scholars abroad have studied these issues, their research information is gathered from Hunter, Shadow or Pioneer serving in military of the USA. Hence, this paper mainly reviews literatures from the USA, contrast to human factor issues with China, and proposes the development trend for Chinese future research.

After initial review, we found some focuses among these articles. Scholars and engineers put on similar emphasis in various workshops, conferences and books. In order to make further investigation, qualitative literatures in hand have been classified according to their research field, namely human factors identification, display and interface, automation and system, crew performance, selection and training and some other issues showing in Table 1.

**Table 1.** The classification of material

| No | Field | The USA | China (English) | China (Chinese) |
|----|-------|---------|-----------------|-----------------|
| 1 | Human factors identification | 19 | 1 | 4 |
| 2 | Displays and interface | 10 | | 5 |
| 3 | Automation and system | 12 | | |
| 4 | Crew performance | 12 | | |
| 5 | Selection and training | 3 | 1 | 7 |
| 6 | Others | 3 | 2 | |
| Total | | 60 | 4 | 16 |

# 4   Discussion

## 4.1   Human Factors Identification

Human factors identification is basic analysis of UAV accidents. Generally, accidents are classified into broad categories based on whether it is related to human factor failures firstly. In the second stage, HFACS is popularly applied. It is a model divided human-related failure into four levels, which are further subdivided into 19 categories.

Tvaryanas (2006) investigated 221 RPA mishaps and identified recurring human factors failures on account of operator, organization, preconditions and supervision levels [2]. In his further review of 95 mishaps, two more factors were recognized, namely fatigue trouble and motivational deficiency [11]. Williams (2004) has found that human error contributed to 61% of UAV mishaps. The largest percentage of accidents causes was attributed to unsafe acts according to HFACS analysis classification [5]. The Department of Defense (DOD) has used the HFACS taxonomy successfully for ten years to recognize the human factors failure in UA mishaps (Oncu and Yildiz 2014). The results of their study revealed that 287 causal factors were attributed to 68 accidents and 65% of the factors were associated with humans [3].

Organizational climate, one of human errors in HFACS, covers kinds of element influencing organization atmosphere, including cultures, policies, relationships, and command and control structure. Cultural difference should be one of organizational climate taken into consideration in human factor analysis. However, existing researches have not referred to this question in Western countries. There is significant cultural difference between Asia and Western countries, especially in China. Chinese scholars hardly pay attention to the gap of national culture. Lei (2014) put forward an associative hazard analysis technique to improve completeness of HFACS [9]. Cui (2015) constructed fuzzy cognitive map to predict UAV accidents [12]. Other Chinese papers mainly review causes analysis based on the US military UAV accidents and emphasize important role of human factors in UAV development. Future work will concern Chinese characteristic for human error elimination.

## 4.2    Displays and Interface

As a typically human-computer system, instrument display and automation system interface are important human factor elements. It is necessary to take these factors into consideration for system design and instrument arrangement.

The pilot of an unmanned aircraft has no access to auditory, tactile, olfactory and sufficient visual information with familiar vestibular cues as conventional aircraft [13]. Prabhala et al. (2003) pointed out although automation is designed for reducing operator workload, the complexity of the system is increased by human factors, such as skill degradation, workload, situational awareness, trust and biases [14]. Developing appropriate interface is able to improve usability and reliability of UAVs. Van Breda (2005) find result that humanized human-machine interfaces design can compensate specific lack of visual information and significantly increase operator performance [15]. Hocraffer and Nam (2016) summarized current situation of UAV management interfaces in terms of the advantages, limitations and assessment method. They have offered proposal to give suggestion about further research on multiple types of feedback, such as tactile, motion, auditory, augmented reality, etc., to improve operator situation awareness [16]. Peschel (2013) researched the human-machine interaction technologies among micro and small UAVs. Significant interface limitations may lead interaction conflicts unexpectedly between mission specialist role and micro UAV operators [17]. In terms of display of UAV, Easier access to information can optimize UAV operations based on the proximity principles [18].

Chinese scholars has conducted several researches on this field. Mi and Yang (2013) has reviewed articles covering current development, limitations, challenges, and provided reference for human-computer interaction in UAV swarms. They had measured relationship between automation and human-computer interaction [19].

### 4.3  Automation and System

Automation systems enables aircraft to be controlled by pilots located remotely. Equipment executes various tasks via different systems, namely "aviate", "navigate", "communicate", and others. Technology development shapes system capabilities and potential in the future. Practical system is critical to assist controller in operating. Reliable automation can help reduce workload, cut down task interference and allow pilots to better handle multiple tasks during flight control [20]. Michael (2012) discussed challenge and opportunities of unmanned air system. The appropriate allocation of crew control and autonomous vehicle control affected mission capability and flexibility of UAVs [21]. It is important to make system easy to use to enable human control reliable. Among the articles we reviewed, various perspectives are considered to address human factors associated to UAV systems.

Gloria (2005) researched the tailoring of synthetic overlay technology [22]. Brandon (2015) analyzed lighting system for safe remote sensing during night time [23]. James (2008)' paper probes into the motion platforms of tele-operated system and employs motion cueing to increase UAV operator performance [24]. Savla (2008) proposed several coordination strategies for target assignments between operators and UAVs [25]. Colombi (2013) identified what system design induced human errors using HFACS and predicts future application areas of new system development [26]. Cooke (2014) made an overview of human systems integrations issues surrounding Remotely Piloted Aircraft System [27]. Kaliardos (2014) identify human factors challenges to integrating different flight systems for UAV operators and other pilots [28]. Feng (2016) proposes an approach to solve uncertainties and imperfections in interactions with human operators [29]. Balog (2017 65) provide a review of recommendations and guidelines adopting in small UAS to improve task efficiency [44].

### 4.4  Crew Performance

Humans are an integral part of the overall UAV system. Crew performance have direct impact on aircraft flying. Since tele-operated or supervisory form of control, there is a time delay between remote control command input and aircraft response. Pilot may be unable to detect and respond to problems in a distance in sufficient time as well. Crew performance faces more challenges among UAV operators than common aviation due to wireless communication control. Crew performance is an important concern. Among articles we review, the amount of papers about this issue is on the second place. Scholars carry out much research on this topic.

It is convinced that split attention, fatigue and inappropriate workload are persistent threats of UAV operations. As early as 1998, MJ Barnes conducted simulation experiments to examine crew performance in controlling the UAV [30]. Split attention is one of reason leading to flight control problems. Walters (2000) develops fatigue algorithm to explore how fatigue, crew size, and rotation schedule have effect on UAV operator workload and performance [31]. The results of this study indicate reduction number of crewmembers results in more crashes, more time to search for targets and less number of targets detected. Tvaryanas (2004)'s paper address crewmember performance in terms of the comprehensive influence of manpower shortage, deficient rest between work shifts, and lower efficiency [32]. Tvaryanas (2009) studies fatigue in pilots before and after shift work adjustment resulting from lack of opportunities for recovery and enough sleep [33]. Mouloua (2001) also addresses workload concern for the development of functional UAV systems [34]. Dixon et al. (2005) argue that the automation involving to work has positive effects on human performance and reduce workload [20]. Murray (2013) provided a mathematical model for simultaneously routing UAVs and scheduling human operators, subject to operator workload considerations [35]. Research proved that time pressure affected autonomous UAV operator task performance and workload [36].

Mental health is another object to research. Chappelle (2014) repeats a survey to assess mental health among United States Air Force aircrew operating Predator/Reaper remotely piloted aircraft [37]. Wohleber (2015) examined the consistency of stress responses to different sources of stress during simulated multiple UAV operation.

There is hardly an article published in China referring to crew performance. According to existing papers, fatigue, split attention, workload and pressure are critical issues to explore for Chinese scholars and engineers. In addition, Chinese operator characteristic need to be considered due to the specific national culture background.

## 4.5 Selection and Training

Base on system interface, instrument display and flight mission, UAV operators need specific selection and training mode, especially differs from traditional aviation pilots [38]. UAV operators hold the similar view that there is cultural difference existing between remotely controlled aircraft and mainstream aviation according to interview UAV operators (Hobbs 2006) [39]. It is important to make careful selection criterion, train high-quality UAV operators and effectively evaluate their training results.

Complex human-computer systems require carefully selected operators, who will interact with the system (Carretta 2015) [40]. And the reliability of automated systems should be taken into consideration when multi-UAV operators test. (Lin 2016) [41]. Analysis of UAV mishaps associated with flight control problems provide theoretical support to maximize operator efficacy and apply to training practice. The research results gave reference to human computer interface design and help to make appropriate business decisions for staffing and training, thereby human workload reduce and system performance improve (Liu 2015) [36]. Menda et al. (2011) conduct experiment and present early findings that Functional Near-Infrared Spectroscopy (fNIR) application could enhance UAV operator training, evaluation and interface development [42]. Li (2015 21) analyze eye-movement experiments and make conclusion that there are individual differences in various aspects of psychological conditions, knowledge levels, hobbies and interests. However, professional training can impose positive influences on the professional skills of trainees in a certain kind of a field [43].

Among articles we review, a number of Chinese scholars regard the training issue as an important topic. Some of them discussed development of selection and training in USA as reference for domestic application. Others explore UAV operators training for military and civilian UAV in China. According the articles that we review, it is necessary to improve practical training in present institution. Systematic training, including theoretical knowledge study, simulated training and practice skill training, is a major tendency of future development.

**Acknowledgement.** This study is supported by the Technical Research Foundation of China, the National Nature Foundation of China grant 71401018, the Social Science Foundation Beijing grant 16YYC04, and China Scholarship Council.

# References

1. Gawron, V.J.: Human factors problems associated with uninhabited aerial vehicles (UAVs). Hum. Factors Ergon. Soc. Ann. Meet. Proc. **42**(23), 1600–1600 (1998)
2. Tvaryanas, A.P., Thompson, W.T., Constable, S.H.: Human factors in remotely piloted aircraft operations: HFACS analysis of 221 mishaps over 10 years. Aviat. Space Environ. Med. **77**(7), 724 (2006)
3. Oncu, M., Yildiz, S.: An analysis of human causal factors in Unmanned Aerial Vehicle (UAV) accidents. Int. J. Med. Sci. **11**(8), 758–64 (2014)
4. Mccarley, J.S., Wickens, C.D.: Human Factors Concerns in UAV Flight
5. Williams, K.W.: A summary of unmanned aircraft accident/incident data: human factors implications, 4 (2004)
6. Hofstede, G.: Dimensions of national cultures in fifty countries and three regions. Immun. Cell Biol. **90**(4), 429–440 (1983)
7. Hofstede, G., Mccrae, R.R.: Personality and culture revisited: linking traits and dimensions of culture. Cross-Cultural Res. **38**(1), 52–88 (2004)
8. Hofstede, G., Bond, M.H.: The confucius connection: from cultural roots to economic growth. Organ. Dyn. **16**(4), 5–21 (1988)
9. Gong, L., Zhang, S., Tang, P., et al.: An integrated graphic-taxonomic-associative approach to analyze human factors in aviation accidents. 中国航空学报(英文版) **27**(2), 226–240 (2014)
10. Hawkins, F.H.: Human factors in flight. Appl. Ergon. **19**(4) (1993)
11. Tvaryanas, A.P., Thompson, W.T.: Recurrent error pathways in HFACS data: analysis of 95 mishaps with remotely piloted aircraft. Aviat. Space Environ. Med. **79**(5), 525–532 (2008)
12. 崔军辉, 魏瑞轩, 崔建汝, 等. 基于 FCM 的 UAV 事故成因预测方法. 系统工程理论与实践 **35**(12), 3258–3264 (2015)
13. Hobbs, A.: Chapter 16–Unmanned Aircraft Systems. Hum. Factors Aviation, 505–531 (2010)
14. Prabhala, S.V., Gallimore, J.J., Narayanan, S.: Human effectiveness issues in simulated uninhabited combat aerial vehicles. In: Proceedings of the Simulation Conference, vol. 1, pp. 1034–1038. IEEE (2004)
15. Van Breda, L., Jansen, C., Veltman, J.A.: Supervising UAVs: improving operator performance by optimizing the human factor (2005)
16. Hocraffer, A., Chang, S.N.: A meta-analysis of human-system interfaces in unmanned aerial vehicle (UAV) swarm management. Appl. Ergon. **58**, 66–80 (2017)

17. Peschel, J.M., Murphy, R.R.: On the human–machine interaction of unmanned aerial system mission specialists. IEEE Trans. Hum.-Mach. Syst. **43**(1), 53–62 (2013)
18. Kamine, T.H., Bendrick, G.A.: Visual display angles of conventional and a remotely piloted aircraft. Aviat. Space Environ. Med. **80**(4) (2009)
19. Mi, Z., Yang, Y.: Human-robot interaction in UVs swarming: a survey. Int. J. Comput. Sci. Issues (2013)
20. Dixon, S.R., Wickens, C.D., Chang, D.: Mission control of multiple unmanned aerial vehicles: a workload analysis. Hum. Fact. **47**(3), 479–487 (2005)
21. Francis, M.S.: Unmanned air systems: challenge and opportunity. J. Aircr. **49**(6), 1652–1665 (2004)
22. Calhoun, G.L., Abernathy, M.F.: Synthetic vision system for improving unmanned aerial vehicle operator situation awareness. In: Proceedings of SPIE - The International Society for Optical Engineering, vol. 5802, pp. 219–230 (2005)
23. Stark, B., Smith, B., Navarrete, N., et al.: The airworthiness and protocol development for night flying missions for small unmanned aerial systems (sUASs). In: International Conference on Unmanned Aircraft Systems, pp. 252–259. IEEE (2015)
24. Hing, J.T., Oh, P.Y.: Development of an Unmanned Aerial Vehicle Piloting System with Integrated Motion Cueing for Training and Pilot Evaluation. Kluwer Academic Publishers (2009)
25. Savla, K., Nehme, C., Temple, T., et al.: On efficient cooperative strategies between UAVs and humans in a dynamic environment (2013)
26. Hardman, N., Colombi, J.: Requirements elicitation through legacy mishap analysis. J. Aerosp. Comput. Inf. Commun. **10**(3), 105–113 (2013)
27. Cooke, N.J., Rowe, L.J., Bennett, W.J., et al.: Remotely piloted aircraft systems: a human systems integration perspective. Proc. Hum. Factors Ergon. Soc. Ann. Meet. **58**(1), 102–104 (2016)
28. Kaliardos, B., Lyall, B.: Human factors of unmanned aircraft system integration in the national airspace system (2015)
29. Feng, L., Wiltsche, C., Humphrey, L., et al.: Synthesis of human-in-the-loop control protocols for autonomous systems. IEEE Trans. Autom. Sci. Eng. **13**(2), 450–462 (2016)
30. Barnes, M.J., Matz, M.F.: Crew simulations for unmanned aerial vehicle (UAV) applications: sustained effects, shift factors, interface issues, and crew size. Hum. Factors Ergon. Soc. Ann. Meet. Proc. **42**(1), 143–147 (1998)
31. Walters, B., French, J., Barnes, M.J.: Modeling the effects of crew size and crew fatigue on the control of tactical unmanned aerial vehicles (TUAVs). In: Simulation Conference, Proceedings, vol. 1, pp. 920–924. IEEE (2000)
32. Tvaryanas, A.P.: Human systems integration in remotely piloted aircraft operations. Aviat. Space Environ. Med. **77**(12), 1278–1282 (2006)
33. Tvaryanas, A.P., Macpherson, G.D.: Fatigue in pilots of remotely piloted aircraft before and after shift work adjustment. Aviat. Space Environ. Med. **80**(5) (2009)
34. Mouloua, M., Gilson, R., Kring, J., et al.: Workload, situation awareness, and teaming issues for UAV/UCAV operations. Hum. Factors Ergon. Soc. Ann. Meet. Proc. **45**(2), 162–165 (2001)
35. Murray, C.C., Park, W.: Incorporating human factor considerations in unmanned aerial vehicle routing. IEEE Trans. Syst. Man Cybern. Syst. **43**(4), 860–874 (2013)
36. Liu, D., Peterson, T., Vincenzi, D., et al.: Effect of time pressure and target uncertainty on human operator performance and workload for autonomous unmanned aerial system. Int. J. Ind. Ergon. **51**, 52–58 (2016)

37. Chappelle, W.L., Mcdonald, K.D., Prince, L., et al.: Symptoms of psychological distress and post-traumatic stress disorder in United States Air Force "drone" operators. Mil. Med. **179**(suppl. 8), 63–70 (2014)
38. Wohleber, R.W., Matthews, G., Reinerman-Jones, L.E., et al.: Individual differences in resilience and affective response during simulated UAV operations **59**(1), 751–755 (2015)
39. Hobbs, A.: Human challenges in the maintenance of unmanned aircraft systems
40. Carretta, T.R., King, R.E.: Personnel selection influences on remotely piloted aircraft human-system integration. Aerosp. Med. Hum. Perform. **86**(8) (2015)
41. Lin, J., Matthews, G., Wohleber, R., et al.: Automation reliability and other contextual factors in multi-UAV operator selection **60**(1), 846–850 (2016)
42. Menda, J., Hing, J.T., Ayaz, H., et al.: Optical brain imaging to enhance UAV operator training, evaluation, and interface development. J. Intell. Robot. Syst. **61**(1–4), 423–443 (2011)
43. Li, X., Pei, H., Sha, F., et al.: Testing research on the professional ability of multi-axial UAV operators based on eye-movement technology (2015)
44. Balog, C.R., Terwilliger, B.A., Vincenzi, D.A., et al.: Examining human factors challenges of sustainable small unmanned aircraft system (sUAS) Operations. In: Savage-Knepshield, P., Chen, J. (eds.) Advances in Human Factors in Robots and Unmanned Systems. AISC, vol. 499. Springer, Cham (2017). https://doi.org/10.1007/978-3-319-41959-6_6

# Culture, Emotions and Design

# Acceptance of Social Robots by Aging Users: Towards a Pleasure-Oriented View

Na Chen[(✉)]

Beijing University of Chemical Technology,
Beijing 100055, People's Republic of China
chenn4@163.com

**Abstract.** The aging population is getting larger and the demands for social robots in providing home-based care services is increasing. As social robots are new technology and have not fully reached domestic fields, this study explored aging adults' acceptance of social robots in a domestic environment. This study adopted the adapted UTAUT to develop aging adults' acceptance. The model in this study involved both utilitarian use and pleasure-oriented use of social robots perceived by aging adults. A questionnaire survey involving 277 valid responses was conducted. This study examined that both pleasure expectancy and the four influencing constructs in UTAUT showed significantly positive effects on user adoption of social robots. In addition, based on the results, aging adults slightly did not think they could get pleasure from social robots whereas they had slightly preference to accept social robots. Implications were discussed for future work.

**Keywords:** Aging adults · Social robots · Home-based elderly care
UTAUT

## 1 Introduction

The aging population is getting larger in China and this results in an increasing demand for elderly care. Population aging is a complex issue which concerns both aging adults and their families. Due to Chinese traditional culture, elderly care depends largely on families. In China, there is a tendency of miniaturization for the sizes of families [1] which will lead to a fact that in a typical core family, two adults (both spouses) should take care of four aging adults (both parents) and at the same time the couple should raise their child/children. Family miniaturization, cultural traditions and the one-child policy in China have caused enormous pressure on the care of aging adults for Chinese society and families. Relying merely on families could not satisfy the demand of elderly care.

Many smart devices and systems have been developed to improve the quality life of aging adults in order to relieve the elderly care pressure, such as wearable devices which detect falls [2], smart home technologies and systems which monitor security [3] and healthcare monitoring systems [4]. Among them, robots show potential in help aging adults both physically and psychologically [5].

On one hand, robots provide utilitarian services for aging adults, such as cleaning house [6], providing information [7] and guiding users in unfamiliar places [8]. On the other hand, some researchers suggested that robots also provide hedonic and pleasure-oriented services [9, 10]. For example, robot can play with [11] and accompany aging adults [12] to reduce their feelings of social alienation and loneliness. In this context, social robots which have both utilitarian functions and pleasure-oriented functions seems to be an important part of home-based elderly care system in the future.

The robots interact with human being via human social rules are considered as social robots [13]. On one hand, social robots have utilitarian functions, such as performing household working. On the other hand, social robots have pleasure-oriented functions, such as interacting with users and building relationships with them. The social robots with pleasure-oriented functions attract users and satisfy users' human social expectation. Users will find the interaction enjoyable and be willing to keep the relationships with social robots. Therefore, it is important to investigate the pleasure-oriented use of social robots in order to get a more comprehensive view of its role in aging adults' acceptance and usage of social robots.

Users' acceptance of technology affects their usage. Among the acceptance models developed by previous studies, the Unified Theory of Acceptance and Usage of Technology (UTAUT) was one of the most accepted models. As an extension of the Technology Acceptance Model (TAM) [14], UTAUT was firstly proposed by [15]. UTAUT indicated that usage behavioral intention and use behaviors of information system were affected mainly by four factors, involving performance expectancy, effort expectancy, social influence and facility conditions. During the fifteen years after the model was proposed, it has been revised to multiple transformation, such as mobile commerce acceptance [16], online banking [17] and interactive whiteboards among teachers [18]. In the field of intelligent robots, extant studies have tried to explain users' acceptance of robots following UTAUT [i.e., 9, 19–21]. UTAUT defined that usage contains two steps – users firstly generated the usage intention and then performed the use behaviors. The constructs of performance expectancy, effort expectancy and social influence directly affected usage intention and indirectly affected use behaviors, whereas only the construct of facility conditions directly affect use behaviors. Use behaviors were usually measured through usage frequencies or duration. However, in this study, because social robots have not reached into home-based care system, this means that it is difficult to obtain data of usage behaviors.

Among the studies following UTAUT, [22] adapted UTAUT – all four constructs directly affect user adoption which measures users' subjective acceptance of technology through questionnaire items. The model of [22] achieved good reliability, validity and model fitness.

Hence, this study aimed to explored the roles of both utilitarian use and pleasure-oriented use of social robots in aging users' acceptance and adopted the adapted UTAUT by [22] to develop aging adults' acceptance of social robots in a domestic environment.

# 2   Research Model

Performance expectancy reflects users' belief of performance improvement by using social robots. Effort expectancy is defined as the perceived ease of using social robots. Social influence reflects the effects of others' opinions on users' behaviors, such as friends, spouses and families. Facility conditions mean users' belief of getting support from organizational and technical infrastructures on their behaviors. According to UTATU and adapted UTAUT, performance expectancy, effort expectancy, social influence and facility conditions positively affect user adoption [15, 22]. Thus, we hypothesize:

**Hypothesis 1**. Performance expectancy has a positive effect on user adoption of social robots.
**Hypothesis 2**: Effort expectancy has a positive effect on user adoption of social robots.
**Hypothesis 3**: Social influence has a positive effect on user adoption of social robots.
**Hypothesis 4**: Facility conditions has a positive effect on user adoption of social robots.

This study defined the perceived pleasure of aging users from using social robots as pleasure expectancy. Pleasure expectancy positively affects their acceptance [9]. Thus, we have:

**Hypothesis 5**: Pleasure expectancy has a positive effect on user adoption of social robots.

The research model is shown in Fig. 1.

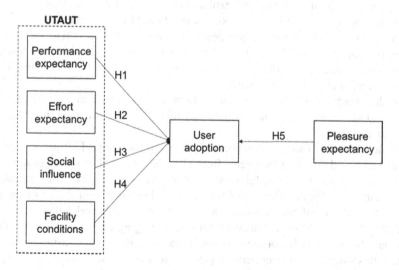

**Fig. 1.**  Research model.

# 3 Method

## 3.1 Questionnaire Design

This study adopted a questionnaire survey to test the research model. The research model included six constructs and each construct was measured using multiple items which were derived from previous studies.

The construct of pleasure expectancy was adapted from [23] which tested users' acceptance of online retailing. Three items about enjoyment in the sub-scale of playfulness were chosen. The evaluation objects of the three items were changed from online retailing to social robots in order to fit this study. An example of the items in the construct was "Using social robots gives me enjoyment".

The items in the construct of user adoption in [22] were based on specific scenarios of using mobile banking which did not fit this study. Hence, this study followed [22] to develop new items for the construct. Targeting the utilitarian use and pleasure-oriented use of social robots, this study developed two items to state the scenarios of using social robots respectively, involving "I will use social robots to help me to do housework" and "I will use social robots to accompany myself". In addition, this study developed two items to generally state the positive effects of using social robots on life quality, involving "I will use social robots to improve my life quality" and "Social robots will make me live better".

Both [15, 22] involved four influencing constructs in UTAUT model, involving performance expectancy, effort expectancy, social influence and facility conditions. After comparing the details of the statement of the two instruments and their applicability for this study, we adapted the constructs of social influence and facility conditions from [15], whereas we adapted the constructs of performance expectancy and effort expectancy from [22]. We will explain the reasons of the selection.

For the construct of performance expectancy, both [15, 22] contained four similar items with each other. However, one item "If I use the system, I will increase my chances of getting a raise" did not fit the scenarios of using social robots in a domestic environment. Hence, this study did not adopt this item and kept the other three items, such as "I feel social robots are useful".

For the construct of effort expectancy, both studies contained four items which fitted this study. Hence, this study adopted all four items and changed the evaluation objects to social robots.

For the construct of social influence, [15] involved four items. [22] just kept two of them and removed the other two items from [15], involving "The senior management of this business has been helpful in the use of the system" and "In general, the organization has supported the use of the system". Due to the small size of the construct, the reliability of the construct in [22] might be negatively affected. Hence, considering that the closest connections for Chinese aging adults were their children who would be the most important persons in teaching aging adults using technology products, this study kept all four items in [15] and revised the two removed by [22] into "My children would be helpful in the use of social robots" and "In general, my family would support the use of robots".

For the construct of facility conditions, [22] removed one items from the four items in [15], which was "The system is not compatible with other systems I use". This statement could be revised to adapted to this study. Hence, we kept this item and revised it into "Social robots are not compatible with my house".

All the items of the six constructs were measured using a 5-point Likert scale with "1 = strongly disagree" and "5 = strongly agree".

In addition, responders' demographic information, involving age, gender and levels of education were measured. Their previous experience with robots and perceived themselves' computer skills were also measured using a 5-point Likert scale as shown in Table 1.

**Table 1.** Profile of responders.

| Measure | Item | Frequency | Percentage (%) |
|---|---|---|---|
| Gender | Male | 99 | 35.74 |
| | Female | 178 | 64.26 |
| Age | 57–60 | 94 | 33.94 |
| | 61–65 | 93 | 33.57 |
| | 66–70 | 62 | 22.38 |
| | 71–74 | 28 | 10.11 |
| Level of education | Under high school degree | 115 | 41.52 |
| | High school degree | 123 | 44.40 |
| | Bachelor degree | 32 | 11.55 |
| | Master degree or above | 7 | 2.53 |
| Experience with robots | Extremely inexperienced | 32 | 11.55 |
| | Inexperienced | 143 | 51.62 |
| | Neutral | 88 | 31.77 |
| | Experienced | 13 | 4.69 |
| | Extremely experienced | 1 | 0.36 |
| Computer skills | Extremely poor | 4 | 1.44 |
| | Poor | 92 | 33.21 |
| | Neutral | 142 | 51.26 |
| | Advanced | 37 | 13.36 |
| | Extremely advanced | 2 | 0.72 |

## 3.2   Responders

Based on the fact that in China the government-regulated retirement age for women is 55 years old and that for mem is 60 years old, the younger aging adults aged from 57 years old to 74 years old were considered as potential responders of the questionnaire survey [24].

This study distributed the questionnaires in two communities in Beijing and a total of 418 questionnaires were collected. Among the collected questionnaires, 277 were valid, taking up 66.27% of the total. The average age of the responders who contributed valid questionnaires was 63.42 years old (standard deviation = 4.69), ranging from 57 years old to 74 years old. Among the valid questionnaires, 99 were answered by male responders, taking up 35.74% of the total valid responds, whereas the other 178 were answered by female responders, taking up 64.26%.

Most of the responders held a degree of high school or lower, taking up more than 80% of the total valid responds; this was in line with the common sense of the academic qualifications of the aging adults in this age group. More than 80% of the responders thought they were inexperienced or had a neutral level of experience with robots; this was in line with the fact that social robots had not been applied in home-based elderly care and few aging adults ever had close contact with robots. More than half of responders reported that they had a neutral level of computer skills.

The distribution of the ages, levels of education, experience with robots and computer skills of the responders is listed in Table 1.

# 4   Results

The research model was analyzed by AMOS and SPSS. The results of descriptive statistics analysis are listed in Table 2.

**Table 2.**  Profile of responders.

| Measure | Average | Standardized deviation |
|---|---|---|
| Pleasure expectancy | 0.27 | 0.70 |
| Performance expectancy | 3.66 | 0.65 |
| Effort expectancy | 2.53 | 0.51 |
| Social influence | 3.31 | 0.44 |
| Facility conditions | 2.16 | 0.55 |
| User adoption | 3.26 | 0.59 |

Based on the results, the average score of the construct of user adoption was 3.26, slightly higher than 3.0 (neutral level); this suggested that responders have slightly preference to accept social robots. The average score of the construct of pleasure expectancy was 0.27, slightly lower than 3.0; this suggested that responders slightly did not think they could get pleasure from using social robots.

Next, this study first analyzed the measurement model to test its reliability and validity and then analyzed the structural model to test the hypotheses [25].

## 4.1   Measurement Model

Cronbach alpha and item-to-total correlations were used to assess the internal consistency reliability. The results are shown in Table 3. The values of item-total correlations ranged from 0.559 (for one item of the construct of social influence) to 0.827 (for one item of the construct of user adoption), whereas the values of Cronbach Alpha ranged from 0.817 (for the construct of social influence) to 0.909 (for the construct of user adoption). The values of item-total correlations which are higher than 0.50 are acceptable [26], whereas the values of Cronbach Alpha which are higher than 0.70 are acceptable [27].

**Table 3.** The results of internal reliability and convergent validity.

| Construct | Items | Internal reliability | | Convergent validity | | |
|---|---|---|---|---|---|---|
| | | Cronbach Alpha | Item-total correlation | Factor loading | Composite reliability | Average variance extracted |
| Pleasure expectancy | 3 | 0.865 | 0.740 | 0.806 | 0.860 | 0.672 |
| | | | 0.738 | 0.814 | | |
| | | | 0.762 | 0.839 | | |
| Performance expectancy | 3 | 0.854 | 0.766 | 0.752 | 0.802 | 0.575 |
| | | | 0.736 | 0.762 | | |
| | | | 0.679 | 0.760 | | |
| Effort expectancy | 4 | 0.888 | 0.802 | 0.803 | 0.867 | 0.620 |
| | | | 0.674 | 0.766 | | |
| | | | 0.737 | 0.770 | | |
| | | | 0.813 | 0.810 | | |
| Social influence | 4 | 0.817 | 0.559 | 0.678 | 0.828 | 0.547 |
| | | | 0.651 | 0.776 | | |
| | | | 0.693 | 0.765 | | |
| | | | 0.649 | 0.734 | | |
| Facility condition | 4 | 0.901 | 0.806 | 0.841 | 0.903 | 0.701 |
| | | | 0.778 | 0.812 | | |
| | | | 0.738 | 0.821 | | |
| | | | 0.796 | 0.873 | | |
| User adoption | 4 | 0.909 | 0.801 | 0.848 | 0.923 | 0.749 |
| | | | 0.827 | 0.865 | | |
| | | | 0.785 | 0.889 | | |
| | | | 0.767 | 0.859 | | |

Factor loadings, composite reliability (CR) and average variance extracted (AVE) were measured to examine the convergent validity of the model. The results are shown in Table 3. Factor loadings of all items ranged from 0.678 (for one item of the construct of user adoption) to 0.889 (for one item of the construct of user adoption); all were larger than 0.70 and significant at .001. CRs ranged from 0.802 (for the construct of performance expectancy) to 0.923 (for the construct of user adoption); all exceeded the recommended lower threshold value of 0.7 [28]. AVEs ranged from 0.575 (for the construct of performance expectancy) to 0.749 (for the construct of user adoption); all exceeded the recommended lower threshold value of 0.50 [29].

Confirmatory factor analysis (CFA) was also used to examine the convergent validity of the instrument. The results indicated that the ratio of the chi-square statistic to the degree of freedom ($\chi^2$/d.f.) was 2.423; this was lower than the recommended upper threshold value of 5 [30]. The goodness-of-fit (GFI) was 0.864; this exceeded the recommended lower threshold value of 0.80 [30].

These results indicated that the internal consistency reliability and the convergent validity of the instrument was acceptable.

## 4.2    Structure Model

Besides $\chi^2$/d.f. and GFI, this study also tested other fit indices of the model, involving root mean square residual, adjusted goodness-of-fit index, Tucker-Lewis index, normed fit index and comparative fit index; all satisfied the recommended threshold values of 0.005, 0.80, 0.90, 0.90 and 0.90 [28]. These indicated a good fit between the model and the data. The values of the fit indices are listed in Table 4.

**Table 4.**  Fit indices of the model.

| Fit index | Scores | Recommended threshold values |
|---|---|---|
| Minimum fit function chi-square ($\chi^2$) | 506.397 (p < .001) | The lower, the better |
| Degree of freedom (d.f.) | 209 | |
| $\chi^2$/d.f. | 2.423 | <5 |
| Goodness-of-fit index (GFI) | 0.864 | >0.80 |
| Root mean square residual (RMSR) | 0.013 | <.005 |
| Adjusted goodness-of-fit index (AGFI) | 0.835 | >0.80 |
| Tucker-Lewis index (TLI) | 0.942 | >0.90 |
| Normed fit index (NFI) | 0.914 | >0.90 |
| Comparative fit index (CFI) | 0.948 | >0.90 |

This study next tested the model hypotheses. The standardized coefficient of all path and their significance are shown in Fig. 2. All the five influencing constructs showed significantly positive effects on the construct of user adoption. All hypotheses were supported (all sig. < .001).

## 5    Discussions

The results of CFA showed that the standardized coefficients of all the path were 1.000; this might be related to the model. This model actually was a linear regression model – all the five influencing constructs of pleasure expectancy, performance expectancy, effort expectancy, social influence and facility conditions were linear correlated to the construct of user adoption. Hence, the reported standardized coefficients in Table 4 were the results of a linear regression test. These indicated that the model has possibility of further improvement. There are two improvement directions. Firstly, after the

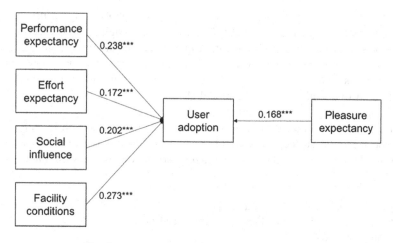

**Fig. 2.** Model estimation results (***$p$ < .001).

social robots are actually applied in the home-based elderly care system in the future, aging adults' intention to use social robots and their actual usage of social robots might be measured, and consequently the effects of the construct of pleasure expectancy on their intention and actual usage could be measured so as that the model might be more in line with UTAUT. Secondly, the relationships between the construct of pleasure expectancy and the constructs of performance expectancy, effort expectancy, social influence and facility conditions could be explored further. However, related literature is still insufficient. More work need to be done to explore the relationships among the constructs.

Although social robots have not reached in home applications, aging adults in this study still thought they had some knowledge of social robots through media campaigns –36.82% of the valid questionnaires reported that they had such knowledge (neutral, experienced or extremely experienced). The proportion of aging adults who thought they had knowledge about computer skills was much higher –65.34% of the valid questionnaire reported that they had neutral, advanced or extremely advanced computer skills, who could be considered to maintain a certain level of basic knowledge about using social robots. All these show that there is a certain possibility that social robots are applied in the field of home-based care system.

Aging adults had slightly preference to use social robots in a domestic environment but they did not think robots could provide them pleasure; this suggested that the images of social robots in aging adults tend more to provide functional services rather than companion or entertaining services.

## 6  Conclusions

Against the background of the rapidly aging population and the dramatic increasing elderly care pressure, the purposes of this study involved investigating Chinese aging adults' acceptance of social robots in a domestic environment and exploring the roles of both utilitarian use and pleasure-oriented use of social robots in aging users' acceptance. This study adopted an adapted UTAUT to develop aging adults' acceptance of social robots in a domestic environment. A questionnaire survey involving 277 valid responses was conducted. This study examined that pleasure expectancy together with other four influencing constructs in UTAUT showed significantly positive effects on user adoption of social robots – the model showed acceptable reliability, convergent validity and model fitness. In addition, based on the results, aging adults slightly did not think they could get pleasure from social robots and they had slightly preference to accept social robots. Further work could be conducted to investigate the effects of the perceived pleasure of social robots by aging adults on their usage intention and behaviors.

**Acknowledgements.** This study was supported by Beijing Natural Science Foundation 9184029, Beijing Social Science Fund 17SRC021, and Fundamental Research Funds for the Central Universities ZY1706.

# References

1. Zhou, L., Wang, C.: Population structure and household debt: Microcosmic evidence from CFPS. Econ. Manag. **31**(3), 31–37 (2017)
2. Wang, Z., Yang, Z., Dong, T.: A review of wearable technologies for elderly care that can accurately track indoor position, recognize physical activities and monitor vital signs in real time. Sensors **17**(2), 341 (2017)
3. Do, H.M., Pham, M., Sheng, W., Yang, D., Liu, M.: RiSH: A robot-integrated smart home for elderly care. Robot. Auton. Syst. **101**, 74–92 (2018)
4. Ahmed, A.B., Abdallah, A.B.: Architecture and design of real-time system for elderly health monitoring. Int. J. Embedded Syst. **9**(5), 484–494 (2017)
5. Ahn, H.S., Lee, M.H., Broadbent, E., MacDonald, B.A.: Gathering healthcare service robot requirements from young people's perceptions of an older care robot. In: 1st IEEE International Conference on Robotic Computing (IRC), pp. 22–27. IEEE, New York City (2017)
6. Takeshita, T., Tomizawa, T., Ohya, A.: A house cleaning robot system-path indication and position estimation using ceiling camera. In: 2006 SICE-ICASE International Joint Conference, pp. 2653–2656. IEEE, New York City (2006)
7. Ombelet, P.J., Kuczerawy, A., Valcke, P.: Employing robot journalists: Legal implications, considerations and recommendations. In: 25th International Conference Companion on World Wide Web, pp. 731–736. ACM, New York City (2016)
8. Karreman, D., Ludden, G., Evers, V.: Visiting cultural heritage with a tour guide robot: a user evaluation study in-the-wild. Social Robotics. LNCS (LNAI), vol. 9388, pp. 317–326. Springer, Cham (2015). https://doi.org/10.1007/978-3-319-25554-5_32
9. Klamer, T., Allouch, S. B.: Acceptance and use of a social robot by elderly users in a domestic environment. In: 4th International Conference on Pervasive Computing Technologies for Healthcare, pp. 1–8. IEEE, New York City (2010)
10. Van der Heijden, H.: User acceptance of hedonic information systems. MIS Q. **28**(4), 695–704 (2004)
11. Tay, B.T., Low, S.C., Ko, K.H., Park, T.: Types of humor that robots can play. Comput. Hum. Behav. **60**, 19–28 (2016)

12. Ferrer, G., Zulueta, A.G., Cotarelo, F.H., Sanfeliu, A.: Robot social-aware navigation framework to accompany people walking side-by-side. Auton. Robots **41**(4), 775–793 (2017)
13. Looije, R., Cnossen, F., Neerincx, M.A.: Incorporating guidelines for health assistance into a socially intelligent robot. In: 15th IEEE International Symposium on Robot and Human Interactive Communication, pp. 515–520. IEEE, New York City (2006)
14. Davis, F.D.: Technology Acceptance Model for Empirically Testing New End-user Information Systems Theory and Results. Unpublished Doctoral Dissertation, MIT (1986)
15. Venkatesh, V., Morris, M.G., Davis, G.B., Davis, F.D.: User acceptance of information technology: Toward a unified view. MIS Q. **27**(3), 425–478 (2003)
16. Min, Q., Ji, S., Qu, G.: Mobile commerce user acceptance study in China: A revised UTAUT model. Tsinghua Sci. Technol. **13**(3), 257–264 (2008)
17. Escobar-Rodríguez, T., Carvajal-Trujillo, E.: Online purchasing tickets for low cost carriers: An application of the unified theory of acceptance and use of technology (UTAUT) model. Tour. Manag. **43**, 70–88 (2014)
18. Šumak, B., Šorgo, A.: The acceptance and use of interactive whiteboards among teachers: Differences in UTAUT determinants between pre-and post-adopters. Comput. Hum. Behav. **64**, 602–620 (2016)
19. Baisch, S., Kolling, T., Schall, A., Rühl, S., Selic, S., Kim, Z., Rossberg, H., Klein, B., Pantel, J., Oswald, F., Knopf, M.: Acceptance of social robots by elder people: Does psychosocial functioning matter? Int. J. Soc. Robot. **9**(2), 293–307 (2017)
20. Broadbent, E., Stafford, R., MacDonald, B.: Acceptance of healthcare robots for the older population: Review and future directions. Int. J. Social Robot. **1**(4), 319–330 (2009)
21. Flandorfer, P.: Population ageing and socially assistive robots for elderly persons: the importance of sociodemographic factors for user acceptance. Int. J. Popul. Res. **2012**, 1–13 (2012)
22. Zhou, T., Lu, Y., Wang, B.: Integrating TTF and UTAUT to explain mobile banking user adoption. Comput. Hum. Behav. **26**(4), 760–767 (2010)
23. Ahn, T., Ryu, S., Han, I.: The impact of Web quality and playfulness on user acceptance of online retailing. Inf. Manag. **44**(3), 263–275 (2007)
24. McDonald-Miszczak, L., Neupert, S.D., Gutman, G.: Younger-old and older-old adults' recall of medication instructions. Can. J. Aging **24**(4), 409–417 (2005)
25. Anderson, J.C., Gerbing, D.W.: Structural equation modeling in practice: A review and recommended two-step approach. Psychol. Bull. **103**(3), 411–423 (1988)
26. Everitt, B., Skrondal, A.: The Cambridge Dictionary of Statistics, 2nd edn. Cambridge University Press, Cambridge (2002)
27. Nunnally, J.C.: Psychometric theory. McGraw-Hill, New York City (1978)
28. Gefen, D., Straub, D.W., Boudreau, M.C.: Structural equation modeling and regression: Guidelines for research practice. Commun. Assoc. Inf. Syst. **4**(7), 1–70 (2000)
29. Bagozzi, R.P., Yi, Y.: On the evaluation of structural equation models. J. Acad. Mark. Sci. **16**(1), 74–94 (1988)
30. Hair, J.F., Black, W.C., Babin, B.J., Anderson, R.E., Tatham, R.L.: Multivariate data analysis. Prentice-Hall, Upper Saddle River (1998)

# Study on Design Principles of Voice Interaction Design for Smart Mobile Devices

Feng Gao[✉], Chaoyang Yu, and Jun Xie

ZTE Shanghai R&D Center, No. 889 Bibo Road, Pudong District, Shanghai, China
gao.feng6@zte.com.cn

**Abstract.** Since the first launch of Star One in 2014, ZTE has been boldly exploring the voice interaction design of smartphones. Through years of practice the ZTE design team gained rich experience. This paper is a brief introduction of eight design principles that have been summarized in the light of its design and a more beautiful user experience, created by the team on the analysis of the advantage and disadvantage of voice interaction. These 8 principles include: Reducing screen domination, eliminating embarrassment, smart scene, complex operations and long command, pause any time, learnability and emotion. Especially the first 3 described the core thinking of voice interaction designs in ZTE mobile phones.

**Keywords:** Voice interaction · Interaction design · Design principle
Intelligent terminal · Human-machine interaction

## 1 Introduction

The journey of exploring voice recognition, understanding and synthesis has never stopped in the past 7 decades. The voice user interaction technology has advanced with the rapid development of smart mobile devices and cloud computing. The speech to text technology used to record in the iFLYTECH 2015 conference has superior accuracy in character and semantic recognition than those of 5 stenographers in the show day.

However, due to the diversity of usage scenarios and the complexity of software/hardware coordination, the user experience of those voice assistants, including 3rd party applications or system layer integrated, is barely satisfactory on those smart mobile devices. The advantages of voice interaction is just as obvious as its disadvantages. Therefore, how to avoid those disadvantages and optimize user experience with smart mobile devices' usage scenarios and hardware configuration, is very worthy of research topic. ZTE design team has made great progress and efforts to lead the industry. This article summarized the thinking in the design process and proposed 8 simple design principles for your reference.

© Springer International Publishing AG, part of Springer Nature 2018
P.-L. P. Rau (Ed.): CCD 2018, LNCS 10911, pp. 398–411, 2018.
https://doi.org/10.1007/978-3-319-92141-9_31

## 2   Disadvantages

It's been a long-standing dream to communicate with machines because voice is a natural way of communication. But VUI (Voice User Interaction) has some fundamental defects compared to mainstream matured GUI (Graphic User Interface).

### 2.1   Uncertainty of Input, Output and Understanding

Human language is very complex. There are over 5000 languages in the world, of which about 140 ones have more than 1 million users. Take Chinese for example, it has numerous dialects. Apart from mandarin, there are 6 other main dialects, Wu, Xiang, Gan, Hakka, Cantonese and Min. It is said that Fujian province itself has 8 non-mutually-intelligible sub-varieties.

Even with the same language and accent, there are other variations such as polyphony, pronunciation and intonation, particle, punctuation, rhetoric and tone which may alter the meaning of the context.

This complexity and uncertainty has significant impacts on three major field of technologies, voice recognition, semantic comprehension and speech synthesis. Those three fields are the foundation of voice interaction technology, including three phases: input, understanding and output. Failures during any of those phases will result in miscommunication or poor user experience. [1]

### 2.2   Weak Guidance

People may take seat when they see a chair, pull or push when seeing a door, and grasp the handrail when riding a subway. Donald Norman tells us that these are signs and some designers can add to the ideogram.

Generally GUI are guidance to users, telling them how to confirm, cancel, or even tell you to follow this interesting WeChat account by a shining animation [2].

Nevertheless, Voice is invisible and you wouldn't know what kind of services are provided until the actual interaction occurs. Even in the process of interaction, you still don't know what the boundary is, what you can or can't do. You need to listen carefully to find whether it provides such service or not.

The lack of guidance further confirms the supporting role of voice interaction.

### 2.3   Picky on Usage Scenarios

Mobile device design needs to consider different usage scenarios. In contrast to GUI, VUI has more using there are more usage scenarios.

Firstly, it will be a lot less efficient when it is used in noisy environment.

Secondly, using voice command may disturb others in quiet public places and it has privacy issues. Therefore to avoid those uncomfortable incidents, voice interactions are usually not used in such places like libraries, meeting rooms, hospitals or banks (Fig. 1).

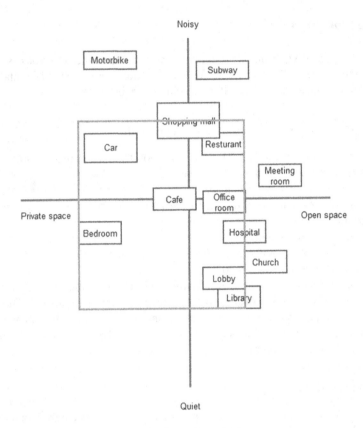

**Fig. 1.** Scenario analysis

### 2.4  Transient (Unrepeatable)

While voice has the characteristics of time and space (vibrate, position, broadcast), and is a four-dimensional 'object', it only shows its time characteristic for a specific receiver. Compared with visual, voice is transient. A distraction will likely to cause misunderstanding. This is the reason why a 'repeat' option is offered in many of the telephony voice services GUI allows users to see the menu at any level and input with no time restrictions but voice doesn't work. This transient applies to not only when users receive information from machine but also when giving orders to machine. Human communications are not like actor's lines because people may forget and repeat words. Yet many of those voice interaction products are designed to end up with a shorter recognition time. That means they consider command completed and start the executions.

## 2.5 High Expectation

Apart from its technology, people have high expectations on how intelligent voice interaction should be. Naturally, there will be strong dissatisfaction when it is not performing as smart as expected causing people against using voice interactions.

# 3 Strength

Voice interaction has some limitations, but it also has many obvious advantages. That's the reason why it becomes the hot spot in modern AI field and IT industry.

## 3.1 More Friendly, Natural and Intuitive

Voice language was emerged earlier than written language and was first used in human communication which helped to establish a larger community to win a better development. Everyone grows up learning how to communicate and learning how to express themselves in writing. So voice language is destined to be more friendly, natural and intuitive than written language.

Aristotle once said "Spoken words are the symbols of mental experience and written words are the symbols of spoken words", although in hieroglyphic system, "Spoken words are the sound of one's heart while writings are the pictures of one's heart." (Fayan. Volume Wenshen, Yangxiong, scholar of the Western Han Dynasty), there are not a lot pictograph characters drawn from heart and they became fewer and fewer as society develops. On the other hand, phonographic characters occupied 90% of all characters in Kangxi dictionary. This indicates that phonographic characters has been the mainstream in new vocabularies in the development of Chinese characters. [3]

It begins from one's mind to sound and then sound to written words. Therefore the GUI based on symbols and words is not as friendly, natural and intuitive as voice based VUI.

## 3.2 Unlimited Display Boundary

GUI has clear display boundaries, whether it shows on a 3" 5" 6" or 10" mobile device, a 15" 21" 40" 50" desktop display, or a bigger projector. Due to limited space, GUI often displays in the form of a muti-level menu tree.

While VUI is not restrained by space, it can theoretically have infinite level 1 menu to where users have direct access without going through levels.

## 3.3 No Visual Disturbance

GUI is the dominate form of user interface and this is not likely be changed in the short term, no matter how well you designed a voice interaction product. However if VUI is used as an auxiliary tool, it will give you an amazing user experience without pop-up windows or having to switch between screens, and no need to interrupt your current operation.

### 3.4  Long Operable Distance

Usually GUI interactions occurs within finger tips unless using a wireless controller or a Bluetooth mouse. For mobile devices discussed in this paper, space is very limited. Take touch screen for example, 15' would be the largest screen you can find on the market, and the common viewing distance is less than 1 m. Gesture control on the other hand, frees some space but requires the user to stay in it's camera or sensor's active area.

By comparison, VUI has a farther operable distance. With enhanced microphone process on smart phones, VUI could reach 3–5 m and over 10 m with a professional meeting system.

## 4  Voice Interaction Principles

We have looked into the strength and weakness of voice interaction which uses sound as the media of communication. Now we introduce below design guidelines attached relevant cases to design a good user experience.

### 4.1  Reduce Screen Domination

On those devices that use GUI as primary user interface, VUI provides a form of interaction with 1 extra dimension. Its advantage is to allow parallel operation and does not occupy your screen, so it can greatly improve efficiency. Reducing interface exclusivity is a very important and easily overlooked design principles.

'hands free' is the word that appears to people's mind when it comes to voice interaction design. Therefore the GUI that supposed to complement each other can be short of consideration. For instance, Apple made such a mistake after activating Siri, it occupies the entire screen and blocked all other usage.

It would bring amazing user experience if screen domination could be avoided.

For example, you are using Wechat or blog on a mobile browser, at this stage you want to play music. With GUI you would have to quit those applications, go back to launcher, find and open the music player and then chose your desired song to play. Not only is it tedious, but it also needs to interrupt the current operation. With VUI help, it is much easier. You may play any songs with just one simple voice command. But you won't feel the convenience if the interface for your voice assistant dominates the screen– you would need to stop and wait for it to disappear.

ZTE smart voice assistant took a very conspicuous but not exclusive interface design: when the voice assistant is activated by voice command or other methods, in addition to the alarm sound there is a notification on the top of the screen only, with tips on the animated wave:"please say voice command". And you can still touch other part of this screen to use your phone (Fig. 2).

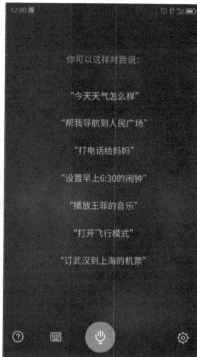

**Fig. 2.** ZTE voice assistant and Siri (picture on the right). Picture on the left is ZTE logo which indicates the combination of sound and touch

Nevertheless, in some cases such as a confirmation page or when no other actions are advised, A clear full screen GUI can speed up interaction process (Fig. 3).

For example, when you are trying to call a contact person with multiple numbers, a simple name voice-command cannot tell which number to call from. So you would need a full screen interface with listed and sorted phone numbers, then you can quickly make the phone call by just a click on that number or saying the voice command via voice assistant (Fig. 4).

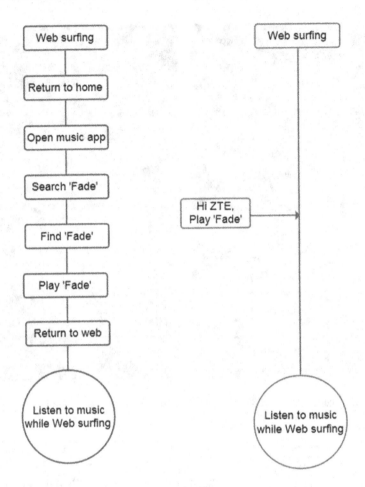

**Fig. 3.** Target oriented design (flow chart comparison)

**Fig. 4.** Librarian and map

## 4.2 Affordance and Guidance

In our real world, we can see the boundaries and sense the affordance. The same thing in the GUI world, you would swipe when you see a slider, click when you see an icon. people already have some conventions and boundaries.

i.e. if you are looking for a book in a library, you would understand all the book index, directions and bathroom locations when you see the library map. but you wouldn't use it to find the way home because the map has a clear boundary. It tells you exactly what it has and what it doesn't. Voice interaction is like when you ask someone how to go to the nearest bathroom or where to find philosophy books. You want everyone you asked is a professional librarian who know everything about this library. But sometimes when he is not you would have to ask a stranger who may not know the library at all. Then this could become difficult in your pathfinding experience. Therefore, making your voice assistant the omniscient 'librarian' is the priority. Try to extend its boundary and improve its knowledge as much as possible.

**All-round Design.** According to different products, try to design the scope of voice interaction as large as possible. This includes functional definition and voice material design.

Take mobile phones for example. Users should be able to use every functions of this phone through VUI such as phone calls, messaging, taking photos, starting and closing applications, changing settings, adding or deleting alarms and calender events etc. Additional cloud service can even provide jokes, weather reports, daily news, reservations, Uber and other services. The more comprehensive VUI can be realized, the more likely the consumer will be in the long-term use.

At the same time, voice materials are equally important. Each user may speak differently to perform the same action. Play music for instance, you may say "play music", "play life in full bloom" or "play WangFeng's song" which are all imperative sentences, while other may say "can you play WangFeng's song?" which is a question. The more complete the voice material is, the more likely a user use it.

**Guidance.** Today GUI as a leading design, proper guidance through visual and audio is what should be carefully designed to help those users achieve a more efficient experience when exploring VUI.

First of all, in addition to regular visual assistance, using scenarized designs give users a very intelligent user experience.

For example, a user is probably looking for an application icon when he is repeatedly swiping on the screen. At this time, a friendly notice helps him find that icon via a simple voice command. This is a great example of scenarized design which can develop users ability to use VUI while it is not disturbing.

Moreover, if the system can tell the possible name of the song or the singer, or even hum the tune when users are searching in music players; or give the user a popup notice 'show me photos taken in Wuxi last month' when exploring albums; or reminds users to quickly call using voice command when he is difficult on finding the right number. Those are tentative guidance designs. If users can try and solve their problems successfully, they will gradually become accustomed to and fall in love with VUI.

Last but not the least is the voice notice, mainly in the first use or error. For instance, when the driver mode is launched for the first time, it will tell the user the basic operations such as how to activate, commands etc. When the system does not fully understand user's command it will ask narrow-down questions based on the recognized words, or ask the user to repeat the voice command, for example 'Sorry I do not understand please say****, or ****'.

To create a good guidance, the time and content of the notice is crucial. It starts with the right time and the correct understanding of the scenario. The content should focus on those scenarios where tasks are much easier to complete through VUI than GUI. So as to rapidly attract users to use voice interactions (Fig. 5).

**Fig. 5.** Screenshots of voice interaction guidance interfaces on ZTE mobile phones

**Show Clear Boundaries.** It is a essential to let users know what voice interaction cannot do and by doing so will give users feelings of control. For example, if a user says 'buy me a blockbuster movie ticket' while the VUI does not support this function, the system should send a distinct message to the user that "I cannot purchase movie tickets yet, now searching on web browser".

### 4.3 Eliminates Embarrassment

Embarrassment is an emotional state and one of the authoritative definitions is: it is a emotional experience when someone has a socially unacceptable act (which has characteristics of time and regions), that was unexpectedly becomes the focus of society (witnessed by or revealed to others) resulting in submissive behavior (loss of honor) to please others [4].

The causes for embarrassment usually are: Poor performance (singing out of tune), clumsy movements (fall on the red carpet), cognitive error (mistaken someone), inappropriate act (dressed badly), unintentionally invasion of privacy (entering the wrong room), attract attention (suddenly become the focus) etc. VUI usually has one or more of the above problems so many considered it as a tricky interaction experience [5].

According to my own experience in design and case study, I believe the most important thing to eliminate embarrassment is to avoid poor performance, inappropriate act and attracting attention.

**Avoid Poor Performance.** Performance relies on the development of voice interaction technologies to improve known issues. For example, failure to voice wake-up, the system is not responding no matter what you say; mistaken suddenly the system speaks "I am here, what can I do for you?" when you are talking to someone; failure to recognize: "sorry, I don't understand what you mean", or the system executed a wrong voice command. Unable to execute: poor network, music not found in local music library etc. Hardware improvements and algorithm optimization is off topic.

However those problems can be partially solved.

For example, narrow down the scope according to scenarios or by selected questions such as 'answer or reject?', 'yes or no?'. the experiments prove that over 80% of the testers use same words from the questions rather than using new words. This significantly reduced the voice recognition difficulty.

**Avoid Inappropriate Act.** Avoiding inappropriate act demands a more natural operation which means additional natural interaction technology is required. For instance, voice call is a classic example of elimination embarrassment by using proximity sensor, gyroscope and VUI. In past VUI users need to say 'hello siri', then say 'call XXX' after receiving respond from the system. Not many people use this function in public because it just looks dumb, even though the rate of successfully made phone calls was high.

Apparently, whether it is an appropriate behavior has strong social and time attributes. A common wear in the Qing Dynasty such as Mandarin jacket looks like costume nowadays. Phone with Bluetooth headset in ancient times would definitely be considered as a crazy talking to himself. Some inhabits of Today's VUI could become popular in the future. And interaction designers' focus shall be gradually moving from GUI to VUI. But in current situation, we can only adapt to the development of social cognition and culture, and design a more natural experience.

**Avoid Attracting Attention.** Avoiding attention is too difficult for VUI because you will always draw attention when speaking to the machine-even when no one is around, you may still feel the concerns.

In my opinion, it is an effective way to reduce short voice-activated materials, code command, natural interaction design.

First of all, a short voice-activated command can significantly lower attentions. Usually users would need a proper respond when a smart terminal was voice-activated, such as "I'm here, how can I help you" and it is hard not to draw attention if it is activated in a public place. So this design is preferably for those tools that are used in a private place such as a driving assistant etc. However it is not applicable when you are entering an underground garage and try to turn on the flashlight. In this situation efficiency matters the most. So it would be ideal to turn on your flashlight (on your mobile phone) with just a 'ting' sound or vibrate without drawing any attention.

Using code is also a good design. This allows users to customize their own activation code for quick access to specific applications. For example, use 'let's go' for opening Google map application, or 'flash light' for flash light. This is not just to avoid attention. When everyone feels panic, you use a simple word command to open your flashlight on your mobile phone and it will turn the embarrassment associated with attention into proud-look, how brilliant my phone is!

As for natural interaction design, we have looked into a case which utilizes proximity sensor gyroscope and voice interaction to make phone calls. So we will not be further discussing this matter.

### 4.4  Smart Scene

It could be very frustrating, if you talk to someone who does not know anything about chemistry, like Ammonium bicarbonate or melamine. So voice and semantic recognition are usually categorized as if professionals have specializations. Because VUI is not a menu choice, it has infinite possibilities. With limited hardware and network on mobile terminals, we can categorize the infinity into specified scenarized design thus to improve the successful rate of VUI interaction. This is the concept of smart scene.

For instance, you may pre-load more music relevant content such as singers, bands, song titles; and you may grant system access to all your contact names. This will make your system smarter and reduce false command caused by voice recognition errors. Suppose you have a contact named Gaofeng while one of your favorite singer is also named Gaofeng (same pronunciation but different characters). So with smart scene the system will understand which Gaofeng you refer to accordingly.

Moreover, context should also be considered in voice recognition. For instance when a user asks 'how about tomorrow?' right after a voice weather query, the system should continue this conversation and give tomorrow's weather forecast. Context is one of the important characteristics in human conversations, thus we must consider this in our designs.

### 4.5  Complex Operation and Long Command

VUI are especially suitable for complex operation and long command because it can reach to targets directly without having to go through menu trees. Such designs can increase user viscosity [6].

For example, 'show me last month's photos taken in Wuxi', 'remind me that there is a meeting with my client at 9 am tomorrow morning', 'set a 5 min alarm', those are all complex operations. In the GUI system, you would need to open the album, go to settings and set it to be sorted by location, then open Wuxi to the last month. This could be the same for setting calenders and alarms which requires multiple clicks after we open an application.

Long command means a command with detailed content. Such as "help me to translate, how to go to the airport", "send a message to my wife, I have to work late tonight and won't be home for dinner" etc. These type of commands are more efficient, and more important. It gives users a more intelligent feeling, making it looks like a private assistant rather than a machine.

### 4.6   Pause Any Time

This principle is very simple to understand. People can interrupt each other at any time, and machine should do, too. However this has not been taken into considerations for product designs and has become the reasons why many users dislike and leave such products. For example, when the voice assistant is reading a new message, users should be able to interrupt or read the next message at any time. Same applies to music player when users want to cut, pause or chose to play the next song.

### 4.7   Learnability

Learnability has become a basic requirement people have for smart products. The longer you use the product, the smarter this product become and the more comfortably you use it.

Learnability in terms of technologies is to adapt to accents or tunes etc. As for interaction design, we focus on how to let the products know more about you.

For instance, when you say "navigate to work", your phone does not know the address. So it should ask "where do you work?". once you have answered it, it will never ask again. This is a simple example of learnability.

So when designing a voice assistant, you would need to plan a user database including locations like home and working place, or lifestyle such as timetables and exercise habits; or work related matters like business trips.

In fact, in additional to the voice interaction itself, a voice assistant should be able to understand users through the use of the mobile device. This can be system applications such as calender, alarm clock and to do list, or 3rd party applications like Taobao, JD. Only then can a voice assistant truly understand the users' need.

### 4.8   Emotion

Emotion is a distant dream for mobile device interaction design because the maturity of artificial psychology is far less than artificial intelligence. Just like many design concepts and principles mentioned earlier in this paper, designers should focus on design methods, with the help of current technologies, to make better products.

Although real emotion is hard to simulate, designs can bring us closer by using rich verbals and personified settings.

Take voice-activated command for example, you would need to call someone's name and received a respond before real communication. So does machine which need an activation code as well. Many of the voice assistant requires a 'voice lock' such as 'hello Siri' or 'hello ZTE'. This feels mechanical and less friendly. It would be much more comfortable if users are allowed to customize the code just like to give a name to a new pet.

Emotional design is usually flexible, independent and creative. In one of my design patent, I designed a multi-theme proposal for naming process–users are able to chose from one of the naming theme where it is presented smartly and full of fun.

## 5  Conclusion

Voice interaction is a more natural and friendly interaction. Although with today's technologies, artificial intelligence and artificial psychology is yet to develop, VUI shall replace GUI as the main interaction interface in the future.

Meanwhile, we should also understand VUI's strength and weakness over GUI. In order to enable more users to get used to VUI, designers must bring up a better user experience. Reduce screen domination, eliminate embarrassment, smart scene, complex operations and long command, pause any time, learnability and emotion are the 8 design principles summarized in this paper. Especially the first 3 described the core thinking of voice interaction designs in ZTE mobile phones.

Apparently, those principles are made based on the current computing abilities, network speed, and voice recognition technologies, and are limited to the development of technologies. In addition, to some extend they are one-sided due to the solo product type involved in the study. Thus peer reviews are very welcomed to continued improvement and perfection.

## References

1. Zhang, Y.: Voice interaction basics, current situation and trends. NUANCE archive, May 2014 (in Chinese)
2. Norman, D.A.: The Design of Everyday Things. CITIC Press, Beijing (2015) (in Chinese)
3. Aristotle (translation by Fangshuchun): Categories Interpretation. The Commercial Press, Beijing (2003) (in Chinese)
4. Sunyanhua, M.: Study on embarrassments. Health Study **29**(16), 484–491 (2009) (in Chinese)
5. Shiota, M.N., Kalat, J.W. (translation by Zhourenlai): Emotion Psychology. China Light Industry Press, Beijing (2015) (in Chinese)
6. Anshunyu: Voice interaction design for mobile phones. UXPA (2015) (in Chinese)

# Trendiness and Emotion, Two Key Factors for Predicting Aesthetic Preference on Automotive Interior Form Design Among Chinese Consumers

Fangzhou Gu[1], Danhua Zhao[2(✉)], and Jianghong Zhao[2]

[1] State Key Laboratory of Advanced Design and Manufacturing for Vehicle Body, Hunan University, Changsha, China
gfz@hnu.edu.cn
[2] School of Design, Hunan University, Changsha, China
bear8213@126.com, zhaomak@126.com

**Abstract.** Semantics reflects what people perceive in product appearance. Previous studies demonstrate that user's description of product appearance can be categorized into three fundamental semantic dimensions (trendiness, complexity, and emotion). Each dimension formed a linear relationship with novelty, which has been proved to be one of the determining factors in aesthetic preference. Although automotive interior design is subordinate to product design, it's unique since interior design is more complicated, more time costing, and growth cycle of interior designers is much longer. In this study, we collected a large number of automotive interior photos, and extracted representative ones from each car category (sedan, SUV, pick-up, and mini-car) by sorting and clustering. Then we conducted a research on Chinese consumers, to explore the relationship between three semantic dimensions and aesthetic preference on interior form design, and built a mathematical expression for them with stepwise regression analysis. The result shows that: for Chinese consumers' aesthetic preference on automotive interior form design, both trendiness and emotion have a significant impact on aesthetic preference; while the impact of complexity is extremely small. Hence, in order to improve design efficiency, designers should take trendiness and emotion factors into account during new aesthetic generation and design revision period.

**Keywords:** Automotive interior design · Aesthetic preference
Aesthetic experience

## 1 Introduction

As a typical industrial product, the appearance of automotive design is the key to success, by increasing the competitive advantage in market. For consumers, automotive interior is not only a space for driving but also an agent for consumers to express their identities, such as status, aesthetic tastes and hobbies. Realizing the fact that Chinese consumers

© Springer International Publishing AG, part of Springer Nature 2018
P.-L. P. Rau (Ed.): CCD 2018, LNCS 10911, pp. 412–422, 2018.
https://doi.org/10.1007/978-3-319-92141-9_32

seem to have a special aesthetic standard on automotive design, many auto companies often launch special versions of new products for Chinese market.

Product appearance is of significant meaning to consumers, usually, customers pay most attention to design and aesthetics when they make decision on purchasing. People often judge products according to the initial visual impression. Aesthetic preference reflects individuals' cognition and judgment to products' visual elements. Due to the diversity of its design elements, automotive interior design has high requirements for the background knowledge, design skills and experience on designers. Therefore, to create products that are more desirable to consumers, car designers need to understand which factors influence the consumer's aesthetic experience on automotive interior design, and improve the effectiveness and credibility of design.

## 2    The Present Research on Aesthetic Preference

Aesthetic refers to the visual form and sensory experience of objects that associated with structure, harmony, rules of style and sense of beauty [17]. By visual communication, aesthetics decides individual's perception on objective things, and further, influences individual's behavior. Vision is the most informative one in five senses, which has the hugest impact on consumers, compared with other senses. Products with higher visual aesthetics, in general, can achieve higher expressiveness, enlightenment and cheerfulness. The generation and perception of visual aesthetics are formed through human evolution in thousands of years prehistoric [23]. It's a way of communication before the formation of language [16]. Consumers get aesthetic experience from aesthetically appealing product designs. Aesthetic experience treated as a high-level cognitive process, mingled with cognitive, imagination, and feelings interact [17].

### 2.1    Aesthetic Experience and Neuroscience

Aesthetic experience is particularly interesting because of their hedonic properties and the possibility to provide self-rewarding cognitive operations [15]. The research in neuroscience has shown that visual stimuli with aesthetics are associated with higher reward values in the brain [19]. Several researches have shown that understanding of artwork results in an activation of the rewarding centers in the brain, and this activation will further influence individuals' preference, judgment and decision-making [6]. If a product has higher aesthetic value, it's more likely to stimulate the reward system in the brain, and receive higher preferences and appreciation as a consequence [21].

### 2.2    Visual Information Processing of Aesthetic Preference

To explain visual information processing in aesthetic appreciation, Leder proposed the model of aesthetic experience [14]. According to Leder's theory (Fig. 1), aesthetic experience is continuing cognitive process, accompanied by up growing emotional state that triggers aesthetic emotion, and this continues consists of five stages: perceptual analysis, internal memory integration, explicit classification, cognitive mastering and

evaluation, affective and emotional processing. In the prior two stages, visual information processing is a spontaneous process, which proceeds quickly, unconsciously and
without effort. In other words, in these two stages, visual information processing is
subliminal and automatic, individuals are not able to manipulate it by will.

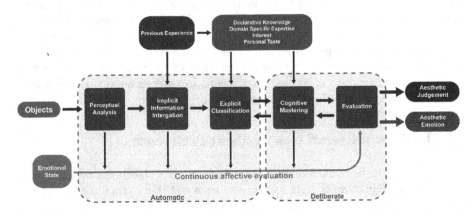

**Fig. 1.** Model of aesthetic experience.

Aesthetic preference is primly determined by the output of these two stages. Perceptual analysis mainly refers to occipital visual processing for basic image information,
including complexity, color, symmetry, grouping, and order of images, can have an
effect on aesthetic experience [14]. The result of implicit memory integration does not
have to become conscious in order to affect aesthetic processing. In this stage, familiarity
and typicality are included. By 'mere-exposure' paradigm, some studies have shown
that familiarity increases the aesthetic experience for a stimulus [12]. Typicality is
defined as an attribute of products that deals with the extent to which the product is
representative in a product category, which has been proved to affect individuals'
aesthetic experience.

To summarize, factors that affect aesthetic preferences can be classified into four
groups: the basic image elements, the underlying visual information including color,
shape and etc.; complexity, which is related with number and variety of basic image
elements; rules of form, the general summary or conclusion of forms, including
symmetry, equilibrium, proportions, rhythm and etc.; background elements, based on
individuals' past experiences, such as novelty, familiarity and typicality.

## 2.3   Aesthetic Preference and Product Design

Novelty is an issue that has always been discussed in studies on aesthetic preference of
product design. Berlyne firstly proposed the theoretical model of inverted U-curve to
explain the relationship between novelty and product aesthetic preference [1]. His model
argues that products with medium level novelty are preferred over both extremely typical
and extremely novel objects. Hekkert measured the effect of novelty and typicality
separately, finding that novelty and typicality have large negative correlations; his study

also shows that novelty and typicality are jointly and equally effective in explaining the aesthetic preference on consumer products, but each of them tend to inhibit the effect of the other one [9]. Hung and Chen verified the inverted U-curve relationship between novelty and aesthetic preference on products, and proposed three dimensions to influence the novelty of product design, trendiness (traditional-trendy), emotion (emotional-rational) and complexity (simple-complex). The three dimensions all have a linear correlation with novelty, and they all contribute to the perception of novelty [11].

## 3    Automotive Interior Design

Automotive interior is the most complicated part in the automotive design, with the so many parts related. Tasks of interior design is about form, texture, color, and material. Since exterior design is often dominated by technical constraints such as the aerodynamics, interior design often allows designers to use more individual and aesthetically justified designs [13]. The perceived quality of automotive interior is influenced by not only user's background information factor but also brand factor [5]. Leder's investigation on attractiveness and interior characteristics indicate that interior attractiveness ratings are particularly affected by curvature and innovativeness, and curved and non-innovative designs were generally preferred [13]. In addition, research on unity-in-variety indicated that, although both unity and variety can be used on prediction for aesthetic appreciation of interior design, unity is much more influential than variety, and automotive design students attribute more appreciation to unity [20].

Car is a classic industrial design product, and users' cognition on cars are highly emotional. The style of the automotive interior reflects brand idea integrated with designers' intention. As for the composition of interior, automotive interior is made up of a variety of parts, including steering wheel, dashboard, rear-view mirror, change gear, multi-media equipment, air-conditioning and wind gap [22]. Design of components are

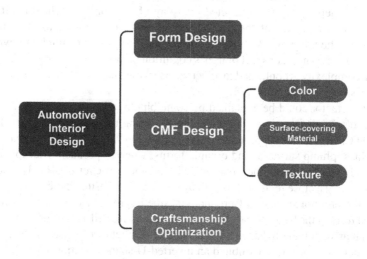

**Fig. 2.**  Tasks in automotive interior design

416 F. Gu et al.

often emphasized the importance of focusing on unity, as the whole must predominate over the parts, and components must be structured into a coherent interior design [20]. Task of interior design consists of form design (Fig. 2), CMF design (including color design, surface-covering material design and texture design) and craftsmanship optimization [8]. The interior design process always starts from a theme defining, accompanied by conceptual design, scale model, digital models, and reverse engineering, ends when real model generated. To summarize, although interior design of the car is subordinate to industrial design, the interior design is unique because of high complexity, the variety of components and long design term.

## 4 Study on Aesthetic Preference on Interior Form

Statements above revealed the fact that there's a significant difference between automotive interior design and consumer products design. Hence, the aim of this study was to assess whether influential factors for aesthetic preference on consumer products, would be applicable for predicting aesthetic preference on automotive interior. Since color design and surface-covering material design are all attached to interior form, in this study, we mainly investigate the effect on form.

We adopted the theory proposed by Hung and Chen that trendiness, emotion, and complexity are three factors for aesthetic preference on products design [11]. They are also semantic dimensions that suitable for describing the emotional response to products [10]. We should make a brief review of three factors before carrying out research.

Trendiness factor, also known as modern sense, contemporary, avant-garde, and young [7]. Trendy, which refers to in a particular time span, to what extent the style is popular. As a result, trendiness is influenced by changing of times. For product design, trendiness refers to an attribute of product designs that deals with the degree to which the product design follows the up-to-date styles and fashion in the market [4].

Complexity factor means that the category, component, factor, and concept are diverse, and there is an interconnected interplay of relationships which is difficult to analyze. The complexity of the product design is mainly related to the number of elements and the unity in design [10]. Complexity is opposite to simplicity, which has been proved to be another aspect of user's cognition on product appearance. By Leder's research, complexity is confirmed to affect the user's aesthetic preference on automotive interior aesthetic appreciation [13].

Emotion factor could be explained by some bipolar adjectives such as, emotional-rational, soft–hard, feminine–masculine. By analyzing the appearance characteristics, Hsiao and Chen found that products with high emotion values are likely to have curved feature lines, plump surfaces, and organic forms; whereas products with low emotion values tend to have straight lines, flat surfaces, and geometric forms [10]. Thus, emotion factor may have a close relationship with the curvature in aesthetic preferences [11]. As a result, the emotional factor of product's aesthetic preference is mainly affected by shape and form of the basic visual elements. Blijlevens created a series of stimuli varying from angular to rounded shapes and found that aesthetic responses to this series of "angular curved" variations exhibited an inverted-U-shaped relationship [2].

## 4.1 Measurements

A 5-point semantic-differential scales were used for measurement on aesthetic preference on automotive interior form, trendiness, emotion, and complexity. The adjective beautiful was selected as rating scale for aesthetic preference on automotive interior form; and for investigating the effects of trendiness, emotion and complexity separately, three additional adjectives were introduced as rating scales, modern for trendiness, emotional for emotion and complex for complexity.

## 4.2 Stimuli

The aim of present research was to explore how trendiness, complexity, and emotion influence the aesthetic preferences of automotive interior form. Thus, stimulus should cover a wider range, and be as representative as possible, rather than be specific to a particular brand or a type of car. The above considerations are based on established fact: cars of the same brand may have family gene features, and cars of the same type may have some type features. For example, every Hyundai car has fluid sculptural exterior surface, and SUV cars have strong and powerful fender. These family gene features and type features may decrease the variety of stimulus.

Many consumers would view automotive interior on Internet before buying cars [18], which suggested that consumers form their first impressions on automotive interiors mainly by photos on websites and smartphone Apps, rather than real cars on road or in sales centers. Therefore, we decided to take photos as stimulus, as this will simulate the condition that they get know of new cars mostly.

The research collected 39 photos of automotive interior from Autohome and NetCar-Show on website. To ensure the representativeness of every sample, and improve the efficiency of questionnaire, samples were refined by two steps. Step one, cars launched between 2005 and 2017 was selected. This mainly because of the time span of 12 years would ensure there is noticeable difference in trendiness, as automakers launch new generation of design, on average, every 4 years. As the service time of cars is 15 years in common, cars launched after 2005 would be able to avoid unfamiliarity of stimulus to participants. The second step, in order to ensure that the samples were differential in emotion and complexity factors, photos were sorted by two Ph.D. students that have studied in automotive design. As for emotion factor, all interior photos are classified into three groups according to the curvature of interior feature line, and plumpness of surface; as for complexity factor, interior photos are classified into three groups, namely "high complexity", "medium complexity" and "low complexity". Then, we chose at least two photos from each group as stimulus.

Finally, eight representative interior photos were selected as stimulus, including 3 concept cars, and 5 mass production cars (including sedan, mini car, SUV, and pickup). To remove the irrelevant variable, such as brand, background of interior photos and angle of camera, research has particular requirement on stimuli photos: the size of photos is 1900 * 1200 pixels, 300 dpi; the background of automotive interior is white; brand logo, images in multi-media devices, name, and other brand identities are removed from stimuli photos (Fig. 3).

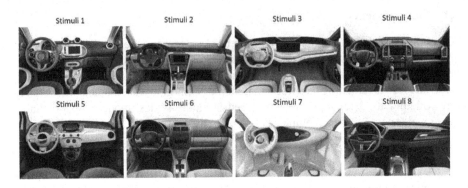

**Fig. 3.** Photos of 8 stimulus.

### 4.3 Subjects

The subjects were 75 participants, they are postgraduates and undergraduate students from Hunan University, in China. Therefore, the results only reflect the cognitive status and aesthetic preference of a group of Chinese people who are young and well educated.

### 4.4 Procedure

The research is a two-step questionnaire.

Step one, subjects were required to watch the 8 stimuli photos, and rate the appearance of every stimuli according to how beautiful its form is, the score of every stimulus reflected participants' aesthetic preference. As mentioned before, interior design consists of three parts, form, color and material, and each part works independently. Thus, to ensure participants' aesthetic preferences for form would not be influenced by color and texture, we created special versions of stimuli photos. For all stimuli photos in step one, color was removed, luminosity values was preserved and texture was erased by Gaussian Blur in Photoshop. Step two, subjects were asked to evaluate the three factors that influenced the aesthetic preference on automotive interior: trendiness, complexity, and emotion.

### 4.5 Result

The average scores of aesthetic preference rating, complexity, trendiness and emotion for eight stimulus are shown in Table 1.

**Table 1.** The average scores of the measurements

|  | Stimuli 1 | Stimuli 2 | Stimuli 3 | Stimuli 4 | Stimuli 5 | Stimuli 6 | Stimuli 7 | Stimuli 8 |
|---|---|---|---|---|---|---|---|---|
| Aesthetic preference | 2.42 | 2.95 | 3.58 | 2.87 | 2.98 | 2.38 | 3.11 | 4.02 |
| Complexity | 3.60 | 2.89 | 2.42 | 3.62 | 2.92 | 2.67 | 2.94 | 2.98 |
| Emotion | 3.84 | 2.42 | 2.91 | 2.22 | 3.36 | 2.67 | 4.31 | 2.44 |
| Trendiness | 2.62 | 2.95 | 4.07 | 2.76 | 3.20 | 2.07 | 3.95 | 4.05 |

## 4.6 Exploratory Analysis

The aim of present study was to explore how three factors (trendiness, complexity, and emotion) influence Chinese consumers' aesthetic preferences on automotive interior form. We added the average scores of trendiness, complexity and emotion for eight stimulus as three variables, and conducted a stepwise linear regression analysis.

At step one of analysis, we only introduced trendiness factor as independent variable to exam the assumption that the aesthetic preference on automotive interior would be affected by trendiness factor. The results supported our hypothesis, indicating that a significant proportion of the variance in aesthetic preference on automotive interior was explained by trendiness ($\beta = 0.650$, $p < 0.01$); $R^2 = 0.749$, $F = 23.193$, $p < 0.01$.

At step two of analysis, we added emotion factor as an independent variable to examine whether aesthetic preference on automotive interior would also be influenced by the curvature of feature line and plumpness of surface. Result suggested that more proportion of the variance in aesthetic preference on automotive interior was explained by not only trendiness ($\beta = 0.713$, $p = <0.01$) but also emotion ($\beta = -0.307$, $p < 0.01$); $R^2 = 0.965$, $F = 68.681$, $p < 0.01$. Two factors account for 96.5% of the variance, which suggests that we could stop adding new variable into regression analysis, but we continue the third step to test the impact of complexity factor.

At step three of analysis, when complexity factor was introduced into multiple regression analysis, explanatory power of both trendiness factor and emotion factor decrease very slightly. The result of analysis showed when complexity factor was added, the explanation didn't increase, which indicate that aesthetic preference on automotive interior is significantly influenced by trendiness factor ($\beta = 0.718$, $p = <0.01$) and emotion factor ($\beta = -0.309$, $p < 0.05$), while complexity factor ($\beta = 0.025$, $p > 0.05$) has no significant effect on aesthetic preference on automotive interior; $R^2 = 0.965$, $F = 36.956$, $p < 0.01$.

## 4.7 Conclusion

Thus, complexity factor was eliminated, and we adopt the result in step two of stepwise regression analysis, and build following regression formula ($R^2 = 0.965$, $F = 68.681$, $p < 0.01$):

$$aesthetic\ preference = 1.677 + 0.713 * (trendiness\ factor) + (-0.307) * (emotion\ factor)$$

Two factors account for 96.5% of the variance in aesthetic preference on automotive interior, which indicate that complexity factor is not applicable for predicting aesthetic preference on automotive interior form. Therefore, trendiness factor, and emotion factor was regarded as predictor variables. In particular, regression coefficient of trendiness factor is 0.713, which suggests that trendiness has a positive linear relationship with aesthetic preference on interior form, in other words, more trendy more preferred. However, regression coefficient of emotion factor is $-0.307$, which shows a negative linear relationship between emotion factor and aesthetic preference. According to the relationship between product semantics and feature that proposed by Hsiao and Chen [10], we may conclude that interior with more curved feature line and plumper surface will be less preferred. Partial regression analysis for both trendiness factor and emotion factor shows significant linear relation (Fig. 4).

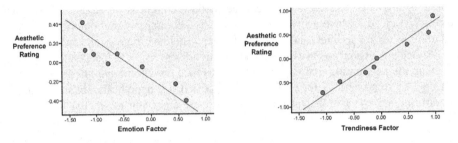

**Fig. 4.** Partial regression analysis for trendiness factor and emotion factor.

## 5   Discussion

In this research, based on literature review, we presented brief statement of the content of visual information processing in every stage of the aesthetic experience, and summary of visual factors that affects individuals' aesthetic preference in general, and then described three factors for aesthetic preference on common consumer products as well as differences between automotive interior design and product design.

We conducted a test among Chinese consumers to evaluate how automotive interior form is preferred, and assessed every automotive interior in three dimensions: trendiness, complexity, and emotion, which have been proved to be three influential factor for aesthetic preference on product design. Also, we took a stepwise linear regression analysis to explore the mathematical relationship between them aesthetic preference on automotive interior form and three influential factors. Analysis of results provided evidence for our assumption that influential factors for aesthetic preference on product design are partly applicable for predicting aesthetic preference on automotive interior, and explanation of every factor differentiates from each other. Complexity factor has a minimal impact on aesthetic preferences of automotive interior, which coincide with Leder's experimental results [13]. Both trendiness factor and emotion factor have significant influence on preference of automotive interior prediction. But, compared with trendiness factor, emotion factor explained a smaller proportion of the variance in aesthetic preference on automotive interior. This finding is not surprising, as trendiness often show up as the most important factor affecting consumer perception of product appearance [3, 10, 11].

Mastering the key impact factors of the aesthetic preference on interior design can provide practical reference for developing automotive interior for Chinese market. In various stages of interior design project, such as theme defining, conceptual design, and design revision, design work are always based on the mapping relationship between semantics and characteristics. Both emotion factor and trendiness factor link to particular type of characteristics. Thus, in theme defining stage, they are assisted to theme words filtering and sorting; in aesthetic generation stage, they have guidance function imagery selection; in the stage of design evaluation and revision, they can provide evaluation index and weight for a structured evaluation system.

## 6  Limitation

Although it has been proved that trendiness is the most influential factor in the aesthetic preference for automotive interior form, the definition and quantization of trendiness factor are among the most difficult tasks in design. One possible reason may be that essence of trendiness changes when times change. Another reason may due to the complicacy of automotive interior design. As mentioned before, interior design is a complicated task, thus, trendiness may be affected by some non-form factors such as material, color, texture and light. Even if stimuli photos being decolorized and texture has been erased, the interior form factor can't be totally separated from non-form factors. So, in the study about aesthetic preference on automotive interior form factor, being disturbed by non-form factors is inevitable.

**Acknowledgments.** We would like to thank National Nature Science Foundation of China (51605154) for providing this research with financial support.

## References

1. Berlyne, D.E.: Novelty, complexity, and hedonic value. Percept. Psychophys. **8**(5), 279–286 (1970)
2. Blijlevens, J., Carbon, C.C., Mugge, R., et al.: Aesthetic appraisal of product designs: independent effects of typicality and arousal. Br. J. Psychol. **103**(1), 44–57 (2012)
3. Blijlevens, J., Creusen, M.E.H., Schoormans, J.P.L.: How consumers perceive product appearance: the identification of three product appearance attributes. Int. J. Des. **3**(3), 27–35 (2009)
4. Blijlevens, J., Mugge, R., Ye, P., et al.: The influence of product exposure on trendiness and aesthetic appraisal. Int. J. Des. **7**(1) (2013)
5. Karlsson, B.S.A., Aonsson, N., Svensson, K.A.: Using semantic environment description as a tool to evaluate car interiors. Ergonomics **46**(13/14), 1408–1422 (2003)
6. Chamberlain, A.T.: On the evolution of human aesthetic preferences (2000)
7. Creusen, M.E.H., Schoormans, J.P.L.: The different roles of product appearance in consumer choice (2005)
8. Ersal, I., Papalambros, P., Gonzalez, R., et al.: Modelling perceptions of craftsmanship in vehicle interior design. J. Eng. Des. **22**(2), 129–144 (2011)
9. Hekkert, P., Leder, H.: Product aesthetics. Prod. Exp. 259–285 (2008)
10. Hsiao, K.A., Chen, L.L.: Fundamental dimensions of affective responses to product shapes. Int. J. Ind. Ergon. **36**(6), 553–564 (2006)
11. Hung, W.K., Chen, L.L.: Effects of novelty and its dimensions on aesthetic preference in product design. Int. J. Des. **6**(2), 81–90 (2012)
12. Kunst-Wilson, W.R., Zajonc, R.B.: Affective discrimination of stimuli that cannot be recognized. Science **207**(4430), 557–558 (1980)
13. Leder, H., Carbon, C.C.: Dimensions in appreciation of car interior design. Appl. Cogn. Psychol. **19**(5), 603–618 (2005)

14. Leder, H., Nadal, M.: Ten years of a model of aesthetic appreciation and aesthetic judgments: the aesthetic episode – developments and challenges in empirical aesthetics. Br. J. Psychol. **105**(4), 443–464 (2014)
15. Levy, E.K.: Inner vision: an exploration of art and the brain. Endeavour **24**(3), 137–138 (2000)
16. Lindgaard, G., Whitfield, T.W.A.: Integrating aesthetics within an evolutionary and psychological framework. Theor. Issues Ergon. Sci. **5**(1), 73–90 (2004)
17. Meamber, L.A.: The aesthetics of consumption and the consumer as an aesthetic subject. Consum. Mark. Cult. **11**(1), 45–70 (2008)
18. Molesworth, M., Suortti, J.P.: Buying cars online: the adoption of the web for high-involvement, high-cost purchases. J. Consum. Behav. **2**(2), 155–168 (2002)
19. Nadal, M., Munar, E., Capó, M.A., et al.: Towards a framework for the study of the neural correlates of aesthetic preference. Spat. Vis. **21**(3–5), 379 (2008)
20. Post, R.A.G., Blijlevens, J., Hekkert, P.P.M.: The influence of unity-in-variety on aesthetic appreciation of car interiors. In: Proceedings of the 5th International Congress of International Association of Societies of Design Research, IASDR 2013, "Consilience and Innovation in Design", Tokyo, Japan, 26–30 August 2013 (2013)
21. Reimann, M., Zaichkowsky, J., Neuhaus, C., et al.: Aesthetic package design: a behavioral, neural, and psychological investigation. J. Consum. Psychol. **20**(4), 431–441 (2010)
22. Yun, M.H., You, H., Geum, W., et al.: Affective evaluation of vehicle interior craftsmanship: systematic checklists for touch/feel quality of surface-covering material. Hum. Factors Ergon. Soc. Annu. Meet. Proc. **48**(6), 971–975 (2004)
23. Rhodes, G.: The evolutionary psychology of facial beauty. Annu. Rev. Psychol. **57**, 199–226 (2006)

# Applying Storyboards to Fashion Design for Empathy

Chien-Chih Ni[1,2(✉)], I-Ting Wang[2], and Hsien-Fu Lo[2]

[1] Hsuan-Chung University, Hsinchu, Taiwan
[2] National Taiwan University of Arts, New Taipei City, Taiwan
etinw@ms43.hinet.net, nancynil008@gmail.com,
hsienfulo@gmail.com

**Abstract.** Taking Pinocchio as the starting point of design, this study applied scenarios to fashion design. Fashion is people's second skin, and wearing clothes is a psychological and physiological reflection as well as an emotional and cognitive reaction. With stories as the main axis, this study designed six sets of fashion for gender transformation. In the questionnaire survey, 111 subjects evaluated the masculinization or feminization of fashion according to nine fashion design elements. According to the analysis of the questionnaire survey results, Fashion D and Fashion F were the most masculine, and proportion of garment, sense of design, and overall image were the most distinctive features of masculinization. The most significant difference in the reaction to the masculinization or feminization of fashion between the male and female subjects occurred with Fashion B, especially in regards to proportion of garment and trousers, sense of design, and overall image. The results can be taken as a reference for the expression of gender in future fashion design.

**Keywords:** Empathy · Empathic design · Fashion design

## 1 Introduction

During the past century, fashion design has gradually separated itself from the concept of the second skin, and the function of fashion has developed from one of physiological demand to social and psychological demands. Aside from leaving a specific impression on others, wearing clothes also has an effect on the individual. The multi-dimensional perceptions, social factors and symbolic correlations of fashion all have influence on the feelings of the people wearing it and those who see it. Corrigan [5] said the order of the society is the order of the dress, one's occupation, class, age, sex, gender, region, and religion can be interpreted by what he/she wears. With the incorporation of diverse cultures into design, fashion has become a medium for self-expression. People indicate sex, age, and identity recognition through fashion. Therefore, fashion can be regarded as an expression of contemporary life and attitude.

In an era where physiological and psychological gender has become blurred, personal sexual awareness has gradually attracted attention. Hence, people have begun self-assertion, self-performance and self-expression through fashion. An increasing number of females are dressing themselves in masculine clothes, and elements which were once considered feminine have been found in clothes for males. Clothes for both sexes now occupy a position in the existing fashion markets for both men and women. This manifests that a person's attitude towards sex identity and the selection of popular fashion has becoming increasingly diverse.

This study was divided into two stages. In the first stage, six sets of fashion were designed on the basis of the design curriculum and the story structure of Pinocchio. The story was adopted to change the style and look of the fashion to discuss key factors for the fashion design based on stories. In the second stage, a questionnaire survey on the six sets of fashion was conducted to find out the factors that influenced consumers' and viewers' evaluation of the masculinization or feminization of the six sets of fashion in terms of style and look, so as to provide a reference for the sexual orientation of future fashion design.

## 2  Story Application

### 2.1  Scenario: Pinocchio

Scenarios are a frequently-used mode in design. The telling of a story creates a scenario for designing products that are suitable for users. Most of the traditional design modes elaborate on the relationship between objects and design functions from the perspective of the designer. However, they neglect the differences caused by various understandings between designers and users of the productions [13]. Scenarios can be used to analyze the interaction between people and products through a true or imaginary story, including features of the users and events, and the relationship between product and environment, in the development of products [14]. Nardi [11] believed that scenarios can be used to describe a future life and how future technologies could help users. It can provide a definite and specific imagination. Carroll [3] argued that scenario plays the role as an instructive tool in the communication of design, helping developers with the procedure and response of design as well as the management of design situations.

Pinocchio tells the story of a piece of wood turning into a living puppet. Brave, honest and selfless, the puppet is transformed into a real boy. The transformation from the puppet's birth to his experiences and the desire to become a boy is like that of cloth and material which expect to be turned into fashion. The design concept of Pinocchio desiring to become a boy reflects the fashion style of self-expression in the combination of two perspectives, fashion and viewing, in current society. In fashion design, scenarios can bring multi-dimensional and instructive design thoughts and make fashion design more suitable for consumers and users.

### 2.2  Elements of Fashion Design

There is a wide range of fashion designs, and different demands and functions will lead to different design thoughts. As far as overall conception is concerned, fashion design can be divided into three layers, namely, functional purpose, form and technique, and the cultural meaning of design. The functional purpose of fashion design emphasizes the occasion and purpose of wearing clothes, such as fashion for athletes, common leisure fashion, and suits for official occasions. The functions of fashion causes designers to think about the form and culture of fashion. The forms and techniques of fashion come after the functions of fashion. According to the literature, color, material, profile, proportion, detail, and integrity are all found in form and technique, which have the most direct effect on consumers' preferences for and evaluation of fashion. The final layer of fashion design lies in cultural meanings or the signs and information that fashion delivers [4, 17, 18]. Therefore, some designers incorporate historical signs and patterns into fashion design, and some adopt popular culture elements, art works or spiritual concepts for fashion design, so as to convey the cultural meaning of design. Fashion design integrates function with design meaning and technique. Apart from satisfying consumers' material demands, fashion must be consistent with consumers' psychological responses. Meanwhile, the popularity of fashion can also be seen as an ideology being understood and recognized in a group. Fashion is not only a daily necessity of life but also a product of cultural creativity showing a humanistic style [18].

In fashion design, designers transform creative ideas into specific popular fashion looks in a systematic way through the sense, style and look of fashion. The presentation of a look is an essential index which guides the creative ideas of fashion and generates popular elements [8]. How designers turn disordered thoughts and creative ideas into a systematic connection, manifest the message of traditional aesthetics through design, and deliver it to consumers and arouse consumers' resonance are challenges facing all fashion designers today. The basic constituents of fashion design include material (selection of cloth), structure (fashion model), form (fashion style), and function (occasion and viewer). Under the interaction between designs, fashion can be taken as a tool to show emotions and express individuality, as well as the interaction with others in society [7].

According to what has been mentioned about the three layers of fashion design, fashion is not only an appearance based on wearing clothes, but also a reflection of the designers' and users' thoughts on fashion.

## 2.3 The Relationship Between Clothes and Humans

In all eras, fashion has been indispensable for humans. The most basic three functions of fashion and Maslow's five basic needs of humans are consistent with the transformation of individuals' psychological demand for fashion. People select the clothes to show their personal traits. For instance, lace indicates feminization. Therefore, fashion influences individuals' thinking and behavior.

Many psychologists, sociologists and anthropologists have tried explaining humans' motives for wearing clothes. According to the theories, three functions of fashion can be found in the history of human evolution: physiological functions, social functions, and psychological functions, which are used to explain the transformation in human's understanding of the importance of fashion.

### Physiological Function: The Second Skin
As a layer between the human body and the external environment, fashion is expected to protect the body and keep it warm. Throughout history, different materials such as

plants and the animal fur have been used for the above purposes. According to Maslow, only after the most basic demands for existence, including food, clothing, accommodation and travel, are satisfied will humans move on to the demands in the next layer. In terms of the demand for safety, fashion can be taken as a safety mechanism to prevent individuals from injury or threat. People's demand for fashion will also change with the environment. Fashion can protect the human body from being harmed in the work-place, natural environment, daily life, or sports. An appropriate fashion will not restrict human movement; instead, it will protect the body in an appropriate way.

**Social Function: Fashion Style**

Fashion has multiple layers of social meaning. Apart from revealing personal traits and identity, fashion manifests itself in eras, region, politics and culture. Hence, individuals can tell the occupation, age and sex of a person through the way he/she is dressed; moreover, they can even imagine the possible social patterns where the fashion user lives. The third demand in Maslow's theory is the demand for belonging and love. Individuals need to belong to a group and hope to be accepted and concerned by the group. They long to love others and be loved. The subtle changes in emotion are significantly more minute and elusive than those for physiological demands. The fourth demand is the demand for respect, which means an individual's social status and recognition of his/her capabilities. When an individual's demand for respect is met, he/she will feel confident and recognize his/her value. Fashion will change with social circumstances, and a person living in society will always want to become part of a group or society and get a sense of belonging. Therefore, he/she will select clothes according to the latest fashion trend, thereby seeking the acceptance of his/her group through fashion.

**Psychological Function: Personalization**

Fashion is not only a part of appearance and an extension of self-will, but also an expression of personal emotions. Hence, an individual will dress himself/herself according to time, space, mood, preference and occasion. The highest demand in Maslow's theory is the demand for self-achievement, which means that an individual tries his/her best to fulfill dreams and aspirations and become the person he/she wants to become. The appearance of clothes is closely related to the way a person views himself/herself. Different people have different life experiences, and there will also be differences in the development of self-recognition. As a result, people will have different opinions on the collocation of clothes. Aside from the differences between individuals, a person's self-recognition will constantly influence his/her clothing choices throughout his/her personal growth. In other words, an individual will reconstruct his/her preferences for clothes according to the information he/she receives in different growth stages. Throughout personal growth, he/she will continuously seek a relationship with fashion.

### 2.4  Design for Empathy

Tim Brown [2] said that "empathy is at the heart of design. Without the understanding of what others see, feel, and experience, design is a pointless task." According to western countries, empathy is a concept which was first proposed by Robert Vischer in the form of Einfühlung in 1873. In 1897, Theodor Lipps adopted experimental psychology to analyze aesthetic empathy, believing that the reason for aesthetic appreciation lay in the mind rather than in objects and in subjective factors rather than objective factors. Scholars have come up with different views on empathy. For example, Lipps proposed the inner imitation and the outward imitation [10]. Edward Bullough, from the University of Cambridge and University of Oxford, put forward the theory of psychological distance [9]. From the perspective of literary psychology, Zhu Guangqian regarded projection as "projecting a person's cognition and emotion onto objects to make them in objects" [9]. It is possible to divide reflections around empathy into two main dimensions. The first may be seen as emotional empathy, which is an instinctive, affective, shared. and mirrored experience. The other dimension of empathy is cognitive, in which an individual understands how other people may experience the world from their point of view [6, 12, 15]. Being empathy or sympathy and being revealed through emotion or cognition, empathy in design can contribute to a closer communication between designers and users, thus allowing designers to get to know the users' demands and make their designs more suitable for users.

According to Froukje Sleeswijk Visser and Kouprie [16], empathy is an individual's ability to identify with and understand another person's feelings, ideas and circumstances. For designers who have not directly been in contact with the users they receive information about, special attention must be given to the communication of user insights. Katja Battarbee, Jane Fulton Suri, and Suzanne Gibbs Howard [1] defined empathy as the ability to be aware of, understanding of, and sensitive to another person's feelings and thoughts without having had the same experience.

Brown [2] stated that individuals build bridges of insight through empathy, including the effort to see the world through the eyes of others, understand the world through their experiences, and feel the world through their emotions. In Emotional Design, Don Norman [13] said that products must be attractive, pleasant, and interesting, and that people's feelings about using products must be valued. Individuals' feelings of beauty and emotion must be considered in design. Therefore, empathy-based design is important for design. In fashion design, empathy means prioritizing users and getting to know consumers' physiological, social and psychological demands for fashion, so as to make clothes that psychologically satisfy users while expressing fashion design and beauty.

## 3   The Framework of the Research

This study was divided into two parts. In the first part, scenarios were applied to fashion design. In the second part, a questionnaire survey was conducted to understand the differences in cognition of the masculinization and feminization of clothes among consumers.

### 3.1   Scenario-Based Fashion Design

The fashion design of this study was based on the graduation projects of four students from August 2015 to June 2016. For each week, four hours were spent on discussion.

After class, the students designed and made clothes according to the results of the discussion. The course lasted for 34 weeks. As a conclusive course for students majoring in fashion design, it aimed to help the students apply the concepts and designs of integrated fashion, develop the ability to work as a learning group according to the fashion trends, and develop design thinking. The story of Pinocchio was taken as the design theme for the four students. The possibility of designing the gender concepts of the story through the reading and analysis of the story was combined with the concept, practice design thinking, and popular trends to lead the students to develop people-oriented thinking. In the design discussion, Pinocchio was integrated with scenarios for the design to reflect that the cognition of gender can change through wearing clothes through the concept of a puppet's desire to become a boy. It was hoped that it will be considered as a demand in fashion design.

As shown in Fig. 1, fashion designers need to take viewers and consumers into consideration to make empathetic design. For consumers, what feeling will the clothes bring? What is the perspective of a viewer? These questions must be considered by designers.

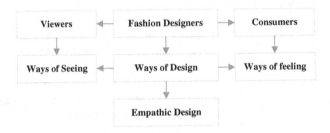

**Fig. 1.** Relationship between the empathetic design of clothes, viewers and consumers.

## 3.2    Scenario-Based Design Procedure

Scenarios were adopted to analyze the story of Pinocchio, which led to three design axes: (1) a girl wanting to become a boy; (2) a man wanting to become a boy; and (3) a puppet wanting to become a boy.

The first scenario (a girl wanting to become a boy) presented a masculine style and visual effects on a woman's clothes. Therefore, masculine factors were added into the fashion design with the concept of uniform. The second scenario (a man wanting to become a boy) consisted of adding a child's factors into the transformation of identity and mind from a man to a boy on a man's clothes, so as to reveal a man's desire to become a boy. The third scenario (a puppet wanting to become a boy) consisted of re-dissembling and reconstructing the process of transforming a puppet into a boy on a man's clothes to show the process of transformation (Table 1).

**Table 1.** Pinocchio scenario-based fashion design concepts

| Design idea | Design concept | Development item | Design factor |
|---|---|---|---|
| A girl wanting to become a boy | Add masculine style into a uniform | A woman's clothes | Use warm colors. Take cotton and linen as the main material. The jacket is short and the trousers fit. Different clothes are adopted to show details. |
| A man wanting to become a boy | Add a child's factors into a uniform | A man's clothes | Combine cold colors with warm ones. Take plain weaving fabric as the main material. The jacket is short and the trousers fit. Loose or straight trousers; show details through the thread. |
| A puppet wanting to become a boy | Re-dissemble the uniform and explore the transformation from a puppet into a boy through deconstruction | A man's clothes | Take blue as the main color. Take jeans as the main material The jacket is long. Show details through the collar and trousers. |

### 3.3   Questionnaire Design

Through a literature review and data analysis, nine evaluation factors of fashion design were chosen for the questionnaire of this study, and six sets of fashion made through empathetic design were applied to the evaluation of masculinization and feminization. The nine evaluation factors were color collocation, material application, proportion of jacket, proportion of trousers, detail, design sense, and overall image. The sample questionnaire was as follows (Table 2).

### 3.4   Experimental Design

The subjects of this study were individuals with a background of fashion, art design, and other professions. The total number of subjects was 111, including 37 males and 74 females. The number of subjects with a fashion background was 32; that of subjects with an art design background was 24, and that of those with a background from other professions was 55. The subjects ranged in age from 18 to 46. The researcher invited subjects to fill the questionnaire, which was distributed and completed on the Internet. It took about 15 min to fill in the questionnaire. The questionnaire included basic

**Table 2.** Questionnaire

| Sample A | |
|---|---|
| | |
| Color collocation | feminization     1----2----3----4----5     masculinization |
| Fabric application | feminization     1----2----3----4----5     masculinization |
| Proportion of jacket | feminization     1----2----3----4----5     masculinization |
| Proportion of trousers | feminization     1----2----3----4----5     masculinization |
| Style of jacket | feminization     1----2----3----4----5     masculinization |
| Style of trousers | feminization     1----2----3----4----5     masculinization |
| Detail | feminization     1----2----3----4----5     masculinization |
| Design sense | feminization     1----2----3----4----5     masculinization |
| Overall image | feminization     1----2----3----4----5     masculinization |

information, such as gender, age, profession, and the nine design factors of the six sets of fashion. A 5-point scale was adopted for the evaluation items, with scores ranging from 1 (highest level of feminization) to 5 (highest level of masculinization). There were altogether 57 evaluation items.

## 4   Results and Discussion

### 4.1   Scenario-Based Design Results

Scenarios can narrow the difference between domains and between thinking and language, and they can increase the efficiency and benefits of communication [14]. Taking the story of Pinocchio as the scenario, the mood of the transformation of roles was reflected in the fashion design. The story was considered to show the design factors of masculinization and feminization in current society. The four students finished the six sets of fashion. A girl's, man's, and puppet's desire to become a boy were shown through color, material and pattern for the transformation of gender design. The analysis of the results for the design concept and form of the six sets of fashion is shown in Table 3.

## 4.2 Questionnaire Survey Results

This study asked the following two questions: (1) Whether the six sets of fashion designed on the basis of a scenario were accepted by viewers and consumers? (2) What are the factors that influence public opinion on the masculinization or feminization of fashion? The analysis of the results of the questionnaire survey was as follows (Table 4):

According to the analysis of the means of the 111 subjects, four factors of Fashion D and five factors of Fashion F had the highest mean among the nine evaluation factors. Specifically, Fashion D scored the highest in fabric application, style of trousers, detail, and design sense. Fashion D represented a man's desire to become a boy. The blue fabric and jeans could fully express the transformation of mind. As for the style of trousers, the masculine waist and colorful thread revealed the details and design sense. Fashion F scored the highest in color collocation, fabric application, proportion of jacket, style of jacket, and overall image. The design axis of Fashion F was a puppet's desire to become a boy. The four different layers of blue fabric showed the transformation of mood, and the asymmetric collar of the jacket and the wide bound design of the waist increased the masculinization of the overall image.

The analysis of the differences of both sexes was as follows (Table 5):

According to the evaluation of the nine factors of the six sets of fashion between the male and female subjects, there was significant difference in color collocation, fabric application, proportion of trousers and style of trousers for Fashion A. This result indicated that the female subjects felt the masculinization of the four evaluation factors of Fashion A was stronger. There was a significant difference in the nine evaluation factors of Fashion B for all subjects, both male and female. The design concept of Fashion B was a man's desire to become a boy, and the design pattern of the fashion was for a man. The most significant difference was found in proportion of jacket, proportion of trousers, style of trousers, design sense, and overall image for the male and female subjects. In terms of proportion of jacket and proportion of trousers, Fashion B was relatively loose. For the female subjects, a loose design was masculine.

Following the overall means, Fashion D and Fashion F were the most masculine for all the subjects. It was also found that proportion of trousers had the lowest mean in masculinization. This result indicated that trousers had the least influence on the difference between masculinization and feminization. However, the T-test on the male and female subjects showed that Fashion B revealed the greatest difference in the masculinization or feminization of fashion, showing significant difference in the nine evaluation factors. This result demonstrated that the female subjects believed Fashion B to be more masculine.

**Table 3.** Pinocchio fashion design results

| Code | Design idea | Image | Design concept | Clothing form and techniques |
|---|---|---|---|---|
| A | A girl↦ A boy | | Hard fabric and masculine colors are adopted to show a girl's desire to become a boy. | Plain woven fabric is adopted; the jacket is made into a short feminine design to reserve female factor in the overall image |
| B | A man →A boy | | Soft fabric is adopted to show a man's desire to become a boy | Loose design; threads is adopted in the jacket to show the suit collar and pocket, representing a hidden man's world. |
| C | A girl↦ A boy | | Hard fabric and masculine colors are adopted to show a girl's desire to become a boy. | The red underclothes are adopted to maintain female factors in the overall image. The lattice fabric and the dark color aim to underline male colors. |
| D | A man →A boy | | Soft fabric is adopted to show a man's desire to become a boy | The collarless jacket shows the interest of a boy. The blue fabric and the jeans reveal the relaxation of a man turning into a boy |
| E | A puppet→A boy | | A fashion profile with intense lines shows the limbs of a puppet | The colorblock lines and the stitched fabric show the image of a puppet's limbs. The blue and green fabric manifest a puppet's desire to become a boy |
| F | A puppet→A boy | | The design concept of dissemblance is adopted to show a puppet's limbs and desire to become a boy. | Take blue as the main color, and adopt four different layers of blue fabric to show the mood of transformation. The asymmetric design reveals the variety of a puppet's limbs. |

**Table 4.** Sample D & F descriptive statistics

| Variables | D (n = 111) | | F (n = 111) | |
|---|---|---|---|---|
| | M | SD | M | SD |
| Color collocation | 4.162 | 0.7204 | **4.18** | 0.8113 |
| Fabric application | **4.045** | 0.7674 | **4.045** | 0.7907 |
| Proportion of jacket | 4.027 | 0.7193 | **4.162** | 0.7925 |
| Proportion of trousers | 3.856 | 0.8826 | 3.622 | 1.0095 |
| Style of jacket | 4.045 | 0.7907 | **4.162** | 0.7573 |
| Style of trousers | **3.865** | 0.8789 | 3.757 | 1.011 |
| Detail | **3.946** | 0.8825 | 3.937 | 0.8558 |
| Design sense | **4.009** | 0.8257 | 3.964 | 0.8304 |
| Overall image | 4.09 | 0.7693 | **4.126** | 0.8215 |

**Table 5.** Difference in the masculinization and feminization of the six sets of fashion between the two sexes T-test (n = 111)

| Sample | Variables | gender | n | M | SD | T value | Difference comparison |
|---|---|---|---|---|---|---|---|
| A | Color collocation | Female | 74 | 2.473 | .8636 | 2.701** | Female > Male |
| | | Male | 37 | 2.000 | .8819 | | |
| A | Fabric application | Female | 74 | 2.635 | .9447 | 2.475* | Female > Male |
| | | Male | 37 | 2.162 | .9578 | | |
| A | Proportion of trousers | Female | 74 | 2.635 | 1.0673 | 1.988* | Female > Male |
| | | Male | 37 | 2.216 | 1.0037 | | |
| A | Style of trousers | Female | 74 | 2.689 | 1.0589 | 2.141* | Female > Male |
| | | Male | 37 | 2.243 | .9833 | | |
| B | Color collocation | Female | 74 | 3.676 | .8618 | 2.819** | Female > Male |
| | | Male | 37 | 3.162 | .9864 | | |
| B | Fabric application | Female | 74 | 3.541 | .8631 | 2.312* | Female > Male |
| | | Male | 37 | 3.135 | .8870 | | |
| B | Proportion of jacket | Female | 74 | 3.743 | .8610 | 3.946*** | Female > Male |
| | | Male | 37 | 3.054 | .8802 | | |
| B | Proportion of trousers | Female | 74 | 3.595 | .9351 | 4.029*** | Female > Male |
| | | Male | 37 | 2.838 | .9284 | | |
| B | Style of jacket | Female | 74 | 3.851 | .8709 | 2.556* | Female > Male |
| | | Male | 37 | 3.378 | 1.0097 | | |
| B | Style of trousers | Female | 74 | 3.608 | .9038 | 3.386*** | Female > Male |
| | | Male | 37 | 2.973 | .9856 | | |
| B | Detail | Female | 74 | 3.635 | .9001 | 3.193** | Female > Male |
| | | Male | 37 | 3.054 | .9112 | | |
| B | Design sense | Female | 74 | 3.568 | .8123 | 3.372*** | Female > Male |
| | | Male | 37 | 3.000 | .8819 | | |

(continued)

434    C.-C. Ni et al.

**Table 5.** (*continued*)

| Sample | Variables | gender | n | M | SD | T value | Difference comparison |
|--------|-----------|--------|---|---|----|---------|-----------------------|
| B | Overall image | Female | 74 | 3.811 | .8708 | 4.021*** | Female > Male |
|   |               | Male | 37 | 3.054 | 1.0527 | | |
| D | Style of jacket | Female | 74 | 4.189 | .6959 | 2.799** | Female > Male |
|   |                 | Male | 37 | 3.757 | .8946 | | |

*p < 0.05, **p < 0.01, ***p < 0.001

## 5 Conclusion

According to the questionnaire survey on the six sets of fashion designed on the basis of Pinocchio, the design featuring story empathy was found to enable the subjects to feel masculine factors. Fashion design requires psychological and physiological appeal; in other words, it needs both rationality and emotion. This study created designs based on a story and incorporated the story into current topics about gender in society to generate three design axes based on the story outline, in order to help students create empathetic designs showing both emotion and cognition.

According to the results of the questionnaire survey, Fashion D and Fashion F scored the highest in masculinization. Style of jacket and proportion of jacket were the most important dimension in the subjects' evaluation of the masculinization or feminization of fashion. The second most important dimension was overall image. It was also found that proportion of trousers did not lead to a significant difference in masculinization or feminization. The difference in masculinization or feminization of fashion was found in proportion of jacket and proportion of trousers. This result indicated that a loose design was considered masculine for the female subjects. Design sense and overall image were also important factors in the evaluation of the masculinization or feminization of fashion.

Gender is an essential social topic today, and thinking and designs featuring empathetic design and designs showing emotion and cognition can better meet consumers' demands for masculinization or feminization in fashion. Revealing more diverse sex identities through fashion is a topic worthy of exploration in the future.

## References

1. Battarbee, K., Fulton Suri, J., Gibbs Howard, S.: Empathy on the Edge, IDEO (2014). https://www.ideo.com/images/uploads/news/pdfs/Empathy_on_the_Edge.pdf. Accessed 6th Dec 2017
2. Brown, T.: Change by Design: How Design Thinking Transforms Organizations and Inspires Innovation. Harper Collins, New York (2009)
3. Carroll, J.M.: Five reasons for scenario-based design. Des. Stud. **13**(1), 43–60 (2000)
4. Cao, J.X.: The creating of the mood of literary works in fashion design. Melliand China **7**, 59–60 (2011). [in Chinese, semantic translation]

5. Corrigan, P.: The Dressed Society: Clothing, the Body and Some Meanings of the World. SAGE Publications Ltd, London (2008)
6. Gasparini, A.A.: Perspective and use of empathy in design thinking. In: The Eighth International Conference on Advances in Computer-Human Interactions, ACHI 2015, Lisbon, pp. 49–54 (2015)
7. Liang, H.E., Chen, B.Y., Cui, R.R.: Jianfnan folk costumes and cultural connotations revelation of modern clothing design. J. Wuhan Univ. Sci. Eng. 22(6), 36 (2009). [in Chinese, semantic translation]
8. Lin, C.H.: A study on the relationship between fashion style and design element-2002/3 A/W Milan women fashion styles as example. J. Nat. Taiwan Coll. Arts 73, 89–97 (2003)
9. Liu, C.Y.: The Introduction of Western Aesthetics. Linking Publishing, Taipei (1986)
10. Liu, W.T.: Contemporary Aesthetics. The Commercial Press, Ltd, Taipei (2003)
11. Nardi, B.A.: The use of scenarios in design. ACM SIGCHI Bull. 24(4), 13–14 (1992)
12. New, S., Kimbell, L.: Chimps, designers, consultants and empathy: a "Theory of Mind" for service design. In: Proceedings of the Cambridge Academic Design Management Conference (2013)
13. Norman, D.A.: Emotional Design: Why We Love (or Hate) Everyday Things. Basic Books, New York (2004)
14. Tang, H.H., Lin, Y.Q.: The influence and problems of scenario design approach on multi-disciplinary collaboration design. J. Des. 16(3), 21–44 (2011)
15. Spencer, E.: The Principles of Psychology. Williams and Norgate, London (1881)
16. Visser, F.S., Kouprie, M.: Stimulating empathy in ideation workshops. In: Proceedings of the Tenth Anniversary Conference on Participatory Design, pp. 174–177. Indiana University (2008)
17. Yeh, L.C.: Clothing Aesthetics. Shinning Culture, Taipei (2006). [in Chinese, semantic translation]
18. Yen, H.Y.: Factors in transforming cultural elements into fashion design: a case study of the fashion exhibition China: through the looking glass at the Metropolitan Museum of Art in New York. J. Des. 22(2), 1–24 (2017)

# A Survey Website Designed for the Older People – A Case Study of Happy Life Survey

Yimeng Xiao and Hsien-Hui Tang[⊠]

National Taiwan University of Science and Technology, Taipei, Taiwan
xiao.easymoe@gmail.com

**Abstract.** The aging problem in Greater China Region is becoming increasingly serious, and the main users of computers have expanded from the young to the elderly. However, most of the interface designs on the market are designed to fulfill the needs of young people, and there is very little research on senior user- friendly interface design especially for online survey. 「Happy Life Survey」 is a responsive online survey website designed for the older people, being accessible via smartphones, tablets, and computers. The website design is created for a user-friendly experience for the older people and in consideration of commercial viability and technical feasibility. Through the case study, this paper studies and analyzes the operational characteristics and user experience of the senior-friendly online survey.

The result of this study provided four major UX problems for older people including eyesight, hand gesture, cognition and memory, digital ability in terms of online survey operation. To resolve these issues, a new design of the system was created with three iterations. The system was tested and used in a public survey of about 36 thousand of older users. The result of this study contributes to the design of the senior-friendly online survey and increases the understanding of older user experience.

**Keywords:** Older people · Online survey · User experience · Survey design

## 1 Introduction

Greater China Region is a rapidly aging society. The aging population in Taiwan is becoming increasingly serious. The United States Census Bureau estimates that the number of people over 65 years old has reached 600 million in 2017, accounting for 8.5% of the world population. An estimated 17% growth is expected by 2050. The United Nations' global population aging report predicts that people over 60 years old will rise up to 44% of Taiwan's population by 2050, which will become the highest percentage in the world. Nowadays, the target users of high technology spreading from the young to the elderly. However, most of the interface designs of products on the market are designed to satisfy the needs of young people and often neglects friendly interface design for older people. Many operational problems are found on smartphones, tablets,and computers, such as confusing abstract icons, interface information complexity, and so on. Zhou Beizhen (2009) pointed out that the decline of physical and cognitive abilities makes the learning process of operating technological products

© Springer International Publishing AG, part of Springer Nature 2018
P.-L. P. Rau (Ed.): CCD 2018, LNCS 10911, pp. 436–448, 2018.
https://doi.org/10.1007/978-3-319-92141-9_34

difficult for them, consequently resulting in decreased learning intention or even rejection. Online surveys are flourishing nowadays, but only a few websites and applications are designed specifically for the elderly, thus limiting their rights to express opinions use online surveys.

Stans Foundation Chinese Consumer Center (CCC) focuses on researching the daily needs of older people in the Greater China. Through a senior-friendly online survey design system, this research and CCC hope to attract older people to participate in the survey. The results collected from the survey will ultimately provide suggestions for the government or relevant industries and insights on the needs of older people in Taiwan, helping to build welfare strategies and product services for them. This multi-disciplinary collaboration project, Happy Life Survey, had members from design, business, and technology, looking for innovative output.

The case study of "Happy Life Survey" emphasizes on the user experience of the online survey and focuses on studying the problematic experiences of the interface of online surveys. With literature review, online survey analysis and experience gathered from the operational behavior of the older people, this research explores the design strategy, the operating characteristics for the older people, and help to establish a new version of a senior-friendly online survey system.

## 2  Literature Review

### 2.1  The Older People Research

**The Middle-ager and the Elder.** The WTO defines 'elder' as being over 65 years of age. According to the Plan on Promoting the Job Redesign among Middle-agers promulgated by the Ministry of Labor of Taiwan in 2015, the 'elder' is defined as nationals aged over 65, while the 'middle-ager' is defined as nationals aged from 45 to 65. In the international arena, the categorization and definition of old age are all different. Zhang Yuhan (1989) also claimed that there is no single standard for "old", which is linked to many aspects. Older people in this paper refer to the middle-aged and people aged 50 and above. By inviting them to participate in the survey, we attempt to understand the needs and demands of these older people who are about to enter or have already entered the old age.

**Visual and Cognitive Mechanism of the Older People.** Shi Yiru (2009) claimed that the ordinary people experience the gradual decline of visual acuity at around 40-45 years of age. The focusing ability required for seeing close objects has gradually diminished the ability to adjust the distance to the objects decreases, and errors appear gradually in the phototaxis process needed to see objects. Adequate focusing becomes difficult, and visual acuity worsens. In addition, the dynamic images captured by the older people are not as clear as they were when they were young. Their sensation of light and shade diminishes, and their color perception and contrast sensitivity also decrease accordingly. Hawthorn (2000) pointed out that the degradation of vision is the most common factor affecting older people's operation of products. Regarding the operation of the online survey, vision is the main channel for receiving information.

Therefore, how to reduce the problems in use caused by vision deterioration of older people via the visual and other media and thereby enhance their experience of online survey operation is one of the major design considerations of this project.

Guo Chenjia (2001) pointed out that the deterioration of visual and cognitive functions in the older people is an important factor affecting their operation of products. After receiving the information, the older people pass it to the brain to generate cognition. Affected by aging, declining execution speed, and other factors, the cognitive abilities of the older people also deteriorate. Attention, discernment, reasoning, memory, and comprehension all begin to decline, leading to difficulties in their operation of products. Moreover, compared to the ordinary operations, the online survey involves more complicated information cognitions and operational interactions, such as understanding the questions in the survey, the logical relationship of the survey and the text input, which are more likely to cause filling-out obstacles among the older people, thereby affecting their experience of using online survey. Hence, how to help the older people deal with the problems resulting from cognitive decline to better complete the online survey is also an important design consideration of this project.

## 2.2    Online Survey Analysis

**Online Survey and Other Survey.** During the twentieth century, there were great advances in the techniques and technologies utilized in survey research, from systematic sampling methods to enhanced survey design and computerized data analysis. The field of survey research became much more scientific, and several leading associations emerged to further enhance industry practices. Technology has revolutionized the way in which surveys are administered – with the advent of the first e-mail surveys in the 1980s and the initial web-based surveys in the 1990s (Schonlau et al., 2001). Joel R. Evans and Anil Mathur (2005) had a detailed description of the advantages and potential disadvantages of the online survey. If done properly, online surveys have significant advantages over other formats. However, it is imperative that the potential weaknesses of online surveys be mitigated and that online surveys only be used when appropriate. In addition, there are three main types of surveys: mail survey, personal survey, telephone survey. According to Joel R. Evans and Anil Mathur (2005)'s research, comparing the advantages and potential disadvantages of the online survey with these three survey methods, as shown in Table 1.

To summarize, in order to reduce the difficulties found within the online survey and consider the particularity of the target group, this campaign simultaneously carries out an online and offline survey. Samples have been enhanced to help the older people with weak digital abilities to smoothly operate each step of the webpage. Therefore, while reducing their operational concerns, this research is also able to gather more information about the older people.

**Survey Cake Online Survey System.** The research uses Survey Cake, a free online survey platform, to customize the official online survey system. Survey Cake system is used because Taiwan 25sprout Company is willing to cooperate with the research by carrying out case studies and providing technical support. Survey Cake online survey

**Table 1.** The advantages and disadvantages of the main survey formats.

|  | Advantages | Disadvantages |
|---|---|---|
| Online survey | Global reach; B-to-B and B-to-C appeal; Flexibility.; Technological innovations; Convenience; Ease of data entry and analysis. Question diversity; Low administration cost; Ease of follow-up; Controlled sampling; Large sample easy to obtain; Control of answer order; Required completion of answers; Go to capabilities; Knowledge of respondent vs. nonrespondent characteristics | Perception as junk mail; Skewed attributes of internet population: upscale, male, etc.; Questions about sample selection (representativeness) and implementation; Respondent lack of online experience/expertise; Technological variations; Unclear answering instructions; Impersonal. Privacy and security issues; Low response rate |
| Mail survey | The ability to use a large sample; the geographic coverage; the lack of interviewer bias; less respondent time pressure; the variety of questions that may be asked; possible respondent anonymity; and the low cost per respondent relative to personal surveys | The time needed for a company to receive all responses; the high non-response rate; unclear instructions; the tendency for some item non-responses – where answers are left blank; incomplete answers; brief answers to open-ended questions; an impersonal approach; and respondent ability to control the order in which questions are answered |
| Personal survey | Personal interaction; clear instructions; question variety; flexibility and adaptability; use of probing techniques; ability to use physical stimuli; capability to observe respondents; and control over the survey environment | Interviewer bias; costs per respondent; limited sample size; geographic limitations; convenience sampling with questionable response rates (such as mall surveys); respondent time pressure; and the difficulty in getting demographics |
| Telephone survey | The possibility of random sampling; good geographic coverage, cost savings from centralized phone banks and discount calling providers; control over the survey process; timeliness and completion speed, personal interaction; and technological enhancements for interviewers that ease data entry and reduce errors | Interviewer bias; the refusal of many of people – leading to low response rates and non-representative samples; the need to be brief; a lack of respondent trust – often related to the unseen nature of interviewers; and an inability to use visual aids |

system has more than ten types of questions format and about twenty professional functions. It provides rich samples of surveys, such as customer satisfaction, market research, and so on. Moreover, results are shown through clear and interactive graphs with advanced features, like exporting results to Excel and SPSS or switch results to different chart display. However, from the pilot test conducted on the recruited old-ages people, eleven usability problems and operation characteristics were found. Therefore, the survey system will be customized according to the design optimization.

## 2.3    User-Friendly Website Design for the Older People

Previous literature on elder-friendly website design has contributed to the understanding of this research, and more importantly, new contributions are made to enhance and produce innovative results. Andrew Arch (2008) summed up the literature regarding website design for the older adults from the year 1999 to 2008. Some of these are driven by theory in academia, while others come from the web industry and practical experience. Examples of experiences derive from the search engine, navigation, and e-Services influence the operation of the elderly. There is no literature related to the older people about online survey research. However, among past literature, the most relevant information found is the format of the surveys. Line and her colleagues (Lines, Patel and Hones, 2004; Lines et al., 2006; Lines, Ikechi and Hones, 2007) proposed seven guidelines related to form design and expanded six requirements with the initial requirements as shown below in Table 2.

**Table 2.**  Guidelines related to form design.

| First study | |
| --- | --- |
| 1. Form layout | Extra space between questions and answer boxes (not confirmed in the second study) |
| 2. Simplified question structure | To avoid creating 'excessive' cognitive loads |
| 3. Question completion assistance | Pop-up messages and/or hyperlinked context-sensitive help with each appropriate questions |
| 4. Additional information | Including a list at the top of what information will be required to complete the form |
| 5. Data entry | Automatic checking and validation during completion |
| 6. Form personalization | Presenting only those questions appropriate to the users, e.g. a widow should not be asked for information about her spouse |
| 7. Form submission | Online submission will be easy for many mobility impaired elderly people and may lead to quicker processing time |
| Second Study | |
| 1. Bullet point instructions | Easier to read than paragraph text |
| 2. Logical information groupings | To ensure that the user does not need to go back-and-forth within a form |
| 3. Justification for personal/sensitive questions | The participants resented providing some information for no apparent good reason |
| 4. Security information | How could the users be sure their data would remain confidential? |
| 5. Help and assistance feature | This second study suggested a 'formal' help page in addition to the pop-up and/or hyperlinks suggested previously |
| 6. Save and return | An advantage of paper-based forms is that you can put them down and finish completing them later; this was requested by users for online forms |

There are many literature studies on the operation experience and the use of different digital devices for the older people. However, there has been no research done on the online survey for the old-aged people using different digital devices. This research is based on the information gathering and results from the relevant literature, the exploration and the improvement of the study of this field.

## 3   Case Study: Happy Life Survey for the Older People

### 3.1   Research Method

The purpose of this case is to help older people successfully complete online survey. Through the case study method, this research explores the user experience of online survey for the elderly. Yin (2003) pointed out that the case study consists of four important stages: narration, exploration, hypothesis verification and interpretation. The content of the study is shown in Table 3.

**Table 3.** Research stage

| Stage | Task | Content |
|-------|------|---------|
| Narration | Narrate question | Nowadays, older people endure bad experiences when they answer online surveys |
| Exploration | Empirical evidence | Through literature review, survey analysis and practical operation experience, this case studies and explores design strategy and mainly focuses on usability problem and user operation characteristics |
| Hypothesis verification | Demonstration | The hypotheses proposed for the design phase are verified during the study and testing stage |
| Interpretation | Analysis | Iterative test hypothesis, analyzing the results from the observations |

### 3.2   Case Introduction

CCC focuses on researching the daily needs of older people in the Greater China. Through an elder-friendly online survey design system, this research aims to attract older people to participate in the survey. This case balances the restrictions of desirability, viability, and feasibility, producing the most innovative design for the older people, yet also meeting the needs of a wide age range of people. CCC is sponsoring and business marketing research center. Design Information and Thinking Lab is responsible for user Design. 25sprout Company and Cyberon Corporation are responsible for the technical support, the survey system and the Voice Output function. It is a responsive online survey website accessible on smartphones, tablets, and computers. Due to the server design challenges of smartphone operators, this paper uses the smartphone as the main device. The research, design and official website and the launch of this project are spanned from March to August of 2017. The online surveys and the 30 offline field tests were carried out simultaneously in Taiwan. The field tests contacted about 1,024 older people. As of October 18, a total of 79,441 responses from older people were collected, 36,032 respondents were over 50 years old and 2,042 respondents over the age of 75 years.

### 3.3    Target User Research and Insight

From data analysis and test observations, the design team discovered that the degree of physiological aging, cognitive competence and digital literacy are the most crucial dimensions in measuring the smoothness of the operation. In order to solve the usability problem of older people, the testers were classified into three types of digital literacy: low digital literacy, medium digital literacy,and high digital literacy. These criteria derive from the 33 participants of this research, based on their degree of physical age and cognitive competence. The purpose is to provide design strategy for the design, thus this standard, as reference only, does not have other applicability. The standard definition of physiological aging is the ability to see the interface information clearly, to hear the voice playback clearly, and to complete the hand operation accurately. Meanwhile, the standard definition of cognitive competence is the ability to recognize and understand the contents of the survey. The older people who can meet these criteria were then further divided into different target groups according to the operational experience, learning ability, and operating attitude, as shown in Table 4.

**Table 4.** Three types of digital literacy

|  | Low digital literacy | Medium digital literacy | High digital literacy |
|---|---|---|---|
| Operational experience | 1. The use individual functions from a single device and the use of only the basic level software 2. They cannot solve operational problems by themselves | 1. Use main functions of one or more devices and use the advanced degree of the software 2. They try and solve most operational problems | 1. The most used functions of many devices and the use of high degree software 2. They can solve most problems through empirical reasoning |
| Learning ability | Need to learn new skills in the use of digital devices for more than 3 times | Need to learn new skills in the use of digital devices for 1 or 2 times | Quickly learns new skills in digital devices |
| Operating attitude | Not used to operating the digital device | Neither rejecting nor very confident in the operation of digital devices | Confidence in the operation of digital devices |

Based on the recruited subjects' everyday usage of digital device functions, the design team roughly rated the older people's digital literacy corresponding to the operational difficulty of these functions. The basic functions frequently used by the older people with low digital literacy includes making phone calls, sending text messages, taking pictures and using search inputs. The older people with medium digital literacy can also make frequent use of advanced functions like finding information, downloading and playing videos or music, using social networking software and playing simple games. As for older people with high digital literacy, aside from the functions used by the former two groups, they also use high-end features such as online forums, sending and receiving e-mails, cloud resource management, and online shopping.

Appropriate design strategies are implemented adapting to the classification of these three groups. The present survey website offers intuitive operation and pleasant design to older people with all three levels of digital literacy. Moreover, for older people with medium digital literacy, an easy-to-operate system, valid prompts and voice assistance are also needed. Finally, there is insufficient time for the older people with low digital literacy to digest their learning, thus the most effective solution would be assisted operation by presenting a one-time submission survey.

By testing and observing the operational behaviors of the older people, it is found that older people in three groups could be classified according to the digital ability. They present the following characteristic issues: **(1) Poor eyesight.** They require larger size fonts when reading; smaller font size or insufficient contrast between the text and the background can reduce readability. **(2) Hand gesture.** The habit of rushing, repeating and rage clicks until a response occurs; trouble hitting interface targets due to limited motor control; finger remains too long or difficult to click accurately. **(3) Cognitive decline and memory limitation.** Having a hard time reading and remembering too much content at a time; weak learning ability for things that they have not experienced before; can easily be disturbed by information unrelated to the operation in a page; memorize forms and steps by rote memorization because they do not understand the operation principle of digital products. **(4) Weak digital ability.** Compared with young people, some of the older people cannot use the advanced function or complex operation, do not understand the meaning of the generic symbols and icons on the internet, do not know that they can browse more information by sliding the page, and moreover, they have difficulties in typing. According to the problems found in the pilot test from the former survey system, the research preceded multiple iterations of the user experience design and test. The research process is shown in Fig. 1.

### 3.4  User Experience Design

The design of this online survey website has experienced three iterations. In the first stage, the design team attempts to solve the problems based on the usability problems found in the pilot test,as shown in Table 5.

### 3.5  User Experience Test

Following two iterative tests and final test, the first stage design was verified and improved for the official online survey website. Details are described as follows.

**Design of Poor Eyesight.** The system uses Voice Output function. The survey offers Voice Output in three languages (Mandarin, Taiwanese, and Hakka dialect) to assist

444    Y. Xiao  and  H.-H. Tang

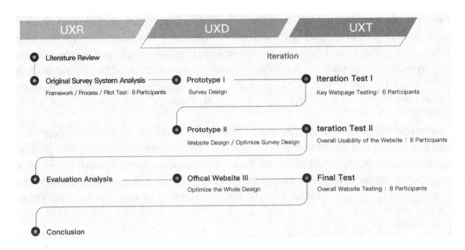

**Fig. 1.** UX research process

older people with poor vision or poor literacy. The test found out that most of the older people did not actively click this button when they were filling in the survey; moreover, they operated through their vision.

**Design of Cognitive Decline and Memory Limitations.** 1. Although the button was clickable, older people often clicked the small checkbox in the edge of the button. It might cause by their written experience of check-signs from paper surveys, so an enlarge checkbox has been provided for them to check. 2. Improved Stage Reminder web pages were added. Considering the number of questions and the variety of the types of questions presented in the survey, we speculated that older people might get lost or inpatient in the process of a survey, so reminders throughout the survey were added to help the users to know the progress and to encourage them to finish. We revised these five reminder pages and made the progress and content clear.

**Table 5.** Characteristic issues and design

| Characteristic issues | Design |
|---|---|
| Design of poor eyesight | 1. Sharp color contrast and larger font size can help the older people easily visit website information |
| | 2. The survey follows the consistent principle so that there is a uniform use pattern for the older people |
| Design of hand gesture | 1. To complete the survey process, clicking and sliding are two simple gestures to replace long presses, dragging and other non-intuitive gestures |
| | 2. Keeping enough distance in the area of input, option, and button to minimize false contacts |
| | 3. The modified size of the button is suitable for older people to click on |

*(continued)*

**Table 5.** (*continued*)

| Characteristic issues | Design |
|---|---|
| Design of cognitive decline and memory limitation | 1. To reduce older people from sliding back and forth, the title is locked in place using a floating-table-header |
| | 2. Encourage webpage helps older people understand the location of the survey. (modification after the test) |
| | 3. The survey follows the consistent principle so that there is a uniform pattern for the older people |
| | 4. Reduce the interference when older people are operating, such as clickable advertising that jumps out of the survey |
| | 5. Require title and life problem title to compromise between cognitive load and frequent operations for older people |
| | 6. Survey answering mechanism is designed such that older people can only click on the next page button at the bottom of the page after making selections or inputs upon browsing all the contents on the page, so as to prevent the answering without browsing complete information |
| Design of weak digital ability | 1. Replace abstract icons or symbols with clear, understanding words |
| | 2. Reduce typing and adding hint for input web pages, like "Click here to type" in input box; the corresponding keyboard will be provided based on their required information input (e.g. character, numbers) |
| | 3. To provide clear error tips to help older people smoothly fill in the survey in time |
| | 4. To provide a friendly-reminder to slide downward in long web pages (modification after the test) |
| | 5. To provide webpage operating tutorial to help older people learn how to operate (modification after the test). |

The test found that the pages would cause some older people to try to click on the reminder box, leading them to stay on the webpage for a long time. Finally, the final version of the reminder design was simplified as one page, only using color to remind them the progress. The final version did help the older people generally feel that the survey would be less time consuming and thus could be finished without fatigue.

**Design of Weak Digital Ability.** 1. On the long page with more than one screen, the reminder for sliding down "More to Read downward slide" was changed to "After finishing, press the next page button to continue." The test found that the original design could be confusing for older people after selecting the answer, and did not know how to continue. As a result, they would try to click the reminder bar, so a more detailed words description was provided for clear reminding.

2. The Operation Instruction page was removed. In the first stage of prototype design, the design team assumed that the operation instruction can assist older people

with weaker technological capability in learning how to fill out the survey. The first version of the operation instruction presented animations before each question. However, the test found out that the older people would either operate on the page following the instructions or unable to understand the instructions due to inability to keep up with the speed of play.

Therefore, the operation instruction was optimized: (1) Dark gray area was added on both sides of the page to separate from the page contents, thus clearly informing its difference from the previous content. (2) Elders were allowed to skip the page quickly. (3) For older people who wanted to browse the instruction, apparent visual guidance was added, such as dividing instruction steps and slowing down the playing speed. Verification of the second version of design found that most of the older people were able to complete the operation smoothly, so the necessity of instruction was reduced. Older people unable to understand the instructions could also continue the survey by skipping the questions. Therefore, we decided to remove the operation instruction.

The revision process made the design team know that the mini animation mode of instruction was inappropriate for the older people who had never used online survey before. Older people with lower digital literacy were unable to learn about the operation by only watching animations in such a short time. However, we assume that the mini animation mode of instruction is suitable in the cases where older people need to use online survey frequently and have time for comprehension.

After six experts evaluated the usability problems of the original survey system and three iteration tests from the 30 participants, the design has been optimized and finalized. Comparing the scores of the original and the final online surveys, we found that the SUS usability scale scores rose from 79.06 to 86.56, and NPS scores rose from 37.5 to 100. This indicates that the redesigned survey has greatly improved usability, moreover, the applicability of research results has also been ensured to some extent.

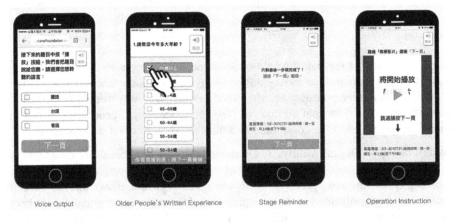

Voice Output          Older People's Written Experience          Stage Reminder          Operation Instruction

**Fig. 2.** Design features

# 4   Conclusion

In summary, this research might have the largest number of participants in the online survey for the older people. It showed that the user experience design has an important role in online survey or the senior. The study found out that, older people suffered from four types of common user experience problems: vision, hand gesture, cognition and memory limitation, or digital ability. In this study, design features were provided to resolve these four issues. After iterative tests, an elder-friendly online survey was designed. The design features of this case include: (1). Try to use Voice Output function to help older people fill in the survey. (2). Continue older people's written experience from the paper survey. (3). Try to use Stage Reminder and Operation Instruction page. The design features are shown in Fig. 2.

Moreover, this design was the first online survey using Voice Output to help older people fill in the online survey. How to use hearing assisting technologies to help the older people could be our future studies.

**Acknowledgments.** The authors would like to thank the DITL design members who participated in the program.

# References

1. Andrew, A.: Web Accessibility for Older Users: A Literature Review.W3C Working Draft, 14 May 2008
2. Buurman, R.D.: User-centred design of smart products. Ergonomics **40**(10), 1159–1169 (1997)
3. Ching, J.C., Chia, W.L.: Understanding older adult's technology adoption and withdrawal for elderly care and education: mixed method analysis from national survey. J. Med. Internet Res. **19**(11), e374 (2017)
4. Cooper, A.: About Face 4: The Essentials of Interaction Design. Publishing House of Electronics Industry (2015)
5. Hawthorn, D.: Possible implications of aging for interface designers. Interact. Comput. **12** (5), 507–528 (2000)
6. Jerry, C.: Mobile Design Trends 2016: Magical Micro-interactions, 29 October 2015. Accessed 29 May 2017
7. Joel, R.E., Anil, M.: The value of online surveys. Internet Res. **15**(2), 195–219 (2005). https://doi.org/10.1108/10662240510590360
8. Wright, K.B.: Researching internet-based populations: advantages and disadvantages of online survey research, online questionnaire authoring software packages, and web survey services. Comput.-mediat. Commun. 10(3), April 2005
9. Lee, C.F, Kuo, C.C.: A pilot study of ergonomic design for elderly Taiwanese people. In: Proceedings of the 5th Asian Design (2001)
10. Lines, L., Ikechi,O., Hones, K.S.: Accessing e-Government Services: Design Requirements for the Older User (2007). https://link.springer.com/chapter/10.1007/978-3-540-73283-9_101

11. Michael, H.: The Difference Between UX And Usability, 24 November 2011. Accessed 29 May 2017
12. Okada, A.: Ergonomics approach in universal design. Special Issue of JSSD **4**(4), 40–45 (1997)
13. Sri, K.,Panayiotis, Z.: Research-Derived Web Design Guidelines for Older People (2005). https://dl.acm.org/citation.cfm?id=1090810
14. Ying, W.B., Wen, C.H., Chun, C.C.: Design and implementation of a four-quadrant and voice interaction user interface of a smartphone for the visually impaired users. In: International Conference on Consumer Electronics-Berlin (2016)

# Constructing and Analyzing a Measurement Model of Product Emotional Design

Hui-Yun Yen[(⊠)]

Department of Advertising, Chinese Culture University, Taipei, Taiwan
pccu.yhy@gmail.com

**Abstract.** The cultural consumer market, characterized by the aesthetic economy, experiential economy, and emotional consumption, has matured with the advent of the Internet and communication technology. This study investigated the commercial design products by professional designers and university students to determine the influences of product emotional design dimensions on consumers' purchase intention of and preference for those products. The differences between currently available design products in the consumer market and the assignments of product design courses were explored and analyzed to identify the prevailing principles of product design at present. In addition to being integrated into design education to cultivate design talents who satisfy market needs, these principles can serve as a reference for related industries in product design. This study reached two conclusions. First, the proposed measuring scale for product emotional design is proven to be feasible. Second, the emotional design of a product influences preference for the product, which subsequently enhances purchase intention of it.

**Keywords:** Product design · Emotional design · Purchase intention
Preference

## 1 Introduction

With the economy of aesthetics on the rise since the turn of the millennium, numerous corporate organizations have advanced from cost-oriented to design-oriented business models and have developed products of cultural and aesthetic value. Because brands are an abstract concept to consumers, products become a channel for brands to connect emotionally with consumers [1]. There is a growing shift in shopping habits from brick-and-mortar to online stores, where consumers can buy high-quality commodities at affordable and even bargain prices and have more convenient and pleasant shopping experiences [2]. Thus, numerous shopping websites that sell design products are built to provide consumers with diverse shopping experiences. This study explored the role of emotional design in consumers' purchase intention of, and preference for, design products, thereby elucidating the differences between currently available design products in the consumer market and the assignments of product design courses. The contents and essence of these two types of design products were further investigated. This study aimed to develop assessment criteria and design models for emotionally engaging products, thereby aiding Taiwanese businesses in improving their competitiveness and brand image.

## 2 Literature Review

### 2.1 Product Design in the Age of the Aesthetic Economy

The concept of aesthetics has been popularized with the rise of the knowledge economy and provides the foundation for incorporating cultural elements into the design process to create profitable cultural businesses. Given the fact that a well-developed cultural market characterized by the aesthetic economy, experiential economy, and Kansei elements-based consumption has been developed, the culture and creative industry can transform to an industry with high added value if adequate investments of resources and brain power are provided [3]. As the world has entered the age of the aesthetic economy, consumer products made to be culturally and aesthetically engaging while retaining their utility have become tremendously popular. Therefore, cultural and art activities are increasingly launched to promote the aesthetic literacy of the public at large. Against this backdrop, today's businesses should design their commodities to be both utilitarian and culturally distinctive; moreover, in brand management, the businesses should simultaneously promote aesthetic lifestyles and adopt profitable business models to achieve ideal balance [4].

### 2.2 Emotional Design of Products

The design, functionality, style, and utility of an emotionally-appealing product in the consumer market together trigger emotions in consumers. These attributes are encapsulated as emotional design [5].

Anderson [6] divided product design into the following dimensions: "functional," "reliable," "usable," "convenient," "pleasurable," and "meaningful." The dimensions of "pleasurable" and "meaningful," in particular, correspond with the stage of self-actualization in the hierarchy of needs of Maslow [7]. Over the past decade or so, numerous methods have been proposed to measure the emotional design of products. For example, Green and Jordan [8] suggested that products should be made to satisfy four types of human pleasure (i.e., ideo-pleasure, socio-pleasure, physio-pleasure, and psycho-pleasure). Norman [9] argued that good product design ensures a balance between beauty and utility, adding that the emotional design of a product can be assessed in terms of pleasure, utility, aesthetics, attractiveness, and beauty. Khalid and Helander [10] classified consumer needs for products into three categories—holistic attributes, functional design, and styling design, of which holistic attributes and styling design are associated with the feelings and emotions of consumers. Hassenzahl [11] maintained that the aesthetics of a product prompt consumers to understand their perceptions of it and imagine using it.

Moreover, the relationship between the aesthetics and utility of a product can be evaluated on the basis of its utilitarianism (or utility), hedonism (or stimulation and identification), goodness (or satisfaction), and beauty. McCarthy and Wright [12] constructed a model of emotion to indicate that emotions play a part in a consumer's experience with a product or service. This model encompassed the overall experience, senses, emotions, the wider socio-cultural context, and the immediate venue for usage. Yen, Lin, and Lin [13] developed a model for measuring qualia, arguing that a consumer's emotions about a product should be explicated on the basis of its appeal, aesthetics, creativity, sophistication, and mechanics. Jagtap [14] designed a measuring scale for the attributes or emotions elicited from the visual appearance of a product, stressing the role of visual appearance in identifying consumer responses to a product and in the commercial success of the product. Jagtap noted that specific attributes and emotions elicited by the visual appearance of a product may help designers in the design process.

### 2.3   Product Preference and Purchase Intention

The visual appearance of a product accounts for its explicit attributes and can trigger emotional responses. Therefore, the aesthetics of products can induce emotions from consumers, and subsequently, their personality traits and behaviors, and people prefer products that match their self-image and personality [15, 16]. Purchase intention can be defined as one's willingness to buy a product and recommend it to one's friends (which can be perceived as a foreseeable behavior after purchase) and used to predict one's purchase decisions for the short term [17–20]. In summary, consumers are normally satisfied with products whose functions meet or exceed their expectations; the design of products is a critical factor in products' commercial success; and consumers are more inclined to choose commodities they prefer, and their purchase intention can be substantially enhanced when such commodities or similar ones have received recommendation [21].

## 3   Methods

### 3.1   Research Framework and Hypotheses

This study was confirmatory in nature. With its framework premised on related theories and "preference" as a mediating variable, this study investigated whether the emotional design of products influences consumers' purchase intention of those products. Creativity, aesthetics, functionality, and pleasure, which constitute the emotional design of products, were used as independent variables; consumers' perceived preference was used as a mediating variable; and purchase intention was used as a dependent variable. Each variable contained several assessment items. On the basis of related theories and the results of a literature review, the following hypotheses were formulated to address the objective of this study:

H1: The elements of product emotional design are important.
H1a: Product emotional design significantly influences purchase intention.
H1b: Product emotional design significantly influences preference.
H1c1: The creative dimension of product emotional design significantly influences purchase intention.

H1c2: The creative dimension of product emotional design significantly influences preference.

H1d1: The aesthetic dimension of product emotional design significantly influences purchase intention.

H1d2: The aesthetic dimension of product emotional design significantly influences preference.

H1e1: The functional dimension of product emotional design significantly influences purchase intention.

H1e2: The functional dimension of product emotional design significantly influences preference.

H1f1: The pleasurable dimension of product emotional design significantly influences purchase intention.

H1f2: The pleasurable dimension of product emotional design significantly influences preference.

To further discuss the interrelationships between product emotional design, preference, and purchase intention, the following hypotheses were proposed:

H2: Preference significantly influences purchase intention.

H3a: Preference mediates between product emotional design and purchase intention.

H3b: Product emotional design influences preference and enhances purchase intention accordingly.

The hypotheses above were tested. Figure 1 shows the conceptual framework and hypothetical model of this study.

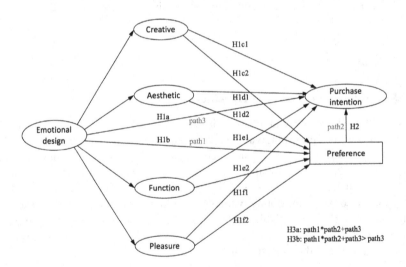

**Fig. 1.** Conceptual framework

## 3.2 Experimental Subjects

Design products were collected from Pinkoi (a Taiwan-based website that sells designer products) and design works from university students. The commodities were respectively designated P2, P4, P6, and P8; whereas the students' works were designated P1, P3, P5, and P7 (Table 1).

**Table 1.** Experimental subjects

| Product name/code | Image | Product name/code | Image |
|---|---|---|---|
| P1. Mobile Power Pack (concept: the root of culture) | | P2. Stereo Puzzle - Stereo Moai Speakers (Pinkoi) | |
| P3. Vampire Pounded Garlic Grater | | P4. Sword Chopsticks (Pinkoi) | |
| P5. Chandelier (concept: read by the light of bagged fireflies or the reflected light of snow) | | P6. Bird's Nest Key Ring (Pinkoi) | |
| P7. Bull Magnet | | P8. Candlestick diamond jewelry sets (Pinkoi) | |

## 3.3    Instrument

A scale was composed on the basis of a literature review and data analysis to measure the effects of different criteria for product emotional design on purchase intention and preference (Table 2). The scale comprised 19 items across five dimensions.

**Table 2.** Scale for measuring the influence of product emotional design on purchase intention and preference

| Dimension | | Item |
|---|---|---|
| Emotional design | Creative | C1 This product is novel.<br>C2 This product is original or innovative.<br>C3 This product is unusual.<br>C4 This product is ingenious in terms of material use. |
| | Aesthetic | A1 This product is fashionable.<br>A2 This product is well-proportioned in shape.<br>A3 This product is properly colored.<br>A4 This product is delicately designed.<br>A5 The surface or decoration of the product is finely designed. |
| | Function | F1 This product is useful.<br>F2 This product is safe to use.<br>F3 This product is convenient. |
| | Pleasure | P1 This product is entertaining.<br>P2 This product reminds me of my certain life experiences.<br>P3 This product makes me happy. |
| Purchase intention | | PI1 I want to buy this product.<br>PI2 If I find something similar to this product that I like, I will buy it.<br>PI3 I will buy the product on others' recommendation. |
| Preference | | PR1 I like this product. |

## 3.4    Experimental Design

Two hundred and thirty five university students with a basic understanding of design (who were potential consumers of design products) were recruited; 59 of them were men and 176 were women. All participants were aged 18–22 years. The students' design works and the design products shown on Pinkoi (which is popular among young people in Taiwan in terms of both social network sharing and actual purchase) were sampled. The 19 items of the measurement scale (Table 2) were rated on a 7-point Likert scale. In total, 231 valid responses were returned.

# 4 Results and Discussion

## 4.1 Structural Equation Modeling and Hypothesis Validation

Structural equation modeling (SEM) was conducted to test the proposed hypotheses, thereby determining the effect sizes of latent and observable variables and the causal relationships among latent variables. Constructed through deduction, the resulting structural model consisted of 19 measurement variables across 4 dimensions, with product emotion design used as an independent variable and purchase intention and preference as dependent variables. Figure 2 shows the structural model and the validation results of the hypotheses.

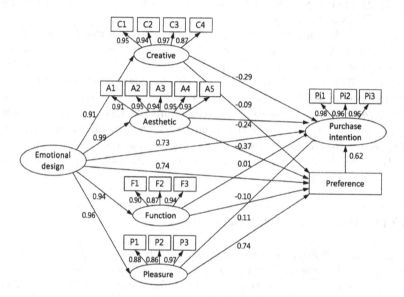

**Fig. 2.** The confirmatory of the SEM analysis

The goodness-of-fit of the model was tested according to the testing procedures proposed in previous studies [22–25]. The results of the test showed that the ratio of the chi-squared value to the degree of freedom (X2/df) of the model was 4.351, which fell within the acceptable range of 1–5. The goodness-of-fit index (GFI) and adjusted GFI of the model were below 0.9; its root mean square error of approximation was approximately 0.121, which only slightly exceeded the acceptable range of 0.05–0.1. Other indices of the model were within acceptable levels (RMR = 0.039 < 0.08; PGFI = 0.571 > 0.5; NFI = 0.920 > 0.9; RFI = 0.902 > 0.9; IFI = 0.937 > 0.9; NNFI (TLI) = 0.923 > 0.9;  CFI = 0.937 > 0.9;  PRATIO = 0.819 > 0.5;  PNFI = 0.753 > 0.5; PCFI = 0.767 > 0.5). With almost all of the indices meeting or approximating acceptable levels, the overall theoretical structure of this study and the empirical data exhibited favorable goodness of fit.

As Fig. 2 (illustrating paths in the structural model) and Table 3 (showing the results of SEM) suggest, H1a, H1b, H1f2, H2, H3a, and H3b were validated, whereas H1c1, H1c2, H1d1, H1d2, H1e1, H1e2, and H1f1 were not. The indirect effect of product emotional design on purchase intention and the mediating effect of preference on the relationship between product emotional design and purchase intention were assessed using the Sobel test [26]. The test yielded a Z-value of 23.92 (higher than the benchmark value of 1.96), indicating that the mediating effect of preference on the relationship between product emotional design and purchase intention was significant. Moreover, the results of bootstrapping showed that at 95% confidence interval for the direct effect path of product emotional design on purchase intention did not include 0 (0.069, 0.256; $p < .05$), indicating that this effect was significant and the mediating effect of preference existed between product emotional design and purchase intention. Therefore, H3a was validated.

The path coefficient for the direct effect of product emotional design on purchase intention was 0.74, whereas that for the indirect effect of product emotional design (with preference as the mediator) on purchase intention was 0.422 (the product of $0.62 \times 0.68$). The total effect of product emotional design on purchase intention was therefore calculated as follows: $0.62 \times 0.68 + 0.74 = 1.16 > 0.74$ (total effect > direct effect). Accordingly, H3b was validated. The results of SEM also suggested that the pleasurable dimension of product emotional design strongly affected preference, but that hypotheses for the other dimensions of product emotional design were not validated. Thus, for a product to appeal to consumers, its emotional design should account for not only pleasure but also functionality, creativity, and aesthetics.

## 5    Conclusions and Recommendations

To distinguish itself from its rivals, build a favorable brand image, and operate sustainably in a market characterized by varying consumer tastes, a business should attune itself to the needs and expectations of consumers. This requires academic research to be conducted; the results of that research must be applied in educational and industrial contexts. The findings of this study can be used to inform the emotional design of future commodities.

This study has the following conclusions. First, the structural equation model for the proposed measurement scale had acceptable goodness-of-fit values, suggesting that the scale may apply well to school courses in product design and to the incorporation of creative elements into commercial products in related businesses. Second, the results of SEM indicated that product emotional design influenced purchase intention; product emotional design, preference, and purchase intention affected each other; the pleasurable dimension of product emotional design had a direct effect on preference, whereas other dimensions did not directly affect preference or purchase intention, except when they were combined with the pleasurable dimension. The results also suggested that preference mediated between product emotional design and purchase intention; therefore, product emotional design affected preference, thereby improving purchase intention.

**Table 3.** Results of structural equation modeling

| Parameter (Variable) | | Standardized path coefficient | CR | p | Hypothesis validation |
|---|---|---|---|---|---|
| H1a | Product emotional design -> Purchase intention | 0.73 | 30.97 | *** | Validated |
| H1b | Product emotional design -> Preference | 0.74 | 35.29 | *** | Validated |
| H1c1 | Creative dimension of product emotional design -> Purchase intention | −0.29 | −4.54 | *** | Invalidated |
| H1c2 | Creative dimension of product emotional design -> Preference | −0.09 | −1.25 | 0.21 | Invalidated |
| H1d1 | Aesthetic dimension of product emotional design -> Purchase intention | −0.24 | −1.70 | 0.09 | Invalidated |
| H1d2 | Aesthetic dimension of product emotional design -> Preference | −0.37 | −2.18 | * | Invalidated |
| H1e1 | Functional dimension of product emotional design -> Purchase intention | 0.01 | 0.13 | 0.90 | Invalidated |
| H1e2 | Functional dimension of product emotional design -> Preference | −0.10 | −1.04 | 0.30 | Invalidated |
| H1f1 | Pleasurable dimension of product emotional design -> Purchase intention | 0.11 | 0.85 | 0.39 | Invalidated |
| H1f2 | Pleasurable dimension of product emotional design -> Preference | 0.74 | 5.74 | *** | Validated |
| H2 | Preference -> Purchase intention | 0.62 | 8.71 | *** | Validated |

Source: Prepared by the researcher. Note: $*p < .05$, $**p < .01$, $***p < .001$.

Businesses in Taiwan are diverse and boast mature production techniques—strengths that enable them to imbue their commodities with cultural value. They can integrate cultural elements such as local lifestyles, Chinese culture, and foreign influences into their products to cement their brand image. By developing high-quality, culturally inspired products that can help to polish brand image, businesses can contribute to the aesthetic economy and become more reputable and competitive.

**Acknowledgements.** The author gratefully acknowledge the support for this research provided by the Ministry of Science and Technology of Taiwan under grant No. MOST- 106-2221-E-034 - 015.

# References

1. Creusen, M.E., Schoormans, J.P.: The different roles of product appearance in consumer choice. J. Prod. Innov. Manag. **22**(1), 63–81 (2005)
2. Kacen, J.J., Hess, J.D., Chiang, W.Y.K.: Bricks or clicks? consumer attitudes toward traditional stores and online stores. Glob. Econ. Manag. Rev. **18**(1), 12–21 (2013)
3. Lin, R.T., Lin, P.H.A.: Study of integrating culture and aesthetics to promote cultural and creative industries. J. National Taiwan Univ. Arts **85**, 81–105 (2009). (in Chinese, semantic translation)
4. Yen, H.Y., Lin, R.: A study of value-added from qualia to business model of cultural and creative industries. J. National Taiwan Univ. Arts **91**, 127–152 (2012). (in Chinese, semantic translation)
5. Ho, A.G., Siu, K.W.M.G.: Emotion design, emotional design, emotionalize design: a review on their relationships from a new perspective. Des. Journal **15**(1), 9–32 (2012)
6. Anderson, S.P.: Seductive Interaction Design: Creating Playful, Fun, and Effective User Experiences. Portable Document. Pearson Education, London (2011)
7. Maslow, A.H.: A theory of human motivation. Psychol. Rev. **50**, 370–396 (1943)
8. Green, W. S., & Jordan, P. W. (Eds.). Pleasure with products: Beyond usability. CRC Press (2003)
9. Norman, D.A.: Emotional design: Why we love (or hate) everyday things. Basic Books, New York (2004)
10. Khalid, H.M., Helander, M.G.: A framework for affective customer needs in product design. Theor. Issues Ergon. Sci. **5**(1), 27–42 (2004)
11. Hassenzahl, M.: The interplay of beauty, goodness, and usability in interactive products. Hum-Comput. Interact. **19**(4), 319–349 (2004)
12. McCarthy, J., Wright, P.: Technology as experience. Interactions **11**(5), 42–43 (2004)
13. Yen, H.Y., Lin, P.H., Lin, R.: The effect of product qualia factors on brand image-using brand love as the mediator. Bull. of Jpn. Soc. Sci. Des. **62**(3), 67–76 (2015)
14. Jagtap, S.: Attributes and emotions in product form design: a survey of professional industrial designers. In: Chakrabarti, A., Chakrabarti, D. (eds.) ICoRD 2017. SIST, vol. 66, pp. 705–714. Springer, Singapore (2017). https://doi.org/10.1007/978-981-10-3521-0_60
15. Batra, R., Seifert, C., Brei, D. (eds.): The Psychology of Design: Creating Consumer Appeal. Routledge, Abingdon (2015)
16. Govers, P.C., Schoormans, J.P.: Product personality and its influence on consumer preference. J. Consum. Mark. **22**(4), 189–197 (2005)
17. Fandos, C., Flavian, C.: Intrinsic and extrinsic quality attributes, loyalty and buying intention: an analysis for a PDO product. Br. Food J. **108**(8), 646–662 (2006)
18. Kotler, P.: Marketing management: Analysis, planning, implementation, and control. Prentice-Hall, Englewood Cliffs (1988)
19. Keller, K.L.: Building customer-based brand equity: a blueprint for creating strong brands. Marketing Science Institute, Cambridge (2001)
20. Schiffman, L.G., Kanuk, L.L.: Consumer behavior, 7th edn. Prentice Hall, New York (2000)
21. Baker, M.J., Churchill Jr., G.A.: The impact of physically attractive models on advertising evaluations. J. Mark. Res. **14**, 538–555 (1977)
22. Blunch, N.J.: Introduction to structural equation modelling using SPSS and AMOS. Sage, London, England (2008)
23. Chen, K.Y., Wang, C.H.: Statistical analysis of practice: Using SPSS and AMOS, 2nd edn. Wu-Nan Book, Taipei (2011). (in Chinese, semantic translation)

24. Hair, J.F., Black, W.C., Babin, B.J., Anderson, R.E., Tatham, R.L.: Multivariate data analysis, 7th edn. Prentice Hall, Upper Saddle River (2010)
25. Jung, T.S.: AMOS and research methods, 4th edn. Wu-Nan Book, Taipei (2011). (in Chinese, semantic translation)
26. Sobel, M.E.: Asymptotic confidence intervals for indirect effects in structural equation models. Sociol. Methodol. **13**(1982), 290–312 (1982)

# Effect of Illumination on Reading Performance and Affect in a Virtual Environment

Xingchen Zhou and Pei-Luen Patrick Rau[(⊠)]

Tsinghua University, Beijing, People's Republic of China
xczhou13@gmail.com, rpl@mail.tsinghua.edu.cn

**Abstract.** The development of virtual reality (VR) technology facilitates reading in a virtual environment. However, how the virtual environmental factors influence users' reading performance has not been studied. Researchers need to compare reading in a virtual environment to the real world situation and to normal digital displays. This paper examined the effect of illumination (dim vs. glaring) in a virtual environment on Chinese text understanding performance, long-term recall performance and affect. The effect of gender is also discussed. The results reveal that in a brightly lit environment, people show better text understanding and logic reasoning performance. However, in a dim environment, people concentrate more and have better long-term memory performance. These findings can be used in guidelines for designers and virtual environment developers. A brightly lit environment is more suitable for understanding and for logical reasoning tasks and a dim environment is suggested for tasks regarding memory and concentration.

**Keywords:** Virtual environment · Reading performance · Illumination

## 1 Introduction

Virtual reality technology has developed quickly in recent years. The application of head-mounted display (HMD) dramatically increased users' immersion in a virtual environment. This technology is now applied in many different fields and researchers have investigated people's performance in different virtual environments [1]. However, the existing work mainly focuses on the performance influenced by the display technology or the rendering software. Few studies have focused on how a virtual environment influences the cognition performance of people working or playing in it. Environmental psychologists have conducted a significant body of research about the effect of real environmental factors on people's cognition and affect. However, these studies are all cases in the real world. Whether the case would be the same in a virtual environment remains to be discovered. In most situations, a virtual environment is formed by an HMD and the device offers mainly visual information. The difference between an HMD and other self-luminous displays need to be examined.

Nowadays, many researchers show an interest in knowing how people read in a virtual environment, and thus the effect of virtual environmental factors on people's reading performance is worth investigating. In reading tasks, text understanding and memory are two important cognition processes. In our study, the effect of light

© Springer International Publishing AG, part of Springer Nature 2018
P.-L. P. Rau (Ed.): CCD 2018, LNCS 10911, pp. 460–471, 2018.
https://doi.org/10.1007/978-3-319-92141-9_36

illumination in a virtual environment on readers' understanding performance and memory were measured. The mood change induced by the light was also studied. This study aims to supply guidelines for designers on how to build virtual environments for a reading activity and other similar cognition tasks.

## 2 Literature Review

Many environmental psychologists have investigated the influence of environmental factors on mood and cognition performance in the real world. Some of these works produced valuable findings. Light illumination in real environments was found to have a significant influence on mood and cognition performance, and the influence differed greatly by gender [2–4]. There are also some other works regarding how ambient illumination affects the performance of a digital display such as on a lap-top or a tablet computer. The head-mounted display, as a new type of display device, should also be contrasted with lap-tops and tablets.

### 2.1 Mood

In an environmental system, many factors influence people's mood, and light is an important factor. A study contrasted the effect of light in several different places in the world where the cultural style and the latitude varied. The result of this research showed that the effect was significantly similar in different places [3]. Knez and his colleagues conducted research on exploring the effect of light on mood and cognition performance [2, 5, 6]. In the experiment performed by Knez, mood change was measured by the difference between the affect before and the affect after the experiment. This had not been measured by earlier researchers [2]. This study showed a significant interaction effect between illumination and light temperature. It also illustrated that a positive mood is preserved best in warm white light with low illumination level and in cool white light with high illumination level. McCloughan et al. discussed the effect of light from two aspects, namely initial effect and long-term effect. They found that many factors change the effect of light, including the light color temperature, the illumination, and gender [4]. Their findings about the interaction between mood and gender are also in accordance with the work by Knez and Enmarker that males are more positive than females [5].

### 2.2 Performance

Daurat et al. compared the different effects of bright light and dim light. They found that, unlike dim light, bright light stimulates subjects' alertness and improves their performance [7]. Another experiment investigated people's cognition performance under different environmental conditions of noise (38 and 58 dB), illumination (300 lx and 1500 lx) and air temperature (21 °C and 27 °C), and the results indicated that subjects have better long-term recall performance in environments with a high illumination level [8]. As for the performance of long-term recall, Knez stated that people perform better in the condition which induces the least negative mood, but he did not establish the relationship between long-term recall performance and objective illumination conditions [2]. However, in a later work examining light and cognition performance, no significant results regarding memory were found [5].

## 2.3    Gender

Some researchers discovered that the degree of illumination of light has an interactive effect with gender. Belcher and Kluczny found that the positive mood of males increases in a bright light environment (2175 lx) while it remains stable in a dim light environment (215 lx). For females, the change is in the opposite direction [9]. Even though gender plays a significant role in affecting mood, the influence of gender on cognition performance such as long-term recall and attention has not been examined. However, for cognition tasks like short-term recall, females performed better than males in a bright illumination condition [8]. In line with former studies, Knez and Enmarker found that, compared to females, males perform much better in decision making tasks [5]. People's perception also differs by gender so that females generally perceive the environment as being more glaring than males do.

## 2.4    Ambient Environment

In recent years, HMD becomes a widely used VR device. To some extent, HMD is more like a display device with a special appearance and it works in a close proximity to the users. It has many characteristics in common with other traditional self-luminous display devices such as tablet computers. In a real indoor environment, the ambient illumination is the light source. However, in the virtual environment, the reading material is self-luminous. In this case, the virtual reading task is similar to the reading activity on a tablet computer in a real environment, especially considering that tablet computers also have backlit displays.

Some researchers focused on the performance on tablet computers used in different ambient illumination environments and they arrived at some conclusions. J.-G. Chen, Wu, Chiu, Tu, and Liu chose 200 lx and 500 lx as their experiment conditions to investigate the influence of ambient illumination when using tablet computers [10]. Their results showed that the ambient illumination had no significant effect on performance, which is in line with previous research [11]. In this case, researchers also found no significant difference when the illumination conditions were respectively 200 lx, 450 lx, and 700 lx. However, Kim et al. stated that the ambient illumination actually impairs the display effect as the illumination level increases [12]. However, all of these research studies focused mainly on the display and the visual expression, when assessing the users' performance. They ignored the influence of the environment on people's cognition performance. On the other hand, the illumination levels they chose were too similar. Therefore the results might not reflect the real case.

# 3   Research Hypothesis

Compared to a desktop, an HMD increases a user's immersion in a virtual environment [13]. People wearing a HMD feel more natural about the virtual environment and are assumed to act in a similar manner to how they would act in the real world. The main hypothesis is that, although virtual environments mainly provide information of visual modality, the effect of visual factors like illumination on mood and cognition of users is similar to its effect in the real world. Based on the main hypothesis, we formulated the following sub-hypotheses.

**Hypothesis 1.** For reading tasks in a virtual environment, the text understanding performance in a condition with high illumination level (glaring) will be better than that in a condition with low illumination level (dim).

**Hypothesis 2.** Content displayed in a condition with a high illumination level (glaring) leaves readers with a deeper impression than content in a condition with a low illumination level. (i.e., people can recall more things that they read in a glaring environment).

**Hypothesis 3.** The mood induced by the environment differs by gender. Males tend to have more a positive mood than females in a glaring reading environment.

# 4   Methods

## 4.1   Experiment Design

A two-parameter mixed-design experiment was designed. Illumination with two levels (dim and glaring), and gender, were chosen as the independent factors. Participants' mood, understanding of the reading materials and their long-term recall performance were chosen as the dependent variables. The mood was measured three times using PANAS scales (before the experiment, after experiment 1 and after experiment 2) [14]. The effect of illumination on mood change was mainly investigated. Participants' understanding of the reading materials was measured by the accuracy of subjects' answers to the reading questions. The long-term recall performance was measured by the number of the topics that subjects recalled after the experiment.

The reading materials were based on the reading questions of the HSK test, which is a standard Chinese language test for foreign language learners similar to the TOFEL/IELTS in English. Two sets of reading material were prepared (The two sets contained respectively 2,872 and 2,893 Chinese characters). Each set of reading material contained eight reading topics and each reading topic was followed by one or two questions. Each set of reading material contained 14 questions in total. The length of each reading topic ranged from 201 Chinese characters to 486 Chinese characters.

Illumination was a within-subject variable and participants of different gender were equally and randomly divided into four different experiment groups (illumination by content). Participants in each group were tested both in the glaring and in the dim illumination conditions.

## 4.2 Subjects

Sixteen participants were recruited for the experiment (eight females and eight males). They were all undergraduate and graduate students in Tsinghua University. The ages of these participants ranged from 20 to 27 (mean = 23.32 and SD = 1.49). All the participants were native Chinese speakers and they all had used VR equipment more than twice and less than ten times. No participant had reading problems.

## 4.3 Apparatus

The experiment in our study was carried out in a laboratory where the noise, the temperature and the humidity were kept stable. The VR equipment used in this experiment was HTC Vive and the virtual experiment environment was developed via Unity 3D. The experiment environment was a virtual indoor environment with two different illumination conditions (dim vs. glaring) shown as Fig. 1. We built the two different illumination conditions by setting the light intensity in Unity 3D (glaring: light intensity = .3, dim: light intensity = 1.6).

In the virtual environment, there was a sofa for the subjects to sit on when answering the reading questions (Fig. 2). A real sofa was placed in the real laboratory and it matched the virtual sofa. This was intended to increase users' immersion during the experiment process. All the reading materials were displayed on a screen in the virtual environment and the readers interacted with the virtual environment via the trigger button of the controller (see Fig. 3). After every test, the program automatically recorded the accuracy and the time remaining (total time for every reading test was 20 min). The experiment set-up is also shown in Fig. 3.

**Fig. 1.** Experimental virtual indoor environment with different illumination levels (dim vs. glaring)

**Fig. 2.** Equipment used to increase participants' immersion in the virtual environment

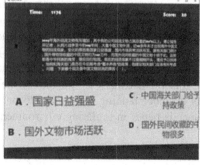

**Fig. 3.** Experiment set-up (above) and interaction interfaces in the virtual environment (below)

## 4.4   Procedures

The experiment took place in the following stages: (1) Before the first stage of the reading test, the subjects were asked to fill in a PANAS scale to measure their mood at the time. (2) Subjects took part in the first stage of the reading test. Before the test began, every participant was shown around the virtual environment and was asked to walk to the sofa and to sit on it. The total test time was 20 min. (3) Subjects were asked to fill in the PANAS scale for a second time. After that, they were invited to close their eyes and to take a rest for five minutes. (4) Subjects took part in the second stage of the reading test. The total test time was also 20 min. (5) Subjects filled in the PANAS scale for the third time. (6) Subjects were required to recall as much as possible of the reading topics (14 in total) within five minutes (After five minutes, participants could choose to continue or not). (7) A semi-structured post experiment interview was conducted and it consisted of four questions ("Which stage was more suitable for reading and why?" "During which stage did you have a more positive mood, and why?" "During which stage were you more able to concentrative, and why?" "Which stage would be your preference for a reading environment?").

The average time for the whole experiment for all subjects was around 55 min.

## 5   Results

### 5.1   Understanding

The result of a mixed ANOVA test showed that participants' understanding of the reading materials in a dim environment and in a glaring environment was different. The main effect of illumination on participants' accuracy in answering reading questions was significant $(F(1,14) = 6.07, p < .05,$ Cohen's $d = 0.95)$. As shown in Fig. 4, participants' accuracy in a glaring environment (Mean $= .77$, SD $= .11$) is higher than that in a dim environment (Mean $= .87$, SD $= .09$). However, the main effect of gender $(F(1,14) = .067, p > .79)$ and the interaction effect between illumination and gender $(F(1,14) = .8, p > .38)$ are not significant.

As for the time spent in each reading stage, the time use of each subject remained similar in each stage of the reading task. The result of a mixed ANOVA test suggested that the main effects of illumination and gender on the use of time were not significant (Illumination: $F(1,14) = .68, p > .42$; Gender: $F(1,14) = 1.68, p > .22$). The interaction effect was also not significant $(F(1,14) = .44, p > .51)$. This result meant that, in the different stages, the time used was almost the same and it also partially supported the results for accuracy by excluding the possible influence of reading speed. The results of understanding are similar to previous research showing that cognition performance is better in a glaring environment, thus hypothesis 1 was proved.

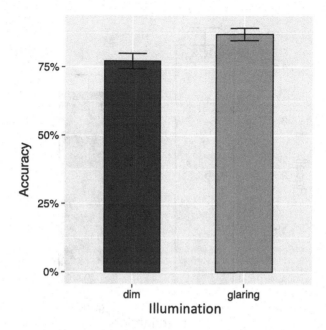

**Fig. 4.** The mean accuracy and standard error in a dim environment and a glaring environment

## 5.2  Long-Term Memory

The total number of reading topics was sixteen and, within each reading stage, the quantity of reading topics was eight. The long-term recall result is shown in Fig. 5. As for the quantity of topics, participants recalled more topics that were displayed in the dim environment (mean = 4.4, SD = 1.26) than topics displayed in the brightly lit environment (mean = 3.5, SD = 1.26). This indicated that long-term memory in a dim environment might be better than that in a bright environment.

A mixed ANOVA test was conducted with gender as a between-subject variable and illumination as a within-subject variable. The result indicated that the main effect of gender was not significant ($F(1,14) = .093$, $p > .76$). However, we can assume the illumination has a relatively significant inclination to influence participants' recall performance ($F(1,14) = 3.77$, $p < .073$, Cohen's $d = .69$).

The result for long-term memory was quite opposite to hypothesis 2, which meant that people had a deeper impression of items displayed in an environment with dim light. Therefore, the reverse of hypothesis 2 was proved.

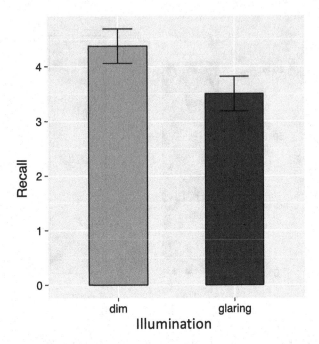

**Fig. 5.** The quantity of topics recalled by participants in different illumination conditions

### 5.3   Mood

We firstly examined the scores for positive and negative affect in test environments with different illumination conditions. The results of a mixed ANOVA test showed that both illumination and gender had no significant influence on the participants' affect as measured after finishing each reading test (For both positive and negative affect, all ps > .5).

We also examined the change in participants' affect. The mood change was defined by the positive state (or negative stage) after the experiment minus the positive state in the beginning. The results showed that, for positive affect, the effect of illumination, gender and interaction between illumination and gender are not remarkable (with all ps > .26). As for the negative state, there were also no remarkable results (with all ps > .55). However, when considering whether the affect was strengthened, the result was different. Subjects' affect was marked as strengthened when the mood change was above zero. The result of the Chi square test showed that males' positive mood is more likely to be induced than that of females ($Chi^2(1) = 5.24$, $p < .05$). As for negative affect, the difference between genders was not significant ($Chi^2(1) = .51$, $p = 0.48$). The result was convincing evidence that the positive affect of males was more likely to be induced which is in line with the findings of previous studies in a real world indoor environment.

# 6   Discussion

## 6.1   Understanding

The results for text understanding performance are in support of the previous findings arrived at in a real world environment. This is a proof that, in a virtual environment, when performing reading tasks, people tend to perform better in a glaring environment. The result is in line with the findings of Daurat et al. [7].

The results of interviews showed that nine of the 16 subjects felt that the glaring environment was more fruitful for the reading tasks (another five preferred the dim environment and two said they had no preference), as they felt "more active in this environment" and "the reading materials seem more clear". This may result from higher arousal state in a glaring environment [8].

## 6.2   Long-Term Memory

The results of long-term recall denied hypothesis 2, but in the opposite direction, the result showed that the main effect of illumination on long-term recall in a virtual environment was significant.

In the post-experiment interview, 10 of the 16 subjects said that they could concentrate more in the dim environment, while five others said that the glaring environment made them more dedicated and one said that there was no difference. The multiple resource theory of Wickens might explain the results [15]. In the glaring environment, the aesthetic features of the virtual indoor environment would have occupied some cognition resources, thus the readers would have received more information than in the dim environment in that less memory capacity was used to remember the reading topics.

The number of reading topics that were mentioned was also in line with the information processing capacity theory of Miller [16]. The average number of recalled topics is 7.79 (SD = 1.32), quite close to the number in Miller's theory. To some extent, it could partially validate the experiment result.

As in the previous study, the effect of light on long-term recall could sometimes be non-significant [5]. We assumed that the effect might not only result from the illumination condition, it might be also caused by the illumination contrast between the environment and the screen. A movie shown in the cinema is a good example. Therefore, further studies may focus more on the effect of contrast between the environment and the reading material since, in a virtual environment, the screen is also self-luminous.

## 6.3   Mood

An analysis of the change of positive mood and negative mood showed no remarkable effect of illumination and gender. However, there is quite possibly a tendency that the positive mood of males will be more likely to be strengthened, which is in line with the findings of Belcher and Kluczny [9]. Considering the definition of arousal, the strengthened positive mood is similar to the arousal state. For the future work, direct concern about the arousal state influenced by illumination and gender may matter more, referring to the discussion of the arousal model influenced by environmental factors [8].

### 6.4   Comparison with Tablet Computers

In an HMD based virtual environment, only information of visual modality was offered to the users. However, in the real world, heat and humidity are all influenced by the light which will in turn influence people's cognitive performance. The results of our study showed that, even with only the visual modality, the influence of the virtual environment established by HMD-based VR did have similar effects as those in the real world.

Tablet computers are another kind of widely used display. The illumination condition of tablet computers was studied. Just as in an HMD, the screen of tablet computers is also self-luminous. When considering the performance of tablet computers, the illumination conditions in former research studies are all no more than 750 lx [10–12]. Researchers found that the effect of illumination conditions was not significant. This may result from experiment conditions that are too similar. In the domain of environmental psychology, the difference between illumination conditions is quite large.

When considering the usage of new digital devices, engineers are concerned more about the display performance. Therefore, they ignore the effect of illumination on users' cognition. As an environmental factor in itself, illumination has a direct influence on people's cognition. Some studies considered it instead from an indirect aspect by examining how illumination affected the screen display and then affected the readers. For HMD equipment, the visual influence from the outer environment was isolated, therefore the virtual environment offered the only visual information that should be considered.

## 7   Conclusion

This study investigated the effect of illumination and gender on reading tasks in a virtual indoor environment. The result showed that in a glaring environment, people had better performance with text understanding and logical reasoning tasks, because they were more aroused in bright conditions. However, while in dim conditions, the subjects felt less interference from the environment, thus they could concentrate more on the items that they would like to keep in mind. Therefore, people recalled more items that they read in dim environment.

This research concentrated mainly on the effect of illumination on reading performance, long-term memory and mood. The other important factor of light environment is color temperature. Considering both illumination and color temperature as well as their interaction effect will be important for future work.

Another important contribution of this study is that it proved the significant effect of a virtual environment established by head-mounted display (HMD) and contrasted its similarity and difference with other self-luminous digital displays. Guidelines can also be given to designers and virtual environment developers that a glaring environment is suitable for arousing users and helping users to deal with understanding and logical reasoning tasks, while a dim environment with little interference can increase concentration and is more suitable for remembering items.

# References

1. Nash, E.B., Edwards, G.W., Thompson, J.A., Barfield, W.: A review of presence and performance in virtual environments. Int. J. Hum.-Comput. Interact. **12**, 1–41 (2000)
2. Knez, I.: Effects of indoor lighting on mood and cognition. J. Environ. Psychol. **15**, 39–51 (1995)
3. Küller, R., Ballal, S., Laike, T., Mikellides, B., Tonello, G.: The impact of light and colour on psychological mood: a cross-cultural study of indoor work environments. Ergonomics **49**, 1496–1507 (2006)
4. McCloughan, C.L.B., Aspinall, P.A., Webb, R.S.: The impact of lighting on mood. Light. Res. Technol. **31**, 81–88 (1999)
5. Knez, I., Enmarker, I.: Effects of office lighting on mood and cognitive performance and a gender effect in work-xrelated judgment. Environ. Behav. **30**, 553–567 (1998)
6. Knez, I., Kers, C.: Effects of indoor lighting, gender, and age on mood and cognitive performance. Environ. Behav. **32**, 817–831 (2000)
7. Daurat, A., Aguirre, A., Foret, J., Gonnet, P., Keromes, A., Benoit, O.: Bright light affects alertness and performance rhythms during a 24-h constant routine. Physiol. Behav. **53**, 929–936 (1993)
8. Hygge, S., Knez, I.: Effects of noise, heat and indoor lighting on cognitive performance and self-reported affect. J. Environ. Psychol. **21**, 291–299 (2001)
9. Belcher, M.C.: The effects of light on decision making: Some experimental results. In: Proceedings of the CIE 21st Session, Venice 1987, pp. 354–357 (1987)
10. Chen, J.G., Wu, S.K., Chiu, H.P., Tu, C.N., Liu, C.H.: Evaluation of three tablet computers at two levels of ambient illumination. Int. J. Hum.-Comput. Interact. **32**, 394–401 (2016)
11. Chen, M.T., Lin, C.C.: Comparison of TFT-LCD and CRT on visual recognition and subjective preference. Int. J. Ind. Ergon. **34**, 167–174 (2004)
12. Chang, Y.K., Hong, S.K., Luo, M.R., Rhodes, P., Lee, S., Park, S.O., Choe, W., Baek, Y., Kim, Y.J.: Factors affecting the psychophysical image quality evaluation of mobile phone displays: the case of transmissive liquid-crystal displays. J. Opt. Soc. Am. A Opt. Image Sci. Vis. **25**, 2215 (2008)
13. Santos, B.S., Dias, P., Pimentel, A., Baggerman, J.W., Ferreira, C., Silva, S., Madeira, J.: Head-mounted display versus desktop for 3D navigation in virtual reality: a user study. Multimed. Tools Appl. **41**, 161–181 (2009)
14. Watson, D., Clark, L.A., Tellegen, A.: Development and validation of brief measures of positive and negative affect: the PANAS scales. J. Pers. Soc. Psychol. **54**, 1063–1070 (1988)
15. Wickens, C.D., Damos, D.L.: Processing resources and attention, Multiple-task Performance, 3–34 (1991)
16. Miller, G.A.: The magical number seven plus or minus two: some limits on our capacity for processing information. Psychol. Rev. **101**, 343 (1994)

# Author Index

Printed in the United States
By Bookmasters